Conversion Tables

Conversion Tables

Volume 3
Subject Headings—LC and Dewey

Second Edition

Mona L. Scott

1999
LIBRARIES UNLIMITED, INC.
Englewood, Colorado

Libraries Unlimited, Inc.
P.O. Box 6633
Englewood, CO 80155-6633
1-800-237-6124
www.lu.com

ISBN 1-56308-596-8 (set)
ISBN 1-56308-850-9 (Vol. 1 LC-Dewey)
ISBN 1-56308-848-7 (Vol. 2 Dewey-LC)
ISBN 1-56308-849-5 (Vol. 3 Subject Headings—LC and Dewey)
ISBN 1-56308-597-6 (Disk version)

Contents

Introduction

Analyzing and compiling the first edition of *Conversion Tables: LC-Dewey; Dewey-LC* proved to be an enormous undertaking and the exigencies of publication precluded inclusion of Library of Congress subject headings. For the second edition, however, LC subject headings are included as a separate section comprising Volume 3. Volumes 1 and 2 now consist of the LC-Dewey conversion table and the Dewey-LC conversion table, respectively. It is hoped the division of the book into three separate volumes will facilitate concurrent use of different volumes which, in turn, will facilitate libraries' conversion projects and daily cataloging activities.

Materials referenced in the *Conversion Tables* are the 21st edition of the *Dewey Decimal Classification*; the most current edition of the various volumes of the Library of Congress classification schedules available to me at the NASA/Goddard Space Flight Center Library and the library of the School of Library and Information Science at Catholic University of America in Washington, D.C.; the 1996 edition of *Library of Congress Subject Headings*; and the 1994 edition of *Library of Congress Free-Floating Subdivisions*. Library of Congress subject authority files were consulted regularly to maintain the currency of country or nation names.

Conversion Tables was conceived as a cataloging tool that could be a standard reference in any cataloging department for daily copy cataloging activities, as well as massive projects of converting from one classification system to the other. For the former, the conversion tables most frequently will be used to convert individual MARC records from bibliographic utilities that include only one classification number. With the addition of the LC subject heading table, *Conversion Tables* also can be used as a call number assigning tool.

The LC and Dewey Decimal classification schemes approach the organization of knowledge from different perspectives. This can been seen in how LC and Dewey view language and the literatures of each language. LC classes them together in the Ps while Dewey separates them, placing language in the 400s and literature in the 800s. Similarly, LC places military and naval sciences in stand-alone classes, U for military science and V for naval science; Dewey places both in the so-called megaclass 300s, which includes virtually all of the social sciences.

As the two schemes differ so greatly in basic concepts, it was necessary to analyze the concepts of each order to select the corresponding numbers or alphanumeric notations to construct the tables. Ultimately, it involved assigning more than 52,000 class notations.

Structure of Tables

This cataloging tool is arranged in three sections each in its own volume: LC to Dewey, Volume 1; Dewey to LC, Volume 2; and Subject Headings with corresponding classifications, Volume 3. Thus, each section contains the same lists of classifications in the two systems and corresponding subject headings but in different arrangements.

Example:

LC to Dewey tables

LC	Dewey	Subject Heading
DS109.93	956.9404	Palestine—History—Partition, 1947

Dewey to LC tables

Dewey	LC	Subject Heading
956.9404	DS109.93	Palestine—History—Partition, 1947

Subject Heading tables

Subject Heading	LC	Dewey
Palestine—History—Partition, 1947	DS109.93	956.9404

The notation for a general concept, such as Philosophy which is 100 in Dewey and B in the Library of Congress Classification, will have divisions and subdivisions broken down into smaller concepts and thus more detailed notations (Philosophy—Congresses is 105 in Dewey and B20 in LC).

The differences discussed above also result in more than one notation corresponding to the other, or even a whole range of numbers and alphanumeric notations corresponding to the other. For example, 951.041 in the Dewey schedule under the history of China corresponds to seven LC notations in these tables, in the range DS773.83 to DS777.45.

Dates in the LC and Dewey schemes have been a problem. The two schemes often do not agree on the date that an event occurred. For example, the LC classification indicates that the Time of Troubles in Russian history was from 1598-1613, but the Dewey scheme uses the dates 1605-1613. However, in other places the dates match perfectly, as in the history of Tunisia. To aid in the conversion, I have often used a range of dates from Table 1 in the Dewey Classification to indicate a century, rather than the single date.

The following conventions have been used:

- Diacritics have not been included in the subject headings.

- Within the class numbers and subject headings, "/" indicates a choice and is usually contained within parentheses or brackets.

- As in conventional cataloging rules, brackets [ ] contain words added by the author.

Instructions for Use of the Tables

To convert a classification from LC to Dewey or Dewey to LC, find the section containing the table from which you wish to convert. Locate the classification from which you wish to convert in the left column. As indicated above, it may be included in a range of "numbers" or alphanumeric notations that correspond to the other classification, or it may fall between two classifications. In these cases, locate the class nearest in concept by using the Subject Headings. The classification to which you wish to convert is in the middle column, with the subject heading on the right.

The Subject Heading section provides a shortcut to the call number assigning process. Using that section, you can search for the subject heading that reflects or approximates the subject matter of the item that is being cataloged and note the appropriate classification next to it. This notation may be the classification that is needed, or will lead you to the appropriate one in the schedules.

Subject Headings—LC and Dewey

Subject Heading	LC	Dewey	Subject Heading	LC	Dewey
AEGIS (Weapons system)	VF347	359.98170973	Abortion in the press	PN4784.A18	363.46
AGATE (Computer war game)	U310	355.480285	Abortion services	RG734-.5	363.46
AIDS (Disease)	RC607.A26	616.9792	Abraham (Biblical patriarch) in the New Testament	BS580.A3	225.92
AIDS (Disease) in adolescence	RJ387.A25	616.979200835	Abscess	RD641	616.047
AIDS (Disease) in children	RJ387.A25	618.929792	Absentee mothers	HQ759.3	306.8743
AIDS (Disease) in infants	RJ387.A25	618.929792	Absentee voting	JF1033	324.65
AIDS (Disease) in mass media	P96.A39	362.1969792	Absolute, The	BD416	111.6
			Absolution (Canon law)	BX1939.A	262.933
AIDS (Disease) in pregnancy	RG580.A44	618.3	Absorption (Physiology)	QP165	612.38
			Absorption of light	QC437	535.326
AIDS-related complex	RA644.A25	614.599392	Absorption of sound	QC233	534.208
Aardvark	QL737.T8	599.31	Abused lesbians	HQ75.3-.6	305.489664
Aaronic Priesthood (Mormon Church)	BX8659.5	262.1	Abused parents	HQ755.85	306.874
			Abuscd wives—Services for	HV697-700.5	362.8292
Aatmna (Hindu deity)	BL1225.A	294.52113	Abused wives—Services for—[By region or country]	HV699-700	362.829209(4-9)
Abaca (Fiber)	SB261.M3	633.571			
Abacus	QA75	513.0284	Abused women—Pastoral counseling of	BV4445.5	259.082
Abalone culture	SH371.5-.52	639.4832			
Abalone fisheries	SH371.5-.52	639.4832	Abyssinian cat	SF449.A28	636.826
Abalones	QL430.5.H34	594.32	Academic costume	LB2389	378.28
Abandoned children	HV873-875.7	362.73	Academic freedom	LC72-.5	371.104
Abandoned children— [By region or country]	HV880-887	362.7309(4-9)	Academic libraries	Z675.U5	027.7
			Academies and learned societies	AS	060
Abandoned children— United States	HV880-885	362.730973	Acala (Buddhist deity)	BQ4860.A4	294.34211
			Accelerometers	TL589.2.A3	629.1352
Abazin language	PK9201.A2	499.962	Acceptances	HG1655	332
Abbasids	DS234-238	953.80099	Accident law—England	KD3510	344.42047
Abbeys	NA4800-6113	726.7	Accident law—United States	KF3970	344.73047
Abbots (Canon law)	BX1939.A	262.932	Accidents—Prevention	HV675-677	363.107
Abbreviations, Persian	PK6395	491.5511	Acclimatization	QH543.2	578.42
Abbreviations, Romanian	PC785	459.11	Accordion	ML1083	788.8609
Abdomen	QM543	611.95	Accordion music	M175.A4	788.86
Abdomen—Cancer	RC280.A2	616.99495	Account books	HF5680-5681	657
Abdomen—Diseases	RC944	617.55	Accounting	HF5601-5689.8	657
Abdomen—Surgery	RD540-548	617.55059	Accounting—Study and teaching (Internship)	HF5630	657.071
Abdomen—Tumors	RC280.A2	616.99495			
Abdomen—Wounds and injuries	RD540-548	617.55044	Accounting machines	HF5679	657.0284
			Accounts current	HF5681.A2	657.72
Abduction	HV6571-6574	364.154	Accounts payable	HF5681.A27	657.74
Abent squirrel	QL737.R68	599.36	Accounts receivable	HF5681.A3	657.72
Abenteeism (Labor)	HD5715-.2	331.2598	Accounts receivable loans	HG3752.3	332.7
Aberration	QB163	522.9	Accreditation (Education)	LB2810-.5	379.158
Abhayagiri (Sect)	BQ8000-8049	294.39	Acetal resins	TP1180.A33	668.423
Ability grouping in education	LB3061	371.254	Acetylene	QD305.H8	547.413
			Acetylene compounds	QD305.H8	547.413
Ability in children	BF723.A25	155.4139	Achaemenid dynasty, 559-330 B.C.	DS281-284.7	935.05
Ability in infants	BF720.A24	155.42239			
Ability—Testing	BF431-433	153.93	Achievement motivation	BF501-505	153.8
Abitibi Indians	E99.A12	973.04971	Achievement tests	LB3060.3	371.271
Abkhaz language	PK9201.A3	499.9623	Acid mine drainage	TD899.M5	628.42
Abkhaz literature	PK9201.A35-.A39	899.9623	Acid precipitation (Meteorology)	QC926.5-.57	551.5771
Abkhazo-Adyghian languages	PK9051	499.962			
			Acid soils	S592.57-.575	631.42
Abnaki Indians	E99.A13	973.04973	Acid sulphate soils	S592.575	631.42
Abortion	HQ767-.4	363.46	Acidosis	RB147	616.3992
Abortion in the press	PN4888.A2	363.460973	Acids	TP213-217	661.2

Subject Heading	LC	Dewey
Ackia, Battle of, 1736	F347.A25	976.202
Acne	RL131	616.53
Acoli language	PL8041	496.5
Acoustical engineering	TA365-367	620.2
Acoustooptical devices	TA1770	621.3828
Acquisition of art catalogs	Z688.A7	025.277
Acquisition of databases	Z692.D38	025.284
Acquisition of maps	Z692.M3	025.286
Acquisition of medical literature	Z688.M4	025.2761
Acquisition of serial publications	Z692.S5	025.28305
Acquistions (Libraries)	Z689-.8	025.2
Acrobatics	GV551-553	796.47
Acromegaly	RC658.3	616.47
Acrostics	PN6366-6377	793.73
Acrylic fiber industry	HD9929.5.A27-.A274	338.476774742
Acrylic painting	ND1535	751.426
Acting	PN2061-2071	792.028
Acting—Vocational guidance	PN2055	792.023
Action research in education	LB1028.24	370.72
Actions and defenses—United States	KF8863-8865	347.73053
Actium, Battle of, 31 B.C.	DG269	937.05
Active childbirth	RG662	618.4
Active oxygen	QD181.01	546.721
Active oxygen in the body	QP535.01	572.53
Activity coefficients	QD541-543	541.34
Actors	PN2205-2217	792.028092
Actors—Professional ethics	PN2056	174.97914
Actresses	PN2205-2217	792.028092
Acupressure	RM723.A27	615.822
Acupressure for children	RJ53.A27	615.822083
Acupuncture	RM184-.5	615.892
Acupuncture for children	RJ53.A27	615.892083
Acupuncture points	RC73.2	615.892
Acute abdomen	RD540-548	617.55
Acute hemorrhagic conjunctivitis	RE320	617.773
Acute leukemia	RC643	616.99419
Acute myelocytic leukemia in children	RJ416.A25	618.9299419
Acute renal failure in children	RJ476.R46	618.92614
Acute toxicity testing	RA1199.4.A38	615.907
Adam (Biblical figure) in the Koran	BP133.7.A3	297.122092
Adamawa languages	PL8024.A33	496.361
Adaptation (Biology)	QH546	578.4
Adaptation (Physiology)	QP82-.2	578.4
Addison's disease	RC659	616.45
Addition	QA115	513.211
Addition polymerization	QD281.P6	547.28
Adelie penguin	QL696.S473	598.47
Adhesives	TP967-970	668.3
Adhesives industry	HD9999.A4-.A44	338.476683
Adipose tissues	QM565	611.0182
Aditi (Hindu deity)	BL1225.A4	294.52114
Adityas (Hindu deities)	BL1225.A42	294.52113
Adjustment (Psychology)	BF335-337	155.24
Adjustment disorders	RC455.4.S87	155.24
Adlerian psychology	BF175.5.A33	150.1953
Administrative law	K3400-3431	342.066
Administrative law—United States	KF5401-5425	342.73066
Administrative responsibility	JF1621	352.35
Administrators apostolic	BX1939.A3	262.02
Admirals	VB190	359.331
Adolescence	GN483-484	305.235
Adolescence	LB1135	155.5
Adolescence	GN63	599.90835
Adolescent analysis	RJ503	618.928917
Adolescent gynecology	RJ478-.5	618.92098
Adolescent medicine	RJ550	616.00835
Adolescent psychiatric nursing	RJ502.3	610.7368
Adolescent psychiatry	RJ503	616.8900835
Adolescent psychology	BF724-.3	155.5
Adolescent psychopathology	RJ503	616.8900835
Adolescent psychotherapy	RJ503	616.891400835
Adolescent psychotherapy—Termination	RJ505.T47	616.891400835
Adonis (Greek deity)	BL820.A25	292.2113
Adoption	HV874.8-875.7	362.734
Adrenal cortex	QP188.A28	612.45
Adrenal glands	QM371	611.45
Adrenal glands	QP188.A3	612.45
Adrenal glands	RJ420.A27	618.9245
Adrenal glands—Diseases	RC659	616.45
Adrenalectomy	RD599.5.A37	617.44
Adrenergic alpha blockers	RC684.A34	616.1206
Adrenergic beta blockers	RC684.A35	616.1206
Adrianople, Battle of, 378	DF559	949.501
Adult children of alcoholics	HV5132	362.2923
Adult education	LC5201-6660	374
Adult education of women	LC1660-1666	374.1822
Adultery	HQ806	306.736
Adulthood	HQ799.95-.97	305.24
Advaita	B132.A3	181.482
Advanced guard (Military science)	U167.5.A35	355.4
Advent calendars	GT4987.5	394.2667
Advent sermons	BV40	252.61
Adventists	BX6101-6193	286.7
Adventists—Biography	BX6191-6193	286.7092
Adventists—History	BX6115-6117	286.709
Adventists—Sermons	BX6123	252.067
Adventure and adventurers	CT9970-9971	904
Adventure and adventurers	G521-539	904
Adventure stories	PN6120.95.A38	808.8387
Adventure stories	PN3448.A3	809.387
Advertising	HF5801-6182	659.1
Advertising—Airlines	HF6161.A38	659.193877
Advertising—Churches	BV653	254.4
Advertising—Directories	HF5804-5808	659.1025
Advertising—Encyclopedias	HF5803	659.103
Advertising—History	HF5811-5813	659.109
Advertising—Periodicals	HF5801-5802	659.105
Advertising—Recruiting and enlistment	UB320-338	355.2236
Advertising—Study and teaching	HF5814-5815	659.1071

Subject Heading	LC	Dewey	Subject Heading	LC	Dewey
Advertising, Direct-mail	HF5861-5863	659.133	Aeronautics—Sanitation	RA615.2	629.1344
Advertising, Newspaper	HF5871-6141	659.132	Aeronautics—Societies, etc.	TL500-504	629.13006
Advertising, Newspaper— [By region or country]	HF5901-6097	659.13209(4-9)	Aeronautics—[By region or country]	TL521-532	629.13009(4-9)
Advertising, Point-of-sale	HF5828	659.157	Aeronautics, Commercial	HE9761-9900	387.7
Advertising agencies	HF6178-6182	659.1125	Aeronautics, Commercial— Freight	TL720.7	387.744
Advertising cards	HF5851	659.132	Aeronautics, Commercial— History	HE9774-9775	387.709
Advertising departments	HF5804-5808	659.1122			
Advertising drinking glasses	HF6146.D75	659.13	Aeronautics, Commercial— Law and legislation— England	KD1804	343.42097
Advertising laws	HF5833	343.082			
Advertising laws—Canada	KE1610-1614	343.71082			
Advertising laws—England	KD2206	343.42082	Aeronautics, Commercial— Passenger traffic	HE9787-.5	387.742
Advertising laws— United States	KF1614-1617	343.73082	Aeronautics, Commercial— Periodicals	HE9761-.9	387.705
Advertising layout and typography	HF5825	659.132	Aeronautics, Commercial— [By region or country]	HE9801-9900	387.709(4-9)
Advertising media planning	HF5826.5	659.111	Aeronautics, Commercial— Africa	HE9882-9888.4	387.7096
Advocacy advertising	HD59.3	659.1	Aeronautics, Commercial— Asia	HE9869.22-9869.27	387.7095
Adygei litcrature	PK9201.A45-.A49	899.9625			
Aeolic Greek dialect	PA550-554	480	Aeronautics, Commercial— Australia	HE9889	387.70994
Aerial photography	TR810	778.35			
Aerial photography in anthropology	GN34.3.A35	301.028	Aeronautics, Commercial— Benelux countries	HE9852-9854.5	387.709492
Aerial photography in geomorphology	GB400.42.A35	551.41028	Aeronautics, Commercial— Canada	HE9815	387.70971
Aerial photography in glaciology	GB2401.72.A37	551.31028	Aeronautics, Commercial— Central America	HE9817-9823	387.709728
Aerial photography in hydrology	GB656.2.A37	551.48028	Aeronautics, Commercial— China	HE9878	387.70951
Aerial reconnaissance	UG760-765	358.45	Aeronautics, Commercial— Europe	HE9842-9867.7	387.7094
Aerial reconnaissance, American	UG763	358.450973			
Aerial reconnaissance, British	UG765.G	358.450941	Aeronautics, Commercial— France	HE9848	387.70944
Aerobic exercises	RA781.15	613.71	Aeronautics, Commercial— Germany	HE9849-.5	387.70943
Aerodynamic measurements	TL573	629.13230287			
Aerodynamic noise	TL574.N6	629.1323	Aeronautics, Commercial— Great Britain	HE9843-9845.5	387.70941
Aerodynamics	QA930	533.62	Aeronautics, Commercial— Greece	HE9867.5	387.709495
Aerodynamics	TL570-574	629.1323			
Aerodynamics, Hypersonic	TL571.5	629.132306	Aeronautics, Commercial— India	HE9871	387.70954
Aerogrammes	HE6184.A35	383.144			
Aeronautical instruments	TL589-.5	629.1300284	Aeronautics, Commercial— Iran	HE9869.2	387.70955
Aeronautical laboratories	TL566-568	629.130072			
Aeronautical libraries	Z675.A5	026.62913	Aeronautics, Commercial— Iraq	HE9869	387.709567
Aeronautical museums	TL506	629.130074			
Aeronautical sports	GV750-770	797.5	Aeronautics, Commercial— Israel	HE9868.45	387.7095694
Aeronautics	TL500-830	629.13			
Aeronautics—Abbreviations	TL509	629.1300148	Aeronautics, Commercial— Italy	HE9851	387.70945
Aeronautics—Biography	TL539-540	629.130092			
Aeronautics—Communi- cation systems	TL692-696	629.135	Aeronautics, Commercial— Japan	HE9877	387.70952
Aeronautics—Congresses	TL505	629.13006	Aeronautics, Commercial— Mexico	HE9816	387.70972
Aeronautics—Flights	TL721	629.13			
Aeronautics—History	TL515-532	629.13009	Aeronautics, Commercial— Middle East	HE9868.2-.95	387.70956
Aerpnautics—Law and legislation	K4091-4124	343.097			
Aeronautics—Patents	TL513	629.1300272	Aeronautics, Commercial— Philippines	HE9876	387.709599
Aeronautics—Pictorial works	TL549	629.1300222			
Aeronautics—Safety measures	TL553.5	629.1300289			

3

Subject Heading	LC	Dewey	Subject Heading	LC	Dewey
Aeronautics, Commercial—Russia	HE9855	387.70947	Affective disorders	RC537-545	616.8527
Aeronautics, Commercial—South America	HE9830-9841	387.7098	Affective disorders in children	RJ506.D4	618.928527
			Affinity credit cards	HG1643	332.178
Aeronautics, Commercial—Spain	HE9861	387.70946	Afforestation	SD409	634.956
			Afghan hounds	SF429.A4	636.7533
Aeronautics, Commercial—Switzerland	HE9863	387.709494	Afghanistan—Census	HA4570.6	315.81
			Afghanistan—Civilization	DS354	939.6/958.1
Aeronautics, Commercial—United States	HE9803-9814	387.70973	Afghanistan—Description and travel	DS352	913.9604/ 915.8104
Aeronautics, Commercial—West Indies	HE9824-9829.9	387.709729	Afghanistan—Economic conditions	HC416-420	330.9581
Aeronautics, Military	UG630-670	358.4	Afghanistan—Gazetteers	DS351	913.96003/ 915.81003
Aeronautics in missionary work	BV2082.A9	266	Afghanistan—History	DS355-371.2	939.6/958.1
			Afghanistan—History—1989-	DS371.3	958.104(5-6)
Aeronautics in wildfire control	SD421.43	634.9618	Afghanistan—History—Soviet occupation, 1979-1989	DS371.2	958.1045
Aerosols	QC882.4-.46	363.7392			
Aerospace engineering	TL500-4050	629.1	Afghanistan—Maps	G2265-2269	912.581
Aerospace industries	HD9711.5	338.4762912	Afghanistan—Maps	G7630-7634	912.581
Aerospace telemetry	TL694.T35	629.437	Afghanistan—Politics and government	JQ1760-1769	320.9581
Aerostatics	QC168	533.61			
Aerotherapy	RM824-827	615.836	Africa	DT	960
Aesculapius (Greek deity)	BL820.A4	292.2113	Africa—Armed Forces—Supplies and stores	UC247-253	355.8096
Aesthetics	BH	111.85			
Aesthetics	N61-79	701.17	Africa—Biography	CT1920-2750	920.06
Aesthetics—Congresses	BH19	111.8506	Africa—Church history	BR1359-1470	276
Aesthetics—Dictionaries	BH56	111.8503	Africa—Civilization	DT14	960
Aesthetics—History	BH81-208	111.8509	Africa—Climate	QC991	551.696
Aesthetics—Periodicals	BH1-8	111.8505	Africa—Colonization	JV246	325.6
Aesthetics—Study and teaching	BH61-62	111.85071	Africa—Commerce	HF3871-3937	380.1096
			Africa—Description and travel	DT6.5-12.25	916.04
Aesthetics, Ancient	BH91-116	111.850901			
Aesthetics, Byzantine	BH221.B	111.8509495	Africa—Economic conditions	HC800-1085	330.96
Aesthetics, Canadian	BH221.C	111.850971	Africa—Emigration and immigration	JV8790-9024.5	325.(26/6)
Aesthetics, Medieval	BH131-137	111.850902			
Aesthetics, Medieval	N61	701.170902	Africa—Gazetteers	DT2	916.003
Aesthetics, Modern	BH151-208	111.850903	Africa—Genealogy	CS1550-1779	929.107206
Aesthetics, Modern—16th century	BH161-168	111.8509031	Africa—History	DT17-39	960
			Africa—History—1884-1918	DT29	960.(23-314)
Aesthetics, Modern—16th century	N61	701.1709031	Africa—History—1884-1960	DT29-30.2	960.(23-326)
			Africa—History—1960-	DT30.5	960.3(26-3)
Aesthetics, Modern—17th Century	N61	701.1709032	Africa—History—To 1498	DT25	960.(1-21)
			Africa—History—To 1884	DT24-28	960.(1-23)
Aesthetics, Modern—17th century	BH171-178	111.8509032	Africa—Manufactures	TS115-119	670.96
			Africa—Maps	G8200-8202	912.6
Aesthetics, Modern—18th century	BH181-188	111.8509033	Africa—Maps	G2445-2739	912.6
			Africa—Politics and government	JQ1870-3981	320.96
Aesthetics, Modern—18th century	N61	701.1709033			
			Africa—Religion	BL2400-2490	299.6
Aesthetics, Modern—19th century	BH191-198	111.8509034	Africa, Central—Church history	BR1430	276.7
Aesthetics, Modern—19th century	N61	701.1709034	Africa, Central—History—1884-1960	DT352.7	967.03(1-25)
Aesthetics, Modern—20th century	BH201-208	111.850904	Africa, Central—History—To 1884	DT352.65	967.0(1-2)
Aesthetics, Modern—20th century	N61	701.170904	Africa, Central—Maps	G2590-2639	912.67
			Africa, East	DT365-469	967.6
Aesthetics, Oriental	BH101-102	111.85095	Africa, East—Church history	BR1440-1445	276.76
Aetolia (Greece)	DF261.A2	938.3	Africa, East—History	DT365.5-.8	967.6
Afar language	PJ2465	493.5	Africa, East—Maps	G2500-2559	912.676

Subject Heading	LC	Dewey
Africa, East—History—To 1886	DT365.65	967.601
Africa, North	DT160-177	939.7/961
Africa, North—Church history	BR1369-1415	276.1
Africa, North—Description and travel	DT163-165.2	913.9704/916.104
Africa, North—History	DT160-176	939.7/961
Africa, North—History—1882-	DT176	961.0(3-5)
Africa, North—History—647-1517	DT172	961.0(22-45)
Africa, North—History—To 647	DT168-171	939.7
Africa, North—Maps	G2455-2499	912.61
Africa, North—Maps	G8220-8222	912.61
Africa, North—Religion	BL2462	299.3
Africa, Northwest	DT179.2-.9	939.71/964
Africa, Southern—Church history	BR1446-1458	276.8
Africa, Southern—History—Mfecane period, 1816-ca. 1840	DT1123	968.0009034
Africa, West	DT470-671	966
Africa, West—Church history	BR1460-1463	276.6
Africa, West—History—1884-1960	DT476.2-.23	966.0(23-326)
Africa, West—History—1960-	DT476.5-.523	966.03(26-3)
Africa, West—History—To 1884	DT476	966.0(1-2)
Africa, West—Maps	G2640-2714	912.66
African buffalo	QL737.U53	599.642
African drama (English)	PR9347	822.008
African drama (English)	PR9343	822
African elephant	QL737.P98	599.674
African essays	AC177-189	089.96
African fiction (English)	PR9344	823
African fiction (English)	PR9347.5	823.009
African fish eagle	QL696.F32	598.942
African gray parrot	QL696.P7	598.71
African languages	PL8000-8008	496
African languages—Grammar	PL8008	496.5
African languages—Study and teaching	PL8004	496.071
African literature	PL8010-8014	896
African literature (English)	PR9340-9408	820.9
African literature (French)	PQ3980-3989.2	840
African literature (Portuguese)	PQ9900-9948	869
African periodicals	PN5450-5499	079.6
African poetry (English)	PR9342	821.009
African poetry (English)	PR9346-.5	821.008
African trypanosomiasis	RC186.T82	616.9363
African violets	QK495.G4	583.95
African wild ass	QL737.U62	599.665
Africander cattle	SF199.A3	636.28
Africanized honeybee	QL568.A6	595.799
Afrikaans drama	PT6520	839.362009
Afrikaans drama	PT6570	839.362008
Afrikaans fiction	PT6525	839.363009
Afrikaans fiction	PT6570	839.363008
Afrikaans language	PF861-884	439.36
Afrikaans literature	PT6500-6593.36	839.36
Afrikaans poetry	PT6560	839.361008
Afrikaans poetry	PT6545	839.361008
Afrikaans poetry	PT6515	839.361009
Afrikaans prose literature	PT6525	839.36808
Afrikaans prose literature	PT6590	839.36808
Afrikaans prose literature	PT6570	839.36808
Afrikaans wit and humor	PN6222.S	839.367
Afro-American artists	N6538.N5	700.08996073
Afro-American authors	PS153.N5	810.9896073
Afro-American Catholics	BX1407.N4	282.08996073
Afro-American children	E185.86	305.2308996073
Afro-American children's games	GR103	394.308996073
Afro-American decorative arts	NK839.3.A35	745.08996073
Afro-American engineers	TA157	620.008996073
Afro-American Episcopalians	BX5979	283.7308996073
Afro-American families	E185.86	306.850896073
Afro-American freemasonry	HS875-895	366.108996073
Afro-American lawyers	KF299.A35	349.7308996073
Afro-American mass media	P94.5.A37	302.2308996073
Afro-American Methodists	BX8435-8473	287.8
Afro-American newspapers	PN4882.5	070.484
Afro-American nurses	RT83.5	615.7308996073
Afro-American pharmacists	RS122.5	615.108996073
Afro-American press	PN4882.5	070.484
Afro-American prints	NE539.3.A35	769.08996073
Afro-American psychologists	BF109	150.8996073
Afro-American theater	PN2270.A35	792.08996073
Afro-Americans—Biography	E185.96-.97	920.009296073
Afro-Americans—Civil rights	E185.61	323.1196073
Afro-Americans—Communication	P94.5.A37	302.208996073
Afro-Americans—Crimes against	HV6250.4.E75	362.8808996073
Afro-Americans—Economic conditions	E185.8	330.9730896073
Afro-Americans—Education	LC2701-2853	371.82996073
Afro-Americans—Education (Elementary)	LC2771	372.182996073
Afro-Americans—Education (Higher)	LC2781	378.1982996073
Afro-Americans—Education (Secondary)	LC2779	373.182996073
Afro-Americans—Health and hygiene	RA448.5.N4	613.08996073
Afro-Americans—History	E185.18-.98	973.0496073
Afro-Americans—History—1863-1877	E185.2	973.(7-82)0496073
Afro-Americans—History—1877-1964	E185.6	973.(83-923)0496073
Afro-Americans—History—1964-	E185.615	973.92(3-9)0496073
Afro-Americans—History—To 1863	E185.18	973.(1-7)0496073
Afro-Americans—Housing	HD7288.72U	363.5908996073
Afro-Americans—Medical care	RA448.5.N4	362.108996073
Afro-Americans—Mental health	RC451.5.N4	616.89008996073
Afro-Americans—Mortality	HB1323.B5	304.6408996073

Subject Heading	LC	Dewey
Afro-Americans—Professional education	LC2785	378.01308996073
Afro-Americans—Psychology	E185.625	155.8496073
Afro-Americans—Scholarships, fellowships, etc.	LC2707	371.22308996073
Afro-Americans—Segregation	E185.61	305.896073
Afro-Americans—Services for	HV3181-3185	362.8496073
Afro-Americans—Social conditions	E185.86	973.0496073
Afro-Americans—Social life and customs	E185.86	973.0496073/ 390.08996073
Afro-Americans—Suffrage	JK1924-1929	324.6208996073
Afro-Americans—Vocational education	LC2780	370.11308996073
Afro-Americans and mass media	P94.5.A37	302.2308996073
Afro-Americans in business	E185.8	338.790896073
Afro-Americans in dentistry	RK60.45	617.6008996073
Afro-Americans in mass media	P94.5.A37	302.2308996073
Afro-Americans in medicine	R695	610.8996073
Afro-Brazilian cults	BL2590.B7	299.891
Afroasiatic languages	PJ990	492
Agates	TN997.A35	622.387
Agave	QK495.A26	584.352
Agave products industry	HD9019.A43-.A434	633.577
Age distribution (Demography)	HB1531-1738	305.2
Age distribution (Demography)—[By region or country]	HB1541-1737	305.209(4-9)
Age distribution (Demography)—United States	HB1545-1567	305.20973
Age distribution (Demography)—[United States, By state]	HB1565	305.2097(4-9)
Aged	HQ1060-1064	305.26
Aged	HV1450-1494	362.6
Aged—Anthropometry	GN59.A35	599.940846
Aged—Crimes against	HV6250.4.A34	362.880846
Aged—Diseases	RC952-954.6	618.97
Aged—Dwellings	NA7195.A4	728.0846
Aged—Education	LC5451-5493	371.8246
Aged—Employment	HD6279-6283	331.398
Aged—Government policy	HQ1060-1064	305.26
Aged—Mental health services	RC451.4.A5	362.20846
Aged—Psychology	BF724.8-.85	155.67
Aged—Recreation	GV184	790.1926
Aged—Religious life	BV4580	248.85
Aged—Sexual behavior	HQ30	306.70846
Aged—Surgery	RD145	617.97
Aged—[By region or country]	HV1457-1494	362.609(4-9)
Aged in mass media	P96.A38	305.26
Aged in the Bible	BS680.A34	220.0846
Agency (Law)—Canada	KE1328-1332	346.7102
Agency (Law)—United States	KF1341-1348	346.73029
Aggada	BM516-.5	296.19
Aggressiveness (Psychology)	BF575.A3	155.232
Agincourt, Battle of, 1415	DC101.5.A2	944.026
Agnus Dei (Sacramental)	BX2310.A	264.0209
Agoraphobia	RC552.A44	616.85225
Agrammatism	RC425.5	616.8552
Agressiveness (Psychology) in adolescence	BF724.3.A34	155.51247
Agressiveness (Psychology) in youth	BF724.3.A34	155.51247
Agricultural chemistry	S583-587.5	631.41
Agricultural colleges	S537-539	630.711
Agricultural conservation	S604.5-.64	631.451
Agricultural cooperative credit associations	HG2041-2051	332.31
Agricultural credit	HD1439-1440	332.71
Agricultural ecology	S441-482	577.55
Agricultural education	S530-539	630.7
Agricultural engineering	S671-760	631
Agricultural exhibitions	S550-559	630.74
Agricultural experimental stations	S541-543	630.724
Agricultural extension work	S544-545	630.715
Agricultural geography	S439-481	630.9(4-9)
Agricultural implements	S676-.3	631.3
Agricultural implements, Prehistoric	GN799.A4	630.901
Agricultural instruments	S676.5	631.3
Agricultural laborers	HD1521-1542	331.763
Agricultural laws and legislation—Canada	KE1671-1745	343.71076
Agricultural laws and legislation—England	KD2241-2295	343.42076
Agricultural laws and legislation—United States	KF1681-1755	343.73076
Agricultural machinery	S671-760	631.3
Agricultural machinery	TJ1480-1496	631.3
Agricultural machinery industry	HD9486-.6	338.76313
Agricultural mechanics	S675.3	631.3
Agricultural museums	S549	630.74
Agricultural pests	SB599-999	632.(6-7)
Agricultural pests—Congresses	SB599.2	632.(6-7)06
Agricultural physics	S589-.6	631.43
Agricultural pollution	TD195.A34	577.273
Agricultural prices	HD1447	338.13
Agricultural surveys	S494.5.E8	630.723
Agricultural surveys	S441-451	630.723
Agricultural systems	S439-481	630.11
Agricultural wages	HD4966.A29	331.283
Agricultural wastes as feed	SF99.A37	636.08556
Agriculture	S1-954	630-638
Agriculture—History	S419-481	630.9
Agriculture—International cooperation	HD1428-1431	338.181
Agriculture—Origin	GN799.A4	630.901
Agriculture—Periodicals	S1-19	630.5
Agriculture—Research	S539.5-542	630.72
Agriculture—Rome	S431	630.945632

Subject Heading	LC	Dewey	Subject Heading	LC	Dewey
Agriculture—Safety measures	S565	630.289	Airplanes—Nuclear power plants	TL708	629.134355
Agriculture—Societies, etc.	S20	630.6	Airplanes—Oxygen equipment	TL697.08	629.1344
Agriculture—Study and teaching	S531-539	630.71	Airplanes—Piloting	TL710-713.5	629.13252
Agriculture—Vocational guidance	S494.5.A4	630.23	Airplanes—Pressurization	TL681.P7	629.13442
			Airplanes—Radio equipment	TL693.R2	629.1355
Agriculture and energy	S494.5.E5	631.37	Airplanes—Take-off	TL711.T3	629.1325212
Agriculture, Cooperative	HD1483-1491.5	334.683	Airplanes—Turbine-propeller engines	TL709.3.T8	629.1343532
Agriculture, Prehistoric	S421-431	630.901			
Agroforestry	S494.5.A45	634.99	Airplanes—Turbojet engines	TL709.3.T83	629.1343533
Agropastoral systems	S494.5.A47	630	Airplanes—Turbojet engines—Air intakes	TL709.5.I5	629.134353
Aid to families with dependent children	HV697-700	362.713			
			Airplanes—Wings	TL672-673	629.13432
Aids to air navigation	TL695-696	629.1352	Airplanes—Wings, Swept-back	TL673.S9	629.13432
Aikido	GV1114.35	796.8154			
Ailanthus moth	QL561.S2	595.78	Airplanes, Company	HE9795-9796	387.7
Ainu	DS832	952.004946	Airplanes, Military	TL685.3	623.746
Ainu language	PL495	494.6	Airplanes, Military	UG1240-1242	358.4183
Air	QC161-166.5	533.6	Airplanes, Military—Turrets	VG90-95	359.94834
Air conditioning	TH7687-7688	697.93	Airplanes, Military—Turrets	UG630-635	623.746
Air defenses	UG730-735	358.414	Airport buildings	NA6300-6307	725.39
Air forces	UG622-1425	358.4	Airport buildings	TL725.3.B8	629.136
Air forces—Congresses	UG623	358.4006	Airport control towers	TL725.3.C64	629.1366
Air forces—History	UG625	358.4009	Airport slot allocation	HE9797.4.S56	387.7364
Air forces—Insignia	UG1180-1185	358.414	Airports	HE9797-.5	387.736
Air forces—Societies, etc.	UG622	358.4006	Airports	TL725-733	629.136
Air interdiction	UG700	358.41422	Airports—Visibility	TL557.V5	629.136
Air mail service	HE6238	383.144	Airships	TL650-668.1	629.13324
Air masses	QC880.4.A5	551.5512	Airways	TL725-733	387.72
Air pilots	TL712	629.13252	Akan language	PL8046.A63	496.3385
Air pilots, Military	UG626-.2	358.40092	Akkadian language	PJ3101	492.1
Air quality	TD883	628.53	Alabama	F321-355	976.1
Air raid shelters	TH1097	690.5	Alabama—Gazetteers	F324	917.61003
Air traffic control	TL725.3.T7	629.1366	Alabama—History—1819-1950	F326	976.10(5-63)
Air traffic controllers	HD8039.A425	629.1366092			
Air warfare	UG630	358.4	Alabama—History—1951-	F330-.3	976.106(3-4)
Air—Pollution	TD881-890	628.53			
Air-brakes	TF420-430	625.25	Alabama—History—To 1819	F326	976.105
Air-compressors	TJ990-992	621.51			
Aircraft cabins	TL681.C3	629.13445	Alabama—Maps	G3970-3974	912.761
Aircraft carriers	V874-875	359.9435	Alabama—National Guard	UA50-59	355.3709761
Aircraft gas-turbines—Combustion chambers	TL709.5.C55	629.134353	Alabama—Periodicals	F321	976.1005
			Alaska	F901-951	979.8
Aircraft industry	HD9711-.2	338.4738773	Alaska—Gazetteers	F902	917.98008
Airdrop	UC330-335	355.83	Alaska—History—1867-1959	F908-909	979.80(3-4)
Airframes	TL671.6	629.13431			
Airlift, Military	UC330-335	355.83	Alaska—History—1959-	F910-.7	979.805
Airlines—Rates	HE9783-.75	387.712	Alaska—History—To 1867	F907	979.80(1-2)
Airplane ambulances	RA996.5	362.188	Alaska—Maps	G4370-4374	912.798
Airplanes	TL670-723	629.13334	Alaska—National Guard	UA60-69	355.3709798
Airplanes—Air conditioning	TL681.A5	629.13442	Alaska—Periodicals	F901	979.8005
Airplanes—Electronic equipment	TL693-696	629.1355	Albania	DR901-998	939.8/949.65
			Albania—Biography	DR928-93	920.0398/ 920.04965
Airplanes—Flight testing	TL671.7	629.13453			
Airplanes—Fuel	TL704.7	629.134351	Albania—Census	HA1620.5	314.965
Airplanes—Inspection	TL671.7	629.13452	Albania—Civilization	DR922	939.8/949.65
Airplanes—Jet propulsion	TL709-.5	629.134353	Albania—Congresses	DR903.5	939.8006/ 949.65006
Airplanes—Landing	TL711.L3	629.1325213			
Airplanes—Landing gear	TL682-683	629.134381			
Airplanes—Motors	TL701-704.7	629.13435			

Subject Heading	LC	Dewey	Subject Heading	LC	Dewey
Albania—Description and travel	DR914-918	913.9804/ 914.96504	Alcoholism	RC564.7-565.9	616.861
			Alcoholism—Periodicals	HV5001-5002	362.29205
Albania—Economic conditions	HC402	330.94965	Alcoholism—Psychological aspects	HV5045	616.8610019
Albania—Gazetteers	DR90	913.98003/ 914.965003	Alcoholism and crime	HV5053-5055	362.292
			Alcoholism and employment	HF5549.5.A4	658.3822
Albania—History	DR927-977.25	939.8/949.65	Alcoholism counseling	HV5275-5283	362.29286
Albania—History	DR965	949.65	Aleut language	PM31-34	497.19
Albania—History— 1501-1912	DR961-969	949.6501	Aleutian Islands (Alaska)	F951	979.84
			Alexandrine War, 48-47 B.C.	DT92-.7	932.021
Albania—History— 1840-1912	DR965.9-969	949.6501	Algae	QK564-580.5	579.8
			Algebra	QA150-272.5	512
Albania—History— 1878-1912	DR966	949.6501	Algebra—Study and teaching	QA159	512.0071
			Algebra, Abstract	QA162	512.02
Albania—History— 1912-1944	DR970-975	949.6502	Algebra, Boolean	QA10.3	511.324
			Algebra, Universal	QA251	512
Albania—History— 1944-1990	DR976-977.25	949.650(2-3)	Algebraic fields	QA247-.45	512.3
			Algebraic functions	QA341	512.74
Albania—History—1990-	DR976-977.25	949.650(3-4)	Algebraic logic	QA10-.3	511.324
Albania—History—Axis occupation, 1939-1944	DR975	949.6502	Algeria	DT271-299	939.71/965
			Algeria—Census	HA4683	316.5
Albania—History—June Revolution, 1924	DR973	949.6502	Algeria—Civilization	DT282	939.71/965
			Algeria—Description and travel	DT277.8-280.2	913.97104/ 916.504
Albania—History—Peasant Uprising, 1914-1915	DR972	949.6502	Algeria—Economic conditions	HC815	330.965
Albania—History—To 1501	DR954-960.5	939.8/949.6501	Algeria—Gazetteers	DT274	913.971003/ 916.5003
Albania—History—Turkish War, 15th century	DR959-960.5	949.6501	Algeria—History	DT283-299	939.71/965
Albania—History— Uprising, 1912	DR969	949.6502	Algeria—History— 1516-1830	DT291-292	965.02
Albania—Maps	G2005-2009	912.4965	Algeria—History— 1830-1962	DT294-295.3	965.03
Albania—Periodicals	DR90	939.8005/ 949.65005	Algeria—History— 1945-1962	DT295-.3	965.03
Albanian language	PG9501-9599	491.991	Algeria—History—1962-	DT295.5-.55	965.05
Albanian literature	PG9601-9665	891.991	Algeria—History— 647-1516	DT289	965.02
Albanian philology	PG9501-9513	491.991	Algeria—History— English Expedition, 1816	DT291	965.02
Alberta—Gazetteers	F1975.4	917.123003			
Alberta—History	F1075-1080	971.23			
Alberta—Maps	G3500-3504	912.7123	Algeria—History—English expedition, 1620-1621	DT291	965.02
Alberta—Periodicals	F1075	971.23005			
Albinos and albinism	GN199	599.945	Algeria—History—Expedition of Charles V, 1541	DT292	965.02
Alchemy	QD13	540.112			
Alchemy	QD23.3-26.5	540.112	Algeria—History—French Expedition, 1830	DT294	965.03
Alcoholism—[Other regions or countries]	HV5301-5722	362.29209(4-9)			
Alcohol	TP593	663.1	Algeria—History— Revolution, 1954-1962	DT295	965.046
Alcohol as fuel	TP358	662.6692			
Alcohol—Law and legislation	K3651-3654	344.042	Algeria—History—Spanish Expedition, 1775	DT291	965.02
Alcohol—Law and legislation—England	KD3466-3480	344.42042	Algeria—History—To 647	DT288	939.71
			Algeria—Maps	G8240-8244	912.65
Alcohol—Law and legislation—United States	KF3901-3925	344.7305	Algonquian Indians	E99.A35	973.04973
			Algonquian languages	PM600-609	497.3
Alcoholic liver diseases	RC848.A42	616.3624	Algonquin Indians	E99.A349	973.04973
Alcoholic psychoses	RC525-527	616.861	Alien labor	HD6300	331.62
Alcoholics' spouses	HV5132	362.2923	Aliens—England	KD4130-4139	342.42083
Alcoholics—Family relationships	HV5132	362.2923	Aliens—United States	KF4800-4848	342.73083
			Alimentary canal	QM301-367	611.3
Alcoholism	HV5001-5722	362.292	Alkali lands	S595	631.42

Subject Heading	LC	Dewey	Subject Heading	LC	Dewey
Alkalies	QD172.A4	546.38	Ambivalence	BF575.A45	152.4
Alkalies	TN895-897	669.725	Ambulance service	RA995-996	362.188
Alkalies	TP222-223	661.03	Ambulances	TL235.8	629.22234
Alkaloids	RM666.A4	615.321	Ambulatory blood pressure	RC683.5.A43	616.132075
Alkaloids	QD421-.7	547.72	monitoring		
All Saints' Day	BV67	263.98	Ambulatory	RC683.5.A45	616.1207547
All Souls' Day	BV50.A4	263.9	electrocardiography		
All Souls' Day	GT4995.A4	394.264	Ambulatory	RC386.6.A45	616.8047547
All terrain cycling	GV1056	796.63	electroencephalography		
Allegiance	JC328	323.6	Ambulatory surgery	RD110-.5	617.024
Allegory	PN56.A5	808.8015	Amebiasis	RC121.A5	616.936
Allergy	RC583-598	616.97	Amebiasis	RA644.A57	614.516
Allergy	RA645.A44	614.5993	America	E	970/980
Allergy	QR188	571.972	America—Biography	E17	920.07/920.08
Allergy in children	RJ386-.5	618.9297	America—Colonization	JV221-231	325.(7-8)
Alligator hunting	SK305.A	799.2798	America—Discovery and	E101-135	970.01/980.01
Alligators	QL666.C925	597.98	exploration		
Alloys	TN690	669.95	America—Gazetteers	E14	917.003/
Alluvial plains	GB591-598	551.453			918.003
Almanacs	AY	030	America—History	E16-18.85	970/980
Almanacs	QC999	551.6365	America—History	F	970-989
Almanacs—History	AY30-39	030.9	America—Maps	G3290-5669	912.7
Almanacs—America	AY51-381	031	America—Periodicals	E11	970.005/
Almanacs—Australia	AY1600-1636	032.0994			980.005
Almanacs—Canada	AY410-425	031.0971	American Samoa	DU819.A1	996.13
Almanacs—Germany	AY850-860	033.1	American Samoa—Census	HA4018.5	319.613
Almanacs—Great Britain	AY830-839	034.1	American bison	QL737.U53	599.643
Almanacs—Italy	AY890-899	035.1	American bison	SF401.A45	636.292
Almanacs—Portugal	AY1010-1019	036.9	American diaries	PS669	818.3
Almanacs—Spain	AY1000-1009	036.1	American diaries	PS409	818.03
Almshouses	HV61	362.585	American drama	PS330-351	812.009
Alpenhorn music	M110	788.92	American drama	PS623-635	812.008
Alpha rays	QC793.5.A22-.A229	539.7232	American drama (Comedy)	PS336.C7	812.052309
			American drama (Tragedy)	PS336.T7	812.051209
Alphabets	P211-214	411	American drama—Study	PS335	812.0071
Alpine gardens	SB459	635.9528	and teaching		
Alps	DQ820-829	949.47	American essays	AC1-8	081
Alps—Maps	G6035-6036	912.4947	American essays	PS420-428	814.009
Altaic lanugages	PL1-9	494	American essays	PS680-688	814.008
Altars	BV195-196	247.1	American fiction	PZ1	813
Altars	NA5060	726.5291	American fiction	PS371-379	813.009
Altars, Buddhist	BQ5070-5075	294.3437	American letters	PS670-678	816.008
Altered states of	BF1045.A48	154.4	American letters	PS410-418	816.009
consciousness			American literature	PS	810
Alternative medicine	R733	615.5	American literature—	PS153-490	810.9
Alternatives to imprisonment	HV9276.5	364.68	History and criticism		
Altitude, Influence of	QP82.2.A4	571.49	American literature—	PS208	810.900(2-3)
Alto horn music	M110	788.974	1783-1850		
Altruism	BJ1474	171.8	American literature—	PS201-214	810.9003
Aluminum alloys	TA480.A6	620.186	19th century		
Aluminum, Structural	TA480.A6	620.186	American literature—	PS221-228	810.9005
Aluminum—Metallurgy	TN775	669.722	20th century		
Alvars	BL1171	294.5213	American literature—	PS508.N3	810.80896073
Alzheimer's disease	RC523-.2	616.831	Afro-American authors		
Amateur circus	GV1838	791.3	American literature—	PS185-191	810.9001
Amateur plays	PN6119.9	792.0222	Colonial period,		
Amateur radio stations	TK9956	621.38416	ca. 1600-1775		
Amateur theater	PN3151-3171	792.0222	American literature—	PS193	810.9002
Amazons	BL820.A6	292.13	Revolutionary period,		
Amazons	HQ1139	305.409	1775-1783		
Amber	TN885	622.339			

Subject Heading	LC	Dewey
American literature—Women authors	PS147-151	810.99287
American literature—Women authors	PS508.W7	810.809287
American loyalists	E277	973.343
American newspapers	PN4840-4899	051
American periodicals	PN4840-4900	071
American poetry	PS	811
American poetry—1783-1850	PS319	811.209
American poetry—19th century	PS316-321	811.309
American poetry—20th century	PS324	811.509
American poetry—Colonial period, ca 1600-1775	PS312	811.109
American poetry—Revolutional period, 1775-1783	PS314	811.209
American poetry—Study and teaching	PS306-.5	811.071
American poetry—Afro-American authors	PS591.N4	811.0080896073
American poetry—Women authors	PS589	811.00809287
American prose literature	PS642-659.2	818.08
American prose literature	PS360-379	818.08
American prose literature—Colonial period, ca. 1600-1775	PS366	818.08
American prose literature—Revolutionary period, 1775-1783	PS367-369	818.08
American wit and humor	PN6157-6162	817.008
American wit and humor	PS430-438	817.009
Americanism (Catholic controversy)	BX1407.A5	282.73
Americanization	JK1758	323.60973
Amicicide (Military science)	U167	355.422
Amines in the body	QP801.A48	572.548
Amino acid sequence	QP551	572.633
Amino acids	QP561-563	572.65
Amino acids	QD431-.7	547.75
Amino acids in human nutrition	QP561	613.282
Amish	BX8129.A5-.A6	289.73092
Ammunition	UF700-770	358.1282
Amnesia	RC394.A5	616.85232
Amniocentesis	RG628.3.A48	618.3204275
Amoeba	QL368.A5	579.432
Amon (Egyptian deity)	BL2450.A45	299.31
Amphibious warfare	U261	355.46
Amplifiers (Electronics)	TK7871.2-.58	621.381535
Amplifiers (Electronics)	TK6565.A55	621.38412
Amputation	RD553	617.58059
Amsterdam (Netherlands)	DJ411.A5-59	949.2352
Amulets	GR600	398.45
Amulets (Buddhism)	BQ4570.A4	294.3437
Amulets (Islam)	BP190.5.A5	297.39
Amusement parks	GV1851-1860	791.068
Amusements—Law and legislation—England	KD3523	344.42099
Amusements—Law and legislation—United States	KF3987	344.73099
Amycus (Greek mythology)	BL820.A63	292.13
Anabaptists	BX4929-4946	284.3
Anaerobic bacteria	QR89.5	579.3149
Anagrams	GV1507.A5	793.734
Analgesics	RM319	615.783
Analog-to-digital converters	TK7887.6	621.39814
Analogy	BD190	169
Analogy (Religion)	BL210	210
Analysis of variance	QA279-.2	519.538
Analytic functions	QA331	515.73
Analytical toxicology	RA1221-1223	615.907
Anarchism	HX821-970.7	335.83
Anarchism—[By region or country]	HX841-970.7	335.8309(4-9)
Anatolian languages	P1001	491.998
Anatomical museums	QM51	611.0074
Anatomy, Artistic	NC760-783.8	743.49
Anatomy, Comparative	QL801-950.9	571.3
Anatomy, Surgical and topographical	QM531-549	611.9
Ancestor worship	BL467	291.213
Anchors	VM791	623.862
Andorra	DC921-930	946.79
Andrology	RC875-899.5	616.65
Anecdotes	PN6259-6268	808.882
Anemia	RC641-.7	616.152
Anesthesia in obstetrics	RG732-733	617.9682
Aneurysms	RC693	616.133
Angels	BT960-968	235.3
Angels	BL477	291.215
Angels (Islam)	BP166.89	297.215
Anger	BF575.A5	152.47
Anger	BJ1535.A6	179.8
Anger	RC569.5.A53	152.47
Angina pectoris	RC685.A6	616.122
Angiocardiography	RC683.5.A5	616.1207572
Angiography	RC691.6.A53	616.1307572
Angioplasty	RD598.5	617.413
Angiosperms	QK495	580
Angiosperms, Fossil	QE980-983	561
Anglican Communion	BX5001-5009	283
Anglican Communion—History	BX5005	283.09
Anglican Communion—Sermons	BX5008	252.03
Anglican orders	BX5178	255.83
Anglo-Dutch War, 1664-1667	DJ180-182	949.204
Anglo-Dutch War, 1780-1784	DJ205-206	949.204
Anglo-French War, 1666-1667	D274.5-.6	940.252
Anglo-Saxon race	CB216-220	941.0042
Anglo-Saxons	DA150-162	941.0892/ 942.017
Angola—Census	HA4710	316.73

Subject Heading	LC	Dewey
Angola—Civilization	DT1302	967.3
Angola—Description and travel	DT1282-1286	916.7304
Angola—Economic conditions	HC950	330.9673
Angola—Gazetteers	DT1264	916.73003
Angola—History	DT1314-1436	967.3
Angola—History— To 1482	DT1357	967.301
Angola—History— 1482-1648	DT1357-1369	967.301
Angola—History— 1648-1885	DT1373-1382	967.302
Angola—History— 1885-1961	DT1385-1396	967.30(2-3)
Angola—History— Civil War, 1975-	DT1428	967.304
Angola—History— Revolution, 1961-1975	DT1398-1417	967.303
Angola—Maps	G8640-8644	912.673
Anguilla	F2033	972.973
Anguilla—Maps	G5045-5049	912.72973
Animal behavior	QL750-795	591.5
Animal biotechnology	SF140.B54	636.0821
Animal breeding	SF105-109	636.082
Animal burrowing	QL756.15	591.5648
Animal communication	QL776	591.59
Animal culture	SF	636
Animal defenses	QL759	591.47
Animal ecology	QH540-549.5	591.7
Animal feeding	SF94.5-99	636.084
Animal flight	QP310.F5	573.798
Animal health	SF600-1100	636.0893
Animal intelligence	QL785	591.513
Animal locomotion	QP301-310	612.76
Animal navigation	QL782	573.87
Animal nutrition	SF94.5-99	636.085
Animal populations	QL752	591.788
Animal products	TS1950-1982	664.9
Animal psychology	QL785-.27	591.5
Animal rights	HV4701-4890.7	179.3
Animal sculpture	NB1940-1942	731.832
Animal sounds	QL765	591.594
Animal tracks	QL768	591.479
Animal training	GV1829-1831	791.32
Animal weapons	QL940	591.47
Animal welfare	HV4701-4959	636.0832
Animal worship	BL439-443	291.212
Animals as carriers of disease	RA639-641	614.43
Animals as carriers of disease	SF740	636.089456
Animals in art	NC780-783.8	743.6
Animals in art	ND1380-1383	758.3
Animals, Fossil	QE760.8-899.2	560
Animals, Mythical	GR820-830	398.369
Animals—Diseases	SF600-1100	636.0896
Animals—Food	QL756.5-.57	591.5(3-4)
Animals—Habitations	QL756-.15	591.564
Animals—War use	UH87-100	355.424
Animated films	NC1765-1766	741.58

Subject Heading	LC	Dewey
Animated films	PN1997.5	741.58
Animation (Cinematography)	TR897.5-.75	778.5347
Animism	GN471	291.21
Annapolis (Md.)	F189.A6	975.256
Annihilation reactions	QC794	539.75
Annihilationism	BT930	236.23
Annuals (Plants)	SB422	635.9312
Annuities	HG8790-8793	368.37
Anorexia nervosa	RC552.A5	616.85262
Antacids	RM365	615.73
Antarctica	G845-890	919.89
Antarctica	HA4020-.5	319.89
Antarctica—Maps	G3100-3102	912.989
Antartica—Maps	G9800-9804	912.989
Antelopes	QL737.U53	599.64
Anthems	M2038-2099	782.265
Anthologies	PN6010-6065	808.8
Anthracite coal	TN820-823	622.335
Anthrax	RC121.A6	616.956
Anthrax	SF787	636.0896956
Anthropologists	GN20-21	301.092
Anthropology	GN	301
Anthropology—Methodology	GN33-34.3	301.01
Anthropology—Research	GN42-46	301.072
Anthropometry	GN51-59	599.94
Anthropomorphism	BL215	211
Anthroposophy	BP595-597	299.935
Anti-Nazi movement	DD256.3-.4	943.086
Antiaircraft guns	UF625	358.1382
Antiallergic agents	RC588.C45	616.97
Antibacterial agents	RM409	615.329
Antibiotics	RM265-267	615.329
Antibiotics in animal nutrition	SF98.A5	636.08557
Antibiotics in veterinary medicine	SF918.A5	636.0895329
Antichrist	BT985	236
Antidepressants	RM332-.3	615.788
Antietam, Battle of, Md., 1862	E474.65	973.73(2-3)
Antifertility vaccines	RG136.85	613.9432
Antigen-antibody reactions	QR187-.3	571.9677
Antigens	QR186.5-.6	571.9645
Antigua	F2035	972.974
Antigua—Maps	G5050-5054	912.72974
Antilles, Greater	F1741-1991	972.9(1-5)
Antilles, Lesser	F2001-2151	972.9(7-8)
Antimony	QD181.S3	546.716
Antineoplastic agents	RC271.C5	616.99406
Antiprotons	QC793.5.P72-.P729	539.72123
Antiques	NK	745.1
Antiques—Dictionaries	NK30	745.103
Antiques—Encyclopedias	NK28	745.103
Antiques—Exhibitions	NK512-520	745.1074
Antiques—Periodicals	NK1-9	745.105
Antiques—Private collections	NK530-570	745.1074
Antiques—Reproduction	NK1128	745.102872
Antiques—Study and teaching	NK50-440	745.1071

Subject Heading	LC	Dewey	Subject Heading	LC	Dewey
Antiquities—Collection and preservation	CC135-137	930.10288	Aquatic animals—Antarctic Ocean	QL126.5	591.777
Antisocial personality disorders	RC555	616.858	Aquatic animals—Arctic Ocean	QL126	591.7732
Antisubmarine aircraft	UG1242.A25	358.4283	Aquatic animals—Atlantic Ocean	QL127-135	591.773
Antitank weapons	UF628	358.12	Aquatic animals—Indian Ocean	QL137	591.775
Antitoxins	RM278	615.375	Aquatic animals—Pacific Ocean	QL138	591.774
Antitrust law—England	KD2218-2220	343.420721	Aquatic biology	QH90-100	578.76
Ants	QL568.F7	595.796	Aquatic ecology	QH541.5.W3	577.6
Anxiety	BF575.A6	152.46	Aquatic exercises	GV838.53.E94	613.716
Anxiety	RC531	616.85223	Aquatic exercises	RA781.17	613.71
Anxiety in children	BF723.A5	155.41246	Aquatic plants	QK102-105	581.76
Anxiety in children	RJ506.A58	618.9285223	Aquatic plants	QK930-935	581.76
Aorta	QM191	611.13	Aquatic sports	GV771-840	797
Aorta—Diseases	RC691	616.138	Aquatint	NE2230	766.3
Aortic aneurysms	RC693	616.138	Aqueducts	TD398	628.15
Apache Indians	E99.A6	973.04972	Arab countries	DS36-39.2	909.0974927
Apartment houses	NA7860-7863	728.314	Arab countries—Civilization	DS36.77-.88	909.0974927
Apartment houses	TX957-959	647.92	Arab countries—History	DS37-39.2	909.0974927
Apes	QL737.P96	599.88	Arab countries—History— 1517-1918	DS38.8	909.09749270 (5-821)
Aphasia	RC425-.7	616.8552			
Aphorisms and apothegms	PN6269-6278	398.9	Arab countries—History— 1798-	DS38.9	909.097492708
Aphrodisiacs	RM386	615.766			
Apnea	RC737-.5	616.2	Arab countries—History— 20th century	DS39	909.0974927082
Apocalyptic literature	BS646	220.046			
Apocryphal books (New Testament)	BS2831-2970	229	Arab countries—History— Arab Revolt, 1916-1918	DS39	909.09749270821
Apologetics	BT1095-1255	239	Arab countries—Politics and government	JQ1850	320.9174927
Apologetics—Early church, ca. 30-600	BT1115	230.1			
Apologetics—History	BT1109-1115	239.09	Arabic alphabet	PJ6123	492.711
Apostles	BS2440	225.92	Arabic drama	PJ7665	892.72008
Apostolic Fathers	BR60-67	270.1092	Arabic drama	PJ7565	892.72009
Appalachian dulcimer music	M142.A7	787.75	Arabic essays	AC105-106	089.927
Apparitions	BF1444-1486	133.1	Arabic language	PJ6001-7144	492.7
Appellate courts—England	KD7132-7216	347.4203	Arabic language—Dialects	PJ6701-6901	492.77
Appellate courts—Scotland	KDC110-113	347.41103	Arabic language— Dialects—Arabian Peninsula	PJ6841-6880	492.77
Appellate procedure	K5495	347.035			
Appellate procedure— United States	KF8741-8752	347.7305	Arabic language— Dialects—Egypt	PJ6771-6799	492.77
Appendectomy	RD542	617.5545			
Appendix (Anatomy)	QM345	611.345	Arabic language— Dialects—Iraq	PJ6821-6830	492.77
Apperception	BF321-323	153.73			
Apperception	LB1067	153.73	Arabic language— Dialects—Lebanon	PJ6810	492.77
Appetizers	TX740	641.812			
Application software	QA76.76.A65	005.3	Arabic language— Dialects—Palestine	PJ6805-6808	492.77
Applications for positions	HF5383	650.14			
Applied human geography	GF24	304.2	Arabic language— Dialects—Spain	PJ6751-6760	492.77
Appomattox Campaign, 1865	E477.67	973.738			
			Arabic language— Dialects—Syria	PJ6811-6820	492.77
Apprentices	HD4881-4885	331.55			
Approximation theory	QA221-224	512.924	Arabic language— Dictionaries	PJ6031	492.73
April Fools' Day	GT4995.A6	394.262			
Aquaculture	SH20.5-191	639.8	Arabic language— Etymology	PJ6172-6199	492.72
Aquaculture—History	SH21	639.809			
Aquaculture—[By region or country]	SH34-133	639.809(4-9)	Arabic language—Grammar	PJ6101-6599	492.75
			Arabic language—Study and teaching	PJ6065-6069	492.7071
Aquariums	SF456-458.83	597.073			
Aquariums, Public	QL78-79	597.073			
Aquarius (Astrology)	BF1727.7	133.5276			
Aquatic animals	QL120-149	591.77	Arabic literature	PJ7501-8518	892.7

Subject Heading	LC	Dewey
Arabic literature—Africa	PJ8195-8390	892.7
Arabic literature—America	PJ8500-8517	892.7
Arabic literature—Asia	PJ8025-8190	892.7
Arabic literature—Europe	PJ8395-8490	892.7
Arabic literature—Middle East	PJ8030-8129	892.7
Arabic philology	PJ6001-6071	492.7
Arabic poetry	PJ7541-7561	892.71009
Arabic poetry	PJ7631-7661	892.71008
Arabic prose literature	PJ7571-7577	892.7808
Arabic prose literature	PJ7671-7677	892.7808
Arachnida	QL451-459.2	595.4
Aramaic language	PJ5201-5329	492.2
Arapaho Indians	E99.A7	973.04973
Arapaho language	PM635	497.3
Arbitration and award—Canada	KE8618	347.7109
Arbitration and award—England	KD7645-7647	347.4209
Arbitration and award—United States	KF9085-9086	347.7309
Arbitration, Industrial	HD5481-5630.7	331.89143
Arbitration, Industrial—[By region or country]	HD5501-5630.7	331.8914309 (4-9)
Arbovirus infections	QR201.A72	571.992562
Arboviruses	QR398	579.2562
Arc measures	QB291	526.30287
Arch dams	TC547	627.8
Archaeological geology	CC77.5	930.1028
Archaeological surveying	CC73-75	930.1028
Archaeologists	CC110-115	930.1092
Archaeology	CC	930.1
Archaeology	GN700-890	930.1
Archaeology—Dictionaries	CC70	930.103
Archaeology—Directories	CC120-125	930.1025
Archaeology—Methodology	CC73-75	930.101
Archaeology—Periodicals	CC1-15	930.105
Archaeology—Philosophy	CC72-81	930.101
Archaeology—Societies, etc.	CC20-39	930.106
Archdeacons	BX5179	262.(12/03)
Archdeacons	BX1911	262.02
Archery	GV1185-1189	799.32
Arches	NA2880	721.41
Architects	NA	720.92
Architects—Professional ethics	NA1995	174.972
Architectural acoustics	NA2800	729.29
Architectural design	NA2750-2793	721
Architectural drawing	NA2700-2780	720.222
Architectural models	NA2790	720.22
Architectural photography	TR659	778.94
Architecture	NA	720
Architecture—Aesthetics	NA2500	720.1
Architecture—Biography	NA40	720.92
Architecture—Competitions	NA2335-2360	720.79
Architecture—Composition, proportion, etc.	NA2760	729.11
Architecture—Conservation and restoration	NA105-112	720.288
Architecture—Designs and plans	NA2600-2635	720.222

Subject Heading	LC	Dewey
Architecture—Details	NA2835-3060	721
Architecture—Directories	NA50-60	720.25
Architecture—Encyclopedias	NA31	720.3
Architecture—History	NA190-1555.5	722-724
Architecture—Periodicals	NA1-9	720.5
Architecture—Societies, etc.	NA10-17	720.6
Architecture—Study and teaching	NA2000-2320	720.71
Architecture—Afghanistan	NA1492-.3	720.9581
Architecture—Africa	NA1580-1599	720.96
Architecture—Africa, East	NA1597-.6	720.9676
Architecture—Africa, West	NA1598-1599	720.966
Architecture—Algeria	NA1588-.3	720.965
Architecture—Argentina	NA830-839	720.982
Architecture—Arid regions	NA2542.A73	720.9154
Architecture—Asiatic Russia	NA1492.6-1499	720.957
Architecture—Australia	NA1600-1605.3	720.994
Architecture—Austria	NA1001 1011.6	720.9436
Architecture—Bahamas	NA800-802	720.97296
Architecture—Belgium	NA1161-1173.3	720.9493
Architecture—Bolivia	NA840-849	720.984
Architecture—Brazil	NA850-859	720.981
Architecture—Bulgaria	NA1381-1393.3	720.9499
Architecture—Burma	NA1512-.3	720.9591
Architecture—Cambodia	NA1515-.3	720.9596
Architecture—Canada	NA740-749.5	720.971
Architecture—Central America	NA760-790	720.9728
Architecture—Chile	NA860-869	720.983
Architecture—China	NA1540-1549.6	720.951
Architecture—Colombia	NA870-879	720.9861
Architecture—Costa Rica	NA773-775	720.97286
Architecture—Cuba	NA803-805	720.97291
Architecture—Czechoslovakia	NA1023-1034.5	720.9437
Architecture—Denmark	NA1211-1223.3	720.9489
Architecture—Ecuador	NA880-889	720.9866
Architecture—El Salvador	NA788-790	720.97284
Architecture—Ethiopia	NA1586-.3	720.963
Architecture—Europe	NA950-1455	720.94
Architecture—Finland	NA1455.F5	720.94897
Architecture—France	NA1041-1059	720.944
Architecture—French Guiana	NA897	720.9882
Architecture—Germany	NA1061-1089	720.943
Architecture—Great Britain	NA961-981	720.941
Architecture—Greece	NA1091-1103	720.9495
Architecture—Guatemala	NA776-778	720.97281
Architecture—Guyana	NA895	720.9881
Architecture—Haiti	NA806-808	720.97294
Architecture—Honduras	NA779-781	720.97283
Architecture—Hungary	NA1012-1022	720.9439
Architecture—Iceland	NA1241-1253.3	720.94912
Architecture—India	NA1501-1510.3	720.954
Architecture—Indonesia	NA1526-.8	720.9598
Architecture—Iran	NA1480-1489	720.955
Architecture—Iraq	NA1467-1469	720.9567
Architecture—Israel	NA1477-1479	720.95694
Architecture—Italy	NA1111-1123.3	720.945
Architecture—Jamaica	NA809-811	720.97292
Architecture—Japan	NA1550-1559.6	720.952
Architecture—Jordan	NA1479.6-.8	720.95695

Subject Heading	LC	Dewey	Subject Heading	LC	Dewey
Architecture—Korea	NA1560-1570.3	720.9519	Architecture, Italian	NA295-340	722.70937
Architecture—Laos	NA1516-.3	720.9594	Architecture, Medieval	NA350-497	723
Architecture—Lebanon	NA1476.6-.8	720.95692	Architecture, Modern	NA500-680	724
Architecture—Libya	NA1589-.3	720.9612	Architecture, Modern—	NA627-640	724.19
Architecture—Malaysia	NA1525-.8	720.9595	17th-18th centuries		
Architecture—Mexico	NA750-759	720.972	Architecture, Modern—	NA645-670	724.5
Architecture—Morocco	NA1590-.3	720.964	19th century		
Architecture—Netherlands	NA1141-1153.3	720.9492	Architecture, Modern—	NA673-682	724.6
Architecture—New Zealand	NA1606-1608	720.993	20th century		
Architecture—Nicaragua	NA782-784	720.97285	Architecture, Norman	NA423-429	723.4
Architecture—Norway	NA1261-1273.3	720.9481	Architecture, Oriental	NA1460-1579	720.95
Architecture—Oceania	NA1610-1613	720.99(5-6)	Architecture, Oriental	NA1460-1570.3	720.95
Architecture—Pakistan	NA1510.7-.73	720.95491	Architecture, Primitive	GN414	722
Architecture—Panama	NA785-787	720.97287	Architecture, Primitive	NA205-207	722
Architecture—Paraguay	NA900-909	720.9892	Architecture, Queen Anne	NA630	720.94209033
Architecture—Peru	NA910-919	720.985	Architecture, Renaissance	NA510-575	724.12
Architecture—Philippines	NA1527-1529	720.9599	Architecture, Rococo	NA590	724.19
Architecture—Poland	NA1466.P6	720.9438	Architecture, Roman	NA310-340	722.7
Architecture—Poland	NA1466.P6	720.9438	Architecture, Romanesque	NA390-419	723.4
Architecture—Portugal	NA1321-1333.3	720.9469	Architecture, Spanish	NA1301-1313.3	720.946
Architecture—Puerto Rico	NA812-814	720.97295	Archive buildings	CD981-986.5	725.15
Architecture—Romania	NA1421-1433.3	720.9498	Archives	CD921-4280	027
Architecture—Russia	NA1181-1199	720.947	Archives—Dictionaries	CD945	027.003
Architecture—Saudi Arabia	NA1470-1472	720.9538	Archives—Directories	CD941	027.0025
Architecture—Scandinavia	NA1201-1293.3	720.948	Archives—History	CD995-4280	027.009
Architecture—South America	NA820-939	720.98	Archives—Law and	KD3753-3755	344.42092
Architecture—Southern	NA1591.7-1596.6	720.968	legislation—England		
Africa			Archives—Law and	KF4325	344.73092
Architecture—Spain	NA1301-1313.3	720.946	legislation—United		
Architecture—Sri Lanka	NA1510.6-.63	720.95493	States		
Architecture—Surinam	NA896	720.9883	Archives—Methodology	CD973	027.0028
Architecture—Sweden	NA1281-1293.3	720.9485	Archives—Periodicals	CD921	027.005
Architecture—Switzerland	NA1341-1353.3	720.9494	Archives—Philosophy	CD947	027.001
Architecture—Syria	NA1489.6-.8	720.95691	Archives—Study and	CD987-988	027.0071
Architecture—Thailand	NA1521-1523	720.9593	teaching		
Architecture—Tunisia	NA1591-.3	720.9611	Archives—[By region	CD1000-4280	027.0(1-9)
Architecture—Turkey	NA1361-1375	720.9561	or country]		
Architecture—United States	NA705-738	720.973	Archives—Africa	CD2300-2491	027.06
Architecture—Uruguay	NA920-929	720.9895	Archives—Asia	CD2001-2291	027.05
Architecture—Venezuela	NA930-939	720.987	Archives—Austria	CD1120-1149.5	027.0436
Architecture—Vietnam	NA1514-.63	720.9597	Archives—Balkan Peninsula	CD1930-1989.5	027.0496
Architecture—West Indies	NA791-815	720.9729	Archives—Belgium	CD1670-1689.5	027.0493
Architecture—Yugoslavia	NA1441-1453.3	720.9497	Archives—Canada	CD3620-3649.6	027.071
Architecture, American	NA702.5-939	720.9(7-8)	Archives—Caribbean area	CD3860-3985	027.0729
Architecture, Ancient	NA210-340	722	Archives—Central America	CD3690-3859.5	027.0728
Architecture, Assyro-	NA220-221	722.51	Archives—China	CD2030-2059.5	027.051
Babylonian			Archives—Czechloslovakia	CD1150-1169.5	027.0437
Architecture, Baroque	NA590	724.16	Archives—Denmark	CD1770-1789.5	027.0489
Architecture, Colonial	NA707	724.1	Archives—Europe	CD1000-2000	027.04
Architecture, Domestic	NA7100-7882	728	Archives—France	CD1190-1219.5	027.044
Architecture, Domestic—	NA7127-7135	728	Archives—Germany	CD1220-1378.195	027.043
Designs and plans			Archives—Great Britain	CD1040-1199.5	027.041
Architecture, Domestic—	NA7201-7333	728.09(4-9)	Archives—Hungary	CD1170-1189.5	027.0439
[By region or country]			Archives—Iceland	CD1790-1809.5	027.04912
Architecture, Egyptian	NA1581-1585.3	720.962	Archives—India	CD2080-2099.5	027.054
Architecture, Egyptian	NA215-216	722.2	Archives—Israel	CD2010-2919.5	027.05694
Architecture, Etruscan	NA300-301	722.62	Archives—Italy	CD1400-1658	027.045
Architecture, Georgian	NA640	724.19	Archives—Japan	CD2160-2189.5	027.052
Architecture, Gothic	NA440-489	723.5	Archives—Mexico	CD3650-3679.5	027.072
Architecture, Greek	NA270-290	722.8	Archives—Netherlands	CD1690-1733.3	027.0492
Architecture, Industrial	NA6400-6589	725.4			

Subject Heading	LC	Dewey
Archives—[New Zealand/ Australia]	CD2500-2529.5	027.09(3/4)
Archives—Norway	CD1810-1829.5	027.0481
Archives—Oceania	CD2795	027.09(5-6)
Archives—Poland	CD1740-1759.5	027.0438
Archives—Portugal	CD1880-1899.5	027.0469
Archives—Russia	CD1710-1739.5	027.047
Archives—South America	CD4000-4279.5	027.08
Archives—Spain	CD1850-1879.5	027.046
Archives—Sweden	CD1830-1849.5	027.0485
Archives—Switzerland	CD1900-1929.5	027.0494
Archives—United States	CD3020-3615	027.073
Archives—[United States, By state]	CD3070-3609	027.07(4-9)
Argentina—History—1515-1535	F2841	982.0(1-22)
Argentina—History—1535-1617	F2841	982.023
Argentina—History—1617-1776	F2841	982.023
Argentina—History—1776-1810	F2841	982.023
Argentina—History—19th century	F2843	982.0(24-5)
Argentina—History—English Invasions, 1806-1807	F2845	982.024
Argentina—History—1810-	F2843	982.0(3-6)
Argentina—History—War of Independence, 1810-1817	F2845	982.03
Argentina—History—1817-1860	F2846	982.0(3-4)
Argentina—History—Revolution, 1833	F2846	982.04
Argentina—History—1860-1910	F2847	982.0(4-5)
Argentina—History—Revolution, 1890	F2847	982.05
Argentina—History—1910-1943	F2848	982.061
Argentina—History—Revolution, 1930	F2848	982.061
Argentina—History—1943-	F2849-.22	982.06(1-4)
Argentina—History—1943-1955	F2849	982.06(1-2)
Asia—History—1945-	DS35.2	950.4(2-3)
Argentina—History—1955-1983	F2849.2	982.06(3-4)
Austria—History—1955-	DB99.2	943.6053
Argentina—History—Revolution, 1955	F2849.2	982.063
Argentina—History—Peronist Revolt, 1956	F2849.2	982.063
Argentina—History—Coup d'etat, 1966	F2849.2	982.063
Argentina—History—1983-	F2849.2	982.064
Argentina—Manufactures	TS36-37	670.982
Argentina—Maps	G5350-5354	912.82
Argentina—Periodicals	F2801	982.005

Subject Heading	LC	Dewey
Argentina—Politics and government	JL2000-2099	320.982
Argentine literature	PQ7600-7798.36	860
Argonne, Battle of the, 1915	D545.A6	940.424
Argonne, Battle of the, 1918	D545.A63	940.434
Arianism	BT1350	273.4
Arid regions	GB611-618	551.415
Arid regions agriculture	S612-619	630.9154
Arid regions climate	QC993.7	551.69154
Arid soils	S592.17.A73	631.49154
Aries (Astrology)	BF1727	133.5262
Aristocracy (Social class)	HT647-653	305.52
Arithmetic	GN476.1	513
Arithmetic	QA101-141.8	513
Arithmetic—Foundations	QA248-.5	513
Arizona	F806-820	979.1
Arizona—Gazetteers	F809	917.91003
Arizona—History—To 1912	F811	979.10(1-4)
Arizona—History—1912-1950	F811	979.105(2-3)
Arizona—History—1951-	F815-.3	979.105(3-4)
Arizona—Maps	G4330-4334	912.791
Arizona—National Guard	UA70-79	355.3709791
Arizona—Periodicals	F806	979.1005
Arkansas	F406-420	976.7
Arkansas—Gazetteers	F409	917.67003
Arkansas—Maps	G4000-4004	912.767
Arkansas—National Guard	UA80-89	355.3709767
Arkansas—Periodicals	F406	976.7005
Arm	QM548	611.97
Arm wrestling	GV1196.5	796.812
Arm—Amputation	RD557	617.574059
Armatures	TK2477	621.316
Armed forces—Procurement	UC260	355.6212
Armed forces—Mobilization	UA910-915	355.28
Armenia (Republic)	DK680-689.5	947.56
Armenia (Republic)—History—Uprising, 1921	DS195.5	947.560841
Armenia	DS161-195.5	947.56
Armenia—Civilization	DS171	947.56
Armenia—Description and travel	DS165	914.75604
Armenia—History	DS173-195.5	947.56
Armenia—History—To 428	DS181-184	947.56
Armenia—History—Arsacid (Arshakuni) dynasty, 66-428	DS181-184	947.56
Armenia—History—428-1522	DS186-188	947.56
Armenia—History—428-640	DS186-188	947.56
Armenia—History—Arab period, 640-885	DS186-188	947.56
Armenia—History—Turkic Mongol Domination, 1045-1522	DS186-188	947.56
Armenia—History—1522-1800	DS191-193	947.5607
Armenia—History—1801-1900	DS194-.5	947.560(7-83)
Armenia—History—1901-	DS195-.3	947.5608(3-6)

Subject Heading	LC	Dewey	Subject Heading	LC	Dewey
Armenia—History— Revolution, 1917-1920	DS195.5	947.560841	Art—Belgium—History	N6967-6973	709.493
Armenian Church	BX120-129	281.62	Art—Canada—History	N6540-6545.5	709.71
Armenian essays	AC132-133	089.91992	Art—Central America— History	N6573.2-6582.5	709.728
Armenian language	PK8001-8454	491.992	Art—Czechoslovakia— History	N6828-6831.5	709.437
Armenian literature	PK8501-8835	891.992	Art—Greece—History	N6897-6898.5	709.495
Armenian literature— Europe	PK8601-8661	891.992	Art—Italy—History	N6915-6923	709.45
Armenian literature— United States	PK8681-8689	891.992	Art—Mexico—History	N6555-.5	709.72
Armenian massacres, 1915-1923	DS195.5	947.560(83-841)	Art—Portugal—History	N7125-7128.5	709.469
			Art—Scandinavia—History	N7007-7088	709.48
Armies	UA	355.31	Art—South America—History	N6635-6735.5	709.8
Armies—Commissariat	UC700-780	355.62	Art—Spain—History	N7105-7108.5	709.46
Armies—Equipment	UC460-465	355.81	Art, Abstract	N6490	709.04052
Armies—Officers	UB410-415	355.332	Art, Ancient	N5315-5899	709.01
Armies, Colonial	UA14	355.352	Art, Arab	N5470	709.394
Armies, Cost of	UA17	355.622	Art, Classical	N5603-5896.3	709.38
Arminianism	BX6195-6197	284.9	Art, Early Christian	N7832	704.9482
Armor	U800-897	623.4409	Art, Egyptian	N5350-5351	709.32
Armor—Exhibitions	U804	623.441074	Art, Greek	N5630-5720	709.38
Armor—[By region or country]	U818-823.5	623.44109(4-9)	Art, Medieval	N5940-6320	709.02
			Art, Modern	N6350-6494	709.03
Armor, Ancient	U805	623.4410901	Art, Modern—17th- 18th centuries	N6410-6425	709.03(2-3)
Armored personnel carriers	UG446.5	358.1883	Art, Modern—19th century	N6450-6465	709.034
Armored trains	UG345	623.63	Art, Modern—20th century	N6480-6494	709.04
Armored vessels	V799-800	359.32	Art, Oriental	N7260-7355.5	709.5
Armories	UA	355.75	Art, Prehistoric	GN799.A	700.901
Arnhem, Battle of, 1944	D763.N4	940.54219218	Art, Prehistoric	N5310-5313	709.011
Aromatic compounds	QD330-341	547.6	Art, Primitive	N5310-5313	709.011
Aromatic plants	SB301-303	633.81	Art, Renaissance	N6370-6375	709.024
Arraignment—United States	KF9645-9650	345.73072	Art, Rococo	N6410	709.0332
Arrest (Police methods)	HV8080.A6	363.232	Art, Roman	N5760-5763	709.37
Arrest—United States	KF9625	345.730527	Art, Romanesque	N6280	709.0216
Arrhythmia	RC685.A65	616.128	Art, Sumerian	N5370	709.35
Arrowheads	GN498.B78	623.441	Art, Syrian	N5460	709.3943
Arroyos	GB561-568	551.442	Art, Turkish	N5480-5560	709.392
Arsenals	UF540-545	355.7	Art and mythology	N7760-7763	704.947
Arson	HV6638-.5	364.164	Art and photography	N72.P5	770
Arson—[By region or country]	HV6638.5	364.16409(4-9)	Art as an investment	N8600	332.63
Art	N	700	Art criticism	N7475-7485	701.18
Art—Biography	N40-43	709.2	Art dealers	N8610-8660	381.457(3-6)
Art—Congresses	N21	706	Art deco	N6494.A7	709.04012
Art—Conservation and restoration	N8554-8585	702.88	Art metal-work	NK6400-8459	739
			Art museums	N400-3990	708
Art—Dictionaries	N33	703	Art museums—Belgium	N1750-1850	708.93
Art—Directories	N50-55	702.5	Art museums—Europe	N1010-3690	708.(2-9)
Art—Exhibitions	N4390-5098	707.4	Art museums—France	N2010-2180	708.4
Art—History	N5300-7418	709	Art museums—Germany	N2210-2406	708.3
Art—Hungary—History	N6819-6820.5	709.439	Art museums—Great Britain	N1020-1560	708.2
Art—Periodicals	N1-9.9	705	Art museums—Greece	N2410-2430	708.95
Art—Philosophy	N61-75	701	Art museums—Italy	N2510-3065	708.5
Art—Private collections	N5198-5299	708	Art museums—Netherlands	N2450-2505	708.92
Art—Private collections— Europe	N5240-5280	708.(2-8)	Art museums—Russia	N3310-3382	708.7
			Art museums—Spain	N3410-3499	708.6
Art—Private collections— United States	N5215-5220	708.1(3-9)	Art museums—United States	N510-880	708.1(3-9)
			Art objects	NK	745
Art—Societies, etc.	N10-17	706	Art objects—Catalogs	NK1133-.26	745.0294
Art—Study and teaching	N81-390	707.1	Art objects—Collectors and collecting	NK1125-1130	745.075
Art—Technique	N7429.7-7433	702.8			
Art—Austria—History	N6805-6808.5	709.436			

Subject Heading	LC	Dewey	Subject Heading	LC	Dewey
Art objects—[By region or country]	NK801-1094.5	745.09(4-9)	Artillery—Japan	UF105-106	358.120952
			Artillery—Mexico	UF28-29	358.120972
Art objects, Ancient	NK610-685	745.0901	Artillery—[New Zealand/ Australia]	UF121-122	358.12099(3/4)
Art objects, Classical	NK665-680	745.0938			
Art schools	N325-335	707.1	Artillery—Oceania	UF123-124	358.12099(5-6)
Art schools—Europe	N332	707.104	Artillery—Portugal	UF83-84	358.1209469
Art schools—United States	N328-330	707.1073	Artillery—Russia	UF85-86	358.120947
Art therapy	RC489.A7	616.891656	Artillery—Scandinavia	UF86.5	358.120948
Art thieves	N8795	364.162	Artillery—South America	UF34-54	358.12098
Arterial catheterization	RD598.5	617.413	Artillery—Spain	UF87-88	358.120946
Arteries	QL835	573.185	Artillery—United States	UF23-25	358.120973
Arteries	QM191	611.13	Artillery—Venezuela	UF54	358.120987
Arteries—Diseases	RC691-697	616.13	Artillery—West Indies	UF32-33	358.1209729
Arteritis	RC694.5.I53	616.13	Artillery, Coast	UF450-455	358.16
Arthritis	RC933	616.722	Artillery, Field and mountain	UF400-445	358.12
Arthropoda	QL434-599.82	595	Artillery drill and tactics	UF157-302	358.124
Arthropoda, Fossil	QE815-832	565	Artists' models	N7574	702.8
Articulation disorders	RC424.7	616.855	Artists' tools	N8543	702.84
Artificial arms	RD756.2-.22	617.574	Arts	NX	700
Artificial corneas	RE336	617.7190592	Arts—Dictionaries	NX80	700.3
Artificial flowers	TT890-894	745.5943	Arts—Encyclopedias	NX70	700.3
Artificial hip joints	RD549	617.4720592	Arts—Endowments	NX700-750	700.79
Artificial horizons (Nautical instruments)	VK584.A7	527.0284	Arts—Forgeries	NX636	702.874
			Arts—Periodicals	NX1-9	700.5
Artificial insemination	SF105.5	636.08245	Arts—[By region or country]	NX501-596.3	700.9(3-9)
Artificial insemination, Human	RG134	618.178	Arts—Afghanistan	NX575.6	700.9581
			Arts—Africa	NX587-589.8	700.96
Artificial intelligence	Q334-342	006.3	Arts—Africa, East	NX588.8-.9	700.9676
Artificial knee	RD561	617.5820592	Arts—Africa, North	NX587.6-588.6	700.961
Artificial limbs	RD756-.42	617.58	Arts—Africa, Southern	NX589.7-.8	700.968
Artificial minerals	TP870	666.86	Arts—Africa, West	NX589-.6	700.966
Artificial reefs	SH157.85.A7	639.92	Arts—Argentina	NX531	700.982
Artificial respiration	RC87.9	617.1806	Arts—Asia	NX572-586	700.95
Artificial satellites	TL796-798	629.46	Arts—Asiatic Russia	NX575.7	700.957
Artificial satellites in navigation	VK562	623.893	Arts—Australia	NX590	700.994
			Arts—Austria	NX548	700.9436
Artificial satellites in telecommunication	HE9719-9721	384.51	Arts—Bahamas	NX524	700.97296
			Arts—Balkan Peninsula	NX566-569	700.9496
Artificial satellites in telecommunication	TK5104-.2	621.3825	Arts—Belgium	NX555	700.9493
			Arts—Bolivia	NX532	700.984
Artillery	UF	358.12	Arts—Brazil	NX533	700.981
Artillery—Dictionaries	UF9	358.1203	Arts—Cambodia	NX578.6.C3	700.9596
Artillery—History	UF15	358.1209	Arts—Canada	NX513-.3	700.971
Artillery—Societies, etc.	UF1	358.12006	Arts—Central America	NX515-522	700.9728
Artillery—[By region or country]	UF21-124	358.1209(4-9)	Arts—Chile	NX534	700.983
			Arts—China	NX583	700.951
Artillery—Africa	UF115-119	358.12096	Arts—Colombia	NX535	700.9861
Artillery—Argentina	UF36-37	358.120982	Arts—Costa Rica	NX517	700.97286
Artillery—Asia	UF99-113	358.12095	Arts—Cuba	NX525	700.97291
Artillery—Canada	UF26-27	358.120971	Arts—Denmark	NX558	700.9489
Artillery—Central America	UF30-31	358.1209728	Arts—Ecuador	NX536	700.9866
Artillery—Chile	UF43-44	358.120983	Arts—Egypt	NX588-.3	700.962
Artillery—China	UF101-102	358.120951	Arts—El Salvador	NX522	700.97284
Artillery—Colombia	UF45-46	358.1209861	Arts—Ethiopia	NX588.7	700.963
Artillery—Europe	UF55-95	358.12094	Arts—Europe	NX542-571	700.94
Artillery—France	UF71-72	358.120944	Arts—France	NX549	700.944
Artillery—Germany	UF73-74	358.120943	Arts—Germany	NX550-.6	700.943
Artillery—Great Britain	UF57-64	358.120941	Arts—Great Britain	NX543-547.6	700.941
Artillery—Greece	UF75-76	358.1209495	Arts—Greece	NX551	700.9495
Artillery—India	UF103-104	358.120954	Arts—Guatemala	NX518	700.97281
Artillery—Italy	UF79-80	358.120945	Arts—Haiti	NX526	700.97294

Subject Heading	LC	Dewey	Subject Heading	LC	Dewey
Arts—Honduras	NX519	700.97283	Asia—Church history	BR1060-1357	275
Arts—Iceland	NX559	700.94912	Asia—Climate	QC990	551.695
Arts—India	NX576	700.954	Asia—Description and travel	DS5.95-10	915.04
Arts—Indonesia	NX580	700.9598	Asia—Economic conditions	HC411-495	330.95
Arts—Iran	NX574	700.955	Asia—Emigration and	JV8490-8758	325.(25/5)
Arts—Israel	NX573.7	700.95694	immigration		
Arts—Italy	NX552	700.945	Asia—Gazetteers	DS4	915.03
Arts—Jamaica	NX527	700.97292	Asia—Genealogy	CS1080-1549.5	929.107205
Arts—Japan	NX584	700.952	Asia—History	DS31-35.2	950
Arts—Korea	NX584.6-.7	700.9519	Asia—History—1945-	DS35.2	950.4(2-3)
Arts—Laos	NX578.6.L3	700.9594	Asia—History—20th century	DS35-.2	950.4
Arts—Malaysia	NX579	700.9595	Asia—Maps	G2200-2444	912.5
Arts—Mexico	NX514	700.972	Asia—Maps	G7400-8198.54	912.5
Arts—Middle East	NX573-.7	700.956	Asia—Periodicals	DS1	950.05
Arts—Netherlands	NX554	700.9492	Asia—Politics and	JQ21-1825	320.95
Arts—New Zealand	NX593	700.993	government		
Arts—Nicaragua	NX520	700.97285	Asia, Central	DK845-860	958
Arts—Norway	NX560	700.9481	Asia, Central	DS327-329.4	939.6/958
Arts—Oceania	NX595-596	700.99(5-6)	Asia, Central—Commerce	HF3770.22-.27	380.10958
Arts—Pakistan	NX576.7	700.95491	Asia, Southeastern—	BR1178-1261	275.9
Arts—Panama	NX521	700.97287	Church history		
Arts—Paraguay	NX538	700.9892	Asia, Southeastern—History	DS524-526.7	959
Arts—Peru	NX539	700.985	Asia, Southeastern—Religion	BL2050-2150	299.5
Arts—Philippines	NX581	700.9599	Asian flu	RC150	616.203
Arts—Portugal	NX563	700.9469	Asian periodicals	PN5360-5449	079.5
Arts—Puerto Rico	NX528	700.97295	Asians—Education	LC3001-3501	371.82995
Arts—Russia	NX556	700.947	Asiatic Russia—	TS109-110	670.957
Arts—Scandinavia	NX557-561	700.948	Manufactures		
Arts—South America	NX530-541	700.98	Asphalt	TN853	622.337
Arts—Spain	NX562	700.946	Asphyxia	RC87.3	617.18
Arts—Sri Lanka	NX576.6	700.95493	Asphyxia	RA1071-1082	617.18
Arts—Sweden	NX561	700.9485	Asphyxia neonatorum	RJ256	618.922
Arts—Switzerland	NX564	700.9494	Aspirin	HD9675.A7-.A74	338.476153137
Arts—Thailand	NX578.7	700.9593	Aspirin	RM666.A82	615.3137
Arts—Turkey	NX565	700.9561	Assamese language	PK1550-1599	491.451
Arts—United States	NX503-512.3	700.973	Assassination	HV6499-6535	364.1524
Arts—Uruguay	NX540	700.9895	Assassination	HV6278	364.1524
Arts—Venezuela	NX541	700.987	Assassins (Ismailites)	BP195.A8	297.822
Arts—Vietnam	NX578.6.V5-.V55	700.9597	Assault and battery	HV6618	364.1555
Arts—West Indies	NX523-529	700.9729	Assault rifles	UD390-395	356.1182425
Arts—[By region or country]	NX501-596.3	700.9(3-9)	Assaying	HG325-329	669.92
Arts, Islamic	NX688	704.9489	Assaying	TN550-580	669.92
Arts and crafts movement	NK1135-1149.5	745	Assertiveness training	RC489.A77	158.2
Aruba—Maps	G5170-5174	912.72986	Assimilation (Sociology)	JV6342	303.482
AS (Coin)	CJ937	737.4937	Assisted suicide	R726	179.7
Asbestos	TN930	622.3672	Association of ideas	BF365-395	153.2
Ascension Day	BV57	263.93	Associations, institutions,	KF1355-1480	346.7306
Ascension Day	GT4995.A8	394.266	etc.—Law and legislation		
Asceticism	BL625	291.447	Assyro-Babylonian literature	PJ3601-3953	892.1
Asceticism	BJ1491	291.447	Asteroids	QB377-379	523.44
Asceticism	BV5015-5068	248.47	Asteroids	QB651	523.44
Asceticism—Buddhism	BQ6200-6240	294.34447	Asteroids	QB516	523.44
Asceticism—Islam	BP190.5.A75	297.576	Asthma	RC591	616.238
Asceticism—History—	BV5023	248.470901	Asthma in children	RJ436.A8	618.92238
Early church, ca. 30-600			Astigmatism	RE932	617.755
Asceticism—History—	BV5025	248.470902	Astral projection	BF1389.A7	133.95
Middle Ages, 600-1500			Astrodynamics	TL1050-1060	629.4
Asia	DS	950	Astrographic catalog	QB6	520.216
Asia—Armed Forces—	UC234-245	355.8095	and chart		
Supplies and stores			Astrology	BF1651-1729	133.5
Asia—Biography	CT1498-1919	920.05	Astrology	QB25-26	520

Subject Heading	LC	Dewey
Astrology and politics	BF1729.P6	133.5832
Astrology, Arab	BF1714.A6	133.593927
Astrometry	QB807	522
Astronautical charts	TL1070	629.453
Astronautical instruments	TL1082	629.474
Astronautics	TL787-4050	629.4
Astronautics—Experiments	TL794.3	629.40724
Astronautics—Study and teaching	TL845-848	629.4071
Astronautics—[By region or country]	TL789.8	629.409(4-9)
Astronomers—Biography	QB35-36	520.92
Astronomical clocks	QB107	522.5
Astronomical geography	QB630-638.8	525
Astronomical instruments	QB84.5-115	522.2
Astronomical models	QB67	520.228
Astronomical observatories	QB81-84	522.29
Astronomical photography	QB121-.5	522.63
Astronomical photometry	QB135	522.62
Astronomical spectroscopy	QB465	522.67
Astronomy	QB	520
Astronomy—Charts, diagrams, etc.	QB65	529.223
Astronomy—Encyclopedias	QB14	520.3
Astronomy—History	QB15-34	520.9
Astronomy—Mathematics	QB47	520.151
Astronomy—Observations	QB4-.9	522.1
Astronomy—Periodicals	QB1	520.5
Astronomy—Philosophy	QB14.5	520.1
Astronomy—Study and teaching	QB61-62.7	520.71
Astronomy, Ancient	QB16-22	520.901
Astronomy, Assyro-Babylonian	QB19	520.935
Astronomy, Chinese	QB17	520.931
Astronomy, Greek	QB21	520.938
Astronomy, Medieval	QB23-26	520.902
Astronomy, Prehistoric	GN799.A8	520.901
Astronomy, Renaissance	QB29	520.90(23-31)
Astronomy in the Bible	BS655	220.852
Astrophysics	QB460-466	523.01
Atheism	BL2700-2790	211.8
Athena (Greek deity)	BL820.M6	292.2114
Athens (Greece)	DF915-936	949.512
Athletes	GV697	796.092
Athletic clubs	GV563	796.068
Athletic fields	GV411-416	796.068
Athletics	GV561-749.5	796
Athletics—Equipment and supplies	GV743-749	796.0284
Atlanta (Ga.)	F294.A8	975.8231
Atlanta Campaign, 1864	E476.7	973.7371
Atlantic Ocean—Maps	G2805-2839	912.1963
Atlantic States—Maps	G3709.3-3933	912.7(4-5)
Atmosphere	QC851-999	551.5
Atmosphere, Upper	QC879-.59	551.514
Atmosphere, Upper—Radiosonde observations	QC879	551.514
Atmospheric chemistry	QC879.6-.85	551.511
Atmospheric circulation	QC880.4.A8	551.517
Atmospheric electricity	QC960.5-969	551.563

Subject Heading	LC	Dewey
Atmospheric ionization	QC966.7.A84	551.561
Atmospheric nucleation	QC921.6.C6	551.5741
Atmospheric pressure	QC885-896	551.54
Atmospheric pressure—Physiological effect	QP82.2.P7	571.437
Atmospheric radiation	QC912.3	551.5273
Atmospheric radio refractivity	QC973.4.R35	551.51
Atmospheric radioactivity	QC913-.2	551.5276
Atmospheric temperature	QC901-912.2	551.525
Atmospheric thermodynamics	QC880.4.T5	551.52
Atmospheric tides	QC883.2.A8	551.4708
Atmospheric turbulence	QC880.4.T8	551.55
Atomic absorption spectroscopy	QC454.A8	535.84
Atomic mass	QD466	541.242
Atomic structure	QC173.4.A87	539.14
Atomic theory	QD461	541.2
Atomic weights	QD463-464	541.242
Atomism	BD646	146.5
Atomism	B193	182
Atoms	QC173	539.7
Atonement	BT263-268	234.5
Atopic dermatitis	RL242-249	616.521
Attack helicopters	UG1230-1235	358.4383
Attack planes	UG1242.A28	358.43
Attention	BF321-323	153.733
Attention	LB1065	153.1532
Attention in newborn infants	BF720.A85	155.42221532
Attention-deficit hyperactivty disorder	RJ506.H9	618.928589
Attitude (Psychology)	BF327	152.4
Attribute (Philosophy)	BD352	111.8
Atum (Egyptian deity)	BL2450.A89	299.31
Auctions	HF5476-5477	381.17
Audiences	P96.A83	302.23
Audio-visual education	LB1043-1044.9	371.335
Audiology	RF286-320	617.8
Audiology—Instruments	RF298-310	617.800284
Audiology—Societies, etc.	RF286	617.8006
Audiometry	RF294-.5	612.85
Auditing	HF5667-5668.25	657.45
Auditing, Internal	HF5668-.25	657.458
Auditoriums	NA6815	725.83
Augmentation mammaplasty	RD539.8	618.190592
Augustinians	BX2901-2956	255.4
Aura	BF1389.A8	133.892
Auroras	QC970-972.5	538.768
Auschwitz (Poland : Concentration camp)	D805.P7	940.53170943
Australia—Armed Forces—Supplies and stores	UC255-256	355.80994
Australia—Biography	CT2800-2808	920.0994
Australia—Census	HA3001-3010	319.4
Australia—Church history	BR1480-1483	279.4
Australia—Climate	QC992	551.6994
Australia—Commerce	HF3941-3950	380.10994
Australia—Description and travel	DU97-5-105.2	919.404
Australia—Economic conditions	HC601-610	330.994

Subject Heading	LC	Dewey	Subject Heading	LC	Dewey
Australia—Emigration and immigration	JV9100-9199	325.(294/94)	Austrian Succession, War of, 1740-1748	D291-294	940.2532
Australia—Gazetteers	DU90	919.4003	Austrian Succession, War of, 1740-1748	DB72	940.2532
Australia—Genealogy	CS2000-2009	929.1072094	Austroasiatic languages	PL4281-4587	495.93
Australia—History	DU108-117.2	994	Austronesian languages	PL5021-6571	499.2
Australia—History—To 1788	DU98.1	994.01	Autarchy	HD82-85	338.9
Australia—History—1788-1851	DU115	994.02	Authoritarianism (Personality trait)	BF698.35.A87	155.232
Australia—History—1788-1900	DU114-115.2	994.0(2-3)	Authority	HM271-276	303.36
Australia—History—20th century	DU116-117.2	994.0(4-65)	Authority—Religious aspects	BT88-92	262.8
Australia—Manufactures	TS121-122	670.994	Authors and publishers—United States	KF3084	070.520973
Australia—Maps	G8960-8964	912.94	Authorship	PN101-249	808.02
Australia—Maps	G2750-2793	912.94	Authorship—Marketing	PN161	380.145808
Australian aborigines—Antiquities	GN871-875	994.01	Autism	RC553.A88	616.8982
			Autism in children	RJ506.A9	618.928982
Australian aborigines—Ethnic identity	GN666	305.89915	Autoantibodies	QR186.82-.83	571.973
			Autobiographies	CT101	920
Australian languages	PL7001-7101	499.15	Autobiography	CT25	920
Australian literature	PR9600-9619.3	820	Autoerotic asphyxia	RC560.A97	616.8583
Australian periodicals	PN5510-5590	079.94	Autographs	Z41-42.5	929.88
Austria	DB1-879	936.3/943.6	Autoharp music	M175.A8	787.75
Austria—Biography	DB36-.7	920.0363/ 920.0436	Autoimmune diseases	RC600	616.978
			Autoimmunity	QR188.3	571.973
Austria—Census	HA1171-1190	314.36	Automatic control	TA165	629.8
Austria—Civilization	DB30	936.3/943.6	Automatic machinery	TJ212.2-225	629.8
Austria—Description and travel	DB21-27.5	913.6304/ 914.3604	Automatic meteorological stations	QC875	551.63
Austria—Economic conditions	HC261-270	330.9436	Automatic pilot (Airplanes)	TL589.5	629.1326
			Automation	T59.5	670.427
Austria—Emigration and immigration	JV7800-7899	325.(2436/436)	Automobile drivers	TL152.5-.55	629.283092
			Automobile driving	TL152.5-.55	629.283
Austria—Gazetteers	DB14	913.63003/ 914.36003	Automobile engineers—Biography	TL139-140	629.222092
Austria—Historiography	DB36.8-.9	936.30072/ 943.60072	Automobile parking	TL154	629.283
			Automobile racing drivers	GV1032	796.72092
Austria—History	DB46-99.2	936.3/943.602	Automobile rallies	GV1029.2	796.73
Austria—History, Military	DB42-44	355.309436	Automobile theft investigation	HV8079.A98	363.25962
Austria—History, Naval	DB45	359.309436			
Austria—History—To 1273	DB51-57	936.3	Automobile travel	GV1021-1025	796.7
Austria—History—1273-1519	DB57-59	943.60(25-3)	Automobiles	TL1-230.5	629.222
			Automobiles—Aerodynamics	TL245	629.231
Austria—History—1519-1740	DB65.2-77	943.603	Automobiles—Bodies	TL255-256.5	629.26
			Automobiles—Catalogs	TL12	629.2220294
Austria—History—Revolution, 1848-1849	DB83	940.284	Automobiles—Congresses	TL6	629.22206
			Automobiles—Conservation and restoration	TL152.2	629.287
Austria—History—1918-1938	DB96-99.2	943.6051	Automobiles—Design and construction	TL240-278	629.23
Austria—History—1938-1945	DB99	943.6052	Automobiles—Electric equipment	TL272	629.2548
Austria—History—1955-	DB99.2	943.6053	Automobiles—Encyclopedias	TL9	629.22203
Austria—Manufactures	TS65-.2	670.9436			
Austria—Maps	G6490-6494	912.436	Automobiles—Heating and ventilation	TL271-.5	629.2772
Austria—Maps	G1935-1939	912.436	Automobiles—History	TL15	629.22209
Austria—Periodicals	DB1	936.3005/ 943.6005	Automobiles—Maintenance and repair	TL152-.2	629.287
Austria—Politics and government	JN1601-2041	320.9436	Automobiles—Marketing	HD9710-.37	380.145388342
			Automobiles—Models	TL237-.2	629.221

Subject Heading	LC	Dewey	Subject Heading	LC	Dewey
Automobiles—Motors	TL210-.7	629.252	Backyard gardens	SB473	635
Automobiles—Museums	TL7	629.222074	Bacon's Rebellion, 1676	F229	975.502
Automobiles—Periodicals	TL1-5	629.22205	Bacteria	QR75-99.5	579.3
Automobiles—Pollution control devices	TL214.P6	629.25	Bacteria—Evolution	QR81.7	579.3138
			Bacteria cell surfaces	QR77.35	571.629
Automobiles—Testing	TL285-295	629.282	Bacterial diseases	QR201.B34	571.993
Automobiles—[By region or country]	TL21-127	629.22209(4-9)	Bacterial diseases	RC115-116	616.92
			Bacterial diseases in children	RJ406.B32	618.9292
Automobiles—France	TL71-72.5	629.2220944			
Automobiles—Germany	TL73-74.5	629.2220943	Bacterial vaccines	QR189.5.B33	615.372
Automobiles—Great Britain	TL57-64	629.2220941	Bacteriological laboratories	QR64-.8	579.3072
Automobiles—Japan	TL105-106	629.2220952	Bacteriology	QR	579.3
Automobiles—Russia	TL85-86	629.2220947	Bacteriology, Agricultural	QR351	579.31755
Automobiles—United States	TL23-25	629.2220973	Bacteriology, Agricultural	QR111	579.31755
Automobiles, Military	UG615-620	623.7472	Bacteriology—Technique	QR65-69	579.3028
Automobiles, Racing	TL236	629.228	Bacteriophages	QR342-.2	579.26
Automobiles, Steam	TL200	629.2292	Badges	CR67-69	929.6
Autopsy	RB57	616.0759	Bagpipe music	M145	788.49
Autopsy	RA1063.4	614.1	Bahai faith	BP300-395	297.93
Auxiliary sciences of history	C	900	Bahai meditations	BP380	297.93435
Auxiliary sciences of history—Congresses	C3	906	Bahamas	F1650-1660	972.96
			Bahamas—Periodicals	F1650	972.96005
Auxiliary sciences of history—Periodicals	C4	905	Bahamas—Census	HA861	317.296
			Bahamas—Civilization	F1654	972.96
Auxiliary sciences of history—Societies, etc.	C2	906	Bahamas—Description and travel	F1651	917.29604
Auxiliary sciences of history—Study and teaching	C20	907.1	Bahamas—Gazetteers	F1650.7	917.296003
			Bahamas—History	F1655.3-1657.2	972.96
			Bahamas—Maps	G4980-4984	912.7296
Avalanches	QC929.A8	551.307	Bahamas—Politics and government	JL610-619	320.97296
Avant-garde (Aesthetics)	BH301.A94	700.411			
Avarice	BJ1535.A8	178	Bahrain—Census	HA4568	315.365
Aversion therapy	RC489.B4	616.89142	Bahrain—Economic conditions	HC415.38	330.95365
Avestan language	PK6101-6109	491.52			
Aviaries	QL677.8	598.073	Bahrain—Maps	G7590-7594	912.5365
Aviation medicine	RC1050-1097	616.980213	Bahrain—Politics and government	JQ1846	320.95365
Aviculture	SF461	636.6			
Avionics	TL695-696	629.135	Bail—United States	KF9632	345.73056
Avitaminosis	RC623.7	616.39	Bailments—Canada	KE970-972	346.71025
Avulsion fractures	RD104.A95	617.15	Bailments—England	KD1679-1685	346.42025
Azerbaijan	DK690-699.5	947.54	Bailments—United States	KF939-951	346.73025
Azerbaijani language	PL311-314	494.361	Bait	SH448	799.10284
Azimuth	QB207	526.63	Bait fishing	SH455.4	799.122
Azimuth	TA597	526.63	Bakers and bakeries	HD9057-9058	641.815
Azimuth	VK563	527	Bakers and bakeries	HD8039.B2	641.815
Azores—Census	HA2280	314.699	Bakers and bakeries	TX761-799	664.02
Azores—Maps	G9130-9134	912.4699	Baking powder	HD9330.B2-.B23	664.68
Aztecs	F1219.73-.75	972.00497452	Balalaika music	M142.B2	787.875
B-52 bomber	UG1242.B6	358.42830973	Balance of payments	HG3882-3890	332.152
Baal (Deity)	BL1671	299.26	Balance of power	D217	327.112
Babism	BP340	297.92	Balance of trade	HF1014	382.17
Baby books	HQ779-.5	305.232	Balconies	NA3070	721.84
Babysitting	HQ769.5	649.10248	Balcony gardening	SB419.5	635.9671
Baccalaureate addresses	BV4255	252.68	Balder (Norse deity)	BL870.B3	293.2113
Bachelor of arts degree	LB2383	378.2	Baldness	RL155-.5	616.546
Bachelors	HQ800.3	305.389652	Balinese language	PL5221-5224	499.22
Bacillus (Bacteria)	QR82.B3	579.362	Balkan Peninsula	DR	949.6
Bacitracin	RM666.B2	615.329	Balkan Peninsula—Biography	CT1399-1458	920.0496
Back	QM540	612.9			
Backache	RD771.B217	617.564	Balkan Peninsula—Biography	DR33	920.0496
Backpacking	GV199.6	796.51			

Subject Heading	LC	Dewey	Subject Heading	LC	Dewey
Balkan Peninsula—Civilization	DR22-23	949.6	Banjo	MT560-570	787.8807
Balkan Peninsula—Congresses	DR1.5	949.6006	Banjo Music	M120-122	787.88
			Bank accounts	HG1660	332.1752
Balkan Peninsula—Description and travel	DR11-16	914.9604	Bank buildings	NA6240-6245	725.24
			Bank capital	HG1616.C34	332.1
Balkan Peninsula—Economic conditions	HC401-407	330.9496	Bank credit cards	HG1643	332.178
			Bank deposits	HG1660	332.1752
Balkan Peninsula—Gazetteers	DR5	914.96003	Bank investments	HG1616.I5	332.1754
			Bank loans	HG1641-1643	332.1753
Balkan Peninsula—History	DR32-48.5	949.6	Bank mergers	HG1722	332.16
Balkan Peninsula—Manufactures	TS95.A2	670.9496	Bank notes	HG348-353.5	332.4044
			Bank notes	HG607-610	332.40440973
Balkan Peninsula—Periodicals	DR1	949.6005	Bank reserves	HG1656	332.1
			Bank stocks	HG1723	332.6722
Balkan Peninsula—Politics and government	JN9600-9689	320.9496	Banking law	HG1725-1778	346.082
			Banking law	K1066-1088	346.082
Ball games	GV861	796.3	Banking law—Canada	KE991-1026	346.71082
Ballads	M1627	782.43	Banking law—England	KD1715-1737	346.42082
Ballet	ML3460	781.55609	Banking law—United States	KF966-1032	346.73082
Ballet	GV1787	792.84	Bankruptcy	HG3760-3769	332.75
Ballet—Costume	GV1789.2	792.8026	Bankruptcy—Canada	KE1491-1506	346.71078
Ballet dancing	GV1788	792.84	Bankruptcy—England	KD2141-2164	346.42078
Ballista	U875	355.8241	Bankruptcy—United States	KF1501-1548	346.73078
Ballistic instruments	UF830	623.510284	Banks and banking	HG1501-3550	332.1
Ballistics	UF820-840	623.51	Banks and banking—Accounting	HG1706-1708	657.8333
Ballistics—Tables	VF550	623.51021			
Ballistics—Tables	UF820	623.51021	Banks and banking—Computer programs	HG1709	332.10285
Balloon ascensions	TL620	629.13322			
Balloon racing	GV763	797.51	Banks and banking—Customer services	HG1616.C87	332.17
Ballooning	GV762-763	797.51			
Balloons	TL609-639	629.13322	Banks and banking—[By region or country]	HG2401-3542.7	332.109(4-9)
Ballot	JF1091-1177	324.65			
Ballot	JK2214-2217	324.650973	Banks and banking—United States	HG2401-2626	332.10973
Ballroom dancing	GV1751	793.33			
Balls (Parties)	GV1746-1750	793.38	Banks and banking, Cooperative	HG2032-2039	334.2
Balls (Parties)	GV1757	793.38			
Balls (Sporting goods)	GV749.B34	796.30284	Bantu languages	PL8025	496.39
Baltic States	DK502.3-.7	947.9	Baptism	BV803-814	265.1
Baltic States—History	DK502.7	947.9	Baptism (Canon law)	BX1939.B3	262.933
Baltimore (Md.)	F189.B1	975.26	Baptism for the dead	BV814	265.1
Baltimore, Battle of, 1814	E356.B2	973.523	Baptism in the Holy Spirit	BT123	234.13
Band music	M1200-1268	784	Baptismal water	BX2307.3	264.02036
Band music—Analysis, appreciation	MT125	784.117	Baptisteries	NA4910	726.4
			Baptists	BX6201-6495	286.(1-5)
Bandages and bandaging	RD113-.4	617.93	Baptists—Biography	BX6493-6495	286.1092
Bandonion music	M175.B2	788.84	Baptists—Catechisms	BX6336	238.6(1-5)
Bands (Music)	ML1300-1354	784.09	Baptists—Creeds	BX6335	238.6
Bangladesh—Census	HA4590.6	315.492	Baptists—Dictionaries	BX6211	286.(1-5)03
Bangladesh—Civilization	DS393.8	934/954.92	Baptists—Doctrines	BX6330-6331.2	230.6(1-5)
Bangladesh—Economic conditions	HC440.8	330.95492	Baptists—Education	BX6219-6227	268.86(1-5)
			Baptists—Government	BX6340-6346.3	262.06(1-5)
Bangladesh—Gazetteers	DS393.3	934.003/ 915.492003	Baptists—History	BX6231-6328	286.(1-5)09
			Baptists—Liturgy	BX6337	264.06(1-5)
Bangladesh—History	DS394.5-395.7	934/954.92	Baptists—Sermons	BX6333	252.06(1-5)
Bangladesh—History—Revolution, 1971	DS395.5	954.92051	Baptists—Societies, etc.	BX6205	286.(1-5)06
			Baptists—Africa	BX6320-6322	286.(1-5)6
Bangladesh—Maps	G2275-2279	912.5492	Baptists—Asia	BX6315-6316	286.(1-5)5
Bangladesh—Maps	G7645-7649	912.5492	Baptists—Australia	BX6325-6326	286.(1-5)94
Bangladesh—Politics and government	JQ630-639	320.95492	Baptists—Canada	BX6251-6253	286.(1-5)71
			Baptists—Europe	BX6275-6310	286.(1-5)4
			Baptists—Oceania	BX6327-6328	286.(1-5)9(5-6)

Subject Heading	LC	Dewey
Baptists—South America	BX6271-6273	286.(1-5)8
Baptists—United States	BX6235-6249	286.(1-5)73
Barbados	F2041	972.981
Barbados—Census	HA865	317.2981
Barbados—Maps	G5140-5144	912.72981
Barbecue cookery	TX840.B3	641.5784
Barbering	TT950-979	646.724
Barbiturates	RM325	615.782
Barges	VM466.B3	623.829
Baritone music	M90-94	788.975
Barns	NA8230	728.922
Barometers	QC886-887	551.540284
Barracks	UC400-440	355.71
Barrel racing	GV1834.45.B35	791.84
Bartending	TX951	641.874
Baryton music	M59	787.6
Bas-relief	NB1280-1291	731.54
Basal cell carcinoma	RC280.S5	616.99477
Base measuring	QB303	526.3
Baseball	GV862-880.6	796.357
Baseball—Records	GV877	796.357
Baseball cards	GV875.3	796.357075
Baseball fields	GV879.5	976.357068
Baseball players	GV865	796.357092
Bashfulness	BF575.B3	155.232
Basic education	LC1035-.8	370
Basket making	GN431	746.412
Basket making	TT879.B3	746.412
Basketball	GV885	796.323
Basketball players	GV884	796.323092
Basketwork	NK3649.5-.55	746.412
Basque language	PH5001-5259	499.92
Basque literature	PH5280-5490	899.92
Basque philology	PH5001-5022	499.92
Bass clarinet music	M70-74	788.65
Bass fishing	SH681	799.1758
Bass guitar music	M125-129	787.87
Bassoon	ML953	788.5807
Bassoon music	M75-79	788.58
Bastille Day	DC167	394.2635
Bathrooms	NK2117.B33	747.78
Bathrooms	TH6485-6500	696.182
Baths	RA780	613.41
Bathtubs	TH6493	696.182
Batik	TT852.5	746.662
Battle cruisers	V820-.5	359.3253
Battles	D25	355.4
Bayonets	UD340-345	356.118241
Bayonets	UD400	356.118241
Bazaars (Charities)	HV544	361.7
Beach volleyball	GV1015.5.B43	796.325
Beaches	GV454.B3	796.53
Beacons	VK1000-1249	623.8944
Beadwork	NK3650-.5	745.582
Beadwork	TT860	745.582
Beard	GT2320	391.5
Beard	RL91	616.546
Bearings (Machinery)	TJ1061-1073.7	621.822
Beatitudes	BT382	226.93
Beauty culture	TT950-979	646.7042
Beauty, Personal	GT49	391
Bedsores	RL675	616.545
Bee culture	SF521-539	638.1
Bee products	SF539	638.16
Beef cattle	SF207	636.213
Beer	TP568-587	663.42
Bees	QL563-569.4	595.799
Beeswax	TP678	638.17
Beet sugar	TP390-391	664.123
Begging	HV6174	364.256
Behavior disorders in children	RJ506.B44	618.92858
Behavior modification	BF637.B4	153.85
Behavior modification	LB1060.2	370.153
Behavior therapy	RC489.B4	616.89142
Behaviorism (Psychology)	BF199	150.1943
Beheading	HV8552-8555	364.66
Belarus	DK507-.95	947.8
Belarus—Gazetteers	DK507.18	914.78003
Belarus—History	DK507.37-.78	947.8
Belgian literature (French)	PQ3810-3858	840
Belgium	DH401-811	936.4/949.3
Belgium—Biography	DH513-516	920.0364/ 920.0493
Belgium—Census	HA1391-1410	314.93
Belgium—Civilization	DH471	936.4/949.3
Belgium—Description and travel	DH431-435	913.6404/ 914.9304
Belgium—Economic conditions	HC311-320	330.9493
Belgium—Emigration and immigration	JV8160-8169	325.(2493/493)
Belgium—Gazetteers	DH414	913.64003/ 914.93003
Belgium—History, Military	DH540-545	355.309493
Belgium—History, Naval	DH551	359.309493
Belgium—History— To 1555	DH571-584	936.4/ 949.30(1-2)
Belgium—History— Charles V, 1506-1555	DH584	949.302
Belgium—History— 1555-1648	DH585-606	949.302
Belgium—History— 1648-1794	DH607-619	949.302
Belgium—History— Revolution, 1789-1790	DH616-618.5	949.302
Belgium—History— 1794-1814	DH620-631	949.302
Belgium—History— Revolution, 1830-1839	DH650-665	949.303
Belgium—History— Leopold II, 1865-1909	DH671-676	949.303
Belgium—History— Albert I, 1909-1934	DH681-685	949.3041
Belgium—History— German occupation, 1914-1918	DH682	949.3041
Belgium—History— German occupation, 1940-1945	DH687	949.3042
Belgium—History— Baudouin I, 1951-	DH690-692	949.304(3-4)

Subject Heading	LC	Dewey	Subject Heading	LC	Dewey
Belgium—Manufactures	TS67-68	670.9493	Bermuda Islands—History	F1635-1637	972.99
Belgium—Maps	G6010-6014	912.493	Bermuda Islands—	F1630	972.99005
Belgium—Periodicals	DH401	936.4005/	Periodicals		
		949.3005	Bermuda Islands—	JL590-599	320.97299
Belgium—Politics and	JN6101-6371	320.9493	Politics and government		
government			Bessarabia (Moldova	DK509.1-.95	947.(6-7)
Belief and doubt	BD215	121.(5/6)	and Ukraine)		
Belize	F1441-1457	972.82	Bessemer process	TN736-738	669.1423
Belize—Census	HA791-800	317.282	Betrothal	GN484.43	392.4
Belize—Civilization	F1443.8	972.82	Betrothal	GT2650	392.4
Belize—Description and	F1444-.3	917.28204	Beverages	TX951	641.2
travel			Beverages	TX815-817	641.87
Belize—History	F1445.5-1448	972.82	Beverages	TP500-660	663
Belize—Maps	G4820-4824	912.7282	Bhakti	BL1214.32.B53	294.5211
Belize—Periodicals	F1441	972.82005	Bhutan—Census	HA4590.3	315.498
Belize—Politics and	JL670-679	320.97282	Bhutan—Maps	G7780-7784	912.5498
government			Bible	BS	220
Bells	CC200-255	786.8848	Bible. English	BS135-198	220.52
Belts and belting	TJ1100-1119	621.852	Bible. Polyglot	BS1-3	220.51
Benediction	BV197.B5	264.13	Bible—Abridgments	BS405-408	220.5
Benediction	BX2048.B5	264.13	Bible—Biography	BS570-580	220.092
Benelux countries	G1850-1874	912.492	Bible—Chronology	BS637	220.9
Benelux countries	DH	936.3/949.2	Bible—Commentaries	BS482-498	220.7
Benelux countries—	JV2500-2899	325.3492	Bible—Concordances	BS420-429	220.(4-5)
Colonies			Bible—Criticism,	BS500-534.8	220.6
Benelux countries—	HF3591-3620.5	380.109492	interpretation, etc.		
Commerce			Bible—Devotional use	BS617.8	242
Benelux countries—	CS780-839	929.10720492	Bible—Evidences,	BS480	220.1
Genealogy			authority, etc.		
Bengali (South Asian	DS432.B4	954.0049144	Bible—Examinatons,	BS612	220.076
people)			questions, etc.		
Bengali language	PK1651-1695	491.44	Bible—History	BS445-460	220.09
Benin—Census	HA4722	316.683	Bible—History of Biblical	BS635-636	220.9
Benin—Civilization	DT541.4	966.83	events		
Benin—Description and	DT541.27	916.68304	Bible—Inspiration	BS480	220.13
travel			Bible—Language, style	BS537	220.(4-5)
Benin—History	DT541.5-.845	966.83	Bible—Parables	BS680.P3	226.8
Benin—History—To 1894	DT541.65-.67	966.8301	Bible—Prayers	BS680.P64	242.5
Benin—History—Coup	DT541.845	966.83051	Bible—Prophecies	BS647-649	220.15
d'etat, 1977			Bible—Study and teaching	BS585-613	220.071
Benin—Maps	G8750-8754	912.6683	Bible—Theology	BS543	230.041
Benzene	QD341.H9	547.611	Bible—Versions	BS450-460	220.(4/5)
Berber languages	PJ2369-2399	493.3	Bible. N.T.	BS1901-2970	225-228
Berber languages	PJ2340-2349	493.3	Bible. N.T. Acts	BS2620-2628	226.6
Berber languages—	PJ2349	493.33	Bible. N.T. Epistles	BS2630-2815.5	227
Dictionaries			Bible. N.T. Gospels	BS2549	226
Berber languages—	PJ2347	493.32	Bible. N.T. Pauline Epistles	BS2640-2815.5	227
Etymology			Bible. N.T.—Commentaries	BS2333-2348	225.7
Berber languages—	PJ2345	493.35	Bible. N.T.—Concordances	BS2301-2308	225.(4-5)
Grammar			Bible. N.T.—Criticism,	BS2350-2393	225.6
Bergen-Belsen (Germany :	D805.G3	940.5318	interpretation, etc.		
Concentration camp)			Bible. N.T.—History	BS2315-2318	225.09
Berlin (Germany)	DD851-900	943.155	Bible. N.T.—Study and	BS2525-2544	225.071
Bermuda Islands	F1630-1640	972.99	teaching		
Bermuda Islands—Census	HA921-930	317.299	Bible. N.T.—Theology	BS2397	230
Bermuda Islands—	F1633	972.99	Bible. N.T.—Versions	BS1901	225.(4-5)
Civilization			Bible. O.T. Apocrypha	BS1691-1830	229
Bermuda Islands—	F1631	917.29904	Bible. O.T. Greek	BS737-765	221.48
Description and travel			Bible. O.T. Latin	BS767-815	221.47
Bermuda Islands—	F1630.7	917.299003	Bible. O.T. Pentateuch	BS1221-1285.5	222.1
Gazetteers			Bible. O.T. Psalms	BS1419-1450	223.2

Subject Heading	LC	Dewey
Bible. O.T. Song of Solomon	BS1481-1490	223.9
Bible. O.T.—Biography	BS580	221.092
Bible. O.T.—Commentaries	BS1143-1158	221.7
Bible. O.T.—Concordances	BS1121-1128	221.(4-5)
Bible. O.T.—Criticism, interpetation, etc.	BS1160-1191.5	221.6
Bible. O.T.—Harmonies	BS1104	221.65
Bible. O.T.—History	BS1130-1134	221.09
Bible. O.T.—Study and teaching	BS1193-1195	221.071
Bible. O.T.—Theology	BS1192.5	230.0411
Bible. O.T.—Versions	BS701-1013	221.(4-5)
Bible as literature	BS535-537	809.93522
Bible stories	BS546-559	220.9505
Biblical cosmology	BS651-652	231.765
Bibliography	Z1001-9000	010
Bibliography, National	Z1201-4980	015
Bibliography, National—Africa	Z3501-3975	015.6
Bibliography, National—Armenia	Z3461-3465	015.4756
Bibliography, National—Asia	Z3126-3415	015.5
Bibliography, National—Asia, Southeastern	Z3221-3415	015.59
Bibliography, National—Asiatic Russia	Z3401-3409	015.47
Bibliography, National—Australia	Z4001-4439	015.94
Bibliography, National—Canada	Z1365-1401	015.71
Bibliography, National—Europe	Z2000-2959	015.4
Bibliography, National—Iran	Z3366-3370	015.55
Bibliography, National—Israel	Z3476-3480	015.5694
Bibliography, National—Lebanon	Z3466-3470	015.5692
Bibliography, National—Mexico	Z1411-1431	015.72
Bibliography, National—Middle East	Z3013-3028	015.56
Bibliography, National—South America	Z1601-1939	015.8
Bibliography, National—Syria	Z3481-3485	015.5691
Bibliography, National—United States	Z1215-1363	015.73
Bibliography, National—West Indies	Z1501-1595	015.729
Bicycle racing	GV1049	796.62
Bicycle touring	GV1044-1046	796.64
Bicycle trails	TE301	625.88
Bicycles	GV1040-1058	796.6(2-4)
Bicycles	HE5736-5739	388.3472
Bicycles	TL410-438	629.2272
Big band music	M1366	784.48
Big bang theory	QB991.B54	523.18
Big business	HD2350.8-2356	338.644
Big game fishing	SH457.5	799.12

Subject Heading	LC	Dewey
Big game hunting	SK295-305	799.26
Bills, Legislative—United States	KF16-22	348.7301
Binomial theorem	QA161.B5	512.942
Bioadhesive drug delivery systems	RS201.B54	615.6
Biochemical engineering	TP248.3	660.63
Biochemistry	QD415-436	572
Biochemistry	QH345	572
Biochemistry	QP501-801	572
Bioclimatology	QH543-.2	577.22
Bioethics	QH332	174.957
Biofertilizers	S654.5	631.847
Biogas	TP359.B48	665.776
Biogeochemistry	QH343.7-344	577.14
Biogeography	QH84-198	578.09
Biographical preaching	BV4235.B56	251
Biography	CT	920
Biography as a literary form	CT21-22	809.93592
Biography—20th century	D1070-1075	920.00904
Biography—Middle Ages, 500-1500	D115	920.00902
Biography—Middle Ages, 500-1500	D107-110.5	920.00902
Biography—To 500	D55	920.00901
Bioinorganic chemistry	QP531-535	572.51
Biological apparatus and supplies	QH324	570.284
Biological control systems	QH508	571.7
Biological diversity conservation	QH75-77	333.95
Biological invasions	QH353	577.18
Biological laboratories	QH321-323.2	570.72
Biological models	QH324.8	570.228
Biological pest control agents	SB975	632.96
Biological productivity	QH541.3	577.15
Biological rhythms	QH527	571.77
Biological rhythms	QP84.6	571.77
Biological rhythms in plants	QK761	571.772
Biological rhythms—Effect of space flight on	RC1151.B54	612
Biological transport	QH509	571.64
Biological warfare	UG447.8	358.38
Biologists	QH26-31	570.92
Biology	QH301-705	570
Biology—Data processing	QH324.2	570.285
Biology—History	QH305-.2	570.9
Biology—Philosophy	QH331	570.1
Biology—Research	QH315-320	570.72
Biology—Study and teaching	QH315-320	570.71
Bioluminescence	QH641	572.4358
Biomagnetism	QH504	154.72
Biomathematics	QH323.5	570.151
Biomechanics	QH513	571.43
Biomedical engineering	R856-857	610.28
Bionics	Q317-321	003.5
Bioorganic chemistry	QP550-801	572
Biophysics	QH505	571.4
Biosphere reserves	QH75-77	333.95
Biotechnology	TP248.13-.65	660.6

Subject Heading	LC	Dewey	Subject Heading	LC	Dewey
Body temperature	QP135	612.01426	Bombings	HV6640	364.164
Body temperature	RC75	616.0754	Bonaire	F2048	972.986
Bodybuilding	GV546.5-.56	646.75	Bonaire—Maps	G5175-5179	912.72986
Bog ecology	QH541.5.B63	577.687	Bonapartism	JC359	321.030944
Bogs	GB621-628	551.41	Bond transfer	HG4028.B6	332.6323
Bohemia (Czech Republic)—History—To 1526	DB2080-2133	943.71023	Bonds	HG4651	332.6323
Bohemia (Czech Republic)—History—1526-1618	DB2135-2151	943.710232	Bone carving	NK6020-6022	736.6
			Bone carving	TT288	745.58
			Bone diseases in children	RJ482.B65	618.9271
Bohemia (Czech Republic)—History—1618-1848	DB2155-2162	943.7102	Bone marrow	QM569	611.0184
Bohemia (Czech Republic)—History—1848-1918	DB2165-2182	943.71024	Bone marrow—Transplantation	RD123.5	617.440592
Boiler-plates	TJ290-291	621.194	Bone wiring (Orthopedics)	RD103.B65	617.471
Boilers	TH7538	697.07	Bone-grafting	RD123	617.4710592
Boilers	TH7588	697.507	Bone-meal	S659	631.85
Boiling (Cookery)	TX685	641.731	Bone-meal	SF99	636.0855
Boiling water reactors	TK9203.B6	621.4834	Boncs	QL821	573.76
Bolivia	F3301-3359	984	Bones	QM101-117	573.76
Bolivia—Census	HA961-970	318.4	Bones—Diseases	RC930-931	616.71
Bolivia—Civilization	F3310	984	Bones—Surgery	RD684	617.471059
Bolivia—Description and travel	F3311-3315	918.404	Bonpo (Sect)	BQ7960-7989	294.39
Bolivia—Economic conditions	HC181-185	330.984	Bonpo incantations	BQ7982.4	294.343
			Bonsai	SB433.5	635.9772
Bolivia—Emigration and immigration	JV7450-7459	325.(284/84)	Bonus system	HD4928.B6	331.2164
			Book burning	Z657-659	323.445
Bolivia—Gazetteers	F3304	918.4003	Book clubs	Z549	070.5
Bolivia—History	F3320.3-3327	984	Book clubs	Z1008	070.5
Bolivia—History—To 1809	F3322	984.0(1-3)	Book collecting	Z987-997.2	026.1
Bolivia—History—War of Independence, 1809-1825	F3323	984.041	Book selection	Z689-.5	025.21
			Book thefts	Z702	025.82
			Bookbinders	Z269-.3	686.30092
Bolivia—History—1825-1879	F3324	984.04(2-5)	Bookbinding	Z266-276	686.3
Bolivia—History—1879-1938	F3324-3325	984.0(45-51)	Bookkeeping	HF5601-5689.8	657.2
			Books and reading	Z1003-.5	028
Bolivia—History—1938-	F3326-3327	984.05(1-2)	Books of hours	BX2080	242.802
Bolivia—History—1938-1982	F3326	984.05(1-2)	Books—Conservation and restoration	Z700.9-701.5	025.7
Bolivia—History—Coup d'etat, 1943	F3326	984.051	Books—Deacidification	Z701.3.D4	025.84
			Books—History	Z4-8	002.09
Bolivia—History—Revolution, 1946	F3326	984.051	Booksellers and bookselling	Z278-550	381.45002
			Boots	TS989-1025	685.31
Bolivia—History—Revolution, 1952	F3326	984.052	Borax	HD9585.B67-.B674	338.27633
Bolivia—History—Revolution, 1964	F3326	984.052	Borax	TN917	622.3633
Bolivia—History—Coup d'etat, 1979	F3326	984.052	Borderline personality disorder	RC569.5.B67	616.85852
Bolivia—History—Coup d'etat, 1980	F3326	984.052	Bores (Tidal phenomena)	GC376	551.4708
			Boring	TN281	622.24
Bolivia—History—1982-	F3327	984.052	Boring	TD412	628.114
Bolivia—Manufactures	TS38-39	670.984	Boroughs	JS261	352.16
Bolivia—Maps	G5320-5324	912.84	Bosnia and Hercegovina	DR1652-1785	939.8/949.742
Bolivia—Periodicals	F3301	984.005	Bosnia and Hercegovina—History	DR1697-1785	949.742
Bolivia—Politics and government	JL2200-2299	320.984	Bosnia and Hercegovina—Maps	G6860-6863	912.49742
			Boston (Mass.)	F73-.9	974.461
Bolivian literature	PQ7801-7820	860	Boston Massacre, 1770	E215.4	973.3113
Bolts and nuts	TJ1330-1333	621.882	Boston Tea Party, 1773	E215.7	973.3115
Bombing and gunnery ranges	U300-305	355.5	Botanical chemistry	QK861-899	572.2
			Botanical gardens	QK71-73	580.73
			Botanists	QK26-31	580.92

Subject Heading	LC	Dewey	Subject Heading	LC	Dewey
Botany	QK	580	Brahmanism	BL1100-1245	294.5
Botany—Anatomy	QK641-707	575	Brahmans	BL1241.46	294.5
Botany—Classification	QK91-97	580.12	Braids (Hairdressing)	TT975	646.724
Botany—Dictionaries	QK9	580.3	Brain	QP376-430	612.82
Botany—Exhibitions	QK79-.5	580.74	Brain	GN181-190.5	599.948
Botany—Folklore	GR780	398.368	Brain—Cancer	RC280.B7	616.99481
Botany—Nomenclature	QK96	580.14	Brain—Degeneration	RC394.D35	616.8
Botany—Pictorial works	QK98	580.222	Brain—Diseases	RC386-395	616.8(1-4)
Botany—Societies, etc.	QK1	580.6	Brain—Surgery	RD594-.15	617.481059
Botany—Study and teaching	QK51-57	580.71	Brain—Tumors	RD663	616.99481
Botany—Terminology	QK10	580.14	Brain—Wounds and injuries	RD594-.15	617.481044
Botany—Africa	QK381-424	580.96	Brain death	RA1063.3	614.1
Botany—Antarctica	QK474.4	580.9989	Brain-damaged children	RJ496.B7	618.928043
Botany—Arctic regions	QK474-.3	580.998	Brainwashing	BF633	153.853
Botany—Asia	QK341-379	580.95	Branding (Punishment)	HV8609	364.67
Botany—Asia, Southeastern	QK360-368	580.959	Brandy	TP599	663.53
Botany—Australia	QK431-461	580.994	Brass	TS564-589	673.3
Botany—Canada	QK201-203	580.971	Brass band music	M1200-1269	784.9
Botany—Central America	QK215-222	580.9728	Brass ensembles	M955-959	785.9
Botany—Europe	QK281-339	580.94	Brass instrument music	M111	788.9
Botany—Mexico	QK211	580.972	Brass instruments	MT418	788.907
Botany—Middle East	QK353	580.956	Brazil	F2501-2656	981
Botany—South America	QK241-274	580.98	Brazil—Census	HA971-990	318.1
Botany—United States	QK115-195	580.973	Brazil—Civilization	F2510	981
Botany—West Indies	QK225-231	580.9729	Brazil—Description and travel	F2511-2517	918.104
Botany, Economic	SB107-109	338.1	Brazil—Economic conditions	HC186-190	330.981
Botany, Medical	QK99	581.634			
Botswana—Census	HA4706	316.883	Brazil—Emigration and immigration	JV7460-7469	325.(281/81)
Botswana—Civilization	DT2452	968.83			
Botswana—Description and travel	DT2448	968.8304	Brazil—Gazetteers	F2504	918.1003
			Brazil—History	F2520.3-2538.5	981
Botswana—Gazetteers	DT2434	916.883003	Brazil—History—To 1822	F2526-2534	981.0(1-33)
Botswana—History	DT2464-2502	968.83	Brazil—History— 1500-1548	F2526	981.03(1-2)
Botswana—History— To 1966	DT2483-2493	968.830(1-2)			
			Brazil—History— 1548-1580	F2528	981.032
Botswana—History—1966-	DT2496-2502	968.8303			
Botswana—Maps	G8600-8604	912.6883	Brazil—History— 1549-1762	F2528	981.032
Bottles	TP866	666.192			
Bottom fishing	SH455.6	799.122	Brazil—History—French colony, 1555-1567	F2529	981.032
Bound states (Quantum mechanics)	QC174.17.B6	530.12			
			Brazil—History— 1580-1640	F2530	981.032
Boundaries	JC323	320.12			
Boundary layer	QA913	532.051	Brazil—History—Dutch Conquest, 1624-1654	F2532	981.032
Boundary layer	TL574.B6	629.13237			
Boundary stones	CC600-605	320.12	Brazil—History—War of the Emboabas, 1707-1709	F2528	981.032
Bow and arrow	GN498.B78	623.441			
Bow and arrow	U877-878	355.8241			
Bowhunting	SK36	799.215	Brazil—History— 1763-1822	F2534	981.033
Bowling	GV901-909	794.6			
Boxing	GV1115-1137	796.83	Brazil—History—United Kingdom, 1815-1822	F2534	981.033
Boy Scouts	HS3312-3316	369.43			
Boy's clothing	TT603	646.40608341	Brazil—History—1822-	F2535-2538.5	981.0(4-6)
Boycotts	HD5461	331.893	Brazil—History—Declaration of Independence, 1822	F2536	981.033
Boys	HQ775	649.132			
Boys	HV877-878	369.42	Brazil—History—Empire, 1822-1889	F2536	981.04
Boys—Prayer-books and devotions	BV283.B7	242.82			
			Brazil—History— Revolution, 1842	F2536	981.04
Boys—Societies and clubs	HV878	369.42			
Boys—Societies and clubs	HS3301-3325	369.42	Brazil—History—Quebra Quilos' Revolt, 1874	F2536	981.04
Boys as soldiers	UB418.B69	355.3308351			
Brackish water biology	QH95.9	578.77			

Subject Heading	LC	Dewey	Subject Heading	LC	Dewey
Brazil—History—Canudos Campaign, 1893-1897	F2537	981.05	Bridal price	GN480.1	392.4
Brazil—History—Naval Revolt, 1893-1894	F2537	981.05	Bridges	HE374-377	388.132
			Bridges	TG	624.2
Brazil—History—1889-1930	F2537	981.05	Bridges—Abutments	TG325	624.28
			Bridges—Congresses	TG5	624.206
Brazil—History—Canudos Campaign, 1893-1897	F2537	981.05	Bridges—Design and construction	TG300-304	624.25
Brazil—History—Naval Revolt, 1893-1894	F2537	981.05	Bridges—Design and construction—Estimates	TG313	624.250299
Brazil—History—Naval Revolt, 1910	F2537	981.05	Bridges—Floors	TG325.6	624.283
Brazil—History—Contestado Insurrection, 1912-1916	F2537	981.05	Bridges—Foundations and piers	TG320	624.284
			Bridges—History	TG15-20	624.209
Brazil—History—Revolution, 1922	F2537	981.05	Bridges—Maintenance and repair	TG315	624.20288
Brazil—History—Revolution, 1924-1925	F2537	981.05	Bridges—Periodicals	TG1-4	624.205
Brazil—History—1930-1945	F2538	981.061	Bridges—[By region or country]	TG21-127	624.209(3-9)
Brazil—History—Revolution, 1930	F2538	981.05	Bridges, Arched	TG327-340	624.6
Brazil—History—Uprising, 1935	F2538	981.061	Bridges, Brick	TG330	624.63
			Bridges, Cantilever	TG385	624.35
Brazil—History—Revolution, 1938	F2538	981.061	Bridges, Concrete	TG335-340	624.63
			Bridges, Continuous	TG413-416	624.33
Brazil—History—1945-1954	F2538	981.061	Bridges, Stone	TG330	624.63
Brazil—History 1954-1964	F2538.2-.22	981.062	Bridges, Truss	TG375-380	624.38
			Bridges, Wooden	TG365	624.32
Brazil—History—1964-1985	F2538.25-.27	981.063	Bridges, Wooden	TG375	624.38
			Bridges (Dentistry)	RK666	617.692
Brazil—History—1985-	F2538.3-.5	981.064	Bridles	SF309.9	636.10837
Brazil—Manufactures	TS41-42	670.981	Brigands and robbers	HV6441-6453	364.1552
Brazil—Maps	G5400-5404	912.81	Bright's disease	RC907	616.612
Brazil—Periodicals	F2501	981.005	Briquets (Fuel)	TP323	662.65
Brazil—Politics and government	JL2400-2499	320.981	British Columbia—Gazetteers	F1086.4	917.11003
Brazilian literature	PQ9500-9699	869	British Columbia—History	F1086-1089.7	971.1
Bread	TX769-770	641.815	British Columbia—Maps	G3510-3514	912.711
Breakfasts	TX733	641.52	British Columbia—Periodicals	F1086	971.1005
Breakwaters	TC333	627.24	British Virgin Islands	F2129	972.9725
Breast	QM495	611.49	British Virgin Islands—Maps	G5020-5024	912.729725
Breast—Diseases	RG491-499	618.19	British literature	PN849.G	820
Breast feeding	RJ216	613.269	Broadcasting	PN1990-1992.92	384.54
Breathing exercises	RA782	613.192	Broiling	TX687	641.76
Breeding	S494	636.082	Brokers	HF5419-5422	381.2092
Bremsstrahlung	QC484.3	539.7222	Bronchitis	RC778	616.234
Breton language	PB2800-2849	491.68	Bronze	TS570	673.3
Breton language—Grammar	PB2811-2847	491.685	Bronze age	GN777-778	930.15
Breton language—Study and teachings	PB2807	491.68071	Bronze sculpture	NB135-143	731.456
			Brotherhoods	BV950-1220	267
Breton literature	PB2856-2932	891.68	Brownian movements	QC183	530.475
Breviaries	BX2000-.68	264.024	Brunei—Civilization	DS650.4	959.55
Bribery	HV6301-6321	364.1323	Brunei—Description and travel	DS650.35	915.95504
Bribery—[By region or country]	HV6303-6321	364.132309(4-9)	Brunei—Gazetteers	DS650.2	915.955003
Bribery—United States	HV6306-6316	364.13230973	Brunei—History	DS650.44-.83	959.55
			Brush drawing	ND2460	741.26
Brick houses	NA7150	728	Brushes, Carbon	TK2484	621.316
Brickmaking	TP826-833	666.737	Brushwork	ND1505	751.4
			Brussels (Belgium)	DH802-809.95	949.332
			Bryophytes	QK532.4-563.87	588
			Brythonic languages	PB2001-2060	491.6

Subject Heading	LC	Dewey	Subject Heading	LC	Dewey
Brythonic languages—Etymology	PB2021	491.6(2-8)2	Buddhism—Thailand	BQ550-568	294.309593
Brythonic languages—Grammar	PB2009-2015	491.6(2-8)5	Buddhism—United States	BQ730-739	294.30973
Brythonic languages—Lexicography	PB2023	491.6(2-8)3028	Buddhism and social problems	BQ5851-5899	294.33783
Brythonic languages—Study and teaching	PB2005	491.6(2-8)071	Buddhist astrology	BF1714.B7	133.59443
Buccaneers	F2161	910.45092	Buddhist education	BQ141-209	294.375
Buccaneers	G535-537	910.45092	Buddhist education of children	BQ171-199	294.375
Buchenwald (Germany : Concentration camp)	D805.G3	940.5318	Buddhist ethics	BJ1289	294.35
Buckling (Mechanics)	TG265	624.252	Buddhist pilgrims and pilgrimages	BQ6400-6495	294.34351
Buckling (Mechanics)	TA410	620.112	Buddhist precepts	BQ5485-5530	294.342
Buckshot War, Harrisburg, Pa., 1838	F153	974.803	Buddhist sects	BQ8000-9800	294.39
Budapest (Hungary)	DB981-999	943.912	Buddhist shrines	BQ6300-6388	294.3435
Buddha (The concept)	BQ4180	294.363	Buddhists—Biography	BQ840-845	294.3092
Buddhas	BQ4670-4690	294.363	Budget	HJ2005-2216	352.48
Buddhism	BQ1-9999	294.3	Budget—Law and Legislation—England	KD5292	343.42034
Buddhism—Apologetic works	BQ4050	294.342	Budget—Law and legislation—United States	KF6221-6227	343.73034
Buddhism—Catechisms	BQ4170	294.32	Building	TH	690
Buddhism—Charities	BQ5851-5899	294.3378	Building—Accidents	TH443	690.22
Buddhism—Creeds	BQ4170	294.32	Building—Congresses	TH5	690.06
Buddhism—Customs and practices	BQ4965-5030	294.344	Building—Details	TH2025-3000	690.1
Buddhism—Doctrines	BQ5485-5530	294.342	Building—Directories	TH12-13	690.025
Buddhism—Doctrines	BQ4061-4570	294.342	Building—Equipment and supplies	TH915	690.0284
Buddhism—Doctrines—History	BQ4080-4125	294.34209	Building—Estimates	TH434-437	692.5
Buddhism—History	BQ251-799	294.309	Building—History	TH15-19	690.09
Buddhism—History—To ca. 100 A.D.	BQ287-296	294.30901	Building—Periodicals	TH1-4	690.05
Buddhism—Liturgical objects	BQ5070-5075	294.3437	Building—Study and teaching	TH165-213	690.071
Buddhism—Missions	BQ5901-5975	294.372	Building—[By region or country]	TH21-127	690.09(3-9)
Buddhism—Periodicals	BQ1-10	294.305	Building—United States	TH23-25	690.0973
Buddhism—Prayer-books and devotions	BQ5535-5594	294.34433	Building, Bombproof	TH1097	693.854
Buddhism—Psychology	BQ4570.P76	294.3375	Building, Brick	TH1301	693.21
Buddhism—Relations	BQ4600-4610	294.3372	Building, Fireproof	TH1061-1093	693.82
Buddhism—Rituals	BQ4965-5030	294.3438	Building, Ice and snow	TH1431	693.91
Buddhism—Sacred books	BQ1100-3340	294.382	Building, Iron and steel	TA684-695	624.182
Buddhism—Societies, etc.	BQ12-93	294.365	Building, Iron and steel	TH1610-1635	693.71
Buddhism—Africa	BQ710-719	294.3096	Building, Stone	TH1201	693.1
Buddhism—America	BQ720-760	294.309(7-8)	Buildings—Additions	TH4816.2	690.24
Buddhism—Asia, Central	BQ570-609	294.30958	Buildings—Earthquake effects	TH1095	693.852
Buddhism—Burma	BQ416-439	294.309591	Buildings—Environmental engineering	TH6014-6085	697
Buddhism—Canada	BQ740-749	294.30971	Buildings—Joints	TH2060	690.1
Buddhism—China	BQ620-649	294.30951	Buildings—Maintenance	TH3351-3361	690.24
Buddhism—East Asia	BQ610-699	294.3095	Buildings—Remodeling for other use	TH3401-3411	690.24
Buddhism—Europe	BQ700-709	294.3094	Buildings—Repair and reconstruction	TH3401-3411	690.24
Buddhism—India	BQ330-349	294.30954	Buildings—Specifications	TH425	692.3
Buddhism—Indonesia	BQ510-539	294.309598	Buildings, Prefabricated	NA8480	721.04497
Buddhism—Japan	BQ670-699	294.30952	Buildings, Prefabricated	TH1098	693.97
Buddhism—Korea	BQ650-669	294.309519	Building fittings	TH6010-6013	696-697
Buddhism—Malaysia	BQ540-549	294.309595	Building management	TX955	647
Buddhism—Nepal	BQ380-396	294.3095496	Building materials	TA401-492	620.1(2-9)
Buddhism—Oceania	BQ770-799	294.3099(3-6)	Bulgaria	DR51-98	939.8/949.9
Buddhism—Sri Lanka	BQ350-379	294.3095493			

Subject Heading	LC	Dewey	Subject Heading	LC	Dewey
Bulgaria—Biography	DR66	920.0398/ 920.0499	Burkina Faso—History	DT555.52-.83	966.25
Bulgaria—Biography	DR66	920.0398/ 920.0499	Burkina Faso—History— Coup d'etat, 1987	DT555.8	966.2505
Bulgaria—Census	HA1621-1630	314.99	Burkina Faso—Maps	G8805-8809	912.6625
Bulgaria—Civilization	DR63	939.8/949.9	Burlesques	PN6231.B84	792.7
Bulgaria—Description and travel	DR57-61	913.9804/ 914.9904	Burma—Census	HA4570.7	315.91
			Burma—Civilization	DS527.9	959.1
Bulgaria—Directories	DR53.7	949.90025	Burma—Description and travel	DS527.5-.7	915.9104
Bulgaria—Economic conditions	HC403	330.9499	Burma—Economic conditions	HC422	330.9591
Bulgaria—Gazetteers	DR53	913.98003/ 914.99003	Burma—History—To 1824	DS527.2-.3	959.102
			Burma—History— 1824-1948	DS529.7-530.32	959.10(2-4)
Bulgaria—Historiography	DR66.7-.97	939.80072/ 949.90072	Burma—History—Peasant Uprising, 1931	DS530	959.104
Bulgaria—History	DR65-93.34	939.8/949.9			
Bulgaria—History, Military	DR70	355.309499	Burma—History— Japanese occupation, 1942-1945	DS530	959.104
Bulgaria—History—To 681	DR74.3	939.8/949.901			
Bulgaria—History— 681-1018	DR74.5	949.9013	Burma—History—1948-	DS530.4	959.105
			Burma—Maps	G2285-2289	912.591
Bulgaria—History— 1018-1185	DR79	949.9014	Burma—Maps	G7720-7724	912.591
			Burma—Politics and government	JQ751	320.9595
Bulgaria—History— 1393-1878	DR82-.5	949.9015	Burmese language	PL3921-3969	495.8
			Burmese literature	PL3970-3988	895.8
Bulgaria—History— 1878-1944	DR84.9-.8	949.902	Burn care teams	RD96.4-.55	617.11
			Burn out (Psychology)	BF481	158.723
Bulgaria—History—1944-	DR89.9-93.34	949.90(2-3)	Burns and scalds	RD96.4-.55	617.11
Bulgaria—Maps	G2040-2044	912.499	Burr Conspiracy, 1805-1807	E334	973.48
Bulgaria—Maps	G6890-6894	912.499	Bursitis	RC935.B8	616.76
Bulgaria—Periodicals	DR51	939.8005/ 949.9005	Burundi—Census	HA4696	316.7572
			Burundi—Civilization	DT450.63	967.572
Bulgarian language	PG801-993	491.81	Burundi—Description and travel	DT450.6	916.757204
Bulgarian language— Dictionaries	PG975-984	491.813	Burundi—Economic conditions	HC880	330.967572
Bulgarian language— Grammar	PG831-925	491.815			
			Burundi—Gazetteers	DT450.515	916.7572003
Bulgarian literature	PG1000-1146	891.8109	Burundi—History	DT450.66-.855	967.572
Bulgarian philology	PG801-823	491.81	Burundi—Maps	G8435-8439	912.67572
Bulimia	RC552.B84	616.85263	Bus drivers	TL232.3	629.22233092
Bulk carrier cargo ships	VM393.B7	623.8245	Bus lanes	HE336.B8	388.12
Bull Run, 1st Battle of, Va., 1861	E472.18	973.731	Bus lines	HE5601-5725	388.322
			Business	HF5001-6182.2	338.7
Bull Run, 2nd Battle of, Va., 1862	E473.77	973.732	Business cards	NE965-.3	741.685
			Business communication	HF5717-5734.7	651.7
Bullfights	GV1107-1108.6	791.82	Business consultants	HD69.C6	658.46
Bungee jumping	GV770.27	797.5	Business cycles	HB3711-3840	338.542
Bunker Hill, Battle of, 1775	E241.B9	973.3312	Business cycles—[By region or country]	HB3741-3840	338.54209(4-9)
Buoys	VK1000-1246	623.8944			
Buoys—[By region or country]	VK1150-1246	623.8944	Business education	HF1101-1186	380.1071
			Business education—[By region or country]	HF1131-1186	380.10710(4-9)
Burglar alarms	TH9739	643.16			
Burglary	HV6646-6665	364.162	Business education—Africa	HF1176	380.107106
Burglary protection	TH9701-9745	643.16	Business education—Asia	HF1171	380.107105
Burial	GT3150-3390.5	393.1	Business education— Australia	HF1181-1182	380.1071094
Burial	RA625-630	614.6			
Burial	GN486	393.1	Business education— Europe	HF1140-1165	380.107104
Burkina Faso—Census	HA4728	316.625			
Burkina Faso—Civilization	DT555.4	966.25	Business education— Latin America	HF1135	380.107108
Burkina Faso—Description and travel	DT555.27	916.62504			
Burkina Faso—Gazetteers	DT555.15	916.625003			

Subject Heading	LC	Dewey
Business education—United States	HF1131-1134	380.1071073
Business enterprises—Finance	HG4001-4285	338.6041
Business ethics	HF5387	174.4
Business etiquette	HF5389	395.52
Business intelligence	HD38.7	658.47
Business law	K1010-1014	346.07
Business law—United States	KF1970-2105	346.7307
Business libraries	Z675.B8	027.69
Business logistics	HD38.5	658.5
Business mathematics	HF5691-5716	650.01513
Business names—England	KD1450	346.42048
Business relocation	HC79.D5	338.7
Business report writing	HF5719	651.74
Business writing	HF5718.3-5734	651.74
Business—Forms	HF5371	651.29
Busing for school integration	LC214.5-.53	379.263
Busts	NB1300	731.74
Butter	SF263-269.5	637.2
Butterflies	QL541-562.4	595.789
Byzantine Empire	DF501-649	949.50(13-3)
Byzantine Empire—Biography	DF506-.5	920.0495
Byzantine Empire—Congresses	DF501.5	949.50(13-3)006
Byzantine Empire—Geography	DF518	914.95
Byzantine Empire—Historiography	DF505-.7	949.50(13-3)0072
Byzantine Empire—History	DF550-649	949.50(13-3)
Byzantine Empire—History, Military	DF543	355.309495
Byzantine Empire—History, Naval	DF544	359.309495
Byzantine Empire—History—To 527	DF553.5-568	949.5013
Byzantine Empire—History—Arcadius, 395-408	DF561	949.5013
Byzantine Empire—History—Theodosius II, 408-450	DF562	949.5013
Byzantine Empire—History—Leo I, 457-474	DF564	949.5013
Byzantine Empire—History—Leo II, 474	DF565	949.5013
Byzantine Empire—History—Zeno, 474-491	DF566	949.5013
Byzantine Empire—History—Justinian I, 527-565	DF572-.8	949.5013
Byzantine Empire—History—Justine II, 565-578	DF573	949.5013
Byzantine Empire—History—Tiberius II, 578-582	DF573.2	949.5013
Byzantine Empire—History—Maurice, 582-602	DF573.5	949.5013
Byzantine Empire—History—Heraclius, 610-641	DF574	949.5013
Byzantine Empire—History—Constans II, 641-668	DF575.3	949.5013
Byzantine Empire—History—Leo III the Isaurian, 717-741	DF582	949.502
Byzantine Empire—History—Constantine V Copronymus, 741-775	DF583	949.502
Byzantine Empire—History—Irene, 797-802	DF586	949.502
Byzantine Empire—History—Basil I, 867-886	DF589	949.502
Byzantine Empire—History—Leo VI, 886-911	DF592	949.502
Byzantine Empire—History—Romanus II, 959-963	DF594	949.502
Byzantine Empire—History—1081-1453	DF604-649	949.50(3-4)
Byzantine Empire—History—Alexius I Comnenus, 1081-1118	DF605	949.503
Byzantine Empire—History—John II Comnenus, 1118-1143	DF606	949.503
Byzantine Empire—History—Manuel I Comnenus, 1143-1180	DF607	949.503
Byzantine Empire—History—Lascarid dynasty, 1208-1259	DF625	949.504
Byzantine Empire—History—John V Palaeologus, 1341-1391	DF638	949.504
Byzantine Empire—Periodicals	DF501	949.50(13-3)005
Byzantine Empire—Politics and government	JC91-93	320.9495
Byzantine Empire—Study and teaching	DF505.8-.82	949.50(13-3)0071
Byzantine drama	PA5190-5194	882.208
Byzantine drama	PA5160-5163	882.209
Byzantine literature	PA5170-5198	880.8002
Byzantine literature	PA5101-5167	880.9002
Byzantine poetry	PA5150-5155	881.209
Byzantine poetry	PA5180-5189	881.208
Byzantine prose literature	PA5165	888.08
Byzantine prose literature	PA5195-5196	888.08
Cab and omnibus service	HE5601-5725	388.413214
Cabala	BF1585-1623	135.47
Cabala	BM525	296.16
Cabinet officers	JK610-616	352.240973

Subject Heading	LC	Dewey	Subject Heading	LC	Dewey
Cabinet system	JF331-341	352.24	Camouflage (Military science)	UG449	355.41
Cabinetwork	TT197	684.16	Camp sites, facilities, etc.	GV198.L3	796.54
Cables, Submarine	HE7709-7741	384.1	Camp-meetings	BX8475-8476	269.24
Cables, Submarine	TK5601-5681	384.1	Camp-meetings	BV3798-3799	269.24
Cabooses (Railroads)	TF485	625.22	Campaign funds	JK1991-.5	324.780973
Cacao	SB267	633.74	Campaign insignia	CJ5806	737.223
Cache memory	TK7895.M4	621.397	Campaign literature	JK2251-2391	324.70973
Cafeteria benefit plans	HD4928.N6	331.255	Camping	GV191.68-198.9	796.54
Cage birds	SF461	636.68	Camps	GV192-198	796.54
Cake	TX771-.2	641.8653	Camps for the handicapped	GV197.H3	796.542087
Calcium	QP535.C2	572.516	Campus parking	LB3253	371.61
Calcium in the body	QP535.C2	572.516	Campus police	HV8290-8291	363.289
Calculators	HF5688-5689	681.145	Canaanites	DS121.4	933.004926/
Calculators	QA75	510.284			956.004926
Calculus	QA303-316	515	Canada	F1001-1040	971
Calculus of variations	QA315-316	515.64	Canada—Armed forces— Supplies and stores	UC90-93	355.80971
Calendar, Assyro-Babylonian	CE33	529.0935	Canada—Biography	CT280-310	920.071
Calendar, Islamic	CE59	529.327	Canada—Census	HA741-750	317.1
Calendar, Jewish	CE35	529.326	Canada—Civilization	F1021-.2	971
Calendar, Julian	CE75	529.42	Canada—Climate	QC985-.5	551.6971
Calendar, Roman	CE46	529.309376	Canada—Commerce	HF3221-3230	380.10971
Calendars	CE73	529.3	Canada—Constitutional law	KE4125-4775	342.71
California	F856-870	979.4	Canada—Description and travel	F1012-1017	917.104
California—Gazetteers	F859	917.94003	Canada—Economic conditions	HC111-120	330.971
California—History— To 1846	F864	979.40(1-3)	Canada—Emigration and immigration	JV7200-7299	325.(271/71)
California—History— 1846-1850	F865	979.40(3-4)	Canada—Foreign relations— Law and legislation	KE4310	342.710412
California—History— 1850-1950	F866	979.40(4-53)	Canada—Gazetteers	F1004	917.1003
California—History—1950-	F866.2-.4	979.405(3-4)	Canada—Genealogy	CS80-90	929.1072071
California, Southern	F867	979.49	Canada—History, Military	F1028	355.30971
Cambodia—History— 1444-1863	DS554.6-.64	959.603	Canada—History, Naval	F1028.5	359.30971
			Canada—History—To 1763 (New France)	F1030-.9	971.01
Cambodia—History— 1863-1953	DS554.7-.73	959.60(3-41)	Canada—History— 1755-1763	F1030.9	971.0188
Cambodia—History— 1953-1975	DS554.8-.83	959.604	Canada—History— 1763-1791	F1031	971.02
Cambodia—History— Civil War, 1970-1975	DS554.84	959.6042	Canada—History— 1763-1867	F1032	971.02(2-49)
Cambodia—History—1975-	DS554.84-.842	959.6042	Canada—History— 1775-1783	F1032	971.024
Cambodia—Maps	G8010-8014	912.596	Canada—History— 1791-1841	F1032	971.03
Cambodia—Maps	G2374.3-.34	912.596	Canada—History— Rebellion, 1837-1838	F1032	971.038
Cambodia—Politics and government	JQ930-939	320.9596	Canada—History— 1841-1867	F1032	971.04
Camcorders	TR882.3	384.558	Canada—History— Fenian Invasions, 1866-1870	F1033	971.048
Cameos	NK5720-5722	736.222			
Cameras	TR250-265	771.3	Canada—History— Confederation, 1867	F1033	971.05
Cameroon—Census	HA4719	316.711			
Cameroon—Civilization	DT569.5	967.11	Canada—History— 1914-1945	F1034	971.06(12-32)
Cameroon—Description and travel	DT566-568	916.71104			
Cameroon—Economic conditions	HC995	330.96711	Canada—History—1945-	F1034.2-.3	971.063(2-48)
Cameroon—Gazetteers	DT563	916.711003	Canada—Manufactures	TS26-27	670.971
Cameroon—History	DT572-578.4	967.11			
Cameroon—History— Coup d'etat, 1984	DT578	967.1104			
Cameroon—Maps	G8730-8734	912.6711			
Camouflage (Military science)	V215	359.41			

Subject Heading	LC	Dewey
Canada—Maps	G1115-1193	912.71
Canada—Maps	G3400-3612	912.71
Canada—Periodicals	F1001	971.005
Canada—Politics and government	JL1-500	320.971
Canada—Politics and government—To 1763	JL41-45	320.971090(1-33)
Canada—Politics and government—1763-1791	JL48	320.97109033
Canada—Politics and government—1791-1841	JL53	320.9710903(3-4)
Canada—Politics and government—1841-1867	JL55	320.97109034
Canada—Politics and government—1867-	JL65	320.97109 (34-511)
Canada. Parliament	JL131-179	354.7299
Canada. Parliament.	KE4533-4665	342.7105
Canadian Invasion, 1775-1776	E231	973.33(1-2)
Canadian periodicals	PN4901-4920	051
Canal-boats	TC765	623.829
Canals	HE526	386.4
Canals	TC601-791	627.13
Canals, Interoceanic	HE528-545	386.42
Canals, Interoceanic	TC601-791	627.1
Canals—Lifts	TC763	627.1353
Canals—Steam-navigation	TC769	623.89229
Canary Islands—Census	HA2287	316.49
Canary Islands—Maps	G9150-9154	912.649
Cancer	RC261-282	616.994
Cancer—Etiology	RC268.48	616.994071
Cancer—Genetic aspects	RC268.4-.44	616.994042
Cancer—Homeopathic treatment	RX261.C3	616.99406
Cancer—Hormone therapy	RC271.H55	616.99406
Cancer—Immunotherapy	RC271.I45	616.99406
Cancer—Nursing	RC266	610.73698
Cancer—Prevention	RC268-.15	616.99405
Cancer—Research	RC267	616.9940072
Cancer—Surgery	RD651-678	616.994059
Cancer—Treatment	RC270.8-271	616.99406
Cancer (Astrology)	BF1727.3	133.5265
Candlesticks	NK3685	745.5933
Candy	TX783-793	641.853
Cannabis	RC568.C2	616.8635
Cannabis	RM666.C266	615.7827
Canned foods	TX552	641.612
Cannibalism in animals	QL756.57	591.53
Canning and preserving	TX599-612	641.4
Canoes and canoeing	GV781-785	797.122
Canoes and canoeing	GN440.2	386.229
Canon law—Early church, ca. 30-600	BV761	262.90901
Canonization	BX2330	235.24
Canonization	BX576	235.24
Cantatas, Sacred	M2020-2036	782.24
Cantatas, Secular	M1530-1546.5	782.48
Cantatas, Secular (Unison)	M1609	782.5

Subject Heading	LC	Dewey
Cantonese dialects	PL1731-1740	495.17
Cantors (Judaism)	BM658.2	296.462
Canvassing	HF5446-5456	380.1
Cape Verde—Census	HA2289	316.658
Cape Verde—Civilization	DT671.C23	966.58
Cape Verde—Description and travel	DT671.C22	916.65804
Cape Verde—History	DT671.C25-.C28	966.58
Cape Verde—History—To 1975	DT671.C265	966.580(1-2)
Cape Verde—History—1975-	DT671.C28	966.5803
Cape Verde—Maps	G9160-9164	912.6658
Capital	HD39-40.7	658.152
Capital	HB501	332.041
Capital	HC79.C3	332.041
Capital gains tax	HJ4653.C3	336.24240973
Capital investments	HG4028.C4	332.0414
Capital movements	HG3891	332.042
Capital punishment—United States	KF9725	345.730773
Capitols	NA4410-4417	725.11
Capricorn (Astrology)	BF1727.65	133.5275
Capstan	VM811	621.864
Capsules (Pharmacy)	RS201.C3	615.43
Car pools	HE5620.C3	388.413212
Carbohydrates	QP701-702	572.56
Carbohydrates	QD320-327	547.78
Carbon	TP245.C4	661.0681
Carbon dioxide	QD181.C1	546.6812
Carbon dioxide—Physiological effect	QP913.C1	612.22
Carbon monoxide	RA1247.C17	615.91
Carbonated beverages	TP628-636	663.62
Carbuncle	RL221	616.523
Carburetors	TJ787	621.437
Carcinogenesis	RC268.5-.7	616.994071
Carcinogens	RC268.6-.7	616.994071
Card games	GV1232-1299	795.4
Card system in business	HF5735-5746	651.53
Card tricks	GV1549	793.85
Cardiac arrest	RC685.C173	616.123025
Cardiac catheterization	RD598.35.C35	617.412
Cardiac pacing	RC684.P3	617.4120645
Cardinal virtues	BV4645	241.4
Carding	TS1485-1487	676.02821
Cardiogenic shock	RC685.C18	616.12
Cardiologists	RC666.7-.72	616.10092
Cardiomyoplasty	RD598.35.C37	617.412
Cardiotonic agents	RM349	615.71
Cardiovascular agents	RM345-349	615.71
Cardiovascular system	QM178-197	611.1
Cardiovascular system	QL835-841	573.1
Cardiovascular system—Abnormalities	RC701	616.1043
Cardiovascular system—Diagnosis	RC670-.5	616.1075
Cardiovascular system—Diseases	RC666-701	616.1

Subject Heading	LC	Dewey
Cardiovascular system—Diseases—Eclectic treatment	RV251-256	616.106
Cardiovascular system—Diseases—Homeopathic treatment	RX311-316	616.106
Cardiovascular system—Diseases—Nursing	RC674	610.73691
Cardiovascular system—Surgery	RD597-598.7	617.41
Career development	HF5381-5382.5	650.1
Career development	HF5549.5.C35	658.3
Career education	LC1037-.8	370.113
Career plateaus	HF5384.5	650.1
Cargo handling	VK235	387.544
Cargo ships	VM391-395	623.8245
Caribbean Area	F2155-2191	972.9
Caribbean Area—Church history	BR655	277.29
Caribbean Area—History	F2173-2191	972.9
Caribbean Area—Maps	G1535-1537	912.729
Caribbean Area—Maps	G4390-4392	912.729
Caricatures and cartoons	NC1300-1766	741.5
Caricatures and cartoons—Exhibitions	NC1310-1312	741.5074
Caricatures and cartoons—Periodicals	NC1300	741.505
Caricatures and cartoons—[By region or country]	NC1400-1762	741.59(4-9)
Carillon music	M172	786.64
Carnivals	GT4180-4299	394.25
Carnivals	GV1834.7-1835.56	791.1
Carnivora	QL737.C2	599.7
Carnivorous plants	QK917	583.75
Carnivorous plants	SB432.7	635.93375
Caroline Islands	DU560-568	996.6
Caroline Islands—History	DU565-567	996.6
Caroline Islands—Maps	G9420-9424	912.966
Carolingians	DD129-134.9	943.014
Carolingians	DQ85-87	949.401
Carpal tunnel syndrome	RC422.C26	616.87
Carpathian Mountains	DJK71-76	947.79
Carpentry	HD9716.C3-.C33	694
Carpentry	TH5601-5695	694
Carpentry drafting	TH5611	694.1
Carpets	NK2775-2898	747.5
Carpets	TS1772-1779.5	677.643
Carriage and wagon-making	TS2001-2035	688.6
Carrier proteins	QP552.C34	572.69
Carriers—Law and legislation—Canada	KE1099-1135	343.71093
Carriers—Law and legislation—England	KD1800-1847	343.42093
Carriers—Law and legislation—United States	KF1091-1137	343.73093
Cartels	HD2757.5	338.87
Cartilage	QM567	611.0183
Cartography	GA101-1999	526
Cartography—History	GA201-246	526.09
Cartography—United States	GA405	526.0973
Cartography—[United States, By state]	GA409-460	526.097(4-9)
Cartons	HF5770	658.7884
Cartridges	UF740-745	358.128255
Carving (Meat, etc.)	TX885	642.6
Cascade Range	F851.7	979.5
Cash management	HG4028.C45	658.15244
Cashew nut	SB401	634.57
Casinos	HV6711	364.17206
Casserole cookery	TX693	641.821
Castanet music	M175.C35	786.873
Caste	GN491.4	305.5122
Caste	DS422.C3	305.51220954
Caste	HT713-725	305.5122
Casting (Fishing)	SH454-.9	799.124
Castles	NA7710-7786	728.81
Castor oil	TP684.C275	665.353
Castor oil	RM666.C375	615.32369
Castration	RD572	617.463059
Castration complex	BF175.5.C37	150.195
Casual labor	HD5855-5856	331.544
Catalan language	PC3801-3899	449.9
Catalan language—Etymology	PC3883-3886	449.92
Catalan language—Grammar	PC3819-3873	449.95
Catalan language—Lexicography	PC3887-3895	449.93028
Catalan literature	PC3900-3976	849.9
Catalogs, Booksellers'	Z998-1000.5	017.4
Catalogs, Union	Z695.83	025.31
Catalysis	QD505	541.395
Catamarans	GV811.57	797.1246
Catamarans	VM311.C3	623.822
Catapult	U875	355.8241
Cataract	RE451	617.742
Catechetics	BX1968	268.82
Catechetics	BX8068-8070	238
Catechetics (Canon law)	BX1939.C3	262.933
Catechisms	BT1029-1040	238
Caterers and catering	TX901-921	642.4
Cathedrals	NA4830	726.6
Cathode ray oscilloscope	TK7878.7	621.3815483
Catholic Church	BX800-4795	282
Catholic Church—Apologetic works	BX1752	230.2
Catholic Church—Biography	BX4650-4705	282.092
Catholic Church—Bishops	BX1905	262.122
Catholic Church—Catechisms	BX1958-1968	238.2
Catholic Church—Clergy	BX1912-1914.5	262.142
Catholic Church—Clergy—Sexual behavior	BX1912.9	253.252
Catholic Church—Dictionaries	BX841	282.03
Catholic Church—Doctrines	BX1746-1755	230.2
Catholic Church—Education	BX895-939	268.82
Catholic Church—Finance	BX1950	254.8
Catholic Church—Government	BX1800-1920	262.02

Subject Heading	LC	Dewey		Subject Heading	LC	Dewey
Catholic Church—History	BX940-1745	282.09/270		Cavalry—History	UE15	357.09
Catholic Church—Liturgy	BX1970.A7-.Z	264.02		Cavalry—Societies, etc.	UE1	357.06
Catholic Church—Liturgy— Texts	BX1999.8-2047	264.02(1-9)		Cavalry—Uniforms	UE440-445	357.04144
Catholic Church—Liturgy— Theology	BX2347-2348	264.02		Cavalry—[By region or country]	UE21-124	357.09(4-9)
Catholic Church—Missions	BV2130-2300	266.2		Cavalry—Africa	UE115-119	357.096
Catholic Church— Periodicals	BX800-806	282.05		Cavalry—Argentina	UE36-37	357.0982
Catholic Church—Prayer- books and devotions	BX2050-2155	242.802		Cavalry—Asia	UE99-113	357.095
				Cavalry—Australia	UE121-122	357.0994
Catholic Church—Sermons	BX1756	252.02		Cavalry—Canada	UE26-27	357.0971
Catholic Church— Societies, etc.	BX808-816	282.06		Cavalry—Central America	UE30-31	357.09728
Catholic Church—[By region or country]	BX4600-4644	282.73		Cavalry—Chile	UE43-44	357.0983
				Cavalry—China	UE101-102	357.0951
Catholic Church—Africa	BX1675-1682	282.6		Cavalry—Colombia	UE45-46	357.09861
Catholic Church—Asia	BX1615-1673	282.5		Cavalry—Europe	UE55-95	357.094
Catholic Church—Canada	BX1419-1424	282.71		Cavalry—France	UE71-72	357.0944
Catholic Church—Central America	BX1432-1447	282.728		Cavalry—Germany	UE73-74	357.0943
Catholic Church—East Asia	BX1662-1670.7	282.5		Cavalry—Great Britain	UE57-64	357.0941
Catholic Church—Europe	BX1490-1612	282.4		Cavalry—Greece	UE75-76	357.09495
Catholic Church—France	BX1528-1533	282.44		Cavalry—India	UE103-104	357.0954
Catholic Church—Germany	BX1534-1539	282.43		Cavalry—Italy	UE79-80	357.0945
Catholic Church—Great Britain	BX1491-1514	282.41		Cavalry—Japan	UE105-106	357.0952
				Cavalry—Mexico	UE28-29	357.0972
Catholic Church—Italy	BX1543-1548	282.45		Cavalry—Oceania	UE123-124	357.099(5-6)
Catholic Church—Mexico	BX1427-1431	282.72		Cavalry—Portugal	UE83-84	357.09469
Catholic Church—Middle East	BX1617-1636	282.56		Cavalry—Russia	UE85-86	357.0947
				Cavalry—Scandinavia	UE86.5	357.0948
Catholic Church—[New Zealand/Australia]	BX1685-1692	282.9(3/4)		Cavalry—South America	UE34-54	357.098
				Cavalry—Spain	UE87-88	357.0946
Catholic Church—Russia	BX1558-1560	282.47		Cavalry—United States	UE23-25	357.0973
Catholic Church—South America	BX1460-1489	282.8		Cavalry—Venezuela	UE54	357.0987
				Cavalry—West Indies	UE32-33	357.09729
Catholic Church—Spain	BX1583-1588	282.46		Cavalry drill and tactics	UE157-302	357.184
Catholic Church— United States	BX1404-1418	282.73		Cave dwellings	GN783-784	930.1
Catholic Church— West Indies	BX1448-1459	282.729		Caves	GN783-.5	930.1
				Caves	GB601-608	551.447
Catholic universities and colleges	LC487	378.07122		Caving	GV200.6-.66	796.525
				Cavitation	TA357.5.C38	620.1064
Cats	SF441-450	636.8		Cayman Islands	F2048.5	972.921
Cats—Pedigrees	SF443	636.80822		Cayman Islands—Maps	G4965-4969	912.72921
Cattle	SF191-219	636.2		Cayman Islands—Politics and government	JL629.5	320.972921
Cattle—Diseases	SF961-967	636.20886				
Cattle—Infections	SF961-967	636.208969		Ceilings	NA2950	721.7
Cattle—Transportation	HE595.L7	387.5448		Ceilings	TH2531-2533	690.17
Cattle—Transportation	HE2321.L7	385.24		Celesta music	M175.C44	786.83
Cattle brands	SF101-103.5	636.20812		Celestial mechanics	QB349-421	521
Cattle breeds	SF198-199	636.2(2-8)		Celibacy	BV4390	253.25
Cattle stealing	HV6646-6665	364.1552		Celibacy	HQ800.15	306.732
Cattle trade	HD9433	380.14162		Cell culture	QH585.2-.45	571.638
Caucasian languages	PK9001-9201	499.96		Cell death	QH671	571.939
Caucasian race	GN537	305.8034		Cell differentiation	QH607	571.835
Caucasian race	HT1575-1577	305.8034		Cell division	QH605-.3	571.844
Caucus	JF2085	324.52		Cell membranes	QH601-602	571.64
Causation	BD530-595	122		Cell metabolism	QH634.5	572.4
				Cell nuclei	QH595	571.66
Causation (Buddhism)	BQ4240	294.34		Cell physiology	QH631-647	571.6
Cavalry	UE	357		Cell respiration	QH633	572.47
				Cells	QH573-671	571.6
				Cells—Effect of radiation on	QH652-.7	571.6345
				Celluar radio	HE9713-9715	384.53
				Celluloid	TP1180.C5	668.44

36

Subject Heading	LC	Dewey	Subject Heading	LC	Dewey
Cellulose	TP1180.C6	668.44	Central America—History	F1435.4-1439.5	972.8
Celtic Church	BR794	274.4	Central America— Manufactures	TS30-31	670.9728
Celtic Church	BR748	274.4	Central America—Maps	G1550-1594	912.728
Celtic harp music	M142.C44	787.95	Central America—Maps	G4800-4884	912.728
Celtic languages	PB1001-1095	491.6	Central America—Periodicals	F1421	972.8005
Celtic languages— Etymology	PB1083-1085	491.6(2-8)2	Central nervous system depressants	RM330	615.788
Celtic languages—Grammar	PB1019-1071	491.6(2-8)5	Centrifuges	QD54.C4	542
Celtic languages— Lexicography	PB1087-1089	491.6(2-8)3028	Ceramic tableware	NK4695.T33	738.38
Celtic languages—Study and teaching	PB1011	491.6071	Cereals, Prepared	TP434-435	664.756
			Cereals, Prepared	TX395	641.331
Celtic philology	PB1001-1095	491.6	Cereals as food	TX393	641.331
Celts	DA140-143	941.089916	Cerebal palsied children	RJ496.C4	618.92836
Celts—History	D70	936.4	Cerebellum	QM455	611.81
Cement	TN945	622.368	Cerebellum	QL937	573.86
Cemeteries	GT3320	393.1	Cerebellum	QP379	612.827
Cemeteries	RA626-630	363.75	Cerebral cortex	QP383-.17	612.825
Censers	BV196.C	264	Cerebral infarction	RC394.I5	616.81
Census	HA175-4737	310	Cerebral palsied	RC388	616.836
Centaurs	BL820.C	292.13	Cerebral palsy	RA645.C47	614.59836
Centers for the performing arts	PN1585-1589	725.83	Cerebrovascular disease	RC388.5	616.81
			Ceres (Roman deity)	BL820.C5	292.2114
Central African Republic— Census	HA4717	316.741	Certainty	BD171	121.63
			Cervix erosion	RG314	618.143
Central African Republic— Civilization	DT546.34	967.41	Cervix uteri—Diseases	RG310-315	618.14
			Cesarean section	RG761	618.86
Central African Republic— Description and travel	DT546.327	916.74104	Chad—Census	HA4718	316.743
			Chad—Civilization	DT546.44	967.43
Central African Republic— Gazetteers	DT546.315	916.741003	Chad—Description and travel	DT546.427	916.74304
			Chad—Economic conditions	HC990	330.96743
Central African Republic— History	DT546.348-.384	967.41	Chad—History	DT546.457-.483	967.43
			Chad—History—1960-	DT546.48-.483	967.4304
Central African Republic— History—To 1960	DT546.365-.37	967.410(1-3)	Chad—History—Civil War, 1965-	DT546.48	967.4304(1-4)
Central African Republic— History—1960-	DT546.375-.384	967.4105	Chad—Maps	G8720-8724	912.6743
			Chain stores	HF5468	381.12
Central African Republic— History—Coup d'etat, 1979	DT546.38	967.4105	Chairs	TS880	684.13
			Chamber music	M177-990	785
			Chamber music—History and criticism	ML1100-1165	785.009
Central African Republic— Maps	G8710-8714	912.6741	Champagne (Wine)	TP555	663.224
Central America	F1421-1577	972.8	Chance	BD595	123.3
Central America— Armed Forces— Supplies and stores	UC98-99	355.809728	Chance	BC141	123.3
			Chance	QA273-274.8	519.2
			Chance compositions	M1470	781.3
Central America—Biography	CT570-638	920.0728	Chancellorsville (Va.), Battle of, 1863	E475.35	973.733
Central America—Church history	BR620-625	277.28	Change	BD373	116
Central America— Civilization	F1430	972.8	Channeling (Spiritualism)	BF1281-1315	133.91
			Channels (Hydraulic engineering)	TC175-.2	532.54
Central America— Commerce	HF3241-3310	380.109728	Chants (Buddhist)	BQ5035-5065	294.3438
Central America— Description and travel	F1431-1433.2	917.2804	Chants (Hindu)	BL1226.2	294.538
			Chapels	NA4870	726.4
Central America— Economic conditions	HC141-148	330.9728	Chaplains	UH20-25	355.347
			Chaplains, Military	VG20-25	359.347
Central America— Gazetteers	F1424	917.28003	Character	BF818-839	155.2
			Character	LC251-301	370.114
Central America— Genealogy	CS120-199	929.10720(72-8)	Character tests	BF818-839	155.2076
			Charades	PN6366-6377	793.24

Subject Heading	LC	Dewey	Subject Heading	LC	Dewey
Charcoal	TP331	662.74	Chemistry, Inorganic—Societies, etc.	QD146	546.06
Charcoal drawing	NC850	741.22	Chemistry, Organic	QD241-441	547
Chariot racing	GV33	798	Chemistry, Organic—Periodicals	QD241	547.005
Charisma (Personality trait)	BF698.35.C45	155.232	Chemistry, Physical and theoretical	QD450-801	541
Charities	HV1-4959	361.7			
Charities, Medical	HV687-694	361.7	Chemistry, Physical and theoretical—Societies, etc.	QD450	541.06
Charity	BV4639	241.4			
Charity organization	HV40-69	361.7			
Charms	GR600	398.45	Chemistry, Technical	TP	660
Charms (Buddhism)	BQ4570.A4	294.3437	Chemistry, Technical—Congresses	TP5	660.06
Chastity	BJ1533.C4	176			
Chastity	BV4647.C5	241.66	Chemistry, Technical—Encyclopedias	TP9	660.03
Chastity belts	GT2810	392.5			
Check collection systems	HG1692	332.76	Chemistry, Technical—History	TP15-20	660.09
Check credit plans	HG1643	332.178			
Check float	HG1692	332.76	Chemistry, Technical—Periodicals	TP1	660.05
Checkers	GV1461-1463	794.2			
Checking accounts	HG1691-1704	332.1752	Chemists	QD21-22	540.92
Cheerfulness	BJ1533.C5	179.9	Chemotherapy	RM260-263	615.58
Cheerfulness	BJ1477-1486	179.9	Cherokee Indians	E99.C5	973.049755
Cheerleading	LB3635	791.64	Cherokee language	PM781-784	497.55
Cheese	SF270-274	637.3	Chess	GV1313-1457	794.1
Chemical apparatus	QD53-54	542	Chest pain	RC941	617.54
Chemical burns	RD96.45	617.11	Chest—Diseases	RC941	617.54
Chemical carriers (Tankers)	VM455.3	623.8(1245/245)	Chest—Diseases—Eclectic treatment	RV293	617.5406
Chemical engineering	TP155-156	660			
Chemical engineering—Equipment and supplies	TP157-159	660.283	Chest—Diseases—Homeopathic treatment	RX360	617.5406
			Chests	TT197	684.16
Chemical engineering laboratories	TP165-183	660.072	Cheyenne Indians	E99.C53	973.04973
			Chicago (Ill.)	F548-.9	977.311
Chemical industry	HD9650-9660	338.4766	Chickenpox	RC125	616.914
Chemical laboratories	QD51-64	540.72	Chickens	SF481-513	636.5
Chemical oceanography	GC109-149	551.4601	Children's museums	AM8	069.083
Chemical plants	TP155.5-.6	660.28	Child abuse	HV6626.5-.54	364.15554
Chemical processes	TP155.7-.75	660.281	Child abuse	RC569.5.C55	616.858223
Chemical reaction, Conditions and law of	QD501-505.5	541.39	Child abuse—Investigation	HV8079.C46	363.2595554
			Child analysis	RJ504.2	618.928917
Chemical senses	QP455-458	612.86	Child development	GN63	612.65
Chemical spills	TD196.C45	628.16836	Child development	LB1101-1139	155.4
Chemical warfare	UG447-.65	358.34	Child development	RJ131-137	612.65
Chemicals	TP200-248	661	Child psychiatry	RJ499-520	618.9289
Chemicals—Safety measures	TP149	660.2804	Child psychology	BF721-723	155.4
			Child psychopathology	RJ499-520	618.9289
Chemistry	QD	540	Child psychopathology—Research	RJ500.2	618.9289027
Chemistry—Dictionaries	QD4-5	540.3			
Chemistry—Experiments	QD43	540.724	Child psychotherapy	RJ504-505	618.928914
Chemistry—History	QD11-18	540.9	Child rearing	HQ768-777.95	392.13/649.1
Chemistry—Nomenclature	QD7	540.14	Child sexual abuse	RC560.C46	616.85836
Chemistry—Societies, etc.	QD1	540.6	Child sexual abuse	RJ506.C48	616.85836
Chemistry—Study and teaching	QD40-49	540.71	Child sexual abuse—Investigation	HV8079.C48	363.2595554
			Child welfare	HV701-1420.5	362.7
Chemistry, Analytic	QD71-142	543	Child welfare—Periodicals	HV701	362.705
Chemistry, Analytic—Periodicals	QD71	543.005	Child welfare—[By region or country]	HV741-804	362.709(4-9)
Chemistry, Analytic—Qualitative	QD81-98	544			
			Child welfare—United States	HV741-743	362.70973
Chemistry, Analytic—Quantitative	QD101-117	545			
Chemistry, Forensic	HV8073-8077.5	363.25			
Chemistry, Forensic	RA1057	614.1			
Chemistry, Inorganic	QD146-197	546			

Subject Heading	LC	Dewey
Child welfare—[Other regions or countries]	HV745-804	362.709(4-9)
Childbirth at home	RG661.5	618.4
Children	HQ767.8-792.2	305.23
Children—Diseases	RJ	618.92
Children—Diseases—Eclectic treatment	RV375-377	618.9206
Children—Diseases—Homeopathic treatment	RX501-531	618.9206
Children—Diseases—Treatment	RJ52-53	615.542
Children—Employment	HD6228-6250.5	331.31
Children—Growth	RJ131-137	612.65
Children—History	HQ767.87	305.2309
Children—Metabolism	RJ128	618.92716
Children—Mortality	HB1323.C5	304.64083
Children—Nutrition	RJ206 235	612.3
Children—Physiology	RJ125-137	612.0083
Children—Sexual behavior	HQ784.S45	306.7083
Children—Surgery	RD137-139	617.98
Children's clothing	TT635-645	646.406
Children's literature	PZ5-90	808.068
Children's parties	GV1205	793.21
Children's sermons	BV4315	252.53
Children of alcoholics	HV5132	362.2923
Children of interracial marriage	HQ777.9	306.843083
Chile	F3051-3285	983
Chile—Census	HA991-1010	318.3
Chile—Civilization	F3060	983
Chile—Description and travel	F3061-3065	918.304
Chile—Economic conditions	HC191-195	330.983
Chile—Emigration and immigration	JV7470-7479	325.(283/83)
Chile—Gazetteers	F3054	918.3003
Chile—History	F3081-3098	983
Chile—History—To 1565	F3091	983.0(1-3)
Chile—History—To 1810	F3091	983.0(1-3)
Chile—History—1565-1810	F3091	983.03
Chile—History—1810-	F3093	983.0(4-6)
Chile—History—War of Independence, 1810-1824	F3094	983.04
Chile—History—1824-1920	F3095	983.0(4-63)
Chile—History—Insurrection, 1851	F3095	983.05
Chile—History—Insurrection, 1859	F3095	983.05
Chile—History—War with Spain, 1865-1866	F3095	983.061
Chile—History—Revolution, 1891	F3098	983.062
Chile—History—20th century	F3099	983.06(3-6)
Chile—History—1920-1970	F3099	983.06(3-45)
Chile—History—Naval Revolt, 1931	F3099	983.0641
Chile—History—Uprising, 1938	F3099	983.0642
Chile—History—1970-1973	F3100	983.0646
Chile—History—1973-1988	F3100	983.065
Chile—History—Coup d'etat, 1973	F3100	983.065
Chile—History—1988-	F3100	984.06(5-6)
Chile—Manufactures	TS43-44	670.983
Chile—Maps	G5330-5334	912.83
Chile—Periodicals	F3051	983.005
Chile—Politics and government	JL2600-2699	320.983
Chilean literature	PQ7900-8098.36	860
Chime music	M172	786.848
Chimneys	NA3040	721.5
Chimneys	TH2281-2288	690.15
Chin	QM535	611.92
China	DS701-799.9	931/951
China—Armed Forces—Management	UB101-102	355.60951
China—Census	HA4631-4640	315.1
China—Church history	BR1280-1297	275.1
China—Civilization	DS721-727	931/951
China—Commerce	HF3831-3840	380.10951
China—Description and travel	DS707-712	913.104/ 915.104
China—Economic conditions	HC426-430	330.951
China—Emigration and immigration	JV8700-8709	325.(251/51)
China—Gazetteers	DS705	931.003/ 915.1003
China—History, Military	DS777.65	355.30951
China—History, Military—1912-1949	DS775.4	355.30951
China—History, Naval—1949-	DS777.7	359.30951090 (45-5)
China—History—To 221 B.C.	DS741-747.23	931.0(1-3)
China—History—Han dynasty, 202 B.C.-220 A.D.	DS748-.164	931.04
China—History—Three Kingdoms, 220-265	DS748.2-.29	931.04
China—History—220-589	DS748.17-.76	931.04
China—History—221 B.C.-960 A.D.	DS747.28-749.76	931.04/951.01
China—History—Ch'in dynasty, 221-207 B.C.	DS747.5-.9	931.004
China—History—Chin dynasty, 265-419	DS748.4-.44	931.04
China—History—Five Hu and the Sixteen kingdoms, 304-439	DS748.45-.48	931.04
China—History—Northern and Southern dynasties, 386-589	DS748.5-.76	951.01
China—History—Northern Wei dynasty, 386-534	DS748.7-.76	931.04/951.015
China—History—Warring States, 403-221 B.C.	DS747.2	931.01
China—History—Liu Sung dynasty, 420-479	DS748.6-.66	951.015
China—History—Ch'i dynasty, 479-502	DS748.6-.66	951.015

Subject Heading	LC	Dewey	Subject Heading	LC	Dewey
China—History—Liang dynasty, 502-557	DS748.6-.66	951.015	China—History—1912-1928	DS776.4-777.46	951.04(1-2)
China—History—Northern Ch'i dynasty, 550-577	DS748.7-.76	951.015	China—History—Revolution, 1913	DS777.2	951.041
China—History—Ch'en dynasty, 557-589	DS748.7-.76	951.01(5-6)	China—History—Revolution, 1915-1916	DS777.25	951.041
China—History—Northern Chou dynasty, 557-581	DS748.7-.76	951.015	China—History—Warlord period, 1916-1928	DS777.36	951.04(1-2)
China—History—Spring and Autumn period, 722-481 B.C.	DS747.15	931.01	China—History—Ch'ing Dynasty Restoration Attempt, 1917	DS777.38	951.041
China—History—An Lu shan Rebellion, 755-763	DS749.46	951.017	China—History—May Fourth movement, 1919	DS777.43	951.041
China—History—Huang Ch'ao Rebellion, 874-884	DS749.47	951.017	China—History—May Thirtieth movement, 1925	DS777.45	951.041
China—History—Earlier Shu kingdom, 907-925	DS749.7-.76	951.018	China—History—1928-1937	DS777.47-.514	951.042
China—History—Five dynasties and the Ten kingdoms, 907-979	DS749.5-.76	951.0(18-24)	China—History—Tsinan Incident, 1928	DS777.462	951.042
China—History—Southern Han kingdom, 917-971	DS749.7-.76	951.0(18-24)	China—History—Long March, 1934-1935	DS777.5132-.5139	951.042
China—History—Later Shu kingdom, 934-965	DS749.7-.76	951.0(18-24)	China—History—December Ninth Movement, 1935	DS775	951.042
China—History—Southern T'ang kingdom, 937-975	DS749.7-.76	951.0(18-24)	China—History—Sian Incident, 1936	DS777.514	951.042
China—History—Liao dynasty, 947-1125	DS751.72-.78	951.0(18-24)	China—History—1937-1945	DS777.518-.5316	951.042
China—History—Hsi Hsia dynasty, 1038-1227	DS751.82-.88	951.024	China—History—Southern Anhui Incident, 1941	DS777.534	951.042
China—History—Chin dynasty, 1115-1234	DS751.92-.98	951.024	China—History—Civil War, 1945-1949	DS777.535-.544	951.042
China—History—Li Tzu ch'eng Rebellion, 1628-1645	DS753.65	951.026	China—History—1949-	DS777.545-779.29	941.0(5-6)
China—History—White Lotus Rebellion, 1796-1804	DS756.3-.37	951.033	China—History—1949-1976	DS777.55	951.05(5-7)
China—History—Opium War, 1840-1842	DS757.4-.7	951.033	China—History—Hundred Flowers Campaign, 1956	DS778.4	951.055
China—History—Taiping Rebellion, 1850-1864	DS758.7-759.4	951.034	China—History—Antirightist Campaign, 1957-1958	DS778.5	951.055
China—History—Nien Rebellion, 1853-1868	DS759.5	951.03(4-5)	China—History—Cultural Revolution, 1966-1969	DS778.7	951.056
China—History—Self-strengthening movement, 1861-1895	DS763.65	951.03(4-5)	China—History—1976-	DS779.15-.29	951.0(57-6)
China—History—1861-1912	DS763.5-773.6	951.03(4-6)	China—History—Tiananmen Square Incident, 1989	DS779.32	951.058
China—History—Boxer Rebellion, 1899-1901	DS770-772.3	951.035	China—History—20th century	DS774	951.0(35-59)
China—History—20th century	DS774	951.0(35-59)	China—Manufactures	TS101-102	670.951
China—History—Hsuan t'ung, 1908-1912	DS773-.6	951.03(5-6)	China—Maps	G2305-2321	912.51
China—History—Revolution, 1911-1912	DS773.32-.6	951.036	China—Maps	G7820-7824	912.51
China—History—Republic, 1912-1949	DS773.83-777.544	951.04	China—Politics and government	JQ1500-1519	320.951
			China—Religion	BL1800-1975	299.51
			Chincoteague pony	SF315.2.C4	636.16
			Chinese drama	PL2356-2393	895.12009
			Chinese drama	PL2566-2603	895.12008
			Chinese essays	AC149-150	089.951
			Chinese essays	PL2606-2623	895.14008
			Chinese essays	PL2395-2413	895.14009
			Chinese fiction	PL2415-2443	895.13009
			Chinese fiction	PL2625-2653	895.13008
			Chinese language	PL1001-2244	495.1

Subject Heading	LC	Dewey
Chinese language—Ancient chinese, 600-1200	PL1079	495.17
Chinese language—Dialects	PL1501-1940	495.17
Chinese language—Dictionaries	PL1420-1498	495.13
Chinese language—Etymology	PL1281-1315	495.12
Chinese language—Grammar	PL1099-1241	495.15
Chinese language—Lexicography	PL1401-1498	495.13028
Chinese language—Middle Chinese, 1200-1919	PL1081	495.17
Chinese language—Modern Chinese, 1919-	PL1083	495.17
Chinese language—Phonology	PL1201-1219	495.115
Chinese language—To 600	PL1077	495.17
Chinese literature	PL2250-3207	895.1
Chinese literature—To 221 B.C.	PL2280	895.1109
Chinese literature—220-589	PL2284.5	895.109002
Chinese literature—Three kingdoms, 220-265	PL2285	895.109002
Chinese literature—221 B.C.-960 A.D.	PL2283	895.10900(2-3)
Chinese literature—Chin dynasty, 265-419	PL2286	895.109002
Chinese literature—Liu Sung dynasty, 420-479	PL2287	895.109002
Chinese literature—Sui dynasty, 581-618	PL2290	895.1090024
Chinese literature—Yuan dynasty, 1260-1368	PL2294	895.1090044
Chinese literature—Ming dynasty, 1368-1644	PL2296	895.1090046
Chinese literature—Ch'ing dynasty, 1644-1912	PL2297	895.1090048
Chinese poetry	PL2306-2355.8	895.11009
Chinese poetry	PL2517-2565.8	895.11008
Chinese-Japanese War, 1894-1895	DS764.4-767.6	951.035
Chiropractic	RZ201-275	615.534
Chiropractic clinics	RZ242	362.12
Chiropractors—Biography	RZ231-232	615.534092
Chiropractors—Directories	RZ233	615.534025
Chivalry	CR	394.7
Choirs (Music)	MT88	782.507
Cholera	RC126-134	616.932
Cholera	RA644.C3	614.514
Choral music	ML1500-1554	782.509
Choral singing	MT875	782.507
Christian art and symbolism	BV150-168	704.9482
Christian art and symbolism	N7810-8189.6	704.9482
Christian communities	BV4405-4406	262.26
Christian doctrinal theology	BT	230
Christian education of children	BV1474-1475.2	268.432
Christian ethics	BV4625-4780	241
Christian ethics	BJ1188.5-1278	241
Christian giving	BV772	254.8
Christian leadership	BV652.1	262.1
Christian life	BV4500-4595	248.4
Christian pilgrims and pilgrimages	BX2323	263.04
Christian saints	BX2325-2333	270.092
Christian saints	BX380	235.2
Christian saints	BX575-577.5	235.2
Christian Science	BX6901-6997	289.5
Christian Science—Biography	BX6990-6996	289.5092
Christian Science—Congresses	BX6905-6907	289.506
Christian Science—Education	BX6917	268.895
Christian Science—Government	BX6958	262.095
Christian Science—History	BX6931-6935	289.509
Christian Science—Liturgy	BX6960	264.095
Christian Science—Societies, etc.	BX6903	289.506
Christian sects	BR157	280
Christian shrines	BX2320-2321	263.042
Christian union	BX1-9.5	280.042
Christianity	BR1-129	230
Christianity—Early church, ca. 30-600	BS2410	270.(1-2)
Christianity and other religions	BR127-128	261.2
Christmas	GT4985	394.2663
Christmas cookery	TX739.2.C45	641.568
Christmas sermons	BV4257	252.615
Christmas trees	GT4989	394.2663
Chromolithography	NE2500-2529	764.2
Chronic active hepatitis	RC848.C4	616.3623
Chronic diseases	RB156	616.044
Chronic diseases	RC108	616.044
Chronic fatigue syndrome	RB150.F37	616.0478
Chronic lymphocytic leukemia	RC643	616.99419
Chronic renal failure	RC918.R4	616.614
Chronology	CE	529
Chronology—Congresses	CE1.5	529.06
Chronology—Dictionaries	CE4	529.03
Chronology—History	CE6	529.09
Chronology—Periodicals	CE1	529.05
Chronology, Assyro-Babylonian	CE33	529.30935
Chronology, Greek	CE42	529.30938
Chronology, Historical	D11-.5	900
Chronology, Oriental	CE31-39.5	529.325
Chronometers	QB107	522.5
Church	BV590-640	262
Church—Authority	BT91	262.8
Church—Catholicity	BV601.3	261
Church and social problems	HN30-39	261.83
Church and state	BV629-631	261.7

Subject Heading	LC	Dewey	Subject Heading	LC	Dewey
Church and state	K3280-3282	322.1	Church of England—Directories	BX5031	283.42025
Church and state—Catholic Church	BX1790-1795	261.7	Church of England—Doctrines	BX5137-5140	230.342
Church and state—United States	KF4865-4869	342.730852	Church of England—Government	BX5150-5182.5	262.0342
Church architecture	NA4790-6113	726.5	Church of England—History	BX5051-5101	283.4209
Church attendance	BV4523	254.5	Church of England—Liturgy	BX5140.5-5147	264.0342
Church buildings	NA4790-5095	726.5	Church of England—Parties and movements	BX5115-5126	283.42
Church buildings—Interdenominational use	BV636	254.7	Church of England—Periodicals	BX5011	283.4205
Church calendar	CE81-83	529.44	Church of England—Prayer-Books and devotions	BX5145	264.03
Church camps	BV1650	796.5422	Church of England—Relations	BX5127-5129.8	283.42
Church camps—Baptists	BX6475-6476	269.24	Church of England—Africa	BX5681-5700.9	283.6
Church charities	HV530	361.75	Church of England—Asia	BX5661-5680.7	283.5
Church colleges	LC427-629	378.071	Church of England—Canada	BX5601-5620	283.72
Church controversies	BV652.9	250	Church of England—Canada—History	BX5610-5613	283.72
Church decoration and ornament	NA5000	726.51	Church of England—[New Zealand/Australia]	BX5701-5720.8	283.9(3/4)
Church decoration and ornament	NK2190-2192	747.86	Church of England—Oceania	BX5721-5740	283
Church etiquette	BJ2018-2019	395.53	Church of England—Wales	BX5596-5598	283.429
Church finance	BV770-777	254.8	Church of Ireland	BX5410-5595	283.415
Church fund raising	BV772.5	254.8	Church of Ireland—Biography	BX5590-5595	283.415092
Church growth	BV652.25	254.5	Church of Ireland—History	BX5500-5510	283.41509
Church history	BR	270	Church of Scotland	BX9075-9095	285.233
Church history—Biography	BR1690-1725	270.092	Church officers	BV705	262.1
Church history—Congresses	BR41-43	270.06	Church orders, Ancient	BV761.A1-.A5	255.00901
Church history—Dictionaries	BR95	270.03	Church publicity	BV652.95-657	254.4
Church history—Middle Ages, 600-1500	BR160-270	270.3	Church renewal	BV600	262.0017
Church history—Modern period, 1500-	BR290-481	270.(5-8)	Church schools	LC427-629	371.071
			Church Slavic language	PG601-698	491.81701
Church history—Periodicals	BR1-9	270.05	Church Slavic language—Grammar	PG661-698	491.817015
Church history—Philosophy	BR138	270.01			
Church history—Primitive and early church, ca. 30-600	BR160-240	270.(1-2)	Church Slavic literature	PG700-716	891.81
			Church societies	BV900-1450	267
Church history—Societies, etc.	BR21-29	270.06	Church vestments	BX2790	390.008822
			Church vestments	BX5180	390.008823
Church history—[By date]	BR160-481	270.(1-8)	Church vestments	BV167	391.04204
Church libraries	Z675.C5	027.67	Church vestments	BX1925	390.008822
Church management	BV652-.9	254	Church work with prostitutes	HQ301-440.7	362.809(4-9)
Church membership	BV820	254.5	Church year	BV30-135	263.9
Church music	ML3869	781.71017	Cigarette habit	HV5740-5745	362.296
Church music	ML3000-3190	781.71009	Cigars	TS2260	679.72
Church music—Catholic Church	ML3002-3051	782.3222009	Cinematography	TR845-899.5	778.53
Church music—Catholic Church (Byzantine rite)	ML3060	782.32215009	Cinematography—Special effects	TR858	778.5345
			Cipher and telegraph codes	HE7669-7679	384.14
Church music—Church of England	ML3166	782.3223009	Circle	QA484	516.15
			Circle—Religious aspects	BL604.C5	291.37
Church music—Episcopal Church	ML3166	782.3223009	Circumcision	GN484	392.1
			Circumcision	RD590	617.463
Church music—Protestant churches	ML3100-3188	782.3224009	Circumpolar medicine	RC955-958	616.9881
Church of England	BX5011-5740	283.42	Circus	GV1800-1831	791.3
Church of England—Biography	BX5619-5620	283.0972092	Cities and towns	HT101-395	307
Church of England—Biography	BX5197-5199	283.42092	Cities and towns	HV6177	364.22
Church of England—Clergy	BX5175-5182.5	262.03	Cities and towns, Ancient	HT114	307.76093

Subject Heading	LC	Dewey
Cities and towns, Medieval	D134	307.760902
Cities and towns, Medieval	HT115	307.760902
Citizens band radio	TK6570.C5	621.38454
Citizenship	JF801	323.6
Citizenship—England	KD4050-4058	342.42083
Citizenship—United States	KF4700-4720	342.73083
Citrus fruits	SB369	634.3
City children	HT206	305.23091732
City churches	BV637	250.91732
City clergy	BV637.5	262.14091732
City halls	NA4430-4437	725.13
City planning	HT165.5-169.5	307.1216
City planning	NA9000-9284	711
City planning and redevelopment law—United States	KF5691-5710	346.73045
City planning—[By region or country]	HT167-169.54	307.121609(4-9)
City planning—[By region or country]	NA9101-9285	711.09(4-9)
City planning—United States	HT167-168	307.12160973
City-states	JC352	321.06
Civil defense	UA926-929	363.35
Civil defense—Law and legislation—England	KD6340	344.420535
Civil defense—Law and legislation—United States	KF7685	344.730535
Civil disobedience	JC328.3	322.4
Civil law	K623-968	346
Civil law—Canada	KE495	347.71
Civil law—England	KD720-721	347.42
Civil procedure	K2201-2385	347.05
Civil procedure—United States	KF8810-9075	347.7305
Civil rights	K3236-3268	342.085
Civil rights	JC571-628	323
Civil rights—Canada	KE4381-4430	342.71085
Civil rights—England	KD4080-4119	342.42085
Civil rights—Religious aspects	BL65.C58	291.177
Civil service	HD8001-8013	352.63
Civil service	K3440-3460	342.068
Civil service	JF1501-1521	351
Civil service	JK631-868	351.73063
Civil service	JS148-153	352.63
Civil service reform	JK681	352.630973
Civil service, Colonial	JV443	353.15
Civil service—Canada	JL106-111	352.630971
Civil service—Pensions	JF1671	353.549
Civil service—Personnel management	JK765-770	352.63
Civil service—United States	KF5336-5398	342.73068
Civil-military relations	JF195	322.5
Civilian-based defense	UA10.7	355.45
Civilization	CB	909
Civilization	HM101	909
Civilization—Dictionaries	CB9	903
Civilization—Extraterrestrial influences	CB156	001.94
Civilization—Historiography	CB15-18	907.2
Civilization—Periodicals	CB3	905

Subject Heading	LC	Dewey
Civilization—Philosophy	CB19	901
Civilization—Pictoral works	CB13	902.22
Civilization—Study and teaching	CB20	907.1
Civilization, Ancient	CB311	930
Civilization, Arab	DS36.77-.88	909.0974927
Civilization, Assyro-Babylonian	DS70.7	935
Civilization, Christian	BR115.C5	230
Civilization, Classical	DE46-61	937/938
Civilization, Germanic	CB213-214	943
Civilization, Hindu	DS423-425	909.097645
Civilization, Islamic	DS35.62	909.097671
Civilization, Medieval	CB351-355	909.07
Civilization, Modern	CB357-430	909.08
Civilization, Oriental	CB253-256	950
Civilization, Western	CB245	909.09812
Clarinet	MT380-388	788.6207
Clarinet music	M70-74	788.62
Class size	LB3013.2	371.251
Classical antiquities	DE	937/938
Classical antiquities	DF	938
Classical antiquities	DG	937
Classical antiquities—Periodicals	DE1	93(7/8).005
Classical antiquities—Study and teaching	DE15-.5	(93(7/8).0071
Classical biography	DE7	920.093(7/8)
Classical drama	PA3461-3466	882.008
Classical drama—History and criticism	PA3024-3029	882.009
Classical education	LC1001-1021	373.242
Classical geography	DE23-31	913.(7-8)
Classical geography	G87	913.(7-8)
Classical languages	PA	480
Classical languages—Dictionaries	PA31	480.03
Classical languages—Grammar, Comparative	PA111	485
Classical literature	PA3301-3671	880.8
Classical literature—Appreciation	PA3013	880.01
Classical literature—History and criticism	PA3001-3045	880.09
Classical philology	PA1-199	480
Classical poetry	PA3431-3459	881.008
Classical poetry	PA3019-3022	881.009
Classicism	PN56.C6	808.80142
Classroom management	LB3013	371.1024
Clavichord	ML649.8-747	786.309
Clavichord music	M20-39	786.3
Clavicle	QM101	611.717
Clay	QE471.3	552.5
Cleaning compounds	TP990-992.5	667.1
Clearcutting	SD387.C58	634.92
Clearinghouses (Banking)	HG2301-2351	332.12
Clergy	BV659-683	262.14
Clergy (Canon law)	BX1939.C665	262.932
Clergy couples	BV675.7	262.14
Clergy—Divorce	BV4395.5	253.2
Clergy—Family relationships	BV4396	253.22

Subject Heading	LC	Dewey	Subject Heading	LC	Dewey
Clergy—Pensions	BV4382	331.252912532	Coats	TT530	687.142
Clergy—Political activity	BV4327	253.2	Coats	TT595-600	687.141
Clerks (Retail trade)	HD8039.M39	381.1092	Cobalt ores	TN490.C6	622.3483
Client-centered	RC481	616.8914	Cobras	QL666.064	597.96
psychotherapy			Coca	QK495.E92	583.79
Cliff-dwellers	E99.P9	973.04974	Coca	RS165.C5	615.32379
Climacteric, Male	RC884	616.693	Cocaine habit	HV5810	362.298
Climatology	QC851-999	551.6	Cocaine habit	RC568.C6	616.8647
Clinical biochemistry	RB112.5	616.0756	Cochlear implants	RF305	617.8820592
Clinical chemistry	RM40	616.0756	Cocktails	TX951	641.874
Clinical medicine	RC31-80	616	Cocoa	TX817.C5	641.877
Clinical psychology	RC466.8-467.95	616.89	Coconut oil	TP684.C7	665.355
Clinics	RA966	362.12	Codependency	RC569.5.C63	616.8619
Cloaks	TT530-535	687.147	Coelenterata	QL375-379	593.5
Clock and watch making	TS540-549	681.11(3-4)	Coevolution	QH372	576.87
Cloning	QH442.2	660.65	Coffee	GT2918	394.12
Close and open communion	BV820	264.36	Coffee	TX415	641.3373
Closed-circuit television	TK6680	384.556	Coffee	TP645	663.93
Clothes moths	QL561.T55	595.78	Coffee	SB269	633.73
Clothing and dress	GN418-419	391	Coffee cakes	TX771	641.8659
Clothing and dress	GT500-2350	391	Coffee habit	RC567.5	616.8526
Clothing and dress	TT507	687	Coffeehouses	TX901-910	642.5
Clothing and dress	TX340	646.3	Coffer-dams	TC198	624.157
Clothing and dress—	TT550	646.408	Cogeneration of electric	TK1041-1078	621.3121
Alteration			power and heat		
Clothing and dress—	TT720-730	646.2	Cognition	BF309-499	153
Repairing			Cognition in animals	QL785	591.513
Clothing and dress—	GT525	391	Cognition in children	BF723.C5	155.413
Social aspects			Cognitive balance	BF337.C62	153
Clothing factories	TT498	687	Cognitive psychology	BF201	153
Clothing trade	TT490-695	687	Cognitive styles	BF311	153
Clothing trade—Periodicals	TT490	646.05	Cognitive therapy	RC489.C63	616.89142
Cloture	JF538	328.34	Cognitive-analytic therapy	RC489.C6	616.89142
Clouds	QC920.7-924	551.576	Coherence (Optics)	QC403	535.2
Clowns	GV1811	791.33	Coinage	HG551-566	332.40420973
Clubhouses	NA7910-7977	728.4	Coinage	HG261-315	332.4042
Clubs	HS2501-3371	367	Coinage, International	HG381-421	332.45
Clubs—Directories	HS2507-2515	367.025	Coins	CJ1-4625	737.4
Clubs—Periodicals	HS2501-2503	367.05	Coins—Congresses	CJ27	737.406
Clubs—[By region or country]	HS2721-3200	367.9(4-9)	Coins—Errors	CJ125	737.4
Clubs—United States	HS2721-2725	367.973	Coins—Exhibitions	CJ39-41	737.4074
Clubs—[Other regions	HS2731-3200	367.9(4-9)	Coins—Grading	CJ101	737.4
or countries]			Coins—History	CJ59	737.409
Cluster headache	RC392	616.8491	Coins—Periodicals	CJ1-9	737.405
Coach horses	SF312	636.14	Coins—Philosophy	CJ53	737.401
Coaching	HE5746-5749	388.228	Coins—Societies, etc.	CJ14-23	737.406
Coaching	SF304.5-307	388.341	Coins, African	CJ3920-4389	737.496
Coaching (Athletics)	GV711	796.077	Coins, American	CJ1800-2449	737.4973
Coal	HD9540-9559	338.2724	Coins, Ancient	CJ201-1397	737.493
Coal	TN799.9-844.7	622.334	Coins, Ancient [By region	CJ1021-1144	737.49(3-9)
Coal gasification	TP759	665.772	or country]		
Coal mine accidents	TN311-320	622.8	Coins, Ancient—Africa	CJ1071-1085	737.496
Coal mines and mining	TN799.9-844.7	622.334	Coins, Ancient—Asian	CJ1087-1099	737.49396
Coal mines and mining—	TN295	622.8	Coins, Ancient—Europe	CJ1101-1147	737.493(6/98)
Safety measures			Coins, Ancient—Italy	CJ1021-1070	737.4937
Coal slurry pipelines	TJ898.5	388.57	Coins, Australian	CJ4400-4419	737.4994
Coal trade	HD9540-9559	380.14224	Coins, Byzantine	CJ1201-1291	737.49398
Coal-tar	TP953	661.803	Coins, Canadian	CJ1860-1879	737.4971
Coaling	VK361	387.54044	Coins, European	CJ2450-3369	737.494
Coast defenses	UG448	358.16	Coins, Greek	CJ425-763	737.4938
Coating processes	TP156.C57	667.9	Coins, Greek	CJ301-763	737.4938

Subject Heading	LC	Dewey
Coins, Italian	CJ517-542	737.4937
Coins, Latin American	CJ1889-2449	737.498
Coins, Medieval	CJ1601-1715	737.40902
Coins, Medieval—[By region or country]	CJ1800-4625	737.49(4-9)
Coins, Oriental	CJ3370-3893	737.495
Coins, Oriental	CJ1301-1397	737.49396
Coins, Roman	CJ801-1147	737.4937
Cold—Physiological effect	QP82.2.C6	571.464
Cold (Disease)	RF361	616.205
Cold regions agriculture	S604.33	630.911
Cold regions agriculture	SB109.7	630.911
Cold storage	TP372.2	664.02852
Cold storage on shipboard	VM485	623.8535
Cold waves (Meteorology)	QC981.8.A5	551.5512
Cold weather clothing	GT529	391
Colic	RJ267	618.9233
Colitis	RC862.C6	616.3447
Collagen diseases in children	RJ520.C64	618.9277
Collars in heraldry	CR41.C5	929.6
Collectibles as an investment	AM237	332.63
Collective bargaining	HD6971.5-.65	331.89
Collective farms	HD1492-.5	334.683
Collectors and collecting	AM200-401	069.5
Collectors and collecting— History	AM221	069.509
Collectors and collecting— [By region or country]	AM301-396	069.509(4-9)
Collectors and collecting— Africa	AM387-389	069.5096
Collectors and collecting— Asia	AM372-385	069.5095
Collectors and collecting— Australia	AM390-391	069.50994
Collectors and collecting— Canada	AM313	069.50971
Collectors and collecting— Central America	AM315-322	069.509728
Collectors and collecting— Europe	AM342-371	069.5094
Collectors and collecting— France	AM349	069.50944
Collectors and collecting— Germany	AM350	069.50943
Collectors and collecting— Great Britain	AM343-347	069.50941
Collectors and collecting— History	AM221	069.509
Collectors and collecting— Mexico	AM314	069.509728
Collectors and collecting— New Zealand	AM393	069.50993
Collectors and collecting— Oceania	AM395-396	069.5099(5-6)
Collectors and collecting— Portugal	AM363	069.509469
Collectors and collecting— Russia	AM356	069.50947
Collectors and collecting— South America	AM330-341	069.5098

Subject Heading	LC	Dewey
Collectors and collecting— Spain	AM362	069.50946
Collectors and collecting— United States	AM303-311	069.50973
Collectors and collecting— West Indies	AM323-329	069.509729
College administrators	LB2341	378.111
College applications	LB2351.5-.52	378.1616
College athletes—Recruiting	GV350.5	796.043
College buildings	NA6600-6605	727.3
College costs	LB2342-.2	378.38
College credits	LB2359.5	378.1618
College sports	GV346-350	796.043
College students— Employment	HD6276.5-.52	331.34
College teachers	LB1778	378.12
Collisions (Nuclear physics)	QC794.6.C6	539.757
Collisions at sea— Prevention	VK371-378	623.8884
Colloquial language	P408	418
Collotype	TR930-937	686.2325
Colombia	F2251-2299	986.1
Colombia—Census	HA1011-1020	318.61
Colombia—Civilization	F2260	986.1
Colombia—Description and travel	F2261-2264.2	918.6104
Colombia—Economic conditions	HC196-200	330.9861
Colombia—Emigration and immigration	JV7480-7489	325.(2861/861)
Colombia—Gazetteers	F2254	918.61003
Colombia—History	F2270.3-2279.22	986.1
Colombia—History— To 1810	F2272	986.10(1-2)
Colombia—History— Insurrection of the Comuneros, 1781	F2272	986.102
Colombia—History— 19th century	F2273	986.1(2-62)
Colombia—History—1810-	F2273	986.10(3-6)
Colombia—History—War of Independence, 1810-1822	F2274	986.10(3-4)
Colombia—History— 1822-1832	F2275	986.104
Colombia—History— 1832-1886	F2276	986.105(2-61)
Colombia—History—Civil War, 1860-1862	F2276	986.1053
Colombia—History— 1886-1903	F2276.5	986.1062
Colombia—History— Revolution, 1899-1903	F2276.5	986.1062
Colombia—History— 1903-1946	F2277	986.106(2-31)
Colombia—History— 1946-1974	F2278	986.1063(2-3)
Colombia—History— Coup d'etat, 1953	F2278	986.10632
Colombia—History—1974-	F2279-.22	986.1063(4-5)
Colombia—Manufactures	TS45-46	670.9861

Cle - Col

Subject Heading	LC	Dewey
Colombia—Maps	G5290-5294	912.861
Colombia—Periodicals	F2251	986.1005
Colombia—Politics and government	JL2800-2899	320.9861
Colombian literature	PQ8160-8180.36	860
Colon—Cancer	RC280.C6	616.994347
Colon—Diseases	RC860-862	616.34
Colon (Anatomy)	QM345	611.347
Colonies	JV	321.08
Colonies—Administration	JV412-461	353.15
Colonies—History	JV61-151	325.309
Colonies—Law and legislation	K3375	341.28
Colonization	JV1-5399	325.3
Color	QC494-496.9	535.6
Color—Psychological aspects	BF789.C7	535.6019
Color—Therapeutic use	RM840	615.831
Color—Therapeutic use	RZ414.6	615.831
Color blindness	RE921	617.759
Color of man	GN197	599.945
Color photography	TR510-545	778.6
Color-printing	Z258	686.23042
Color prints	NE1850-1879	769
Color television	TK6670	621.38804
Color vision—Testing	RE918-921	617.759075
Colorado	F771-785	978.8
Colorado—Gazetteers	F774	917.88003
Colorado—History—To 1876	F780	978.80(1-2)
Colorado—History—1876-1950	F781	978.803(1-3)
Colorado—History—1951-	F781.2-.3	978.803(3-4)
Colorado—Maps	G4310-4314	912.788
Colorado—Periodicals	F771	978.8005
Colors	QC494-496.9	535.6
Colors, Liturgical	BV165	246.6
Columbia River Valley	F853	979.7
Columns	TH2252-2253	690.13
Columns, Corinthian	NA2860-2875	721.3
Columns, Ionic	NA2860	721.3
Coma	RB150.C6	616.849
Comanche Indians	E99.C85	973.049745
Combinations	QA165	512.925
Combinatorial analysis	QA164-167.2	511.6
Combined operations (Military science)	U260	355.46
Combustion	QD516	541.361
Combustion, Spontaneous	TN313-315	622.82
Combustion chambers	TJ254.7	621.43
Comets	QB717-732	523.6
Comets—Orbits	QB357	523.63
Comic books, strips, etc.	PN6700-6790	070.444
Command of troops	UB210	355.33041
Commandments of the church	BV4720-4730	241.5
Commando troops	U262	355.422
Commerce	GT6010-6070	395.52
Commerce	HF	380.1
Commerce—Directories	HF54	380.1025
Commerce—Encyclopedias	HF1001-1002.5	380.103
Commerce—Periodicals	HF1-53	380.105
Commercial art	NC997-1003	741.6
Commercial art—Periodicals	NC997.A1	741.605
Commercial art—Study and teaching	NC1000	741.6071
Commercial associations	HF294-343	380.106
Commercial buildings	NA6210-6280	725.2
Commercial buildings—Design and construction	TH4311-4315	690.52
Commercial catalogs	HF5861-5863	659.133
Commercial correspondence	HF5721-5734	651.75
Commercial credit	HG3751-3754.5	332.742
Commercial geography	HF1021-1027	330.9
Commercial law	K3840-4375	343.07
Commercial law	K1001-1388	346.07
Commercial law—Canada	KE1935-1999	343.7107
Commercial law—England	KD2455-2530	343.4207
Commercial law—Ireland	KDK550-769	343.41507
Commercial law—Northern Ireland	KDE235-282	343.41607
Commercial law—United States	KF1600-2940	343.7307
Commercial loans	HG1641-1643	332.1753
Commercial policy	HF1410-1411	380.13
Commercial products	HF1040-1044	380.1
Commercial statistics	HF1016-1017	380.1021
Commission merchants	HF5422	381.2092
Commodity exchanges	HG6046-6051	332.644
Commodity exchanges—Law and legislation—United States	KF1085-1087	343.7308
Commodity futures	HG6046-6051	332.6328
Commons	HD1286-1289	333.2
Commonwealth countries	KD5020-5025	349.42
Commonwealth countries—Economic conditions	HC246	330.917241
Commonwealth countries—History	DA10-18.2	909.0971241
Communal living	HQ970-975.7	307.774
Communicable diseases	RC109-216	616.9(01-6)
Communicable diseases	RA643-644	614.5
Communicable diseases in animals	SF781-809	636.08969
Communication	P87-96	302.2
Communication, Prehistoric	GN799.T73	302.2
Communication policy	P95.8	302.2
Communications, Military	VG70-85	623.8567
Communications, Military	UA940-945	355.85/623.73
Communications software	TK5105.9	005.3
Communicative disorders	RC423-428.8	616.855
Communion of saints	BT972	262.73
Communion sermons	BV4257.5	252
Communism and agriculture	HX550.A37	334.683
Communist countries	D847-.2	940.54217
Communist ethics	BJ1390-.5	171.7
Communist leadership	HX518.L4	335.4092
Communist state	JC474	321.92
Community-based corrections	HV9279	365.34
Community centers	HN41-46	790.068

Subject Heading	LC	Dewey
Community centers—[By region or country]	HN43-46	790.068(4-9)
Community centers—United States	HN43-45	790.06873
Community colleges	LB2328	378.1543
Community development	HN49.C6	307.14
Community life	HM131-134	307
Community psychiatry	RC455	362.22
Community psychology	RA790.55	362.22
Community service (Punishment)	HV9277.5	364.68
Comoro Islands—Census	HA2303	316.94
Comoro Islands—Maps	G9210-9214	912.694
Compact discs	TK7882.C56	621.3976
Comparative law	K583-591	340.2
Comparative linguistics	P123	410
Compass	VK577	623.8932
Compassion (Buddhism)	BQ4360	294.342
Compensatory education	LC213-.3	370.111
Competition	HF1414	338.6048
Competition	HD41	338.6048
Competition (Biology)	QH546.3	577.83
Competition, Imperfect	HB238	338.6048
Competition, Unfair—England	KD2225-2226	343.42072
Competition, Unfair—United States	KF1601-1611	343.73072
Competition, Unfair—United States	KF3195-3198	343.73072
Compilers (Computer programs)	QA76.76.C65	005.453
Complex carbohydrate diet	RM237.58	613.283
Complexes (Psychology)	RC569.5.C68	154.24
Composition (Art)	N7429.7-7433	701.8
Composition (Music)	MT40-67	781.307
Composition (Music)	ML430-455	781.309
Compost	TD796.5	363.728
Compost	S661	631.875
Compressed air	TJ981-1009	621.51
Compressed air—Therapeutic use	RM827	615.836
Compressors	TJ990-992	621.51
Compromise of 1850	E423	973.(64/7113)
Compulsive behavior	RC533	616.8584
Compulsive eating	RC552.C65	616.8526
Compulsive gambling	RC569.5.G35	616.85841
Computer algorithms	QA76.9.A43	005.1
Computer architecture	QA76.9.A73	004.22
Computer-assisted instruction	LB1028.5-.7	371.334
Computer crimes	HV6772-6773.3	364.168
Computer crimes—Investigation	HV8079.C65	363.25968
Computer engineering	TK7885-7895	621.39
Computer games	GV1469.15-.25	794.8
Computer graphics	T385	006.6
Computer interfaces	TK7887.5	621.398
Computer networks	TK5105.5-.9	004.6
Computer security	QA76.9.A25	005.8
Computer simulation	QA76.9.C65	003.3
Computer software	QA76.75-.9	005.3

Subject Heading	LC	Dewey
Computer stores	HF5468.2	380.145004
Computer terminals	TK7887.8.T4	621.3985
Computer viruses	QA76.76.C68	005.84
Computer war games	U310	355.480285
Computers	QA75.5-.95	004
Computers	TK7885-7895	621.39
Computers—Dictionaries	QA76.15	004.03
Computers—History	QA76.17	004.09
Computers—Maintenance and repair	TK7887	621.390288
Conception	QP251-281	612.63
Conception	RG133	618.2
Concertina music	M154	788.84
Concord, Battle of, 1775	E241.C7	973.3311
Concrete	TA439-446	620.136
Concrete construction	NA4125	721.0445
Concrete construction	TA680-683.94	624.1834
Concrete construction	TH1461-1501	693.5
Concrete dams	TC547	627.82
Concrete houses	NA7160	728
Concrete sculpture	NB1215	731.2
Concrete walls	TA683.5.W34	624.1834
Concrete walls	TH2245	690.12
Condensation (Meteorology)	QC921.6.C6	551.574
Condensation products (Chemistry)	QD341	547.28
Condiments	GT2870	394.12
Condiments	TX819	641.3382
Conditional immortality	BT919-925	236.23
Conduct disorders in children	RJ506.C65	618.9289
Conduct of life	BJ1545-1697	170.44
Conducting	MT85	781.4507
Confectionery	TX783-799	641.853
Confederate Memorial Day	E645	394.26975
Confederate States of America	E482-489	973.713/975
Confederate States of America—Defenses	UA580-585	355.450975
Confederate States of America—History	E487-488	973.713/975
Confederate States of America—History, Military	E470.2	973.742
Confederate States of America—History, Military	E545	973.742
Confederate States of America—History, Naval	E591-600	359.30975
Confederate States of America—Politics and government	JK9661-9993	320.0975
Confederate States of America—Social conditions	E487	973.713/975
Confederate States of America. Army	UA580-585	355.30975
Confederate States of America. Army—Commissariat	UC85-86	355.620975

Subject Heading	LC	Dewey	Subject Heading	LC	Dewey
Confederate States of America. Army—Field service	U173.5	355.350975	Conformal mapping	QA646	515.9
			Conformal mapping	QA360	515.9
Confederate States of America. Army—Firearms	UD383.5	355.82420975	Confucianism	BL1830-1875	299.512
			Congenital heart disease	RC687	616.12043
Confederate States of America. Army—Prisons	E611-612	973.771	Conglomerate corporations	HD2756-.2	338.8042
			Congo (Brazzaville)—Census	HA4716	316.724
Confederate States of America. Navy—History	E591-600	359.30975	Congo (Brazzaville)—Civilization	DT546.24	967.24
Confederate States of America. Navy—Organization	VA393-395	359.30975	Congo (Brazzaville)—Description and travel	DT546.227	916.72404
Confession	BX2262-2267	264.020862	Congo (Brazzaville)—Economic conditions	HC980	330.96724
Confession	BX5949.C6	234.166/265.62			
Confession	BX5149.C6	264.03562	Congo (Brazzaville)—Gazetteers	DT546.215	916.724003
Confession	BV845-847	265.62	Congo (Brazzaville)—History	DT546.25-.283	967.24
Confessors	BV845-847	265.62			
Confessors	BX2262-2267	264.020862	Congo (Brazzaville)—History—To 1960	DT546.265-.275	967.240(1-3)
Confirmation	BV815	265.2			
Confirmation (Buddhist rite)	BQ5005	294.3438	Congo (Brazzaville)—Maps	G8700-8704	912.6724
Confirmation (Canon law)	BX1939.C72	262.933	Congregational churches	BX7101-7260	285.8
Confirmation (Jewish rite)	BM707-.4	296.4424	Congregational churches—Congresses	BX7106-7109	285.806
Conflict of laws	K7000-7720	342.042			
Conflict of laws—Arbitration and award	K7690	347.09	Congregational churches—Creeds	BX7235-7236.2	238.58
Conflict of laws—Banking	K7380-7384	340.982	Congregational churches—Education	BX7119-7127	268.858
Conflict of laws—Commercial law	K7340-7512	340.97	Congregational churches—Government	BX7240-7246	262.058
Conflict of laws—Contracts	K7350-7444	340.97	Congregational churches—History	BX7131-7228	285.809
Conflict of laws—Contracts	K7265-7305	340.92			
Conflict of laws—Copyright licenses	K7555-7557	340.9482	Congregational churches—Liturgy	BX7237	264.058
Conflict of laws—Corporations	K7490-7495	340.966	Congregational churches—Sermons	BX7233	252.058
Conflict of laws—Domestic relations	K7155-7197	340.915	Congregational churches—Societies, etc.	BX7105	285.806
Conflict of laws—Guardian and ward	K7197	340.918	Congregational churches—Africa	BX7220-7222	285.86
Conflict of laws—Industrial property	K7570-7582	340.948	Congregational churches—Asia	BX7215-7216	285.85
Conflict of laws—Inheritance and succession	K7230-7245	340.952	Congregational churches—Australia	BX7225-7226	285.894
Conflict of laws—Insurance	K7470	340.986	Congregational churches—Canada	BX7151-7153	285.871
Conflict of laws—Intellectual property	K7550-7582	340.948	Congregational churches—Europe	BX7175-7210	285.84
Conflict of laws—Juristic persons	K7145-7148	340.913	Congregational churches—United States	BX7135-7149	285.873
Conflict of laws—Maritime law	K7449-7460	343.096	Congregationalism	BX7101-7260	285.8
Conflict of laws—Negotiable instruments	K7360-7370	340.996	Congregationalist—Biography	BX7259-7260	285.8092
Conflict of laws—Obligations	K7260-7335	340.92	Congresses and conventions	AS6	060
Conflict of laws—Parent and child	K7181-7197	340.917	Congruences (Geometry)	QA608	516.2
			Congruences and residues	QA242-244	512.72
Conflict of laws—Persons	K7120-7197	340.912	Conjunctiva—Diseases	RE310-326	617.773
Conflict of laws—Property	K7200-7218	340.94	Conjunctivitis	RE321	617.773
Conflict of laws—Quasi contracts	K7310	340.929	Conjunctivitis, Infantile	RJ296	618.92097773
			Conjuring	GV1541-1561	793.8
Conflict of laws—Sales	K7350	340.972	Connecticut—Gazetteers	F92	917.46003
Conflict of laws—Torts	K7315-7335	340.93	Connecticut—History	F91-105	974.6

Subject Heading	LC	Dewey	Subject Heading	LC	Dewey
Connecticut—History—Colonial period, ca. 1600-1775	F97	974.60(1-2)	Consumer credit	HG3755-3756	332.743
			Consumer education	TX335	640.73
			Consumers	HC79.C6	339.47092
Connecticut—History—1775-1865	F99	974.60(2-3)	Consumers' leagues	HD3271-3575	334.5
			Consumption (Economics)	HB801-843	339.47
Connecticut—History—1865-1950	F100	974.604(1-3)	Consumption (Economics)	HC79.C6	339.47
			Contact dermatitis	RL244	616.51
Connecticut—History—1951-	F101	974.604(3-4)	Contact lenses	RE977.C6	617.7523
			Container gardening	SB418-.4	635.986
Connecticut—Maps	G3780-3784	912.746	Containers	TS197.5	688.8
Connecticut—National Guard	UA100-109	355.3709746	Containers—Law and legislation—England	KD2230-2231	343.42075
Connecticut—Periodicals	F91	974.6005			
Connective tissues	QM563	611.74	Contemplation	BV5091.C7	248.34
Connective tissues—Diseases	RC924-.5	616.77	Contempt of court	JK1543	364.1340973
			Continuing education	LC5201-6660	374
Connective tissue diseases in children	RJ482.C65	618.9277	Contraception	RG136-137.6	613.94
			Contraceptive drugs	RG137.4-.6	613.9432
Conscience	BV4615	241.1	Contraceptives	RG137-.6	613.9432
Conscience	BJ1471	170	Contraceptives, Vaginal	RG137.2	613.9435
Conscience, Examination of	BX2377	241.1	Contract labor	HD4871-4875	331.542
Conscientious objectors	UB341-342	355.224	Contracting out	HD2365-2385	331.542
Consciousness	BF309-499	153	Contracts	K840-917	346.02
Consecration	BV4501	265.92	Contracts	K1024-1132	346.02
Consecration of virgins	BX2305	264.02092	Contracts—Canada	KE850-1225	346.7102
Conservation of natural resources	S900-954	333.72/631.45	Contracts—England	KD1554-1920	346.4202
			Contracts—Ireland	KDK370-437	346.41502
Conservation of natural resources—United States	KF5505-5510	346.73044	Contracts—United States	KF801-1241	346.7302
			Contracts, Aleatory—United States	KF1241	344.730542
Conservative Judaism	BM197.5	296.8342			
Consolation	BV4900-4911	242.4	Contracts for work and labor—United States	KF898-905	344.7301542
Consolation (Judaism)	BM729.C6	296.72			
Consolidation and merger of corporations	HD2746.5-.55	338.83	Contradiction	BC199.C6	165
			Control theory	QA402.3-.37	515.64
Consolidation and merger of corporations	HG4028.M4	338.83	Controlled fusion	QC791.7-.775	539.764
			Convection oven cookery	TX840.C65	641.58
Consolidation of land holdings	HD1334-1335	333.33	Convenience stores	HF5469.25-.55	381.147
			Convention facilities	NA6880-.5	725.91
Conspiracies	HV6275	364.1	Conversation	BJ2120-2128	395.59
Constables	HV7981	363.2	Conversion	BV4912-4950	248.24
Constellations	QB63	523.1	Conversion	BT780	248.24
Constipation	RC861	616.3428	Conversion	BR110	248.24
Constitutional conventions	JF71-99	342.0292	Converts	BV4930-4935	248.24
Constitutional conventions	JK301	342.73024	Conveying machinery	TJ1385-1418	621.867
Constitutional history	K3161	342.029	Convict labor	HV8888-8931	365.65
Constitutional law	K3154-3367	342	Convulsions	RC394.C77	616.845
Constitutions, State	JK2413-2428	342.0297(4-9)	Cook Islands—Census	HA4017.5	319.623
Construction equipment	TH900-915	690.0284	Cook Islands—Maps	G9600-9604	912.9623
Construction industry	HD9715-9717.5	338.47624	Cookery	TX642-840	641.5
Construction industry—Law and legislation	KD2435	343.42078624	Cookery—History	TX645	641.509
			Cookery—Study and teaching	TX661-669	641.5071
Construction industry—Law and legislation—Canada	KE1915	343.71078624	Cookery, French	TX719-.2	641.5944
			Cookery, German	TX721	641.5943
			Cookery, Japanese	TX724.5.J3	641.5952
Construction industry—Law and legislation—United States	KF1950	343.73078624	Cookery, Marine	VC370-375	641.57
			Cookery, Mexican	TX716.M4	641.5972
			Cookery, Military	UC720-735	641.57
Consumer affairs departments	HF5415.5	381.3	Cookery (Canned foods)	TX821	641.612
			Cookery (Fish)	TX747	641.692
Consumer cooperatives	HD3271-3575	334.5	Cookery (Meat)	TX749-.5	641.66
Consumer cooperatives—[By region or country]	HD3281-3410.9	334.509	Cookery (Poultry)	TX750-.5	641.665
			Cookery (Seafood)	TX747	641.692

Subject Heading	LC	Dewey	Subject Heading	LC	Dewey
Cookery (Vegetables)	TX801-807	641.65	Corporation law—England	KD2057-2127	346.42066
Cookies	TX772	641.8654	Corporation law—United	KF1384-1480	346.73066
Cooks	TX649	641.5092	States		
Cooperation	HD2951-3575	334	Corporations	HD2709-2932	338.74
Cooperation—History	HD2956	334.09	Corporations—Accounting	HF5686.C7	657.95
Cooperation—Societies, etc.	HD2952	334.06	Corporations—Corrupt	HV6763-6771	364.168
Coopers and cooperage	HD9750-9769	674.82	practices		
Coopers and cooperage	HD4966.C82	331.287482	Corporations—Finance	HG4001-4285	338.74
Coopers and cooperage	TS890	674.82	Corporations—Investor	HD59	338.74
Copenhagen (Denmark)	DL276	948.913	relations		
Copper	TA480.C7	620.182	Corporations—Law and	KF1396-1477	346.73066
Copper—Metallurgy	TN780	669.3	legislation—United States		
Copper age	GN777-778	930.15	Corporations—Taxation	HD2753	336.207
Coptic language	PJ2001-2187	493.2	Corporations—[By region	HD2770-2930.7	338.7409
Coptic language—Etymology	PJ2161	493.22	or country]		
Coptic language—Grammar	PJ2029-2113	493.25	Corporations—Africa	HD2917-2929.3	338.74096
Coptic language—	PJ2181	493.23028	Corporations—Australia	HD2930	338.740994
Lexicography			Corporations—Benelux	HD2865.5-	338.7409492
Coptic language—Study	PJ2019	493.2071	countries	2873.5	
and teaching			Corporations—Canada	HD2807-2810	338.740971
Coptic literature	PJ2190-2199	893.2	Corporations—Central	HD2813.5-2819	338.7409728
Copying processes	Z48	686.4	America		
Copyright	K1411-1485	346.0482	Corporations—China	HD2910	338.740951
Copyright	Z551-656	351.824	Corporations—Europe	HD2844-2891.84	338.74094
Copyright—England	KD1281-1325	346.420482	Corporations—France	HD2853-2856	338.740944
Copyright—Transfer	Z649.T7	346.0482	Corporations—Germany	HD2857-2860.5	338.740943
Copyright—United States	KF2986-3080	346.730482	Corporations—Great Britain	HD2845-2847.5	338.740941
Coral Sea, Battle of the,	D774.C	940.5426	Corporations—Greece	HD2891.83	338.7409495
1942			Corporations—India	HD2897-2900	338.740954
Coral fisheries	SH399.C6	639.32	Corporations—Indonesia	HD2904	338.7409598
Coral reef biology	QH95.8	578.7789	Corporations—Iran	HD2892.56	338.740955
Coral reef ecology	QH541.5.C7	577.789	Corporations—Iraq	HD2892.55	338.7409567
Coral reefs and islands	GB461-468	551.424	Corporations—Israel	HD2892.2	338.74095694
Coral reefs and islands	QE565-566	551.424	Corporations—Italy	HD2862-2865	338.740945
Cordage	TS1784-1787	677.71	Corporations—Japan	HD2907	338.740952
Cordage, Prehistoric	GN799.C49	623.8620901	Corporations—Mexico	HD2811	338.740972
Corinthian League	DF233.2	938.0(1-8)	Corporations—Philippines	HD2905	338.7409599
Cornea—Diseases	RE336-340	617.719	Corporations—Portugal	HD2889	338.7409469
Cornet music	M85-89	788.96	Corporations—Russia	HD2874-2877	338.740947
Cornish language	PB2501-2549	491.67	Corporations—South	HD2827-2843	338.74098
Cornish language—	PB2511-2547	491.675	America		
Grammar			Corporations—Spain	HD2885-2888	338.740946
Cornish language—Study	PB2507	491.67071	Corporations—Turkey	HD2891.93	338.7409561
and teaching			Corporations—United States	HD2771-2798.5	338.740973
Cornish literature	PB2551-2621	891.67	Corporations—West Indies	HD2820.5-2825.9	338.7409729
Coronary artery bypass	RD598.35.C67	617.413	Corporations, Government	HD3850	352.266
Coronary circulation	QP108	612.17	Corporations, Government—	KF1480	346.73067
Coronary heart disease	RC685.C6	616.123	Law and legislation—		
Coronations	D127	394.4	United States		
Coronations	GT5050	394.4	Corporations, Government—	HD3881-4420.8	352.2660973
Coronations	JC391	321.6	United States		
Corporal punishment	HQ770.4	364.67	Corporations, Government—	HD4001-4420.7	352.26609(4-9)
Corporal punishment	HV8609-8621	364.67	[Other regions or countries]		
Corporal punishment	UB810-815	355.13325	Correlation (Statistics)	HA31.3	310.72
Corporal punishment	VB910	359.13325	Correlation (Statistics)	QA273-281	519.537
Corporal works of mercy	BV4647.M4	241.4	Corrosion and	TA418.74-.76	620.11223
Corporate governance	HD2741-2749	658.4	anti-corrosives		
Corporate image	HD59.2	338.74	Corrosion resistant alloys	TA486	620.16
Corporate state	JC478	321.94	Corsets	GT2075	391.42
Corporate state	HD3611-4730.9	321.94	Corsica (France)—History	DC611.C8-.C839	944.945
Corporation law—Canada	KE1369-1465	346.71066	Cosmetics	GT2340-2341	391.63

Subject Heading	LC	Dewey
Cosmetics	TP983-986	668.55
Cosmic dust	QB791	523.1125
Cosmic magnetic fields	QC809.M25	538.7
Cosmic physics	QC801-809	550
Cosmic physics	QC883.2.S6	551.5276
Cosmic rays	QC484.8-485.9	539.7223
Cosmochemistry	QB450-.5	523.02
Cosmogony	QB980-991	523.12
Cosmology	BD493-708	113
Cosmology	QB980-991	523.1
Cosmology—History	BD494-497	113.09
Cosmology, Ancient	BD495	113.0901
Cosmology, Medieval	BD495.5	113.0902
Cost accounting	HF5686.C8	657.42
Cost and standard of living	HD6977-7080	339.42
Cost control	HD47.3	658.1552
Cost effectiveness	HD47.4	658.1554
Costa Rica	F1541-1557	972.86
Costa Rica—Census	HA801-810	317.286
Costa Rica—Civilization	F1543.8	972.86
Costa Rica—Description and travel	F1544	917.28604
Costa Rica—Emigration and immigration	JV7413	325.(27286/7286)
Costa Rica—Gazetteers	F1542	917.286003
Costa Rica—History—To 1821	F1547	972.860(1-3)
Costa Rica—History—1821-1948	F1547.5	972.8604
Costa Rica—History—Uprising, 1932	F1547.5	972.86044
Costa Rica—History—1948-1986	F1548	972.8605
Costa Rica—History—1986-	F1548.2-.23	972.8605
Costa Rica—Maps	G4860-4864	912.7286
Costa Rica—Periodicals	F1541	972.86005
Costa Rica—Politics and government	JL1440-1459	320.97286
Costa Rican literature	PQ7480-7489.2	860
Costume	GT500-2370	391
Costume—History	GT530-596	391.0090(1-5)
Costume—History—To 500	GT530-560	391.00901
Costume—History—Medieval, 500-1500	GT575	391.00902
Costume—History—[16th/18th] century	GT585	391.00903(1-3)
Costume—[By region or country]	GT601-1605	391.009(3-9)
Costume—Africa	GT1580-1589	391.0096
Costume—Asia	GT1370-1570	391.0095
Costume—Europe	GT720-1330	391.0094
Costume—[New Zealand/Australia/Oceania]	GT1590-1599	391.0099(3-6)
Costume—North America	GT603-648	391.0097
Costume—South America	GT675-716	391.0098
Costume, Jewish	GT540	391.0088296
Cote d'Ivoire—Census	HA4725	316.668
Cote d'Ivoire—Civilization	DT545.4	966.68
Cote d'Ivoire—Description and travel	DT545.27	916.66804
Cote d'Ivoire—Economic conditions	HC1025	330.96668
Cote d'Ivoire—Gazetteers	DT545.15	916.668003
Cote d'Ivoire—History	DT545.52-.83	966.68
Cote d'Ivoire—Maps	G8780-8784	912.6668
Cottage industries	HD2336.2-.25	338.634
Cottages	NA7551-7555	728.37
Cotton	TS1542	677.21
Cotton growing	HD9070-9093	338.17351
Cotton-picking machinery	S715.C64	631.37
Cotton trade	HD9070-9089	380.141351
Cotton trade	HD9870-9889	380.141351
Councils and synods	BV710	262.(4-5)
Councils and synods, Episcopal (Catholic)	BX820-838	262.52
Counseling	BF637.C6	158.3
Counted thread embroidery	TT778.C65	746.442
Counter-Reformation	D220-271	943.03
Counter-Reformation	BR430	270.6
Counter-Reformation	DD176-189	943.03
Counterfeits and counterfeiting	HG641-645	332.490973
Counterfeits and counterfeiting	HG335-341	332.90973
Counterinsurgency	U241	355.0218
Counterrevolutions	JC492	321.09
Countertransference (Psychology)	RC489.C68	616.8914
Counting	QA113	513.211
Counting-out rhymes	GR485	398.8
Country life	GT3470	390.091734
Country music	ML3523-3524	784.164209
County agricultural agents	S533-534	630.715092
County government—United States	JS411	352.150973
County school systems	LB2813	379.123
Couple-owned business enterprises	HD62.27	338.7
Coups d'etat	JC494	321.09
Courage	BJ1533.C8	179.6
Court rules—United States	KF8816-8821	347.73051
Courtesy	BJ1533.C9	177.1
Courtesy	BJ1520-1688	177.1
Courthouses	NA4470-4477	725.15
Courtly love	GT2620	392.4
Courts and courtiers	GT3510-3530	390.23
Courts of honor	UB880	394.(7-8)
Courts of love	DC611.P961	396.70944
Courts—Canada	KE8200-8605	347.7101
Courts—Canada	KE4775	347.7101
Courts—England	KD4645	347.4201
Courts—United States	JK1606	347.7301
Courts—United States	KF101-153	347.7301
Courts—United States—Officials and employees	KF8771-8807	347.731(4-6)
Courts—Wales	KD9480-9484	347.42901
Courts-martial and courts of inquiry	VB800-807	343.0143
Courts-martial and courts of inquiry	UB850-857	343.0143

Subject Heading	LC	Dewey	Subject Heading	LC	Dewey
Courts-martial and courts of inquiry—United States	KF7625-7659	343.730143	Criminal justice, Administration of— [By region or country]	HV9950-9960	345 0509(4-9)
Covenant theology	BT155	231.76	Criminal justice, Administration of— United States	HV9950-9956	345.050973
Covenants (Church polity)	BT1010	262			
Covenants—Judaism	BM612.5	296.31172			
Coverlets	TT835	746.46	Criminal law	K5011-5316	345
Cows	SF191-219	636.2	Criminal law—Canada	KE8801-9112	345.71
Crab culture	SH380.4-.45	639.56	Criminal law—England	KD7850-8090	345.42
Cracking process	TP690.4	665.533	Criminal law—Ireland	KDK1750-1782	345.415
Cradles	GN415.C8	645.4	Criminal law—Scotland	KDC910-920	345.411
Cranes, derricks, etc.	TJ1363-1365	621.87	Criminal law—United States	KF9201-9479	345.73
Craniology	GN71-131	599.948	Criminal law—Wales	KD9490	345.429
Craniotomy	RD529	617.514	Criminal liability	K5064-5083	345.04
Craniotomy	RG781	618.83	Criminal procedure	K5401-5570	345.05
Crayon drawing	NC855-875	741.23	Criminal procedure—England	KD8220-8464	345.4205
Creation	BL224-226	213	Criminal procedure— Northern Ireland	KDE550-557	345.41675
Creation	BS651-652	231.765			
Creation (Literary, artistic, etc.)	BH301.C84	153.35	Criminal psychology	HV6080-6113	364.3
Creation (Literary, artistic, etc.)	BF408-426	153.35	Criminal statistics— [By region or country]	HV7245-7400	364.09(4-9)021
Creationism	BS651-652	231.7652	Criminal statistics—Africa	HV7382-7388.4	364.096021
Creative ability	BF408	153.3	Criminal statistics—Asia	HV7368-7381	364.0995021
Creative ability in children	BF723.C7	155.4133	Criminal statistics—Australia	HV7389	364.0994021
Creative thinking	BF408-426	153.3	Criminal statistics—Canada	HV7315	364.0971021
Creative thinking	LB1062	370.157	Criminal statistics—Central America	HV7317-7323	364.09728021
Credit	HG3691-3769	332.7			
Credit control	HG3705-3711	332.75	Criminal statistics—China	HV7378	364.0951021
Credit ratings	HG3751.5-.9	332.7	Criminal statistics—Europe	HV7342-7367.7	364.094021
Credit unions	HG2032-2039	334.22	Criminal statistics—France	HV7348	364.0944021
Creeds	BT990-1010	238	Criminal statistics— Germany	HV7349-.5	364.0943021
Creeds, Ecumenical	BT990	238			
Creek War, 1813-1814	E83.813	975.903	Criminal statistics—Great Britain	HV7343-7345.5	364.0941021
Cremation	GT3330	393.2			
Cremation	RA631-636.7	614.6	Criminal statistics—India	HV7371	364.0954021
Creole dialects	PM7831-7875	447.9	Criminal statistics—Italy	HV7351	364.0945021
Crests	CR55-57	929.6	Criminal statistics—Japan	HV7377	364.0952021
Crete (Greece)—History	DF901.C78-.C89	949.59	Criminal statistics—Mexico	HV7316	364.0972021
Cretinism	RC657	616.858848043	Criminal statistics—Russia	HV7355	364.0947021
Crime	HV6251-6773.3	364	Criminal statistics—South America	HV7330-7341	364.098021
Crime	HV6001-7220.5	364			
Crime analysis	HV7936.C88	363.256	Criminal statistics—Spain	HV7361	364.0946021
Crime and age	HV6163	364.24	Criminal statistics—United States	HV7245-7300	364.0973021
Crime in mass media	P96.C74	364			
Crime prevention	HV7431	364.4	Criminal statistics—[United States, By state]	HV7250-7300	364.097(4-9)021
Crime stoppers programs	HV7936.C58	364.4			
Crimean War, 1853-1856	DR567	956.1015	Criminal statistics—West Indies	HV7324-7329.9	364.09729021
Crimean Tatar language	PL65.C74	494.388			
Crimean War, 1853-1856	DK214-215	947.0738	Criminals	GT6550-6710	390.406927
Crimes without victims	HV6705-6738	364.1	Criminals	HV6001-7220.5	364.3
Criminal anthropology	HV6001-6197	364.2	Criminals—Identification	HV6065-6079	363.258
Criminal behavior— Genetic aspects	HV6047	364.24	Criminals—Rehabilitation	HV9261-9430.7	364.601
			Criminals—[By region or country]	HV6774-7220.5	364.(1/3)09(4-9)
Criminal investigation	HV8073-8079.3	363.25			
Criminal jurisdiction	K5036-5048	345.01	Criminals—United States	HV6774-6795	364.(1/3)0973
Criminal jurisidiction	K5423	345.01	Criminals—[Other regions or countries]	HV6801-7220.5	364.(1/3)09(4-9)
Criminal justice, Administration of	HV7231-9960	345.05			
			Criminology	HV6001-7220.5	364
Criminal justice, Administration of— Research	HV7419.5	345.05072	Criminology—History	HV6021-6023	364.09
			Criminology—Periodicals	HV6001-6006	364.05
			Criminology—Research	HV6024.5	364.072

Subject Heading	LC	Dewey	Subject Heading	LC	Dewey
Criminology—Study and teaching	HV6024	364.071	Crustacea	QL435-445.2	595.3
Crinolines	GT2075	391.42	Crutches	RD756	617.9
Critical care medicine	RC86-88.9	616.028	Cryobiology	QH324.9.C7	571.4645
Criticism, Textual	P47	801.959	Cryochemistry	QD515	541.3686
Criticism, Textual	PA47	880.9	Cryptogams	QK504-635	586
Croatia	DR1502-1645	939.8/949.72	Cryptography	Z102.5-104.5	652.8
Croatia—History	DR1547-1598	939.8/949.72	Crystal growth	QD921-926	548.5
Croatia—Maps	G2030-2032	912.4972	Crystalline lens—Diseases	RE401-461	617.742
Croatia—Maps	G6870-6873	912.4972	Crystallization	QD901-999	548.5
Crocheting	TT820-829	746.434	Crystallography	QD901-999	548
Crocodiles	QL666.C925	597.98	Crystallography, Mathematical	QD911-919	548.7
Crop improvement	SB106.I47	631.52	Ctenophora	QL380-.8	593.8
Crop rotation	S603	631.582	Cuba	F1751-1854.9	972.91
Crop science literature	SB45.65	630	Cuba—Census	HA871-880	317.291
Crops	SB1-317	630	Cuba—Civilization	F1760	972.91
Crops—Congresses	SB16	630.6	Cuba—Description and travel	F1761-1765.3	917.29104
Crops—Effect of acid precipitation on	SB745	632.19	Cuba—Emigration and immigration	JV7370-7379	325.(27291/7291)
Crops—Effect of air pollution on	SB745	632.19	Cuba—Gazetteers	F1754	917.291003
Crops—Evolution	SB106.074	631.52	Cuba—History	F1751-1849	972.91
Crops—Genetic engineering	SB123.57	631.5233	Cuba—History—To 1810	F1779	972.910(1-4)
Crops—Periodicals	SB1-13	630.5	Cuba—History—British occupation, 1762-1763	F1781	972.9103
Crops—Research	SB51-56	630.72	Cuba—History—1810-1899	F1783	972.9105
Cross-country skiing	GV855-.5	796.932	Cuba—History—Black Eagle Conspiracy, 1830	F1783	972.9105
Cross-cousin marriage	GN480.4	306.81			
Cross-cultural orientation	GN345.65	303.482	Cuba—History—Negro Conspiracy, 1844	F1783	972.9105
Cross, Sign of the	BV197.S5	264.9			
Crosses	BV160	246.558	Cuba—History—Insurrection, 1849-1851	F1783	972.9105
Crosses	CC300-350	246.558			
Crosses	BL406.C7	291.37	Cuba—History—Insurrection, 1868-1878	F1785	972.9105
Crossword puzzles	GV1507.C7	793.732			
Croup	RC746	616.201	Cuba—History—1878-1895	F1785	972.9105
Crow Indians	E99.C92	973.049752			
Crow language	PM1001	497.52	Cuba—History—Revolution, 1879-1880	F1785	972.9105
Crowds	HM281-283	302.33			
Crowns	CR4480.C7	929.7	Cuba—History—1895-	F1786-1788.22	972.910(5-6)
Crowns (Dentistry)	RK666	617.692	Cuba—History—Revolution, 1895-1898	F1786	972.9105
Crucifixion	HV8569	364.66			
Cruelty	BJ1535.C7	179	Cuba—History—1899-1906	F1787	972.9106(1-2)
Cruise missiles	UG1312.C7	358.428251	Cuba—History—1909-1933	F1787	972.91062
Crusades	D151-173	909.07	Cuba—History—American occupation, 1906-1909	F1787	972.91062
Crusades—Biography	D156-.5	909.07092			
Crusades—Eighth, 1270	D168	909.07	Cuba—History—Revolution, 1933	F1787.5	972.91063
Crusades—Fifth, 1218-1221	D165	909.07			
Crusades—First, 1096-1099	D161-.5	909.07	Cuba—History—Moncada Barracks Attack, 1953	F1787.5	972.91063
Crusades—Fourth, 1202-1204	D164-.5	909.07			
			Cuba—History—Revolution, 1959	F1788	972.91064
Crusades—Historiography	D156.58	909.07072			
Crusades—Later, 13th, 14th, and 15th centuries	D171-173	909.07	Cuba—History—Invasion, 1961	F1788	972.91064
			Cuba—Maps	G4920-4924	912.7291
Crusades—Second, 1147-1149	D162-.5	909.07	Cuba—Periodicals	F1751	972.91005
			Cuba—Politics and government	JL1000-1019	320.97291
Crusades—Seventh, 1248-1250	D167	909.07			
			Cuban literature	PQ7370-7390	860
Crusades—Sixth, 1228-1229	D166	909.07	Culture	CB	306
			Culture	GN400-406	306
Crusades—Third, 1189-1192	D163-.5	909.07	Culture	HM101-121	306
Crushing machinery	TJ1345	621.914			

Subject Heading	LC	Dewey
Dairy products—Marketing	HD9275-9283.7	380.1417
Dairy products industry	HD9275-9283.7	338.47637143
Dairy schools	SF241-245	636.21420711
Dairying	SF221-250	636.2142
Dairying—Accounting	SF261	636.21420681
Dairying—Equipment and supplies	SF247	636.21420284
Dairying—Study and teaching	SF241-245	636.2142071
Daisies	QK495.C74	583.99
Daisies	SB413.D	635.93399
Daisy Girl Scouts	HS3359	369.463
Dajo, Mount, Battle of, 1906	DS685	959.9032
Dakini (Buddhist deity)	BQ4750.D33	294.34211
Dakota Indians	E99.D1	973.049752
Dakota Indians—Wars, 1862-1865	E83.86	978.02
Dakota Indians—Wars, 1876	E83.876	978.02
Dakota Indians—Wars, 1890-1891	E83.89	978.02
Dakota language	PM1021-1024	497.52
Dalai lamas	BQ7930	294.361
Dall Porpoise	QL737.C434	599.53
Dallas (Tex.)	F394.D21	976.42812
Dalmatia (Croatia)—Maps	G2025-2027	912.4972
Dalmatian dog	SF429.D3	636.72
Dalmatian language (Romance)	PC890	457.994972
Dalmatian poetry	PG1654-.5	891.821008
Dalmatian poetry	PG1650-.5	891.821009
Dalton laboratory plan	LB1029.L3	371.382
Dam-tshig-rdo-rje (Buddhist deity)	BQ4890.D33-.D334	294.34211
Damage control (Warships)	V810	623.888
Dampness in buildings	TH9031	693.892
Dams	TC540-558	627.8
Dams—Design and construction	TC540	627.8
Dams—Earthquake effects	TC542.5	627.8
Damselflies	QL520-.42	595.733
Dan literature	PL8123.5-.9	896.34
Dance	GV1580-1799.4	792.8
Dance—Biography	GV1785	792.8092
Dance criticism	GV1600	792.809
Dance for children	GV1799	793.083
Dance for the aged	GV1799.3	793.0846
Dance for the handicapped	GV1799.2	793.087
Dance in art	N8217.D3	704.9497928
Dance music—History and criticism	ML3400-3451	781.55409
Dance of death	N7720	700.4548
Dance-orchestra music	ML3518	784.4809
Dance-orchestra music	M1356	784.48
Dance therapy	RC489.D3	616.891655
Dance therapy for children	RJ505.D3	615.85155083
Dancing mice	QL737.R6	599.35
Dandelions	QK495.C74	583.99
Dandie Dinmont terrier	SF429.D33	636.755
Dandruff	RL91	616.546
Dangerous animals	QL100	591.65

Subject Heading	LC	Dewey
Dangerous birds	QL677.75	598.165
Dangerous fishes	QL618.7	597.165
Dangerous reptiles	QL645.7	597.9165
Danish—Study and teaching	PD3065	439.81071
Danish Americans	E184.S19	973.043981073
Danish drama	PT7800-7832	839.812009
Danish drama	PT7999-8020	839.812008
Danish fiction	PT8022-8024	839.813008
Danish fiction	PT7835-7862	839.813009
Danish language	PD3001-3929	439.81
Danish language—Dialects	PD3700-3929	439.817
Danish language—Dictionaries	PD3625-3693	439.813
Danish language—Etymology	PD3571-3599	439.812
Danish language—Grammar	PD3101-3400	439.815
Danish language—Lexicography	PD3601-3693	439.813028
Danish language—Slang	PD3901-3929	439.817
Danish letters	PT7866	839.816009
Danish letters	PT8030	839.816008
Danish literature	PT7601-8260	839.81
Danish literature—18th century	PT7741-7747	839.810900(4-5)
Danish literature—19th century	PT7751-7756	839.8109006
Danish literature—20th century	PT7760	839.8109007
Danish literature—Study and teaching	PT7640-7644	839.81071
Danish literature—To 1500	PT7721-7737	839.8109001
Danish newspapers	PN5281-5289	078.489
Danish periodicals	PN5281-5290	058.81
Danish philology	PD3001-3071	439.81
Danish poetry	PT7770-7795	839.811009
Danish poetry	PT7975-7994	839.811008
Danish prose literature	PT8021-8024	839.81808
Danish prose literature	PT7835-7862	839.81808
Dano-Swedish War, 1643-1645	DL190	948.9701
Dano-Swedish Wars, 1657-1660	DL192	948.9701
Danube River Valley	DJK76.2-.8	943.3
Dardanelles, Battle of the, 1656	DR534.5.D3	956.1015
Dardic languages	PK7001-7070	491.499
Dargwa language	PK9201.D3	499.964
Dargwa literature	PK9201.D35-.D39	899.964
Dari language	PK6871-6879	491.56
Dark matter (Astronomy)	QB791.3	523.1126
Darters (Fishes)	QL638.P4	597.75
Darts (Game)	GV1564-1565	794.3
Data compression (Computer science)	QA76.9.D33	005.746
Data recovery (Computer science)	QA76.9.D348	005.86
Data tape drives	TK7887.55	621.3976
Data transmission systems	TK5105-.42	621.38216
Database design	QA76.9.D26	005.74

Subject Heading	LC	Dewey	Subject Heading	LC	Dewey
Database industry	HD9696.D36-.D364	338.4702504	Death—Proof and certification	RA405	353.596
Database management	QA76.9.D3	005.74	Death—Psychological aspects	BF789.D4	155.937
Database marketing	HF5415.126	380.14502504	Death, Apparent	RA1063	614.1
Database security	QA76.9.D314	005.8	Death instinct	BF175.5.D4	155.937
Databases	QA76.9.D32	005.74	Deathbed hallucinations	BF1063.D4	133.9013
Date	SB364	634.62	Debates and debating	PN4177-4191	808.53
Date palm	SB364	634.62	Debit cards	HG1710.5	332.76
Date palm	QK495.P17	584.5	Debris avalanches	QE599	551.307
Dating violence	HQ801.83	306.73	Debts, External	HJ8003-8899	336.3
Dattatreya (Hindu deity)	BL1225.D3	294.52113	Debts, Public	HJ8001-8899	336.3
Dauntless (Dive bomber)	UG1242.A28	358.42	Debts, Public—Law and legislation—England	KD5300	343.42037
David, King of Israel, in the Koran	BP133.7.D38	297.122092	Debts, Public—Law and legislation—United States	KF6241-6245	343.73037
Davits	VM831	623.86	Debts, Public—[By region or country]	HJ8101-8899	336.3409(4-9)
Davits	VM801	623.86	Decadrachma	CJ359	737.4938
Dawah (Islam)	BP170.85	297.74	Decalcomania	NK9510	745.74
Dawn redwood	QK494.5.T3	585.5	Decapoda (Crustacea)	QL444.M33	595.38
Dawn redwood	SD397.D37	634.9758	Decay schemes (Radioactivity)	QC793.3.D4	539.752
Day care centers	HQ778.5-.7	362.712	Decay schemes (Radioactivity)	QC795.8.D4	539.752
Day care centers for mentally handicapped children	HV891-901	362.38	Decca navigation	VK560	623.89
Day care centers for the aged	HV1455-.2	362.68	Decentralization in government	JS113	352.283
Day care centers for the developmentally disabled	HV3004-3009.5	362.1968	Decentralization in management	HD50	658.402
Day care centers for the handicapped	HV1568.7-.8	362.48	Decidability (Mathematical logic)	QA9.65	511.3
Daylighting	NA2794	729.28	Decimal fractions	QA242	513.26
Daylilies	QK495.L72	584.32	Decimal system	HG393	332.4048
Days	GR930	398.33	Decimal system	QC90.8-94	530.812
Daytona International Speedway Race	GV1033.5.D	796.72068759	Decision-making	BF448	153.83
Daza language	PL8127	496.5	Decision-making	HD30.23	658.403
De facto school segregation	LC212.6-.63	379.263	Decision-making	QA279.4-.7	519.542
Deaconesses	BV4423-4425	262.14	Decision-making	T57.95	658.5036
Deacons	BX1912	262.02	Decision-making—Psychic aspects	BF1045.D42	133.3
Deacons	BV680	262.14	Deck machinery	VM781	623.86
Dead	GR455	393	Decks (Architecture, Domestic)	TH4970	690.893
Dead	GT3150-3390	393	Decomposition method	QA402.2	519.4
Dead	RA619-640	614.6	Decompression sickness	RC103.C3	616.9894
Dead loads (Mechanics)	TA648.2	624.172	Decoration and ornament	NK1160-1590	745.4
Deadly sins	BV4626	241.3	Decoration and ornament, Ancient	NK1180-1250	745.442
Deaf	HV2350-2990.5	362.42	Decoration and ornament, Architectural	NA3310-4050	729
Deaf—Education	HV2417-2500	371.912	Decoration and ornament, Baroque	NK1345	745.443
Deaf—Marriage	HQ1040	306.810872	Decoration and ornament, Buddhist	NK1676	745.40882943
Deaf—[By region or country]	HV2510-2990.5	362.4209(4-9)	Decoration and ornament, Byzantine	NK1652.25	745.442
Deaf—United States	HV2510-2561	362.420973	Decoration and ornament, Gothic	NK1295	745.442
Deafness	RF286-320	617.8			
Deafness, Noise induced	RF293.5	617.8			
Deans (Education)	LB2341	371.4			
Death	GT3150-3390.5	393			
Death	GR455	393			
Death	HQ1073-.5	306.9			
Death	RA1063-.5	616.078			
Death	QH671	571.936			
Death	QP87	571.939			
Death—Causes	RA1063	614.1			

Subject Heading	LC	Dewey	Subject Heading	LC	Dewey
Decoration and ornament, Islamic	NK1270-1275	745.442088297	Delphinium	SB413.D4	635.93334
Decoration and ornament, Medieval	NK1260-1295	745.442	Deltas	GB591-598	551.456
			Deluge	BS658	222.11
Decoration and ornament, Primitive	NK1177	745.441	Demand for money	HG226.5	332.414
			Deme	JC75.D	320.938
Decoration and ornament, Renaissance	NK1330	745.443	Dementia	RC521-524	616.8983
			Demeter (Greek deity)	BL820.C5	292.2114
Decoration and ornament, Rococo	NK1355	745.443	Demidoff's galago	QL737.P93	599.83
			Democracy	JC421-423	321.8
Decoration and ornament, Romanesque	NK1285	745.442	Democratic centralism	HX77	335.43
			Demographic anthropology	GN33.5	304.6
Decorations of honor	CR4501-6305	929.81	Demographic libraries	Z675.D28	026.3046
Decorations of honor	UB430-435	355.1342	Demographic transition	HB887	304.6
Decoys (Hunting)	TT199.75	745.5936	Demography	HB848-3697	304.6
Decoys (Hunting)	SK335	799.2028	Demography—Afghanistan	HB3636.6	304.609581
Dedekind rings	QA251.3	512.4	Demography—Albania	HB3626.5	304.6094965
Dedication services	BV199.D4	265.92	Demography—Algeria	HB3661.4	304.60965
Deductive databases	QA76.9.D32	006.33	Demography—American Samoa	HB3693.7	304.6099613
Deep diving	GV840.S78	797.23			
Deep-sea drilling ships	VM453	623.828	Demography—Angola	HB3664.4	304.609673
Deep-sea ecology	QH541.5.D35	577.7	Demography—Anguilla	HB3556.72	304.60972973
Deep-sea temperature	GC175	551.4601	Demography—Antigua	HB3556.74	304.60972974
Deepwater rice	QK495.G74	584.9	Demography—Arctic Regions	HB3695	304.60998
Deer	QL737.U55	599.65	Demography—Argentina	HB3559-3560	304.60982
Deer farming	SF401.D3	636.29401	Demography—Aruba	HB3557.35	304.60972986
Deer hunting	SK301	799.2765	Demography—Australia	HB3675-3676	304.60994
Defecation disorders	RC866.D43	616.342	Demography—Austria	HB3591-3592	304.609436
Defense Mechanisms Inventory	RC473.D43	155.2	Demography—Azores	HB3667.5	304.6094699
			Demography—Bahamas	HB3547-3548	304.6097296
Defense industries	HD9743-9744	338.47355	Demography—Bahrain	HB3635.9	304.6095365
Defense industries— Employees	HD8039.M9	338.47355092	Demography—Bangladesh	HB3640.6	304.6095492
			Demography—Barbados	HB3556.57	304.60972981
Deferred tax	HF5681.D39	657.46	Demography—Belgium	HB3603-3604	304.609493
Deficiency diseases	RC623.5-627	616.39	Demography—Belize	HB3535-3536	304.6097282
Deformations (Mechanics)	TA417.6	620.11232	Demography—Benin	HB3665.7	304.6096683
Degree of freedom	QC174.52.D43	530.143	Demography—Bermuda Islands	HB3668	304.6097299
Degrees, Academic	LB2381-2391	378.2			
Delaware—Gazetteers	F162	917.51003	Demography—Bhutan	HB3640.3	304.6095498
Delaware—History	F161-175	975.1	Demography—Biography	HB855-865	304.6092
Delaware—History— Revolution, 1775-1783	E263.D3	975.10(2-3)	Demography—Bolivia	HB3561-3562	304.60984
			Demography—Bonaire	HB3557.36	304.60972986
Delaware—History— War of 1812	E359.5.D3	975.103	Demography—Botswana	HB3663.9	304.6096883
			Demography—Brazil	HB3563-3564	304.60981
Delaware—History—Civil War, 1861-1865	E500	975.103	Demography—Bulgaria	HB3627-3628	304.609499
			Demography—Burkina Faso	HB3666.4	304.6096625
Delaware—History— 1865-1950	F169	975.14(1-3)	Demography—Burma	HB3636.7	304.609591
			Demography—Burundi	HB3662.8	304.60967572
Delaware—History—1951-	F170	975.104(3-4)	Demography—Cambodia	HB3644.3	304.609596
Delaware—Maps	G3830-3834	912.751	Demography—Cameroon	HB3665.4	304.6096711
Delaware—National Guard	UA110-119	355.3709751	Demography—Canada	HB3529-3530	304.60971
Delaware—Periodicals	F161	975.1005	Demography—Canary Islands	HB3669	304.609649
Delegation of authority	HD50-.5	658.402			
Delegation of powers	JF225	352.283	Demography—Cape Verde	HB3669.5	304.6096658
Delftware	NK4295-.5	738.37	Demography—Chad	HB3665.3	304.6096743
Delirium tremens	RC526	616.861	Demography—Chile	HB3565-3566	304.60983
Delivery of goods	HF5761-5780	658.788	Demography—China	HB3654	304.60951
Delmarva Peninsula— History—Revolution, 1775-1783	E263.D3	975.210(2-3)	Demography—Colombia	HB3567-3568	304.609861
			Demography—Comoro Islands	HB3672.5	304.609694
Delphian oracle	DF261.D35	133.32480938	Demography—Congo (Brazzaville)	HB3665	304.6096724

Subject Heading	LC	Dewey	Subject Heading	LC	Dewey
Demography—Cook Islands	HB3693.65	304.6099623	Demography—Kerguelen Islands	HB3674	304.609699
Demography—Costa Rica	HB3537-3538	304.6097286	Demography—Kiribati	HB3692.9	304.6099681
Demography—Cote d'Ivoire	HB3666	304.6096668	Demography—Korea	HB3652.5-.6	304.609519
Demography—Cuba	HB3549-3550	304.6097291	Demography—Kuwait	HB3636	304.6095367
Demography—Curacao	HB3557.37	304.60972986	Demography—Laos	HB3644.4	304.609594
Demography—Cyprus	HB3633.5	304.6095693	Demography—Lebanon	HB3633.9	304.6095692
Demography—Czechoslovakia	HB3592.3	304.609437	Demography—Lesotho	HB3663.7	304.6096885
Demography—Denmark	HB3611-3612	304.609489	Demography—Liberia	HB3667.2	304.6096662
Demography—Djibouti	HB3662.3	304.6096771	Demography—Libya	HB3661.6	304.609612
Demography—Dominica	HB3556.93	304.609729841	Demography—Liechtenstein	HB3592.9	304.60943648
Demography—Dominican Republic	HB3552	304.6097293	Demography—Luxembourg	HB3606.5	304.6094935
			Demography—Macao	HB3655	304.6095126
Demography—Ecuador	HB3569-3570	304.609866	Demography—Madagascar	HB3663.2	304.609691
Demography—Egypt	HB3661.7	304.60962	Demography—Madeira Islands	HB3668.5	304.6094698
Demography—El Salvador	HB3544	304.6097284			
Demography—England and Wales	HB3585-3586	304.60942(9)	Demography—Malawi	HB3664	304.6096897
			Demography—Malaysia	HB3644.6	304.609595
Demography—Equatorial Guinea	HB3664.6	304.6096718	Demography—Maldives	HB3671.5	304.6095495
			Demography—Mali	HB3666.3	304.6096623
Demography—Ethiopia	HB3662	304.60963	Demography—Martinique	HB3557.9	304.60972982
Demography—Falkland Islands	HB3671	304.6099711	Demography—Mauritania	HB3666.6	304.609661
			Demography—Mauritius	HB3673	304.6096982
Demography—Fiji	HB3693.5	304.6099611	Demography—Mexico	HB3531-3532	304.60972
Demography—Finland	HB3608.3	304.6094897	Demography—Monaco	HB3594.5	304.60944949
Demography—France	HB3593-3594	304.60944	Demography—Mongolia	HB3652.8	304.609517
Demography—French Guiana	HB3572.7	304.609882	Demography—Montserrat	HB3556.76	304.60972975
			Demography—Morocco	HB3661.3	304.60964
Demography—French Polynesia	HB3693.9	304.609962	Demography—Mozambique	HB3663	304.609679
			Demography—Namibia	HB3664.2	304.6096881
Demography—Gabon	HB3664.9	304.6096721	Demography—Nepal	HB3636.9	304.6095496
Demography—Gambia	HB3667	304.6096651	Demography—Netherlands	HB3605-3606	304.609492
Demography—Germany	HB3595-3596.5	304.60943	Demography—New Caledonia	HB3693.3	304.6099597
Demography—Ghana	HB3666.8	304.609667			
Demography—Greece	HB3632.5	304.609495	Demography—New Zealand	HB3692.5	304.60993
Demography—Greenland	HB3696	304.609982	Demography—Nicaragua	HB3541	304.6097285
Demography—Grenada	HB3556.95	304.609729845	Demography—Niger	HB3665.9	304.6096626
Demography—Guadeloupe	HB3557.7	304.60972976	Demography—Nigeria	HB3666.7	304.609669
Demography—Guam	HB3692.7	304.609967	Demography—Northern Ireland	HB3588.5	304.609416
Demography—Guatemala	HB3539	304.6097281			
Demography—Guinea	HB3666.2	304.6096652	Demography—Norway	HB3615-3616	304.609481
Demography—Guinea-Bissau	HB3667.3	304.6096657	Demography—Oman	HB3635.3	304.6095353
			Demography—Pakistan	HB3640.5	304.6095491
Demography—Guyana	HB3572.3	304.609881	Demography—Panama	HB3542-3543	304.6097287
Demography—Haiti	HB3551	304.6097294	Demography—Papua New Guinea	HB3692.8	304.609953
Demography—Honduras	HB3540	304.6097283			
Demography—Hong Kong	HB3657	304.6095125	Demography—Paraguay	HB3573-3574	304.609892
Demography—Hungary	HB3592.5	304.609439	Demography—Periodicals	HB848	304.605
Demography—Iceland	HB3613-3614	304.6094912	Demography—Peru	HB3575-3576	304.60985
Demography—India	HB3639-3640	304.60954	Demography—Philippines	HB3649-3650	304.609599
Demography—Indonesia	HB3647-3648	304.609598	Demography—Poland	HB3608.7	304.609438
Demography—Iran	HB3636.4	304.60955	Demography—Portugal	HB3621-3622	304.609469
Demography—Iraq	HB3636.3	304.609567	Demography—Qatar	HB3635.7	304.6095363
Demography—Ireland	HB3589-3590	304.609415	Demography—Reunion	HB3673.5	304.6096981
Demography—Israel	HB3634	304.6095694	Demography—Romania	HB3631-3632	304.609498
Demography—Italy	HB3599-3600	304.60945	Demography—Russia	HB3607-3608.2	304.60947
Demography—Jamaica	HB3553-3554	304.6097292	Demography—Rwanda	HB3662.7	304.60967571
Demography—Japan	HB3651-3652	304.60952	Demography—Saba (Netherlands Antilles)	HB3557.38	304.60972977
Demography—Jordan	HB3634.3	304.6095695			
Demography—Kenya	HB3662.5	304.6096762			

Subject Heading	LC	Dewey	Subject Heading	LC	Dewey
Demography—Saint Eustatius (Netherlands Antilles)	HB3557.385	304.60972977	Demography—Zaire	HB3664.5	304.6096751
			Demography—Zambia	HB3663.6	304.6096894
Demography—Saint Helena	HB3670	304.609973	Demography—[United States, By City]	HB3527	304.6097(4-9)
Demography—Saint Kitts and Nevis	HB3556.78	304.60972973	Demography—[United States, By State]	HB3525	304.6097(4-9)
Demography—Saint Lucia	HB3556.97	304.609729843	Demolition, Military	UG370	358.23
Demography—Saint Martin	HB3557.39	304.60972977	Demoniac possession	BF1555	133.426
Demography—Saint Vincent	HB3556.99	304.609729844	Demonology	GR540	398.45
Demography—Sao Tome and Principe	HB3664.7	304.6096715	Demonology	BL480	291.216
			Demonology	BF1501-1562	133.42
Demography—Saudi Arabia	HB3634.7	304.609538	Demonology, Islamic	BP166.89	297.216
Demography—Scotland	HB3587-3588	304.609411	Demurrage (Car service)	HE1826	385.22
Demography—Senegal	HB3666.5	304.609663	Demythologizcation	BS2378	225.68
Demography—Seychelles	HB3672	304.609696	Dendrobium	SB409	635.9344
Demography—Sierra Leone	HB3666.9	304.609664	Dengue	RA644.D4	614.571
Demography—Solomon Islands	HB3693	304.6099593	Dengue	RC137	616.921
Demography—Somalia	HB3662.2	304.6096773	Denkyira (Kingdom)	DT532.12	966.68
Demography—South Africa	HB3663.4	304.60968	Denmark—Census	HA1471-1490	314.89
Demography—Spain	HB3619-3620	304.60946	Denmark—Civilization	DL131-133	936.3/948.9
Demography—Sri Lanka	HB3636.8	304.6095493	Denmark—Colonies	JV3300-3399	325.3489
Demography—Sudan	HB3661.8	304.609624	Denmark—Description and travel	DL115-120	913.6304/ 914.8904
Demography—Surinam	HB3572.5	304.609883			
Demography—Swaziland	HB3663.8	304.6096887	Denmark—Economic conditions	HC351-360	330.9489
Demography—Sweden	HB3617-3618	304.609485			
Demography—Switzerland	HB3623-3624	304.609494	Denmark—Emigration and immigration	JV8200-8209	325.(2489/489)
Demography—Syria	HB3633.7	304.6095691			
Demography—Taiwan	HB3656	304.60951249	Denmark—Gazetteers	DL105	913.63003/ 914.89003
Demography—Tanzania	HB3662.9	304.609678			
Demography—Thailand	HB3644.55	304.609593	Denmark—History	DL101-291	936.3/948.9
Demography—Togo	HB3665.8	304.6096681	Denmark—History— To 1241	DL162-173.8	948.901
Demography—Tonga	HB3693.6	304.6099612			
Demography—Trinidad and Tobago	HB3557	304.60972983	Denmark—History— 1241-1397	DL174-183.9	948.90(1-2)
			Denmark—History— Waldemar IV, 1340-1375	DL176	948.9015
Demography—Tristan da Cunha	HB3670.5	304.609973			
Demography—Tunisia	HB3661.5	304.609611	Denmark—History— 1397-1448	DL179-181.6	948.902
Demography—Turkey	HB3633.4	304.609561			
Demography—Ubangi-Shari	HB3665.2	304.6096741	Denmark—History— 1448-1660	DL182-192.3	948.90(2-3)
Demography—Uganda	HB3662.6	304.6096761			
Demography—United Arab Emirates	HB3635.5	304.6095357	Denmark—History— Frederick I, 1523-1533	DL185-192.8	948.903
Demography—United States	HB3505-3527	304.60973	Denmark—History— Frederick I, 1523-1533	DL186	948.903
Demography—[United States, By City]	HB3527	304.6097(4-9)	Denmark—History— Christian III, 1534-1559	DL187	948.903
Demography—[United States, By State]	HB3525	304.6097(4-9)	Denmark—History— The Count's War, 1534-1536	DL187	948.903
Demography—Uruguay	HB3577-3578	304.609895			
Demography—Vanuatu	HB3693.4	304.6099595	Denmark—History— Coup d'etat, 1536	DL187	948.903
Demography—Venezuela	HB3579-3580	304.60987			
Demography—Vietnam	HB3644.5	304.609597	Denmark—History— Frederick II, 1559-1588	DL188-.8	948.903
Demography—Virgin Islands of the United States	HB3556.3	304.609729722			
			Denmark—History— Christian IV, 1588-1648	DL189-.5	948.903
Demography—Western Sahara	HB3667.4	304.609648			
Demography—Western Samoa	HB3693.8	304.6099614	Denmark—History— Frederick III, 1648-1670	DL191.8	948.903
Demography—Yemen	HB3634.9-3635	304.609533	Denmark—History—Coup d'etat, 1660	DL192.3	948.903
Demography—Yugoslavia	HB3628.5	304.609497			

Subject Heading	LC	Dewey
Denmark—History—Christian V, 1670-1699	DL195-.8	948.903
Denmark—History—Fredrick IV, 1699-1730	DL196-.8	948.903
Denmark—History—18th century	DL197-199	948.903
Denmark—History—Coup d'etat, 1784	DL199-.8	948.903
Denmark—History—War of 1807-1814	DL206	948.903
Denmark—History—Frederick VI, 1808-1839	DL205-208	948.90(3-4)
Denmark—History—Christian VIII, 1839-1848	DL209-212	948.904
Denmark—History—Frederick VII, 1848-1863	DL213-228	948.904
Denmark—History—1849-1866	DL217-241	948.904
Denmark—History—Christian IX, 1863-1906	DL234-249	948.904
Denmark—History—1900-	DL248-263	948.90(4-7)
Denmark—History—Christian X, 1912-1947	DL255-257	948.905(1-5)
Denmark—History—German occupation, 1940-1945	DL256.5-257	948.9051
Denmark—Manufactures	TS69-70	670.9489
Denmark—Maps	G6920-6924	912.489
Denmark—Maps	G2055-2059	912.489
Denmark—Periodicals	DL101	936.3005/948.9005
Denmark—Politics and government	JN7101-7367	320.9489
Densitometer (Meteorological instrument)	QC880	551.50284
Density matrices	QC174.17.D44	530.122
Dental adhesives	RK652.7-.8	617.695
Dental amalgams	RK519.A4	617.675
Dental anthropology	GN209	599.943
Dental auxiliary personnel	RK60.5	617.60233
Dental bonding	RK652.7-.8	617.69
Dental calculus	RK328	617.6
Dental caries	RK331	617.67
Dental cavity preparation	RK515	617.672
Dental cements	RK652.7-.8	617.695
Dental ceramic metals	RK653.5	617.675
Dental ceramics	RK655	617.675
Dental clinics	RK3-.5	362.11
Dental clinics—[By region or country]	RK3.5	362.1109(4-9)
Dental deposits	RK328	617.6
Dental drilling	RK515	617.672
Dental enamel—Diseases	RK340-341	617.634
Dental enamel microabrasion	RK320.E53	617.634
Dental ethics	RK52.7	174.2
Dental health education	RK60.8	617.60071
Dental instruments and apparatus	RK681-686	617.600284
Dental jurisprudence	RA1062	614.1
Dental libraries	Z675.D3	026.6176
Dental materials	RK652.5-655	617.695
Dental metallurgy	RK653	617.675
Dental plaque	RK328	617.6
Dental Prophylaxis	RK60.7-.8	617.601
Dental public health	RK52-.45	614.5996
Dental surveys	RK52-.45	617.600723
Dental therapeutics	RK318-320	617.606
Dentistry	RK	617.6
Dentistry—Congresses	RK21	617.6006
Dentistry—Examinations, questions, etc.	RK57	617.60076
Dentistry—Formulae, receipts, prescriptions	RK701-715	617.606
Dentistry—History	RK29-34	617.60901
Dentistry—Periodicals	RK16	617.6005
Dentistry—Practice	RK58-59.3	617.6023
Dentistry—Psychological aspects	RK53	617.60019
Dentistry—Research	RK80	617.60072
Dentistry—Societies, etc.	RK1	617.6006
Dentistry—Study and teaching	RK71-231	617.60071
Dentistry—Study and teaching—[By region and country]	RK86-231	617.600710(4-9)
Dentistry—Study and teaching—United States	RK91-97	617.6071073
Dentistry—Terminology	RK28	617.60014
Dentistry—Vocational guidance	RK60-.5	617.60023
Dentists	RK	617.60232
Dentists	RK	617.60092
Dentists—Directories	RK37	617.60025
Denture attachments	RK656	617.69
Dentures	RK656-666	617.692
Dentures, Immediate	RK656-666	617.692
Denver (Colo.)	F784.D4	978.883
Department stores	HF5460-5469.5	381.141
Dependency (Psychology)	BF575.D34	155.232
Dependency (Psychology)	RC569.5.D47	155.232
Deposit insurance	HG1662	368.854
Depository libraries	Z675.D4	025.26
Depreciation	HF5681.D5	657.73
Depression, Mental	RC537-545	616.8527
Depression in adolescence	RJ506.D4	616.852700835
Depression in children	RJ506.D4	618.928527
Depression in infants	RJ506.D4	618.928527
Depression in old age	RC537.5	616.852700846
Depressions	HB3711-3840	338.542
Depth charges	VF509	359.8251
Dermatoglyphics	GN192	599.945
Dermatologic nursing	RL125	610.736
Dermatologists	RL46.2-.3	616.50092
Dermatologists—Directories	RL43	616.50025
Dermatology	RV381-391	616.506
Dermatology	RX561-581	616.506
Dermatology	RL	616.5

Subject Heading	LC	Dewey	Subject Heading	LC	Dewey
Dermatology—Apparatus and instruments	RL55	616.500284	Detective and mystery stories	PZ1-3	808.83872
Dermatology—Congresses	RL31	616.5006	Detective and mystery stories—Technique	PN3377.5.D4	809.3872
Dermatology—History	RL46	616.5009	Detectives in mass media	P96.D4	363.25092
Dermatology—Periodicals	RL26	616.5005	Detergent pollution of rivers, lakes, etc.	TD427.D4	628.1682
Dermatology—Societies, etc.	RL1	616.5006	Determinants	QA191	512.9432
Dermatology—Study and teaching	RL77	616.50071	Determination (Personality trait)	BF698.35.D48	155.234
Dermatology—Terminology	RL39	616.50014	Determinism (Philosophy)	B105.D47	123
Dermatology, Experimental	RL79	616.5027	Deterrence (Strategy)	U162.6	355.0217
Dermis	QM484	611.77	Detonation waves	QC168.85.D46	532.593
Dermis	QL941-943	573.5	Detroit (Mich.)	F574.D4	977.434
Dermis	QP88.5	573.5	Detroit (Mich.)—Surrender to the British, 1812	E356.D4	973.523
Description (Rhetoric)	PE1427	820.8022	Deuterium	QD181.H1	546.212
Description (Rhetoric)	PR1285	820.8022	Deuteron magnetic resonance spectroscopy	QC762	538.362
Descriptive cataloging	Z693-695.83	025.32	Devanagari alphabet	PK119	491.(2-4)
Desert animals	QL116	591.754	Devanarayana (Hindu deity)	BL1225.D48	294.52113
Desert biology	QH88	578.754	Developing countries—History	D880-888	909.09724
Desert ecology	QH541.5.D4	577.54			
Desert gardening	SB427.5	635.9525	Developing countries—Population	HB884	304.6091724
Desert kangaroo rat	QL737.R66	599.35987			
Desert locust	QL508.A2	595.726	Development banks	HG1975-1976	332.28
Desert plants	SB427.5	635.9525	Developmental psychology	BF712-724.85	155
Desert plants	QK938.D4	581.754	Developmental reading	LB1050.53	418.4
Desert plants	QK922	581.754	Developmentally disabled	HV1570-.5	362.1968
Desert reclamation	HD1711-1741	333.736153	Developmentally disabled children	HV891-901	362.1968
Desert reclamation	S612-619	631.6			
Desert reclamation	TC801-957	333.736153	Deventer, Surrender of, 1587	DH199.D4	949.203
Desert soils	S592.17.D47	631.49154			
Desert soils	S599-.9	631.49154	Devices (Heraldry)	CR67-69	929.6
Desert tortoise	QL666.C584	597.92	Devil	BT980-981	235.4
Desertification	GB611-618	551.415	Devil	BL480	291.216
Desertification—Control	GB611-618	551.415	Devil	BF1546-1561	133.422
Desertion—United States	HQ833-836	306.880973	Devil (Islam)	BP166.89	297.216
Desertion—[Other regions and countries]	HQ837-960.9	306.8809(4-9)	Devil in literature	PN57.D4	808.8038291216
			Devon cattle	SF199.D38	636.226
Desertion, Military	UB788	355.1334	Devotion	BV4815	242
Desertion, Naval	VB870-875	359.1334	Devotion (Buddhism)	BQ5595-5630	294.344
Desertion and non-support	HQ805	306.88	Devotional calendars	BV4810-4812	242.3
Deserts	GB611-618	551.415	Devotional exercises	BV4800-4897	248
Deserts	QH88	578.754	Devotional literature	BX2177-2198	242
Design	NC703	745.4	Devotional literature	BV4800-4895	242
Design	NK1160-1590	745.4	Dew	QC929.D5	551.5744
Design—Study and teaching	NK1170	745.4071	Dew-ponds	TD395	628.13
Design protection—England	KD1345	346.420484	Dewar flasks	QD535	542
Design protection—United States	KF3086	346.730484	Dexter cattle	SF199.D4	636.225
			Dextrose	QD321	547.7813
Designer drugs	RM316	616.86	Dge-lugs-pa (Sect)	BQ7530-7950	294.39
Desirade (Guadeloupe)	F2050	972.976	Dharma (Buddhism)	BQ4195-4250	294.34
Desks	TS880	684.14	Dhat al-Sawari, Battle of, 655	DS38.1	956.013
Desks	TT197.5.D4	684.14			
Desktop publishing	Z253.53-.532	686.22544416	Dhows	VM371	623.8226
Desktop publishing	Z286.D47	686.22544416	Diabetes	RA645.D5	614.59462
Despotism	JC375-392	321.6	Diabetes	RC660-662.4	616.462
Desserts	TX773	641.86	Diabetes	RC658.5	616.462
Destroyers (Warships)	V825-.5	359.3254	Diabetes clinics	RC660.7	362.12
Detective and mystery plays	PN6120.M9	808.82527	Diabetes in adolescence	RJ420.D5	616.46200835
Detective and mystery stories	PN3448.D4	809.3872			

Subject Heading	LC	Dewey	Subject Heading	LC	Dewey
Diabetes in children	RJ420.D5	618.92462083	Differential equations, Linear	QA372	515.354
Diabetes in pregnancy	RG580.D5	618.326			
Diabetes in youth	RJ420.D5	618.92462083	Differential equations, Partial	QA374-377	515.353
Diabetic retinopathy	RE661.D5	617.735			
Diagnosis	RC71-78.7	616.075	Differential forms	QA381	515.37
Diagnosis, Differential	RC71.5	616.075	Differential invariants	QA381	515.37
Diagnosis, Fluoroscopic	RC78.7.F5	616.07572	Differential relays	TK2861	621.317
Diagnosis, Laboratory	RB37-56.5	616.075	Differential topology	QA613.6-.66	514.72
Diagnosis, Noninvasive	RC71.6	616.075	Diffraction	QC414.8-417	535.4
Diagnosis, Radioscopic	RC78-.5	616.0757	Diffusion	QC185	530.475
Diagnosis, Ultrasonic	RC78.7.U4	616.07543	Diffusion processes	QA274.75	519.233
Diagnostic equipment industry	HD9995.D54-.D544	338.47681761	Digambara (Jaina sect)	BL1380.D	294.493
			Digestion	QP145-159	612.3
Diagnostic imaging	RC78.7.D53	616.0754	Digestive organs	QM301-367	611.3
Dialectical materialism	B809.8	146.32	Digestive organs	QL856-867	573.3
Dialing	QB215	529.7	Digestive organs—Cancer	RC280.D5	616.99434
Dialogue	PN1551	808.8026	Digestive organs—Diseases	RC799-869	616.3
Dialogue sermons	BV4307.D5	252	Digestive organs—Diseases—Eclectic treatment	RV271-276	616.306
Diamagnetism	QC771	538.42			
Diathermy	RM874	615.8323			
Diatomaceous earth	TN948.D5	622.36	Digestive organs—Diseases—Homeopathic treatment	RX331-336	616.306
Dice	GV1303	795.1			
Dice games	GV1303	795.1			
Dicetyledons, Fossil	QE983	561.3	Digestive organs—Radiography	RC804.A5	616.307572
Dicotyledons	QK495.A12	583			
Dicotyledons	QK108-474.5	583	Digestive organs—Surgery	RD540-547	617.55059
Dictating machines	HF5548	651.74	Digital audiotape recorders and recording	TK7881.65	621.3883
Dictators	JC495	321.9092			
Dictionaries, Polyglot	P361	413	Digital communications	TK5103.7-.8	621.382
Dictionaries, Polyglot	PB331	413	Digital computer industry	HD9696.D54-.D544	338.47004
Dictograph	HF5548	651.74			
Didgora Mountain (Georgia), Battle of, 1121	DK511.G44	947.02	Digital integrated circuits	TK7874-.8	621.395
			Digital subtraction angiography	RJ423.5.D54	618.92107572
Diegueno Indians	E99.D5	973.049757	Digitalis	RS165.D5	615.711
Dielectric measurements	QC584	537.240287	Digitalis	RM666.D5	615.711
Dielectrics	QC584-585.8	537.24	Dikes (Engineering)	TC337	627.24
Dien Bien Phu (Vietnam), Battle of, 1954	DS553.3.D5	959.7042	Dikes (Geology)	QE611-.5	551.88
			Diktynna (Greek deity)	BL820.D54	292.2114
Dieppe Raid, 1942	D756.5.D5	940.54214	Dill	QK495.U48	583.849
Dies (Metal-working)	TS253	621.984	Diluted magnetic semiconductors	QC611.8.M25	537.6223
Diesel fuels	TP343	665.5384			
Diesel fuels industry	HD9579.D5-.D54	338.476655384	Dining room furniture	NK2117.D5	747.76
Diesel locomotives	TJ619-.7	625.266	Dining room furniture	TT197.5.D5	684.13
Diet	RA784	613.2	Dining rooms	NK2117.D5	747.76
Diet	TX551-560	641.563	Dining rooms	TX855-859	643.4
Diet in disease	RM214-258	615.854	Dinka language	PL8131	496.5
Diet kitchens	HV694	363.883	Dinners and dining	TX737	641.54
Diet therapy	RM214-258	615.854	Dinosaurs	QE862.D5	567.9
Diet therapy for children	RJ53.D53	618.9200654	Dinosaurs in mass media	P96.M6	567.9
Dietaries	TX551-560	641.563	Dinwiddie Court House, Battle of, Dinwiddie, Va., 1865	E477.67	973.738
Dietetics	RM214-258	615.854			
Difference algebra	QA247.4	512.56			
Difference equations	QA431	515.625	Diocesan pastoral councils	BX838	262.3
Differential-algebraic equations	QA372.5	512.56	Diodes, IMPATT	TK7871.89.A94	621.381522
			Diodes, Switching	TK7871.89.S95	621.381522
Differential Aptitude Tests	BF432.5.D53	153.94	Diola language	PL8134	496.32
Differential-difference equations	QA373	515.38	Dionysia	BL820.B2	292.2113
			Diophantine analysis	QA242	512.74
Differential equations	QA370-380	515.35	Diophantine equations	QA242	512.72
Differential equations	TA347.D45	515.35	Diorama	ND2880-.5	751.74

Subject Heading	LC	Dewey
Diorite	QE462.D56	552.3
Diphtheria	RC138-.9	616.9313
Diphtheria—Prevention	RA644.D6	614.5123
Diplomatics	CD1-724	327.2
Diplomatics—[By region or country]	CD50-79	327.2090(1-5)
Diplopia	RE738	617.762
Dippers (Birds)	QL696.P235	598.832
Direct costing	HF5686.C8	657.42
Direct energy conversion	TK2896	621.3124
Direct marketing	HF5415.126	381.1
Direct taxation	HJ3863-3925	336.294
Direct taxation—[By region or country]	HJ3925.A-.Z	336.29409(4-9)
Directories	AY2001	011.7
Directors of religious education	BV1531	268.3
Disappeared persons	HV6322-.7	362.87
Disappointment	BF575.D57	152.4
Disarmament—Inspection	UA12.5	327.1747
Disaster nursing	RT108	610.7349
Disaster relief	HV553-639	363.348
Disaster relief—Law and legislation—United States	KF3750	344.7305348
Disaster relief—[By region or country]	HV555	363.34809(4-9)
Disasters—Psychological aspects	BF789.D5	155.935
Disasters in the press	PN4784.D57	904
Disbudding	SB125	631.54
Discernment of spirits	BV5083	248.29
Discernment of spirits (Islam)	BP166.89	297.21
Disciples of Christ	BX7301-7343	286.6
Discipline of children	HQ770.4	649.64
Discipline of children	LB3025	371.5
Disco dancing	GV1796.D57	793.33
Discount	HG1651-1654	332.84
Discount brokers	HG4621	332.62
Discount houses (Finance)	HG1651-1654	332.84
Discount houses (Retail trade)	HF5429.2-.215	381.149
Discourse analysis	P302-.87	401.41
Discoveries in geography	G200-336	910.9
Discrete-time systems	QA402	003.83
Discretion	BV4647.D6	241.4
Discriminant analysis	QA278.65	519.535
Discrimination in education	LC212-.863	379.26
Discrimination in employment	HD4903-.5	331.133
Diseases—Chiropractic treatment	RZ260-275	615.534
Diseases—Reporting	RA404	614.4
Diseases and history	R702	616.009
Disfigured children	HV903-907	362.4083
Disguise	GT1747-1748	391
Disguised unemployment	HD5708.7-.75	331.137
Disinfection markings (Philately)	HE6184.D56	769.56
Dislocations	RD106	617.16
Dislocations in crystals	QD945	548.842
Disorderly conduct	HV6486-6491	364.143
Dispensaries	RA960-993	362.12
Dispensatories	RS151.2-.9	615.13
Dispensatories, Eclectic	RV431	615.53
Dispersion	QC431-435	535.4
Displacement (Ships)	VM157	623.81
Display of merchandise	HF5845-5849	659.152
Displays in education	LB1043.6	371.33
Disposal tableware industry	HD9971.5.T32-.T324	338.4767634
Dissecting aortic aneurysms	RD598.5	617.413
Dissecting aortic aneurysms	RC693	617.413059
Disseminated intravascular coagulation	RC647.D5	616.157
Dissenters, Religious—England	BX5200-5207	280.40941
Dissertations, Academic	AC801-895	Varies
Dissertations, Academic	LB2369	378.242
Dissociation	QD562.I65	541.3722
Dissociation	QD517	541.364
Dissociative disorders	RC553.D5	616.8523
Distance education	LC5800-5808	371.35
Distances—Tables	G109-110	910.21
Distemper	SF991.D5	636.70896
Distillation	TP156.D5	660.28425
Distillation	QD63.D6	542.4
Distilled water	VM505	623.854
Distilleries	TH4532	690.54
Distillers feeds	SF99.D5	636.0855
Distilling industries	HD9390-9395	338.4766316
Distinguished Conduct Medal (Great Britain)	UB435.G	355.13420941
Distinguished Service Cross (U.S.)	UB433	355.13420973
Distributed databases	QA76.9.D3	005.758
Distributed operating systems (Computers)	QA76.76.O63	005.4476
Distribution (Probability theory)	QA273.6	519.24
Ditch, Battle of the, 627	DS232	953.8
Ditches	TC970	627.54
Diuretics	RM377	615.761
Diuretics	RS431.D58	615.761
Dive bombers	UG1242.A28	358.4283
Divehi language	PK1836	491.487
Diversification in industry	HD2756-.2	338.6
Dividend reinvestment	HG4028.D5	332.63221
Divination	BF1745-1779	133.3
Divination	BL613	291.32
Divine right of kings	JC389	321.6
Diving	GV837	797.24
Diving—Jackknife dive	GV838.65.J32	797.24
Diving—Swan dive	GV838.65.S84	797.24
Diving bells	VM987	623.827
Diving for men	GV838.62.M45	797.24081
Diving for women	GV838.62.W65	797.24082
Division	QA115	513.214
Division algebras	QA247.45	512.3
Divorce	HQ811-960.7	306.89
Divorce—[By region or country]	HQ831-960.7	306.8809(4-9)

Subject Heading	LC	Dewey	Subject Heading	LC	Dewey
Divorce therapy	RC488.6	616.89156	Dolomite	QE471.15.D6	552.58
Divorced fathers	HQ756	306.874208653	Dolphins	QL737.C432	599.53
Dixieland music	M1366	781.653	Dolphins, Fossil	QE882.C5	569.5
Dixieland music	ML3505.8-3509	784.165309	Domain-referenced tests	LB3060.32.D65	371.271
Djibout	DT411-.9	967.71	Domes	NA2890	721.46
Djibouti—Census	HA4691	316.771	Domes	TH2170-.7	690.146
Djibouti—Civilization	DT411.4	967.71	Domestic animals	GN407.6-.7	636
Djibouti—Description and travel	DT411.27	916.77104	Domestic animals—Diseases	SF600-1100	636.0896
Djibouti—Gazetteers	DT411.15	916.771003	Domestic animals—Genetic engineering	SF756.5	636.0821
Djibouti—History	DT411.5-.83	967.71	Domestic animals—Parasites	SF810	636.089696
DNA	QP624-.75	572.86	Domestic asses	SF360.6-361.75	636.1
DNA ligases	QP619.D53	572.86	Domestic drama, English	PR635.D45	822.009
DNA topoisomerase I	QP616.D56	572.86	Domestic relations	K670-709	346.015
DNA topoisomerase II	QP616.D56	572.86	Domestic relations—Canada	KE531-606	346.71015
Doberman pinschers	SF429.D6	636.736	Domestic relations—England	KD750-785	346.42015
Docks	HE951-953	387.15	Domestic relations—United States	KF501-553	346.73015
Docks	HE550-560	387.15			
Docks	VK361-365	387.15	Domestication	GT5870-5899	392.3
Docks	TC355-365	627.31	Domestication	SF41	636.082
Doctor of philosophy degree	LB2386	378.2	Domestics	HD8039.D5	640.46
Doctrine and covenants stories	BX8628.A5	289.32	Domestics	HD6072-.2	640.46
			Domestics	TX331-334	640.46
Documentary credit	HG3746	332.7	Dominica	F2051	972.9841
Documentary hypothesis (Pentateuchal criticism)	BS1225	222.106	Dominica, Battle of, 1782	E271	973.338
			Dominica—Maps	G5100-5104	912.729841
Documents on microfilm	Z265-.5	686.43	Dominican Americans	E184.D6	973.04687293073
Dodder	QK495.C98	583.94	Dominican Republic	F1931-1941	972.93
Dodo	QL696.C67	598.65	Dominican Republic—Census	HA886-890	317.293
Dog Mass	BX2015.5.H	264.02			
Dog collars	SF427.15	636.70837	Dominican Republic—Civilization	F1935	972.93
Dog industry	SF434.5-435	338.1767			
Dog racing	SF439.5-440.2	798.8	Dominican Republic—Description and travel	F1936-.3	917.29304
Dog rescue	HV4746	636.0832			
Dog shows	SF425-.8	636.70811	Dominican Republic—Emigration and immigration	JV7395	325.(27293/7293)
Dog walking	SF427.46	636.7083			
Dogfish	QL638.9	597.36			
Dogma	BT19-33	230	Dominican Republic—Gazetteers	F1932	917.293003
Dogmatism	BF698.35.D64	155.232			
Dogs	GR720	398.3699772	Dominican Republic—History	F1937-1938.58	972.93
Dogs	QL737.C2	599.77			
Dogs	SF421-440.2	636.7	Dominican Republic—History—To 1844	F1938.3	972.930(1-4)
Dogs—Diseases	SF991-992	636.70896			
Dogs—Obedience trials	SF425.7	636.70811	Dominican Republic—History—1844-1930	F1938.4	972.930(4-52)
Dogs—Pedigrees	SF423	636.70822			
Dogs—Training	SF431	636.70835	Dominican Republic—History—American occupation, 1916-1924	F1938.45	972.93052
Dogs as carriers of disease	RA641.D6	614.56			
Dolgan dialect	PL364.Z9.D	494.332			
Doll clothes—Patterns	TT175.7	745.5922	Dominican Republic—History—1930-	F1938.5-.58	972.9305(3-4)
Doll furniture	TT175.5	745.5923			
Doll industry	HD9993-.D65-.D654	338.476887221	Dominican Republic—History—1930-1961	F1938.5	972.93053
			Dominican Republic—History—Invasion, 1959	F1938.5	972.93053
Dollhouses	GV1220	790.133			
Dollhouses	NK4891.3-4894.4	745.5923	Dominican Republic—History—1961-	F1938.55-.58	972.93054
Dollhouses	TT175.3	745.5923			
Dolls	GV1219	790.133			
Dolls	NK4891.3-4894.4	745.59221			
Dolls	TS2301.T7	688.7221			
Dolls	TT175-.7	745.59221			
Dolomite	TN967	622.3516			
Dolomite	QE391.D6	549.782			

Subject Heading	LC	Dewey
Dominican Republic— History—Coup d'etat, 1963	F1938.55	972.93054
Dominican Republic— History—Revolution, 1965	F1938.55	972.93054
Dominican Republic— History—Revolution, 1973	F1938.55	972.93054
Dominican Republic— History—Uprising, 1984	F1938.55	972.93054
Dominican Republic—Maps	G4950-4954	912.7293
Dominican Republic— Periodicals	F1931	972.93005
Dominican Republic— Politics and government	JL1120-1139	320.97293
Dominican literature	PQ7400-7409.2	860
Dominican poetry	PQ7406	861.008
Dominican poetry	PQ7402	861.009
Dominican sisters	BX4337-.5	255.972
Dominican-Haitian Conflict, 1937	F1938.5	972.93053
Dominicans	BX3501-3556	255.2
Dominion theology	BT82.25	230.046
Dominoes	GV1467	795.32
Donation of Pepin	DD126.5	943.0(13-25)
Donation of organs, tissues, etc.	RD129.5	362.1783
Donatists	BT1370	273.4
Dong Khe (Vietnam), Battle of, 1950	DS553.3	959.7041
Doniphan's Expedition, 1846-1847	E405.2	973.623
Donkey breeders	SF361	636.182092
Donkeys	SF361	636.182
Door fittings	TH2279	690.1822
Doors	TH2278	690.1822
Doorways	NA3010	721.822
Doped semiconductors	QC611.8.D66	537.6223
Doppler echocardiography	RC683.5.U5	616.1207543
Doppler radar	TK6592.D6	621.3848
Doric Greek dialect	PA530-539	480
Dormancy in plants	QK761	571.782
Dormice	QL737.R656	599.3596
Dormitories	LB3226-3229	371.871
Dornach, Battle of, 1499	DQ107.S8	949.403
Dorr Rebellion, 1842	F83.4	974.503
Double bass	MT320-334	787.5107
Double cropping	S603.7	631.58
Double descent (Kinship)	GN480	306.83
Double flowers	QK830	575.6
Double flowers	QK653	575.6
Double pinochle	GV1295.P6	795.416
Double salts	QD191	546.343
Double stars	QB421	523.841
Double stars	QB821-830	523.841
Double-bass music	M55-58	787.5
Doubloons	CJ3188	737.4946
Douglas fir	QK494.5.P66	585.2
Douglas fir	SD397.D7	634.9754
Douglas fir beetle	QL596.S35	595.76
Dowisng	BF1628	133.323
Down's syndrome	RC571	616.858842
Down's syndrome	RJ506.D68	618.92858842
Downhill ski racing	GV854.9.R3	796.935
Downhill skiing	GV854-.87	796.935
Downy mildew diseases	SB741.D68	632.446
Dowry	HQ1017	392.4
Dowsers	BF1628	133.323
Doxology	BV194.D	242.72
Doxorubicin	RC271.D68	616.994061
Draft	UB340-355	355.22363
Draft	UB350-355	355.225
Draft Riot, New York, N.Y., 1863	F128.44	974.703
Draft animals	SF180	636.0882
Draft horses	SF311-.3	636.15
Draft-gear	TF413	625.21
Drafts	HG1685-1704	332.55
Drag racing	GV1029.3	796.72
Dragonflies	QL520-.42	595.733
Dragons	GR830.D7	398.469
Drain-gages	S594	631.62
Drain-tiles	TA447	620.14
Drain-tiles	TP839	666.733
Drainage	TC970-978	627.54
Drainage	S621	631.62
Drainage, House	TD929	628.742
Drainage, House	TH6571-6675	696.13
Drama	PN1600-1861	808.2
Drama—Collections	PN6110.5-6120	808.82
Drama—History and criticism	PN1720-1861	809.2
Drama—Study and teaching	PN1701	808.20071
Drama—Technique	PN1660-1692	808.2
Drama in Christian education	BV1534.4	268.67
Dramatic criticism	PN1707	809.2
Dramatic music	M1500-1527.8	782.1
Dramatic music	ML3857-3862	781.552
Dramatic music	ML1699-2100	782.109
Drapery	NK3175-3296.3	746.94
Drapery	TT390	646.21
Drapery in art	NC775	743.5
Drapery in interior decoration	NK2115.5.D73	747.5
Drapery industry	HD9939	338.476453
Dravidian languages	PL4601-4794	494.8
Dravidian philology	PL4601	494.8
Drawbacks	HF1715-1718	382.7
Drawbridges	TG420	624.8
Drawing	NC	741
Drawing—17th century	NC86	741.09032
Drawing—18th century	NC87-.5	741.09033
Drawing—19th century	NC90-.5	741.09034
Drawing—20th century	NC95-.5	741.0904
Drawing—Catalogs	NC37-38.5	741.0294
Drawing—Copying	NC1920-1940	741.217
Drawing—Exhibitions	NC15-17	741.074
Drawing—Periodicals	NC1	741.05
Drawing—Private collections	NC30-33	741.074
Drawing—Study and teaching	NC390-670	741.071
Drawing—Technique	NC730-758	741.2

Subject Heading	LC	Dewey	Subject Heading	LC	Dewey
Drawing—[By region or country]	NC101-377	741.09(3-9)	Drawing—Scandinavia	NC270-284	741.0948
			Drawing—South America	NC189-224	741.098
Drawing—Afghanistan	NC324.6	741.09581	Drawing—Spain	NC285	741.0946
Drawing—Africa	NC360-368.6	741.096	Drawing—Sri Lanka	NC330	741.095493
Drawing—Africa, East	NC366-6	741.09676	Drawing—Sweden	NC282-284	741.09485
Drawing—Africa, North	NC361-365.6	741.0961	Drawing—Switzerland	NC291-293	741.09494
Drawing—Africa, Southern	NC368-.6	741.0968	Drawing—Thailand	NC335	741.09593
Drawing—Africa, West	NC367-.6	741.0966	Drawing—Turkey	NC294-296	741.09561
Drawing—Argentina	NC192-194	741.0982	Drawing—United States	NC105-139.3	741.0973
Drawing—Asia	NC315-359	741.095	Drawing—Uruguay	NC219-221	741.09895
Drawing—Asiatic Russia	NC325	741.0957	Drawing—Venezuela	NC222-224	741.0987
Drawing—Australia	NC369-371	741.0994	Drawing—Vietnam	NC334.V5-.V55	741.09597
Drawing—Bahamas	NC171-173	741.097296	Drawing—West Indies	NC168-186	741.09729
Drawing—Balkan Peninsula	NC297-308	741.09496	Drawing, Medieval	NC70-75	741.0902
Drawing—Bolivia	NC195-197	741.0984	Drawing, Renaissance	NC85	741.090(24-31)
Drawing—Brazil	NC198-200	741.0981	Drawing ability in children	BF723.D7	155.4133
Drawing—Cambodia	NC334.C3	741.09596	Drawing instruments	NC845-915	741.2
Drawing—Canada	NC141-143.3	741.0971	Drawing instruments	T375-377	604.20284
Drawing—Central America	NC147-167	741.09728	Drawing-room management	T352	604.2068
Drawing—China	NC348-350	741.0951	Drawing-room practice	T352	604.24
Drawing—Colombia	NC204-206	741.09861	Dreams	BF1074-1099	135.3
Drawing—Costa Rica	NC153-155	741.097286	Dreams	RC499.D7	154.63
Drawing—Cuba	NC174-176	741.097291	Dredges	TC188	627.73
Drawing—Denmark	NC273-275	741.09489	Dredging	TC187-188	627.73
Drawing—Ecuador	NC207-209	741.09866	Dredging spoil	TC187	627.73
Drawing—Egypt	NC363-.3	741.0962	Dresden, Battle of, 1813	DC236.7.D8	940.27
Drawing—El Salvador	NC167	741.097284	Dresden, Peace of, 1745	DD407.5	943.054
Drawing—Ethiopia	NC365.7	741.0963	Dressage	SF309.48-.658	798.23
Drawing—Europe	NC225-312	741.094	Dressage horses	SF309.65-.653	636.13
Drawing—France	NC246-248	741.0944	Dressmaking	TT500-560	687.112
Drawing—Germany	NC249-251.6	741.0943	Dried foods	TX609	641.44
Drawing—Great Britain	NC228-242	741.0941	Dried milk	SF259	637.143
Drawing—Greece	NC252-254	741.09495	Dried milk industry	HD9282	338.7637143
Drawing—Guatemala	NC156-158	741.097281	Dried skim milk	TX556.M5	641.37143
Drawing—Haiti	NC177-179	741.097294	Driftwood sculpture	NB1250	731.2
Drawing—Honduras	NC159-161	741.097283	Drill (Agricultural implement)	S687-689	631.3
Drawing—Iceland	NC276-278	741.094912	Drill presses	TJ1260	621.952
Drawing—India	NC327-329	741.0954	Drilling and boring	TJ1260-1270	621.952
Drawing—Indonesia	NC339-341	741.09598	Drinking and traffic accidents	HE5620.D7	363.12514
Drawing—Iran	NC321-323	741.0955	Drinking cups	GT2940-2947	394.1(2/3)
Drawing—Israel	NC320	741.095694	Drinking customs	GT2850-2930	394.1
Drawing—Italy	NC255-257	741.0945	Drinking glasses	NK5440.D75	748.83
Drawing—Jamaica	NC180-182	741.097292	Driveways	TE279.3	625.889
Drawing—Japan	NC351-353	741.0952	Driving of horse-drawn vehicles	SF304.5-307	388.341
Drawing—Korea	NC353.6-.7	741.09519			
Drawing—Laos	NC334.L3	741.09594	Dropouts	LC142-145	371.2913
Drawing—Malaysia	NC336-338	741.09595	Drought-tolerant plants	SB439.8	635.9525
Drawing—Mexico	NC144-146	741.0972	Droughts	HV625-626	363.34929
Drawing—Middle East	NC318-320	741.0956	Droughts	QC929.2-.28	551.5773
Drawing—New Zealand	NC372-374	741.0993	Drowning	RA1076	617.18
Drawing—Nicaragua	NC162-164	741.097285	Drug abuse	HV5800-5840	362.29(3-8)
Drawing—Norway	NC279-281	741.09481	Drug abuse—Prevention	HV5800-5840	362.29(3-8)7
Drawing—Oceania	NC375-376	741.099(5-6)	Drug abuse—[By region or country]	HV5825-5840	362.29(3-8)09 (4-9)
Drawing—Pakistan	NC331	741.095491			
Drawing—Panama	NC165	741.097287	Drug abuse—United States	HV5825-5833	362.29(3-8)0973
Drawing—Paraguay	NC213-215	741.09892	Drug abuse—[Other regions or countries]	HV5840	362.29(3-8)09 (4-9)
Drawing—Peru	NC216-218	741.0985			
Drawing—Philippines	NC342-344	741.09599	Drug abuse in pregnancy	RG580.D76	618.3268
Drawing—Portugal	NC288-290	741.09469	Drug allergy	RC598.D7	616.9758
Drawing—Puerto Rico	NC183-185	741.097295	Drug delivery devices	RS210	615.6
Drawing—Russia	NC267-269	741.0947	Drug delivery systems	RS199.5-210	615.6

Subject Heading	LC	Dewey
Drug factories	TH4541	690.54
Drug interactions	RM302-.4	615.7045
Drug resistance in microorganisms	QR177	616.01
Drug stability	RS424	615.18
Drug traffic—Investigation	HV8079.N3	363.25977
Drugs	RM300-671.5	615.1
Drugs—Administration	RM147-180	615.6
Drugs—Analysis	RS189-190	615.1901
Drugs—Controlled release	RS201.C64	615.6
Drugs—Dosage forms	RS200-201	615.14
Drugs—Law and legislation—Canada	KE3714-3725	344.7104233
Drugs—Law and legislation—England	KD3460-3462	344.4204233
Drugs—Packaging	RS159.5	615.18
Drugs—Prescribing	RM138	615.14
Drugs—Preservation	RS159	615.18
Drugs—Psychic aspects	BF1045.D76	154.4
Drugs—Side effects	RM302.5	615.7042
Drugs—Standards	RS189	615.10128
Drugs—Testing	RM301.27	615.1901
Drugs—Vehicles	RS201.V43	615.6
Drugs, Nonprescription	RM671-.5	615.1
Drugs and employment	HF5549.5.D7	658.3822
Drugs in motion pictures	PN1995.9.D78	791.43655
Drugstore employees	HD8039.D7	615.1092
Drum	ML1035	786.909
Drum Point Lighthouse (Md.)	VK1025.D	623.89420916347
Drunk driving—Investigation	HV8079.D76	363.25947
Drunkenness (Philosophy)	B105.D78	362.29201
Druzes	BL1695	297.85
Dry cleaning	TP932-.6	667.12
Dry docks	TC361	627.31
Dry farming	SB110	631.586
Dry-goods	TS1760-1770	677
Dry-point	NE2220-2225	767.3
Dryads	BL820.D	292.13
Drying apparatus—Food	TX609	641.44
Dual-purpose cattle	SF211	636.226
Duala language	PL8141	496.3962
Dualism	B812	147.4
Dualism (Religion)	BL218	211.33
Duchenne muscular dystrophy	RJ482.D78	618.92748
Duck shooting	SK333.D8	799.244
Duckpin bowling	GV910.5.D8	794.6
Ducks	SF504.7-505.63	636.597
Ducks	QL696.A52	598.41
Dude ranches	GV198.945-.975	796.56
Dudley's Defeat, 1813	E356.D8	973.523
Dueling	CR4571-4595	394.8
Duets	M177-298.5	785.12
Dugout canoes	GN440.2	386.229
Dugout canoes	VM353	623.8202
Dukhobors	BX7433	289.9
Dulcimer	ML1015-1018	787.7409
Dulcimer music	M142.D8	787.74
Dumbbells	GV547.4	613.7130284
Dump trucks	TL230	629.224
Dumping (International trade)	HF1425	382.6
Dune buggies	TL236.7	629.222
Dune buggy racing	GV1029.9.D8	796.72
Dunes, Battle of the, 1658	DC124.45	944.033
Dung beetles	QL596.S3	595.7649
Dunkerque (France), Battle of, 1940	D756.5.D8	940.5421428
Dunmore's Expedition, 1774	E83.77	975.502
Duodecimal system	QA141.5	513.56
Duodenoscopy	RC804.D79	616.3407545
Duodenum	QM345	611.341
Duodenum	QL863	573.378
Duodenum	QP156	612.33
Duodenum—Radiography	RC804.R6	616.3407572
Duplex ultrasonography—Diagnostic use	RC78.7.D86	616.07543
Duplex ultrasonography—Diagnostic use	RC691.6.D87	616.1307543
Duplicate contract bridge	GV1282.8.D86	795.415
Duplicate whist	GV1283	795.413
Durazzo, Battle of, 48 B.C.	DG266	937.05
Durga (Hindu deity)	BL1225.D8	294.52114
Durga-puja (Hindu festival)	BL1213.D87	294.536
Durmast oak	SD397.D87	634.9721
Durmast oak	QK495.F14	583.46
Durnstein, Battle of, 1805	DC227.5.D8	940.27
Duroc Jersey swine	SF393.D9	636.483
Durum wheat	SB191.W5	633.11
Durum wheat	QK495.G74	584.9
Durum wheat industry	HD9049.W3-.W5	633.11
Dusky seaside sparrow	QL696.P2438	598.883
Dust	QC882.5	551.5113
Dust storms	QC958-959	551.559
Dutch Americans	E184.D9	973.043931073
Dutch War, 1672-1678	DJ190-191	949.204
Dutch War, 1672-1678	D277-278.5	940.252
Dutch drama	PT5490-5515	839.312008
Dutch drama	PT5250-5295	839.312009
Dutch essays	AC16-19	083
Dutch essays	PT5539	839.314008
Dutch fiction	PT5320-5336	839.313009
Dutch fiction	PT5520-5530	839.313008
Dutch language	PF1001-1184	439.31
Dutch language	PF1-979	439.31
Dutch language—Dialects	PF700-979	439.317
Dutch language—Dictionaries	PF1175-1184	439.313
Dutch language—Dictionaries	PF620-693	439.313
Dutch language—Etymology	PF1161-1167	439.312
Dutch language—Grammar	PF1033-1125	439.315
Dutch language—Grammar	PF97	439.315
Dutch language—History	PF1015	439.3109
Dutch language—History	PF51-60	439.3109
Dutch language—Lexicography	PF601-693	439.313028
Dutch language—Morphology	PF171-197	439.315

Subject Heading	LC	Dewey
Dutch language—Parts of speech	PF199-335	439.315
Dutch language—Phonology	PF131-168	439.3115
Dutch language—Rhetoric	PF410-497	808.043931
Dutch language—Slang	PF951-979	439.317
Dutch language—Study and teaching	PF65-69	439.31071
Dutch language—Study and teaching	PF1019	439.31071
Dutch languages—Etymology	PF571-599	439.32
Dutch literature	PT5001-5980	839.31
Dutch literature—To 1500	PT5121-5137	839.3109001
Dutch literature—1500-1800	PT5141-5165	839.310900(2-4)
Dutch literature—19th century	PT5170-5175	839.3109005
Dutch literature—20th century	PT5180-5185	839.3109006
Dutch literature—Study and teaching	PT5040-5044	839.31071
Dutch philology	PF1-979	439.31
Dutch poetry	PT5470-5488	839.311008
Dutch poetry	PT5201-5245	839.311009
Dutch prose literature	PT5517-5547	839.31808
Dutch prose literature	PT5300-5336	839.31808
Dutch rabbits	SF455.D8	636.9322
Dutch wit and humor	PT5541	839.317008
Dutch wit and humor	PT5346	839.317009
Dutch wit and humor	PN6222.N	839.317008
Dwarf Novae	QB843.D85	523.8446
Dwarf ale glasses	NK5440.D85	748.83
Dwarf hamsters	QL737.R638	599.356
Dwarf hamsters as pets	SF459.H3	636.93560887
Dwarf irises	SB413.I8	635.93438
Dwarf irises	QK495.I75	584.38
Dwarf pelargoniums	SB413.G35	635.93379
Dwarf rabbits	SF455.D85	636.9322
Dwarf sea horse	QL638.S9	597.6798
Dwarf stars	QB843.D9	523.88
Dwarf trees	SB435-.8	635.9772
Dwarfism, Pituitary	RJ420.P58	618.9247
Dwarfs	GN69.3-.5	599.949
Dwellings	GR490-497	392.36
Dwellings	GT165-476	392.36
Dwellings	NA7100-7884	728
Dwellings	TH4805-4890	690.8
Dwellings—Air conditioning	TH7688.H6	697.938
Dwellings—Social aspects	GT170	392.36
Dwellings—[By region or country]	GT201-384	392.36009(4-9)
Dwellings—Africa	GT373-377	392.360096
Dwellings—Argentina	GT261-262	392.3600982
Dwellings—Asia	GT349-350	392.360095
Dwellings—Asia	GT343-372	392.360095
Dwellings—Australia	GT379-380	392.3600994
Dwellings—Austria	GT295-296	392.36009436
Dwellings—Bahamas	GT249-250	392.360097296
Dwellings—Balkan Peninsula	GT331-341	392.36009496
Dwellings—Belize	GT235-236	392.360097282
Dwellings—Bolivia	GT263-264	392.3600984
Dwellings—Brazil	GT265-266	392.3600981
Dwellings—Canada	GT228-229	392.3600971
Dwellings—Chile	GT267-268	392.3600983
Dwellings—China	GT365-366	392.3600951
Dwellings—Colombia	GT269-270	392.36009861
Dwellings—Costa Rica	GT237-238	392.360097286
Dwellings—Cuba	GT251-252	392.360097291
Dwellings—Denmark	GT315-316	392.36009489
Dwellings—Ecuador	GT271-272	392.36009866
Dwellings—Egypt	GT375-376	392.3600962
Dwellings—El Salvador	GT246-.5	392.360097284
Dwellings—France	GT297-298	392.3600944
Dwellings—Germany	GT298.9-300.5	392.3600943
Dwellings—Great Britain	GT285-294	392.3600941
Dwellings—Greece	GT301-302	392.36009495
Dwellings—Guatemala	GT239-240	392.360097281
Dwellings—Haiti	GT253-254	392.360097294
Dwellings—Honduras	GT241-242	392.360097283
Dwellings—Hungary	GT296.5-.6	392.36009439
Dwellings—Iceland	GT317-318	392.360094912
Dwellings—India	GT351-352	392.3600954
Dwellings—Indonesia	GT359-360	392.36009598
Dwellings—Iran	GT347-348	392.3600955
Dwellings—Iraq	GT346.5-.6	392.36009567
Dwellings—Ireland	GT294.5-.6	392.36009415
Dwellings—Italy	GT303-304	392.3600945
Dwellings—Jamaica	GT255-256	392.360097292
Dwellings—Japan	GT367-368	392.3600952
Dwellings—Korea	GT369-370	392.36009519
Dwellings—Malaysia	GT357-358	392.36009595
Dwellings—Mexico	GT231-232	392.3600972
Dwellings—Netherlands	GT307-308	392.36009492
Dwellings—New Zealand	GT381-382	392.3600993
Dwellings—Nicaragua	GT243-244	392.360097285
Dwellings—Norway	GT319-320	392.36009481
Dwellings—Oceania	GT383-384	392.360099(5-6)
Dwellings—Panama	GT245-.5	392.360097287
Dwellings—Paraguay	GT275-276	392.36009892
Dwellings—Peru	GT277-278	392.3600985
Dwellings—Philippines	GT361-362	392.36009599
Dwellings—Portugal	GT325-326	392.36009469
Dwellings—Puerto Rico	GT257-.5	392.360097295
Dwellings—Russia	GT311-312	392.3600947
Dwellings—Spain	GT323-324	392.3600946
Dwellings—Sri Lanka	GT352.5-.6	392.360095493
Dwellings—Sweden	GT321-322	392.36009485
Dwellings—Switzerland	GT327-328	392.36009494
Dwellings—Syria	GT344-.2	392.360095691
Dwellings—Thailand	GT355-356	392.36009593
Dwellings—Turkey	GT345-346	392.36009561
Dwellings—United States	GT205-227	392.3600973
Dwellings—Uruguay	GT279-280	392.36009895
Dwellings—Venezuela	GT281-282	392.3600987
Dye industry	HD9660.D84-.D844	338.4754786
Dye lasers	TA1690	621.3664
Dye plants	SB285-287	633.86
Dye plants	QK98.7	581.636
Dyes and dyeing	TT853-854.5	746.6
Dyes and dyeing	TP897-929	667.2

Subject Heading	LC	Dewey	Subject Heading	LC	Dewey
Dyes and dyeing—Chemistry	TP890-929	667.2	Earthworms	QL391.A6	592.64
Dynamic personality inventory	BF698.8.D9	155.283	East Armenian dialect	PK8451-8499	491.9927
			East Asia	DS501-519	950
Dynamics	QA845-871	531.11	East Asia—History—1945-	DS518.1	950.4(2-3)
Dynamics of a particle	QA851-855	531.16	East Asia—Strategic aspects	UA830	355.03305
Dynamics, Rigid	QA861-863	531.11			
Dynamite	TP285	662.27	East Asian literature	PL491-494	895
Dynix (Computer system)	Z678.93.D85	025.3132	East Coast fever	SF967.E3	636.208969
Dysentery	RC140	616.935	East European Americans	E184.E17	973.04917073
Dyslexia	LB1050.5	371.9144	East Indian Americans	E184.E2	973.04914073
Dyslexia	RC394.W6	616.8553	East Prussian cattle	SF199.E2	636.23
Dyslexic children	LC4708-4710	371.9144	East-West trade	HF4050	382
Dyslexic children	RJ496.A5	618.928553	Easter	CE83	529.44
Dysmenorrhea	RG181	618.172	Easter	BV55	263.93
Dzongkha language	PL3651.D96	495.4	Easter	GT4935	394.2667
E document (Biblical criticism)	BS1181.2	220.6	Easter—Sermons	BV4259	252.63
			Easter cookery	TX739.2.E37	641.568
E region	QC881.2.E2	551.5145	Easter decorations	TT900.E2	745.5941
EGPS (Computer program language)	QA76.5	005.13	Easter Island	F3169	996.18
			Easter lily	QK495.L72	584.32
Eagle dance	E98.D2	299.74	Easter Offensive, 1972	DS557.8.E23	959.704342
Eagles	QL696.F32	598.942	Eastern bluebird	QL696.P288	598.842
Ear	QL948	573.89	Eastern chipmunk	QL737.R68	599.364
Ear	QP460-471.2	612.85	Eastern churches	BX100-189	281.5
Ear	QM507	611.85	Eastern diamondback rattlesnake	QL666.069	597.96
Ear—Diseases	RF110-320	617.8			
Ear—Surgery	RF126-127	617.8059	Eastern Hemisphere	G680-700	910.021811
Ear—Tumors	RC280.E2	616.99485	Eastern Hemisphere— History	D890-893	909.09811
Ear, External	QM507	611.85			
Ear, External	QL948	573.89	Eastern Hemisphere—Maps	G1780-2799	912.19811
Ear training	MT35	781.424	Eastern hemlock	QK494.5.P66	585.2
Eared dove	QL696.C63	598.65	Eastern hemlock	SB413.E27	635.97752
Eared seals	QL737.P63	599.79	Eastern hemlock	SD397.E27	634.9753
Early childhood education	LB1139.2-.4	372.21	Eastern Indians, Wars with, 1722-1726	E83.72	974-975 + .02
Early childhood educators	LB1775.6	372.11			
Early retirement	HD7110-.5	306.38	Eastern question (Far East)	DS740.6-.63	950.(3-41)
Early stars	QB843.E2	523.88	Eastern redcedar	QK494.5.C975	585.4
Earrings	GT2265	391.7	Eastern tent caterpillar	QL561.L3	595.78139
Earth	QB630-638.8	525	Eating disorders	RC552.E18	616.8526
Earth—Age	QE508	551.701	Eating disorders in adolescence	RJ506.E18	616.852600835
Earth—Internal structure	QE509	551.11			
Earth—Origin	QB632	523.12	Ebisu (Japanese deity)	BL2211.E24	299.56
Earth—Rotation	QB633	525.35	Ecclesiastical geography	BR97-99	262.009
Earth construction	TH1421	690.8370473	Ecclesiastical law	BV759-763	262.9
Earth currents	QC845	538.748	Echinococcosis	SF810.H8	636.0896964
Earth dams	TC543	627.83	Echinococcosis	RC184.T6	616.964
Earth houses	TH4818.A3	690.8370473	Echinodermata	QL381-385.2	593.9
Earth movements	QE598-600.3	551.307	Echo	QC233	534.204
Earth science instruments	QE49.5	550.284	Echo sounding	VK584.S6	623.8938
Earth sheltered houses	NA7531	728.370473	Echocardiography	RG628.3.E34	618.326107543
Earth sheltered houses	TH4819.E27	690.8370473	Echocardiography	RJ423.5.U46	618.921207543
Earth temperature	QE509	551.12	Echocardiography	RC683.5.U5	616.1207543
Earthmoving machinery	TA725	624.1520284	Eclampsia	RG576	618.75
Earthquake engineering	TA654.6	624.1762	Eclectic psychotherapy	RC489.E24	616.8914
Earthquake resistant design	TA658.44	624.1762	Eclecticism	B271	186.3
Earthquakes	HV599-600	363.3495	Eclecticism	B814	148
Earthquakes	QE531-541	551.22	Eclipses	QB175-185	523.99
Earths, Rare	QD172.R2	546.41	Eclipsing binaries—Orbits	QB835.E4	523.8444
Earthwork	TA715-772	624.152	Ecology	QH540-549.5	577
Earthworks (Archaeology)	GN789	930.1028	Econometric models	HB141	330.011
Earthworm culture	SF597.E3	639.75	Econometrics	HB139-141	330.015195

Subject Heading	LC	Dewey	Subject Heading	LC	Dewey
Economic anthropology	GN448-450.7	306.3	Ecuador—History—Coup d'etat, 1925	F3737	986.6072
Economic development	HD72-88	338.9	Ecuador—History—1944-	F3738	986.607(2-4)
Economic development—Methodology	HD108-.8	338.901	Ecuador—History—Coup d'etat, 1944	F3738	986.6072
Economic forecasting	HB3730	330.0112	Ecuador—Manufactures	TS47	670.9866
Economic geography	HF1021-1027	330.9	Ecuador—Maps	G5300-5304	912.866
Economic history	HC	330.9	Ecuador—Periodicals	F3701	986.6005
Economic history—1945-	HC59-60.5	330.09044	Ecuador—Politics and government	JL3000-3099	320.9866
Economic history—20th century	HC54-60.5	330.0904	Ecuador-Peru Conflict, 1941	F3737	986.6072
Economic history—Medieval, 500-1500	HC41-42	330.0902	Ecuador-Peru Conflict, 1981	F3738	986.6074
Economic policy	HD87-88	338.9	Ecuadorian fiction	PQ8212	863
Economic sanctions	HF1413.5	327.117	Ecuadorian fiction	PQ8216.F5	863
Economic stabilization	HB3732	339.5	Ecuadorian literature	PQ8200-8220.36	860
Economics	HB1-130	330	Ecuadorian poetry	PQ8210	861
Economics—Congresses	HB21	330.06	Ecuadorian poetry	PQ8214-.5	861
Economics—Dictionaries	HB61	330.03	Ecumenical liturgies	BV186.7	264
Economics—Directories	HB63	330.025	Ecumenical movement—African influences	BX9.5.A37	280.042
Economics—History	HB75-130	330.09	Ecumenists	BX6.7-.8	262.0011092
Economics—History—To 1800	HB77-83	330.090(1-33)	Eczema	RL251	616.521
Economics—History—19th century	HB85	330.09034	Eczema in children	RJ516.E35	618.92521
			Eddy currents (Electric)	TK2271	621.31042
Economics—History—20th century	HB87	330.0904	Edema	RB144-.5	616.047
			Eden	BS1237	222.11
Economics—Methodology	HB131	330.01	Edible dormouse	QL737.R656	599.3596
Economics—Periodicals	HB1-9	330.05	Editing	PN162	808.027
Economics—Sociological aspects	HM35	306.3	Education	L	370
Economics—Statistical methods	HB137	330.0727	Education—Aims and objectives	LB41	370.1
Economics in the Bible	BS670	220.8330	Education—Congresses	L106-107	370.6
Ecotones	QH514.15.E27	577	Education—Curricula	LB1570-1571	375
Ecstasy	BV5091.E3	248.29	Education—Data processing	LB1028.43	371.334
Ecstasy	BL626	291.42	Education—Directories	L900-991	373/378.0 + (025)
Ectoparasitic infestations	RC119.5	616.968	Education—Experimental methods	LB1027.3	371.3
Ectopic pregnancy	RG586	618.31			
Ecuador	F3701-3799	986.6	Education—Finance	LB2824-2830	371.206
Ecuador—Census	HA1021-1030	318.66	Education—Finance—Law and legislation—United States	KF4125-4143	344.73076
Ecuador—Civilization	F3710	986.6			
Ecuador—Description and travel	F3711-3716	918.6604	Education—Forecasting	LB41.5	370.112
Ecuador—Economic conditions	HC201-204.5	330.9866	Education—Graduate work	LB2372.E3	378.155
			Education—History	LA	370.9
Ecuador—Emigration and immigration	JV7490-7499	325.(2866/866)	Education—Museums	L797-898	370.74
			Education—Periodicals	L7-101	370.5
Ecuador—Gazetteers	F3704	918.66003	Education—Peru—History	LA595-599	370.985
Ecuador—History	F3723.3-3738.4	986.6	Education—Philosophy	LB125-875	370.1
Ecuador—History—To 1809	F3733	986.60(1-2)	Education—Research	LB1028-.25	370.72
Ecuador—History—Wars of Independence, 1809-1830	F3734	986.60(2-4)	Education—Simulation methods	LB1029.S53	371.397
			Education—[By region or country]	L111-791	370.9(4-9)
Ecuador—History—1830-1895	F3736	986.60(5-6)	Education—Africa	L651-742	370.96
Ecuador—History—1895-1944	F3737	986.60(6-72)	Education—Asia	L561-642	370.95
			Education—Austria	L361-366	370.9436
Ecuador—History—Revolution, 1895	F3736	986.606	Education—Belgium	L431-436	370.9493
			Education—Bulgaria	L541-542	370.9499
Ecuador—History—20th century	F3737	986.607	Education—Canada	L221-223	370.971
			Education—Central America	L231-249	370.9728

Subject Heading	LC	Dewey	Subject Heading	LC	Dewey
Education—China	L571-573	370.951	Education, Primary—Activity programs	LB1537	372.11
Education—Czechoslovakia	L385-387	370.9437			
Education—Denmark	L471-476	370.9489	Education, Rural	LC5146-5148	370.91734
Education—Developing countries	LC2601-2611	370.91724	Education, Urban	LC5101-5143	370.91732
			Education and crime	HV6166	364.25
Education—Europe	L341-551	370.94	Education and state	LC71-188	379
Education—France	L391-396	370.944	Education in mass media	P96.E29	370
Education—Germany	L401-410	370.943	Education in the Bible	BS680.E3	220.837
Education—Great Britain	L341-359	370.941	Education in the Bible	BS1199.E38	221.837
Education—Greece	L411-416	370.9495	Education of princes	JC393	371.82621
Education—Hungary	L381-383	370.9439	Educational acceleration	LC1049-.8	371.28
Education—Iceland	L481	370.94912	Educational accountability	LB2806.22	379.158
Education—India	L577-578	370.954	Educational anthropology	LB45	306.43
Education—Indochina	L585-586	370.959(4-7)	Educational counseling	LB1027.5-.8	371.4
Education—Indonesia	L597-598	370.9598	Educational equalization	LC213-.3	379.26
Education—Iran	L615-616	370.955	Educational evaluation	LB2822.75	379.158
Education—Iraq	L627-628	370.9567	Educational exchanges	LB2283-2286	370.116
Education—Ireland	L346-348	370.9415	Educational exchanges	LB2375-2378	378.016
Education—Israel	L631-632	370.95694	Educational fund raising	LC241-245	371.206
Education—Italy	L421-426	370.945	Educational fund raising	LB2335.95-2337	378.106
Education—Japan	L611-612	370.952	Educational games	LB1029.G3	371.337
Education—Korea	L613-614	370.9519	Educational innovations	LB1027	371.3
Education—Mexico	L227-229	370.972	Educational law and legislation	KD3600-3689	344.4207
Education—Netherlands	L441-446	370.9492			
Education—[New Zealand/ Australia/Oceania]	L750-791	370.99(3-6)	Educational law and legislation	K3740-3762	344.07
Education—Norway	L491-496	370.9481	Educational law and legislation—Canada	KE3805-3917	344.7107
Education—Pakistan	L578.5-.6	370.95491			
Education—Portugal	L521-526	370.9469	Educational law and legislation—United States	KF4101-4257	344.7307
Education—Romania	L545-546	370.9498			
Education—Russia	L451-466	370.947			
Education—Siberia	L617-620	370.957	Educational law and legislation—United States	KF4195-4223	344.7307
Education—South America	L291-335	370.98			
Education—Spain	L511-516	370.946			
Education—Sweden	L501-506	370.9485	Educational leave	HD5257-.2	331.25763
Education—Switzerland	L531-536	370.9494	Educational planning	LC71.2	371.207
Education—Turkey	L539-540	370.9561	Educational psychology	LB1051-1091	370.15
Education—United States	L111-219	370.973	Educational sociology	LC189-214.53	306.43
Education—[United States, By state]	L116-219	370.97(4-9)	Educational statistics	LB2846	370.21
			Educational surveys	LB2823	370.723
Education—West Indies	L251-267	370.9729	Educational tests and measurements	LB3051-3060.87	371.271
Education—Yugoslavia	L549-550	370.9497			
Education—Zaire	LA1910-1914	370.96751	Educational toys	LB1029.T6	371.337
Education, Ancient	LA31-81	370.901	Educators	LA2301-2397	370.92
Education, Bilingual	LC3701-3743	370.1175	Educators	LB51-875	370.92
Education, Compulsory	LC129-139	379.23	Eel fisheries	SH351.E4	639.2743
Education, Egyptian	LA37	370.932	Eel fishing	SH691.E4	799.1743
Education, Elementary	LB1555-1601	372	Efik language	PL8147	496.3642
Education, Greek	LA75	370.938	Egg decoration	TT896.7	745.5944
Education, Higher	LA173-186	378.009	Egg-free diet	RM232	613.26
Education, Higher—Law and legislation—United States	KF4225-4257	344.73074	Eggplant	QK495.S7	583.952
			Eggplant	SB351.E5	635.646
			Eggs	SF490-.8	636.5142
Education, Humanistic	LA106-108	370.11209024	Eggs—Incubation	SF495	636.5082
Education, Humanistic	LC1001-1024	370.112	Eggs—Production	SF490-.8	636.5142
Education, Medieval	LA177	378.00902	Ego Function Assessment	RC473.E36	154.22
Education, Medieval	LA91-98	370.902	Egoism	BJ1474	171.9
Education, Minoan	LA77	370.938	Egungun (Cult)	BL2480.Y6	299.6869
Education, Preschool	LB1140-.5	372.21	Egypt in the Koran	BP134.E5	297.12209
Education, Primary	LB1501-1547	372	Egypt—Census	HA4686	316.2
			Egypt—Civilization	DT70	932/962

Subject Heading	LC	Dewey	Subject Heading	LC	Dewey
Egypt—Description and travel	DT49.98-56	913.204/ 916.204	Egyptian language— Demotic, ca. 650 B.C.-450 A.D.	PJ1801-1921	493.17
Egypt—Economic conditions	HC830	330.962	Egyptian language— Dictionaries	PJ1423-1439	493.13
Egypt—French occupation, 1798-1801	DT103	962.03	Egyptian language— Dictionaries	PJ1031	493.13
Egypt—Gazetteers	DT45	913.2003/ 916.2003	Egyptian language— Etymology	PJ1350-1371	493.12
Egypt—History	DT43-154	932/962	Egyptian language— Grammar	PJ1121-1201	493.15
Egypt—History—To 332 B.C.	DT83-91	932.0(1-2)	Egyptian language— Inscriptions	PJ1501-1819	493.111
Egypt—History—To 640 A.D.	DT83-93	932	Egyptian language— Lexicography	PJ1401-1439	493.13028
Egypt—History—30 B.C.- 640 A.D.	DT93	932.02(2-3)	Egyptian language—Papyri	PJ1501-1921	493.111
Egypt—History— 332-30 B.C.	DT92-.7	932.021	Egyptian language—Writing	PJ1051-1109	493.111
Egypt—History—Greco Roman period, 332 B.C.-640 A.D.	DT92-93	932.02	Egyptian language— Writing, Demotic	PJ1107	493.111
Egypt—History—640-1250	DT95-.88	962.02	Egyptian language— Writing, Hieratic	PJ1105	493.11
Egypt—History—640-1882	DT95-107.4	962.0(2-3)	Egyptian language— Writing, Hieroglyphic	PJ1091-1097	493.111
Egypt—History— Saladin, 1171-1193	DT95.8-.88	962.02	Egyptian literature	PJ1481-1989	893.1
Egypt—History—Invasion of Saint Louis, 1249	DT95.8	962.02	Egyptian philology	PJ1001-1109	493.1
Egypt—History— 1250-1517	DT96-.7	962.02	Eider	QL696.A52	598.415
Egypt—History— 1517-1882	DT97-107.4	962.03	Eidetic imagery	BF367	153.32
Egypt—History—Eighteenth dynasty, ca. 1570-1320	DT87-.5	932.014	Eight-hour movement	HD5106-5267	331.25723
Egypt—History—1798-	DT100-107.87	962.0(3-55)	Eighth house (Astrology)	BF1716.28	133.52
Egypt—History— Mohammed Ali, 1805-1849	DT104	962.03	Eileithyia (Greek deity)	BL820.E5	292.2114
			Ejector pumps	TJ901	621.6
Egypt—History— Ismail, 1863-1879	DT106	962.03	El Alamein, Battle of, Egypt, 1942	D766.9	940.5423
Egypt—History— Tewfik, 1879-1892	DT107-.4	962.0(3-4)	El Caney, Battle of, 1898	E717.1	973.893
			El Ebano, Battle of, 1915	F1234	972.0816
Egypt—History—British occupation, 1882-1936	DT107.3-.8	962.0(4-51)	El Jigue (Cuba), Battle of, 1958	F1787.5	972.91063
Egypt—History—Fuad, 1917-1936	DT107.8	962.0(4-51)	El Nino Current	GC296.8.E	551.4701
Egypt—History—1919-	DT107.8-.87	962.0(4-55)	El Salvador	F1481-1497	972.84
Egypt—History— Insurrection, 1919	DT107.8	962.04	El Salvador—Census	HA841-850	317.284
			El Salvador—Civilization	F1483.8	972.84
Egypt—History—1952-	DT107.821-.87	962.05(3-5)	El Salvador—Description and travel	F1484-.3	917.28404
Egypt—History— Revolution, 1952	DT107.82	962.052	El Salvador—Emigration and immigration	JV7423	325.(27284/ 7284)
Egypt—History— Intervention, 1956	DT107.83	962.053	El Salvador—Gazetteers	F1482	917.284003
Egypt—Manufactures	TS117-118	670.962	El Salvador—History	F1485.5-1488.53	972.84
Egypt—Maps	G8300-8304	912.62	El Salvador—History— To 1838	F1487	972.840(1-42)
Egypt—Politics and government	JC66	320.932	El Salvador—History— 1838-1944	F1487.5	972.840(4-52)
Egypt—Religion	BL2420-2460	299.31	El Salvador—History— 1944-1979	F1488	972.84052
Egyptian drama	PJ1571	893.12	El Salvador—History— Revolution, 1944	F1487.5	972.84052
Egyptian fiction	PJ1487	893.13	El Salvador—History— Revolution of 1948	F1488	972.84052
Egyptian language	PJ1001-1479	493.1	El Salvador—History— 1979-	F1488.3-.53	972.84053
			El Salvador—History— 1979-1992	F1488.3	972.84053

Subject Heading	LC	Dewey
El Salvador—History—1992-	F1488.5-.53	972.84053
El Salvador—Maps	G4840-4844	912.7284
El Salvador—Periodicals	F1481	972.84005
El Salvador—Politics and government	JL1560-1579	320.97284
El Salvador-Honduras Conflict, 1969	F1488	972.84052
Elamite language	P943	499.93
Elands	QL737.U5	599.642
Elastic plates and shells	QA935	531.382
Elastic solids	QC191	531.382
Elastic solids	QA935	531.382
Elastic tissue	QM563	611.0182
Elastic waves	QE539	551.22
Elastic waves	QA935	531.382
Elastic waves	QC191	531.382
Elasticity	QA931-939	531.382
Elasticity	QC191	531.382
Elastomer industry	HD9662.E42-.E423	338.47678
Elbow—Fractures	RD558	617.157
Election (Theology)	BT809-810.2	234
Election sermons	BV4260-4261	252.68
Elections	JK1965-2217	324.620973
Elections	JF1001-1048	324
Elections—Corrupt practices	JF1081-1083	324.66
Elections—Corrupt practices	JK1994	324.66
Elections—Corrupt practices	JK2249	324.660973
Elections—Corrupt practices	JN1088	324.660941
Electors (Kurfursten)	JN3250.C83	324.630943
Electric alarms	TK7241	621.38928
Electric apparatus and appliances	QC543-544	537.0284
Electric apparatus and appliances	RM889	610.284
Electric arc	QC705	537.52
Electric batteries	TK2896-2986	621.31242
Electric boats	VM345-347	623.8726
Electric cables	TK3301-3351	621.31934
Electric charge and distribution	QC581.E4	537.21
Electric circuit-breakers	TK2842	621.317
Electric circuits	TK3001-3521	621.3192
Electric conductivity	QC610.3-635	537.62
Electric conductors	TK3301-3351	537.62
Electric contactors	TK2861	621.317
Electric controllers	TF930	621.33
Electric controllers	TK2851	629.8043
Electric countershock	RC684.E4	616.120645
Electric cranes	TJ1363-1365	621.873
Electric current converters	TK2796	621.313
Electric current rectifiers	TK7872.R35	621.3137
Electric currents	QC601-641	537.6
Electric currents, Alternating	QC641	537.6
Electric currents, Alternating	TK1141-1168	621.31913
Electric currents—Heating effects	QC623	537.6
Electric detonators	UF780	358.1282
Electric drafting	TK431	621.30221
Electric driving	TK4058-4059	629.2293
Electric engineering	TK	621.3
Electric engineering—Congresses	TK5	621.306
Electric engineering—Dictionaries	TK9	621.303
Electric engineering—Directories	TK12	621.3025
Electric engineering—History	TK15-18	621.309
Electric engineering—Museums	TK6	621.3074
Electric engineering—Periodicals	TK1-4	621.305
Electric engineering—Study and teaching	TK165-213	621.3071
Electric engineering—[By region or country]	TK21-127	621.309(4-9)
Elcctric generators	TK2411-2491	621.313
Electric heating	TK4601-4661	621.402
Electric inverters	TK2699	621.3815322
Electric inverters	TK7872.I65	621.3815322
Electric laboratories	QC541	537.072
Electric lamps, Arc	TK4321-4335	621.325
Electric lamps, Portable	TN307	622.473
Electric light fixtures	TK4198	621.320284
Electric lighting	TK4125-4399	621.32
Electric lighting—[By region or country]	TK4134-4156	621.3209(4-9)
Electric lighting, Arc	TK4311-4335	621.325
Electric lighting, Incandescent	TK4341-4367	621.326
Electric lines	TK3201-3261	621.3192
Electric lines—Poles and towers	TK3242-3243	621.3192
Electric locomotives	TF975	625.263
Electric machinery	TK2000-2891	621.31042
Electric machinery—Alternating current	TK2711-2799	621.3133
Electric machinery—Direct current	TK2611-2699	621.3132
Electric measurements	QC535-537	537.0287
Electric measurements	TK275-399	621.37
Electric meters	TK301-399	621.373
Electric motors	TK2781-2789	621.46
Electric motors	TK2681	621.46
Electric motors	TK2511-2541	621.46
Electric motors—Design and construction	TK2435	621.46
Electric motors, Alternating current	TK2781-2789	621.46
Electric network topology	TK454.2	621.3192
Electric networks	TK3226	621.3192
Electric networks, Active	TK454.2	621.3192
Electric networks, Passive	TK454.2	621.3192
Electric power	TK3001-3511	621.31
Electric power	TK4001-9971	621.31
Electric power	TK1001-1841	621.31
Electric power distribution	TK3001-3521	621.319
Electric power distribution—Alternating current	TK3141-3171	621.31913

Subject Heading	LC	Dewey	Subject Heading	LC	Dewey
Electric power distribution— Direct current	TK3111	621.31912	Electrochemistry	QD273	541.37
Electric power distribution— High tension	TK3144	621.31913	Electrochemistry, Industrial	TP250-261	660.297
			Electroculography	RE79.E39	617.707547
Electric power factor	TK153	621.31	Electrocution	HV8696	364.66
Electric power failures	TK3091	621.319	Electrodes	QD571-572	541.3724
Electric power-plants	TK1191-1841	621.3121	Electrodiagnosis	RC77-.5	616.07547
Electric power-plants— Testing	TK1831	621.31210287	Electrodynamics	QC630-648	537.6
			Electroencephalography	RC386.6.E43	616.8047547
Electric power production	TK1001-1841	621.3121	Electrohomeopathy	RZ420	615.532
Electric power transmission	TK3001-3521	621.319	Electroluminescence	QC480	535.357
Electric power transmission— Alternating current	TK3141-3171	621.31913	Electrolysis in medicine	RM886	615.845
			Electrolytes	QD549	541.372
Electric railroads	HE5351-5600	388.42	Electrolytes	QD553-585	541.372
Electric railroads—Brakes	TF949.B7	625.25	Electrolytes	QC541-543	541.372
Electric railroads—Cars	TF920-952	625.2	Electrolytes—Conductivity	QD565	541.372
Electric railroads—Design and construction	TF863-952	621.33	Electrolytic corrosion	TD491	628.15
			Electrolytic oxidation	QD281.09	547.23
Electric railroads— Equipment and supplies	TF920-952	621.330284	Electrolytic oxidation	QD63.09	541.393
			Electrolytic reduction	QD281.R4	547.23
Electric railroads—Freight	TF970	385.24	Electrolytic reduction	QD63.R4	541.393
Electric railroads—Rails	TF872	625.15	Electromagnetic fields	QC665.E4	539.2
Electric railroads—Third rail	TF890	625.15	Electromagnetic interactions	QC794.8.E4	539.7546
Electric railroads—Wires and wiring	TF880-900	621.33	Electromagnetic theory	QC669-675.8	537
			Electromagnetic waves— Diffraction	QC665.D5	539.2
Electric railroads—[By region or country]	TF1021-1127	621.3309(4-9)	Electromagnetic waves— Transmission	QC665.T7	539.2
Electric railroads, Miniature	TF857	625.19			
Electric railway motors	TF935	621.33	Electromagnetism	QC759.6-761.3	537
Electric resistance	QC611	537.62	Electromagnets	QC760-.3	538
Electric resistors	TK6565.R426	621.384133	Electrometallurgy	TN681-687	669.0284
Electric rheostats	TK2851	621.317	Electron Tubes	TK7871.7-.84	621.38151
Electric rocket engines	TL783.54-.63	629.4755	Electron accelerators	QC787.E39	539.73
Electric shavers	TT967	646.724	Electron beams— Therapeutic use	RM862.E4	615.845
Electric signs	TK4399.S6	621.3229			
Electric substations	TK1751	621.3126	Electron microscopes	QH212.E4	570.2825
Electric switchgear	TK2821-2846	621.317	Electron microscopic immunocytochemistry	RB46.7	616.0758
Electric testing	TK401	621.37			
Electric transformers	TK2551	621.314	Electron microscopy	QH212.E4	570.2825
Electric utilities	HD9685-9695	333.7932	Electron optics	QC793.5.E62-.E629	537.56
Electric waves	QC660.5-665	537.534			
Electric welding	TK4660	671.521	Electron paramagnetic resonance	QC763	538.364
Electric wire	TK3301-3351	621.31933			
Electric wiring	TK3201-3285	621.31933	Electronic analog computers	TK7888	621.3919
Electric wiring, Interior	TK3271-3285	621.31933	Electronic apparatus and appliances	TK7869-7872	621.3810284
Electrical burns	RD96.5	617.122			
Electrical injuries	RA1091	617.122	Electronic behavior control	BF210	153.85
Electricians	QC514-515	537.092	Electronic circuits	TK7867-7868	621.3815
Electricians	TK139-140	621.31924092	Electronic counter- countermeasures	UG485	623.043
Electricity	QC501-721	537			
Electricity—Experiments	QC527	537.0724	Electronic countermeasures	UG485	623.043
Electricity—Experiments	QC533-534	537.0724	Electronic data interchange	HF5548.33	651.8
Electricity in aeronautics	TL690-691	629.1354	Electronic data processing—Backup processing alternatives	QA76.9.B32	005.86
Electricity in military engineering	UG480	623.76			
Electricity in mining	TN343	622.48	Electronic data processing—Data entry	QA76.9.D337	005.72
Electro-acoustics	TK5981-5990	621.3828			
Electro-diesel locomotive	TF980	625.263	Electronic data processing—Data preparation	QA76.9.D345	005.72
Electrocardiography	RC683.5.E5	616.1207547			
Electrochemical analysis	QC115-116	543.0871			
Electrochemistry	QD551-575	541.37			

Subject Heading	LC	Dewey	Subject Heading	LC	Dewey
Electronic data processing—Distributed processing	QA76.9.D5	004.36	Electrotyping	Z252	686.221
			Elementary school administration	LB2822.5	372.12
Electronic data processing documentation	QA76.9.D6	004	Elementary school dropouts	LC145.5-.8	372.12913
			Elementary school principals	LB2831.9-.976	372.12012
Electronic digital computers	TK7888.3-.4	621.39	Elementary school teachers	LB1776	372.11
Electronic digital computers—Circuits	TK7888.4	621.395	Elephant hunting	SK305.E3	799.2767
			Elephant seals	QL737.P64	599.794
Electronic digital computers—Programming	QA76.6-.66	004.1	Elephant shrews	QL737.M242	599.336
			Elephantiasis	RC142.5	616.9652
Electronic drafting	TK7866	621.3810221	Elephants	QL737.P98	599.67
Electronic filing systems	HF5738	651.53	Eles (Firm) Strike, Bleidenstadt, Ger., 1975	HD5379.C6	331.89290943
Electronic funds transfer	HG1710-.5	332.10285			
Electronic games	GV1469.2	794.8	Elevators	TJ1370-1380	621.877
Electronic harpsichord music	M20-32	786.4	Elevators (Airplanes)	TL677.E6	629.13433
Electronic instruments	TK7870	621.3810284	Elixirs	RS201.E4	615.42
Electronic keyboard (Synthesizer)	ML1092	786.7409	Elk	QL737.U55	599.657
			Elk farming	SF401.E4	636.965701
Electronic measurements	TK7878-7879.4	621.3810287	Elk hunting	SK303	799.27657
Electronic news gathering	PN4784.E53	070.435	Elliptic functions	QA343	515.983
Electronic office machine industry	HD9801	338.476816	Elvas, Linhas de, Battle of, 1659	DP635	946.9032
			Embalming	GT3340	393.3
Electronic organ music	M14.8	786.59	Embankments	TC337	627.24
Electronic surveillance	TK7882.E2	621.38928	Embankments	TA760-772	624.162
Electronic systems	TK7870	621.381	Embankments	TC759	627.133
Electronic traffic controls	TE228	625.794	Embankments	TC533	627.42
Electronic transformers	TK7872.T7	621.314	Embargo, 1807-1809	E336.5	973.48
Electronics	TK7800-8360	621.381	Embarrassment	BF575.E53	152.4
Electronics—Charts, diagrams, etc.	TK7866	621.3810223	Embassy buildings	NA4440-4447	725.17
			Embezzlement	HV6675-6685	364.162
Electronics—Congresses	TK7801	621.38106	Emblems	BL603	291.37
Electronics—Graphic methods	TK7825	621.3810728	Emblems, National—England	KD4650	344.4209
Electronics—Periodicals	TK7800	621.38105	Emblems, National—United States	KF5150	344.7309
Electronics—Research	TK7855	621.381072			
Electronics in military engineering	UG485	623.043	Embroidery, Hmong	NK9206.4.H56	746.44
			Embryology	QL951-991	571.86
Electronics in navigation	VK560	623.893	Embryology, Experimental	QL961	571.860724
Electronics in sanitary engineering	TH6025	648	Embryology, Human	QM601-695	611.013
			Emeralds	TN997.E5	622.386
Electrons	QC793.5.E462-.E4629	539.72112	Emergency medical personnel	RA645.5-.8	616.025
			Emergency medical services	RA645.5-.9	362.18
Electrons—Polarization	QC793.5.E628	539.72112	Emergency medical technicians	RA645.5-.7	616.025
Electrooptical devices	TA1750	623.7314			
Electrophoresis	QD272.E43	541.372	Emergency medicine	RC86-88.9	616.025
Electrophoresis	QD117.E45	541.372	Emergency nursing	RT120.E4	610.7361
Electrophoresis	QD79.E44	541.372	Emery-wheels	TJ1290	621.923
Electrophotography	TR1035-1050	686.44	Emetics	RM359	615.731
Electrophysiology	QH517	572.437	Emigration and immigration	JV6001-9500	325.(2/1)
Electrophysiology	QP341	572.437	Emigration and immigration—Economic aspects	JV6118	325.(2-1)
Electrophysiology of plants	QK845	572.4372			
Electroplating	TS670-693	671.732			
Electroretinography	RE79.E4	617.707547	Emigration and immigration—History	JV6021-6032	325.(1-2)09
Electroslag process	TN686.5.E4	669.0284			
Electroslag welding	TK4660	671.521	Emin Pasha Relief Expedition, 1887-1889	DT363	967.0312
Electrostatic accelerators	QC787.E4	539.732			
Electrostatic microphone	TK5986	621.38284	Eminent domain	K3511-3512	343.0252
Electrostatics	QC570-596.9	537.2	Eminent domain—England	KD1185-1189	343.420252
Electrotherapeutics	RM869-890	615.845			

Subject Heading	LC	Dewey	Subject Heading	LC	Dewey
Eminent domain—United States	KF5599	343.730252	Endangered species	QH75-77	578.68
Emission spectroscopy	QC454.E46	535.84	Endemic goiter in children	RJ420.G65	618.92442
Emotions	BF511-593	152.4	Endocarditis	RC685.E5	616.11
Emotions	B815	128.37	Endocrine glands	QM371	611.4
Emotions (Philosophy)	B105.E3	128.37	Endocrine glands	QL868	573.4
Emotions in adolescence	BF724.3.E5	155.512	Endocrine glands	QM576	611.4
Emotions in children	BF720.E45	155.412	Endocrine glands	QP187-.6	612.4
Emotions in children	BF723.E6	155.412	Endocrine glands—Diseases	RC648-665	616.4
Emotions in infants	BF720.E45	155.42224	Endocrine gynecology	RG159-208	618.17
Empathy	BF575.E55	152.41	Endocrine manifestations of general diseases	RB48.5	616.047
Emperor penguin	QL696.S473	598.47	Endocrinology	QP187-.6	612.4
Emperor worship	BL465	291.213	Endocrinology	RC648-665	616.4
Emperor worship, Rome	DG124	291.2130937	Endocrinology, Comparative	QL868	573.4
Emperor worship—Japanese	BL2211.E46	299.56	Endocrinology, Comparative	QP187-.6	612.4
			Endodontics	RK351-356	617.6342
Emperors—Byzantine Empire	DF506-.5	949.50(13-3) 0099	Endogamy and exogamy	GN480.3	306.82
			Endometrium—Diseases	RG316	618.1
Emperors—Rome	DG270-365	937.0099	Endoscopic ultrasonography	RG107.5.E48	618.107543
Emphysema, Pulmonary	RC776.E5	616.248	Endoscopy	RC78.7.E5	616.07545
Empiricism	B816	146.44	Endowment of research	Q180.55.G7	001.40681
Employee discounts	HD4928.E4	331.255	Endowments	LB2336-2337	378.106
Employee fringe benefits	HD4928.N6	331.255	Endpapers	Z272	686.3
Employee fringe benefits—Accounting	HF5681.N65	657.74	Energy levels (Quantum mechanics)	QC795.8.E5	539.725
Employee motivation	HF5549.5.M63	658.314	Energy minerals	TN263.5	333.79
Employee orientation	HF5549.5.I53	658.31242	Energy policy	HD9502-.5	333.79
Employee ownership	HD5650-5660	338.7	Engagement (Philosophy)	B105.E5	392.4
Employee rights	HD6971.8	331.011	Engineering	TA	620
Employee stock options	HD4928.S74	331.2164	Engineering—Congresses	TA5	620.006
Employee theft	HF5549.5.E43	658.473	Engineering—Dictionaries	TA9	620.003
Employees' buildings and facilities	NA6598	725.4	Engineering—Equipment and supplies	TA213-215	620.00284
Employees—Counseling of	HF5549.5.C8	658.3151	Engineering—Graphic methods	TA337-338	620.00728
Employees—Drug testing	HF5549.5.D7	658.3112	Engineering—History	TA15-19	620.009
Employees—Effect of technological innovations on	HD6331-.2	331.25	Engineering—Management	TA190-194	620.0068
			Engineering—Notation	TA11	620.00148
Employees—Recruiting	HF5549.5.R44	658.3111	Engineering—Periodicals	TA1-4	620.005
Employees-Rating of	HF5549.5.R3	658.3125	Engineering—Research	TA160-.6	620.0072
Employment (Economic theory)	HD5701.5-.75	331.125	Engineering—Specifications	TA180-182	620.00212
			Engineering—Statistical methods	TA340	620.00727
Employment agencies	HD5860-6000.7	331.128	Engineering—Supplies	T13	620.00284
Employment agencies—[By region or country]	HD5871-6000.7	331.12809(4-9)	Engineering—[By region or country]	TA21-127	620.009(4-9)
Employment interviewing	HF5549.5.I6	658.31124	Engineering—Africa	TA115-119	620.0096
Employment tests	HF5549.5.E5	658.3112	Engineering—Arctic regions	TA125-.5	620.00998
Emporia (Va.)—History—Civil War, 1861-1865	F234.E	975.503	Engineering—Argentina	TA36-37	620.00982
			Engineering—Asiatic Russia	TA109-110	620.00957
Emulsions	TP156.E6	660.294514	Engineering—Australia	TA121-122	620.00994
Emulsions (Pharmacy)	RS201.E5	615.45	Engineering—Austria	TA65-.2	620.009436
Emus	QL696.C34	598.53	Engineering—Balkan Peninsula	TA95.A2	620.009496
Enamel and enameling	NK4997-5024	738.4	Engineering—Belgium	TA67-68	620.009493
Enameled glass	NK5439.E5	748.6	Engineering—Bolivia	TA38-39	620.00984
Encaustic painting	ND2480	751.46	Engineering—Brazil	TA41-42	620.00981
Encyclicals, Papal	BX860	262.91	Engineering—Canada	TA26-27	620.00971
End of the universe	QB991.E53	523.19	Engineering—Central America	TA30-31	620.009728
End of the world	BT875-891	236.9			
End play (Football)	GV951.25	796.3322	Engineering—Chile	TA43-44	620.00983
Endangered plants	QK86	581.68			
Endangered species	QL81.5-84.77	578.68			

Subject Heading	LC	Dewey
Engineering—China	TA101-102	620.00951
Engineering—Colombia	TA45-46	620.009861
Engineering—Congresses	TA5	620.006
Engineering—Czechoslovakia	TA65.3-.4	620.009437
Engineering—Denmark	TA69-70	620.009489
Engineering—Ecuador	TA47	620.009866
Engineering—Egypt	TA117-118	620.00962
Engineering—Finland	TA95.F5	620.0094897
Engineering—France	TA71-72.5	620.00944
Engineering—French Guiana	TA50	620.009882
Engineering—Germany	TA73-74.5	620.00943
Engineering—Great Britain	TA57-64	620.00941
Engineering—Greece	TA75-76	620.009495
Engineering—Guyana	TA48	620.009881
Engineering—Hungary	TA65.5-66	620.009439
Engineering—India	TA103-104	620.00954
Engineering—Indonesia	TA113.I55	620.009598
Engineering—Iran	TA107-108	620.00955
Engineering—Iraq	TA113.I7	620.009567
Engineering—Israel	TA113.I75	620.0095694
Engineering—Italy	TA79-80	620.00945
Engineering—Japan	TA105-106	620.00952
Engineering—Mexico	TA28-29	620.00972
Engineering—Netherlands	TA77-78	620.009492
Engineering—New Zealand	TA122.5-.6	620.00993
Engineering—Norway	TA81-82	620.009481
Engineering—Oceania	TA123-124	620.0099(5-6)
Engineering—Pakistan	TA104.5-.6	620.0095491
Engineering—Paraguay	TA51	620.009892
Engineering—Peru	TA52	620.00985
Engineering—Philippines	TA113.P6	620.009599
Engineering—Portugal	TA83-84.5	620.009469
Engineering—Russia	TA85-86	620.00947
Engineering—Scandinavia	TA88.5	620.00948
Engineering—Spain	TA87-88	620.00946
Engineering—Sri Lanka	TA104.7-.8	620.0095493
Engineering—Surinam	TA49	620.009883
Engineering—Sweden	TA89-90	620.009485
Engineering—Switzerland	TA91-92	620.009494
Engineering—Turkey	TA111-112	620.009561
Engineering—United States	TA23-25	620.00973
Engineering—Uruguay	TA53	620.009895
Engineering—Venezuela	TA54	620.00987
Engineering—West Indies	TA32-33	620.009729
Engineering—Yugoslavia	TA95.Y8	620.009497
Engineering design	TA174	620.0042
Engineering economy	TA177.4-185	620.00681
Engineering ethics	TA157	174.962
Engineering experiment stations	TA416-417	620.0072
Engineering firms	TA216-217	620.006
Engineering firms	TA157	620.006
Engineering firms—Directories	TA12	620.0025
Engineering geology	TA703-705.4	624.151
Engineering geology—[By region or country]	TA705.2-.4	624.15109(3-4)
Engineering inspection	TA191	620.0044
Engineering instruments	TA165	620.00284
Engineering laboratories	TA416-417	620.0072
Engineering mathematics	TA329-348	620.00151
Engineering models	TA177	620.00228
Engineers	TA157-158.3	620.0023
Engineers—Biography	TA139-140	620.0092
Engines	TJ250-255	621.4
England	DA20-690	936.2/942
England—Church history—449-1066	BR749	274.109021
England—Church history—1066-1485	BR745-754	274.10902
England—Church history—1485-	BR750	274.10903
England—Church history—16th century	BR755-757	274.109031
England—Church history—17th century	BR756	274.109032
England—Church history—20th century	BR759	274.10904
England—Constitutional history	KD3931-3966	342.42029
England—Constitutional law	KD3931-4645	342.42
England—Description and travel	DA600-632	913.6204/914.204
England—Economic conditions	HC251-260	330.942
England—Foreign relations—Law and legislation	KD4030	342.420412
England—Maps	G5750-5754	912.42
England—Periodicals	DA20	936.2005/942.005
England. Royal Air force	DA89.5	358.400942
English West Indian Expedition, 1654-1655	F1621	972.903
English West Indian Expedition, 1695	F1621	972.903
English West Indian Expedition, 1739-1742	F2272.5	986.102
English West Indian Expedition, 1759	F2151	972.903
English West Indian Expedition, 1793-1794	F1621	972.903
English West Indian Expedition, 1795-1796	F1621	972.903
English cocker spaniel	SF429.E47	636.7524
English diaries	PR1330	828.03
English diaries	PR908	828.03
English drama	PR621-739	822.009
English drama	PR1241-1273	822.008
English drama (Comedy)	PR631	822.052309
English drama (Comedy)	PR1248	822.052308
English drama (Tragedy)	PR633	822.051209
English drama (Tragedy)	PR1257	822.051208
English drama—To 1500	PR641-644	822.(1-2)09
English drama—To 1500	PR1260	822.(1-2)08
English drama—Early modern and Elizabethan, 1500-1600	PR646-658	822.(2-3)09

Emi - Eng

Subject Heading	LC	Dewey
English drama—Early modern and Elizabethan, 1500-1600	PR1262-1263	822.(2-3)08
English drama—17th century	PR671-698	822.409
English drama—17th century	PR1265.3-1266	822.408
English drama—18th century	PR1269	822.508
English drama—18th century	PR701-719	822.509
English drama—19th century	PR721-734	822.809
English drama—19th century	PR1271	822.808
English drama—20th century	PR736-739	822.909
English drama—20th century	PR1272	822.908
English essays	PR921-927	824.009
English essays	PR1361-1369	824.008
English fiction	PR1281-1309	823.008
English fiction	PR821-888	823.009
English fiction—20th century	PR881-888	823.909
English fiction—Women authors	PZ1	823.00809287
English-horn music	M110.E5	788.53
English language	PE1001-3729	420
English language—Dialects	PE1700-3601	427
English language—Dictionaries	PE1704	423
English language—Early modern, 1500-1700	PE1079-1081	427.00903(1/2)
English language—Etymology	PE1571-1599	422
English language—Grammar	PE1097-1105	425
English language—Grammar—1950-	PE1112	425
English language—History	PE1079-1087	427.9
English language—Lexicography	PE1601-1693	423.028
English language—Morphology	PE1171	425
English language—Parts of speech	PE1199-1359	425
English language—Phonology	PE1133-1168	421.5
English language—Phonology, Historical	PE1133	421.509
English language—Rhetoric	PE1402-1497	808.042
English language—Slang	PE3701-3729	427
English language—Study and teaching	PE1065-1069	420.71
English language—Synonyms and antonyms	PE1591	423.1
English language—United States	PE2801-3102	427.73
English language—Old English, ca. 450-1100	PE101-299	429
English language—Old English, ca. 450-1100—Dialects	PE287-299	429.7
English language—Old English, ca. 450-1100—Dictionaries	PE275-285	429.3
English language—Old English, ca. 450-1100—Etymology	PE261-269	429.2
English language—Old English, ca. 450-1100—Grammar	PE129-231	429.5
English language—Old English, ca. 450-1100—Lexicography	PE274-285	429.3028
English language—Old English, ca. 450-1100—Philology	PE101-123	429
English language—Middle English, 1100-1500	PE501-685	427.02
English language—Middle English, 1100-1500—Dialects	PE688	427.027
English language—Middle English, 1100-1500—Dictionaries	PE575-585	427.023
English language—Middle English, 1100-1500—Etymology	PE561-569	427.022
English language—Middle English, 1100-1500—Grammar	PE529-531	427.025
English language—Middle English, 1100-1500—Lexicography	PE574-585	427.023028
English language—Middle English, 1100-1500—Philology	PE524-531	427.02
English language—18th century	PE1083	427.009033
English language—19th century	PE1085	427.009034
English letters	PR911-917	826.009
English letters	PR1341-1349	826.008
English literature	PR1-9680	820
English literature—Catholic authors	PR1110.C3	820.809222
English literature—Criticism, Textual	PR57-78	820.9
English literature—Dictionaries	PR19	820.3
English literature—History and criticism	PR1-978	820.9
English literature—Irish authors	PR8700-8821	820.99415
English literature—Irish authors	PR8831-8893	820.809415
English literature—Japanese authors	PR9900.J	820.80952
English literature—Outlines, syllabi, etc.	PR87	820.0202

Subject Heading	LC	Dewey
English literature—Scottish authors	PR8500-8621	820.99411
English literature—Scottish authors	PR8631-8693	820.809411
English literature—Study and teaching	PR31-55	820.71
English literature—Welsh authors	PR8900-8997	820.809429
English literature—Women authors	PR1110.W6	820.809287
English literature—Women authors	PR111-119	820.99287
English literature—Old English, ca. 450-1100	PR171-236	829.009
English literature—Middle English, 1100-1500	PR1119-1131	820.8001
English literature—Middle English, 1100-1500	PR251-369	820.900(1-2)
English literature—Early modern, 1500-1700	PR1119-1131	820.800(3-4)
English literature—Early modern, 1500-1700	PR401-439	820.900(2-4)
English literature—18th century	PR1134-1139	820.8005
English literature—18th century	PR441-449	820.9005
English literature—19th century	PR1301-1304	820.8008
English literature—19th century	PR451-469	820.9008
English literature—19th century	PR1143-1145	820.8008
English literature—20th century	PR1149	820.8008
English literature—20th century	PR471-479	820.9009
English newspapers	PN5111-5129	072.(1-8)
English oak	QK495.F14	583.46
English oak	SD397.E54	634.9721
English periodicals	AP2-9	051
English periodicals	PN5111-5130	052
English philology	PE	420
English poetry	PR1170-1227	821
English poetry	PR500-611	821.009
English poetry—History and criticism	PR500-609	821.009
English poetry—Irish authors	PR8848-8863	821.00809415
English poetry—Irish authors	PR8761-8781	891.0099415
English poetry—Irish authors	PR8848-8863	821.00809415
English poetry—Scottish authors	PR8649-8663	821.00809411
English poetry—Scottish authors	PR8561-8581	821.0089411
English poetry—Welsh authors	PR8955-8969	821.00809429
English poetry—Welsh authors	PR8926-8932	821.00909429
English poetry—Women authors	PR111-119	821.0099287
English poetry—Women authors	PR1177	821.00809287
English poetry—Old English, ca. 450-1100	PR1490-1508	829.1
English poetry—Old English, ca. 450-1100	PR201-217	829.1009
English poetry—Early modern, 1500-1700	PR521-549	821.(2-4)09
English poetry—Early modern, 1500-1700	PR1204-1213	821.(3-4)08
English poetry—18th century	PR551-579	821.509
English poetry—18th century	PR1215-1219	821.508
English poetry—19th century	PR581-599	821.809
English poetry—19th century	PR1221-1224	821.808
English poetry—20th century	PR1224-1227	821.908
English poetry—20th century	PR601-609	821.909
English prose literature	PR750-888	828.08
English prose literature	PR1281-1300	828.08
English prose literature—Scottish authors	PR8597-8607	828.08
English prose literature—Scottish authors	PR8672-8687	828.08
English prose literature—Old English, ca. 450-1100	PR221-236	829.808
English prose literature—Early modern, 1500-1700	PR1293-1295	828.08
English prose literature—Early modern, 1500-1700	PR767-769	828.08
English prose literature—18th century	PR1297	828.08
English prose literature—18th century	PR769	828.08
English saddles	SF309.9	636.13037
English springer spaniels	SF429.E7	636.7524
English wit and humor	PR931-937	827.009
English wit and humor	PN6173-6175	827.008
English wit and humor, Pictorial	NC1470-1479	827.0222
Engravers	NE800	769.92
Engravers' marks	NE820	760.278
Engraving	NE	760
Engraving—Exhibitions	NE1410-1412	760.074
Engraving—Printing	NE2800-2890	760
Engraving—Themes, motives	NE886	760.04
Engraving—14th century	NE1638	760.09023
Engraving—15th century	NE1655-1656	760.09024

Subject Heading	LC	Dewey
Engraving (Metal)—16th century	NE1665-1666	760.09031
Engraving—17th century	NE1670-1690	760.09032
Engraving—18th century	NE1710-1719	760.09033
Engraving—19th century	NE1720.5-1739	760.09034
Engraving—20th century	NE1740-1749	760.0904
Engraving (Metal-work)	NE2700-2710	765
Enki (Sumarian deity)	BL1616.E54	299.9295
Enlightenment	B802	190
Ensemble playing	MT728	785.143807
Entebbe Airport Raid, 1976	DS119.7	956.94054
Enteritis	RC862.E5	616.344
Enterobacterial vaccines	QR189.5.E53	615.372
Entertainers—Diseases	RC965.P46	616.0088791
Entertainers in motion pictures	PN1995.9.E77	791.4092
Entertaining	BJ2021-2078	395.3
Entertaining	GV1470-1521	793.2
Entertaining	TX851-885	642.(6-8)
Entertaining	TX731-739	642.4
Enthusiasm	BF575.E6	153.1533
Enthusiasm	BR112	248.2
Entomology—Research	QL468.5	595.7072
Entrees (Cookery)	TX740	641.82
Entrepreneurship	HB615	338.04
Enuresis	RC569.5.E5	616.849
Enuresis	RJ476.E6	618.92849
Envelopment (Military science)	U167.5.E57	355.422
Environmental chemistry	TD193-.5	577.14
Environmental degradation	GE140-160	639.9
Environmental education	S946	333.72071
Environmental education	GE70-90	333.7071
Environmental education	QH541.2-.264	577.071
Environmental impact analysis	TD194.6	363.7
Environmental impact statements	TD194.5-.58	363.7
Environmental monitoring	QH541.15.M64	363.7063
Environmental protection	TD169-171.8	628
Environmental psychology	BF353-.5	155.9
Environmentally induced diseases	RB152	616.98
Enzymes	QP601-619	572.7
Eoliths	GN775-776	930.11
Ephedra	SB295.E63	633.8858
Ephemerides	QB7-9	528
Epic literature, French	PQ201-205	841.03209
Epic poetry	PN1301-1333	808.8132
Epic poetry	PN6110.E6	808.8132
Epic poetry, English	PR321-347	821.03209
Epic poetry, German	PT1411-1418	831.03208
Epic poetry, German	PT1179-1181	831.03208
Epic poetry, Greek	PA3105-3107.5	881.03209
Epic poetry, Greek	PA3437-3439	881.03208
Epic poetry, Latin	PA6125	871.032108
Epidemic encephalitis	RA644.E52	614.59832
Epidemic encephalitis	RC141.E6	614.832
Epidemics	RA648.5-654	614.4
Epidemics—[By region or country]	RA650-650.9	614.42(4-9)

Subject Heading	LC	Dewey
Environmental impact analysis	TD194.6	363.7
Environmental impact statements	TD194.5-.58	363.7
Environmental monitoring	QH541.15.M64	363.7063
Environmental protection	TD169-171.8	628
Environmental psychology	BF353-.5	155.9
Environmentally induced diseases	RB152	616.98
Enzymes	QP601-619	572.7
Eoliths	GN775-776	930.11
Ephedra	SB295.E63	633.8858
Ephemerides	QB7-9	528
Epic literature, French	PQ201-205	841.03209
Epic poetry	PN1301-1333	808.8132
Epic poetry	PN6110.E6	808.8132
Epic poetry, English	PR321-347	821.03209
Epic poetry, German	PT1411-1418	831.03208
Epic poetry, German	PT1179-1181	831.03208
Epic poetry, Greek	PA3105-3107.5	881.03209
Epic poetry, Greek	PA3437-3439	881.03208
Epic poetry, Latin	PA6125	871.032108
Epidemic encephalitis	RA644.E52	614.59832
Epidemic encephalitis	RC141.E6	614.832
Epidemics	RA648.5-654	614.4
Epidemics—[By region or country]	RA650-650.9	614.42(4-9)
Environmental impact analysis	TD194.6	363.7
Environmental impact statements	TD194.5-.58	363.7
Environmental monitoring	QH541.15.M64	363.7063
Environmental protection	TD169-171.8	628
Environmental psychology	BF353-.5	155.9
Environmentally induced diseases	RB152	616.98
Enzymes	QP601-619	572.7
Eoliths	GN775-776	930.11
Ephedra	SB295.E63	633.8858
Ephemerides	QB7-9	528
Epic literature, French	PQ201-205	841.03209
Epic poetry	PN1301-1333	808.8132
Epic poetry	PN6110.E6	808.8132
Epic poetry, English	PR321-347	821.03209
Epic poetry, German	PT1411-1418	831.03208
Epic poetry, German	PT1179-1181	831.03208
Epic poetry, Greek	PA3105-3107.5	881.03209
Epic poetry, Greek	PA3437-3439	881.03208
Epic poetry, Latin	PA6125	871.032108
Epidemic encephalitis	RA644.E52	614.59832
Epidemic encephalitis	RC141.E6	614.832
Epidemics	RA648.5-654	614.4
Epidemics—[By region or country]	RA650-650.9	614.42(4-9)
Epidemics—Africa	RA650.8	614.426
Epidemics—America	RA650-.55	614.42(7-8)
Epidemics—Asia	RA650.7	614.425
Epidemics—Australia	RA650.9.A8	614.4294
Epidemics—Europe	RA650.6	614.424
Epidemiology	RA648.5-654	614.4
Epidermis	QL941-943	573.5

Subject Heading	LC	Dewey
Epidermis	QP88.5	573.5
Epidermis	QM484	611.77
Epidermis	QM561	611.77
Epiglottis	QM255	611.22
Epigrams	PN6279-6288	808.882
Epigrams	PN1441	808.882
Epigrams, French	PN6282	848.02
Epilepsy	RC372-374.5	616.853
Epilepsy in adolescence	RJ496.E6	616.85300835
Epilepsy in children	RJ496.E6	618.92853
Epilepsy in pregnancy	RG580.E64	618.3268
Epinal (France), Battle of, 1870	DC309.E8	944.0812
Epiphany	BV50.E7	263.915
Epirus (Greece and Albania)	DF261.E65	949.53
Episcopacy	BX5176-5178	262.12
Episcopacy	BV669-670.2	262.12
Episcopal Church	BX5949	264.035
Episcopal Church—Creeds	BX5939	238.373
Episcopal Church—Creeds	BX6074	238.373
Episcopal Church—Doctrines	BX5929-5930.2	230.373
Episcopal Church—Education	BX5850-5876	268.8373
Episcopal Church—Education	BX6061-6064.5	268.8373
Episcopal Church—Government	BX6076	262.0373
Episcopal Church—Government	BX5950-5968	262.0373
Episcopal Church—History	BX6065-6069	283.7309
Episcopal Church—History	BX5879-5919	283.7309
Episcopal Church—Liturgy	BX5947-5948	264.03
Episcopal Church—Liturgy	BX6075	264.03
Episcopal Church—Liturgy	BX5940-5948	264.03
Episcopal Church—Missions	BX5969	266.373
Episcopal Church—Periodicals	BX6051	283.7305
Episcopal Church—Prayer-books and devotions	BX5943-5945	264.03
Episcopal Church—Relations	BX5926-5928.5	283.73
Episcopal conferences (Catholic)	BX837.5	262.3
Episcopalians	BX5800-6093	283.73092
Episcopalians—Biography	BX6091-6093	283.73092
Episcopalians—Biography	BX5990-5995	283.73092
Epistemics	B820.3	121
Epitaphs	CN528.E6	929.50937
Epitaphs	CN375.E6	929.50938
Epizootic catarrh in sheep	SF969.E	636.308969
Epoxy resins	TP1180.E6	668.374
Epstein-Barr virus diseases	QR201.E75	571.992
Epstein-Barr virus diseases	RC141.5	616.925
Equality	JC575-578	323.42
Equality	HM146	305
Equality—Religious aspects	BL65.E68	291.17834
Equations	QA211-218	512.94
Equations, Abelian	QA215	512.2
Equations, Binomial	QA245	512.942

Subject Heading	LC	Dewey
Equations, Cubic	QA215	512.942
Equations, Quadratic	QA161	512.942
Equations, Quartic	QA215	512.942
Equations, Theory of	QA211-218	512.94
Equatorial Guinea—Maps	G8660-8664	912.6718
Equatorial Guinea—Census	HA4712	316.718
Equatorial Guinea—Civilization	DT620.4	967.18
Equatorial Guinea—Description and travel	DT620.27	967.1804
Equatorial Guinea—Gazetteers	DT620.15	916.718003
Equatorial Guinea—History	DT620.46-.83	967.18
Equestrian statues	NB1312-1313	731.81
Equilibrium (Economics)	HB145	339.5
Equity—Canada	KE457	346.71004
Equity—England	KD674	346.42004
Equity—United States	KF398-400	346.73004
Ergodic theory	QA313	515.42
Ergodic theory	QA611.5	514
Erie, Lake, Battle of, 1813	E356.E6	973.5254
Erinyes (Greek mythology)	BL820.F8	292.13
Erosion	QE571-597	551.302
Erotic art	N8217.E6	704.9428
Erotic drawing	NC825.E76	743.828
Erotic literature	HQ450-472	809.933538
Erotic literature	PN6071.E7	808.803538
Error analysis (Mathematics)	QA275	511.43
Errors, Popular	AZ999	001.96
Escalators	TJ1376	621.8676
Escapes	HV8657-8658	365.641
Eschatology	BT819-891	236
Eschatology	BL500-547	291.23
Eschatology, Buddhist	BQ4475-4525	294.3423
Eschatology, Islamic	BP166.8	297.23
Eskimo dogs	SF429.E8	636.73
Eskimo languages	PM50-94	497.1
Eskimos	E99.E7	973.04971
Esophageal varices	RC815.7	616.32
Esophagectomy	RD539.5	617.548
Esophagus	QL861	573.359
Esophagus	QM331	611.32
Esophagus	QP146	612.315
Esophagus—Abnormalities	RC815.7	616.32043
Esophagus—Atresia	RJ456.E83	618.9232
Esophagus—Cancer	RC280.E8	616.99432
Esophagus—Diseases	RC815.7	616.32
Esophagus—Foreign bodies	RF545	616.32
Esophagus—Surgery	RD539.5	617.548059
Esophagus—Tumors	RC280.E8	616.99432
Esophagus—Wounds and injuries	RD539.5	617.548044
Esopus Indians—Wars, 1655-1660	E83.655	973.23
Esopus Indians—Wars, 1663-1664	E83.663	973.23
Esperanto	PM8201-8298	499.992
Essay	PN4500	808.4
Essays	PN6141-6145	808.84
Essays and proofs (Philately)	HE6184.D4	769.56

Subject Heading	LC	Dewey	Subject Heading	LC	Dewey
Essence and essential oils	TP958-959	661.806	Ethics, Modern—19th century	BJ315	170.9034
Essenes	BM175.E8	296.814	Ethics, Modern—20th century	BJ319	170.904
Essential fatty acids	QP752.E84	572.57	Ethics, Oriental	BJ961-977	170.95
Essential hypertension	RC685.H8	616.132	Ethics, Polish	BJ847-850	170.9438
Estate planning—England	KD1497	346.4205	Ethics, Positivist	BJ1365-1385	171.2
Estates (Law)—England	KD841-960	346.420432	Ethics, Renaissance	BJ271-285	170.90(23-31)
Estill's Defeat, 1782	F454	976.902	Ethics in the Bible	BS680.E84	220.817
Estimation theory	QA276.8	519.544	Ethiopia	DT371-398	963
Estonia	DK503-.95	947.98	Ethiopia—Census	HA4689	316.3
Estonia—Gazetteers	DK503.18	914.798003	Ethiopia—Civilization	DT379.5	963
Estonia—History—1944-1991	DK503.75-.77	947.98	Ethiopia—Description and travel	DT375-378.3	916.304
Estonia—History—1991-	DK503.8-.85	947.9808	Ethiopia—Economic conditions	HC845	330.963
Estonia—Maps	G7030-7033	912.4798	Ethiopia—Gazetteers	DT371.5	916.3003
Estonian language	PH601-629	494.545	Ethiopia—History	DT380.5-387.954	963
Estonian literature	PH630-671	894.545	Ethiopia—History—To 1490	DT383	963.0(1-2)
Estuaries	GC96-97.8	551.4609	Ethiopia—History—1490-1889	DT384-386.73	963.0(2-4)
Estuarine ecology	QH541.5.E8	577.786	Ethiopia—History—1889-1974	DT387-.92	963.0(43-6)
Estuarine oceanography	GC96-97.8	551.4609	Ethiopia—History—Rebellion, 1928-1930	DT387.7-.8	963.054
Estuarine plants	QK108-474.5	581.7786	Ethiopia—History—Coup d'etat, 1960	DT387.9	963.06
Estuarine plants	QK938.E	581.7786	Ethiopia—Maps	G8330-8334	912.63
Etchers	NE2110	767.2092	Ethiopian languages	PJ8991-8999	492.8
Etching	NE1940-2232.5	767.2	Ethiopic language	PJ9001-9087	492.81
Etching—18th century	NE1990-1992	767.209033	Ethiopic literature	PJ9090-9101	892.81
Etching—19th century	NE1994-1995	767.209034	Ethnic groups	GN495.4	305.8
Etching—20th century	NE1997-1998	767.20904	Ethnic groups—Africa	GN643-661	305.80096
Etching—Catalogs	NE1960	767.20294	Ethnic groups—Asia	GN625-635	305.80095
Etching—Exhibitions	NE1950-1955	767.2074	Ethnic groups—Europe	GN575-585	305.80094
Etching—History	NE1980-2055.5	767.209	Ethnic groups—North America	GN550-560	305.80097
Etching—[By region or country]	NE2001-2096.3	767.209(4-9)	Ethnic groups—Oceania	GN662-671	305.80099(5-6)
Eternity	BT910-912	236.21	Ethnic groups—South America	GN562-564	305.80098
Ethical culture movement	BJ10.E8	171	Ethnic mass media	P94.5.M55	302.23089
Ethics	BJ170	170	Ethnic radio broadcasting	PN1991.8.E84	384.54089
Ethics—Congresses	BJ19	395.06	Ethnic relations	GN496-498	305.8
Ethics—Dictionaries	BJ63	170.3	Ethnic schools	LC3800-3806	371.829
Ethics—History	BJ101-214	170.901	Ethnicity	GN495.6	305.8
Ethics—History	BJ71-982	170.9	Ethnology—Bulgaria	DR64	939.8004/ 949.9004
Ethics—Outlines, syllabi, etc.	BJ1075-1077	170.202	Ethnology—Burma	DS528-.2	959.1004
Ethics—Periodicals	BJ1-8	170.5	Ethnology—Egypt	DT71-72	932.004/ 962.004
Ethics—Philosophy	BJ37-60	170.1	Ethnology—Germany	DD73-78	943.004
Ethics—Societies, etc.	BJ10-11	170.6	Ethnology—Libya	DT223-.2	961.2004
Ethics—Study and teaching	BJ66-68	170.71	Ethnology—Slovakia	DB2740-2743	943.73004
Ethics—Textbooks	BJ991-1185	170	Ethnohistory	GN345.2	305.8009
Ethics, Assyro-Babylonian	BJ136-138	170.935	Ethnological museums and collections	GN35-41	305.80074
Ethics, Chinese	BJ116-118	170.95			
Ethics, Chinese	BJ965-968	170.951	Ethnology	GN301-673	305.8
Ethics, Evolutionary	BJ1298-1335	171.7	Ethnology—Afghanistan	DS354.5-.6	939.6004/ 958.1004
Ethics, French	BJ701-704	170.944			
Ethics, Germanic	BJ751-759	170.943	Ethnology—Africa	DT15-16	960.04
Ethics, Greek	BJ160-224	170.938			
Ethics, Greek	BJ801-804	170.9495			
Ethics, Indic	BJ121-123	170.954			
Ethics, Japanese	BJ969-971	170.952			
Ethics, Jewish	BJ1279-1287	296.36			
Ethics, Korean	BJ973-976	170.9519			
Ethics, Medieval	BJ231-255	170.902			
Ethics, Modern	BJ301-982	170.903			
Ethics, Modern—18th century	BJ311	170.9033			

Subject Heading	LC	Dewey	Subject Heading	LC	Dewey
Ethnology—Albania	DR923-925	939.8004/ 949.65004	Ethnology—Guinea-Bissau	DT613.42-.45	966.57004
Ethnology—Algeria	DT283-.6	939.71004/ 965.004	Ethnology—Hawaii	DU624.6-.7	996.9004
			Ethnology—Hungary	DB919-.2	939.8004/ 943.9004
Ethnology—Angola	DT1304-1308	967.3004	Ethnology—Iceland	DL331-334	949.12004
Ethnology—Armenia	DS172	947.56004	Ethnology—India	DS430-432.5	934.004/ 954.004
Ethnology—Asia	DS13-28	950.04			
Ethnology—Australia	DU120-125	994.004	Ethnology—Indonesia	DS631-632	959.8004
Ethnology—Austria	DB33-34.5	936.3004/ 943.6004	Ethnology—Iran	DS268-269	935.004/ 955.004
Ethnology—Balkan Peninsula	DR24-27	949.6004	Ethnology—Iraq	DS70.8	935.004/ 956.7004
Ethnology—Bangladesh	DS393.82-.8	934.004/ 954.92004	Ethnology—Israel	DS113.2-.8	933.004/ 956.94004
Ethnology—Belgium	DH491-492	936.4004/ 949.3004	Ethnology—Italy	DG455-457	937.004/ 945.004
Ethnology—Benin	DT541.42-.45	966.83004	Ethnology—Japan	DS830-832	952.004
Ethnology—Botswana	DT2454-2458	968.83004	Ethnology—Jordan	DS153.5-.55	933.004/ 956.95004
Ethnology—Brunei	DS650.42-.43	959.55004			
Ethnology—Burkina Faso	DT555.42-.45	966.25004	Ethnology—Kenya	DT433.542-.545	967.62004
Ethnology—Burma	DS538-539	959.1004	Ethnology—Korea	DS904.5-.7	951.9004
Ethnology—Burundi	DT450.64-.65	967.572004	Ethnology—Laos	DS555.44-.45	959.4004
Ethnology—Byzantine Empire	DF542-.4	949.50(13-3)004	Ethnology—Lebanon	DS80.5	939.44004/ 956.92004
Ethnology—Cambodia	DS554.44-.46	959.6004	Ethnology—Lesotho	DT2592-2596	968.85004
Ethnology—Cameroon	DT570-571	967.11004	Ethnology—Liberia	DT630-.5	966.62004
Ethnology—Cape Verde	DT671.C242-.C245	966.58004	Ethnology—Madagascar	DT469.M276-.M277	969.1004
Ethnology—Central African Republic	DT546.342-.345	967.41004	Ethnology—Malawi	DT3189-3192	968.97004
			Ethnology—Malaysia	DS595-.2	959.5004
Ethnology—Chad	DT546.422-.445	967.43004	Ethnology—Mali	DT551.42-.45	966.23004
Ethnology—China	DS730-731	931.004/ 951.004	Ethnology—Mauritania	DT554.42-.45	966.1004
			Ethnology—Mauritius	DT469.M442-.M445	969.82004
Ethnology—Congo (Brazzaville)	DT546.242-.245	967.24004			
Ethnology—Cote d'Ivoire	DT545.42-.45	966.68004	Ethnology—Morocco	DT313-.6	939.71004/ 964.004
Ethnology—Cyprus	DS54.4-.44	939.37004/ 956.93004	Ethnology—Mozambique	DT3324-3328	967.9004
			Ethnology—Namibia	DT1554-1558	968.81004
Ethnology—Czechoslovakia	DB2040-2043	943.7004	Ethnology—Nepal	DS493.8-.9	954.96004
Ethnology—Denmark	DL141-142	936.3004/ 948.9004	Ethnology—Netherlands	DJ91-92	936.3004/ 949.2004
Ethnology—Djibouti	DT411.42-.45	967.71004	Ethnology—Netherlands	DH91-92	936.3004/ 949.2004
Ethnology—Equatorial Guinea	DT620.42-.45	967.18004	Ethnology—New Zealand	DU422.5-424.5	993.004
Ethnology—Ethiopia	DT380-.4	963.004	Ethnology—Niger	DT547.42-.45	966.26004
Ethnology—Europe	D1056-.2	940.55004	Ethnology—Nigeria	DT515.42-.45	966.9004
Ethnology—Europe, Central	DAW1026-1028	943.004	Ethnology—Norway	DL441-442	936.3004/ 948.1004
Ethnology—Europe, Eastern	DJK26-28	947.0004			
Ethnology—Finland	DL1018-1020	948.97004	Ethnology—Pakistan	DS380.A1-.A2	934.004/ 954.91004
Ethnology—France	DC34-.5	936.4004/ 944.004	Ethnology—Poland	DK4120-4122	943.8004
Ethnology—Gabon	DT546.142-.145	967.21004	Ethnology—Portugal	DP533-534.5	936.6004/ 946.9004
Ethnology—Gambia	DT509.42-.45	966.51004			
Ethnology—Germany	DD73-78	943.004	Ethnology—Reunion	DT469.R38-.R39	969.81004
Ethnology—Ghana	DT510.42-.43	966.7004	Ethnology—Romania	DR213-214	939.8004/ 949.8004
Ethnology—Great Britain	DA120-125	936.1004/ 942.004			
Ethnology—Greece	DF135	938.004/ 949.5004	Ethnology—Russia (Federation)	DK33-35	947.004
Ethnology—Greece	DF745-747	949.50(4-9)004	Ethnology—Rwanda	DT450.24-.25	967.571004
Ethnology—Guinea	DT543.42-.45	966.52004	Ethnology—Sao Tome and Principe	DT615.42-.45	967.15004

Subject Heading	LC	Dewey	Subject Heading	LC	Dewey
Ethnology—Saudi Arabia	DS218-219	939.49004/ 953.8004	Euphonium music	M110.B33	788.975
Ethnology—Scandinavia	L41-42	936.3004/ 948.004	Euro-bond market	HG3896	337.14
			Europa Cup (Soccer)	GV943.5	796.33466
Ethnology—Senegal	DT549.42-.45	966.3004	Europe—Armed Forces— Supplies and stores	UC158-233	355.8094
Ethnology—Seychelles	DT469.S442- .S443	969.6004	Europe—Biography	CT759-1495	920.04
			Europe—Census	HA1107-1650	314
Ethnology—Sierra Leone	DT516.42-.45	966.4004	Europe—Civilization— 18th century	CB411	940.2(526-7)
Ethnology—Somalia	DT402.3-.45	967.73004			
Ethnology—South Africa	DT1754-1770	968.004	Europe—Civilization— 19th century	CB204	940.2(7-87)
Ethnology—Spain	DP52-53	936.6004/ 946.004	Europe—Climate	QC989	551.694
Ethnology—Sri Lanka	DS489.2-.25	954.93004	Europe—Commerce	HF3491-3750.7	380.1094
Ethnology—Sudan	DT155-.2	962.4004	Europe—Description and travel	D901-980	914
Ethnology—Swaziland	DT2744-2746	968.87004			
Ethnology—Sweden	DL639-641	936.3004/ 948.5004	Europe—Economic conditions	HC240-407	330.94
Ethnology—Switzerland	DQ48-49	936.4004/ 949.4004	Europe—Foreign relations—1989-	D2009	327.4
Ethnology—Syria	DS94.7-.8	939.43004/ 956.91004	Europe—Genealogy	CS410-1059	929.107204
			Europe—Historical geography—Maps	G1791-1799	911.4
Ethnology—Taiwan	DS799.42-.43	931.004/ 951.249004	Europe—History	D900-1075	940
Ethnology—Tanzania	DT443-.3	967.8004	Europe—History— 1789-1815	D301-309	940.27
Ethnology—Thailand	DS569-570	959.3004			
Ethnology—Togo	DT582.42-.45	966.81004	Europe—History—1945-	D1050-1075	940.5(5-6)
Ethnology—Tunisia	DT253-.2	939.73004/ 961.1004	Europe—History— 1945- —Periodicals	D1050	940.(55-56)005
Ethnology—Turkey	DR434-435	939.2004/ 956.1004	Europe—History— 1945- —Study and teaching	D1050.8-.82	940.(55-56)0071
Ethnology—Uganda	DT433.242-.245	967.61004			
Ethnology—United States	E184-185.98	973.04	Europe—Intellectual life—19th century	CB204	940.2(7-87)
Ethnology—Vietnam	DS556.44-.45	959.7004			
Ethnology—Yugoslavia	DR1229-1230	939.8004/ 949.7004	Europe—Intellectual life—20th century	CB203-231	940.(288-559)
Ethnology—Zaire	DT649.5-650	967.51004	Europe—Maps	G5700-7153	912.4
Ethnology—Zambia	DT3054-3058	968.94004	Europe—Politics and government—1945-	D1058-1065	320.94090 (44-511)
Ethnology—Zimbabwe	DT2910-2913	968.91004			
Ethnology in the Bible	BS661	220.83058	Europe—Politics and government—1989-	D2009	320.940948
Ethnomethodology	HM24	305.8001			
Ethnomusicology	ML3797.7-3799	780.89	Europe—Politics and government— 20th century	JN12	320.94
Ethnophilosophy	GN468	305.8001			
Ethnopsychology	GN502-517	155.82			
Ethnopsychology	GN270-279	155.82	Europe—Religion	BL690-980	200.94
Ethologist	QL26-31	590.92	Europe, Central	DAW	943
Etiquette	BJ1801-2195	395	Europe, Central— Civilization	DAW1024	943
Etiquette—Dictionaries	BJ1815	395.03			
Etiquette—History	BJ1821	395.09	Europe, Central— Congresses	DAW1004	943.0006
Etiquette—Periodicals	BJ1801	395.05			
Etiquette for men	BJ1855	395.142	Europe, Central— Description and travel	DAW1014-1015	914.304
Etiquette for women	BJ1856	395.144			
Etruscan language	P1078	499.94	Europe, Central—History	DAW1031-1051	943
Etruscans—Religion	BL740-760	299.9294	Europe, Central—Periodicals	DAW1001	943.0005
Eucalyptus	QK495.M9	583.766	Europe, Eastern	DJK	947
Eucalyptus	SD397.E8	634.973766	Europe, Eastern—Biography	DJK31	920.047
Eucharistic congresses	BX2215.A1	264.02036	Europe, Eastern—Civilization	DJK24	947
Euclid's Elements	QA451-469	516.2	Europe, Eastern— Congresses	DJK1.5	947.0006
Eugenics	HQ750-755.5	363.92			
Euler's numbers	QA246	515.52	Europe, Eastern— Description and travel	DJK11-18	914.704
Euphonium	ML990.E	788.97509			

Subject Heading	LC	Dewey
Europe, Eastern—Gazetteers	DJK6	914.70003
Europe, Eastern—Historiography	DJK32-34	947.00072
Europe, Eastern—History—1918-1945	DJK49	947.000904(1-4)
Europe, Eastern—History—1945-	DJK50	947.00090(44-5)
Europe, Eastern—History—1945-1989	DJK50	947.000904(4-8)
Europe, Eastern—History—1989-	DJK51	947.00090(48-5)
Europe, Eastern—Periodicals	DJK1	947.0005
Europe, Eastern—Study and teaching	DJK35-36	947.00071
European Americans	E184.E95	973.04(2-8)073
European Economic Community literature	HC241.2-.25	341.2422
European federation	D1060	321.04094
European federation	JN15	321.04094
European periodicals	PN5110-5355	073-078
Eustachian tube	QP461	612.854
Eustachian tube	QM507	611.85
Eustachian tube	QL948	573.89
Eustachian tube—Diseases	RF230	617.86
Eutaw Springs, Battle of, 1781	E241.E	973.337
Euthanasia	R726	179.7
Evacuation Day, Nov. 25, 1783	E239	973.339
Evangelical Revival	BR758	274.109033
Evangelical academies	BV4487.E9	269.2
Evangelicalism and Christian union	BX9.5.E94	280.042
Evangelicalism—Episcopal Church	BX5925	269.2
Evangelistic invitations	BV3793	269.2
Evangelistic sermons	BV3797	252.3
Evangelistic work	BV3750-3799	269.2
Evangelists	BV3780-3785	269.2092
Evaporation	QC304	536.44
Evaporation (Meteorology)	QC915-917	551.572
Evapotranspiration	QC915.5-.7	551.572
Evapotranspiration	QK873	575.8
Even language	PL481.E92	494.1
Evening and continuation schools	LC5501-5560	374.8
Evenki language	PL451-459	494.1
Event horses	SF295.7	636.10811
Evergreens	SB435	635.9775
Everlasting flowers	SB447	635.973
Everlasting flowers	SB428.5	635.973
Evidence	BC171-173	121.65
Evidence (Law)—United States	KF8931-8969	347.7306
Evidence, Criminal	K5465-5490	345.06
Evidence, Criminal—United States	KF9660-9678	345.7306
Evil eye	BF1553	133.425
Evil eye	GN475.6	133.425

Subject Heading	LC	Dewey
Evil, Non-resistance to	BR115.W2	241.3
Evolution	B818	146.7
Evolution (Biology)	QH359-425	576.8
Evolution—Religious aspects	BL263	213
Ewe language	PL8161-8164	496.3374
Ex-monks	BX4668.2-.3	255.(1-7)
Ex-smokers	HV5725-5770	362.296
Examinations	LC1070-1071	378.013076
Examinations	LB2366-2367	378.241
Examinations	LB1762-1765	370.711
Examinations	LB3050-3060	371.271
Examinations—Design and construction	LB3060.65	371.27
Examinations—Questions	LB3051-3059	371.271
Examinations—Scoring	LB3060.77	371.27
Examinations—Study guides	LB3060.57	371.27
Exanthemata	RC106	616.91
Excavation	TH5101	624.152
Excavation	TA730-748	624.152
Excavations (Archaeology)	CC165	930.10283
Excavations (Archaeology)	CC75	930.10283
Excess profits tax	HJ4653.E8	336.24320973
Excise tax	HJ5730-5731	336.271
Excise tax—Law and legislation	K4572-4580	343.0553
Excision of ankle	RD562	617.584059
Exciton theory	QC176.8.E9	530.416
Excretion	QP159	612.46
Excretion	QP211	612.46
Excretory organs	QL872-875	573.49
Execution sermons	BV4262	252.68
Executions and executioners	HV8551-8586	364.66
Executive ability	HD38.2-.25	658.409
Executive departments—Canada	JL87-111	347.71
Executive departments—Confederate States of America	JK9717-9719	351.75
Executive departments—United States	KF5050-5125	342.7306
Executive power	K3332-3351	342.062
Executive power	JF251-289	352.235
Exercise	GV460-548	613.71
Exercise	QP301-336	613.71
Exercise	RA781-.85	613.71
Exercise—Physiological aspects	QP301-310	612.044
Exercise for men	GV482.5	613.71081
Exercise therapy	RM725-727	615.82
Exercise therapy for children	RJ53.E95	618.920062
Exercise therapy for the aged	RC953.8.E93	615.820846
Exgot alkaloids	RS431.E73	615.321
Exhibition buildings	NA6750-6751	725.91
Exhibitions	T391-999	607.34
Exhibitions—Czechoslovakia	DB2001-2002	943.70074
Existential ethics	BJ1340	171.2
Existential phenomenology	B818.5	142.78
Existential psychology	BF204.5	150.192
Existential psychotherapy	RC489.E93	616.8914

Subject Heading	LC	Dewey	Subject Heading	LC	Dewey
Existentialism	B819	142.78	Extortion	HV6688	364.165
Exocrine glands	QP187.7	612.4	Extraction (Chemistry)	TP156.E8	660.284248
Exorcism	BX2340	264.02094	Extradition	JF781	345.052
Exorcism	BF1559	133.427	Extradition—United States	KF9635	345.73052
Exorcism	BV873.E8	265.94	Extrasensory perception in animals	QL785.3	591.5
Exorcism	GR540	398.45			
Expansion (Heat)	QC281.5.E9	536.41	Extreme unction	BX2290	264.0207
Expansion of gases	QC164	536.412	Extremities (Anatomy)	QM548-549	611.9(7-8)
Expansive concrete	TA439	620.136	Extremities (Anatomy)— Abnormalities	RD775-789	616.71043
Expectorants	RM390	615.72			
Expedition antarctique belge, 1897-1899	G850	919.890409034	Extremities (Anatomy)— Diseases	RC951	617.58
Expedition of the Thousand, Italy, 1860	DG554.5.E96	945.083	Extremities (Anatomy)— Fractures	RD551-563	617.158
Expenditures, Public— [By region or country]	HJ7537-7977	336.3909(4-9)	Extremities (Anatomy)— Surgery	RD551-563	617.58059
Expenditures, Public— United States	HJ7537-7654	336.390973	Extremities (Anatomy)— Transplantation	RD551-563	617.580592
Expenditures, Public— [Other regions or countries]	HJ7663-7977	336.3909(4-9)	Extremities (Anatomy)— Wounds and injuries	RD551-563	617.58044
Experience (Religion)	BR110	248.2	Exultets (Liturgy)	BX2045.E96	264.02
Experience (Religion)	BV4912-4915	248.2	Eye	QP475-495	612.84
Experience (Religion)	BL53	291.42	Eye	QM511	611.84
Experiential research	BF76.6.E94	150.724	Eye	QL949	573.88
Experimental immunology	QR180-183.5	571.960724	Eye—Abnormalities	RE906	617.7043
Experimental Volunteer Army Training Progam	U408.3	355.50973	Eye—Accommodation and refraction	RE925-939	617.755
Expert systems (Computer science)	QA76.76.E95	006.33	Eye—Diseases—Eclectic treatment	RV321-331	617.706
Exploding wire phenomena	QC703.7	537.5	Eye—Diseases— Homeopathic treatment	RX410-431	617.706
Exploratory fishing	SH343.5	639.2072	Eye—Examination	RE75-79	617.7075
Explosions	QD516	541.361	Eye—Foreign bodies	RE835	617.74
Explosives	TP267.5-301	662.2	Eye—Infections	RE96	617.74
Explosives—Safety measures	TP297	662.20289	Eye—Inflammation	RE96	617.74
			Eye—Movement disorders	RE731-780	617.762
Explosives—Transportation	HE2321.E8	385.24	Eye—Movements	QP477.5	612.846
Explosives, Military	TP268-299	623.452	Eye—Muscles	RE731-780	617.762
Export controls	HF1414.5-.55	382.64	Eye—Paralysis	RE760	617.762
Export credit	HG3753-3754	332.742	Eye—Radiography	RE79.R3	617.707572
Export subsidies	HF2701	382.63	Eye—Refractive errors	RE925-939	617.755
Exports	HF1414.4-1417.3	382.6	Eye—Surgery	RE80-87	617.7059
Exposition (Rhetoric)	PN205	808.066	Eye—Wounds and injuries	RE831-840	617.713
Express service	HE5880-5990	388.044	Eye banks	RE89	362.1783
Express service—[By region or country]	HE5893-5990	388.04409(4-9)	Eye-sockets	GN131	599.948
			Eye-sockets—Diseases	RE711	617.78
Express service—United States	HE5893-5904.5	388.0440973	Eyeglasses	GT2370	391.44
			Eyeglasses	RE940-981	617.7522
Express service—[Other regions and countries]	HE5905-5990	388.04409(4-9)	Eyelashes	QM488	611.78
			Eyelids	QM511	611.84
Expressionism (Art)	ND1265	709.04042	Eyelids	QL949	573.88
Extemporaneous preaching	BV4235.E8	251	Eyelids—Diseases	RE121-155	617.771
Exterior lighting	TK4188	621.3229	Eyes, Artificial	RE986-988	617.79
Exterior walls	TH2235-2238.7	690.12	Eyestrain	RE51	617.75
External skeletal fixation (Surgery)	RD103.E88	617.471059	Eyestrain	RE48	617.755
			F region	QC879	551.5145
Extinct animals	QL88-.15	560	Faba bean	SB205.F3	633.3
Extinct birds	QL676.8	597.168	Facades	NA2840-2841	729.1
Extinct mammals	QL707	569	Face	NC770	743.42
Extinction (Biology)	QE721.2.E97	576.84	Face	QM535	611.92
Extinction (Biology)	QH78	576.84	Face—Surgery	RD523-527	617.52059

Subject Heading	LC	Dewey
Face—Wounds and injuries	RD523	617.52044
Facelift	RD119.5.F33	617.520592
Facing heads (Numismatics)	CJ161.F3	737.4
Facsimile transmission	TK6710-7620	621.38235
Factor analysis	QA278.5	519.5354
Factor tables	QA51	513.23021
Factories	HD7406-7510	338.4767
Factories	NA6396-6589	725.4
Factories	TH4511-4591	690.54
Factories—Air conditioning	TH7684.F2-.F3	697.9354
Factories—Design and construction	TH4511-4591	690.54
Factories—Soundproofing	TH1725	693.834
Factors (Algebra)	QA161.F3	512.923
Factors (Algebra)	QA242	512.923
Factory and trade waste	TD896-899	628.51
Factory inspection	HD3656-3790.9	658.568
Factory inspection—[By region or country]	HD3661-3790.9	658.56809(4-9)
Factory management	TS155-194	658.5
Factory sanitation	TD895	628.51
Factory system	HD2350.8-2356	338.65
Faculty advisors	LB2343	378.194
Fafnir (Germanic mythology)	BL870.F28	293.13
Failure to thrive syndrome	RJ135	618.92
Fairies	GR549-552	398.45
Fairies	BF1552	398.21
Fairness doctrine (Broadcasting)	HE8689.7.F34	384.54
Fairs	HF5469.7-5481	381.18
Fairs	GT4580-4699	394.6
Fairs	HF5481	381.18
Fairy tales	GR550-552	398.2
Fairy tales	PZ8	398.2
Faith	BV4637	241.4
Faith	BT770-772	234.23
Faith (Islam)	BP166.78	297.22
Faith (Judaism)	BM729.F3	296.32
Falconry	SK321	799.232
Falcons	QL696.F34	598.96
Falkland Islands—Census	HA2295	319.71
Falkland Islands—Maps	G9175-9179	912.9711
Falkland Islands—Politics and government	JL690-699	320.99711
Falkland Islands, Battle of the, 1914	D582.F2	940.423
Fall of man	BT710	233.14
Fallacies (Logic)	BC175	165
Fallopian tubes	QM421	611.65
Fallopian tubes—Diseases	RG421-433	618.12
Falls Fight, 1676	E83.67	973.24
Familial behavior in animals	QL761.5	591.563
Family	GT2420	392
Family	HQ503-1064	306.8
Family	GN480-.65	306.85
Family—Biblical teaching	BS680.F3	220.830685
Family—Health and hygiene	RA418.5.F3	613.04
Family—Religious life	BV200	249
Family demography	HQ759.98	304.634
Family in dreams	BF1099.F34	154.63
Family-owned business enterprises	HD62.25	338.7
Family psychotherapy	RC488.5-.6	616.89156
Family recreation	GV182.8	790.191
Family size	HQ760-767.7	304.634
Family size—[By region or country]	HQ762	304.63409(1-9)
Family violence	HV6626-.23	364.1555(3-4)
Family violence	RC569.5.F3	616.85822
Famine compact, 1765	HC275	330.944
Famines	HC79.F3	363.8
Famines	HV630-635	363.8
Famines in the Bible	BS680.F32	220.83638
Fanaticism	BR114	248.2
Fanconi's anemia	RC641.7.F36	616.152
Fancy work	TT740-897	746.4
Fang language	PL8167.F3	496.396
Fans	GT2150	391.44
Fans	NK4870	745.594
Fans (Machinery) industry	HD9705.5.F35-.F354	338.4762161
Fantasy in children	BF723.F28	155.41332
Fantasy in mass media	P96.F36	154.3
Fanti language	PL8167.F4	496.3385
Far ultraviolet radiation	QC459.5	535.014
Farce	PN1940-1949	808.825232
Farces	PN6120.F3	808.825232
Farm buildings	NA8200-8260	728.92
Farm buildings	TH4911-4935	690.892
Farm equipment	S671-760	631.3
Farm life	HT421	305.555
Farm life	S521	390.463
Farm management	S560-572	630.68
Farm manure	S655	631.861
Farm produce	HD9000-9019	338.17
Farm produce—Marketing	HD9000-9019	380.141
Farm produce—Marketing	S571-.5	380.141
Farm tractors	S711-713	631.372
Farm tractors	TL233-.8	629.2252
Farm trucks	S711-713	631.373
Farmer's lung	RC776.F33	616.24
Farmhouses	NA8208-8210	728.6
Farmhouses	TH4920	690.86
Farms	HD1401-2210	338.16
Farms	HD1471	338.16
Farms	S560-575	630
Farms, Size of	HD1470-1476	338.16
Farms—Valuation	HD1393	333.76
Faroese language	PD2483	439.699
Fasciae (Anatomy)	QM563	611.74
Fascism	JC481	320.533
Fascism	DG571	945.091
Fashion	GT500-2370	391
Fashion drawing	TT509	741.672
Fashion merchandising	HD9940-9949.5	380.145391
Fashoda Crisis, 1898	DT156.6	962.403
Fast draw pistol shooting	GV1175.5	799.31
Fast-day sermons	BV4270	252.6
Fasteners	TJ1320-1340	621.88
Fasting	BV5055	248.47
Fasting	RM226-228	613.25

Subject Heading	LC	Dewey	Subject Heading	LC	Dewey
Fasting (Hinduism)	BL1215.F3	294.5447	Feminist theology	BT83.55	230.082
Fasting (Islam)	BP179	297.53	Feminist theory	HQ1190	305.42
Fastnet Yacht Race	GV832	797.14091631	Femur	QM117	611.718
Fasts and feasts	GT3920-4995	394.2	Fencers	GV1144-.2	796.86092
Fasts and feasts	CE81	263.9	Fences	NA8390-8392	631.27
Fasts and feasts	BL590	291.(447/36)	Fences	S790-.3	631.27
Fasts and feasts	BV30-135	263.9	Fencing	GV1143-1150.6	796.86
Fasts and feasts—Buddhism	BQ5700-5720	294.3438	Feng-shui	BF1779.F4	133.3337
Fasts and feasts—Hinduism	BL1239.72-.82	294.538	Fenians	DA954	941.7081
Fasts and feasts—Islam	BP186	297.53	Feral children	GN372	155.4567
Fasts and feasts—Jainism	BL1355.5	294.438	Feral children	RJ507.F47	155.4567
Fasts and feasts—Judaism	BM690-720	296.43	Fermat's theorem	QA244	512.74
Fasts and feasts—Samaritan religion	BM970	296.43	Fermented foods	TP371.44	664.024
Fatherhood	HQ756-.7	306.8742	Fermions	QC793.5.F42-.F429	539.721
Fathers	HQ756-.7	306.8742	Ferns, Ornamental	SB429	635.9373
Fathers of the church	BR60-67	270.092	Ferreting	SK293	799.23
Fathers of the church	BR1705	270.092	Ferries	HE5751-5870	386.6
Fatigue	BF482	152.1886	Ferroelectric devices	TK7872.F44	537.2448
Fatigue	QP321	612.744	Ferroelectricity	QC596-.9	537.2448
Fatigue	T57.72	658.544	Fertility, Human	HB901-1108	304.632
Fatigue testing machines	TA413-.5	620.11260287	Fertility, Human—[By region or country]	HB901-1108	304.63209(1-9)
Fatty acids	QP752.F35	572.57	Fertility, Human—Developing countries	HB1108	304.632091724
Fatty acids in human nutrition	QP752.F35	572.57	Fertilization (Biology)	QH485	571.864
Faults (Geology)	QE606-.5	551.872	Fertilization in vitro, Human	RG135	618.178059
Fear	BF575.F2	152.46	Fertilization of plants	QK828	571.8642
Fear in children	BF723.F4	155.412	Fertilization of plants by insects	QK926	571.8642
Feast of Jesus Christ the King	BV64.J4	263.97	Fertilizers	S631-667	631.8
Feast of the Assumption of the Blessed Virgin	BV50.A7	263.97	Fescue	QK495.G74	584.9
Feast of the Holy Innocents	BV50.H6	263.97	Festival-day sermons	BV4254.3	252.6
Feast of the Immaculate Conception	BV50.I6	263.97	Festivals	GT3930-4995	394.26
Feast of the Sacred Heart	BV64.S3	263.97	Fetal death	RG631-633	618.32
Feathers	QL697	598.147	Fetal growth disorders	RG629.G75	618.32
Feathers as feed	SF99.F37	636.0855	Fetal growth retardation	RG629.G76	618.32
Febrile convulsions	RJ496.C7	618.92845	Fetal heart rate monitoring	RG628.3.H42	618.3261075
Fecal incontinence	RC866.D43	616.342	Fetal heart—Abnormalities	RJ269	618.3261043
Fecal incontinence in children	RJ456.F43	618.92342	Fetal malnutrition	RG627.6.M34	618.32
Federal Reserve banks	HG2559-2565	332.110973	Fetal monitoring	RG628-.3	618.32075
Federal aid to education	LB2825-2826.6	379.121	Fetal presentation	RG671-693	618.42
Federal government	K3285	321.02	Fetishism	GN472	291.21
Federal government	JC355	321.02	Fetishism (Sexual behavior)	HQ79	306.77
Federal government—United States	KF4600-4629	342.73042	Fetterman Fight, Wyo., 1866	F761	978.701
Feed additives	SF98.A2	636.08557	Fetus	RG600-650	618.32
Feed mills	TS2158	664.76	Fetus—Abnormalities	RG626-629	618.32043
Feedback control systems	TJ216	629.83	Fetus—Diseases	RG626-629	618.32
Feedback oscillators	TK7872.O7	621.381533	Fetus—Effect of drugs on	RG627.6.D79	618.32
Feedlot runoff	TD930.2	628.16846	Fetus—Growth	RG613	612.647
Feeds	SF94.5-99	636.0855	Fetus—Immunology	RG613.7	618.32
Feeds—Fiber content	SF98.F	636.0855	Fetus—Metabolism	RG615	618.326
Feeds—Flavor and odor	SF97.7	636.0855	Fetus—Physiology	RG610-621	612.647
Fehmarn, Battle of, 1644	DL190	948.9701	Fetus—Respiration and cry	RG620	618.4
Fehrbellin, Battle of, 1675	DD394.3	943.044	Fetus—Ultrasonic imaging	RG628.3.U58	618.3207543
Feldspar	QE391.F3	549.68	Feudal law—England	KD834-839	340.550942
Felt	TS1825	677.6(2/3)	Feudalism	D131	321.3
			Feudalism	JC109-121	321.3
			Fever	RB129	616.047
			Fever therapy	RM868-.5	615.8325
			Fever—Eclectic treatment	RV211	616.04706

Subject Heading	LC	Dewey	Subject Heading	LC	Dewey
Fever—Homeopathic treatment	RX211	616.04706	Finance—History	HG171	332.09
			Finance—Periodicals	HG1-61	332.05
Fever therapy	RM868-.5	615.8325	Finance—Statistics	HG176-.5	332.021
Few-body problem	QB362.F47	521.4	Finance—Study and teaching	HG152-.5	332.071
Few-body problem	QC174.17.P7	530.14			
Fiber in animal nutrition	SF98.F	636.0852	Finance, Personal	HG179	332.024
Fiber in human nutrition	TX553.F53	613.263	Finance, Public	HJ	336
Fiber optics	QC447.9-448.2	621.3692	Finance, Public—Accounting	HJ9701-9995	657.61
Fiber plants	SB241-261	633.5	Finance, Public—Auditing—Law and legislation	KF6231-6239	343.73034
Fiberglass craft	NB1270.G5	731.2			
Fibrin	QP91	612.115			
Fibromyalgia	RC927.3	616.723	Finance, Public—History	HJ210-240	336.09(4-9)
Fibrous dysplasia of bone	RC931.F5	616.71	Finance, Public—Law and legislation	K4430-4675	343.03
Fibula (Archaeology)	CC400	611.718			
Fiction	PN3311-3503	808.3	Finance, Public—Law and legislation—Canada	KE5600-6328	343.7103
Fiction—History and criticism	PN3329-3503	809.3			
			Finance, Public—Law and legislation—England	KD5280-5752	343.4203
Fiction—Technique	PN3355-3383	808.3			
Fictions, Theory of	BC199.F5	165	Finance, Public—Law and legislation—Ireland	KDK1430-1526	343.41503
Fictions, Theory of	BL51	210			
Field theory (Physics)	QC173.68-.75	530.14	Finance, Public—Law and legislation—Scotland	KDC807-825	343.41103
Fielding (Baseball)	GV870	796.35724			
Fife	MT356	788.3307	Finance, Public—Law and legislation—United States	KF6200-6795	343.7303
Fife music	M60-62	788.33			
Fifth Monarchy Men	DA420-429	941.063			
Fifth generation computers	QA76.85	004.1	Finance, Public—Periodicals	HJ9-99.8	336.005
Fig	QK495.M73	583.45	Finance, Public—United States	HJ241-785	336.73
Fig	SB365	634.37			
Fighter pilots	UG626-.2	358.43092	Finance, Public—[United States, By state]	HJ285-785	336.7(4-9)
Fighter plane combat	UG700-705	358.434			
Fighter planes	TL685.3	358.4383	Financial crises	HB3722-3725	338.542
Fighter planes	UG1242.F5	358.4383	Financial futures	HG6024.3-.9	332.645
Figure drawing	NC765-778	743.4	Financial institutions	HG1-9999	332
Figure painting	ND2190-2192	751.42242	Financial planners	HG179.5	332.024092
Figure painting	ND1290-1293	757	Financial statements	HF5681.B2	657.3
Figure sculpture	NB1930-1936	731.82	Financial statements, Unaudited	HF5667.65	657.3
Figureheads of ships	VM308	623.84			
Fiji	DU600	996.11	Fines (Penalties)	HV9277	364.68
Fiji—Census	HA4016	319.611	Finger spelling	HV2477-2480	419
Fiji—Maps	G9380-9384	912.9611	Fingerprints	HV6074	363.24
Fijian language	PL6235	499.5	Fingerprints	GN192	599.945
Filariasis	RC142.5	616.9652	Fingers	QM548	611.97
Filariasis	RA644.F5	614.5552	Finish carpentry	TH5640-5695	694.6
File organization (Computer science)	QA76.9.F5	005.741	Finishes and finishing	TP934-945	677.02825
			Finite element method	TA347.F5	620.00151535
File processing (Computer science)	QA76.9.F53	005.74	Finite, The	BD411	111.6
			Finland	DL1002-1180	948.97
Fili (Irish poets)	PB1321	891.621009	Finland—Biography	DL1024	920.04897
Filibusters (Political science)	JF519	328.34	Finland—Census	HA1450.5	314.897
			Finland—Civilization	DL1017	948.97
Filing systems	HF5735-5746	651	Finland—Congresses	DL1004	948.97006
Filipino Americans	E184.F4	973.049921073	Finland—Description and travel	DL1015-.4	914.89704
Fillings (Dentistry)	RK517-519	617.675			
Filmstrips in education	LB1043.8	371.3352	Finland—Gazetteers	DL1007	914.897003
Filters and filtration	QD63.F5	542.6	Finland—Historiography	DL1025	948.970072
Filters and filtration	TD441-449	628.164	Finland—History—To 1523	DL1050-1052.9	948.9701
Filters and filtration	TP156.F5	660.284245	Finland—History—1523-1611	DL1055-1141.6	948.9701
Finance	HG	332			
Finance—Congresses	HG63	332.06	Finland—History—Gustavus II Adolphus, 1611-1632	DL1058-1063	948.9701
Finance—Directories	HG64-96	332.025			
Finance—Encyclopedias	HG151	332.03			

Subject Heading	LC	Dewey	Subject Heading	LC	Dewey
Finland—History—Charles X Gustavus, 1654-1660	DL1060-.5	948.9701	Fire lookout stations	SD421.375	634.93
			Fire prevention	TH9111-9599	693.82
Finland—History—18th century	DL1063-.9	948.9701	Fire prevention—Law and legislation—United States	KF3975-3977	344.7305377
Finland—History—1809-1917	DL1065-.8	948.9702	Fire prevention—Research	TH9120	628.922072
			Fire resistant materials	TH1065	693.82
Finland—History—20th century	DL1066-1141.6	948.970(2-3)	Fire sprinklers	TH9336	628.9252
			Fire-worshipers	BL453	291.212
Finland—History—Revolution, 1917-1918	DL1070-1075	948.97031	Firearms	UD380-415	356.1182
			Firearms	VD360-390	359.824
Finland—History—1918-1939	DL1084	948.97031	Firearms	TS532-537.5	683.4
			Firearms—Identification	HV8077	363.2565
Finland—History—1939-	DL1090-1105	948.9703(2-4)	Firearms—Sights	UD390	356.1182
Finland—Manufactures	TS95.F5	670.94897	Firearms—Sights	UF854	623.46
Finland—Maps	G6960-6964	912.4897	Firearms industry and trade	HD9744.F55-.F554	338.476834
Finland—Maps	G2075-2079	912.4897	Firearms ownership	HV8059	683.4
Finland—Periodicals	DL1002	948.97005	Fireboats	TH9391	628.9259
Finland—Politics and government	JN7390-7399	320.94897	Firecrackers	TP300-301	662.1
Finnic languages	PH91-98	494.54	Firedamp	TN305-306	622.82
Finnish Americans	E184.F5	973.0494541073	Fireplaces	NA3050-3055	721.8
Finnish language	PH101-293	494.541	Fireplaces	TH7421-7434.7	697.1
Finnish language—Grammar	PH131-225	494.5415	Fireproofing	TH1061-1093	693.82
			Fires	HV620	363.37
Finnish literature	PH300-405	894.54109	Fires	TH9448-9449	628.92
Finnish philology	PH101-123	494.541	Fires—Casualties	RA1085	617.11
Finno-Ugric essays	AC80-85	089.945	Fireworks	TP300-301	662.1
Finno-Ugric languages	PH	494.5	First aid for animals	SF914.3	636.08960252
Finno-Ugric languages—Grammar	PH21-41	494.55	First aid in illness and injury	RC86-88.9	616.0252
Finno-Ugric languages—Study and teaching	PH11	494.5071	First-born children	HQ777.2	306.87
			First communion	BX2237	264.02036
Finno-Ugric philology	PH1-11	494.5	First day covers (Philately)	HE6184.F57	769.56
Fins	QL639	597.1479	First of June, 1794, Battle of	DA87.5 1794	941.073
Finsler spaces	QA689	516.375			
Fir	QK494.5.P66	585.2	Fish as food	TX385	641.392
Fir	SD397.F5	634.9754	Fish-culture	SH151-179	639.3
Fire	TP265-267	660.2961	Fish culturists	SH20	639.2092
Fire alarms	TH9271-9275	628.9225	Fish decoys	SH451.3	799.10284
Fire ants	QL568.F7	595.796	Fish habitat improvement	SH157.8-.85	639.92
Fire-clay	TN941-943	622.367	Fish inspection	SH335	363.1929064
Fire-clay	TA455.F5	620.143	Fish kills	SH171-179	639.96
Fire control (Gunnery)	UF848-856	623.558	Fish meal as feed	SF99.F5	636.0855
Fire control (Gunnery)—Optical equipment	UF849	623.5580284	Fish oils	TP676	665.2
			Fish populations	QL618.3	597.1788
Fire control (Naval gunnery)	VF520-530	359.422	Fish traps	SH344.6.T67	639.20284
Fire detectors	TH9271	628.9225	Fisheries	SH	639.2
Fire doors	TH2278	690.1822	Fisheries—Congresses	SH3	639.206
Fire engines	TH9371-9377	628.9259	Fisheries—Equipment and supplies	SH344-.8	639.20284
Fire-escapes	TH2274	628.922			
Fire extinction	TH9111-9599	628.925	Fisheries—History	SH211	639.209
Fire extinction—Chemical systems	TH9338	628.9254	Fisheries—Periodicals	SH1	639.305
			Fisheries—Safety measures	SH343.9	639.20289
Fire extinction—Water-supply	TH9311-9334	628.9252	Fisheries—Asia	SH295-307	639.2095
			Fisheries—Atlantic Ocean	SH213-.77	639.209163
Fire extinguishers	TH9362	628.9254	Fisheries—Australia	SH317-318	639.20994
Fire fighters—Physical training	TH9128	363.37092	Fisheries—Canada	SH223-229	639.20971
			Fisheries—Central America	SH232	639.209728
Fire insurance claims adjusters	HG9711-9715	368.11014	Fisheries—China	SH297-298	639.20951
			Fisheries—Denmark	SH267-268	639.209489

Subject Heading	LC	Dewey	Subject Heading	LC	Dewey
Fisheries—Europe	SH253-293	639.2094	Fishhooks	SH452.9.H	799.10284
Fisheries—Great Britain	SH255-260	639.20941	Fishhooks	SH344.8.H6	639.20284
Fisheries—Greece	SH273-274	639.209495	Fishing	GT5904-5905	394.3
Fisheries—Greenland	SH268.G83	639.209982	Fishing	SH401-691	799.12
Fisheries—Indian Ocean	SH216-.55	639.209165	Fishing—Equipment and supplies	SH447-453	799.10284
Fisheries—Ireland	SH261-262	639.209415	Fishing—History	SH421	799.109
Fisheries—Italy	SH277-278	639.20945	Fishing—Periodicals	SH401	799.1205
Fisheries—Japan	SH301-302	639.20952	Fishing—Canada	SH571-572	799.10971
Fisheries—Korea	SH302.5-.7	639.209519	Fishing—North America	SH462	799.1097
Fisheries—Mexico	SH231	639.20972	Fishing—United States	SH463-565	799.10973
Fisheries—Netherlands	SH275-276	639.209492	Fishing—West Indies	SH577-578	799.1209729
Fisheries—New Zealand	SH318.5	639.20993	Fishing knots	SH452.9.K6	799.1028
Fisheries—Norway	SH279-280	639.209481	Fishing nets	SH344.8.N4	639.20284
Fisheries—Oceania	SH319	639.2099(5-6)	Fishing ports	SH337.5	387.1
Fisheries—Pacific Ocean	SH214-215	639.209164	Fishing rods	SH452-.2	799.10284
Fisheries—Portugal	SH281-282	639.209469	Fishing tackle	SH447-453	799.10284
Fisheries—Russia	SH283-284	639.20947	Fishways	SH153	639.92
Fisheries—South America	SH234-251	639.2098	Five Civilized Tribes	E78.I5	973.0497(3/55)
Fisheries—Spain	SH285-286	639.20946	Five Civilized Tribes	E78.045	973.0497(3/55)
Fisheries—Sweden	SH287-288	639.209485	Five Precepts (Buddhism)	BQ5485-5525	294.342
Fisheries—Turkey	SH291-292	639.209561	Fjords	GB454.F5	551.44
Fisheries—United States	SH221-222	639.20973	Flag Day	JK1761	394.26973
Fisheries—United States	SH11	639.20973	Flagella (Microbiology)	QR78	571.672
Fisheries—West Indies	SH233	639.209729	Flagellata	QL368.F5	579.82
Fisheries navigation	SH343.8	623.89	Flagellation	HV8613-8621	364.67
Fisheries subsidies	SH334	338.3727	Flags	CR101-115	929.92
Fishers	HD8039.F65	639.2092	Flags	UC590-595	355.15
Fishers	SH414-415	799.1092	Flags	V300-305	359.15
Fishery conservation	SH327.7	639.977	Flags—United States	V303-304	359.150973
Fishery law and legislation—Canada	KE1760-1765	343.7107692	Flags—[Other countries]	V305	359.1509(4-9)
Fishery law and legislation—England	KD2310-2315	343.4207692	Flame	QD516	541.361
			Flaps (Airplanes)	TL673.F6	629.13433
Fishery law and legislation—United States	KF1770-1773	343.7307692	Flat roofs	TH2409	690.15
			Flax	TS1700-1735	677.11
			Flea markets	HF5482.15	381.192
Fishery management	SH328-329	639.2068	Fleet ballistic missile weapons systems	V990-995	359.981782
Fishery processing	SH334.9-336.5	664.94	Flemish drama	PT6350-6360	839.312008
Fishery products—Preservation	SH335-337	664.94(1-8)	Flemish literature	PT6000-6466.36	839.31
Fishery products—Preservation	TX612.F5	641.494	Flemish literature—Study and teaching	PT6040	839.31071
Fishery research stations	SH332-.2	639.2072	Flemish poetry	PT6140	839.311009
Fishery research vessels	SH343.4	338.372072	Flemish poetry	PT6330-6348	839.311008
Fishery resources	SH327.5	333.7	Flemish prose literature	PT6365-6397	839.31808
Fishery schools	SH332-.2	639.2071	Fleurus, Battle of, 1794	DC222.F6	940.27
Fishery technology	SH334.5-344.8	639.2028	Flexible weapons (Hand-to-hand fighting)	U167.5.H3	355.824
Fishes	QL614-639.8	597	Flexure	TG265	624.252
Fishes—Classification	QL618	597.012	Flight	TL570-578	629.132
Fishes—Diseases	SH171-179	639.964	Flight	TL570-578	629.13
Fishes—Folklore	GR745	398.3697	Flight training	TL712-.8	629.1325071
Fishes—Genetics	QL638.99	597.135	Flights around the world	G445	910.41
Fishes—Geographical distribution	QL619-637	597.09(4-9)	Floating batteries	V890	359.32
Fishes—Infections	SH171-179	639.964	Floating bodies	QA907	532.25
Fishes—Locomotion	QL639.4	597.1479	Floating bodies	QC147	532.25
Fishes—Migration	QL639.5	597.1568	Floating harbors	TC363	623.83
Fishes—Parasites	SH175	639.96	Flodden, Battle of, 1513	DA784.6	941.104
Fishes—Pathogens	SH171-179	639.964	Flood dams and reservoirs	TC167	627.4
Fishes—Research	QL618.5-.55	597.072	Flood dams and reservoirs	TC540-558	627.8
Fishes—Spawning	QL639.2	597.562	Flood forecasting	GB1399.2	551.4890112

Subject Heading	LC	Dewey	Subject Heading	LC	Dewey
Flood routing	GB1203	551.489	Fluidization	TP156.F65	660.284292
Floodplains	GB561-568	551.442	Fluidized-bed furnaces	TH7140	697.07
Floods	GB1399-.5	551.489	Fluids	QA901-930	532
Floods	HV609-610	363.34938	Fluids	QC138-168.86	532
Floods	SD425	634.9617	Flumes	TC933	627.52
Floor traders (Finance)	HG4621	332.642	Fluorescence	QC477-.4	535.352
Flooring	TH2521-2529	690.16	Fluorescent lamps	TK4386	621.3273
Floors	NA2970	721.6	Fluorine	QD181.F1	546.731
Floriculture	SB403-450.87	635.9	Fluorine	TP245.F6	661.0731
Florida—Gazetteers	F309	917.59003	Flute	MT340-348	788.307
Florida—History	F306-320	975.9	Flute music	M60-64	788.3
Florida—History—To 1565	F314	975.901	Flutter (Aerodynamics)	TL574.F6	629.132362
Florida—History—To 1821	F314	975.90(1-3)	Fly casting	SH454.2	799.124
Florida—History—Huguenot colony, 1562-1565	F314	975.901	Fly fishing	SH456-.2	799.124
			Flying-machines	TL670-724	629.13334
			Foals	SF277-359.7	636.101
Florida—History—Spanish colony, 1565-1763	F314	975.901	Focal infection, Dental	RK305	617.63
			Focal infection, Dental	RK351	617.63
Florida—History—English colony, 1763-1784	F314	975.90(2-3)	Focused group interviewing	H61.28	361.322
			Fog	QC929.F7	551.575
Florida—History—Spanish colony, 1784-1821	F314	975.903	Fog—Control	TL557.F6	629.1324
			Folds (Geology)	QE606-.5	551.875
Florida—History—Cession to the United States, 1819	F314	975.903	Foliage plants	SB431	635.975
			Foliations (Mathematics)	QA613.62	514.72
			Folk art	N5312-5313	745
Florida—History—1821-1865	F315	975.90(4-5)	Folk dancing	GV1580-1799	793.31
			Folk literature	GR72-390	398.2
Florida—History—Civil War, 1861-1865	E558.1-.9	975.905	Folk literature—History and criticism	PN905-1008	398.209
Florida—History—1865-	F316-.23	975.906	Folk literature, Afrikaans	PT6540-6545	398.2043936
Florida—History—1951-	F316.2-.23	975.906(3-4)	Folk literature, American	PS451-478	398.20973
Florida—Maps	G3930-3934	912.759	Folk literature, Arabic	PJ7580	398.204927
Florida—National Guard	UA140-149	355.3709759	Folk literature, Arabic	PJ7680	398.204927
Florida—Periodicals	F306	975.9005	Folk literature, Chinese	PL2445-2446	398.204951
Florists	SB442.8-445	380.14159	Folk literature, Danish	PT7900-7930	398.2043981
Flossenburg (Germany : Concentration camp)	D805.G3	940.5318	Folk literature, Dutch	PT5351-5395	398.2043931
			Folk literature, English	PR951-981	398.2042
Flour	TX393	641.331	Folk literature, Flemish	PT6200-6230	398.2043931
Flour	TS2120-2159	664.7207	Folk literature, French	PQ781-841	398.20441
Flour-mills	TS2120-2159	664.7207	Folk literature, German	PT881-951	398.20431
Flow meters	TC177	532.510284	Folk literature, Greek	PA3285	398.2048
Flower arrangement	SB449-450.87	745.92	Folk literature, Hebrew	PJ5048	398.204924
Flower gardening	SB403-450.87	635.9	Folk literature, Icelandic	PT7420-7438	398.20439691
Flower language	GR780-790	302.222	Folk literature, Italian	PQ4186-4199	398.20451
Flower shows	SB441-.75	635.9074	Folk literature, Japanese	PL748-749	398.204956
Flowering woody plants	SB435-437	635.97713	Folk literature, Korean	PL968.2-.4	398.204957
Flowers	SB403-450	635.9	Folk literature, Low German	PT4829-4830	398.204394
Flowers	QK	582.13	Folk literature, Norwegian	PT8600-8635	398.2043982
Flowers in heraldry	CR41.F6	929.6	Folk literature, Persian	PK6426	398.2049155
Flowers—Anatomy	QK653-661	575.633	Folk literature, Portuguese	PQ9121-9128	398.20469
Flowers—Morphology	QK653-661	575.633	Folk literature, Scandinavian	PT7088-7089	398.204395
Flue gases	TD885	628.532	Folk literature, Spanish	PQ6155-6167	398.20461
Fluegelhorn	MT493	788.9707	Folk literature, Swedish	PT9509-9542	398.204397
Flues	TH2281-2288	697.8	Folk poetry	PN1341-1347	398.2
Fluid copying processes	Z48	686.4	Folk songs	M1627	782.42162
Fluid dynamic measurements	TA357.5.M43	620.10640287	Folklore	GR	398
			Folklore—[By region or country]	GR100-390	398.09(3-9)
Fluid dynamics	QA911-930	530.42	Folklore—Africa	GR350-360	398.096
Fluid dynamics	QC150-159	532.5	Folklore—Asia	GR265-345	398.095
Fluid dynamics	TA357-359	620.106	Folklore—Europe	GR135-263	398.094
Fluid therapy for children	RJ53.F5	618.9200653			

Subject Heading	LC	Dewey
Folklore—North America	GR101-118	398.097
Folklore—Performance	GR72.3	398
Folklore—South America	GR130-133	398.098
Folklore—[New Zealand/ Australia/Oceania]	GR365-385	398.099(3-6)
Folklorists	GR50	398.092
Fon dialect	PL8164.Z9	496.337
Fonts	NA5070	726.5291
Food	GN407-411.5	641.592
Food	TX341-641	641.3
Food—Bacteriology	QR115-129	664.001579
Food—Biotechnology	TP248.65.F66	664.024
Food—Caloric content	TX551	613.23
Food—Carbohydrate content	TX553.C28	613.283
Food—Cholesterol content	TX553.C43	613.284
Food—Drying	TX609	641.44
Food—Microbiology	QR115-129	664.001579
Food—Preservation	TX599-613	641.4
Food—Toxicology	RA1258-1260	615.954
Food additives	TX553.A3	641.3
Food adulteration and inspection	HD9000.9	363.192
Food adulteration and inspection	TX501-597	363.192064
Food allergy	RC596	616.975
Food allergy in children	RJ386.5	618.92975
Food allergy in infants	RJ386.5	618.92975
Food allergy—Diet therapy	RC588.D53	616.9750654
Food crops	SB175-177	635
Food habits	GT2850-2960	394.1
Food in the Koran	BP134.F58	297.12286413
Food law and legislation	K3626-3633	344.04232
Food law and legislation— Canada	KE1867-1906	344.7104232
Food law and legislation— England	KD2405-243	343.4207833847664
Food law and legislation— United States	KF1900-1944	344.7304232
Food of animal origin	GT2865-2866	394.12
Food of animal origin	TX743-759.5	641.36
Food preservatives	TX599-612	641.47
Food processor cookery	TX840.F6	641.589
Food relief	HV696.F6	363.883
Food service	TX901-946.5	658.383
Food service management	TX911.3.M27	658.383068
Food stamps	HV696.F6	363.882
Food supply	HD9000-9019	363.8
Food warmers	NK4695.F6	738.8
Foodborne diseases	RA601.5	614.5
Foot	QM549	611.98
Foot—Abnormalities	RD781-789	617.585043
Foot—Amputation	RD563	617.5850592
Foot—Diseases	RC951	617.585
Foot—Dislocation	RD781	617.585044
Foot—Examination	RD563	617.585075
Foot—Reimplantation	RD563	617.5850592
Foot—Surgery	RD563	617.585059
Foot—Wounds and injuries	RD563	617.585044
Foot washing (Rite)	BV873.F7	265.9
Football	GV937-960	796.332
Football—Defense	GV951.18	796.3322
Football—Offense	GV951.8	796.3322
Football—Rules	GV955	796.33202022
Football for children	GV959.55.C45	796.332083
Football players	GV939	796.332092
Footprints	HV8077.5.F6	363.2562
Forage plants	SB193-207	633.2
Forbes Expedition against Fort Duquesne, 1758	E199	973.26
Forbidden fruit	BS1237	222.11
Force and energy	QC72-73.8	531.6
Forcing (Model theory)	QA9.7	511.801
Forearm	QM548	611.97
Forecasting	CB158-161	003.2
Foreign exchange	HG3810-4000	332.45
Foreign exchange futures	HG3853	332.645
Foreign exchange— Encyclopedias	HG3810.5	332.4503
Foreign exchange—History	HG3811-3815	332.4509
Foreign exchange—Law and legislation—England	KD5288	343.42032
Foreign exchange—[By region or country]	HG3901-4000	332.4509(4-9)
Foreign films	PN1995.9.F67	791.43
Foreign trade promotion	HF1417.5	382
Forensic ballistics	HV8077	363.2562
Forensic pathology	RA1063.4	614.10973
Forensic psychiatry	RA1151-1152	614.1
Forest animals	QL112	591.73
Forest conservation	SD411-428	333.75/634.9
Forest ecology	QH541.5.F6	577.3
Forest ecology	QK938.F6	581.73
Forest fire detection	SD421	634.9618
Forest fires	SD420.5-421.5	634.9618
Forest fires—Prevention and control	SD421	634.9618
Forest genetics	SD399.5	634.956
Forest insects	SB761	634.96
Forest landscape design	SB475.9.F67	719.33
Forest machinery	SD388	634.90284
Forest plants	QK108-474.5	581.73
Forest plants	QK938.F6	581.73
Forest products	HD9750-9769	634.98
Forest protection	SD411-428	634.93
Forest reserves	SD426-428	333.75
Forest reserves— Recreational use	GV191.67.F6	333.784
Forest roads	TE229.5	625.709152
Forest thinning	SD396.5	634.953
Forestry schools and education	SD250-381.5	634.9071
Forests and forestry	SD	634.9
Forests and forestry— Research	SD356-.54	634.9072
Forests and forestry— Safety measures	SD411	634.93
Forests and forestry— Societies, etc.	SD1	634.906
Forests and forestry—[By region or country]	SD11-115	634.909(4-9)
Forests and forestry— United States	SD11-12	634.90973

Subject Heading	LC	Dewey	Subject Heading	LC	Dewey
Forests and forestry—[United States, By state]	SD12	634.9097(4-9)	France—Description and travel	DC21-29.3	913.6404/914.404
Forgery	HV6675-6685	364.163	France—Description and travel—1945-1974	DC29	914.4040904
Forgery	HG1696-1698	332.9	France—Directories	DC15	944.0025
Forgery of antiquities	CC140	364.163	France—Economic conditions	HC271-280	330.944
Forging	TS225	671.332	France—Emigration and immigration	JV7900-7999	325.(244/44)
Forgiveness	BJ1476	177.7			
Forgiveness of sin	BT795	234.5	France—Gazetteers	DC14	913.64003/914.4003
Forms (Law)—England	KD318	347.42055			
Forms (Mathematics)	QA201	512.944	France—History	DC35-423	936.4/944
Forms (Mathematics)	QA243	512.944	France—History, Military	DC44-47	355.30944
Fornovo, Battle of, 1495	DG541	945.06	France—History, Naval	DC49-53	359.30944
Fort Harrison (Va), Battle of, 1864	E477.21	973.737	France—History—To 987	DC60-81.5	944.01
			France—History—14th century	DC97.5-101.7	944.02(4-6)
Fort Henry (Tenn.), Battle of, 1862	E472.96	973.731	France—History—Charles VI, 1380-1422	DC101-.7	944.026
Fort Oswego (Oswego, N.Y.)—Capture, 1756	E199	973.26	France—History—Cabochien Uprising, 1413	DC101.5.C33	944.026
Fort William Henry (N.Y.)—Capture, 1757	E199	973.26	France—History—Charles VII, 1422-1461	DC102-105.9	944.026
Fortification	UG400-442	623.1	France—History—Louis XI, 1461-1483	DC106-.9	944.027
Fortification, Field	UG403	623.1	France—History—Charles VIII, 1483-1498	DC107-.2	944.027
Fortuna (Roman diety)	BL820.F7	292.2114			
Fortune-telling	BF1845-1891	133.3	France—History—Louis XII, 1498-1515	DC108-109	944.027
Forums (Discussion and debate)	LC6501-6560	371.396	France—History—Francis I, 1515-1547	DC113-.5	944.028
Fossil man	GN282-286.7	569.9	France—History—Henry II, 1547-1559	DC114-.5	944.028
Fossils—Collection and preservation	QE718	560.75	France—History—Francis II, 1559-1560	DC115	944.029
Foundation garments	TT677	687.22	France—History—Charles IX, 1560-1574	DC116-118	944.029
Foundations	TH5201	690.11			
Foundations	TH2101	690.11	France—History—War of the Huguenots, 1562-1598	DC116-118	944.0(29-3)
Foundations	TA775-787	624.15			
Founding	TS228.97-239	671.2	France—History—Henry III, 1574-1589	DC119-120	944.029
Founding	TS228.99-240	671.2	France—History—Bourbons, 1589-1789	DC120.8-138	944.03
Foundlings	HV835-847	362.73			
Fountains	NA9400-9425	714	France—History—Henry IV, 1589-1610	DC122-.9	944.031
Four Horsemen of the Apocalypse	BS2820-2827	228	France—History—Louis XIII, 1610-1643	DC123-.9	944.032
Fourier analysis	QA403.5-404.5	515.2433	France—History—Louis XIV, 1643-1715	DC124.5-130	944.033
Fowling	SK311-335	799.24	France—History—Louis XV, 1715-1774	DC133-135	944.034
Fox hunting	SK284-287	799.259775			
Foxes	QL737.C22	599.775	France—History—Louis XVI, 1774-1793	DC136-137.5	944.035
Fractions	QA117	513.26	France—History—Revolution, 1789-1799	DC139-190.8	944.04(1-2)
Fractions—Study and teaching	QA135-139	513.26071			
Fracture mechanics	TA409	620.1126	France—History—Consulate and First Empire, 1799-1815	DC191.2-249	944.0(46-5)
Fractures	RD101-104	617.15			
Fractures in animals	SF914.4	636.089715			
Fractures, Spontaneous	RD101	617.15			
Fragile X syndrome	RJ506.F73	618.928588			
Framing (Building)	TH2301-2311	694.2			
France	DC	936.4/944			
France—Biography	DC36-.8	920.0364/920.044			
France—Census	HA1211-1230	314.4			
France—Church history	BR840-849	274.4			
France—Civilization	DC33-.9	936.4/944			
France—Colonies	JV1800-1899	325.344			
France—Commerce	HF3551-3560	380.10944			

France—History—Louis XVIII, 1814-1824	DC256-260	944.05	Free will and determinism (Islam)	BP166.3	297.227
France—History—Louis Philip, 1830-1848	DC265-269	944.063	Freedom Train	JK4	353.00074
France—History—July Revolution, 1830	DC261-262	944.063	Freedom of religion	BV741	323.442
			Freedom of religion	BL640	323.442
France—History—Second Republic, 1848-1852	DC271.5-274.5	944.07	Freedom of the seas	D580	940.45
France—History—Coup d'etat, 1851	DC274-.5	944.07	Freehand technical sketching	T359	604.2
France—History—Second Empire, 1852-1870	DC275-292	944.07	Freemasonry	HS351-929	366.1
			Freemasonry—Rituals	HS455-459	366.12
France—History—Third Republic, 1870-1940	DC342.8-396	944.081	Freemasons	HS351-929	336.1
			Freemasons—Directories	HS381-390	366.1025
France—History—German occupation, 1914-1918	DC385	944.0814	Freemasons—History	HS403-420	366.109
			Freemasons—Periodicals	HS351-359	366.105
France—History—German occupation, 1940-1945	DC397	944.0816	Freemasons—[By region or country]	HS501-680.7	366.109(4-9)
France—History—1945-	DC398-423	944.08(2-4)	Freemasons—United States	HS503-539	366.10973
France—Manufactures	TS71-72.5	670.944	Freemasons—[Other regions or countries]	HS557-680.7	366.109(4-9)
France—Maps	G1837-1844.24	912.44			
France—Maps	G5830-5834	912.44	Freeze fracturing	QH236.2	570.2827
France—Periodicals	DC1	936.4005/ 944.005	Freight and freightage	HE199-.5	388.044
			Freight and freightage	HE593-597	387.544
France—Politics and government	JN2301-3007	320.944	Freight and freightage	HE2301-2547	385.24
			French Guiana	F2441-2471	988.2
France—Politics and government— 1969-1974	DC421	944.083(6-7)	French Guiana	JL810-819	320.9882
			French Guiana—Census	HA1037	318.82
			French Guiana—Civilization	F2449.8	988.2
France—Politics and government— 1974-1981	DC422	944.083(7-8)	French Guiana—Description and travel	F2450-2452	918.8204
			French Guiana—Gazetteers	F2444	918.82003
France—Politics and government—1981-	DC423	944.0838	French Guiana—History	F2460.3-2464	988.2
			French Guiana— Manufactures	TS50	670.9882
Franciscans	BX4361-4364	255.973	French Guiana—Maps	G5270-5274	912.882
Franciscans	BX3601-3656	255.3	French Guiana—Periodicals	F2441	988.2005
Franco-Provencal dialects	PC3081-3148	449	French drama	PQ1211-1241	842.008
Franco-Prussian War, 1870-1871	DC281-326.5	944.0812	French drama—To 1500	PQ1341-1385	842.(1-2)08
			French essays	AC20-25	084.1
Franco-Spanish War, 1635-1659	DC124.45	944.03(2-3)	French fiction	PQ631-671	843.009
			French fiction	PQ1261-1279	843.008
Franking privilege	HE6148	383.1202	French fiction—20th century	PQ671	843.909
Franking privilege— United States	HE6448	383.12020973	French language	PC2001-3761	440
			French language—Dialects	PC2700-3761	447
Franks	DG515-519	945.02	French language—Etymology	PC2761	442
Fraud	HV6691-6699	364.163	French language—Etymology	PC2571-2591	442
Fraud investigation	HV8079.F7	363.25963	French language—Grammar	PC2101-2400	445
Fredericksburg (Va.), Battle of, 1862	E474.85	973.733	French language—Grammar	PC2721-2746	445
			French language— Lexicography	PC2766	443.028
Free choice of employment	HD4903-.5	331.702	French language— Lexicography	PC2620-2693	443.028
Free electron lasers	TA1693	621.366			
Free enterprise	HB95	330.122	French language— Morphology	PC2171-2175	445
Free love	HX546	306.735	French language—Parts of speech	PC2201-2321	445
Free love	HQ961-967	306.735			
Free piston engines	TJ779	621.4335	French language— Phonology	PC2131-2151	441.5
Free ports and zones	HF1418-.5	387.13			
Free radicals (Chemicals)	RB170	541.224	French language—Readers	PC2113-2117	448.6
Free radicals (Chemistry)	QD471	541.224	French language—Study and teaching	PC2065	440.71
Free radicals (Chemistry)	QP527	541.224			
Free schools	LB1029.F7	371.04			

Subject Heading	LC	Dewey	Subject Heading	LC	Dewey
French language—To 1500	PC2801-2896	447.0(1-2)	Friendship	GN486.3	302.34
French language—To 1500—Etymology	PC2883-2886	447.01(1-2)2	Friendship	BJ1533.F8	177.62
			Friendship	BF575.F66	158.25
French language—To 1500—Grammar	PC2821-2873	447.0(1-2)5	Friendship—Sociological aspects	HM132.5	302.34
French language—To 1500—Lexicography	PC2887-2895	447.0(1-2)3028	Friendship in children	HQ784.F7	302.34083
			Fries Rebellion, 1798-1799	E326	973.44
French literature	PQ1-3999	840	Frisian language	PF1401-1497	439.2
French literature—To 1500	PQ151-221	840.900(1-2)	Frisian language—Philology	PF1401-1411	439.2
French literature—To 1500	PQ1300-1595	840.800(1-2)	Frisian literature	PF1501-1541	839.2
French literature—16th century	PQ1121-1125	840.8003	Frisians	DJ401.F5-.F59	949.213
			Frog culture	SH185	639.3789
French literature—16th century	PQ230-239	840.9003	Frogs	QL668.E2-.E275	597.89
			Frontal sinus	QM505	611.21
French literature—17th century	PQ241-251	840.9004	Fronts (Meteorology)	QC880.4.F7	551.5512
			Frost	QC929.H6	551.38
French literature—17th century	PQ1126-1130	840.8004	Frozen foods	TP372.3	664.02853
			Frozen foods	TX610	641.453
French literature—18th century	PQ1131-1135	840.8005	Fructose	QD321	547.7813
			Fruit	SB354-399	634
French literature—18th century	PQ261-276	840.9005	Frustration	BF575.F7	152.47
			Frustration in children	BF723.F7	155.41247
French literature—19th century	PQ281-299	840.9007	Fuel	TP315-360	662.6
			Fuel cells	TK2931	621.312429
French literature—19th century	PQ1136-1139	840.8007	Fuelwood	TP324	662.65
			Fula language	PL8181-8184	496.322
French literature—20th century	PQ1141	840.80091	Fuladu (Kingdom)	DT532.128	966.(3/51)
			Fumigation	SB955	632.94
French literature—20th century	PQ301-307	840.90091	Fumigation	RA761-767	614.48
			Functional analysis	QA319-329.9	515.7
French literature—Foreign countries	PQ3809	840	Functionalism (Linguistics)	P147	410.18
			Functions	QA331-355	515.25
French literature—Study and teaching	PQ51-65	840.71	Functions of complex variables	QA331.7	515.9
French periodicals	AP20-28.7	054.1	Functions of real variables	QA331.5	515.8
French periodicals	PN5171-5790	054.1	Functions, Zeta	QA351	515.56
French philology	PC2001-2071	440	Fund raising	HG177-.5	658.15224
French poetry	PQ1160-1193	841.008	Fund raising	HV41.2-.9	361.70681
French poetry	PQ400-491	841.009	Fundamental education	LC5161-5163	370.111
French poetry—16th century	PQ416-418	841.309	Fundamentalism	BT82.2	270.82
French poetry—17th century	PQ421-423	841.409	Funds-flow statements	HF5681.B2	657.3
French poetry—18th century	PQ426-428	841.509	Funeral orations	PA3482	885.008
French poetry—19th century	PQ431-439	841.709	Funeral rites and ceremonies	GN486	393
French poetry—20th century	PQ441-443	841.9109	Funeral rites and ceremonies	GT3150-3390.5	393
French poetry—To 1500	PQ1300-1391	841.(1-2)08	Funeral rites and ceremonies, Ancient	GT3170	393.0901
French prose literature	PQ601-657	848.08			
French prose literature	PQ1243-1279	848.08	Funeral rites and ceremonies, Buddhist	BL1477.8.F8	294.3438
French prose literature—To 1500	PQ151-216	848.08	Funeral rites and ceremonies, Islamic	BP184.9.F8	297.385
French-Canadian literature	PQ3900-3919.2	840			
French-Canadians	F1027	971.004114	Funeral sermons	BV4275	252.1
Freshwater animals	QL141-149	591.76	Funeral service	BV199.F8	265.85
Freshwater biology	QH96-100	578.76	Fungal diseases of plants	SB733	632.4
Freshwater ecology	QH541.5.F7	577.6	Fungal viruses	QR343	579.27
Freshwater microbiology	QR105.5	579.176	Fungi	QK600-635	579.5
Freshwater plants	QK105	581.76	Fungi—Genetics	QK602	579.5135
Freshwater plants	QK932-.7	581.76	Fungi, Edible	SB353-.5	635.8
Friars	BX2820	255.(2-3)	Fungi in agriculture	SB733	632.4
Friction	QC197	531.1134	Fungicides	SB951.3	632.952
Friendly societies	HG9201-9245	334.7	Fur	TS1060-1070	675.3
Friendly societies	HS1501-1510	334.7	Fur-bearing animals	SF403-405	636.97

Subject Heading	LC	Dewey
Fur-bearing animals	SK283-.6	799.2597
Fur farming	SF402-405	636.9701
Fur garments	TT525	685.24
Furies (Roman mythology)	BL820.F8	292.13
Furnaces	TH7400	697.07
Furnaces	TJ320-358	621.183
Furniture	GT450	392.36
Furniture	NK2200-2750	749
Furniture	TS880-889	684.1
Furniture	TT194-199.4	684.104
Furniture—Exhibitions	NK2210-2211	747.074
Furniture—Private collections	NK2220	749.074
Furniture—Repairing	TT199	684.00288
Furniture—Styles	NK2235	749
Furniture—[By region or country]	NK2401-2694.5	749.2(1-9)
Furniture making	TS880-889	684.1
Furniture making	TT194-199.4	684.1
Furuncle	RL221	616.523
Fusion	QC303	536.42
Fusion reactors	TK9204	621.484
Future life	BL535-547	291.23
Future life	BT899-940	236.2
Futures	HG6024-6051	332.645
G-spaces	QA689	516.375
Ga language	PL8191	496.3378
Gables	NA2920	721.5
Gabon—Census	HA4715	316.721
Gabon—Civilization	DT546.14	967.21
Gabon—Description and travel	DT546.127-.128	916.72104
Gabon—Economic conditions	HC975	330.96721
Gabon—Gazetteers	DT546.115	916.721003
Gabon—History	DT546.15-.183	967.21
Gabon—History—To 1839	DT546.165	967.2101
Gabon—History—1839-1960	DT546.165-.175	967.2102
Gabon—History—1960-	DT546.18-.183	967.2104
Gabon—Maps	G8690-8694	912.6721
Gadaba language (Dravidian)	PL4627	494.82
Gaelic language	PB1501-1599	491.6(2-3)
Gaelic language—Etymology	PB1583-1584	491.6(2-3)2
Gaelic language—Grammar	PB1521-1573	491.6(2-3)5
Gaelic language—Lexicography	PB1187-1189	491.6(2-3)3028
Gaelic language—Lexicography	PB1587-1595	491.6(2-3)3028
Gaelic language—Study and teaching	PB1511	491.6(2-3)071
Gaelic literature	PB1605-1709	891.63
Gaelic philology	PB1101-1113	491.6(2/3)
Gaelic philology—Study and teaching	PB1111	491.6(2-3)071
Gain sharing	HD4928.G34	331.2164
Gaita	ML980	788.4909
Galaxies	QB856-858.8	523.112
Galician dialect	PC5411-5414	469.794
Galician literature	PQ9450-9469.2	869
Gallbladder	QL867	573.38
Gallbladder	QM352	611.36

Subject Heading	LC	Dewey
Gallbladder	QP185	612.35
Gallbladder—Diseases	RC849-853	616.365
Gallbladder—Surgery	RD546-547	617.5565
Galleys	HV8647-8649	365.3
Gallo-Italian dialects	PC1851-1874	457
Galls (Botany)	SB767	632.2
Galois theory	QA171	512.3
Galois theory	QA211	512.3
Galois theory	QA214	512.3
Gambai dialect	PL8197	496.5
Gambia—Census	HA4734	316.651
Gambia—Civilization	DT509.4	966.51
Gambia—Description and travel	DT509.27	916.65104
Gambia—History	DT509.5-.83	966.51
Gambia—History—Coup d'etat, 1981	DT509.8	966.51031
Gambia—Maps	G8870-8874	912.6651
Gambling	HV6708-6722	364.172
Gambling	GN454.6	306.482
Gambling	GV1301-1311	795
Gambling—Law and legislation—England	KD3527	344.42099
Gambling systems	GV1302	795
Game and game-birds, Dressing of	SK36.2	799.24
Game bird culture	SF508-510	636.63082
Game fowl	SF502.8-503.52	636.63
Game reserves	SK357	639.95
Game theory	QA269-272.5	519.3
Game theory	T57.92	519.3
Games	GV1199-1570	790.1
Games	GN454.8-455	394.3
Games	GR480-485	394.3
Games—Rules	GV1201.42	790.102022
Games of chance (Mathematics)	QA273	519.2
Gamma functions	QA353.G3	515.52
Gamma ray bursts	QB471.7.B85	522.6862
Gamma ray sources	QC793.5.G322	539.7222
Ganda language	PL8201	496.3957
Gang rape	HV6558-6569	364.1532
Gangrene	RD153	616.047
Gangrene	RD628	616.047
Gangs	HV6437-6439	364.106
Gantry cranes	TJ1365	621.873
Garage sales	HF5482.3	381.195
Garages	NA8348	725.38
Garden cities	HT161-165	307.76
Garden ecology	QH541.5.G37	577.554
Garden fertilizers	S633	631.8
Garden lighting	SB476	621.3229
Garden ornaments and furniture	SB473.5	645.8
Garden pests	SB603.5	635.92
Garden pests—[By region or country]	SB605	632.09(4-9)
Garden tools	SB454.8	635.0284
Gardening	SB450.9-467.8	635
Gardening in the shade	SB434.7	635.9543
Gardens	SB450.9-467	635

Subject Heading	LC	Dewey	Subject Heading	LC	Dewey
Generative organs, Female—Surgery	RG104-.7	618.145	Geology—Antartica	QE350	559.89
Generative organs, Male	QP253-257	612.61	Geology—Arctic regions	QE70	559.8(1/2)
Generative organs, Male	QL878	573.65	Geology—Asia	QE289-319	555
Generative organs, Male	QM416	611.63	Geology—Australia	QE340-348	559.4
Genes	QH447-.8	572.86	Geology—Canada	QE185-199	557.1
Genetic disorders	RB155.5-.8	616.042	Geology—Central America	QE210-217	557.28
Genetic disorders in children	RJ47.3-.4	618.920042	Geology—Europe	QE260-288	554
Genetic engineering	QH442-.6	660.65	Geology—Mexico	QE201-203	557.2
Genetic engineering	TP248.6	660.65	Geology—North America	QE71-217	557
Genetic psychology	BF699-711	155.7	Geology—South America	QE230-251	558
Genetic recombination	QH443-450.6	572.877	Geology—United States	QE72-182	557.3
Genetic regulation	QH450-.6	572.865	Geology—[United States, By state]	QE81-182	557.(4-9)
Genetic transcription	QH450.2	572.8845	Geology—West Indies	QE220-226	557.29
Genetic translation	QH450.5	572.645	Geology, Economic	TN260	553
Genetics	QH426-470	576.5	Geology, Stratigraphic	QE640-699	551.7
Geneva (Switzerland)—History—1536-1603	DQ458	949.451	Geology, Stratigraphic—Cenozoic	QE690-699	551.78
Genius	BF412-426	153.98	Geology, Stratigraphic—Mesozoic	QE675-688	551.76
Genoa (Italy)	DG631-645	945.182	Geology, Stratigraphic—Paleozoic	QE654-674	551.72
Genocide	HV6322.7	364.151	Geomagnetic observatories	QC818	538.79
Genomes	QH447	572.86	Geomagnetism	QC811-849	538.7
Genre painting	ND1450-1452	754	Geomagnetism—Maps	QC822	538.70223
Gentry	HT657	305.5232	Geometry	QA440-699	516
Geochemistry	QE514-516.5	551.9	Geometry, Algebraic	QA564-609	516.35
Geodesy	QB275-343	526.1	Geometry, Analytic	QA551-563	516.3
Geodesy—Computer programs	QB297	526.10285	Geometry, Descriptive	QA501-521	516.6
Geodesy—Encyclopedias	QB279	526.103	Geometry, Differential	QA641-672	516.36
Geodesy—History	QB280.5	526.109	Geometry, Infinitesimal	QA615-639	516.36
Geodetic astronomy	QB201-205	526.6	Geometry, Modern	QA473-475	516.04
Geodetic satellites	TL798.G4	629.46	Geometry, Plane	QA451-485	516.22
Geodynamics	QE500-639.5	551.(2-3)	Geometry, Solid	QA457	516.23
Geographers—Biography	G67-69	910.92	Geometry, Solid	QA491	516.23
Geographical myths	GR940-941	398.32	Geomorphology	GB400-649	551.41
Geographical myths	GR650-690	398.32	Geophysics	QC801-809	550
Geography	GN476.4	910	Geophysics	QE500-511.7	550
Geography	G-GF	910	Geopolitics	JC319-323	320.12
Geography—History	G80-99	910.9	Georgia	F281-295	975.8
Geography—Methodology	G70-.4	910.01	Georgia—Gazetteers	F284	917.58003
Geography—Societies, etc.	G2-55	910.6	Georgia—History—1775-1865	F290	975.80(2-3)
Geography—Study and teaching	G72-76.5	910.71	Georgia—History—Revolution, 1775-1783	E263.G3	975.80(2-3)
Geography, Ancient	G83-88	913	Georgia—History—War of 1812	E359.5.G4	975.803
Geography, Medieval	G89-95	911.0902	Georgia—History—Civil War, 1861-1865	E559	975.803
Geological modeling	QE43	551.0228	Georgia—History—Civil War, 1861-1865	E503	975.803
Geological museums	QE51	551.074	Georgia—History—1865-	F291-.3	975.804
Geological surveys	QE61-350.62	551.0723	Georgia—Maps	G3920-3924	912.758
Geological time	QE508	551.701	Georgia—National Guard	UA150-159	355.3709758
Geologists	QE21-22	551.092	Georgia—Periodicals	F281	975.8005
Geology	QE	551	Georgia (Republic)	DK670-679.5	947.58
Geology—Computer programs	QE48.8	551.0285	Georgian language	PK9101-9151	499.969
Geology—History	QE11-13	551.09	Georgian language—Grammar	PK9106-9115	499.965
Geology—Maps	QE36	551.0223	Georgian literature	PK9160-9169	899.969
Geology—Societies, etc.	QE1	551.06	Gergovie, Battle of, 52 B.C.	DC62	936.402
Geology—Study and teaching	QE40-48	551.071			
Geology—Terminology	QE7	551.014			
Geology—Africa	QE320-339	556			

Subject Heading	LC	Dewey	Subject Heading	LC	Dewey
Geriatric anesthesia	RD145	617.9600846	German language—Old High German, 750-1050—Grammar	PF3831-3931	437.015
Geriatric nursing	RC954	610.7365			
Geriatric pharmacology	RC953.7	615.10846	German language—Middle High German, 1050-1500	PF4043-4350	437.02
Geriatric psychiatry	RC451.4.A5	618.9789			
Geriatrics	RC952-954.6	618.97	German language—Middle High German, 1050-1500—Lexicography	PF4327-4345	437.023028
German American literature (German)	PT3900-3919	830			
German drama	PT605-709	832.009	German language—Middle High German, 1050-1500—Dictionaries	PF4333-4345	437.023
German drama	PT1251-1299	832.008			
German drama (Comedy)	PT1275-1277	832.052308			
German drama (Tragedy)	PT1271-1273	832.051208	German language—Middle High German, 1050-1500—Grammar	PF4061-4171	437.025
German essays	AC30-35	083.1			
German essays	PT831	834.009			
German essays	PT1354	834.008	German language—Early modern, 1500-1700	PF4501-4596	437.09
German Expedition to China, 1900-1901	DS771.5	951.035			
German fiction	PT741-772	833.009	German language dictionaries	PT41	830.3
German fiction	PT1321-1340	833.008			
German fiction—Early modern, 1500-1700	PT753-756	833.(3-5)09	German letters	PT811	836.009
			German letters	PT1348-1352	836.008
German fiction—18th century	PT1315	833.608	German literature	PT1100-1479	830.8
			German literature	PT1-1021	830
German fiction—18th century	PT759	833.609	German literature—Congresses	PT31	830.6
German fiction—19th century	PT1332	833.708	German literature—Czechoslovakia	PT3830-3837.5	830
German fiction—19th century	PT763-771	833.709	German literature—Foreign countries	PT3808-3809	830
German fiction—20th century	PT1334	833.908	German literature—Study and teaching	PT51-65	830.71
German fiction—20th century	PT772	833.909	German literature—Old High German, 750-1050	PF3985-3991	839
German language	PF3001-5999	430	German literature—Old High German, 750-1050	PT183	830.9001
German language—Dialects	PF5000-5951	437			
			German literature—Middle High German, 1050-1500	PT175-230	830.9002
German language—Dictionaries	PF3620-3693	433			
			German literature—Middle High German, 1050-1700	PT1375-1479	830.8002
German language—Etymology	PF3571-3599	432			
German language—Grammar	PF3097-3400	435	German literature—Early modern, 1500-1700	PT238-281	830.900(3-5)
German language—History	PF3051-3060	437	German literature—Early modern, 1500-1700	PT1121-1126	830.800(3-5)
German language—Lexicography	PF3601-3693	433.028			
			German literature—18th century	PT1131	830.8006
German language—Morphology	PF3171-3197	435			
			German literature—18th century—History and criticism	PT285-321	830.9006
German language—Parts of speech	PF3199-3335	435			
German language—Phonology	PF3131-3168	431.5	German literature—19th century	PT1136	830.8007
German language—Rhetoric	PF3410-3497	808.0431	German literature—19th century—History and criticism	PT341-395	830.9007
German language—Slang	PF5971-5999	437			
German language—Study and teaching	PF3065-3069	430.71			
			German literature—20th century	T401-403	830.9009
German language—Old High German, 750-1050	PF3801-3991	437.01			
			German literature—20th century	PT1141	830.8009
German language—Old High German, 750-1050—Philology	PF3801-3823	437.01			
			German periodicals	AP30-36.7	053.1
			German periodicals	PN5201-5220	053.1
			German poetry	PT1151-1241	831.008
			German poetry	PT500-597	831.009

Subject Heading	LC	Dewey
German poetry—Middle High German, 1050-1500	PT175-227	831.209
German poetry—Middle High German, 1050-1500	PT1391-1429	831.(1-3)08
German poetry—Early modern, 1500-1700	PT1163-1165	831.(3-5)08
German poetry—Early modern, 1500-1700	PT525-531	831.(4-5)09
German poetry—18th century	PT533-535	831.609
German poetry—18th century	PT1167-1169	831.608
German poetry—19th century	PT541-547	831.709
German poetry—19th century	PT1171-1173	831.708
German poetry—20th century	PT551-553	831.909
German poetry—20th century	PT1174-1175	831.908
German prose literature	PT1301-1340	838.08
German prose literature	PT711-871	838.08
Germanic fiction	PN836	839.3009
Germanic languages	PF	430
Germanic languages	PD	430
Germanic languages—Dialects	PD700-777	430.047
Germanic languages—Dictionaries	PD625-660	430.043
Germanic languages—Etymology	PD571-599	430.042
Germanic languages—Grammar	PD99-321	430.045
Germanic languages—History	PD51-60	437
Germanic languages—Lexicography	PD601-660	430.043028
Germanic languages—Periodicals	PD1-9	430.05
Germanic languages—Study and teaching	PD65-69	430.071
Germanic peoples	GN549.G4	305.83
Germanic peoples—Religion	BL830-875	293
Germany	DD	936.3/943
Germany (East)	DD280-289	943.1087
Germany (West)	DD258-262	943.087
Germany—Armed Forces—Management	UB73-74	355.60943
Germany—Armed Forces—Supplies and stores	UC180-183	355.80943
Germany—Biography	CT1050-1099.8	920.043
Germany—Biography	DD85-.8	920.0363/ 920.043
Germany—Census	HA1231-1349	314.3
Germany—Church history	BR850-856.35	274.3
Germany—Civilization	DD60-68	936.3/943
Germany—Commerce	HF3561-3570.5	380.10943
Germany—Description and travel	DD21.5-43	913.6304/ 914.304
Germany—Directories	DD15.5	943.0025
Germany—Economic conditions	HC281-290.795	330.943
Germany—Emigration and immigration	JV8000-8099	325.(243/43)
Germany—Gazetteers	DD14	913.63003/ 914.3003
Germany—Genealogy	CS610-699	929.1072043
Germany—Historiography	DD86-.7	936.30072/ 943.0072
Germany—History	DD84-257.4	936.3/943
Germany—History, Military	DD99-104	355.30943
Germany—History, Naval	DD106	355.30943
Germany—History—To 843	DD121-134.2	936.3/ 943.01(1-4)
Germany—History—843-918	DD134.3-135	943.021
Germany—History—Saxon House, 919-1024	DD136-140.7	943.022
Germany—History—Franconian House, 1024-1125	DD141-144	943.023
Germany—History—Hohenstaufen, 1138-1254	DD145-155	943.024
Germany—History—1273-1517	DD156-174.6	943.02(6-9)
Germany—History—1618-1648	DD188-.5	943.041
Germany—History—1648-1740	DD190-.8	943.0(43-52)
Germany—History—18th century	DD191-199	943.05
Germany—History—1789-1900	DD197-231	943.0(57-84)
Germany—History—1815-1866	DD206-214	943.07
Germany—History—Revolution, 1848-1849	DD207-209	940.284
Germany—History—1866-1871	DD214-216	943.081
Germany—History—William I, 1871-1888	DD223-.9	943.083
Germany—History—1871-1918	DD217-231	943.08(3-4)
Germany—History—Frederick III, 1888	DD224-226	943.084
Germany—History—William II, 1888-1918	DD228-231	943.084
Germany—History—20th century	DD232-257.4	943.08(4-79)
Germany—History—Allied occupation, 1918-1930	DD650.M5	943.085
Germany—History—Revolution, 1918	DD248	943.085
Germany—History—Kapp Putsch, 1920	DD249	943.085
Germany—History—March Uprising, 1921	DD249	943.085
Germany—History—Beer Hall Putsch, 1923	DD249	943.085

Subject Heading	LC	Dewey	Subject Heading	LC	Dewey
Germany—History—1933-1945	DD253-256.5	943.086	Girls	HV879-887	369.46
Germany—History—Night of the Long Knives, 1934	DD247.R56	943.086	Girls	GT2540	390.08342
			Gisu language	PL8207.G55	496.395
Germany—History—Kristallnacht, 1938	DD135.G3315	943.086	Glacial epoch	QE697-698	551.792
			Glacial erosion	QE575-579	551.313
Germany—History—1945-1955	DD257-.4	943.087(4-5)	Glacial landforms	GB581-588	551.315
			Glaciers	GB2401-2598	551.312
Germany—History—1990-	DD257.4	943.09(79-8)	Gladiators	GV35	796.8092
Germany—History—Unification, 1990	DD257-.4	943.0879	Glands	QM325-371	611.4
			Glands	QP186-246	612.4
Germany—Manufactures	TS73-74.5	670.943	Glands	QL865-868	573.4
Germany—Maps	G1907-1924	912.43	Glass	TA450	620.144
Germany—Maps	G6080-6428	912.43	Glass	NK5100-5440	748
Germany—Politics and government	JN3201-4944	320.943	Glass blowing and working	TP859	666.122
			Glass construction	TH1560	693.96
Germination	QK740	571.862	Glass construction	NA4140	721.04496
Gerrymander	JK1347-1343	328.33455	Glass engraving	NE2690	748.62
Gestalt psychology	BF203	150.1982	Glass manufacture	TP845-869	666.1
Gettysburg (Pa.), Battle of, 1863	E475.53	973.7349	Glass painting and staining	NK5300-5430	748.50282
			Glass sculpture	NB1270.G4	731.2
Geysers	GB1198.5-.8	551.23	Glass shoes	NK5440.S49	748.8
Ghana—Census	HA4732	316.67	Glass, Optical	QC375	666.156
Ghana—Civilization	DT510.4	966.7	Glass-workers	HD8039.G5	666.1092
Ghana—Description and travel	DT510.2	916.6704	Glassware	NK5100-5440	748.2
			Glassware	TP865-868	666.19
Ghana—History	DT510.5-512.34	966.7	Glaucoma	RE871	617.741
Ghana—History—To 1957	DT511-.3	966.70(1-3)	Glazes	TP812	666.427
Ghana—History—Portuguese rule, 1469-1637	DT511	966.7016	Glazes	TP823	666.427
			Glazing	TH8251-8275	698.5
			Gleaning	HD1549	338.163
Ghana—History—Danish Settlements, 1659-1850	DT511	966.701(6-8)	Gliders (Aeronautics)	TL760-769	629.13333
			Gliding and soaring	GV764-766	797.55
			Global analysis (Mathematics)	QA614-.97	514.74
Ghana—History—1957-	DT512-.34	966.705			
Ghana—History—Coup d'etat, 1966	DT512	966.705	Global warming	QC981.8.G56	363.73874
			Glockenspiel music	M147	786.843
Ghana—History—Coup d'etat, 1972	DT512	966.705	Glory of God	BT180.G6	231
			Glottis	QM255	611.22
Ghana—History—Coup d'etat, 1979	DT512.32	966.705	Gloves	GT2170	391.412
			Gloves	TS2160	685.4
			Glucose	QD321	547.7813
Ghana—History—Coup d'etat, 1981	DT512.32	966.705	Glue	TP967-970	668.3
			Glue-sniffing	HV5822.G5	362.299
Ghana—Maps	G8850-8854	912.667	Glycerin	HD9660.G58-.G6	338.476682
Ghosts	GR580	398.47	Glycerin	RA766.G6	614.48
Ghosts	BF1444-1486	133.1	Glycerin	TP973	668.2
Ghouls and ogres	GR525	398.45	Gnosticism	BT1390	273.1
Ghouls and ogres	GR560	398.45	Goats	SF380-388	636.39
Gifted children	BF723.G5	155.455	God	BT98-180	231
Gifted children	HQ773.5	649.155	God—Attributes	BT130-157	231.4
Gifted children	LC3991-4000	371.8279	God—Biblical teaching	BT99	231
Gifts	GT3050	394	God—Goodness	BT137	231.8
Gifts, Spiritual	BT767.3	234.13	God—History of doctrines	BT98	231.09
Gingivitis	RK410	617.632	God—Omnipotence	BT133	231.4
Ginseng	SB295.G5	633.88384	God—Omniscience	BT131	231.4
Ginseng	QK495.A6853	583.84	God—Proof, Cosmological	BT98-102	231.765
Giraffe	QL737.U56	599.638	God—Proof, Ontological	BT98-101	231.042
Girders	TA492.G5	624.17723	God (Greek religion)	B398.G6	184
Girders	TG350-362	624.37	God (Hinduism)	BL1200-1225	294.5211
Girders, Continuous	TG355	624.33	God (Islam)	BP166.2	297.211
Girl Scouts	HS3353.G5	369.463	God (Judaism)	BM610	296.311

Subject Heading	LC	Dewey	Subject Heading	LC	Dewey
Goddesses, Hindu	BL1216	294.52114	Government publications—Mexico	CD333-334	025.17340972
Gods	BL473	291.21	Government publications—Oceania	CD291	025.1734099 (5-6)
Gods, Egyptian	BL2450.G6	299.31	Government publications—South America	CD365-392	025.1734098
Going concern (Accounting)	HF5681.G55	657	Government publications—United States	CD309-311	025.17340973
Going public (Securities)	HG4028.S7	658.15224			
Goiter	RC656-.3	616.442	Government securities	HG4701-4726	332.63232
Gold	HG289	332.4042	Government securities—United States	HG4931-4955	332.632320973
Gold	HG551	332.40420973			
Gold—Metallurgy	TN760-769	669.22	Governors—United States	JK2447-2454	352.232130973
Gold—Minting	HG321	332.4042	Grace (Theology)	BT760-769	234
Gold alloys	RK653	617.675	Grace at meals	BV283.G7	242.2
Gold dredging	TN422	622.3422	Graces, The	BL820.G8	292.13
Gold mines and mining	HD9536	622.3422	Grading and marking (Students)	LB3051-3063	371.272
Gold mines and mining	TN410-429	622.3422			
Gold ores	TN420-429	622.3422	Grafting	SB123.65	631.54
Gold standard	HG297	332.4222	Grain	SB189-192	633.1
Golden Horde	DS22.7	304.82/ 950.04942	Grain trade	HD9030-9049	380.1431
			Grain trade	HF2651.G8	380.14133
Golden rule	BV4715	241.54	Grammar, Comparative and general	P151-299	415
Golden rule	BJ1286.G64	296.36			
Golf	GV961-987	796.352	Gramme dynamos	TK2441	621.3132
Good Friday	BV95	263.925	Granada (Kingdom)—History	DP115-118	946.82
Good Samaritan (Parable)	BT378.G6	226.8			
Good and evil	BJ1400-1408.5	170	Granada—Maps	G5130-5134	912.729845
Gorgons (Greek mythology)	BL820.G7	292.13	Granaries	NA8240	728.92
Gorilla	QL737.P96	599.884	Granaries—Design and construction	TH4461	690.53
Gospel music	M2198-2199	782.254			
Gossip	BJ1535.G6	177.2	Grand Alliance, War of the, 1689-1697	D279-280.5	940.2525
Gothic language	PD1101-1211	439.9			
Gothic language—Dictionaries	PD1193	439.93	Grand National Handicap Steeplechase	SF359.7.G7	798.450942753
			Grand Prix racing	GV1029	796.73
Gothic language—Grammar	PD1119-1167	439.95	Grand unified theories (Nuclear physics)	QC794.6.G7	530.142
Gout	RC629-.5	616.3999			
Government, Resistance to	JC328.3	323.044	Grandparenting	HQ759.9	306.8745
Government liability	JF1621	352.885	Granite	QE462.G7	552.3
Government libraries	Z675.G7	027.5	Granite	TN970	622.352
Government ownership	HD3840-4420.8	352.266	Grapefruit	SB370.G7	634.32
Government property	JF1525.P7	352.5	Grapes	SB387-399	634.8
Government property	K3558-3560	343.02	Grapes	QK495.V84	583.86
Government property—Canada	KE5105-5420	343.7102	Graph theory	QA166-.24	511.5
			Graphology	BF889-905	137
Government property—England	KD1034-1107	343.4202	Graphology	RC473.G7	155.282
			Grasses	SB197-202	633.2
Government property—United States	KF5500-5865	343.7302	Grasses	QK495.G74	584.9
			Grassland ecology	QH541.5.P7	577.4
Government publications—[By region or country]	CD101-392	025.173409(1-9)	Grassland fauna	QL115.3-.5	591.74
			Grasslands	QK938.P7	581.74
Government publications—Africa	CD255-269	025.1734096	Grasslands	QH541.5.P7	577.4
			Gratitude	BJ1533.G8	179.9
Government publications—Asia	CD221-254	025.1734095	Graves' disease	RC657.5.G7	616.443
			Gravimeters (Geophysical instruments)	QB331	526.0284
Government publications—Australia	CD271-272	025.1734094			
			Gravitation	QB341	526.7
Government publications—Canada	CD331-332	025.17340971	Gravitation	QC178	531.14
			Gravitational fields	QC178	531.14
Government publications—Caribbean Area	CD351-362	025.173409729	Gravity	QP82.2.G7	571.435
			Gravity	QB330-339	526.7
Government publications—Central America	CD335-350	025.173409728			
Government publications—Europe	CD101-215	025.1734094			

Subject Heading	LC	Dewey	Subject Heading	LC	Dewey
Gravity	QH657	571.63435	Great Britain—History—20th century	DA566-592	941.082
Gravity waves	QA927	532.59	Great Britain—Kings and rulers	JN331-389	352.2330941
Graz (Austria), Battle of, 1809	DC234.65	940.27	Great Britain—Manufactures	TS57-64	670.941
Grazing	HD241	333.740973	Great Britain—Maps	G1805-1829.24	912.41
Great Awakening	BR520	277.3081	Great Britain—Maps	G5740-5814	912.41
Great Britain	DA	941/936.1	Great Britain—Politics and government	JN101-1371	320.941
Great Britain—Armed Forces—Supplies and stores	UC184-187	355.80941	Great Britain—Politics and government—1066-1485	JN137-158	20.9410902 (1-4)
Great Britain—Biography	CT770-858	920.041	Great Britain—Politics and government—1485-	JN175-231	320.941090 (3-511)
Great Britain—Biography	DA28-.9	920.0361/ 920.041	Great Britain. Parliament	JN500-678	328.41
Great Britain—Census	HA1121-1170	314.1	Great Britain. Parliament.	KD4190-4381	341.4205
Great Britain—Church history	BR740-799	274.1	Great Britain. Royal Navy	VC184-187	359.80941
Great Britain—Civilization	DA110-115	936.1/941	Great Pyrenees	SF429.G75	636.73
Great Britain—Colonies	JV1000-1099	325.341	Great White Brotherhood	BP605.G68	299.93
Great Britain—Commerce	HF3501-3530.5	380.10941	Great circle sailing	VK571	387.52
Great Britain—Emigration and immigration	JV7600-7699	325.(241/41)	Great supper (Parable)	BT378.G7	226.8
Great Britain—Gazetteers	DA640	914.2003	Grebo language	PL8221	496.33
Great Britain—Genealogy	CS410-479.5	929.1072041	Greece	DE	938
Great Britain—Historical geography—Maps	G5741	911.41	Greece	DF	938/949.5
Great Britain—History	DA28-690	936.1/941	Greece	DF701-854.32	949.50(4-9)
Great Britain—History, Military	DA49-69.3	355.30941	Greece—Census	HA1351-1359	314.95
Great Britain—History, Naval	DA70-89.1	359.30941	Greece—Commerce	HF3750.5	380.109495
Great Britain—History—To 1066	DA134-162	936.2/941.01	Greece—Description and travel	DF27-30	913.804/ 914.9504
Great Britain—History—To 1485	DA170-260	941.0(2-46)	Greece—Description and travel	DF721-728	914.9504
Great Britain—History—Modern period, 1485-	DA300-591	941.0(5-8)	Greece—Economic conditions	HC291-300	330.9495
Great Britain—History—Tudors, 1485-1603	DA310-360	941.05	Greece—Emigration and immigration	JV8110-8119	325.(2495/495)
Great Britain—History—Henry VIII, 1509-1547	DA331-339	941.052	Greece—History	DF750-854.32	949.50(4-9)
Great Britain—History—Elizabeth, 1558-1603	DA350-360	941.055	Greece—History, Military	DF765	355.309495
Great Britain—History—Early Stuarts, 1603-1649	DA370-419.5	941.06	Greece—History—To 146 B.C.	DF218-238.9	938.0(1-8)
Great Britain—History—Civil War, 1642-1649	DA410-429	941.062	Greece—History—Dorian Invasions, ca. 1125-1025 B.C.	DF221-.3	938.01
Great Britain—History—1660-1714	DA430-463	941.06(6-9)	Greece—History—Geometric period, ca. 900-700 B.C.	DF221.5	938.01
Great Britain—History—George I, 1714-1727	DA499	941.071	Greece—History—Age of Tyrants, 7th-6th centuries, B.C.	DF222-224	938.01
Great Britain—History—George II, 1727-1760	DA500	941.072	Greece—History—Persian Wars, 500-449 B.C.	DF225-226	938.03
Great Britain—History—George III, 1760-1820	DA505-522	941.073	Greece—History—Ionian Revolt, 499-494 B.C.	DF225.3	938.03
Great Britain—History—George IV, 1820-1830	DA537-538	941.074	Greece—History—Athenian supremacy, 479-431 B.C.	DF227-228	938.04
Great Britain—History—William IV, 1830-1837	DA539-542	941.075	Greece—History—Peloponnesian War, 431-404 B.C.	DF229-230	938.05
Great Britain—History—Victoria, 1837-1901	DA550-565	941.081	Greece—History—Expedition of Cyrus, 401 B.C.	DF231.32	938.05

Subject Heading	LC	Dewey
Greece—History—Macedonian Expansion, 359-323 B.C.	DF232.5-234.9	938.07
Greece—History—Third Sacred War, 355-346 B.C.	DF233.4	938.07
Greece—History—Macedonian Hegemony, 323-281 B.C.	DF235.3-.85	938.08
Greece—History—281-146 B.C.	DF236-238.9	938.08
Greece—History—Galatian Invasion, 279-278 B.C.	DF236.4	938.08
Greece—History—Chremonidean War, 267-262 B.C.	DF236.5	938.08
Greece—History—146 B.C.-323 A.D.	DF239-241	938.09
Greece—Manufactures	TS75-76	670.9495
Greece—Maps	G2000-2004	912.495
Greece—Maps	G6810-6814	912.495
Greece—Periodicals	DF10	938.005/ 949.5005
Greece—Periodicals	DF701	949.5(4-9)005
Greece—Politics and government	JN5001-5191	320.9495
Greece—Politics and government—To 146 B.C.	JC71-75	320.938
Greece—Religion	BL780-795	292.08
Greek drama	PA3131-3239	882.009
Greek drama	PA3461-3468	882
Greek drama (Comedy)	PA3465-3466	882.052308
Greek drama (Comedy)	PA3161-3199	882.052309
Greek drama (Tragedy)	PA3461-3463	882.051208
Greek drama (Tragedy)	PA3131-3159	882.051209
Greek drama, Modern	PA5290-5294	889.2008
Greek drama, Modern	PA5260-5263	889.2009
Greek language	PA201-1179	489.3
Greek language—Dialects	PA500-581	489
Greek language—Dictionaries	PA441-465	489.33
Greek language—Etymology	PA421-430	489.32
Greek language—Grammar	PA251-379	489.35
Greek language—Lexicography	PA431-465	489.33028
Greek language—Morphology	PA283-287	489.35
Greek language—Parts of speech	PA303-361	489.35
Greek language—Phonology	PA265-281	489.315
Greek language—Study and teaching	PA231-241	489.3071
Greek language—Style	PA401-407	889.309
Greek language—Syntax	PA367-379	489.35
Greek language, Biblical	PA695-895	487.4
Greek language, Biblical—Dictionaries	PA881	487.43
Greek language, Biblical—Grammar	PA813-857	487.45
Greek language, Hellenistic (300 B.C.-600 A.D.)	PA600-895	487.4
Greek language, Medieval and late	PA1000-1179	489
Greek language, Modern	PA1000-1179	489.3
Greek language, Modern—Dialects	PA1151-1159	489.37
Greek language, Modern—Dictionaries	PA1031	489.33
Greek language, Modern—Dictionaries	PA1123-1145	489.33
Greek language, Modern—Etymology	PA1111-1114.5	489.32
Greek language, Modern—Grammar	PA1051-1099	489.35
Greek language, Modern—Morphology	PA1076	489.35
Greek language, Modern—Parts of speech	PA1081-1089	489.35
Greek language, Modern—Phonology	PA1061-1072	489.315
Greek language, Modern—Study and teaching	PA1041-1049	489.3071
Greek language, Modern—Syntax	PA1091-1097	489.35
Greek letter societies	LJ	371.85
Greek literature	PA3300-3516	880.8
Greek literature	PA3051-4505	880
Greek literature—Criticism, Textual	PA3520-3564	880.9
Greek literature, Hellenistic	PA3081-3084	880
Greek literature, Hellenistic—Criticism, Textual	PA3527	880.9
Greek literature, Modern	PA5201-5660	889
Greek literature, Modern—1453-1800	PA5301-5395	889.08001
Greek literature, Modern—History and criticism	PA5230-5269	889.09
Greek periodicals	AP85	059.89
Greek poetry	PA3092-3125	881.009
Greek poetry, Hellenistic—Criticism, Textual	PA3537-3543	881.009
Greek poetry, Modern	PA5259-5255	889.1009
Greek poetry, Modern	PA5280-5289	889.1008
Greek prose literature	PA3473-3475	888.08
Greek prose literature	PA3255-3273	888.08
Greek prose literature, Modern	PA5265	888.08
Greek prose literature, Modern	PA5295	889.808
Green Revolution	S439-481	333.7316
Green manuring	S661	631.874
Green movement	GE195-199	333.72
Green movement	JA75.8	333.72
Greenbacks	HG604	332.40440973
Greenhouse gardening	SB415	635.9823
Greenhouse gases	TD885.5.G73	628.532
Greenhouse plants	SB414.6-416.3	635.9823
Greenhouses	SB415-416.3	631.583
Greenland—Census	HA740	319.82

Subject Heading	LC	Dewey	Subject Heading	LC	Dewey
Greenland—Economic conditions	HC110.5	330.9982	Guatemala—Politics and government	JL1480-1499	320.97281
Greenland—Maps	G3380-3384	912.982	Guatemalan literature	PQ7490-7499.2	860
Greenland—Maps	G1110-1114	912.982	Guava	QK495.M9	583.765
Greenland—Politics and government	JN7380-7389	320.9982	Guernsey cattle	SF199.G8	636.224
Grenada	F2056	972.9845	Guerrilla warfare	U240	355.0218
Grenada—Politics and government	JL629.6	320.9729845	Guerrillas	D25.5	355.0218
Grenades	UF765	358.1282	Guide dog schools	HV1780-.6	362.418071
Grievance procedures	HD6972.5	331.8896	Guides (Spiritualism)	BF1275.G85	133.9
Grievance procedures	HF5549.5.G7	658.3155	Guidons	UC590-595	355.15
Grinding and polishing	TJ1280-1298	621.92	Guild socialism	HD6479	335.15
Groceries	TX341-357	641	Guilford Court House, Battle of 1781	E241.G9	973.337
Ground controlled approach	TL696.L33	629.1325213	Guillotine	HV8555	364.66
Ground support systems (Astronautics)	TL4000-4050	629.478	Guilt	BF575.G8	152.4
Groundhog Day	GT4995.G	394.261	Guinea (Coin)	CJ2484	737.4941
Groundwater	GB1001-1199.8	551.49	Guinea pigs	QL737.R634	599.3592
Groundwater—Pollution	TD426-.8	628.168	Guinea pigs	SF401.G85	636.93592
Group counseling	BF637.C6	158.35	Guinea—Census	HA4726	316.652
Group extensions (Mathematics)	QA171	512.4	Guinea—Civilization	DT543.4	966.52
Group homes for children	HV862-866	362.732	Guinea—Description and travel	DT543.27	916.65204
Group marriage	HQ981-996	306.842	Guinea—Economic conditions	HC1030	330.96652
Group ministry	BV675	262.14	Guinea—History	DT543.5-.827	966.52
Group psychoanalysis	RC510	616.8917	Guinea—History—Portuguese Invasion, 1970	DT543.8	966.5205
Group psychotherapy	RC488-.6	616.89152			
Group theory	QA174-183	512.2	Guinea—History—Coup d'etat, 1984	DT543.822	966.5205
Growth	QH511	571.8			
Growth	QP84	612.6	Guinea—Maps	G8790-8794	912.6652
Growth (Plants)	QK731-745	571.82	Guinea-Bissau—Census	HA4736	316.657
Growth disorders	RB140-.5	616.47	Guinea-Bissau—Civilization	DT613.4	966.57
Guadeloupe	F2066	972.976	Guinea-Bissau—Description and travel	DT613.2	916.65704
Guadeloupe—Census	HA918.7	317.2976			
Guadeloupe—Maps	G5070-5074	912.72976	Guinea-Bissau—History	DT613.5-.83	966.57
Guadeloupe—Politics and government	JL820-829	320.972976	Guinea-Bissau—History—Revolution, 1963-1974	DT613.78	966.5702
Guam—Census	HA4012	319.67	Guinea-Bissau—History—Coup d'etat, 1980	DT613.8	966.5703
Guaranteed annual wage	HD4928.A5	331.21			
Guard duty	U190-195	355.422	Guinea-Bissau—Maps	G8890-8894	912.6657
Guard troops	UA12.8	355.35	Guitar	MT580-588	787.8707
Guatemala	F1461-1477	972.81	Guitar music	M125-129	787.87
Guatemala—Census	HA811-820	317.281	Gujarati language	PK1841-1847	491.47
Guatemala—Civilization	F1463.5	972.81	Gujarati literature	PK1850-1888	891.47
Guatemala—Description and travel	F1464-.3	917.28104	Gulf States—History	F296	976
			Gulf Stream	GC296.G9	551.4701
Guatemala—Emigration and immigration	JV7416	325.(27281/ 7281)	Gums—Diseases	RK401-410	617.632
			Gums and resins	SB289-291	633.895
Guatemala—Gazetteers	F1462	917.281003	Gums and resins	QD419-.7	547.8434
Guatemala—History	F1465-1466.7	972.81	Gums and resins	TP977-979.5	668.37
Guatemala—History—To 1821	F1466.4	972.810(1-3)	Gums and resins, Synthetic	TP977-979.5	668.374
			Gun control	HV7435-7439	363.33
Guatemala—History—1821-1945	F1466.45	972.810(4-52)	Gunantuna (Melanesian people)	GN671.B5	305.8995
Guatemala—History—1945-1985	F1466.5	972.81052	Guncotton	TP276	662.26
			Gunnery	UF800-805	623.55
Guatemala—History—1985-	F1466.7	972.8105(2-3)	Gunpowder	TP272	662.26
Guatemala—Maps	G4810-4814	912.7281	Gunpowder Plot, 1605	DA392-.1	941.061
Guatemala—Periodicals	F1461	972.81005	Gunshot wounds	RD96.3	617.145
			Gunsmithing	TS535-.4	683.4

Subject Heading	LC	Dewey	Subject Heading	LC	Dewey
Gurjara-Pratihara dynasty	DS451.8	954.02	Haiti—Description and travel	F1917	917.29404
Gushers	TN871	622.3382	Haiti—Emigration and immigration	JV7393	325.(27294/7294)
Guyana	F2361-2391	988.1	Haiti—Gazetteers	F1913	917.294003
Guyana—Census	HA1033	318.81	Haiti—History	F1918-1939	972.94
Guyana—Civilization	F2369.8	988.1	Haiti—History—To 1791	F1923	972.940(1-3)
Guyana—Gazetteers	F2364	918.81003	Haiti—History— Revolution, 1791-1804	F1923	972.9403
Guyana—History	F2380.3-2391	988.1	Haiti—History—1804-1844	F1924	972.9404
Guyana—History—To 1803	F2383	988.101	Haiti—History— Revolution, 1843	F1938.3	972.9404
Guyana—History— 1803-1966	F2384	988.10(1-31)	Haiti—History—1844-1915	F1926	972.9404
Guyana—History—1966-	F2385	988.1032	Haiti—History—American occupation, 1915-1934	F1927	972.9405
Guyana—Manufactures	TS48	670.9881	Haiti—History—1934-1986	F1927-1928	972.940(6-72)
Guyana—Maps	G5250-5254	912.881	Haiti—History—1986-	F1928.2-.23	972.94073
Guyana—Periodicals	F2361	988.1005	Haiti—History—Coup d'etat, 1991	F1928.2	972.94073
Guyana—Politics and government	JL680-689	320.9881	Haiti—Maps	G4940-4944	912.7294
Guyanese literature	PR9320-.9	820	Haiti—Periodicals	F1900	972.94005
Gymnasiums	GV403-405	796.068	Haiti—Politics and government	JL1080-1099	320.97294
Gymnastics	GV461-475	796.44	Half-dollar	CJ1835	737.4973
Gymnosperms	QK494-.5	585	Half-life (Nuclear physics)	QC795.8.H3	539.752
Gymnosperms, Fossil	QE975-978	561.5	Half-timbered houses	NA7175	728
Gynecologic emergencies	RG158	618.1025	Half-track vehicles, Military	UG446.5	358.1883
Gynecologic examination	RG107-.5	618.1075	Halide minerals	QE389.4	549.4
Gynecologic nursing	RG105	610.73678	Hall effect	QC612.H3	537.6
Gynecologic pathology	RG77	618.07	Halley's comet	QB723.H2	523.642
Gynecologists	RG71-76	618.1092	Halloween	GT4965	394.2646
Gynecologists—Directories	RG32-33	618.10025	Hallucinations and illusions	BF491-493	154.4
Gynecology	RG	618.1	Hallucinations and illusions	RC553.H3	616.8634
Gynecology—Congresses	RG31	618.1006	Hallucinogenic drugs	RM324.8	615.7883
Gynecology—Periodicals	RG26	618.1005	Halocarbons	TD887.H3	628.532
Gynecology—Psychological aspects	RG103.5	618.10019	Halogen compounds	QD165	546.73
Gynoplasty	RG104.5	618.1059	Halogen compounds	QD412	547.62
Gypsies	DX	909.0491497	Hamiltonian systems	QA614.83	514.74
Gypsies—Biography	DX125-127	920.009291497	Hammerhead sharks	QL638.95.S7	597.3
Gypsies—Education	LC3503-3520	371.82991497	Hammers	TJ1201.H3	621.973
Gypsies—History	DX135-145	909.0491497	Hammond organ	ML597	786.509
Gypsum	TN946	622.3635	Hampton Roads (Va.), Battle of, 1862	E473.2	973.752
Gyro compass	TL589.2.C58	629.1352	Hamsters	QL737.R666	599.356
Gyro compass	VK577	623.8932	Hand	QM548	611.97
Gyroscopes	QA862.G9	531.34	Hand	BF908-940	133.6
HIV (Viruses)	QR414.6.H58	616.979201	Hand—Surgery	RD778-.5	617.575059
Habit	BF335-337	152.33	Hand spinning	TT847	746.12
Habit breaking	BF337.B74	152.33	Hand-to-hand fighting	GV1111-1141	796.81
Haciendas	HD1471	333.335	Hand weaving	TT848-849.2	746.14
Hacksaws	TJ1233	621.93	Handbell music	M147	786.88485
Hadith	BP135	297.124	Handbell ringing	MT710	786.8848507
Hadith (Shiites)	BP193.25-.28	297.124	Handbooks, vade-mecums, etc.	AG103-190	028.7
Hadrons	QC793.5.H32-.H329	539.7216	Handcuffs	HV7936.E7	363.20284
Hague, Treaty of, 1717	D283.5	940.253	Handgun hunting	SK39.3	799.213
Hail	QC929.H15	551.5787	Handicapped	HV1551-3024	362.(3-4)
Hailstorms	QC929.H15	551.554	Handicapped—Marriage	HQ1036-1043	306.81087
Hair	QM488	611.78	Handicapped—Sexual behavior	HQ30.5	306.70816
Hair	QL942	573.58	Handicapped children— Education	LC4001-4100	371.91
Hair preparations	TT969	646.7240284			
Hair—Dyeing and bleaching	TT973	646.724			
Hairweaving	TT975	646.724			
Haiti	F1900-1930	972.94			
Haiti—Census	HA881-885	317.294			
Haiti—Civilization	F1916	972.94			

Subject Heading	LC	Dewey	Subject Heading	LC	Dewey
Handicapped children—Services for	HV888-907	362.(3-4)	Hawaii—Maps	G4380-4384	912.969
Handicapped parents	HQ759.912	306.874087	Hawaii—National Guard	UA159.1-.9	355.3709969
Handicraft	TT	745.5	Hay fever	RC590	616.202
Handicraft—Encyclopedias	TT9	745.503	Hazardous occupations	T54	363.11
Handicraft—Exhibitions	TT6	745.5074	Hazardous substances	T55.3.H3	604.7
Handicraft—Periodicals	TT1	745.505	Hazing	LB3604-3615	371.8
Handicraft—Therapeutic use	RM735.7.H35	615.85156	Hazing	U410.E9	355.0071073
Handicraft—[By region or country]	TT15-127	745.509(4-9)	Head	QM535	611.91
Hanging	HV8579-8581	364.66	Head—Diseases	RC936	617.51
Hanging baskets	SB418-.4	635.986	Head—Diseases—Eclectic treatment	RV291	617.5106
Hankel functions	QA408	515.53	Head-gear	GT2110	391.43
Hanukkah	BM695.H3	296.435	Headache	RB128	616.8491
Hanukkah cookery	TX739.2.H35	641.5676435	Headache	RC392	616.8491
Hanukkah lamp	BM657.H3	296.435	Heads of state	JF251-289	321
Happiness	BF575.H27	152.42	Heads of state—Succession	JF285	321.8042
Happiness	BJ1480-1486	170	Heads of state—Term of office	JF286	352.23
Harbor of Refuge Lighthouse (Del.)	VK1025.H	623.894209751	Healers	RZ407-408	615.851092
Harbors	HE550-560	387.1	Healing gods	BL325.H4	291.31
Harbors	TC353-365	627.2	Health	RA773-790	613
Harbors	TC203-327	387.1	Health boards	RA10-388	353.606
Harbors	VK321-369.8	387.1	Health boards—Africa	RA345-352	353.60606
Harbors—Law and legislation	K4198-4200	343.0967	Health boards—Asia	RA303-340	353.60605
			Health boards—Australia	RA371-372	353.606094
Harbors of refuge	VK369-.8	387.1	Health boards—Canada	RA184-186	353.606071
Hard-core unemployed	HD5708.8-.85	331.137	Health boards—Central America	RA191	353.6060728
Hard materials	TA418.45	620.1126			
Hardanger fiddle music	M59	787.6	Health boards—Europe	RA239-299	353.60604
Hardness	TA418.42	620.1126	Health boards—Mexico	RA187-188	353.606072
Hardware	TS400-455	683	Health boards—South America	RA198-235	353.60608
Hare hunting	SK341.H3	799.259328			
Harmonic analysis	QA403-.3	515.2433	Health boards—United States	RA11-182	353.606073
Harmonic functions	QA405	515.53			
Harmonica	ML1088	788.8209	Health boards—[United States, cities]	RA13	353.60607(4-9)
Harmonica music	M175.M8	788.82			
Harmony	ML3836	781.25	Health boards—[United States, by state]	RA15-182	353.60607(4-9)
Harmony	ML3852	781.25			
Harmony	ML3815	781.25	Health maintenance organizations	RA413-.7	362.104258
Harmony (Aesthetics)	BH301.H3	701.8			
Harmony of the spheres	BD645	113	Health promotion	RA427.8	613
Harness racehorses	SF343	636.12	Health resorts	RA794-954	613.122
Harness racing	SF338.7-345	798.46	Health surveys	RA407.3-408	614.42
Harp music	M115-119	787.9	Hearing	BF251-.5	152.15
Harpsichord music	M20-39	786.4	Hearing	QP460-469.3	612.85
Harvest festivals	GT4380-4499	394.26	Hearing aids	RF300-310	617.89
Harvesting	GT5810-5856.995	390.463	Hearing disorders	RF286-320	617.8
Harvesting	SB129	631.55	Hearing impaired	HV2350-2990.5	362.42
Harvesting time	SB185.8	631.55	Heart	QP111-114	612.17
Harvesting time	S600.7.H37	631.55	Heart—Anatomy	QL838	573.17
Hashish	RC568.C2	616.8635	Heart—Anatomy	QM181	611.12
Hashish	RS165.H3	633.79	Heart—Diseases	RC681-688	616.12
Hasidism	BM198	296.8332	Heart—Surgery	RD598-.35	617.412
Hastings, Battle of, 1066	DA196	941.021	Heart—Transplantation	RD598.35.T7	617.4120592
Hate	BF575.H3	152.4	Heart, Artificial	RD598.35.A78	617.4120592
Hats	GT2110	391.43	Heart valves—Diseases	RC685.V2	616.125
Haunted houses	BF1475	133.122	Heat	QC251-338.5	536
Hawaii—Civilization	DU624.5	996.9	Heat—Transmission	QC319.8-338.5	536.2
Hawaii—Gazetteers	DU622	919.69003	Heat-engines	TJ255-265	621.4025
Hawaii—History	DU625-629	996.9	Heat pumps	TJ262	621.4025

Subject Heading	LC	Dewey	Subject Heading	LC	Dewey
Heat pumps	TH7638	697.3	Hemorrhoids	RC865	616.35
Heating	GT420-425	392.36	Hepatitis	RC848.H42	616.3623
Heating	TH7005-7699	697	Hepatitis, Neonatal	RJ272	618.923623
Heating plants	TH7461	697.03	Heracles (Greek mythology)	BL820.H5	292.13
Heaven	BT844-849	236.24	Heraldry	CR	929.6
Heavy ions	QC702.7.H42	539.7234	Heraldry—Congresses	CR2	929.606
Heavy water reactors	TK9203.H4	621.4834	Heraldry—Dictionaries	CR13	929.603
Hebrew essays	AC101-102	089.924	Heraldry—Directories	CR11	929.6025
Hebrew language	PJ4501-4937	492.4	Heraldry—Exhibitions	CR9	929.6074
Hebrew language—Dialects	PJ4855-4937	492.47	Heraldry—History	CR151-159	929.609
Hebrew language—Dictionaries	PJ4825-4847	492.43	Heraldry—Periodicals	CR1	929.605
Hebrew language—Dictionaries	PJ4935-4937	492.43	Heraldry—Philosophy	CR14-16	929.601
Hebrew language—Etymology	PJ4801-4819	492.42	Heraldry, Ornamental	CR29-69	929.6
Hebrew language—Etymology	PJ4931-4933	492.42	Heralds	CR183-185	929.6
Hebrew language—Grammar	PJ4911-4925	492.475	Heralds	GT5020	394.23
Hebrew language—Grammar	PJ4553-4731	492.45	Herb gardens	SB351.H5	635.7
Hebrew language—Lexicography	PJ4820-4847	492.43028	Herbal teas	TX415	641.357
Hebrew language—Lexicography	PJ4934-4937	492.43028	Herbaria	QK75-77	580.74
Hebrew language—Morphology	PJ4601-4677	492.45	Herbicides	SB951.4	632.954
Hebrew language—Phonology	PJ4576-4583	492.415	Herbs	TX406-407	641.657
Hebrew language, Talmudic	PJ4901-4950	492.47	Herbs	SB351.H5	635.7
Hebrew literature	PJ5001-5060	892.4	Herbs—Therapeutic use	RM666.H33	615.321
Hebrew literature—Study and teaching	PJ5007	892.4071	Heredity	HM121	304.5
Hebrew literature, Medieval	PJ5016	892.409002	Heredity	HV6121-6125	364.24
Hebrew literature, Medieval	PJ5037	892.408002	Heresies, Christian	BT20-30	262.8
Hebrew literature, Modern	PJ5038	892.408003	Hermaphroditism	RC883	616.694
Hebrew literature, Modern	PJ5017-5021	892.409003	Hermeneutics	BD240-241	121.68
Hebrew philology	PJ4501-4541	492.4	Hernia	RD621-626	617.559059
Hebrew poetry, Biblical	BS1401-1405.5	223	Heroin	HV5822.H4	362.293
Hedges	SB437	635.976	Herpes genitalis	RA644.H45	614.547
Hedonism	BJ1491	171.4	Herpes genitalis	RC203.H45	616.9518
Hedonism	B279	183	Heterocyclic compounds	QD399-406	547.59
Heisenberg uncertainty principle	QC174.17.H4	530.122	Hewitt-Nachbin spaces	QA611.234	514.3
Helicopters	TL716-.9	629.133352	Hibernation	QL755	591.565
Heliograph	UG582.H4	623.7312	Hibiscus	QK495.M27	583.685
Helium	QD181.H4	546.751	Hibiscus	SB413.H6	635.933685
Helium	TP245.H4	665.822	Hides and skins	HD9778-.5	675.2
Hell	BT834-838	236.25	Hides and skins	TS967	675.2
Hell	BL735	292.28	Hieroglyphic Bibles	BS560	220.49
Hell	BL545	291.23	Hieroglyphics	PH1091-1097	493.111
Helmets	U825	355.81	Hieroglyphics	PJ1091	493.1
Help-wanted advertising	HF6125.5	659.19658311	High-calcium diet	RM237.56	613.285
Helsinki	DL1175-.95	948.971	High-carbohydrate diet	RM237.59	613.283
Hematological oncology	RC280.H47	616.99419	High-fiber diet	RM237.6	613.263
Hematology, Experimental	RC636	616.15027	High-frequency ventilation (Therapy)	RC735.H54	616.206
Hematology, Experimental	RB145	616.15027	High Holiday sermons	BM746	296.4731
Hemoglobin	QP96.5	612.1111	High Holidays	BM693.H5	296.431
Hemophilia	RC642	616.1572	High occupancy vehicle lanes	HE336.B8	388.12
Hemorrhage	RB144-.5	616.157	High-protein diet	RM237.65	613.282
			High school dropouts	LC146.5-.8	373.12913
			High school enrollment	LC146	373.1219
			High school equivalency certificates	LB1627.7	373.238
			High school principals	LB2831.9-.976	373.12012
			High school teachers	LB1777-.4	373.11
			High schools	LB1603-1694	373.238
			High schools—United States	LD7501	373.73
			High temperatures	QC276-277	536.57

Subject Heading	LC	Dewey	Subject Heading	LC	Dewey
Highway capacity	HE336.H48	388.314	History, Modern	D101-110.5	909.08
Highway engineering	TE	625.7	History, Modern	D205-1075	940.2
Highway law	K4028-4042	343.0942	History, Modern—16th	D219-234	909.5
Highway law	K3492	343.0942	century		
Highway law—England	KD1040-1048	343.420942	History, Modern—17th	D242-283.5	909.6
Highway law—United	KF5521-5536	343.730942	century		
States			History, Modern—1945-	D839-850	909.08
Hiking	GV199-.5	796.51	History, Modern—	D839	909.8(24-3)05
Hillside planting	S627.H5	631.455	1945- —Periodicals		
Hindi language	PK1931-1939	491.43	History, Modern—20th	D410-893	909.82
Hindu astrology	BF1714.H5	133.59445	century		
Hindu pilgrims and	BL1239.32	294.5351	History, Modern—	D205	909.0803
pilgrimages			Dictionaries		
Hindu saints	BL1171	294.5213	History (Theology)	BR115.H5	230
Hindu sects	BL1245.A1	294.55	Hittite language	P945	491.998
Hinduism	B130-133	181.4	Hobbies	GV1201	790.13
Hinduism	BL1100-1270	294.5	Hockey	GV847	796.962
Hinduism	BL2000-2030	294.5	Hodgkin's disease	RC644	616.99446
Hinduism—Doctrines	BL1213.32-1215	294.52	Hoisting machinery	TJ1350-1383	621.862
Hindustani language	PK1931-1937	491.43	Hokan-Coahuiltecan	PM1343	497.57
Hindustani literature	PK2030-2142	891.43	languages		
Hinomoto (Sect)	BL2222.H5	299.5619	Holding patterns	TL711.H65	629.13252
Hip joint—Dislocation,	RD772	617.71043	(Aeronautics)		
Congenital			Holiday cookery	TX739-.2	641.568
Hippocampus (Brain)	QL938.H56	573.86	Holiday pay	HD4928.H	331.2576
Hippocampus (Brain)	QM455	611.81	Holidays	GT3930-4995	394.26
Hispanic Americans	E184.S75	973.0468073	Holiness	BT767	234.8
Hispanic Americans—	LC2667-2688	370.8968073	Holography	QC449-.3	774.0153
Education			Holy Cross	BT465	232.963
Histochemistry	QH613	572	Holy Roman Empire—History	DD125-198.7	943.02
Histology	QM550-577.8	611.018	Holy Shroud	BT587.S4	232.966
Histology	QL807	571.5	Holy Spirit	BT117-123	231.3
Historians	D14-15	907.202	Holy Week	GT4930	394.2667
Historic buildings—Law	KF4310-4312	344.73094	Holy Week	BT414	263.925/232.96
and legislation—			Holy Week	BV90-95	263.925
United States			Home	GT2420	392.3
Historical fiction	PN3441	809.381	Home	HQ503-1064	306.8
Historical geography	G141	911	Home economics	TX	640
Historical geology	QE28.3	551.09	Home economics—	TX5	640.6
Historical jurisprudence	K325-328	340.09	Congresses		
Historical lexicology	P326	401.409	Home economics—	TX11	640.3
Historical linguistics	P140	417.7	Encyclopedias		
Historical models	D16	902.28	Home economics—	TX298-299	640.284
Historical sociology	HM104	301.09	Equipment and supplies		
Historicism	D16.9	901	Home economics—History	TX15-19	640.9
Historiography	D206	909.08072	Home economics—	TX1	640.5
Historiography	D13-15	907.2	Periodicals		
History	D	900	Home economics—	TX165-286	640.71
History—Congresses	D3	906	Study and teaching		
History—Dictionaries	D9	903	Home economics—[By	TX21-127	640.9(4-9)
History—Methodology	D16-.18	901	region or country]		
History—Periodicals	D1	905	Home banking services	HG1711-1712	332.17
History—Philosophy	D16.7-.9	901	Home care services	RA645.3-.37	362.14
History—Study and teaching	D16.2-.5	907.1	Home equity loans	HG2040.45	332.722
History, Ancient	D51-95	930	Home improvement loans	HG2040.4	332.722
History, Ancient—	D54	930.03	Home labor	HD2331-2336.35	338.634
Dictionaries			Home missions	BV2650	266.022
History, Ancient—	D56-.52	930.072	Home ownership	HD7287.8-.82	363.5
Historiography			Home schooling	LC40	371.042
History, Ancient—	D51	930.05	Home-based businesses	HD2331-2336.35	338.634
Periodicals			Homelands (South Africa)	DT1760	968.29

Subject Heading	LC	Dewey	Subject Heading	LC	Dewey
Homeless students	LC5144-.3	371.826942	Hong Kong—Census	HA4651-4655	315.125
Homeopathic physicians—Biography	RX61-66	615.532092	Hong Kong—Maps	G7940-7944	912.5125
			Hopi Indians	E99.H7	973.049745
Homeopathic physicians—Directories	RX46	615.532025	Hopi language	PM1351	497.45
			Hormone therapy	RM283-298	615.36
Homeopathy	RX	615.532	Hormones	QP801.H7	573.44
Homeopathy—Attenuations, dilutions, and potencies	RX81	615.532	Hormones, Sex	QP572.S4	612.405
			Horology	TS540-549	681.11(3-4)
Homeopathy—Congresses	RX21	615.53206	Horse farms	SF290-291	636.1
Homeopathy—History	RX51	615.53209	Horse racing	SF321-359.7	798.4
Homeopathy—Hospitals and dispensaries	RX6-.5	362.11	Horse railroads	TF830	625.66
			Horse railroads	TF16	625.1
Homeopathy—Materia medica and therapeutics	RX601-675	615.532	Horse shows	SF294.5-297.7	636.10811
			Horse sports	SF294.2-294.35	798
Homeopathy—Periodicals	RX11	615.53205	Horsemanship	SF309	798.2
Homeopathy—Societies, etc.	RX1	615.53206	Horsemanship	UE460-475	357.2
			Horses	HV4749-4755	364.187
Homeopathy—Study and teaching	RX91-101	615.532071	Horses	UE460-475	357.2
			Horses	SF277-359.7	636.1
Homeostasis	QP90.4	571.75	Horses	UC600-695	357.2
Homeowner's insurance	HG9986	368.096	Horticultural crops	SB317.5-319.77	635
Homeowners' associations	HD7287.8-.82	363.506	Hosiery	GT2128	391.413
Homestead law—United States	KF5670-5673	343.730253	Hosiery	TT679-695	687.3
			Hospice care	RT87.T45	610.7361
Homework	LB1048	371.30281	Hospices (Terminal care)	R726.8	362.1756
Homo erectus	GN284-.7	569.9	Hospital libraries	Z675.H7	027.662
Homo habilis	GN283.9	569.9	Hospitality	BJ2021-2028	395.3
Homogenized milk	SF259	636.2142	Hospitals	RA960-996	362.11
Homology theory	QA612.3-.77	514.23	Hospitals—Administration	RA971-.8	362.11068
Homosexuality	HQ75-76.95	306.766	Hospitals—Emergency service	RA975.5.E5	362.18
Homosexuality	RC558-.5	616.8583			
Honduran literature	PQ7500-7509.2	860	Hospitals—Outpatient services	RA974-.5	362.12
Honduras	F1501-1517	972.83			
Honduras—Census	HA821-830	317.283	Hospitals—Research	RA964.5	362.11072
Honduras—Civilization	F1503.8	972.83	Hospitals—[By region or country]	RA980-993	362.1109(4-9)
Honduras—Description and Travel	F1504	917.28304			
			Hospitals—Africa	RA991	362.11096
Honduras—Emigration and immigration	JV7419	325.(27283/7283)	Hospitals—Arab countries	RA990.5	362.1109174927
			Hospitals—Asia	RA990	362.11095
Honduras—Gazetteers	F1502	917.283003	Hospitals—Australia	RA992-.3	362.110994
Honduras—History	F1505.5-1508.33	972.83	Hospitals—Canada	RA983	362.110971
Honduras—History—To 1838	F1507	972.830(1-4)	Hospitals—Europe	RA985-989	362.11094
			Hospitals—Great Britain	RA986-988	362.110941
Honduras—History—1838-1933	F1507.5	972.8305(1-2)	Hospitals—New Zealand	RA992.5-.7	362.110993
			Hospitals—Oceania	RA993	362.11099(5-6)
Honduras—History—Coup d'etat, 1904	F1507.5	972.83051	Hospitals—United States	RA981-982	362.110973
			Hospitals, Gynecologic and obstetric	RG12-16	362.11
Honduras—History—Revolution, 1919	F1507.5	972.83051			
			Hospitals, Medieval	RA964	362.110902
Honduras—History—1933-1982	F1508-.22	972.8305(2-3)	Hospitals, Naval and marine	VG410-450	359.72
Honduras—History—1982-	F1508.3-.33	972.83053	Hospitals, Ophthalmic and aural	RF5-6	362.11
Honduras—Maps	G4830-4834	912.7283			
Honduras—Periodicals	F1501	972.83005	Hospitals, Ophthalmic and aural—[By region or country]	RF6	362.1109(4-9)
Honduras—Politics and government	JL1520-1539	320.97283			
			Hostility (Psychology)	BF575.H6	152.47
Honesty	BJ1533.H7	179.9	Hot air balloons	TL638	629.13322
Honey	SF539	638.16	Hot-air heating	TH7601-7635	697.3
Honey	TX560.H7	641.38	Hot springs	QE528	551.23
Honeybee	QL568.A6	595.799	Hot springs	GB1198-.4	551.23
Honeybee	SF521-539	638.12			

Subject Heading	LC	Dewey
Hot-water heating	TH7511-7549	697.4
Hot-water supply	TH6551-6568	696.6
Hotels	GT3770-3896	395.53
Hotels	NA7800-7853	728.5
Hotels	TX901-946	647.94
Hotels—Personnel management	TX911.3.P4	647.940683
Hounds	SF429.H6	636.753
Hour-glasses	QB214	529.7
Hours of labor	HD5106-5267	331.257
Hours of labor, Flexible	HD5109-.2	331.2572
Hours of labor, Staggered	HD5108-.2	331.257
House cleaning	TX324	648.5
House construction	TH4805-4890	690.8
House painting	TT320-324	698.1
House plants	SB419-.3	635.965
Houseboats	GV836	797.129
Houseboats	VM335	728.78
Household appliances, Electric	TK7018-7301	643.6
Household ecology	QH541.5.H67	577.554
Househusbands	HQ756.6	640.92
Houses (Astrology)	BF1716-.28	133.52
Housing	HD7285-7391	363.5
Housing—Law and legislation—United States	KF5721-5740	344.73063635
Housing—[By region or country]	HD7291-7391	363.509(4-9)
Housing—Africa	HD7372-7378.4	363.5096
Housing—Asia	HD7359.6	363.5095
Housing—Australia	HD7379	363.50994
Housing—Benelux countries	HD7342-7344.5	363.509492
Housing—Canada	HD7305	363.50971
Housing—Central America	HD7307-7313	363.509728
Housing—China	HD7368	363.50951
Housing—Developing countries	HD7391	363.5091724
Housing—Europe	HD7332-7357.7	363.5094
Housing—France	HD7338	363.50944
Housing—Germany	HD7339-.5	363.50943
Housing—Great Britain	HD7333-7335.5	363.50941
Housing—Greece	HD7357.5	363.509495
Housing—India	HD7361	363.50954
Housing—Iran	HD7359.2	363.50955
Housing—Iraq	HD7359	363.509567
Housing—Israel	HD7358.45	363.5095694
Housing—Italy	HD7341	363.50945
Housing—Japan	HD7367	363.50952
Housing—Mexico	HD7306	363.50972
Housing—Philippines	HD7366	363.509599
Housing—Russia	HD7345	363.50947
Housing—South America	HD7320-7331	363.5098
Housing—Spain	HD7351	363.50946
Housing—Switzerland	HD7353	363.509494
Housing—Turkey	HD7358.25	363.509561
Housing—United States	HD7293—7304	363.50973
Housing—West Indies	HD7314-7319.9	363.509729
Housing, Cooperative	HD7287.7-.72	334.1
Housing, Rural	HD7289	363.5091734
Houston (Tex.)	F394.H8	976.41411
Howitzers	UF560-565	358.1282
Howitzers	UF470-475	358.12822
Hsiang dialects	PL1861-1870	495.17
Hsiung-nu	DS25	950.04
Huguenots	BX9450-9459	284.5
Hula (Dance)	GV1796.H8	792.319969
Human acts	BV4618	241
Human anatomy	QM	611
Human anatomy—Atlases	QM25	611.0022
Human anatomy—Laboratory manuals	QM34	611.0078
Human anatomy—Variation	QM24	599.94
Human-animal communication	QL776	591.59
Human capital	HD4904.7	331.11
Human chromosome abnormalities	RB155.5-.8	616.042
Human-computer interacton	QA76.9.H85	004.019
Human ecology	GF1-900	304.2
Human ecology—[By region or country]	GF500-895	304.209(4-9)
Human ecology—Tropics	GF895	304.20913
Human ecology—United States	GF503-504	304.20973
Human evolution	GN281-289	599.938
Human experimentation in medicine	R853.H8	619.98
Human growth	QP84	612.6
Human immunogenetics	QR184.2	616.0796
Human information processing	BF444	153
Human mechanics	QP301-336	612.76
Human physiology	QP34-38	612
Human reproduction	QP251-285	612.6
Human reproductive technology	RG133.5-135	618.178
Human rights	K3236-3268	342.085
Human rights	JC571-628	323
Human settlements	GF101-127	307.14
Human settlements	HT51-65	307
Human skeleton	QM101-117	611.71
Humanism	B778	144
Humanism	B821	144
Humanistic Judaism	BM197.8	296.834
Humanistic ethics	BJ1360	171.2
Humanistic psychology	BF204	150.198
Humanitarianism	BJ1475.3	171.2
Humidity	QC915-917	551.571
Hummel figurines	NK4660	738.82
Humor in education	LA23	370.207
Humorists	PN6147	808.87092
Hundred Years War, 1339-1453	DC96-105	944.025
Hungarian language	PH2001-2800	494.511
Hungarian language—Dictionaries	PH2625-2693	494.5113
Hungarian language—Grammar	PH2097-2410	494.5115
Hungarian language—Lexicography	PH2601-2693	494.5113028

Subject Heading	LC	Dewey	Subject Heading	LC	Dewey
Hungarian language—Slang	PH2800	494.5117	Hunting—[United States, By state]	SK47-145	799.297(4-9)
Hungarian literature	PH3001-3445	894.511	Hunting—West (U.S.)	SK45	799.2978
Hungarian literature (German)	PT3840-3848	830	Hunting, Prehistoric	GN799.H84	639.0901
Hungary	DB901-999	939.8/943.9	Hunting and fishing clubs	SK3	799.206
Hungary—Biography	DB922	920.0398/ 920.0439	Hunting and fishing clubs	SH403	799.1206
Hungary—Census	HA1201-1210	314.39	Hunting customs	GT5810-5850	394.3
Hungary—Civilization	DB920.5	939.8/943.9	Hunting guns	SK274	799.20283
Hungary—Description and travel	DB906.9-917.3	913.9804/ 914.3904	Hupertrichosis	RL431	616.546
Hungary—Gazetteers	DB904	913.98003/ 914.39003	Hurdy-gurdy music	M175.H9	787.69
			Hurricanes	QC944-948	551.552
Hungary—History—To 896	DB927-928.9	939.8/943.901	Hussites	BX4913-4918	284.3
Hungary—History—896-1301	DB929-.9	943.902	Hyaline membrane disease	RJ274	618.922
Hungary—History—Charles Robert, 1308-1342	DB930.2	943.903	Hydrants	TH9365	628.9252
			Hydraulic engineering	TC	621.2
Hungary—History—Louis I, 1342-1382	DB930.3	943.903	Hydraulic engineering—Dictionaries	TC9	621.203
Hungary—History—Sigismund, 1387-1437	DB930.4	943.903	Hydraulic engineering—History	TC15-20	621.209
Hungary—History—Turkish occupation, 1529-1699	DB931.94-932.48	943.9041	Hydraulic engineering—Periodicals	TC1	621.205
			Hydraulic engineering—Study and teaching	TC157-.5	621.1071
Hungary—History—1699-1848	DB932.3-934	943.9043	Hydraulic engineering—[By region or country]	TC21-127	621.109(4-9)
Hungary—History—Francis Joseph, 1848-1916	DB940-953	943.9042	Hydraulic engineers—Biography	TC139-140	621.2092
Hungary—History—20th century	DB947-957	943.90(43-54)	Hydraulic fluids	TJ844	621.20424
Hungary—History—1918-1945	DB955	943.905(1-2)	Hydraulic jacks	TJ1435	621.2
			Hydraulic laboratories	TC158	621.2072
Hungary—History—1945-	DB956-957	943.905(3-4)	Hydraulic machinery	TJ836-935	621.2
Hungary—History—Revolution, 1956	DB957	943.9052	Hydraulic mining	TN278	622.2927
			Hydraulic motors	TJ855-857	621.2
Hungary—Manufactures	TS65.5-66	670.9439	Hydraulics	TC160-179	532
Hungary—Maps	G6500-6504	912.439	Hydrocarbons	QD305.H5-.H9	547.41
Hungary—Maps	G1940-1944	912.439	Hydrocarbons	QD341.H9	547.61
Hungary—Periodicals	DB901	939.8005/ 943.9005	Hydrocephalus	RC391	616.858843
			Hydrodynamics	QC150-159	532.5
Hunger	QP141	612.391	Hydrodynamics	QA911-930	532.5
Hunt riding	SF295.65	799.23	Hydrodynamics	TC171-179	532.5
Hunters	SK15-17	799.2092	Hydroelectric power plants	TK1081-1083	621.312134
Hunters—Directories	SK12	799.292025	Hydrofoil boats	VM362	623.8204
Hunting	GT5810-5895	395.5	Hydrogen	QD181.H1	546.2
Hunting	SK	799.2	Hydrogen peroxide	RA766.H9	614.48
Hunting—Equipment and supplies	SK273-275	799.2028	Hydrographic surveying	VK588-597	551.4607
			Hydrography	VK	551.46
Hunting—History	SK21	799.209	Hydrology	GB651-2998	551.48
Hunting—Museums	SK276	799.2074	Hydrometallurgy	TN688	669.0283
Hunting—Periodicals	SK7	799.205	Hydrometeorology	GB2801-2998	551.57
Hunting—Societies, etc.	SK1	799.206	Hydroponics	SB126.5-.57	631.585
Hunting—[By region or country]	SK40-267	799.29(4-9)	Hydrotherapy	RM801-822	615.853
			Hygiene	RA770.5	613
Hunting—Africa	SK251-255	799.296	Hygiene	RA780	613
Hunting—North America	SK40-157	799.297	Hygiene, Sexual	RA788	613.95
Hunting—Southern States	SK43	799.2975	Hygienists	RA424.4-.5	613.092
Hunting—United States	SK41-145	799.2973	Hymns	M2115-2145	782.27
			Hymns	BV301-530	246.75
			Hyperbolic navigation	VK560	623.89
			Hyperborean languages	PM1-95	494.6
			Hypertension	RC685.H8	616.132
			Hypnotics	RM325	615.782

Subject Heading	LC	Dewey
Hypnotism	BF1111-1156	133.89
Hypnotism	RC490-499	154.7
Hypocrisy	BV4627.H8	241.3
Hypotension	RC685.H93	616.13
Hypothalamic hormones	QP572.H9	612.8262
Hypothalamus	QM455	611.81
Hypothesis	BC183	167
Hypothyroidism	RC657	616.444
Hysterectomy	RG391	618.1453
Hysteria	RC532	616.8524
Ia Drang Valley (Vietnam), Battle of, 1965	DS557.8.I	959.704342
Iatrogenic diseases	RC90	615.5
Ice	GB2401-2597	551.31
Ice-boats	GV843	796.97
Ice-breaking vessels	VM451	623.828
Ice cream, ices, etc.	TX795	641.86(2-3)
Ice fog	QC929.F7	551.575
Ice sheets	GB2401-2598	551.31
Icebergs	GB2401-2597	551.342
Iceland	DL301-398	949.12
Iceland—Census	HA1491-1500	314.912
Iceland—Description and travel	DL309-315	914.91204
Iceland—Gazetteers	DL304	914.912003
Iceland—History	DL351-380	949.12
Iceland—History—To 1262	DL357-360	949.1201
Iceland—History—1918-1945	DL375	949.120(4-5)
Iceland—Maps	G2060-2064	912.4912
Iceland—Maps	G6930-6934	912.4912
Iceland—Periodicals	DL301	949.12005
Iceland—Politics and government	JN7370-7379	320.94912
Icelandic drama	PT7411	839.692009
Icelandic drama	PT7470-7477	839.692008
Icelandic fiction	PT7413	839.693009
Icelandic fiction	PT7485-7487	839.693008
Icelandic language	PD2401-2447	439.69
Icelandic language—Dictionaries	PD2437	439.693
Icelandic language—Etymology	PD2431	439.692
Icelandic language—Grammar	PD2411-2423	439.695
Icelandic language—Slang	PD2447	439.697
Icelandic language—Study and teaching	PD2407	439.69071
Icelandic literature	PT7351-7550	839.69
Icelandic literature—Study and teaching	PT7370-7373	839.69071
Icelandic poetry	PT7465-7467	839.691008
Icelandic prose literature	PT7480-7495	839.69808
Icelandic prose literature	PT412-418	839.69808
Ichthyosis	RL435	616.544
Idaho	F741-755	979.6
Idaho—Gazetteers	F744	917.96003
Idaho—History—1951-	F750-.22	979.603(3-4)
Idaho—Maps	G4270-4274	912.796
Idaho—National Guard	UA160-169	355.3709796
Idaho—Periodicals	F741	979.6005
Idea (Philosophy)	B398.I3	184
Idealism	B823	141
Ideals (Algebra)	QA247	512.4
Identification	HV8073-.8	363.258
Identity	BD236	111.82
Ideology	B823.3	145
Idols and images—Worship	BL485	291.218
Illegitimacy	HQ998-999	305.906945
Illinois	F536-550	977.3
Illinois—History—To 1778	F544	977.30(1-2)
Illinois—History—1778-1865	F545	977.30(2-3)
Illinois—History—1865-	F546-.4	977.304
Illinois—History—1951-	F546.2-.4	977.304(3-4)
Illinois—Gazetteers	F539	917.73003
Illinois—Maps	G4100-4104	912.773
Illinois—National Guard	UA170-179	355.3709773
Illinois—Periodicals	F536	977.3005
Illumination of books and manuscripts	ND2889-3416	745.67
Illumination of books and manuscripts—Exhibitions	ND2893	745.67074
Illumination of books and manuscripts—Renaissance	ND2990	745.67090(24-31)
Illumination of books and manuscripts—[By region or country]	ND3001-3294.5	745.6709(4-9)
Illumination of books and manuscripts, Ancient	ND2910	745.670901
Illumination of books and manuscripts, Medieval	ND2920-2980	745.670902
Illustration of books	NC960-995.8	741.6
Image processing	TA1637	621.367
Imagery (Psychology)	BF367	153.32
Imaginary wars and battles	U313	355.48
Imaginary wars and battles	V253	359.48
Imagination	BF408-426	153.32
Imaging systems in astronomy	QB51.3.I45	522
Imgination	N61-79	701.15
Imitation	BF357	153.1523
Immaculate Conception	BT620	232.911
Immanence of God	BT124	231
Immersion method (Language teaching)	P53.44	407.1
Immortality	BT919-925	236.22
Immune response	QR186-.3	571.964
Immunization of children	RJ240	613.0432
Immunodeficiency	QR188.35	571.974
Immunogenetics	QR184-.4	571.9648
Immunoglobulins	QR186.7-.85	971.967
Immunological deficiency symdromes	RC606-607	616.979
Immunology	QR180-189.5	571.96
Immunopharmacology	RM370-373	615.37
Immunosuppressive agents	RM373	615.37
Immunotherapy	RM270-282	615.37
Impasse (Psychotherapy)	RC489.I45	616.8914
Imperialism	JC359	325.32
Impetigo	RL283	616.524

Subject Heading	LC	Dewey	Subject Heading	LC	Dewey
Implant dentures	RK667.I45	617.6920592	India—History—British occupation, 1765-1947	DS463-480.83	954.0(296-4)
Imports	HF1419-1420	382.5	India—History—Mysore War, 1790-1792	DS474.1	954.0311
Imposition of hands	BV873.L3	265.9	India—History—Mysore War, 1799	DS475.3	954.0312
Impotence	RC889	616.692			
Impotence	RC560.I45	616.85832	India—History—Mutiny, 1809	DS475.5	954.0313
Impressment	E357.2-.3	973.525			
Imprinting (Psychology)	QL763.2	591.563	India—History—Sepoy Rebellion, 1857-1858	DS478-.3	954.0317
Imprisonment	HV8705-8749	365			
Improvisation (Acting)	PN2071.I5	792.028	India—History—Quit India movement, 1942	DS480.82	954.0359
Impulsive personality	RC569.5.I46	616.8584			
Inauguration Day	JK536	394.40973	India—History—1947-	DS480.832-481	954.0(4-5)
Inbreeding	SF105	636.082	India—Manufactures	TS103-104	670.954
Inbreeding	S494	636.082	India—Maps	G7650-7654	912.54
Incandescent lamps	TK4351-4367	621.326	India—Maps	G2280-2284	912.54
Incantations	BF1558	133.44	India—Politics and government	JQ200-620	320.954
Incantations	GR540	398.45			
Incarnation	BT220	232.1	India-Pakistan Conflict, 1947-1949	DS385.9	954.904
Incentives in industry	HF5549.5.I5	658.3142			
Incest	GN480.3	306.877	Indian essays	AC195	089.97
Incest	HQ71	306.877	Indiana	F521-535	977.2
Incest	RC560.I53	616.85836	Indiana—Gazetteers	F524	917.72003
Incest victims	RC560.I53	618.9285836	Indiana—History—To 1787	F526	977.20(1-2)
Incineration	TD796-.2	628.4457	Indiana—History—1951-	F530-.22	977.204(3-4)
Income	HB522-715	331.21	Indiana—Maps	G4090-4094	912.772
Income tax	HJ4621-4830	336.24	Indiana—National Guard	UA180-189	355.3709772
Income tax—Law and legislation	K4501-4550	343.052	Indiana—Periodicals	F521	977.2005
			Indianapolis (Ind.)	F534.I3	977.252
Income tax—Law and legislation—United States	KF6351-6499	343.73052	Indians	E51-73	970.00497
			Indians—Costume	E59.C6	391.08997
			Indians—Folklore	E59.F6	398.08997
Indentured servants	HD4871-4875	306.363	Indians—History	E58	970.00497
Independent Order of Odd Fellows	HS951-1179	366.3	Indians of Central America	F1434-1435.3	972.800497
			Indians of Central America—Languages	PM3001-4566	497.9
Independent Order of Odd Fellows—Directories	HS963-975	366.3025			
			Indians of Mexico	F1219-1221	972.00497
Independent Order of Odd Fellows—History	HS987-991	366.309	Indians of North America	E75-99	973.0497
			Indians of North America—Employment	E98.E6	331.125008997
Independent Order of Odd Fellows—Periodicals	HS951-953	366.305			
			Indians of North America—Languages	PM1-7356	497
Independent Order of Odd Fellows—Rituals	HS1019-1021	728.4			
			Indians of North America—Legal status, laws, etc.	KF8201-8228	342.730872
Independent Order of Odd Fellows—[By region or country]	HS1041-1051	366.309(4-9)			
			Indians of North America—Psychology	E98.P95	155.8497
Independent Order of Odd Fellows—United States	HS1041-1045	366.30973			
			Indians of North America—Religion	E98.R3	299.7
Independent study	LB1049	371.3943			
Index theorems	QA614.92	514.74	Indians of North America—Social life and customs	E98.S7	973.0497/ 390.08997
Indexes	AI	016			
India	DS421-486.8	934/954			
India—Census	HA4581-4590	315.4	Indians of North America—Wars	E81-83.895	973.(1-8)
India—Church history	BR1150-1156	275.4			
India—Civilization	DS421-428.2	934/954	Indians of North America—Wars—1600-1750	E82	973.(1-26)
India—Commerce	HF3781-3790	380.10954			
India—Economic conditions	HC431-440	330.954	Indians of North America—Wars—1750-1815	E81	973.(26-53)
India—Emigration and immigration	JV8500-8509	325.(254/54)			
			Indians of North America—Wars—1775-1783	E83.775	973.3
India—History—324 B.C-1000 A.D.	DS451-.9	934/954.0(2-223)			
			Indians of North America—Wars—1790-1794	E83.79	973.41
India—History—1000-1526	DS457-460	954.02(23-25)			
India—History—1000-1765	DS452-462.8	954.02(23-96)			

Subject Heading	LC	Dewey	Subject Heading	LC	Dewey
Indians of North America—Wars—1812-1815	E83.812	973.52	Indo-Iranian languages—Dictionaries	PK14	491.13
Indians of North America—Wars—1815-1875	E81	973.(53-82)	Indo-Iranian languages—Grammar	PK21-41	491.15
Indians of North America—Wars—1862-1865	E83.863	973.7	Indo-Iranian literature	PK80-85	891.1
Indians of North America—Wars—1866-1895	E83.866	973.8(1-7)	Indo-Iranian philology	PK1-17	491.1
Indians of North America—Wars—1868-1869	E83.866	973.81	Indo-Iranian philology—Study and teaching	PK11-13	491.1071
Indians of South America	F2229-2290	980.00498	Indochina—Maps	G8000-8198.54	912.59
Indians of South America—Languages	PM5001-7356	497/498	Indochina—Religion	BQ440-509	294.30959
Indians of the West Indies	F1619	972.900497	Indonesia—Census	HA4601-4610	315.98
Indians of the West Indies—Languages	PM5071-5079	497	Indonesia—Civilization	DS625	959.8
Indictments	K5425	345.072	Indonesia—Description and travel	DS617-620	915.9804
Indictments—United States	KF9640-9642	345.73072	Indonesia—Economic conditions	HC446-450	330.9598
Indigenous peoples	GN380	306.08	Indonesia—Gazetteers	DS614	915.98003
Indigestion	RC827	616.332	Indonesia—History	DS633-644.4	959.8
Indigestion disorders	RC815.2	616.332	Indonesia—History—To 1478	DS641	959.8012
Indirect taxation	HJ5250-5255	336.294	Indonesia—History—1478-1798	DS641.5-642.22	959.80(15-21)
Indirect taxation	KF6598-6609	343.730526	Indonesia—History—1798-1942	DS643-.22	959.8022
Individualism	JC571-605	323	Indonesia—History—British occupation, 1811-1816	DS643	959.8022
Individualism	B824	141.4	Indonesia—History—Java War, 1825-1830	DS643	959.8022
Individualism	HM136-146	302.54			
Individuality	BF697-.5	155.2	Indonesia—History—Achinese War, 1873-1904	DS643	959.8022
Indo-Aryan languages	PK101-2899	491.(2-4)			
Indo-Aryan languages, Modern	PK1501-2845	491.4	Indonesia—History—Japanese occupation, 1942-1945	DS643.5	959.8022
Indo-Aryan languages, Modern—Dialects	PK1550-2899	491.4(1-9)			
Indo-Aryan languages, Modern—Dictionaries	PK1537	491.13	Indonesia—History—Revolution, 1945-1949	DS644	959.8035
Indo-Aryan languages, Modern—Grammar	PK1511-1523	491.15	Indonesia—History—1950-1966	DS644-.1	959.803(5-6)
Indo-Aryan philology	PK101-119	491.(2-4)	Indonesia—History—Coup d'etat, 1965	DS644.32	959.8036
Indo-Aryans	DS425	934.02	Indonesia—History—1966-	DS644.4	959.8036
Indo-European languages	P501-769	410	Indonesia—Manufactures	TS113.I55	670.9598
Indo-European languages—Congresses	P505	410.6	Indonesia—Maps	G8070-8074	912.598
Indo-European languages—Etymology	P721-725	412	Indonesia—Politics and government	JQ760-779	320.9598
Indo-European languages—Grammar, Comparative	P575-769	415	Indonesian essays	AC168-169	089.99221
Indo-European languages—Lexicography	P761-769	413.028	Indonesian langue	PL5071-5079	499.221
			Indoor games	GV1221-1229	793
Indo-European languages—Morphology	P611-627	415	Indoor gardening	SB419-.3	635.965
Indo-European languages—Parts of speech	P631-663	415	Indoor gardens	SB419-.3	635.965
			Induction (Logic)	BC80-99	161
Indo-European languages—Phonology	P583-610	414	Induction heating	TK4601	621.4028
Indo-European languages—Syntax	P671-675	415	Indulgences	BX2279-2283	264.020866
			Industrial accidents	HD7262-.5	363.11
Indo-European philology	P501-769	410	Industrial archaeology	T37	930.1
Indo-European philology—Periodicals	P501	413.028	Industrial buildings	NA6396-6589	725.4
			Industrial capacity	T58.7-.8	338/670.42
Indo-Iranian languages	PK1-9201	491.1	Industrial districts	HD1393.5	333.77
Indo-Iranian languages—Dictionaries	PK75-77	491.13	Industrial efficiency	T58.8	658.515
			Industrial engineering	T55.4-60.8	670

Subject Heading	LC	Dewey	Subject Heading	LC	Dewey
Industrial engineering—History	T55.6	670.9	Infrared spectroscopy	QC457	535.842
Industrial engineering—Statistical methods	T57.35	670.21	Infrared technology	TA1570	621.362
			Inheritance and succession	K805-821	346.052
Industrial engineers	T56.3	670.92	Inheritance and succession	K4568	343.0532
Industrial hygiene	RC967	613.62	Inheritance and succession—Canada	KE806-833	346.71052
Industrial hygiene—[By region or country]	HD7651-7780.8	613.6209(4-9)	Inheritance and succession—England	KD1500-1534	346.42052
Industrial hygienists	RC963	613.62092	Inheritance and succession—Ireland	KDK360-365	346.415052
Industrial life insurance	HG9251-9262	368.362	Inheritance and succession—Northern Ireland	KDE145-151	346.416052
Industrial microbiology	QR53-.5	660.62			
Industrial mobilization	UA18	355.26			
Industrial procurement	HD39.5	658.72	Inheritance and succession—Scotland	KDC462-470	346.411052
Industrial productivity	HD56-57.5	338.06	Inheritance and succession—United States	KF753-780	346.73052
Industrial property	K1500-1578	346.048			
Industrial psychiatry	RC967.5	158.7			
Industrial relations	HD6958.5-6976	331			
Industrial safety	T55-.3	363.11	Inheritance and transfer tax	HJ5801-5823	336.276
Industrial sociology	HD6951-6957	306.36	Injections	RM163-176	615.6
Industrial toxicology	RA1229-.5	615.902	Injections, Hypodermic	RM169	615.6
Industrialization	HD2329	338	Injunctions	K2320	344.01893
Industries	HD2321-4730.9	338	Ink	TP946-950	667.4
Inequalities (Mathematics)	QA295	515.26	Inland navigation	HE617-720	623.89229
Inertial navigation systems	VK583.5	623.89	Inland navigation	TC601-791	623.89229
Infant baptism	BV813-.2	265.12	Inland navigation—Law and legislation	K4182-4194	343.0967
Infant psychiatry	RJ502.5	616.890932			
Infant psychology	BF719-720	155.422	Inland navigation—[By region or country]	HE623-720	623.89229(4-9)
Infanticide	HV6537-6541	364.1523			
Infantry	UD	356.1	Inland navigation—[By region or country]	TC615-727	627.109(4-9)
Infantry—Equipment	UD370-375	356.118			
Infantry—History	UD15	356.109	Inland navigation—United States	HE623-633	623.8922973
Infantry—Societies, etc.	UD1	356.106			
Infantry drill and tactics	UD157-302	356.1154	Inland navigation—[Other regions or countries]	HE635-720	623.89229(4-9)
Infants	HQ774	305.232			
Infants (Premature)	RJ250-.3	618.92011	Inland waterway vessels	VM396	623.82436
Infants—Care	RJ101-103	649.122	Inlets	GB454.I54	551.44
Infants—Care	RJ61	618.9201	Innate ideas (Philosophy)	B105.I54	121.4
Infants—Development	HQ774	305.232	Inner child	BF698.35.I55	155.2
Infants—Development	RJ134	612.654	Inner cities	HT156	307.76
Infection	RB153-154	616.047	Inorganic acids	TP213-217	661.2
Infertility	RC889	616.692	Inorganic acids	QD167	546.24
Infertility, Female	RG201-205	618.178	Input-output analysis	HB142	339.23
Infertility, Male	RC889	616.692	Inquiry (Theory of knowledge)	BD183	121.6
Infinite	BD411	111.6			
Infinite	QA9	515.24	Inquisition	BX1700-1745	272.2
Infinite groups	QA171	512.3	Insane, Criminal and dangerous	HV6133	364.24
Inflationary universe	QB991.I54	523.18			
Influenza	RA644.I6	614.518	Insanity	HV4975-4977	362.2
Influenza	RC150-.9	616.203	Inscriptions	CN	411.7
Information services	Z674.2-.5	025.52	Inscriptions—Collectors and collecting	CN25-30	411.7074
Information storage and retrieval systems—Social service	HV29.2-.5	361.10285			
			Inscriptions—Congresses	CN15	411.706
Information technology	HC79.I55	303.4833	Inscriptions—Dictionaries	CN70	411.703
Information theory	Q350-390	003.54	Inscriptions—History	CN55	411.709
Infrared astronomy	QB470	522.683	Inscriptions—Periodicals	CN1	411.705
Infrared photography	TR755	778.34	Inscriptions—Philosophy	CN40-42	411.701
Infrared radiation—Military applications	UG487	623.042	Inscriptions—Study and teaching	CN50	411.7071
Infrared sources	TA1570	621.362	Inscriptions—[By region or country]	CN870-1355	411.709
Infrared spectra	QC457	535.842			

Subject Heading	LC	Dewey	Subject Heading	LC	Dewey
Inscriptions—Africa	CN1300-1320	411.7096	Institution management	TX147	647
Inscriptions—Asia	CN1150-1230	411.7095	Institutional care	HV59-63	361.05
Inscriptions—Australia	CN1340-1345	411.70994	Instructional materials centers	LB3044.7-.74	027.7
Inscriptions—Austria	CN910-915	411.709436			
Inscriptions—Central America	CN882-884	411.709728	Instrument flying	TL711.B6	629.1325214
			Instrumental music	M5-1459	784
Inscriptions—China	CN1160-1161	411.70951	Insubordination	VB880	359.1334
Inscriptions—Europe	CN900-1130	411.7094	Insubordination	UB789	355.1334
Inscriptions—France	CN945-948	411.70944	Insulation (Heat)	TH1715-1718	621.4024
Inscriptions—Germany	CN950-957	411.70943	Insulin	QP572.I5	612.34
Inscriptions—Great Britain	CN960-997	411.70941	Insurance	HG8011-9999	368
Inscriptions—India	CN1170-1175	411.70954	Insurance—[By region or country]	HG8501-8745	368.9(4-9)
Inscriptions—Israel	CN1193-1194	411.7095694			
Inscriptions—Italy	CN1010-1015	411.70945	Insurance—United States	HG8501-8540	368.973
Inscriptions—Japan	CN1180-1181	411.70952	Insurance—[Other regions or countries]	HG8550-8740.5	368.9(4-9)
Inscriptions—Mexico	CN877-878	411.70972			
Inscriptions—Russia	CN1060-1065	411.70947	Insurance, Accident	HG9301-9343	368.384
Inscriptions—South America	CN886-888	411.7098	Insurance, Agricultural	HG9966-9969	368.121
Inscriptions—Spain	CN1090-1095	411.70946	Insurance, Automobile	HG9970	368.092
Inscriptions—United States	CN870-872	411.70973	Insurance, Aviation	HG9972	368.093
Inscriptions, Ancient	CN120-730	411.7	Insurance, Burial	HG9466-9479	368.366
Inscriptions, Arabic	PJ7593-7600	492.711	Insurance, Business	HG8059	368.094
Inscriptions, Aramaic	PJ5208-5209	492.211	Insurance, Casualty	HG9956-9969	368.5
Inscriptions, Byzantine	CN455	487.311	Insurance, Child	HG9271	368.32
Inscriptions, Christian	CN750-753	487.4	Insurance, Disability	HD7105.2-.25	368.382
Inscriptions, Etruscan	CN479	499.9411	Insurance, Disaster	HG9979	368.122
Inscriptions, Greek	CN350-455	481.1	Insurance, Earthquake	HG9981	368.1226
Inscriptions, Greek	CN1000-1005	481.1	Insurance, Fire	HG9651-9899	368.11
Inscriptions, Greek—Asia	CN400	481.1095	Insurance, Fire—History	HG9660	368.11009
Inscriptions, Greek—Crete	CN420	481.1094959	Insurance, Fire—Law and legislation	HG9733-9735	346.086
Inscriptions, Greek—Cyprus	CN430	481.1095693			
Inscriptions, Greek—Egypt	CN440-441	481.0932	Insurance, Fire—Statistics	HG9663	368.110021
Inscriptions, Greek— Middle East	CN440-441	481.10953	Insurance, Fire—[By region or country]	HG9751-9899	368.11009(4-9)
Inscriptions, Greek—Turkey	CN410-415	481.109561	Insurance, Fire—United States	HG9751-9780	368.1100973
Inscriptions, Greek—[By region or country]	CN380-455	481.109(3-9)			
			Insurance, Fire—[Other regions or countries]	HG9781-9866	368.11009(4-9)
Inscriptions, Hebrew	PJ5034.4-.9	492.411			
Inscriptions, Islamic	CN1153	492.71	Insurance, Flood	HG9983	368.1222
Inscriptions, Japanese	PL750-751	495.611	Insurance, Government	HG8205-8220	368.4
Inscriptions, Jewish	CN745	492.411	Insurance, Group	HG8058	368.3
Inscriptions, Korean	PL969.2-.4	495.711	Insurance, Health	HG9371-9399	368.382
Inscriptions, Latin	CN510-740	471	Insurance, Hospitalization	HG9389	368.3827
Inscriptions, Semitic	PJ3081-3095	492.0411	Insurance, Inland marine	HG9903-9905	368.23
Insect pests	SB818-945	632.7	Insurance, Liability	HG9990	368.5
Insect rearing	SF518	638	Insurance, Life	HG8751-9271	368.32
Insecticides	SB951.5-.54	632.9517	Insurance, Life—Law and legislation	HG8901-8914	346.08632
Insects	GR750	398.36957			
Insects	QL461-599.82	595.7	Insurance, Life— Mathematics	HG8779-8793	368.3200151
Insects as carriers of disease	RA639.5	614.432			
			Insurance, Life—[By region or country]	HG8941-9200.5	368.32009(4-9)
Insignia	CR4480-4485	929.9			
Insignia	HS159-160	366.6027	Insurance, Malpractice	HG8053.5-8054.45	368.564
Insignia	VC345	359.1342			
Insignia	UC530-535	355.14	Insurance, Marine	HE961-971	368.2(2/3)
Insomnia	RC548-.5	616.8498	Insurance, Marine—England	KD1845-1847	346.420862
Inspiration	BF410	153.3	Insurance, Maternity	HG9291-9295	368.424
Installation (Clergy)	BV4290	252.7	Insurance, No-fault automobile	HG9970.A4-.A68	368.5728
Installment plan	HG3755.5	332.743			
Instant photography	TR269	770	Insurance, Physicians' liability	HG8054	368.5642
Instinct	QL781	591.512			

Subject Heading	LC	Dewey	Subject Heading	LC	Dewey
Insurance, Products liability	HG9995	368.562	Internal medicine	RC	616
Insurance, Surety and fidelity	HG9997	368.8(3/4)	Internal medicine—Dictionaries	RC41	616.003
Insurance, Title	HG9999	368.88	Internal revenue law—United States	KF6251-6708	343.73036
Insurance, Unemployment	HD7095-7096	331.2550973	Internal revenue—United States	HJ2361	336.200973
Insurance companies	HG8075-8107	368.0065	Internal security—United States	KF4850-4856	344.7305
Insurance crimes	HV6763-6771	364.168			
Insurance law	K1241-1287	346.086	International airports	TL726.15	629.136
Insurance law—Canada	KE1141-1220	346.71086	International cooperation	JC362	327.17
Insurance law—England	KD1851-1913	346.42086	International economic relations	HF1351-1532.935	337
Insurance law—United States	KF1146-1238	346.73086	International economic relations—[By region or country]	HF1451-1647	337.(4-9)
Intangible property—England	KD1238-1450	346.42048	International finance	HG3879-4000	332.042
Integrals	QA308-311	515.4	International law	K540-5570	341
Integrals, Generalized	QA312	515.4	International trade	HF1371-1385	382
Integrated logistic support	U168	355.411	Internationalism	JC361-363	327.17
Integrated optics	TA1660	621.3693	Internet (Computer network)	TK5105.875.I57	004.678
Intellect	BF431-433	153.9	Interns (Medicine)	RA972	610.6952
Intellectual life	GN451-477.7	306.42	Interpersonal communication	BF637.C45	158.2
Intellectual property	K1401-1578	346.048	Interpersonal relations	HM132	302
Intellectual property—Canada	KE2771-2998	346.71048	Interplanetary voyages	TL789-790	629.455
Intellectual property—England	KD1261-1450	346.42048	Interpreters (Computer programs)	QA76.6	005.452
Intellectual property—United States	KF2971-3193	346.73048	Interpreters for the deaf	HV2402	362.4283
Intellectuals	HM213	306.42	Interracial dating	HQ801.8	306.73
Intelligence service	VB230-250	359.3432	Interracial marriage	HQ1031	306.846
Intelligence tests	BF431-432.5	153.93	Interstate agreements	JK2441	352.133
Intelligent control systems	TJ217.5	629.89	Interstellar matter	QB790-792	523.1125
Intensive care nursing	RT120.I5	610.7361	Interviewing	BF761-768	158.39
Intensive care units	RA975.5.I56	362.174	Interviewing in psychiatry	RC480.7	616.8910028
Intentionality (Philosophy)	B105.I56	128	Intestinal absorption	QP165	612.38
Interactive multimedia	QA76.76.I59	006.7	Intestines	QL863	573.37
Interactive video	LB1028.75	371.334	Intestines	QM345	611.34
Interactive video	TK6687	006.7	Intestines	QP156	612.33
Intercontinental ballistic missiles	UG1312.I2	358.175482	Intramural sports	GV710	796.042
Intercountry adoption	HV875.5	362.734	Intraocular lenses	RE988	617.7524
Intercropping	S603.5	631.58	Intrauterine contraceptives	RG137.3	613.9435
Intercultural communication	GN345.6	303.482	Intravenous therapy	RM170-180	615.855
Intercultural communication	HM258	303.482	Intrenchments	UG403	623.1
Interdenominational cooperation	BV625	280.042	Intrenchments	UG446	355.44
Interest (Psychology)	BF321.I5	153.1533	Intrusions (Geology)	QE611-.5	551.88
Interest (Psychology)	LB1065	153.1533	Intuition (Psychology)	BF315.5	153.44
Interest rates	HB531-549	332.6323	Inuit language	PM50-64	497.12
Interest rates	HG1621-1623	332.82	Inventions	T201-339	608
Interface circuits	TK7868.I58	621.3981	Inventions—History	T15-31	609
Interfaith marriage	HQ1031	306.843	Inventors	T39-40	609.2
Interference (Light)	QC411	535.47	Inversions (Geometry)	QA473	516.9
Interferon	QR187.5	571.9644	Invertebrates	QL360-599	592
Interferon inducers	QR187.5	571.9644	Invertebrates, Fossil	QE770-832	562
Interior architecture	NA2850-2856	729.24	Investment clubs	HG4530	332.6
Interior decoration	NK1700-3505	747	Investments	HG4501-6051	332.6
Interior decoration	TX311-317	645	Investments—Law and legislation	K1112-1116	346.092
Interior decoration—[By region or country]	NK2000-2096.3	747.2(1-9)	Investments—Law and legislation—Canada	KE1060-1089	346.71092
Intermediate state	BT830	236.4	Investments—Law and legislation—England	KD1774-1787	346.42092
Internal combustion engines	TJ751-805	621.43			

Subject Heading	LC	Dewey	Subject Heading	LC	Dewey
Investments—Law and legislation—United States	KF1066-1084	346.73092	Iran—Maps	G7620-7624	912.55
			Iran—Politics and government	JQ1780-1789	320.955
Investments—[By region or country]	HG4901-5993	332.609(4-9)	Iran—Religion	BL2270-2280	299.155
			Iranian languages	PK6001-6996	491.5
Investments—United States	HG4905-5131	332.60973	Iranian languages, Middle	PK6135	491.53
			Iranian philology	PK6001-6996	491.5
Investments—[Other regions or countries]	HG5151-5993	332.609(4-9)	Iraq—Antiquities	DS69-70.5	935
			Iraq—Census	HA4569	315.67
Investments, Foreign	HG4538	332.673	Iraq—Civilization	DS70.7	935/956.7
Iodine	QD181.I1	546.734	Iraq—Commerce	HF3770	380.109567
Ion exchange	QD562.I63	541.3723	Iraq—Economic conditions	HC415.4	330.9567
Ion rockets	TL783.63	629.4755	Iraq—Gazetteers	DS67.8	913.5003/ 915.67003
Ionian Islands (Greece)	DF901.I57-.I69	949.55			
Ionization	QD561-562	541.3722	Iraq—History	DS70.82-79.66	935/956.7
Ionization	QC701.7-702.7	530.444	Iraq—Manufactures	TS113.I7	670.9567
Ionization chambers	QC787.I6	539.772	Iraq—Maps	G7610-7614	912.567
Ionization of gases	QC702-721	530.44	Iraq—Maps	G2250-2254	912.567
Ionosphere	QC881.2.I6	551.5145	Iraq—Politics and government	JQ1849	320.9567
Ions	QD561-562	541.372			
Iowa	F616-630	977.7	Ireland—Census	HA1170.1-.5	314.15
Iowa—Gazetteers	F619	917.77003	Ireland—Constitutional law	KDK1200-1350	342.415
Iowa—History—Civil War, 1861-1865	E507	977.702	Ireland—Description and travel	DA969-988	913.6104/ 914.1504
Iowa—History—1951-	F625-.42	977.703(3-4)	Ireland—Emigration and immigration	JV7710-7719	325.(2415/415)
Iowa—Maps	G4150-4154	912.777			
Iowa—National Guard	UA190-199	355.3709777	Ireland—History	DA900-995	936./941.5
Iowa—Periodicals	F616	977.7005	Ireland—History—To 1172	DA930-932.6	936.1/ 941.50(1-2)
Iran	DS251-326	935/955			
Iran-Iraq War, 1980-1988	DS318.85	955.0542	Ireland—History— 1172-1603	DA933-937.5	941.50(3-5)
Iran—Census	HA4570.2	315.5			
Iran—Commerce	HF3770.2	380.10955	Ireland—History—17th century	DA940-946	941.506
Iran—Description and travel	DS255-259.2	913.504/ 915.504	Ireland—History—18th century	DA947-949.5	941.507
Iran—Economic conditions	HC471-480	330.955	Ireland—History—19th century	DA949.7-958	941.5081
Iran—Gazetteers	DS253	913.5003/ 915.5003	Ireland—History—20th century	DA959-965	941.5082
Iran—History	DS270-318.85	935/955	Ireland—Maps	G5780-5784	912.415
Iran—History—To 640	DS276	935	Ireland—Periodicals	DA900	936.1005/ 941.5005
Iran—History—Macedonian Conquest, 334-325 B.C.	DS276	935.06			
Iran—History—640-1256	DS287.8-288.9	955.02	Ireland—Politics and government	JN1405-1571.5	320.9415
Iran—History—640-1500	DS288-290	955.02	Irish language	PB1201-1299	491.62
Iran—History—1256-1500	DS288.95-289.8	955.02	Irish language—Etymology	PB1283-1284	491.622
Iran—History—16th-18th centuries	DS292-297	955.03	Irish language—Grammar	PB1221-1273	491.625
			Irish language— Lexicography	PB1287-1295	491.623028
Iran—History—Qajar dynasty, 1794-1925	DS298-316	955.04	Irish language—Slang	PB1299	491.627
Iran—History—War with Great Britain, 1856-1857	DS307.5	955.04	Irish language—Study and teaching	PB1211	491.62071
Iran—History—1905-1911	DS313	955.0(4-51)	Irish language—To 1100	PB1218	491.627
Iran—History—Paklavi dynasty, 1925-1979	DS316.2-318.7	955.05(2-3)	Irish language—Middle Irish, 1100-1550	PB1218	491.627
Iran—History—Mohammed Reza Pahlavi, 1941-1979	DS318-.7	955.053	Irish literature	PB1306-1449	891.62
Iran—History—1979-	DS318.72-.85	955.054	Iron	QE391.I7	546.621
Iran—History—Revolution, 1979	DS318.72-.85	955.054	Iron Cross	CR5351	929.8143
			Iron alloys	TN756-757	669.141
Iran—Manufactures	TS107-108	670.955	Iron mines and mining	TN400-409	622.341
Iran—Maps	G2255-2259	912.55	Iron sculpture	NB1240.I75	731.2

Subject Heading	LC	Dewey
Iroquoian Indians	E99.I69	973.049755
Iroquoian languages	PM1381-1384	497.55
Irrigation	S612-619	631.587
Irrigation canals and flumes	TC930-933	627.52
Irrigation farming	S612-619	631.587
Islam	BP1-223	297
Islam—Congresses	BP10-15	297.65
Islam—Dictionaries	BP40	297.03
Islam—Doctrines	BP165.5-166.94	297.2
Islam—Periodicals	BP1-9	297.05
Islamic Empire—History—661-750	DS38.5	956.013
Islamic Empire—History—750-1258	DS38.6	956.01(3-4)
Islamic Empire—History—1258-1517	DS38.7	956.01(4-5)
Islamic ethics	BJ1291-1292	297.5
Islamic law	BP140-165	340.59
Islamic preaching	BP184.25	297.37
Islamic religious education	BP42-48	297.77
Islamic sermons	BP183.6	297.37
Islands	GB471-478	551.42
Islands of the Atlantic—Economic conditions	HC585-595.5	330.997
Islands of the Pacific—Economic conditions	HC681-688	330.99(5-6)
Isolation (Hospital care)	RA975	614.45
Isotopes	QD466.5	541.388
Israel	DS101-151	933/956.94
Israel-Arab War, 1948-1949	DS126.9-.99	956.042
Israel-Arab War, 1967	DS127-.9	956.046
Israel-Arab War, 1973	DS128.1-.19	956.048
Israel—Census	HA4560	315.694
Israel—Commerce	HF3760	380.1095694
Israel—Description and travel	DS103-108.5	913.304/915.69404
Israel—Economic conditions	HC415.25	330.95694
Israel—History	DS114-128.19	933/956.94
Israel—History—1948-1949	DS126.5-126.99	956.94052
Israel—History—Declaration of Independence, 1948	DS126.5	956.9405
Israel—Manufactures	TS113.I75	670.95694
Israel—Maps	G2235-2239	912.5694
Israel—Maps	G7500-7504	912.5694
Israel—Politics and government	JQ1830	320.95694
Istanbul (Turkey)—History	DR716-741	949.618
Italian drama	PQ4133-4160	852.009
Italian essays	AC40-45	085.1
Italian essays	PQ4183.E8	854.009
Italian language	PC1001-1977	450
Italian language—Dialects	PC1700-1977	457
Italian language—Dictionaries	PC1620-1645	453
Italian language—Etymology	PC1571-1580	452
Italian language—Grammar	PC1099-1400	455
Italian language—Lexicography	PC1620-1693	453.028
Italian language—Slang	PC1951-1977	457

Subject Heading	LC	Dewey
Italian language—Study and teaching	PC1065	450.71
Italian letters	PQ4183.L4	856.009
Italian literature	PQ4001-5999	850
Italian literature—15th century	PQ4075	850.9003
Italian literature—16th century	PQ4079-4080	850.9004
Italian literature—17th century	PQ4081-4082	850.9005
Italian literature—18th century	PQ4083-4084	850.9006
Italian literature—19th century	PQ4085-4086	850.9007
Italian literature—20th century	PQ4087	850.90091
Italian literature—History and criticism	PQ4001-4199	850.9
Italian literature—Study and teaching	PQ4013-4023	850.71
Italian periodicals	AP37-39	055.1
Italian periodicals	PN5241-5250	055.1
Italian philology	PC1001-1977	450
Italian poetry	PQ4091-4131	851.009
Italian prose literature	PQ4161-4185	858.08
Italic languages and dialects	PA2420-2915	470
Italy	DG	937/945
Italy	DG401-583	937/945
Italy—Biography	DG463-.8	920.037/920.045
Italy—Census	HA1361-1379	314.5
Italy—Civilization	DG441-453	937/945.006
Italy—Colonies	JV2200-2299	325.345
Italy—Commerce	HF3581-3590	380.10945
Italy—Description and travel	DG421.5-430.2	913.704/914.504
Italy—Directories	DG413	945.0025
Italy—Economic conditions	HC301-310	330.945
Italy—Emigration and immigration	JV8130-8139	325.(245/45)
Italy—Gazetteers	DG415	913.7003/914.5003
Italy—Historiography	DG465-.7	937.0072/945.0072
Italy—History	DG461-583	937/945
Italy—History, Military	DG480-484	355.30945
Italy—History—476-774	DG503-514.7	945.01
Italy—History—Gothic War, 535-555	DG509	945.02
Italy—History—Carolingian rule, 774-887	DG515-517	945.02
Italy—History—Period of the Italian Kings, 887-962	DG517.5-518	945.02
Italy—History—Germanic rule, 962-1268	DG520-529	945.0(3-4)
Italy—History—1268-1492	DG530-537.8	945.0(4-5)
Italy—History—1492-1870	DG538-551.8	945.0(5-84)
Italy—History—16th century	DG539-541.8	945.0(6-7)
Italy—History—1789-1815	DG546-549	945.0(7-83)

Subject Heading	LC	Dewey	Subject Heading	LC	Dewey
Italy—History—1789-1870	DG550.5-551.8	945.0(7-8)	Japan	DS801-897	952
Italy—History—Uprising, 1831	DG551	945.083	Japan—Armed Forces—Management	UB105-106	355.60952
Italy—History—1849-1870	DG552-554.5	945.08(3-4)	Japan—Armed Forces—Supplies and stores	UC241	355.80952
Italy—History—War of 1860-1861	DG554.5	945.083	Japan—Census	HA4621-4630	315.2
Italy—History—1870-1915	DG555-569	945.0(84-91)	Japan—Church history	BR1300-1317	275.2
Italy—History—1914-1945	DG570-572	945.091	Japan—Civilization	DS820.8-827	952
Italy—History—March on Rome, 1922	DG571.75	945.091	Japan—Colonies	JV5200-5299	325.352
			Japan—Commerce	HF3821-3830	380.10952
Italy—History—Allied occupation, 1943-1947	DG572	945.09(1-24)	Japan—Description and travel	DS807-811	915.204
Italy—History—German occupation, 1943-1945	DG572	945.091	Japan—Economic conditions	HC461-465	330.952
Italy—History—Grand Council, 1943	DG572	945.091	Japan—Emigration and immigration	JV8720-8729	325.(252/52)
Italy—History—1945-1976	DG577.5-579	945.09(1-27)	Japan—Gazetteers	DS805	915.2003
Italy—History—1976-	DG581-583	945.092(7-9)	Japan—History—To 1185	DS850-856.72	952.01
Italy—Manufactures	TS79-80	670.945	Japan—History—To 794	DS855-.73	952.01
Italy—Maps	G1983-1989.53	912.45	Japan—History—Taika Reform, 645-710	DS855.6	952.01
Italy—Maps	G6710-6714	912.45	Japan—History—Nara period, 710-794	DS855.7-.73	952.01
Italy—Periodicals	DG401	937.005/ 945.005	Japan—History—Heian period, 794-1185	DS855.87-856.72	952.01
Italy—Politics and government	JN5201-5690	320.954	Japan—History—Earlier Nine Years' War, 1051-1062	DS854	952.01
Italy—Study and teaching	DG465.8	937.0071/ 945.0071	Japan—History—Later Three Years' War, 1083-1087	DS856.3	952.01
Italy, Central	DG691-694	945.6			
Italy, Northern	DG600-609	945.(1-3)			
Italy, Southern	DG819-831	945.7	Japan—History—1185-1600	DS856.75-869.6	952.02(1-4)
Iwo Jima, Battle of, 1945	D767.99.I9	940.5426	Japan—History—Kamakura period, 1185-1333	DS858-861	952.021
Jacobites	DA813-814	941.10(69-72)	Japan—History—Jokyu Revolt, 1221	DS861	952.021
Jaina astrology	BF1714.J28	133.59444			
Jaina mantras	BL1377.3	294.437	Japan—History—Attempted Mongol Invasions, 1274-1281	DS861	952.021
Jaina philosophy	B162.5	181.044			
Jainism	BL1300-1365	294.4			
Jainism—Doctrines	BL1356-1375	294.42	Japan—History—Genko Incident, 1331-1333	DS861	952.021
Jainism—Sacred books	BL1310-1314.2	294.482			
Jains	BL1300-1365	294.4	Japan—History—Kenmu Restoration, 1333-1336	DS863	952.02(1-2)
Jamaica	F1861-1896	972.92			
Jamaica—Census	HA891-900	317.292	Japan—History—Muromachi period, 1336-1573	DS863.75-869.6	952.02(2-3)
Jamaica—Civilization	F1874	972.92			
Jamaica—Description and travel	F1870-1872.2	917.29204			
Jamaica—Gazetteers	F1864	917.292003	Japan—History—Period of civil wars, 1480-1603	DS868-869.6	952.02(3-4)
Jamaica—History	F1878-1887	972.92			
Jamaica—History—To 1962	F1884-1886	972.920(1-5)	Japan—History—Tokugawa period, 1600-1868	DS870-881.84	952.02(4-5)
Jamaica—History—Maroon War, 1795-1796	F1884	972.92034			
Jamaica—History—Slave Insurrection, 1831	F1886	972.92034	Japan—History—Keicho Peasant Uprising, 1614-1615	DS871.5	952.025
Jamaica—History—Insurrection, 1865	F1886	972.9204			
Jamaica—History—1962-	F1887	972.9206	Japan—History—Ako Vendetta, 1703	DS871.5	952.025
Jamaica—Maps	G4960-4964	912.7292			
Jamaica—Periodicals	F1861-1896	972.92005	Japan—History—19th century	DS881-.84	952.0(25-31)
Jamaica—Politics and government	JL630-639	320.97292			
Jameson's Raid, 1895-1896	DT1889	968.045			
Jansenists	BX4718.5-4735	284.84			

Subject Heading	LC	Dewey	Subject Heading	LC	Dewey
Japan—History—Restoration, 1853-1870	DS881.2-.84	952.0(25-3)	Japanese literature	PL700-889	895.6
			Japanese literature	PL755.12	895.608
Japan—History—1868-	DS881.85-890.3	952.0(3-5)	Japanese literature—To 1185	PL726.1185-.1186	895.609001
Japan—History—Civil War, 1868	DS881.83-.84	952.025	Japanese literature—To 794	PL726.12	895.609001
Japan—History—Kobe Incident, 1868	DS881.4	952.031	Japanese literature—Heian period, 794-1185	PL787-789	895.6108001
Japan—History—Meiji period, 1868-1912	DS881.98-884	952.031	Japanese literature—1185-1600	PL790-792	895.608002
Japan—History—Sakai Incidnet, 1868	DS881.4	952.025	Japanese literature—Edo period, 1600-1868	PL793-799	895.608003
Japan—History—Kioizaka Incident, 1878	DS882.5	952.031	Japanese literature—Meiji period, 1868-1912	PL800-820	895.6080042
Japan—History—Takehashi Incident, 1878	DS882.5	952.031	Japanese literature—Showa period, 1926-1989	PL821-866	895.60800(44-5)
Japan—History—20th century	DS884.5-890.3	952.0(31-49)	Japanese poetry	PL757-763	895.61008
Japan—History—Taisho period, 1912-1926	DS885.8-888	952.032	Japanese poetry	PL727-733	895.61009
Japan—History—Showa period, 1926-1989	DS888.15-890.3	952.033	Japanese tea ceremony	GT2910-2916	394.120952
Japan—History—1926-1945	DS888.4-.5	952.033	Jargon (Terminology)	P409	417.2
Japan—History—March and October Incidents, 1931	DS888.5	952.033	Jason (Greek mythology)	BL820.A8	292.13
			Jaundice	RC851	616.3625
Japan—History—May Incident, 1932 (May 15)	DS888.5	952.033	Jaundice, Neonatal	RJ276	618.923625
Japan—History—February Incident, 1936 (February 26)	DS888.4-.5	952.033	Java Sea, Battle of the, 1942	D774.J	940.5426
			Java man	GN284.6	569.9
Japan—History—1945-	DS888.84-890.3	952.0(33-5)	Javanese language	PL5161-5169	499.222
Japan—History—Allied occupation, 1945-1952	DS889.16	952.04(4-5)	Javanese literature	PL5170-5179	899.222
			Jaws	QM105	611.716
Japan—History—Heisei period, 1989-	DS890.3	952.0(48-5)	Jaws	QP311	612.92
Japan—Manufactures	TS105-106	670.952	Jazz	M1366	781.65
Japan—Maps	G2355-2359	912.52	Jealousy	BF575.J4	152.48
Japan—Maps	G7960-7964	912.52	Jehovah's Witnesses	BX8525-8528	289.92
Japan—Politics and government	JQ1600-1699	320.952	Jerusalem	DS109-.94	933/956.9442
			Jerusalem—History	DS109.85-.94	933/956.9442
Japan—Religion	BL2200-2228	299.56	Jerusalem—History—Siege, 70 A.D.	DS122.8	956.9402
Japanese drama	PL734-739	895.62009			
Japanese drama	PL764-769	895.62008	Jerusalem—History—Latin Kingdom, 1099-1244	D175-195	956.944203
Japanese essays	AC145-146	089.956			
Japanese essays	PL772-.83	895.408	Jesus Christ	BT198-590	232
Japanese essays	PL742-.83	895.6009	Jesus Christ—Biography	BT300-302	232.901
Japanese fiction	PL740-747	895.63009	Jesus Christ—Biography—Public life	BT340-500	232.95
Japanese fiction	PL770-777	895.63008	Jesus Christ—Character	BT304-.97	232.903
Japanese language	PL501-700	495.6	Jesus Christ—Messiahship	BT230-245	232.1
Japanese language—Dictionaries	PL674.5-677.6	495.63	Jesus Christ—Miracles	BT363-367	232.955
			Jesus Christ—Parables	BT373-378	226.8
Japanese language—Grammar	PL531.3-532.5	495.65	Jesus Christ—Passion	BT430-470	232.96
			Jesus Christ—Person and offices	BT198-590	232.8
Japanese language—To 794	PL525.2	495.67			
			Jesus Christ—Relics	BT587	232.966
Japanese language—Edo period, 1600-1868	PL525.5	495.67	Jesus Christ—Teachings	BS2415-2417	232.954
			Jesus Christ—Transfiguration	BT410	232.956
Japanese languae—Meiji period, 1868-1912	PL525-.6	495.67	Jesus Christ—Words	BT306	232
			Jet lag	RC1076.J48	616.980213
			Jet stream	QC935	551.5183
			Jet transports	TL685.7	358.44

Subject Heading	LC	Dewey	Subject Heading	LC	Dewey
Jew's harp	ML1087	786.88709	Jordan—History— Intervention, 1958	DS154.55	956.95043
Jewelry	NK7300-7695	739.27	Jordan—Maps	G2240-2244	912.5695
Jewelry	GT2250-2281	391.7	Jordan—Maps	G7510-7514	912.5695
Jewelry making	TS740-770	739.27	Jordon—Politics and	JQ1833	320.95695
Jewish cosmology	B157.C65	181.06	government		
Jewish messianic	BM615	296.336	Journalism	PN4700-5650	070.4
movements			Journalism—Editing	PN4778	070.41
Jewish periodicals	AP91-93	059.924	Journalism—Exhibitions	PN4720	070.4074
Jewish preaching	BM730	296.47	Journalism—Political	PN4751	070.44932
Jewish sects	BM175	296.8	aspects		
Jewish way of life	BM723	296.7	Journalism—Social aspects	PN4749	070.4
Jewish women	HQ1172	305.48696	Journalism—Study and	PN4785-4823	070.4071
Jews	GN547	305.8924	teaching		
Jews	DS101-151	933/956.94	Journalism, Military	VG500-505	359.342
Jews—Civilization	DS112-113	933/956.94	Journalism, Military—	VG503	359.3420973
Jews—Dietary laws	BM710	296.73	United States		
Jews—Education	BM70-135	296.68	Judaism—Congresses	BM21-30	296.67
Jews—History—To 1200 B.C.	DS109.912	933.01	Judaism—Customs and practices	BM650-747	296.7
Jews—History—To 953 B.C.	DS109.912	933.02	Judaism—Dictionaries	BM50	296.03
Jews—History— 1200-953 B.C.	DS121.55	933.02	Judaism—Directories	BM55-65	296.025
			Judaism—Doctrines	BM600-603	296.3
Jews—History— 953-586 B.C.	DS121.6	933.03	Judaism—History	BM150-449	296.09
Jews—History—Babylonian captivity, 598-515 B.C.	DS109.912	933.03	Judaism—History— To 70 A.D.	BM165-178	296.09014
Jews—History— 586 B.C.-70 A.D.	DS109.912	933.0(3-5)	Judaism—History— Medieval and early modern period, 425-1789	BM180-185	296.0902
Jews—History— 168 B.C.-135 A.D.	DS121.7-.8	933.0(4-5)/ 956.9402	Judaism—History— Modern period, 1750-	BM190-199	296.09033
Jews—History— Rebellion, 66-73	DS109.913	933.05/ 956.9402	Judaism—Liturgy	BM184	297.38
Jews—History—70-638	DS123.5	956.9402	Judaism—Periodicals	BM11	296.05
Jews—History—Bar Kokhba Rebellion, 132-135	DS122.9	956.9402	Judaism—Societies, etc.	BM1	296.67
			Judaism	BM	296
Jews—History—1789-1945	DS109.92-.93	956.940(3-4)	Judaism—Afghanistan	BM400	296.09581
Jews—Politics and government	JC67	320.933	Judaism—Africa	BM432-440	296.096
			Judaism—Arabia	BM393-395	296.0953
Jews—Restoration	BS649.J5	909.04924	Judaism—Asia	BM377-431	296.095
Jihad	BP182	297.72	Judaism—[Australia/ New Zealand]	BM443-445	296.099(3/4)
Jitterbug (Dance)	GV1796.J6	793.33	Judaism—Austria	BM307-309	296.09436
Job analysis	HF5549.5.J6	658.306	Judaism—Belgium	BM310-312	296.09493
Job descriptions	HF5549.5.J613	658.306	Judaism—Bulgaria	BM364-366	296.09499
Job hunting	HF5382.7-.75	650.14	Judaism—Canada	BM227-229	296.0971
Job security	HD5708.4-.45	331.2596	Judaism—Central America	BM233-247	296.09728
Job stress	HF5548.85	158.72	Judaism—China	BM423-425	296.0951
Job vacancies	HD5710.5	331.124	Judaism—Denmark	BM342-344	296.09489
Joinery	TH5662-5663	694.6	Judaism—Egypt	BM434-436	296.0962
Joints	QM131-142	611.72	Judaism—Europe	BM290-376	296.094
Joints	QL825	573.78	Judaism—Finland	BM334-336	296.094897
Jordan	DS153-154.9	933/956.95	Judaism—France	BM313-315	296.0944
Jordan—Census	HA4561	315.695	Judaism—Germany	BM316-318	296.0943
Jordan—Civilization	DS153.4	933/956.95	Judaism—Great Britain	BM292-305	296.0941
Jordan—Description and travel	DS153.2	913.304/ 915.69504	Judaism—Greece	BM319-321	296.09495
			Judaism—India	BM406-410	296.0954
Jordan—Economic conditions	HC415.26	330.95695	Judaism—Iran	BM396-398	296.0955
			Judaism—Iraq	BM386.4-.6	296.09567
Jordan—History	DS153.7-154.55	933/956.95	Judaism—Israel	BM390-392	296.095694
Jordan—History—20th century	DS154.5-.55	956.950(3-44)	Judaism—Italy	BM322-324	296.0945
			Judaism—Japan	BM426-428	296.0952

Subject Heading	LC	Dewey
Judaism—Mexico	BM230-232	296.0972
Judaism—Netherlands	BM325-327	296.09492
Judaism—Norway	BM348-350	296.09481
Judaism—Oceania	BM447-449	296.099(5-6)
Judaism—Poland	BM337-339	296.09438
Judaism—Portugal	BM328-330	296.09469
Judaism—Romania	BM370-372	296.09498
Judaism—Russia	BM331-333	296.0947
Judaism—Scandinavia	BM340-353	296.0948
Judaism—South Africa	BM437	296.0968
Judaism—South America	BM261-289	296.098
Judaism—Spain	BM354-356	296.0946
Judaism—Sweden	BM351-353	296.09485
Judaism—Switzerland	BM357-359	296.09494
Judaism—[Syria/Palestine]	BM387-389	296.09569(1/4)
Judaism—United States	BM205-225	296.0973
Judaism—West Indies	BM248-260	296.09729
Judaism—Yugoslavia	BM373-375	296.094971
Judgment (Logic)	BC181	121
Judgment Day	BT880-882	236.9
Judgment Day (Islam)	BP166.85	297.23
Judgments, Foreign	K7680	340.9
Judgments—United States	KF8990-9002	347.73077
Judicial power	K3367	347.012
Judicial power—United States	KF5130	347.73012
Judicial review	JF711	347.012
Judicial statistics—Canada	KE198-206	347.71013
Judicial statistics—England	KD327-332	347.42013
Judicial statistics—United States	KF180-185	347.73013
Judo	GV1114	796.8152
Junction transistors	TK7871.92	621.3815282
Jungle warfare	U167.5.J8	355.423
Junior colleges	LB2328	378.1543
Junior colleges—United States	LD6501	378.15430973
Junior high schools	LB1623	373.236
Junks	VM101	623.810951
Jupiter (Planet)	QB661	523.45
Jupiter (Planet)	QB384	523.45
Jupiter (Roman deity)	BL820.J8	292.2113
Jurisdiction—United States	KF8858-8861	347.73051
Jury	K5492	345.075
Jury—United States	KF8971-8984	347.730752
Jury—United States	KF9680	345.73075
CRIMINAL Justice	JC578	320.011
Justice (Virtue)	BV4647.J	241.62
Justification	BT763-764.2	234.7
Juvenile courts	K5575-5582	345.08
Juvenile delinquency	HV9051-9230.7	364.36
Juvenile delinquency—Study and teaching	HV9068	364.36071
Juvenile delinquency—United States	HV9103-9106	364.360973
Juvenile delinquency—[By region or country]	HV9101-9230.7	364.3609(4-9)
Juvenile delinquency—[Other regions or countries]	HV9107-9230.7	364.3609(4-9)
Juvenile delinquents	HV9051-9230.7	364.36

Subject Heading	LC	Dewey
Kabardian language	PK9201.K3	499.9624
Kabardian literature	PK9201.K35-.K39	899.9624
Kabardians	DK34.K13	947.52004
Kabuki	PN2924.5.K3	792.0952
Kallitype	TR400	772.16
Kalmar, Union of, 1397	DL694	948.5018
Kalmar, Union of, 1397	DL485	948.9701
Kalmar, Union of, 1397	DL179	948.9701
Kalmar War, 1611-1613	DL710	948.502
Kalmyks	DK34.K14	947.48
Kannada language	PL4641-4649	494.814
Kansas—Gazetteers	F679	917.81003
Kansas—History	F676-690	978.1
Kansas—History—1854-1861	F685	978.102
Kansas—History—Civil War, 1861-1865	E508	978.1031
Kansas—Maps	G4200-4204	912.781
Kansas—National Guard	UA200-209	355.3709781
Kansas—Periodicals	F676	978.1005
Kaons	QC793.5.M42-.M429	539.72162
Karachay-Balkar language	PL65.B2	494.38
Karaites	BM185-.4	296.81
Karate	GV1114.3	796.8153
Karelian language	PH501-509	494.54
Karen language	PL4051-4054	495
Karma	BL2015.K3	294.5175
Karst	GB599-609.2	551.447
Kashmiri language	PK7021-7029	491.499
Kashmiri literature	PK7031-7037	891.499
Kassr-el-Kebir, Battle of, 1578	DT322	964.02
Kassr-el-Kebir, Battle of, 1578	DP614	946.902
Katyn Forest Massacre, 1940	D804.S65	940.5405
Kayaking	GV781-790.3	797.1224
Kazakhstan	DK901-909.5	958.45
Kearny's Expedition, 1846	E405.2	973.623
Keewatin—History	F1106-1110.5	971.94
Keewatin—Periodicals	F1106.A1	971.94005
Kelly's Ford (Va.), Battle of, 1863	E475.3	973.734
Kennels	SF428	636.70831
Kentucky Derby, Louisville, Ky.	SF357.K4	798.400976944
Kentucky and Virginia resolutions of 1798	E328	973.44
Kentucky bluegrass	SB201.K4	633.21
Kentucky—Gazetteers	F449	917.69003
Kentucky—History	F446-460	976.9
Kentucky—History—To 1792	F454	976.90(1-2)
Kentucky—History—1792-1865	F455	976.903
Kentucky—History—1865-	F456-.26	976.904
Kentucky—Maps	G3950-3954	912.769
Kentucky—National Guard	UA210-219	355.3709769
Kentucky—Periodicals	F446	976.9005
Kenya—Census	HA4693	316.762

Subject Heading	LC	Dewey	Subject Heading	LC	Dewey
Kenya—Civilization	DT433.54	967.62	Knowledge, Theory of	BD143-237	121
Kenya—Description and travel	DT433.527	916.76204	Knowledge, Theory of (Religion)	BL51	210
Kenya—Economic conditions	HC865	330.96762	Kongo Wars, 1928-1931	DT546.37	967.4103
Kenya—Gazetteers	DT433.515	916.762003	Koniagmiut Eskimos	E99.E7	973.04971
Kenya—History	DT433.552-.584	967.62	Koran	BP100-134	297.122
Kenya—History—To 1895	DT433.565-.567	967.6201	Korea (North)	DS930-937	951.93
Kenya—History—To 1963	DT433.565-.577	967.620(1-3)	Korea (South)—History— April Revolution, 1960	DS922-.42	951.95
Kenya—History—1895-1963	DT433.57-.577	967.6203	Korea (South)—May Revolution, 1961	DS922.44	951.95
Kenya—History—1963-	DT433.58-.584	967.6204	Korea—Census	HA4630.5-.6	315.19
Kenya—Maps	G8410-8414	912.6762	Korea—Church history	BR1320-1337	275.19
Keratosis	RL435	616.544	Korea—Civilization	DS904	951.9
Kerchiefs	TT657	687.19	Korea—Description and travel	DS902.2-.4	915.1904
Kerguelen Islands—Census	HA2309	316.99	Korea—Economic conditions	HC466-470.2	330.9519
Kerosene	TP692.4.K4	665.5383	Korea—Gazetteers	DS901.8	915.19003
Kerosene heaters	TH7450.5	697.24	Korea—History—To 935	DS911-.78	951.901
Kerr black holes	QB843.B55	523.8875	Korea—History—Koryo period, 935-1392	DS912-.43	951.901
Kettle Creek (Ga.), Battle of, 1779	E241.K48	973.335	Korea—History—Mongolian Invasions, 1231-1270	DS912.4-.43	951.901
Keyboard instruments	MT180-258	786.07	Korea—History—Yi dynasty, 1392-1910	DS913-915.5	951.902
Khalsa (Sect)	BL2018.7.K44	294.69	Korea—History—Japanese Invasions, 1592-1598	DS913-.45	951.902
Khe Sanh, Battle of, 1968	DS557.8.K5	959.704342	Korea—History—Manchu Invasions, 1627-1637	DS913.615-.675	951.902
Khilji dynasty	DS459.2	954.0234	Korea—History— 1864-1910	DS915-.5	951.902
Khowar language	PK7070	491.499	Korea—History—20th century	DS915.56-922.42	951.90(2-3)
Kibbutzim	HX742.2	335.1209694	Korea—History—Japanese occupation, 1910-1945	DS916.525-.58	951.903
Kidnapping	HV6595-6604	364.154	Korea—History—1945-	DS916.6-922.42	951.904
Kidneys	QM404	611.61	Korea—History—Allied occupation, 1945-1948	DS917.5-.55	951.9041
Kidneys	QP249	612.463	Korea—Maps	G2330-2334.34	912.519
Kidneys	QL873	573.496	Korea—Politics and government	JQ1720-1729.5	320.9519
Kidneys—Diseases	RC902-918	616.61	Korea—Religion	BL2230-2240	299.957
Kidneys—Diseases— Diagnosis	RC904-.5	616.61075	Korean Demilitarized Zone (Korea)	DS921.7	951.90422
Kiev (Ukraine)	DK508.92-.939	947.77	Korean War, 1950-1953	DS918-921.8	951.9042
Kilns	TP841-842	666.43	Korean War, 1950-1953— Aerial operations	DS920.2	951.904248
Kimonos	GT1560	391.00952	Korean War, 1950-1953— Armistices	DS921.7	951.90422
Kindergarten	LB1141-1499	372.218	Korean War, 1950-1953— Atrocities	DS920.8-.9	951.90428
Kindness	BJ1533.K5	177.7	Korean War, 1950-1953— Campaigns	DS918.2	951.904242
Kinematics	QA841-842	531.112	Korean War, 1950-1953— Prisoners and prisons	DS921-.2	951.90427
Kinematics	QC231	534.5			
Kinematics	QA913	532.5	Korean drama	PL962-964	895.72009
Kinesiology	QP303	613.7	Korean drama	PL977-979	895.72008
Kinetic theory of gases	QC175-.16	533.7	Korean fiction	PL980-981.5	895.73008
Kinetic theory of liquids	QC175.3-.36	532.5	Korean fiction	PL965-967	895.73009
Kingdom of God	BT94	231.72	Korean language	PL901-949	495.7
Kings and rulers	JC374-408	321			
Kings and rulers	GN492.7	321			
Kings and rulers, Ancient	GN495.5	321.60901			
Kinship	GN480-.65	306.83			
Kiribati	DU615	996.81			
Kiribati—Census	HA4016.7	319.681			
Kiribati—Maps	G9480-9484	912.9681			
Kissing	GT2640	394			
Kitchens	TX653-655	643.3			
Kites	TL759-.7	629.13332			
Knights and knighthood	CR	929.71			
Knitting	TT819-829	746.432			
Knots and splices	VM533	623.8882			
Knowledge representation (Information theory)	Q387-.5	006.332			

Subject Heading	LC	Dewey	Subject Heading	LC	Dewey
Korean language—Dictionaries	PL935-.6	495.73	Labor laws and legislation—England	KD3001-3177	344.4201
Korean literature	PL950-998	895.7	Labor laws and legislation—United States	KF3301-3580	344.7301
Korean poetry	PL974-976.4	895.71008			
Korean poetry	PL959-961.4	895.71009	Labor market	HD5701-5852	331.12
Krakow (Poland)	DK4700-4735	943.86	Labor market—[By region or country]	HD5723-5851	331.1209(4-9)
Krugerrand (Coin)	CJ3948	737.4968			
Kung fu	GV1114.7	796.8159	Labor market—Afghanistan	HD5812.6	331.1209581
Kuwait—Economic conditions	HC415.39	330.95367	Labor market—Africa	HD5837-5849.3	331.12096
			Labor market—Australia	HD5850	331.120994
Kuwait—Maps	G7600-7604	912.5367	Labor market—Benelux countries	HD5785.5-5793.5	331.1209492
Kuwait—Politics and government	JQ1848	320.95367			
			Labor market—Canada	HD5727-5729	331.120971
Kwangju Uprising, Kwangju-si, Korea, 1980	DS922.445	951.95	Labor market—Central America	HD5733-5739	331.1209728
			Labor market—China	HD5830	331.120951
Kwanzaa	GT4403	394.26	Labor market—Europe	HD5764-5811.84	331.12094
Kyrgyzstan	DK911-919.5	958.43	Labor market—France	HD5773-5776	331.120944
Labels—Law and legislation	KF1619-1620	343.73082	Labor market—Germany	HD5777-5780.5	331.120943
Labels—Law and legislation—Canada	KE1616-1618	343.71082	Labor market—Great Britain	HD5765-5767.5	331.120941
			Labor market—Greece	HD5811.83	331.1209495
Labels—Law and legislation—England	KD2208-2209	343.42082	Labor market—India	HD5817-5820	331.120954
			Labor market—Iran	HD5812.56	331.120955
Labor	HD4801-8943	331	Labor market—Iraq	HD5812.55	331.1209567
Labor—[By region or country]	HD8045-8942.5	331.09(4-9)	Labor market—Israel	HD5812.2	331.12095694
Labor—Afghanistan	HD8670.6	331.09581	Labor market—Italy	HD5782-5785	331.120945
Labor—Africa	HD8771-8837	331.096	Labor market—Japan	HD5827	331.120952
Labor—Australia	HD8841-8850	331.0994	Labor market—Mexico	HD5731	331.120972
Labor—Benelux countries	HD8491-8520.5	331.09492	Labor market—Philippines	HD5825	331.1209599
Labor—Canada	HD8101-8110	331.0971	Labor market—Russia	HD5794-5797	331.120947
Labor—Central America	HD8126-8190	331.09728	Labor market—South America	HD5746-5763	331.12098
Labor—China	HD8731-8740	331.0951			
Labor—Europe	HD8371-8650.7	331.094	Labor market—Spain	HD5805-5808	331.120946
Labor—France	HD8421-8440	331.0944	Labor market—Switzerland	HD5810	331.1209494
Labor—Germany	HD8441-8460.5	331.0943	Labor market—Turkey	HD5811.93	331.1209561
Labor—Great Britain	HD8381-8400	331.0941	Labor market—United States	HD5723-5726	331.120973
Labor—Greece	HD8650.5	331.09495			
Labor—India	HD8681-8690	331.0954	Labor market—West Indies	HD5740-5745.9	331.1209729
Labor—Iran	HD8670.2	331.0955	Labor movement	HD4801-4854	331.8
Labor—Iraq	HD8670	331.09567	Labor policy	HD7795-8013	331.12042
Labor—Israel	HD8660	331.095694	Labor supply	HD5701-5852	331.12
Labor—Italy	HD8471-8490	331.0945	Labor theory of value	HB206	335.412
Labor—Japan	HD8721-8730	331.0952	Labor turnover	HF5549.5.T8	331.126
Labor—Mexico	HD8111-8120	331.0972	Laboratories	Q183-.4	507.2
Labor—Middle East	HD8656-8669	331.0956	Laboratory animals	SF405.5-407	636.0885
Labor—Philippines	HD8711-8720	331.09599	Labrador (Nfld.)—Gazetteers	F1135.4	917.182003
Labor—Russia	HD8521-8530	331.0947	Labrador (Nfld.)—History	F1135-1139	971.82
Labor—South America	HD8251-8370	331.098	Labrador (Nfld.)—Periodicals	F1135	971.82005
Labor—Spain	HD8581-8590	331.0946	Labrador(Nfld.)—Maps	G3610-3612	912.7182
Labor—Switzerland	HD8601-8610	331.09494	Labyrinth (Ear)	QL948	579.89
Labor—United States	HD8051-8085	331.0973	Labyrinth (Ear)	QP471-.2	612.858
Labor—West Indies	HD8191-8250	331.09729	Labyrinth (Ear)	QM507	611.85
Labor, Induced (Obstetrics)	RG734	618.4	Labyrinth (Ear)—Diseases	RF260-275	617.882
Labor, Premature	RG649	618.397	Lace and lace making	TT800-810	746.22
Labor (Obstetrics)	RG651-791	618.4	Lacquer and lacquering	NK9900-.7	745.726
Labor (Obstetrics)—Complications	RG701-721	618.5	Lacrimal apparatus—Diseases	RE201-216	617.764
Labor contract—Canada	KE928-936	344.710189			
Labor contract—England	KD1638-1642	344.4201542	Lacrosse	GV989	796.347
Labor demand	HD5701-5852	331.123	Lactation	QP246	612.664
Labor laws and legislation	K1701-1841	344.01	Lactation disorders	RG861-866	618.71

Subject Heading	LC	Dewey	Subject Heading	LC	Dewey
Lactose intolerance	RC632.L33	616.3998	Land use—Brazil	HD491-500	333.730981
Ladon (Greek mythology)	BL820.L25	292.13	Land use—Bulgaria	HD811-820	333.7309499
Lagoon ecology	QH541.5.L27	577.63	Land use—Burkina Faso	HD1018	333.73096625
Lagoons	GB2201-2398	551.482	Land use—Burma	HD860.7	333.7309591
Laity	BV687	262.15	Land use—Burundi	HD986	333.730967572
Laity—Catholic Church	BX1920	262.152	Land use—Cambodia	HD890.3	333.7309596
Lake ecology	QH541.5.L3	577.63	Land use—Cameroon	HD1009	333.73096711
Lake of the Woods Massacre, 1736	F1030	971.018	Land use—Canada	HD311-320	333.730971
			Land use—Canary Islands	HD1028.7	333.7309649
Lake steamers	VM460	623.82436	Land use—Cape Verde	HD1028.9	333.73096658
Lake-dwellers and lake-dwellings	GN785-786	569.9	Land use—Central African Republic	HD1007	333.73096741
Lakes	GB1601-1798.9	551.482	Land use—Chad	HD1008	333.73096743
Lakes	QH98	578.763	Land use—Chile	HD501-510	333.730983
Lamaism	BQ7530-7950	294.3923	Land use—China	HD921-930	333.730951
Lamanites (Mormon Church)	BX8627.A3-Z	289.32	Land use—Colombia	HD511-520	333.7309861
Lambda calculus	QA9.5	511.3	Land use—Comoro Islands	HD1030	333.7309694
Lambs	SF376.5	636.3	Land use—Congo (Brazzaville)	HD1006	333.73096724
Laminar flow	QA929	532.0525			
Laminated plastics	TP1183.L3	668.492	Land use—Cook Islands	HD1127.5	333.73099623
Laminated wood	TS869	674.835	Land use—Costa Rica	HD341-350	333.73097286
Lamps	GT445	392.36	Land use—Cote d'Ivoire	HD1015	333.73096668
Lances	U872	623.441	Land use—Cuba	HD411-420	333.73097291
Land, Nationalization of	HD1301-1339	333.14	Land use—Curacao	HD456.7	333.730972986
Land banks	HG2041-2051	332.31	Land use—Cyprus	HD847	333.73095693
Land capability for agriculture	HD101-1131	333.76	Land use—Czechoslovakia	HD640.3	333.7309437
			Land use—Denmark	HD731-740	333.7309489
Land capability for agriculture	S590-599.9	631.4	Land use—Djibouti	HD981	333.73096771
			Land use—Dominica	HD454.3	333.7309729841
Land grants—Law and legislation—United States	KF5675-5677	343.730253	Land use—Dominican Republic	HD426-430	333.73097293
Land reform	HD1332-1333.5	333.31	Land use—Ecuador	HD521-530	333.7309866
Land tenure	HD1241-1339	333.3	Land use—Egypt	HD976	333.730962
Land tenure—Law and legislation—England	KD833-960	346.420432	Land use—El Salvador	HD391-400	333.73097284
			Land use—England	HD601-610	333.730942
Land use	HD101-1131	333.73	Land use—Equatorial Guinea	HD1002	333.73096718
Land use—Afghanistan	HD860.6	333.7309581	Land use—Ethiopia	HD979	333.730963
Land use—Albania	HD810.5	333.73094965	Land use—Falkland Islands	HD1029.5	333.7309971
Land use—Algeria	HD973	333.730965	Land use—Fiji	HD1126	333.73099611
Land use—American Samoa	HD1128	333.73099613	Land use—Finland	HD721-725	333.73094897
Land use—Angola	HD1000	333.7309673	Land use—France	HD641-650	333.730944
Land use—Anguilla	HD453.2	333.730972973	Land use—French Guiana	HD540.7	333.7309882
Land use—Antigua	HD453.4	333.730972974	Land use—French Polynesia	HD1129.5	333.7309962
Land use—Arctic regions	HD1130	333.730998(1-8)	Land use—Gabon	HD1005	333.73096721
Land use—Argentina	HD471-480	333.730982	Land use—Gambia	HD1024	333.73096651
Land use—Aruba	HD456.5	333.730972986	Land use—Germany	HD651-660.5	333.730943
Land use—Australia	HD1031-1040	333.730994	Land use—Ghana	HD1022	333.7309667
Land use—Austria	HD631-640	333.7309436	Land use—Greece	HD840.5	333.7309495
Land use—Azores	HD1028	333.73094699	Land use—Greenland	HD1130.5	333.7309982
Land use—Bahamas	HD406-410	333.73097296	Land use—Grenada	HD454.5	333.7309729845
Land use—Bahrain	HD858	333.73095365	Land use—Guadeloupe	HD458	333.730972976
Land use—Bangladesh	HD880.6	333.73095492	Land use—Guam	HD1121.5	333.7309967
Land use—Barbados	HD451.5	333.730972981	Land use—Guatemala	HD351-360	333.73097281
Land use—Belgium	HD691-700	333.7309493	Land use—Guinea	HD1016	333.73096652
Land use—Belize	HD336-340	333.73097282	Land use—Guinea Bissau	HD1026	333.73096657
Land use—Benin	HD1012	333.73096683	Land use—Guyana	HD540.3	333.7309881
Land use—Bermuda Islands	HD1028.3	333.73097299	Land use—Haiti	HD421-425	333.73097294
Land use—Bhutan	HD880.3	333.73095498	Land use—History	HD113-156	333.7309
Land use—Bolivia	HD481-490	333.730984	Land use—Honduras	HD361-370	333.73097283
Land use—Bonaire	HD456.6	333.730972986	Land use—Hong Kong	HD941-945	333.73095125
Land use—Botswana	HD996	333.73096883	Land use—Hungary	HD640.5	333.7309439

Subject Heading	LC	Dewey	Subject Heading	LC	Dewey
Land use—Iceland	HD741-750	333.73094912	Land use—Portugal	HD781-790	333.7309469
Land use—India	HD871-880	333.730954	Land use—Puerto Rico	HD441-450	333.73097295
Land use—Indonesia	HD891-900	333.7309598	Land use—Qatar	HD857	333.73095363
Land use—Iran	HD860.2	333.730955	Land use—Reunion	HD1030.5	333.73096981
Land use—Iraq	HD860	333.7309567	Land use—Rhodesia	HD992	333.7309689
Land use—Ireland	HD621-630	333.7309415	Land use—Romania	HD831-840	333.7309498
Land use—Israel	HD850	333.73095694	Land use—Russia	HD711-720	333.730947
Land use—Italy	HD671-680	333.730945	Land use—Rwanda	HD985	333.730967571
Land use—Jamaica	HD431-440	333.73097292	Land use—Saba	HD456.8	333.730972977
Land use—Japan	HD911-920	333.730952	(Netherlands Antilles)		
Land use—Jordan	HD851	333.73095695	Land use—Saint Eustatius	HD456.85	333.730972977
Land use—Kenya	HD983	333.73096762	(Netherlands Antilles)		
Land use—Kerguelen	HD1030.7	333.7309699	Land use—Saint Helena	HD1029	333.7309973
Islands			Land use—Saint Kitts	HD453.8	333.730972973
Land use—Kiribati	HD1122.3	333.73099681	and Nevis		
Land use—Korea	HD920.5-.6	333.7309519	Land use—Saint Lucia	HD454.7	333.7309729843
Land use—Kuwait	HD859	333.73095367	Land use—Saint Martin	HD456.9	333.730972977
Land use—Laos	HD890.4	333.7309594	Land use—Saint Vincent	HD454.9	333.7309729844
Land use—Lebanon	HD849	333.73095692	Land use—Sao Tome and	HD1003	333.73096715
Land use—Lesotho	HD994	333.73096885	Principe		
Land use—Liberia	HD1025	333.73096662	Land use—Saudi Arabia	HD853	333.7309538
Land use—Libya	HD975	333.7309612	Land use—Scotland	HD611-620	333.7309411
Land use—Liechtenstein	HD640.9	333.730943648	Land use—Senegal	HD1019	333.7309663
Land use—Luxembourg	HD710.5	333.73094935	Land use—Seychelles	HD1029.9	333.7309696
Land use—Macao	HD931-935	333.73095126	Land use—Sierra Leone	HD1023	333.7309664
Land use—Madagascar	HD989	333.7309691	Land use—Solomon Islands	HD1123	333.73099593
Land use—Madeira Islands	HD1028.5	333.73094698	Land use—Somalia	HD980	333.73096773
Land use—Malawi	HD997	333.73096897	Land use—South Africa	HD991	333.730968
Land use—Malaysia	HD890.6	333.7309595	Land use—Spain	HD771-780	333.730946
Land use—Maldives	HD1029.7	333.73095495	Land use—Sri Lanka	HD860.8	333.73095493
Land use—Mali	HD1017	333.73096623	Land use—Sudan	HD977	333.7309624
Land use—Martinique	HD459	333.730972982	Land use—Surinam	HD540.5	333.7309883
Land use—Mauritania	HD1020	333.7309661	Land use—Swaziland	HD995	333.73096887
Land use—Mauritius	HD1030.3	333.73096982	Land use—Sweden	HD761-770	333.7309485
Land use—Mexico	HD321-330	333.730972	Land use—Switzerland	HD791-800	333.7309494
Land use—Monaco	HD650.5	333.730944949	Land use—Syria	HD848	333.73095691
Land use—Mongolia	HD920.8	333.7309517	Land use—Taiwan	HD936-940	333.730951249
Land use—Montserrat	HD453.6	333.730972975	Land use—Tanzania	HD987	333.7309678
Land use—Morocco	HD972	333.730964	Land use—Thailand	HD890.55	333.7309593
Land use—Mozambique	HD988	333.7309679	Land use—Togo	HD1013	333.73096681
Land use—Namibia	HD998	333.73096881	Land use—Tonga	HD1127	333.73099612
Land use—Nepal	HD860.9	333.73095496	Land use—Trinidad and	HD455	333.730972983
Land use—Netherlands	HD701-710	333.7309492	Tobago		
Land use—New Caledonia	HD1124	333.73099597	Land use—Tristan da Cunha	HD1029.3	333.7309973
Land use—New Zealand	HD1120.5	333.730993	Land use—Tunisia	HD974	333.7309611
Land use—Nicaragua	HD371-380	333.73097285	Land use—Turkey	HD846.5	333.7309561
Land use—Niger	HD1014	333.73096626	Land use—Uganda	HD984	333.73096761
Land use—Nigeria	HD1021	333.7309669	Land use—United Arab	HD856	333.73095357
Land use—Northern Ireland	HD620.5	333.7309416	Emirates		
Land use—Norway	HD751-760	333.7309481	Land use—United States	HD170-279	333.730973
Land use—Oman	HD855	333.73095353	Land use—Uruguay	HD561-570	333.7309895
Land use—Pakistan	HD880.5	333.73095491	Land use—Vanuatu	HD1125	333.73099595
Land use—Panama	HD381-385	333.73097287	Land use—Venezuela	HD571-580	333.730987
Land use—Panama Canal	HD386-390	333.730972875	Land use—Vietnam	HD890.5	333.7309597
Zone			Land use—Virgin Islands	HD450.3	333.7309729722
Land use—Papau New	HD1122	333.7309953	of the United States		
Guinea			Land use—Western Sahara	HD1027	333.7309648
Land use—Paraguay	HD541-550	333.7309892	Land use—Yemen	HD854-.5	333.7309533
Land use—Peru	HD551-560	333.730985	Land use—Yugoslavia	HD821-825	333.7309497
Land use—Philippines	HD901-910	333.7309599	Land use—Zaire	HD1001	333.73096751
Land use—Poland	HD726-729.5	333.7309438	Land use—Zambia	HD993	333.73096894

Subject Heading	LC	Dewey	Subject Heading	LC	Dewey
Landforms	GB400-649	551.41	Lapp literature	PH731-735	894.55
Landing aids (Aeronautics)	TL696.L3	629.1351	Lard	TS1980-1981	664.34
Landing operations	U200	355.422	Lard oil	TP676	664.34
Landscape	BH301.L3	700.42	Laryngoscopy	RF514-.5	616.2207545
Landscape architecture	SB469-476.4	712	Larynx	QP306	612.2
Landscape design	SB472.45	712	Larynx	QM255	611.22
Landscape drawing	NC790-800	743.836	Larynx—Surgery	RF516-517	617.533059
Landscape painting	ND2240-2243	751.422436	Lasers	TA1671-1715	621.366
Landscape painting	ND1340-1367	758.1	Last Supper	BT420	232.957
Landscape painting—[By region or country]	ND1351-1367	758.10973	Latent structure analysis	QA278.6	519.535
			Lathes	TJ1218-1222	621.942
Landscape painting—Asia	ND1365-.96	758.1095	Latin America—Civilization	F1408.3-.4	980
Landscape painting—Europe	ND1353-1364	758.1094	Latin America—Description and travel	F1409-.3	918.04
Landscape painting—France	ND1356-.6	758.10944			
Landscape painting—Germany	ND1357-.6	758.10943	Latin America—Gazetteers	F1406	918.003
			Latin America—Periodicals	F1401	980.005
Landscape painting—Great Britain	ND1354-.6	758.10941	Latin Empire, 1204-1261	DF610-629	949.504
			Latin drama	PA6137	872.08
Landscape painting—Italy	ND1358-.6	758.10945	Latin drama—History and criticism	PA6067-6075	872.09
Landscape painting—Spain	ND1362-.6	758.10946			
Landscape painting—United States	ND1351-.6	758.109(3-9)	Latin drama, Medieval and modern	PA8073-8079	872.(3-4)09
Landscape painting—[Other American countries]	ND1352	758.109(71-8)	Latin drama, Medieval and modern	PA8135-8140	872.(3-4)08
Landscape photography	TR660-.5	778.936	Latin language	PA2001-2995	470
Landslides	QE599	551.307	Latin language—Dictionaries	PA2361-2390	473
Language, Universal	PM8008	401.3	Latin language—Etymology	PA2341-2350	472
Language acquisition	P118-.7	401.93	Latin language—Grammar	PA2071-2310	475
Language and languages	P1-410	400	Latin language—Lexicography	PA2351-2390	473.028
Language and languages—Dictionaries	P29	403			
			Latin language—Metrics and rhythmics	PA2329-2340	871.6
Language and languages—Etymology	P321-324.5	412			
			Latin language—Morphology	PA2133-2158	475
Language and languages—Grammars	P207	415	Latin language—Parts of speech	PA2161-2281	475
Language and languages—Periodicals	P1-10	405	Latin language—Phonology	PA2111-2131	475
			Latin language—Study and teaching	PA2061-2067	470.71
Language and languages—Study and teaching	P51-59	407.1			
			Latin language—Syntax	PA2285-2297	475
Language arts (Elementary)	LB1576	372.6	Latin language, Postclassical	PA2300-2309	477
Language disorders	RC423-428.5	616.855			
Languages, Artificial	PM8001-9021	499.99	Latin language, Preclassical to ca. 100 B.C.	PA2510-2519	477
Languages, Secret	PM9001-9021	417.2			
Langue d'oc	PC3371-3420	449	Latin language, Vulgar	PA2600-2748	477
Langue d'oc literature	PC3381-3420.5	849	Latin literature	PA6101-6139	870.8001
Lanterns	GR950.L4	398.355	Latin literature—History and criticism	PA6001-6098	870.9001
Lanterns	GT445	392.36			
Laos—Census	HA4600.4	315.94	Latin literature, Medieval and modern	PA8001-8595	870.900(3-4)
Laos—Civilization	DS555.42	959.4			
Laos—Description and travel	DS555.34-.382	915.9404	Latin philology	PA2001-2067	470
Laos—Economic conditions	HC443	330.9594	Latin poetry	PA6121-6135	871.08
Laos—Gazetteers	DS555.25	915.94003	Latin poetry	PA6045-6063	871.09
Laos—History	DS555.5-86	959.4	Latin poetry, Medieval and modern	PA8120-8133	871.(3-4)08
Laos—History—1975-	DS555.84-.86	959.4042			
Laos—Maps	G2374.5-.54	912.594	Latin poetry, Medieval and modern—History and criticism	PA8050-8065	871.(3-4)09
Laos—Maps	G8015-8019	912.594			
Laos—Politics and government	JQ950-959	320.9594			
			Latin prose literature	PA6138-6139	878.08
Laparoscopy	RG107.5.L34	618.107545	Latin prose literature—History and criticism	PA6081-6095.5	878.08
Laplace transformation	QA432	515.723			
Lapp language	PH701-729	494.55			

Subject Heading	LC	Dewey	Subject Heading	LC	Dewey
Latin prose literature, Medieval and modern	PA8081-8096	878.08	Law—Colorado	KFC1800-2399	349.788
Latin prose literature, Medieval and modern	PA8145-8149	878.08	Law—Columbia	KHH	349.861
			Law—Confederate States of America	KFZ8600-9199	349.75
Latitude	QB231-237	526.61	Law—Connecticut	KFC3600-4199	349.746
Latitude	VK565	527.1	Law—Costa Rica	KGB	349.7286
Lattice dynamics	QC176.8.L3	530.411	Law—Cuba	KGN	349.7291
Lattice theory	QA171.5	511.33	Law—Curacao	KGP0-499	349.72986
Lattice theory	QD911-919	548.7	Law—Cyprus	KJN	349.5645
Lattices, Distributive	QA171.5	512.7	Law—Czechoslovakia	KJP	349.437
Latvia	DK504-.95	947.96	Law—Delaware	KFD0-599	349.751
Latvia—Gazetteers	DK504.18	914.796003	Law—Denmark	KJR	349.489
Latvia—History	DK504.37-.79	947.96	Law—Dominica	KGP2000-2499	349.729841
Latvia—Maps	G7040-7043	912.4796	Law—Dominican Republic	KGQ	349.7293
Latvian language	PG8801-8993	491.93	Law—Ecuador	KHK	349.866
Latvian literature	PG8998-9146	891.93	Law—El Salvador	KGC	349.7284
Latvian philology	PG8801-8993	491.93	Law—England	KD	349.42
Launches	GV835	797.125	Law—England—Dictionaries	KD313	349.4203
Launches	VM340-349	623.81	Law—England—History	KD530-632	349.4209
Laundries	TT980-999	648.1	Law—Falkland Islands	KHL	349.9711
Lava	QE461	552.22	Law—Finland	KJT	349.4897
Law	K	340-349	Law—Florida	KFF0-599	349.759
Law—Biography	K170	340.092	Law—France	KJV	349.44
Law—Dictionaries	K50-54	340.03	Law—French Guiana	KHM	349.882
Law—History	K140-165	340.09	Law—Georgia	KFG0-599	349.758
Law—Humor	K183-184.7	340.0207	Law—Germany	KK	349.43
Law—International unification	K7051-7054	341.7	Law—Greece	KKE	349.495
			Law—Greenland	KDZ3000-3499	349.982
Law—Sources	K280-286	340.11	Law—Grenada	KGR4000-4499	349.729845
Law—Study and teaching	K100-103	340.071	Law—West Indies, French	KGR3000-3499	349.72976
Law—Study and teaching—Canada	KE273-322	349.71071	Law—Guadeloupe	KGR5000-5499	349.72976
			Law—Guatemala	KGD	349.7281
Law—Study and teaching—England	KD419-452	349.42071	Law—Guernsey (Channel Islands)	KDG421-440	349.42342
Law—Alabama	KFA0-599	349.761	Law—Haiti	KGS	349.7294
Law—Alaska	KFA1200-1799	349.798	Law—Hawaii	KFH0-599	349.969
Law—Albania	KJG	349.4965	Law—Honduras	KGE	349.7283
Law—Alberta	KEA	349.7123	Law—Hungary	KKF	349.439
Law—Anguilla	KGJ7000-7499	349.72973	Law—Iceland	KKG	349.4912
Law—Antiguilla	KGK0-499	349.72974	Law—Idaho	KFI0-599	349.796
Law—Argentina	KHA	349.82	Law—Illinois	KFI1200-1799	349.773
Law—Arizona	KFA2400-2999	349.791	Law—Iowa	KFI4200-4799	349.777
Law—Arkansas	KFA3600-4199	349.767	Law—Ireland	KDK	349.415
Law—Aruba	KGK1000-1499	349.72986	Law—Ireland—Dictionaries	KDK84	349.41503
Law—Austria	KJJ	349.436	Law—Isle of Man	KDG26-170	349.4279
Law—Bahamas	KGL0-499	349.7296	Law—Jamaica	KGT0-499	349.7292
Law—Barbados	KGL1000-1499	349.72981	Law—Jersey (Channel Islands)	KDG220-380	349.42341
Law—Belgium	KJK	349.493			
Law—Belize	KGA	349.7282	Law—Kansas	KFK0-599	349.781
Law—Bermuda	KDZ2000-2499	349.7299	Law—Kentucky	KFK1200-1799	349.769
Law—Bolivia	KHC	349.84	Law—Liechtenstein	KKJ	349.43648
Law—Bonaire	KGL2000-2499	349.72986	Law—Louisiana	KFL0-599	349.763
Law—Brazil	KHD	349.81	Law—Luxembourg	KKK0-499	349.4935
Law—British Columbia	KEB	349.711	Law—Maine	KFM0-599	349.741
Law—British Virgin Islands	KGL4000-4499	349.729725	Law—Malta	KKK1000-1499	349.4585
Law—Bulgaria	KJM	349.499	Law—Manitoba	KEM	349.7127
Law—California	KFC0-1199	349.794	Law—Martinique	KGT1000-1499	349.72982
Law—Canada	KE	349.71	Law—Maryland	KFM1200-1799	349.752
Law—[Canada, cities]	KEZ	349.71(1-9)	Law—Massachusetts	KFM2400-2999	349.744
Law—Channel Islands	KDG	349.4234	Law—Mexico	KGF	349.72
Law—Chile	KHF	349.83	Law—Michigan	KFM4200-4799	349.774

131

Subject Heading	LC	Dewey
Law—Minnesota	KFM5400-5999	349.776
Law—Mississippi	KFM6600-7199	349.762
Law—Missouri	KFM7800-8399	349.778
Law—Monaco	KKL	349.44949
Law—Montana	KFM9000-9599	349.786
Law—Montserrat	KGT2000-2499	349.72975
Law—Nebraska	KFN0-599	349.782
Law—Netherlands	KKM	349.492
Law—Nevada	KFN600-1199	349.793
Law—New Brunswick	KEN0-599	349.7151
Law—New Hampshire	KFN1200-1799	349.742
Law—New Jersey	KFN1800-2399	349.749
Law—New Mexico	KFN3600-4199	349.789
Law—New York (State)	KFN5000-6199	349.747
Law—Newfoundland	KEN1200-1799	349.718
Law—Nicaragua	KGG	349.7285
Law—North America	KDZ	349.7
Law—North Carolina	KFN7400-7999	349.756
Law—North Dakota	KFN8600-9199	349.784
Law—Northern Ireland	KDE	349.416
Law—Norway	KKN	349.481
Law—Nova Scotia	KEN7400-7999	349.716
Law—Ohio	KFO0-599	349.771
Law—Oklahoma	KFO1200-1799	349.766
Law—Ontario	KEO	349.713
Law—Oregon	KFO2400-2999	349.795
Law—Panama	KGH	349.7287
Law—Paraguay	KHP	349.892
Law—Pennsylvania	KFP0-599	349.748
Law—Peru	KHQ	349.85
Law—Poland	KKP	349.438
Law—Portugal	KKQ	349.469
Law—Prince Edward Island	KEP	349.717
Law—Puerto Rico	KGV	349.7295
Law—Quebec	KEQ	349.714
Law—Rhode Island	KFR0-599	349.745
Law—Romania	KKR	349.498
Law—Saba (Netherlands Antilles)	KGW0-499	349.72977
Law—Saint Eustatius	KGW7000-7499	349.72977
Law—Saint Kitts and Nevis	KGW2000-2499	349.72973
Law—Saint Lucia	KGW3000-3499	349.729843
Law—Saint Martin	KGW8000-8499	349.72977
Law—Saint Vincent	KGW5000-5499	349.729844
Law—Sasketchewan	KES	349.7124
Law—Scotland	KDC	349.411
Law—Scotland—Dictionaries	KDC152	349.411003
Law—South America	KH	349.8
Law—South Carolina	KFS1800-2399	349.757
Law—South Dakota	KFS3000-3599	349.783
Law—Spain	KKH	349.45
Law—Spain	KKT	349.46
Law—St. Pierre and Miquelon	KDZ4000-4499	349.7188
Law—Surinam	KHS	349.883
Law—Sweden	KKV	349.485
Law—Switzerland	KKW	349.494
Law—Tennessee	KFT0-599	349.768
Law—Texas	KFT1200-1799	349.764
Law—Trinidad and Tobago	KGX0-499	349.72983

Subject Heading	LC	Dewey
Law—Turkey	KKX	349.561
Law—United States	KF	349.73
Law—United States—Dictionaries	KF156	349.7303
Law—United States—History	KF350-374	349.7309
Law—United States—Study and teaching	KF261-292	349.73071
Law—United States—Territories and possessions	KF4635	342.730413
Law—[United States, cities]	KFX	349.7(4-9)
Law—Uruguay	KHU	349.895
Law—Utah	KFU0-599	349.792
Law—Venezuela	KHW	349.87
Law—Vermont	KFV0-599	349.743
Law—Virginia	KFV2400-2999	349.755
Law—Virginia Islands of the United States	KGZ0-499	349.729722
Law—Wales	KD9400-9500	349.429
Law—Wales—Dictionaries	KD9420	349.42903
Law—Wales—Study and teaching	KD9460	344.429071
Law—Washington	KFW0-599	349.797
Law—Washington, D.C.	KFD1200-1799	349.753
Law—West Indies	KGJ-KGZ	349.729
Law—West Virginia	KFW1200-1799	349.754
Law—Wisconsin	KFW2400-2999	349.775
Law—Wyoming	KFW4200-4799	349.787
Law—Yugoslavia	KKZ	349.497
Law—Yukon Territory	KEY	349.7191
Law, Primitive	K190-195	340.52
Law (Theology)	BT95-97	241.2
Law and art—Canada	KE3968	344.71097
Law reporting—United States	KF255	348.73041
Law reports, digests, etc.—Canada	KE132-156	348.71041
Law reports, digests, etc.—England	KD187-291	348.42041
Law reports, digests, etc.—Ireland	KDK61-80	348.41504
Law reports, digests, etc.—Northern Ireland	KDE55-60	348.416041
Law reports, digests, etc.—Wales	KD9410-9417	348.429041
Law School Admission Test	KF285	341.0711
Law schools	LC1101-1261	340.0711
Lawns	SB433-.34	635.9647
Lawyer referral service—United States	KF338	340.0973
Lawyers—Canada	KE335-355	349.71
Lawyers—England	KD460-472	349.42
Lawyers—Ireland	KDK120-134	349.415
Lawyers—Scotland	KDC225-247	349.411
Lawyers—United States	KF297-338	349.73
Laxatives	RM357	615.732
Lay preaching	BV4235.L3	251
Lay readers	BV677	262.15
Layettes	TT637	646.4060832
Le Cateau, Battle of, 1914	D545.L3	940.421

Subject Heading	LC	Dewey	Subject Heading	LC	Dewey
Lead ores	TN450-459	622.344	Lebanon—History— Israeli intervention, 1982-1984	DS87.53	956.92044
Leadership	BF637.L4	158.4			
Leadership	HD57.7	658.4			
Leadership	HM141	303.34	Lebanon—Maps	G7470-7474	912.5692
Leadership	UB210	355.33041	Lebanon—Maps	G2225-2229	912.5692
Lear jet aircraft	TL686.G	629.133340422	Lebanon—Politics and government	JQ1828	320.95692
Learned institutions and societies	AS	060	Lectionary preaching	BV4235.L43	251
Learned institutions and societies—History	AS5	060.9	Lecture method in teaching	LB2393	378.1796
			Lectures and lecturing	LC6501-6560.4	080
Learning	LB1060	153.15	Leeward Islands (West Indies)	F2006	972.97
Learning, Psychology of	BF318-319.5	153.15			
Learning, Psychology of	LB1060-1091	153.15	Leeward Islands (West Indies)—Census	HA866-.9	317.297
Learning ability	LB1134	153.9			
Learning and scholarship	AZ	001.2	Leeward Islands (West Indies)—Maps	G5030-5059	912.7297
Learning and scholarship— History	AZ200-361	001.2090			
Learning and scholarship— History—Medieval, 500-1500	AZ321	001.20902	Leeward Islands (West Indies)—Politics and government	JL640-649.7	320.97297
			Left- and right-handedness	LB1123	152.335
Learning and scholarship— Philosophy	AZ101-111	001.201	Leg	QL950.7	573.79
			Leg	QM549	611.98
Learning and scholarship— Africa	AZ800-821	001.2096	Leg—Abnormalities	RD779-789	616.71043
			Legal photography	HV6071	363.24
Learning and scholarship— Asia	AZ770-795	001.2095	Legal research—Canada	KE250-259	349.71072
			Legal research—England	KD392-400	349.42072
Learning and scholarship— Australia	AZ850-881	001.2099	Legal research—United States	KF240-247	349.73072
Learning and scholarship— Europe	AZ600-765	001.2094	Legal tender	HG361-363	332.42042
			Legends	PN683-687	398.20902
Learning and scholarship— Latin America	AZ517-588	001.2098	Legends, Islamic	BP137-.5	297.18
			Legislation	JF491-619	328
Learning and scholarship— North America	AZ501-516	001.2097	Legislation—Canada	KE78-125	328.3771
			Legislation—England	KD125-180	328.3742
Learning and scholarship— United States	AZ503-513	001.20973	Legislation—Ireland	KDK38-50	328.37415
			Legislation—Northern Ireland	KDE42-50	328.37416
Learning disabilities	LC4704-4706	371.9	Legislation—Scotland	KDC70-90	328.37411
Learning disabled	LC4818-.53	371.9	Legislative bodies	JF501-619	328
Least squares	QA275	511.42	Legislative bodies— Lower chambers	JF601-619	328.32
Leather	TS940-1047	675			
Leatherwork	NK6200-6210	745.531	Legislative bodies— United States	KF4930-5005	342.7305
Leatherwork	TT290	745.531			
Leave of absence	HD5255-5257.3	331.25763	Legislative bodies— Upper chambers	JF541-549	328.31
Leaves	QK649	575.57			
Lebanon—Census	HA4559	315.692	Legumes	SB203-205	633.3
Lebanon—Civilization	DS80.4	939.44/956.92	Legumes as food	TX558.L4	641.6565
Lebanon—Description and travel	DS80.2	913.94404/ 915.69204	Leisure	GV1-200	790.0135
			Leisure	BJ1498	175
Lebanon—Economic conditions	HC415.24	330.95692	Lend-lease operations (1941-1945)	D753.2	940.531
			Lenses	QB84.5-135	522
Lebanon—Gazetteers	DS80.A5	913.944003/ 915.692003	Lenses	QC385	535.324
			Lent	BV85-95	263.92
Lebanon—History	DS80.7-87.53	939.44/956.92	Leo (Astrology)	BF1727.35	133.5266
Lebanon—History— 035-1510	DS83	939.44/ 950.9232	Leprosy	RC154-.9	616.998
			Leptons (Nuclear physics)	QC793.5.L42- .L429	539.7211
Lebanon—History— 1516-1918	DS84	956.9203(2-4)			
			Lesbianism	HQ75.3-.6	306.7663
Lebanon—History—Civil War, 1975-	DS87.5	956.92044	Lesbianism	RC558.5	616.8583
			Lesotho—Census	HA4704	316.885
			Lesotho—Civilization	DT2582	968.85

Subject Heading	LC	Dewey	Subject Heading	LC	Dewey
Lesotho—Description and travel	DT2572	916.88504	Library rules and regulations	Z704	025.56
			Library science	Z665-720	020
Lesotho—Gazetteers	DT2554	916.885003	Library statistics	Z711.3	027.0021
Lesotho—History	DT2604-2660	968.85	Library statistics	Z683	027.0021
Lesotho—History—To 1966	DT2630-2648	968.850(1-2)	Library use studies	Z711.3	025.58
Lesotho—History—1966-	DT2652-2660	968.8503	Librettos	ML48-49	780
Lesotho—Maps	G8580-8584	912.6885	Libya	DT211-239	939.74/961.2
Letter writing	BJ2100-2115	395.4	Libya—Census	HA4685	316.12
Lettering	NK3600-3640	745.61	Libya—Civilization	DT222	939.74/961.2
Lettering	TT360	745.61	Libya—Description and travel	DT218-220.2	913.97404/ 916.1204
Letters	PN4400	809.6			
Letters	PN6130-6140	808.86	Libya—Economic conditions	HC825	330.9612
Letters of credit	HG3745	332.77	Libya—History	DT223.2-236	939.74/961.2
Letters, Papal	BX863	262.91	Libya—History—To 642	DT228	939.74
Leukemia	RC643	616.99419	Libya—History—642-1551	DT229	939.74/961.202
Levees	TC533	627.42	Libya—History—1551-1912	DT231	961.202
Levees	TC337	627.24	Libya—History—1912-1951	DT235	961.203
Levitation	BF1385	133.92	Libya—History—1951-1969	DT235.5	961.20(3-41)
Lexington, Battle of, 1775	E241.L6	973.3311	Libya—History—1969-	DT236	961.2042
Libel and slander	HV6631	364.156	Libya—History—Coup d'etat, 1969	DT236	961.2042
Liberalism (Religion)	BR1615-1617	230.046			
Liberation theology	BT83.57	230.0464	Libya—History— Bombardment, 1986	DT236	961.2042
Liberia—Census	HA4735	316.662			
Liberia—Civilization	DT629	966.62	Libya—Maps	G8260-8264	912.612
Liberia—Description and travel	DT625-627	916.66204	Licenses	HJ5301-5508	336.16
			Licenses—[By region or country]	HJ5321-5510	336.1609(4-9)
Liberia—Gazetteers	DT623	916.66203			
Liberia—History	DT630.8-636.53	966.62	Licenses—United States	HJ5321-5374	336.160973
Liberia—History—To 1847	DT633-.3	966.6201	Lichens	QK580.7-597.7	579.7
Liberia—History— 1847-1944	DT634-.3	966.6202	Lie algebras	QA252.3	512.55
			Lie detectors and detection	HV8078-.5	363.254
Liberia—History— 1944-1971	DT635-636	966.620(2-3)	Lie groups	QA387	512.55
			Liechtenstein	DB881-898	936.3/943.648
Liberia—History— 1971-1980	DT636.2-.4	966.6203	Liechtenstein—Census	HA1210.5	314.3648
			Liechtenstein—Description and travel	DB888	913.6304/ 914.364804
Liberia—History—1980-	DT636.5-.53	966.6203			
Liberia—History—Coup d'etat, 1980	DT636.5	966.6203	Liechtenstein—History	DB891-894	936.3/943.648
			Liechtenstein—Maps	G6050-6054	912.43648
Liberia—History—Civil War, 1989-	DT636.5	966.6203	Liechtenstein—Periodicals	DB881	936.3005/ 943.648005
Liberia—Maps	G8880-8884	912.6662	Lieutenant governors— United States	JK2459	352.2390973
Liberty	JC585-599	323.44			
Liberty of conscience	BV741	323.442	Life	BD430-435	113.8
Libra (Astrology)	BF1727.45	133.5272	Life (Biology)	QH325-349	570.1
Librarians	Z682-.4	023.2	Life (Biology)	QP81-87	570.1
Librarians	Z720	020.92	Life-boats	VK1473	387.29
Libraries	Z662-664	027	Life on other planets	QB54	999
Libraries—Automation	Z678.9-.93	025.3132	Life-preservers	VK1477	623.865
Libraries—History	Z721-871	027.009	Life-saving	GV838.68-.76	797.21
Libraries, Governmental, administrative, etc.	Z675.G7	027.5	Life-saving	VK1300-1481	623.8887
			Life-saving—History	VK1315	623.888709
Library administration	Z678-.88	025.1	Life-saving—[By region or country]	VK1321-1424	623.888709(4-9)
Library administrators	Z682.4.A45	023.4			
Library catalogs	Z710	025.31	Life-saving apparatus	VK1460-1481	623.8887
Library consultants	Z682.4.C65	023.2	Life support systems (Space environment)	TL1500-1575	629.477
Library finance	Z683-.2	025.11			
Library information networks	Z674.7-.83	021.65	Ligaments	QM141	611.72
Library legislation—England	KD3746	344.42092	Ligaments	QL827	573.78356
Library legislation—United States	KF4315-4319	344.73092	Ligaments	QM563	611.72
			Light	QC350-467	535
Library orientation	Z711.2	025.56	Light—Physiological effect	RM838	615.831

Subject Heading	LC	Dewey
Light—Physiological effect	QH651	571.63455
Light, Colored	RM835-844	615.831
Light, Corpuscular theory of	QC402	535.12
Light, Wave theory of	QC403	535.13
Light beating spectroscopy	QC454.L63	535.843
Light metals	TS551-552	669.72
Lighthouses	VK1000-1246	623.8942
Lighthouses	TC375-381	627.922
Lighthouses—History	VK1015	623.894209
Lighthouses—[By region or country]	VK1021-1124	623.894209(4-9)
Lighthouses—Canada	VK1026-1027	623.89420971
Lighthouses—United States	VK1023-1025	623.89420973
Lighting	GT440-445	392.36
Lighting	TH7700-7975	621.32
Lighting, Architectural and decorative	TH7703	729.28
Lightning	GR630	398.363
Lightning	QC966-.7	551.5632
Lightning-conductors	TH9057-9092	693.898
Lightning protection	TH9057-9092	693.898
Lightning war	U167.5.L5	355.422
Lightships	VK1000-1246	623.8943
Limanova, Battle of, 1914	D557.L5	940.422
Limbo	BT850-860	235.4
Limericks	PN6231.L5	808.8175
Limited war	UA11.5	355.0215
Lincoln, Abraham, 1809-1865	E456-459	973.7
Lindy (Dance)	GV1796.L5	793.33
Line geometry	QA608	516.183
Line Islands	DU650	996.4
Line Islands—Maps	G9530-9534	912.964
Line-throwing guns	VK1481.L55	623.865
Line-throwing rockets	VK1479	623.865
Linear accelerators	QC787.L5	539.733
Linear integrated circuits	TK7874	621.395
Linear programming	T57.74-.79	519.72
Linear topological spaces, Ordered	QA322	515.73
Lingerie	TT669-670	687.22
Lingerie industry	HD9948.3	338.4739142
Lingua francas	PM7801-7895	401.3
Linguistic geography	P375-381	409
Linguistic paleontology	P35	417.7
Linguistics	P121-143.3	410
Linguistics, Experimental	P128.E94	417.24
Linguists	P121-149	410.92
Linotype	Z253	686.22542
Lipids	QP751-752	572.57
Lips	QM306	611.317
Lips	QL857	573.355
Liqueurs	TP611	663.55
Liquid crystal displays	TK7872.L56	621.3815422
Liquid fertilizers	S662-.5	631.8
Liquid metal fast breeder reactors	TK9203.B7	621.4834
Liquid propellant rockets—Control systems	TL784.C63	629.47522
Liquidation	HD2747	658.1
Liquids	QC141-159	532

Subject Heading	LC	Dewey
Liquors	TP589-618	663.5
Lisbon (Portugal)	DP752-776	946.9425
Lisbon Expedition, 1589	DA86.22.D7	941.055
Listening	BF323.L5	153.(68/733)
Listening (Philosophy)	B105.L54	153.68
Literacy	LC149-160	379.24
Literary agents	PN163	070.52
Literary ethics	PN154	174.98
Literary forgeries and mystifications	PN171.F6-.F7	098.3
Literary movements	PN597	809.91
Literary recreations	GV1493	790.138
Literature—Aesthetics	PN45	801.93
Literature—Collections	PN6010-6078	808
Literature—History and criticism	PN75-99	809
Literature—History and criticism	PN441-595	809
Literature—Periodicals	PN1-9	805
Literature—Philosophy	PN45	801
Literature—Societies, etc.	PN20-29	806
Literature—Stories, plots, etc.	PN44	808.8024
Literature—Study and teaching	PN59-72	807.1
Literature, Ancient	PN611-630	809.01
Literature, Medieval	PN665-694	808.8002
Literature, Modern	PN695-779	808.800(3-4)
Lithographers	NE2410	763.092
Lithography	NE2250-2529	763
Lithography—Catalogs	NE2280	763.0294
Lithography—Exhibitions	NE2272-2275	763.074
Lithography—History	NE2295-2396.3	763.09
Lithography—19th century	NE2297	763.09034
Lithography—20th century	NE2298	763.0904
Lithography—[By region or country]	NE2301-2396.3	763.09(4-9)
Lithuania	DK505-.95	947.93
Lithuania—Gazetteers	DK505.18	914.793003
Lithuania—History	DK505.37-.79	947.93
Lithuanian language	PG8501-8693	491.92
Lithuanian literature	PG8701-8772	891.92
Lithuanian philology	PG8501-8693	491.92
Litter (Trash)	TD813-870	628.44
Little Bighorn, Battle of the, Mont., 1876	E83.876	978.602
Little League baseball	GV880.5	796.357083
Little Red Riding Hood (Tale)	GR75.L56	398.245
Little theater movement	PN2267	792.02230973
Liturgical language	BX1970	264.02
Liturgics	BV169-199	264
Liturgics and Christian union	BX9.5.L55	280.042
Liturgies	BV198-199	264
Liturgies, Early Christian	BV185	264.01
Liver	QP185	612.35
Liver	QM351	611.36
Liver	QL867	573.38
Liver—Diseases	RC845-848	616.362
Liver function tests	RC847-.5	616.362075
Livery	TT626	687.16
Livestock	SF1-140	636

Subject Heading	LC	Dewey	Subject Heading	LC	Dewey
Livestock—Diseases	SF600-1100	636.0896	Local government—Germany	JS5301-5598	351.43
Livestock brands	SF101-103.5	636.20812	Local government—Great Britain	JS3001-4295	351.41
Livestock protection dogs	SF428.6	636.70886			
Living room furniture	NK2117.L5	747.75	Local government—Hungary	JS4661-4696	351.439
Livonian language	PH581-589	494.54	Local government—India	JS7001-7090	351.54
Load-line	VK237	387.544	Local government—Italy	JS5701-5925	351.45
Loans—Law and legislation—Canada	KE1030-1034	346.71073	Local government—Japan	JS7371-7385	351.52
			Local government—Mexico	JS2101-2143	351.72
Loans—Law and legislation—England	KD1740-1742	346.42073	Local government—Middle East	JS7435-7520	351.056
Loans—Law and legislation—United States	KF1035-1040	346.73073	Local government—Netherlands	JS5931-5998	351.492
			Local government—New Zealand	JS8331-8399	351.93
Loans, Personal	HG3755-3756	332.743	Local government—Oceania	JS8450-8490	351.9(5-6)
Lobbying	JK2498	328.38097(4-9)	Local government—Philippines	JS7301-7335	351.599
Lobbying	JK1118	328.380973			
Local area networks (Computer networks)	TK5105.7-.85	004.68	Local government—Portugal	JS6341-6375	351.469
			Local government—Russia	JS6051-6109	351.47
Local church councils	BV626	262.5	Local government—South America	JS2300-2778	351.8
Local finance	HJ9103-9695	336.014			
Local finance—Law and legislation	K4650-4675	343.03	Local government—Spain	JS6301-6335	351.46
			Local government—Sweden	JS6251-6285	351.485
Local finance—Law and legislation—England	KD5710-5752	343.42(1-9)03	Local government—Switzerland	JS6401-6889	351.494
Local finance—Law and legislation—United States	KF6770-6795	343.73043	Local government—United States	JS300-1583	351.7(4-9)
			Local government—West Indies	JS1840-2058	351.729
Local finance—Periodicals	HJ9103	336.01405			
Local finance—[By region or country]	HJ9141-9695	336.014(4-9)	Local service airlines	HE9785	387.7
			Local transit—Law and legislation	K4080	343.098
Local finance—United States	HJ9141-9343	336.01473			
			Locks and keys	TS519-531	683.32
Local finance—[Other regions or countries]	HJ9350-9695	336.014(4-9)	Locks and keys	TH9735	683.32
			Locks and keys	TH2279	683.32
Local government	JS	352.14	Locksmithing	TS519-531	683.3
Local government—History	JS55-67	352.1409	Locomotion	QP301-336	612.76
Local government—Law and legislation—Canada	KE4900-4995	342.7109	Locomotives	TJ603-695	625.26
			Log cabins	NA8470	728.73
Local government—Law and legislation—England	KD4746-4840	342.4209	Log cabins	TH4840	690.873
			Logarithms	QA55-59	512.922
Local government—Law and legislation—United States	KF5300-5332	342.7309	Logging	SD537-538.83	634.98
			Logic	BC	160
Local government—Societies, etc.	JS42	352.1406	Logic—Congresses	BC5	160.6
			Logic—History	BC11-39	160.9
Local government—Study and teaching	JS49	352.14071	Logic—Methodology	BC50-57	160.1
			Logic—Periodicals	BC1	160.5
Local government—Africa	JS7525-7819	351.6	Logic—Study and teaching	BC59	160.71
Local government—Asia	JS6950-7520	351.5	Logic, Ancient	BC25-32	160
Local government—Australia	JS8001-8310	351.94	Logic, Medieval	BC34-35	160
Local government—Austria	JS4501-4655	351.436	Logic, Modern	BC38-39	160
Local government—Balkan Peninsula	JS6899.5-6949.8	351.496	Logic, Symbolic and mathematical	BC131-135	511.3
Local government—Belgium	JS6001-6048	351.493	Logic, Symbolic and mathematical	QA9-10.3	511.3
Local government—Canada	JS1701-1800	351.71			
Local government—Central America	JS2145-2219	351.728	Logic circuits	TK7888.4	621.395
			Logic devices	TK7872.L64	621.395
Local government—China	JS7351-7365	351.51	Logic machines	BC137-138	006.3
Local government—Denmark	JS6151-6185	351.489	Logic programming	QA76.63	005.115
Local government—Europe	JS3000-6949.8	351.4	Logical positivism	B824.6	146.42
Local government—France	JS4801-5250	351.44			

Subject Heading	LC	Dewey	Subject Heading	LC	Dewey
Logistics	U168	355.411	Low-fat diet	RM237.7	613.284
Logistics, Naval	V179	359.411	Low German drama	PT4837-4838	839.42008
Logos	BT210	232.2	Low German drama	PT4821	839.42009
Logs (Nautical instruments)	VK581	623.890284	Low German language	PF5601-5844	439.4
Lollards	BX4900-4906	284.3	Low German literature	PT4801-4897	839.4
Lombards	D145	304.8	Low German literature— Study and teaching	PT4803	839.4071
Lombards	DG511-514.7	945.01			
Lombardy (Italy)	DG651-664.5	945.2	Low German literature— To 1500	PT4813	839.409001
London (England)—History	DA675-689	942.1			
Loneliness	BF575.L7	155.92	Low German poetry	PT4817-4820	839.41009
Long distance swimming	GV838.53.L65	797.21	Low German poetry	PT4834-4836	839.41008
Long-range weather forecasting	QC997	551.6365	Low impact aerobic exercises	RA781.15	613.71
Long-term care facilities	RA997-999	362.16	Low power television	HE8700.7-.72	384.55
Long waves (Economics)	HB3729	338.542	Low temperature engineering	TP480-482	621.56
Longevity	QP85	612.68			
Longevity	RA776.75	612.68	Low temperature research	QC277.9-278.6	536.56072
Longitude	VK565-567	527.2	Low temperature research	QD536	541.3686072
Longitude	QB225-229.5	526.62	Low vision	RE91	617.712
Looms	TS1493	677.02854	LSD (Drug)	BF209.L9	154.4
Loran	VK560-561	623.8932	LSD (Drug)	HV5822.5.L9	362.294
Lord's Supper	BV823-828	264.36	LSD (Drug)	RM666.L88	615.788
Lord's Supper	BX5149.C5	264.03	Lubrication and lubricants	TJ1075-1081	621.89
Lord's Supper	BX2215-2239	264.02036	Lucid dreams	BF1099.L82	154.63
Los Angeles (Calif.)	F869.L8	979.494	Luddites	DA535	941.073
Loss (Psychology)	BF575.D35	155.93	Lumber	TS800-915	674
Loss (Psychology)	RC455.4.L67	155.93	Lumbering	SD538-557	634.98
Loss (Psychology) in children	BF723.L68	155.93083	Luminescence	QC476.4-480.2	535.35
Lost continents	GN750-751	001.94	Lunar eclipses	QB579	523.38
Lotteries	HG6105-6270.9	336.17	Lunar geology	QB592	523.3
Lotteries—Law and legislation—United States	KF3992	344.730542	Lunar soil	QB592	523.3
			Lunar surface vehicles	TL480	629.295
Lotteries—United States	HG6126-6134	336.170973	Lunar theory	QB391-399	523.3
Louisiana	F366-380	976.3	Luncheons	TX735	641.53
Louisiana Purchase	E333	973.46	Lungs	QM261	611.24
Louisiana Purchase	F351-353	976.204	Lungs	QP121-125	612.2
Louisiana—Gazetteers	F367	917.63003	Lungs	QL848	573.22
Louisiana—History— To 1803	F372-373	976.30(1-3)	Lungs—Cancer	RC280.L8	616.99424
			Lungs-Diseases	RC756-776	616.24
Louisiana—History— Revolution, 1775-1783	E263.L	976.30(2-3)	Lute music	M140-141	787.83
			Lutheran Church	BX8001-8080	284.1
Louisiana—History— 1803-1865	F374	976.30(4-5)	Lutheran Church—Clergy	BX8071-.2	262.041
			Lutheran Church—History	BX8018-8063	284.109
Louisiana—History—War of 1812	E359.5.L8	976.304	Lutheran Church—Liturgy	BX8067	264.041
			Lutheran Church— Periodicals	BX8001	284.104
Louisiana—History—Civil War, 1861-1865	E565	976.305			
			Lutheran Church—Sermons	BX8066	252.041
Louisiana—History—Civil War, 1861-1865	E510	976.305	Lutheran Church—Europe	BX8020-8040.5	284.14
			Lutheran Church—Germany	BX8020-8023	284.143
Louisiana—History— 1865-1950	F375	976.306(1-3)	Lutheran Church—United States	BX8041-8061	284.173
Louisiana—History—1951-	F376-.3	976.306(3-4)			
Louisiana—Maps	G4010-4014	912.763	Lutherans—Biography	BX8079-8080	284.1092
Louisiana—National Guard	UA220-229	355.3709763	Luxembourg	DH901-925	949.35
Louisiana—Periodicals	F366	976.3005	Luxembourg—Biography	DH904	920.04935
Love	BD436	128.46	Luxembourg—Description and travel	DH906-907	914.93504
Love	GT2600-2640	392.4			
Love	BF575.L8	152.41	Luxembourg—Gazetteers	DH903	914.935003
Low-calorie diet	RM222.2	613.25	Luxembourg—History	DH908-918.5	949.35
Low-carbohydrate diet	RM237.73	613.283	Luxembourg (Luxembourg)— History—Siege, 1684	DH913	949.3502
Low-Cholesterol diet	RM237.75	613.284			
			Luxembourg—Periodicals	DH901	949.35005

Subject Heading	LC	Dewey	Subject Heading	LC	Dewey
Luxembourg—Census	HA1411-1420	314.935	Madagascar—History— 1885-1960	DT469.M34-.M342	969.10(1-3)
Luxembourg—Economic conditions	HC330	330.94935	Madagascar—History— French Invasion, 1895	DT469.M34	969.103
Luxembourg—Emigration and immigration	JV8175	325.(24935/ 4935)	Madagascar—History— Menalamba Rebellion, 1895-1899	DT469.M34	969.103
Luxemburg—Maps	G6020-6024	912.4935			
Luxuries—Taxation	HJ5771-5797	336.271	Madagascar—History— Revolution, 1947	DT469.M34	969.103
Lying down position	GT2995	394.12			
Lymphatics	QL841	573.16	Madagascar—Maps	G8460-8464	912.691
Lymphatics	QM197	611.42	Madeira Islands—Census	HA2285	314.698
Lymphatics	QP115	612.42	Madeira Islands—Maps	G9140-9144	912.4698
Lymphocytic leukemia	RC643	616.99419	Madeira wine	TP559.P8	663.223
Lynchburg (Va.), Battle of, 1864	E476.65	973.736	Madrid (Spain)	DP350-374	946.41
			Madrigals	PR1195.M2	782.43
Lynching	HV6455-6471	364.134	Mafia	HV6441-6453	364.106
Lyric poetry	PN691	808.814	Magahi language	PK1821-1824	491.454
Lyric poetry	PN1351-1389	808.14	Magazine design	Z253.5	686.2252
M1 (Tank)	UG446.5	358.1883	Magi	BT315	232.923
M1 carbine	UD395.M17	356.11824250973	Magic	BF1585-1623	133.43
Macadamia nut	SB401.M32	634.5	Magic	GN475.3	291.3/133.43
Macao—Census	HA4641-4645	315.126	Magic squares	QA165	511.64
Macao—Maps	G7945-7947	912.5126	Magicians	GV1545	793.8092
Macedonia	DR2152-2285	949.76	Magnanimity	BV4647.M2	241.4
Macedonia—History	DR701.M13-.M14	949.76	Magnet schools	LB2818	373.241
Macedonia—History— To 168 B.C.	DF233-238	938.0(1-8)	Magnetic bubble devices	TK7872.M25	621.39763
			Magnetic healing	RZ422	615.845
Macedonia—History— Karpos Uprising, 1689	DR2211	949.98	Magnetic induction	QC754.2.M33	538.4
			Magnetic levitation vehicles	TF1600	625.4
Macedonian language	PG1161-1164	491.819	Magnetic measurements	QC818-849	538.0287
Macedonian War, 1st, 215-205 B.C.	DG251	937.04	Magnetic measurements	QC761	538.0287
			Magnetic recorders and recording	TK7881.6	621.38932
Macedonian War, 2nd, 200-196 B.C.	DG251	937.04			
			Magnetic resonance imaging	RC78.7.N83	616.07548
Macedonian War, 3rd, 171-168 B.C.	DG251.6	937.04	Magnetic separation of ores	TN530	622.77
			Magnetic storms	QC835	538.744
Machine design	TJ227-240	621.815	Magnetic tapes	TK5984	621.38234
Machine-guns	UF620	358.1282	Magnetism	QC750-776	538
Machine-guns	VF410	359.82424	Magnetohydrodynamics	QC809.M3	538.6
Machine learning	Q325.5-.78	006.31	Magnetohydrodynamics	QC718.5.M36	538.6
Machine-readable bibliographic data	Z699-.5	025.3132	Magnetosphere	QC809.M35	538.766
			Magnetospheric radio wave propagation	QC973.4.M33	551.514
Machine sewing	TT713	646.2044			
Machine theory	QA267-268.5	511.3	Magnetrons	TK7871.75	621.381334
Machine-tools	TJ1180-1313	621.902	Magnets	QC757	538.4
Machine translating	P307-310	418.020285	Magyars	DB919	943.900494511
Machinery	TJ	621.8	Mah jong	GV1299.M3	795.34
Machinery—Testing	TJ148	621.80287	Maharashtri language	PK1231-1239	491.1
Machinery—Vibration	TJ177	621.81	Mahayana Buddhism	BQ7300-7522	294.392
Machinery industry	HD9705-9705.5	338.476218	Mahican Indians	E99.M12	973.04973
Macro processors	QA76.6	005.45	Mail receiving and forwarding services	HE5999	383.1
Madagascar—Census	HA4699	316.91			
Madagascar—Civilization	DT469.M274	969.1	Mail-order business	HF5465.5-5467	381.142
Madagascar—Economic conditions	HC895	330.9691	Maine—Gazetteers	F17	917.41003
			Maine—History	F16-30	974.1
Madagascar—Gazetteers	DT469.M24	916.91003	Maine—History—War of 1812	F24	974.103
Madagascar—History	DT469.M282-.M345	969.1			
Madagascar—History— To 1810	DT469.M31-.M313	969.101	Maine—History—Colonial period, ca. 1600-1775	F23	974.10(1-2)
Madagascar—History— Hova rule, 1810-1885	DT469.M32-.M335	969.101			

Subject Heading	LC	Dewey	Subject Heading	LC	Dewey
Maine—History—King William's War, 1689-1697	F23	974.102	Malta	DG987-999	945.85
			Malta—History	DG989.8-994.8	945.85
			Mammal pests	SB993.5-994	632.69
Maine—History—King George's War, 1744-1748	F23	974.102	Mammal populations	QL708.6	599.1788
			Mammals	QL700-739.8	599
Maine—History— 1775-1865	F24	974.10(1-3)	Mammals, Fossil	QE881-882	569
			Mammaplasty	RD539.8	618.19059
Maine—Maps	G3730-3734	912.741	Mammary glands	QP188.M3	612.664
Maine—National Guard	UA230-239	355.3709741	Mammary glands	QM495	611.49
Maine—Periodicals	F16	974.1005	Mammary glands	QL944	573.679
Maitreya (Buddhist deity)	BQ4690.M3	294.34211	Man	GN	301
Maiya language	PK7045.M3	491.499	Man—Influence of climate	GF71	304.25
Majorities	JF1051-1075	324.63	Man—Influence of environment	GF51-71	304.2
Malabsorption syndromes	RC862.M3	616.3423	Man—Influence of environment	BF353-.5	155.9
Malaria	RA644.M2	614.532			
Malaria	RC156-166	616.936	Man—Migrations	GN370	304.8
Malawi—Census	HA4707	316.897	Man—Origin	GN281-.4	599.938
Malawi—Civilization	DT3187	968.97	Man, Prehistoric	GN700-890	569.9
Malawi—Description and travel	DT3182	916.89704	Man, Primitive	GN307-499	569.9
			Man (Christian theology)	BT700-745	233
Malawi—Gazetteers	DT3169	916.897003	Man (Hinduism)	BL1215.M3	294.522
Malawi—History	DT3194-3237	968.97	Man (Islam)	BP166.7	297.22
Malawi—History—To 1891	DT3211-3214	968.9701	Man (Theology)	BT700-745	233
Malawi—History— 1891-1953	DT3216-3225	968.9702	Man (Theology)	BS661	233
			Man (Theology)	BL256	291.22
Malawi—History— Chilembwe Rebellion, 1915	DT3225	968.9702	Man-machine systems	TA167	621.3984
			Man-woman relationships	HQ801-.83	306.7
			Managed care plans (Medical care)	RA413-.5	362.104258
Malawi—History— 1953-1964	DT3227-3230	968.970(3-4)			
			Management	HD28-70	658
Malawi—History—1964-	DT3232-3240	968.9704	Management science	T55.4-60.8	658
Malawi—Maps	G8610-8614	912.6897	Management—Employee particpation	HD5650-5660	331.0112
Malay language	PL5101-5129	499.28			
Malaya—History	DS595.8-597.215	959.5	Managerial accounting	HF5657.4	658.1511
Malaya—History—Japanese occupation, 1942-1945	DS596.6	959.503	Managerial economics	HD30.22	338.068
			Manchu language	PL471-479	494.1
Malaya—History—Malayan Emergency, 1948-1960	DS597	959.504	Manchuria (China)	DS781-784.2	951.8
			Manchus	DS781-784.2	951.8
Malayalam language	PL4711-4719	494.812	Manchus	DS753.82-773.6	951.03
Malaysia—Census	HA4600.6	315.95	Mandailing dialect	PJ5401	492.37
Malaysia—Civilization	DS594	959.5	Mandarin dialects	PL1891-1900	495.1
Malaysia—Description and travel	DS592.4-.6	915.9504	Mandates	D650.T4-651	940.31426
			Mandolin music	M130-134	787.84
Malaysia—Gazetteers	DS591.5	915.95003	Manic-depressive psychoses	RC516	616.895
Malaysia—Maps	G8030-8034	912.595	Manicuring	RL94	646.727
Maldives—Census	HA2300	315.495	Manila Bay, Battle of, 1898	E717.7	973.895
Maldives—Maps	G9215-9219	912.5495	Manipulation (Therapeutics)	RM724	615.82
Mali—Census	HA4727	316.623	Manipulation (Therapeutics)	RD736.M25	615.82
Mali—Civilization	DT551.4	966.23	Manitoba—Gazetteers	F1061.4	917.127003
Mali—Description and travel	DT551.27	916.62304	Manitoba—History	F1061-1065	971.27
Mali—Gazetteers	DT551.15	916.623003	Manitoba—Maps	G3480-3484	912.7127
Mali—History	DT551.5-.82	966.23	Manitoba—Periodicals	F1061	971.27005
Mali—History—Coup d'etat, 1968	DT551.8	966.23051	Manna	BS1245	222.12
			Manned undersea research stations	GC66	551.46072
Mali—Maps	G8800-8804	912.6623			
Malnutrition	RA645.N87	614.5939	Manners and customs	GT	390
Malnutrition	RC623	616.39	Manpower	UA17.5	355.22
Malnutrition in children	RJ399.M26	618.9239	Manpower planning	HF5549.5.M3	658.301
Malnutrition in pregnancy	RG580.M34	618.3	Manual training	LB1595-1599	372.5
Malocclusion	RK523	617.643	Manual training	TT161-170.7	373.246

Subject Heading	LC	Dewey	Subject Heading	LC	Dewey
Manufactures	HD9720-9739	338.4767	Marine engineering—[By region or country]	VM621-724	623.809(4-9)
Manufactures	TS	670	Marine engines	VM731-779	623.87
Manures	S655	631.861	Marine laboratories	QH91.6-.65	578.77072
Manus (Hindu mythology)	BL1225.M	294.513	Marine meteorology	QC993.83-994.9	551.65162
Manuscripts, Greek (Papyri)	PA3301-3371	091.09495	Marine microbiology	QR106-.5	579.177
Manx language	PB1801-1847	491.64	Marine mineral resources	TN264	333.8509162
Manx literature	PB1851-1867	891.64	Marine nuclear reactor plants	VM774-777	623.8728
Many-body problem	QB362.M3	521.4	Marine painting	ND2270-2272	751.422437
Many-body problem	QC174.17.P7	530.144	Marine painting	ND1370-1375	758.2
Maori language	PL6465	499.442	Marine parks and reserves	QH91.75	578.77
Map drawing	GA130	526.0221	Marine photography	TR670-.5	778.937
Map projection	GA110-115	526.8	Marine pollution	GC1080-1581	363.7394
Maps	G3200-9980	912	Marine refrigeration	VM485	623.8535
Maps, Military	UA985-997	355.47	Marine resources	GC1000-1023	333.9164
Maps, Military	UG470-474	623.71	Marine resources conservation	GC1018	333.916416
Maps, Statistical	GA109.8	310.0223	Marine sediments	GC380-399	551.46083
Maratha War, 1775-1782	DS473	954.029	Marine steel	VM146	623.81821
Maratha War, 1816-1818	DS475.6	954.0313	Marines	VE	359.96
Marathi language	PK2351-2378	491.46	Marines—Barracks and quarters	VE420-425	359.9671
Marathon running	GV1065-.23	796.4252	Marines—Firearms	VE350-390	359.96824
Marathon, Battle of, 490 B.C.	DF225.4	938.03	Marines—Handbooks, manuals, etc.	VE150-155	359.9633
Marble sculpture	NB1218	731.2	Marines—History	VE15	359.9609
Marble sculpture, Ancient	NB69-169	732.2	Marines—Insigna	VE345	359.961342
Marble sculpture, Classical	NB144	733.3	Marines—Uniforms	VE400-405	359.9614
Marbles (Game)	GV1213	796.2	Marines—[By region or country]	VE21-124	359.96309(4-9)
Marches (Band)	M1247	784.1897	Marines—Africa	VE115-119	359.963096
Marches (Band)	M1260	784.1897	Marines—Asia	VE99-113	359.963095
Marching	UD310-315	356.114	Marines—Australia	VE121-122	359.9630994
Marching bands	MT733.4	784.8307	Marines—Canada	VE26-27	359.9630971
Marduk (Babylonian deity)	BL1625.M37	299.21	Marines—Central America	VE30-31	359.96309728
Margarine	TP684.M3	664.32	Marines—Europe	VE55-96	359.963094
Marginal utility	HB201-205	330.157	Marines—France	VE71-72	359.9630944
Mari language	PH801-807	494.56	Marines—Germany	VE73-74.5	359.9630943
Mariana Islands	DU640-648	996.7	Marines—Great Britain	VE57-64	359.9630941
Mariana Islands—Maps	G9410-9414	912.967	Marines—Italy	VE79-80	359.9630945
Mariculture	SH138	639.8	Marines—Japan	VE105-106	359.9630952
Marie Galante	F2076	972.976	Marines—Mexico	VE28-29	359.9630972
Marihuana	HV5822.M3	362.295	Marines—New Zealand	VE122.5	359.9630993
Marimba music	M175.X6	786.843	Marines—Russia	VE85-86	359.9630947
Marinas	TC328	627.38	Marines—Scandinavia	VE86.5	359.9630948
Marinas	VK369-.8	387.15	Marines—South America	VE34-54	359.963098
Marine algae as feed	SF99.M33	636.0855	Marines—Spain	VE87-88	359.9630946
Marine algae as fertilizer	S661.2.M3	631.87	Marines—West Indies	VE32-33	359.96309729
Marine aquariums	SF457.1	597.177073	Marital psychotherapy	RC488.5-.6	616.89156
Marine aquariums, Public	QL78.5	597.073	Marital status—Statistics	HB1111-1317	306.81021
Marine biology	QH91-95.59	578.77	Marital status—[By region or country]	HB1121-1317	306.8109
Marine biology—Antarctic Ocean	QH95.58	578.777	Marital status—United States	HB1125-1126	306.810973
Marine biology—Atlantic Ocean	QH92-93.9	578.773	Marital status—[United States, By city]	HB1147	306.81097(4-9)
Marine biology—Indian Ocean	QH94-.7	578.775	Marital status—[United States, By state]	HB1145	306.81097(4-9)
Marine biology—Pacific Ocean	QH95-.55	578.774	Maritime Provinces—History	F1035.8	971.5
Marine compressors	VM821	623.8501	Maritime Provinces—Maps	G3410-3444	912.715
Marine diesel motors	VM770	623.87236			
Marine engineering	VM595-989	623.87			
Marine engineering—History	VM615-619	623.809			
Marine engineering—Study and teaching	VM725-728	623.8071			

Subject Heading	LC	Dewey	Subject Heading	LC	Dewey
Market surveys	HF5415.3	380.1/658.83	Marriage with deceased wife's sister	HQ1028	306.84
Marketing	HF5410-5417.5	380.1	Married students	LB3613.M3	371.82655
Marketing (Home economics)	TX356	641.31	Mars (Planet)	QB641	523.43
Marketing research	HF5415.2-5415.34	380.1072/658.83	Mars (Planet)	QB376	523.43
			Marshall Islands	DU710	996.83
Markets	HF5469.7-5481	381.18	Marshall Islands—Maps	G9460-9464	912.9683
Markov processes	QA274.7-.76	519.233	Marshes	QH87.3	578.768
Marlin spike seamanship	VM531-533	623.88	Marshes	TC975	627.54
Marquesas Islands	DU700-701	996.31	Marsyas (Greek diety)	BL820.M26	292.2113
Marquesas Islands—Maps	G9620-9624	912.9631	Martial artists	GV1113	796.8092
Marriage	BV835-838	265.5	Martinique	F2081	972.982
Marriage	GR465	392.5	Martinique—Census	HA918.9	317.2982
Marriage	HQ503-1064	306.81	Martinique—Maps	G5080-5084	912.72982
Marriage	GN480	306.81	Martinique—Politics and government	JL830-839	320.972982
Marriage—History	HQ503-518	306.8109			
Marriage—[By region or country]	HQ531-727.9	306.8109(4-9)	Martinis	TX951	641.874
			Martyrs—Legends	BX4654-4662	282.0922
Marriage—China	HQ684	306.810951	Marxian economics	HB97.5	335.4
Marriage—Africa	HQ691-697.4	306.81096	Mary, Blessed Virgin, Saint	BT595-680	232.91
Marriage—Asia	HQ663-690.5	306.81095	Mary, Blessed Virgin, Saint—Apparitions and miracles	BT650-654	232.917
Marriage—Australia	HQ705-706	306.810994			
Marriage—Benelux Countries	HQ631-636.5	306.8109492			
			Mary, Blessed Virgin, Saint—Theology	BT610-660	232.91
Marriage—Canada	HQ559-560	306.810971			
Marriage—Central America	HQ563-574	306.8109728	Maryland Campaign, 1862	E474.61	973.7336
Marriage—Europe	HQ611-662.7	306.81094	Maryland Campaign, 1864	E476.66	973.737
Marriage—France	HQ623-624	306.810944	Maryland—Gazetteers	F179	917.52003
Marriage—Germany	HQ625-626.5	306.810943	Maryland—History	F176-190	975.2
Marriage—Great Britain	HQ613-618.5	306.810941	Maryland—History—Colonial period, ca. 1600-1775	F184	975.20(1-2)
Marriage—Greece	HQ662.5	306.8109495			
Marriage—India	HQ669-670	306.810954			
Marriage—Iran	HQ666.4	306.810955	Maryland—History—Revolution, 1775-1783	E263.M3	975.20(2-3)
Marriage—Iraq	HQ666.3	306.8109567			
Marriage—Israel	HQ664	306.81095694	Maryland—History—War of 1812	E359.5.M2	975.203
Marriage—Italy	HQ629-630	306.810945			
Marriage—Japan	HQ681-682	306.810952	Maryland—Maps	G3840-3844	912.752
Marriage—Mexico	HQ561-562	306.810972	Maryland—National Guard	UA240-249	355.3709752
Marriage—Philippines	HQ679-680	306.8109599	Maryland—Periodicals	F176	975.2005
Marriage—Russia	HQ637-638	306.810947	Mascarene Islands	DT469.M39	969.8
Marriage—South America	HQ588-610	306.81098	Masculinity (Psychology)	BF692.5	155.332
Marriage—Spain	HQ649-650	306.810946	Masks	GN419.5	391.434
Marriage—Switzerland	HQ653-654	306.8109494	Masks	GT1747-1748	391.434
Marriage—United States	HQ535-557	306.810973	Masks (Sculpture)	NB1310	731.75
Marriage—West Indies	HQ575-587.9	306.8109729	Masochism	RC553.M36	616.85835
Marriage, Companionate	HQ803	306.84	Masonry	TA670-683.94	624.183
Marriage customs and rites	GT2660-2800	392.5	Masonry	TH1199-1301	693.1
Marriage customs and rites, Hindu	BL1226.82.M3	294.5441	Masonry	TH5311-5701	693.1
			Mass	BX2230-2234	264.02
Marriage customs and rites, Islamic	GT2695.M8	392.50882971	Mass media policy	P95.8	302.23
			Mass suicide	HV6547	364.1522
Marriage customs and rites, Jewish	BM713	296.444	Mass transfer	QC318.M3	530.475
			Mass-wasting	QE598-600.3	551.307
Marriage customs and rites, Medieval	GT2680	392.50902	Massachusetts—Gazetteers	F62	917.44003
			Massachusetts—History	F61-75	974.4
Marriage customs and rites—[By region or country]	GT2701-2796	392.509(3-9)	Massachusetts—History—Colonial period, ca. 1600-1775	F67	974.40(1-2)
Marriage service	BX2250-2254	264.02085	Massachusetts—History—New Plymouth, 1620-1691	F68	974.402
Marriage service	HQ745	392.5/395.22			

Subject Heading	LC	Dewey	Subject Heading	LC	Dewey
Massachusetts—History—Queen Anne's War, 1702-1713	E197	974.403	Mathematics—[By region or country]	QA27	510.9(4-9)
Massachusetts—History—King George's War, 1744-1748	E198	974.402	Mathematics, Ancient	QA22	510.901
			Mathematics, Babylonian	QA22	510.935
			Mathematics, Chinese	QA27.C	510.931
Massachusetts—History—French and Indian War, 1755-1763	E199	974.402	Mathematics, Greek	QA22	510.938
			Mathematics, Medieval	QA23	510.902
Massachusetts—History—1775-1865	F69	974.40(2-3)	Mathematics, Medieval	QA32	510.902
			Mathieu functions	QA405	515.54
Massachusetts—History—Revolution, 1775-1783	E263.M4	974.40(2-3)	Matriarchy	GN497.5	306.859
			Matrices	QA188-196	512.9434
Massachusetts—History—War of 1812	E359.5.M3	974.403	Matrix mechanics	QC174.3-.35	530.122
			Matter	BD331	117
Massachusetts—History—Civil War, 1861-1865	E513	974.403	Matter	BD493-708	117
			Matter	QC170-197	530
Massachusetts—History—1865-	F70-71	974.404	Maturation (Psychology)	BF710	155.51
			Matwork plants	SB281-283	633.58
Massachusetts—Maps	G3760-3764	912.744	Mauritania—Census	HA4730	316.61
Massachusetts—National Guard	UA250-259	355.3709744	Mauritania—Civilization	DT554.4	966.1
			Mauritania—Description and travel	DT554.27	916.6104
Massachusetts—Periodicals	F61	974.4005	Mauritania—Gazetteers	DT554.15	916.61003
			Mauritania—History	DT554.52-.83	966.1
Massacres—India—Amritsar	DS480.5	954.0357	Mauritania—History—1960-	DT554.8-.83	966.105
Massage	RM721-723	615.822	Mauritania—Maps	G8820-8824	912.661
Massage	RA780.5	615.822	Mauritius—Census	HA2305	316.982
Mastectomy	RD667.5	616.99449059	Mauritius—Civilization	DT469.M44	969.82
Master of arts degree	LB2385	378.2	Mauritius—Description and travel	DT469.M429	916.98204
Mastoid process—Diseases	RF235	617.87	Mauritius—Gazetteers	DT469.M415	916.982003
Masts and rigging	VM531-533	623.862	Mauritius—History	DT469.M45-.M497	969.82
Masturbation	HQ447	306.772	Mauritius—History—To 1810	DT469.M465-.M467	969.8201
Matches	TP310	662.5			
Materia medica	RS153-185	615.1	Mauritius—Maps	G9185-9189	912.6982
Materialization	BF1378	133.92	Maxima and minima	QA306	511.66
Materials	TA401-492	620.11	Maxims	PN6299-6308	398.9
Materials—Creep	TA418.22	620.11233	May Day	GT4945	394.2627
Materials—Dictionaries	TA402	620.1103	May-pole	GT4945	394.2627
Materials—Periodicals	TA401	620.1105	Mayaguez Incident, 1975	E865	973.925
Materials—Research	TA404.2	620.11072	Mayan lanuagages	PM3961-3969	497.4152
Materials management	TS161	658.7	Mayors	JS143-163	352.23216
Maternal and infant welfare	HV697-700	362.83	Meadow ecology	QH541.5.M4	577.46
Maternity nursing	RG951	610.73678	Meadow plants	QK938.M4	581.746
Mathematical geography	GA1-87	526	Meadows	SB199	633.202
Mathematical geography—Tables	GA4	526.021	Meal	TS2120-2159	664.7207
			Meaning (Philosophy)	B105.M4	121.68
Mathematical instruments	QA71-90	510.284	Measles	RA644.M5	614.523
Mathematical physics	QC19.2-20.85	530.15	Measles	RC168.M4	616.915
Mathematical physics—Study and teaching	QC20.8-.82	530.15071	Measuring instruments	QC100.5-.8	530.7
			Measuring-tapes	TA579-581	526.90284
Mathematical statistics	QA276-280	519.5	Meat	TX371-389	641.36
Mathematicians	QA28-29	510.92	Meat	TX555-556	641.36
Mathematics	QA	510	Mechanical drawing	T351-385	604.2
Mathematics—Dictionaries	QA5	510.3	Mechanical engineering	TJ	621
Mathematics—History	QA21-27	510.9	Mechanical engineering—Congresses	TJ5	621.06
Mathematics—Periodicals	QA1	510.5			
Mathematics—Philosophy	QA8-10.5	510.1	Mechanical engineering—History	TJ15-20	621.09
Mathematics—Study and teaching	QA11-20	510.71	Mechanical engineering—Periodicals	TJ1-4	621.05

Subject Heading	LC	Dewey	Subject Heading	LC	Dewey
Mechanical engineering—Philosophy	TJ14	621.01	Medical geography—United States	RA804-807	614.4273
Mechanical engineering—Study and teaching	TJ158-159	621.071	Medical geography—West Indies	RA815-816	614.42729
Mechanical engineering—[By region or country]	TJ21-127	621.09(4-9)	Medical history taking	RC65	616.0751
Mechanical engineers—Biography	TJ139-140	621.092	Medical informatics	R858-859.7	610.285
Mechanical engineers—Directories	TJ11-13	621.025	Medical instruments and apparatus	R856-858	610.284
Mechanical movements	TJ181-210	621.81	Medical jurisprudence	RA1001-1171	614.1
Mechanical organs	ML1058	786.6609	Medical jurisprudence—History	RA1021-1022	614.109
Mechanics	QC120-168.86	530	Medical jurisprudence—Statistics	RA1018.5-.56	614.1021
Mechanics, Analytic	QA801-871	531.01515	Medical jurisprudence—Study and teaching	RA1027-.5	614.107
Mechanics, Applied	TA350-359	620.1	Medical laboratories	R860-862	610.72
Mechanotherapy	RM719-727	615.822	Medical laws and legislation—Canada	KE3646-3660	344.71041
Medal of Honor	UB433	355.13420973	Medical laws and legislation—England	KD3395-3413	344.4204
Medals	CJ5501-6661	737.22	Medical laws and legislation—Ireland	KDK926-932	344.415041
Medals—Periodicals	CJ5501	737.2205	Medical laws and legislation—Scotland	KDC690-695	344.411041
Medals—Study and teaching	CJ5525	737.22071	Medical laws and legislation—United States	KF3821-3829	344.73041
Medals—[By Region or country]	CJ5795-6661	737.2209(3-9)			
Medals—Africa	CJ6491-6559	737.22096	Medical microbiology	QR46	616.01
Medals—Asia	CJ6381-6485	737.22095	Medical microscopy	RB43-.6	616.0758
Medals—Australia	CJ6561-6569	737.220994	Medical offices	R728	610.6
Medals—Central America	CJ5841-5905	737.2209728	Medical parasitology	QR251-255	616.96
Medals—Europe	CJ6091-6380	737.22094	Medical personnel—Malpractice	RA1056.5	344.0411
Medals—United States	CJ5801-5812	737.220973	Medical referral	R727.5	362.172
Medals, Ancient	CJ5581-5690	737.22093	Medical rehabilitation	RM930-950	617.03
Medals, Greek	CJ5625	737.220938	Medical screening	RA427.5-.6	362.177
Medals, Roman	CJ5641-5685	737.220937	Medical secretaries	R728	651.3741
Medea (Greek mythology)	BL820.M37	292.13	Medical social work	HV687-688	362.10425
Media programs (Education)	LB1028.4	371.33	Medical statistics	RA407-409.5	610.21
Medical assistants	R728.8	610.737	Medical supplies	UH440-445	355.88
Medical astrology	BF1718	133.5861	Medical supplies	VG290-295	359.88
Medical bacteriology	QR46	616.014	Medical thermometers	RC75	610.284
Medical climatology	RA791-954	616.988	Medicated feeds	SF98.M4	636.08557
Medical colleges	R735-845	610.711	Medici, House of	DG737.42	945.05
Medical economics	RA410-415	338.473621	Medicinal plants	QK99	581.634
Medical emergencies	RC86-88.9	616.025	Medicinal plants	SB293-295	633.88
Medical ethics	R724-726	174.2	Medicine	R	610
Medical genetics	RB155-.8	616.042	Medicine—Congresses	R106	610.6
Medical geography	RA791-954	614.42	Medicine—Dictionaries	R121	610.3
Medical geography—[By region or country]	RA801-954	614.42(3-9)	Medicine—Examinations	R837.E9	616.075
			Medicine—Formulae, receipts, prescriptions	RS125-131.9	615.13
Medical geography—Africa	RA943-949	614.426	Medicine—History	R131-684	610.9
Medical geography—Asia	RA891-934	614.425	Medicine—Periodicals	R5-101	610.5
Medical geography—Australia	RA951-952	614.4294	Medicine—Philosophy	R723-.5	610.1
Medical geography—Canada	RA809-810	614.4271	Medicine—Pictural works	R120	610.222
Medical geography—Central America	RA813-814	614.42728	Medicine—Practice	R729.5	610.6
Medical geography—Europe	RA845-887	614.424	Medicine—Religious aspects	BL65.M4	291.175
Medical geography—Mexico	RA811-812	614.4272			
Medical geography—New Zealand	RA952.5	614.4293	Medicine—Societies, etc.	R10-99.7	610.6
Medical geography—Oceania	RA953-954	614.429(5-6)			
Medical geography—South America	RA817-844	614.428			

Subject Heading	LC	Dewey	Subject Heading	LC	Dewey
Medicine—Study and teaching	R735-845	610.71	Medicine, Industrial	RC963-969	616.9803
			Medicine, Medieval	R141-144	610.902
Medicine—Terminology	R123	610.14	Medicine, Military	RC970-971	616.98023
Medicine—Africa	R651-654	610.96	Medicine, Military	UH201-515	355.345
Medicine—Asia	R581-644	610.95	Medicine, Military— Biography	UH341-347	355.345092
Medicine—Asiatic Russia	R635-638	610.957			
Medicine—Australia	R671-674	610.994	Medicine, Military— Congresses	UH205	355.34506
Medicine—Austria	R499-502	610.9436			
Medicine—Belgium	R521-524	610.9493	Medicine, Military—History	UH215-324	355.34509
Medicine—Canada	R461-464	610.971	Medicine, Military—Study and teaching	UH398-399	355.345071
Medicine—Central America	R469-472	610.9728			
Medicine—China	R601-604	610.951	Medicine, Military—Africa	UH315-319	355.345096
Medicine—Denmark	R539-542	610.9489	Medicine, Military— Argentina	UH236-237	355.3450982
Medicine—Europe	R484-575	610.94			
Medicine—France	R504-507	610.944	Medicine, Military—Asia	UH299-313	355.345095
Medicine—Germany	R509-512.5	610.943	Medicine, Military— Australia	UH321-322	355.345094
Medicine—Great Britain	R486-498.4	610.941			
Medicine—Greece	R513-516	610.9495	Medicine, Military—Canada	UH226-227	355.3450971
Medicine—Iceland	R543-546	610.94912	Medicine, Military—Central America	UH230-231	355.34509728
Medicine—India	R605-608	610.954			
Medicine—Indochina	R609-612	610.959(3-7)	Medicine, Military—Chile	UH243-244	355.3450983
Medicine—Indonesia	R614-617	610.9598	Medicine, Military—China	UH301-302	355.3450951
Medicine—Iran	R631-634	610.955	Medicine, Military— Colombia	UH245-246	355.34509861
Medicine—Ireland	R498.6-.9	610.9415			
Medicine—Italy	R517-520	610.945	Medicine, Military—Europe	UH255-295	355.345094
Medicine—Japan	R623-626	610.952	Medicine, Military—France	UH271-272	355.3450944
Medicine—Korea	R627-630	610.9519	Medicine, Military—Germany	UH273-274	355.3450943
Medicine—Mexico	R465-468	610.972	Medicine, Military—Great Britain	UH257-264	355.3450941
Medicine—Netherlands	R526-529	610.9492			
Medicine—New Zealand	R675-678	610.993	Medicine, Military—Greece	UH275-276	355.34509495
Medicine—Norway	R547-550	610.9481	Medicine, Military—India	UH303-304	355.3450954
Medicine—Oceania	R681-684	610.99(5-6)	Medicine, Military—Italy	UH279-280	355.3450945
Medicine—Pakistan	R604.2-.5	610.95491	Medicine, Military—Japan	UH305-306	355.3450952
Medicine—Philippines	R618-621	610.9599	Medicine, Military—Mexico	UH228-229	355.3450972
Medicine—Poland	R535-538	610.9438	Medicine, Military—Oceania	UH323-324	355.345099(5-6)
Medicine—Portugal	R559-562	610.9469	Medicine, Military—Portugal	UH283-284	355.34509469
Medicine—Russia	R531-534	610.947	Medicine, Military—Russia	UH285-286	355.3450947
Medicine—Saudi Arabia	R591-594	610.9538	Medicine, Military— Scandinavia	UH286.5	355.3450948
Medicine—South America	R480-483	610.98			
Medicine—Spain	R555-558	610.946	Medicine, Military— South America	UH234-254	355.345098
Medicine—Sri Lanka	R608.2-.5	610.95493			
Medicine—Sweden	R551-554	610.9485	Medicine, Military—Spain	UH287-288	355.3450946
Medicine—Switzerland	R563-566	610.9494	Medicine, Military—United States	UH223-224	355.3450973
Medicine—Turkey	R640-643	610.9561			
Medicine—United States	R151-363	610.973	Medicine, Military— Venezuela	UH254	355.3450987
Medicine—[United States, by state]	R155-363	610.97(4-9)			
			Medicine, Military—West Indies	UH232-233	355.34509729
Medicine—West Indies	R473-476	610.9729			
Medicine, Ancient	R135-138.5	610.901	Medicine, Naval	RC981-986	616.98024
Medicine, Arab	R143	610.089927	Medicine, Naval	VG100-475	359.345
Medicine, Botanic	RV1-9	615.53	Medicine, Naval—Biography	VG226-228	359.345092
Medicine, Chronothermal	RZ414	615.53	Medicine, Naval—Study and teaching	VG230-235	359.345071
Medicine, Eclectic	RV11-431	615.53			
Medicine, Eclectic— Congresses	RV21	615.5306	Medicine, Naval—[By region or country]	VG121-224	359.34509(4-9)
Medicine, Eclectic—History	RV61	615.5309	Medicine, Naval—Africa	VG215-219	359.345096
Medicine, Eclectic— Periodicals	RV15	615.5305	Medicine, Naval—Asia	VG199-213	359.345095
			Medicine, Naval—Australia	VG221-222	359.3450994
Medicine, Eclectic—Study and teaching	RV100-181	615.53071	Medicine, Naval—Canada	VG126-127	359.3450971
			Medicine, Naval—Central America	VG130-131	359.34509728
Medicine, Experimental	R850-854	619			

Subject Heading	LC	Dewey
Medicine, Naval—Europe	VG155-196	359.345094
Medicine, Naval—France	VG171-172	359.3450944
Medicine, Naval—Germany	VG173-174.5	359.3450943
Medicine, Naval—Great Britain	VG157-164	359.3450941
Medicine, Naval—Italy	VG179-180	359.3450945
Medicine, Naval—Japan	VG205-206	359.3450952
Medicine, Naval—Mexico	VG128-129	359.3450972
Medicine, Naval—New Zealand	VG222.5	359.3450993
Medicine, Naval—Russia	VG185-186	359.450947
Medicine, Naval—Scandinavia	VG186.5	359.3450948
Medicine, Naval—South America	VG134-154	359.345098
Medicine, Naval—Spain	VG187-188	359.3450946
Medicine, Naval—United States	VG123-125	359.3450973
Medicine, Naval—West Indies	VG132-133	359.4509729
Medicine, Oriental	R581	610.95
Medicine, Persian	R135	610.935
Medicine, Physical	RM695-951	615.82
Medicine, Preventive	RA421-790	613
Medicine, Psychosomatic	RC49-52	616.08
Medicine and psychology	R726.5-.8	601.9
Meditation	BL627	291.435
Meditations	BV4800-4870	248.34
Meditations	BX2177-2198	248.34
Mediterranean Region—Historiography	DE8-9	907.201822
Medulla oblongata	QP377	612.828
Medulla oblongata	QL933-937	573.86
Medulla oblongata	QM455	611.81
Meekness	BV4647.M3	241.4
Megarians (Greek philosophy)	B285	183.6
Meiosis	QH605	571.845
Melanesia	DU490	995
Melanesia—Maps	G2870-2894	912.95
Melanesia—Maps	G9260-9262	912.95
Melanesian languages	PL6201-6209	499.5
Melanoma	RC280.M37	616.99477
Melatonin	QP572.M44	612.02
Melodeon music	M175.M38	788.863
Melodrama	PN1910-1919	808.82527
Melody	ML3834	781.24
Melody	MT47	781.2407
Melody	ML3851	781.24
Melons	SB339	635.61
Membrane reactors	TP248.25.M45	660.28424
Membrane separation	TP248.25.M46	660.28424
Memorial Day	E642	394.26973
Memory	BF370-387	153.12
Memory	LB1063-1064	370.1522
Memory	QP406	612.82
Memory (Philosophy)	BD181.7	128.3
Memory disorders	BF376	153.12
Memory disorders	RC394.M46	616.84
Men's furnishing goods	TT570-630	646.402
Men's studies	HQ1088-1090.7	305.31

Subject Heading	LC	Dewey
Menageries	QL73	590.73
Menarche	RJ145	612.662
Meninges	QM469	611.81
Meninges	QL933-937	573.86
Meningitis	RC124	616.82
Meningitis	RC376	616.82
Meningitis	SF799	636.089682
Mennonites	BX8101-8143	289.7092
Mennonites—Biography	BX8141-8143	289.7092
Mennonites—History	BX8115-8119	289.709
Mennonites—Parties and movements	BX8129.A1	252.097
Mennonites—Sermons	BX8127	252.097
Mennonites—Canada	BX8118.5-.7	289.771
Mennonites—United States	BX8116-8118	289.773
Menominee Indians	E99.M44	973.04973
Menopause	RG186	618.175
Menorah	BM657.M35	296.435
Menstrual cycle	RG161-186	618.172
Menstrual regulation	RG734	618.172
Menstruation disorders	RG161-186	618.172
Mensuration	QA465	516.15
Mensuration	T50-51	530.8
Mental fatigue	LB1075	152.1886
Mental healing	RZ400-408	615.851
Mental health	RA790-.95	362.2
Mental health care teams	RC440.7	616.89
Mental health counseling	RC466-.3	158.3
Mental health services	RA790-.95	362.2
Mental illness—Classification	RC455.2.C4	616.89075
Mental retardation	HV3004-3009	362.3
Mental retardation	RC569.7-571	616.8588
Mental retardation	RJ506.M4	618.9285884
Mental retardation facilities	HV3004-3008	362.385
Mental suggestion	BF1156.S8	154.7
Mentally handicapped—[By region or country]	HV3006-3008	362.30973
Mentally handicapped children—Education	LC4601-4700	371.92
Mentally handicapped children—Education (Secondary)	LC4604	371.9573
Mentally ill children—Education	LC4165-4184	371.94
Menus	TX727-739.2	642
Mercantile system	HB91	330.1513
Merchant banks	HG1970-1971	332.37
Merchant marine	HE730-943	387.5
Merchant marine	VK	387.5
Merchant marine—Congresses	VK5	387.506
Merchant marine—Developing countries	HE943	387.5091724
Merchant marine—History	VK15-20	387.509
Merchant marine—Officers	VK221	387.5092
Merchant marine—Periodicals	VK1-4	387.505
Merchant marine—Safety measures	VK200	623.888
Merchant marine—Signaling	VK381-397	387.54

Subject Heading	LC	Dewey
Merchant marine—Vocational guidance	VK160	387.5023
Merchant marine—[By region or country]	HE745-943	387.509(4-9)
Merchant marine—[By region or country]	VK21-124	387.509(4-9)
Merchant marine—United States	HE745-767	387.50973
Merchant marine—United States	VK23-25	387.50973
Merchant marine—[Other regions and countries]	HE769-937	387.509(4-9)
Merchant mariners—Biography	VK139-140	387.5092
Mercury	QD181.H6	546.663
Mercury (Planet)	QB371	523.41
Mercury (Planet)	QB611	523.41
Mercy	BV4647.M4	241.4
Merit (Christianity)	BT773	234
Mermaids	GR910	398.45
Merovingians	DD128	943.013
Mesas	GB571-578	551.434
Mescaline	BF209.M4	154.4
Mesmerism	BF1111-1156	154.7
Mesons	QC793.5.M42-.M429	539.72162
Messenger RNA	QP623.5.M47	572.88
Messengers	HE9751-9756	651.3743
Messiah	BL475	291.61
Messiah—Judaism	BM615	296.336
Metabolism	QP171-177	612.39
Metabolism	QH521	572.4
Metabolism—Disorders	RB147	616.39
Metabolism—Disorders	RC627.5-632	616.39
Metabolism, Inborn errors of	RC627.8	616.39043
Metal insulator semiconductors	TK7871.99.M4	621.38152
Metal sculpture	NB1220	731.2
Metal trade	HD9506-9624	380.1424
Metal-work	NK6400-8459	739
Metal-work	TT205-273	745.56
Metal-work	TS200-770	671
Metal-work—Periodicals	TS200	671.05
Metal-working machinery	TS215	671.0284
Metalanguage	P128.M48	410.1
Metallography	TN689-693	669.95
Metallurgical analysis	TN565	669.92
Metallurgical furnaces	TN677-.5	669.0282
Metallurgy	TN600-799	669
Metallurgy—History	TN615-620	669.09
Metallurgy—Periodicals	TN600-605	669.05
Metallurgy—Study and teaching	TN675.3	669.071
Metallurgy—[By region or country]	TN621-655	669.09(4-9)
Metals	QD171-172	546.3
Metals	TN400-580	622.34
Metals—Fatigue	TA460	620.166
Metals—Finishing	TS653-719	671.7
Metals—Testing	TA459-492	620.160287
Metals in the body	QP532	572.52

Subject Heading	LC	Dewey
Metamathematics	QA9	510.1
Metamorphism (Geology)	QE475.A2	552.4
Metamorphosis	QL981	571.876
Metaphysics	BD95-131	110
Meteorite craters	QB754.8-759	551.397
Meteorites	QB754.8-759	523.51
Meteoroids	QB738	523.51
Meteorological instruments	QC875.5-876.7	551.50284
Meteorological optics	QC974.5-976	551.56
Meteorological services	QC875	354.37
Meteorological stations	QC875	551.63
Meteorologists—Biography	QC858	551.5092
Meteorology	QC851-999	551.5
Meteorology—History	QC855-857	551.509
Meteorology—Periodicals	QC851	551.505
Meteorology—Terminology	QC854.2	551.5014
Meteorology, Agricultural	S600	630.2515
Meteorology in aeronautics	TL556-558	629.1324
Meteors	QB740-753	523.51
Methodism	BX8201-8495	287
Methodist Church	BX8201-8495	287
Methodist Church—[Catechisms/Creeds]	BX8335	238.7
Methodist Church—Doctrines	BX8330-8331.2	230.7
Methodist Church—Education	BX8219-8227	268.87
Methodist Church—Government	BX8340-8345.5	262.07
Methodist Church—History	BX8231-8328	287.09
Methodist Church—Liturgy	BX8337	264.07
Methodist Church—Sermons	BX8333	252.7
Methodist Church—Societies, etc.	BX8207	287.06
Methodist Church—Africa	BX8320-8322	287.(1-8)6
Methodist Church—Asia	BX8315-8316	287.(1-8)5
Methodist Church—[Australia/New Zealand]	BX8325-8326	287.(1-8)9(3/4)
Methodist Church—Canada	BX8251-8253	287.(1-8)71
Methodist Church—Europe	BX8275-8310	287.(1-8)4
Methodist Church—Great Britain	BX8276-8293	287.(1-8)41
Methodist Church—South America	BX8271-8273	287.(1-8)8
Methodist Church—United States	BX8235-8249	287.(1-8)73
Methodist Episcopal Church	BX8380-8389	287.63(2/3)
Methodists—Biography	BX8491-8495	287.092
Metric spaces	QA611.28	514.3
Metric system	QC90.8-94	530.812
Metropolitan government—United States	JS422	352.16097(4-9)
Mexican Americans	E184.M5	973.046872073
Mexican War, 1846-1848	E401-415.2	973.62
Mexican literature	PQ7100-7298.36	860
Mexico	F1201-1392	972
Mexico—Armed forces—Supplies and stores	UC94-97	355.80972
Mexico—Biography	CT550-558	920.072
Mexico—Census	HA761-770	317.2

Subject Heading	LC	Dewey	Subject Heading	LC	Dewey
Mexico—Church history	BR610-615	277.2	Micronesia—Maps	G9400-9494	912.965
Mexico—Civilization	F1210	972	Micronesia—Maps	G2905-2934	912.965
Mexico—Climate	QC986	551.6972	Micronesian languages	PL6191-6195	499.52
Mexico—Commerce	HF3231-3240	380.10972	Micronesians	GN669	305.89952
Mexico—Description and travel	F1211-1216.5	917.204	Microorganisms	QR	579
Mexico—Economic conditions	HC131-140	330.972	Microorganisms—Evolution	QR13	579.138
			Microscopes	QH211-212	570.282
Mexico—Emigration and immigration	JV7400-7409	325.(272/72)	Microscopy	QH201-278.5	570.282
			Microwave cookery	TX832	641.5882
Mexico—Gazetteers	F1204	917.2003	Microwave devices	TK7876	621.3813
Mexico—Genealogy	CS100-110	929.372	Microwave heating	TK4601	621.4028
Mexico—History—To 1519	F1228.98	972.01	Microwave ovens	TX657.064	641.5882
Mexico—History—To 1810	F1229-1231	972.0(1-2)	Microwave transmission lines	TK7876	621.38131
Mexico—History—Conquest, 1519-1540	F1230	972.02	Middle Ages	CB351-355	909.07
Mexico—History—Spanish colony, 1540-1810	F1231	972.02	Middle Ages—History	D111-203	909.07
			Middle Atlantic States	F106	974
Mexico—History—1810-	F1231.5-1236.6	972.0(3-83)	Middle Atlantic States—Maps	G3790-3854	912.74
Mexico—History—Wars of Independence, 1810-1821	F1232	972.03	Middle East	DS41-66	939.4/956
			Middle East—Biography	CT1870-1919	920.056
			Middle East—Commerce	HF3756-3770.2	380.10956
Mexico—History—1821-1861	F1232-.5	972.0(3-6)	Middle East—Description and travel	DS44.98-49.7	913.9404/ 915.604
Mexico—History—European intervention, 1861-1867	F1233	972.07	Middle East—Emigration and immigration	JV8739-8751	325.(256/56)
Mexico—History—1867-1910	F1233.5	972.081(2-4)	Middle East—Gazetteers	DS43	913.94003/ 915.6003
Mexico—History—1910-1946	F1234	972.08(16-26)	Middle East—History—To 622	DS38	939.4
Mexico—History—Revolution, 1910-1920	F1234	972.08(16-21)	Middle East—Maps	G7420-7624	912.56
			Middle East—Religion	BL660-687	200.956
Mexico—History—Decena Tragica, 1913	F1234	972.0816	Middle age	HQ1059.4-.5	305.244
Mexico—History—Revolution, 1923-1924	F1234	972.0822	Middle age—Psychological aspects	BF724.6-.65	155.66
Mexico—History—1946-1970	F1235-.5	972.08(27-31)	Middle class	HT680-690	305.55
Mexico—History—1970-1988	F1236	972.083(2-4)	Middle class—[By region or country]	HT690	305.5509(4-9)
			Middle ear	QM507	611.85
Mexico—History—1988-	F1236	972.083(5-6)	Middle ear	QL948	573.89
Michigan—History—1837-	F566	977.40(3-4)	Middle ear	QP461	612.854
Michigan—History—1951-	F570-.2	977.404(3-4)	Middle ear—Diseases	RF220-229	617.84
Michigan—Maps	G4110-4114	912.774	Middle schools	LB1623	373.236
Michigan—National Guard	UA260-269	355.3709774	Midgets	GN69.3-.5	599.949
Michigan—Periodicals	F561	977.4005	Midrash	BM511-518	296.14
Microbial biotechnology	TP248.27.M53	660.6	Midshipmen	V415	359.0071073
Microbial ecology	QR100-130	576.15	Midway, Battle of, 1942	D774.M5	940.5426
Microbiologists	QR30-31	579.092	Midwives	RG950	618.2
Microbiology	QR	579	Migrant agricultural laborers	HD1521-1542	331.544
Microbiology—Classification	QR12	579.012	Migrant labor	HD5855-5856	331.544
Microbiology—History	QR21-22	579.09	Migrations of nations	D135-149	304.8
Microbiology—Periodicals	QR1	579.05	Migratory locust	QL508.A2	595.726
Microbiology—Pictorial works	QR54	579.0222	Mildew	SB741.M65	632.43
Microbiology—Research	QR61-63	579.072	Mile, Nautical	VK572	527.015308
Microbiology—Technique	QR65-69	579.028	Mile, Roman	G86	530.8
Microbiology—Terminology	QR11	579.014	Militarism	U21	355.0213
Microfilm readers	TR835	302.23	Militarism	UA10	355.0213
Micrographics	Z265	686.43	Military administration	UB	355.6
Micrometeorology	QC883.7-.86	551.66	Military administration—History	UB15	355.609
Micronesia	DU500	996.5			

Subject Heading	LC	Dewey	Subject Heading	LC	Dewey
Military administration—Periodicals	UB1	355.605	Military engineering—History	UG15	358.2209
Military architecture	NA490-497	725.18	Military engineering—Societies, etc.	UG1	358.2206
Military art and science	U	355	Military engineering—Study and teaching	UG157	358.22071
Military art and science—Biography	U51-55	355.0092	Military engineering—[By region or country]	UG21-124	358.2209(4-9)
Military art and science—Congresses	U7	355.006	Military engineers	UG	358.22092
Military art and science—Dictionaries	U24-26	355.003	Military field engineering	UG360-390	358.22
Military art and science—Exhibitions	U13	355.0074	Military fireworks	UF860-880	623.452
Military art and science—History	U27-43	355.009	Military geography	UA985-997	355.47
Military art and science—History—To 500	U29-35	355.00901	Military history	D25-.4	355.009
			Military history—Medieval	D128	355.00902
Military art and science—Officers' handbooks	U130-135	355	Military history—Modern	D214	355.00903
			Military hospitals	UH460-485	355.72
Military art and science—Soldiers' handbooks	U110-115	355.5	Military hygiene	UH600-629.5	355.345
			Military inspectors general	UB240-245	355.685
Military bridges	UG335	623.67	Military intelligence	UB250-271	355.3432
Military calls	UH40-45	781.599	Military law—[By region and country]	UB461-736	343.(3-9)01
Military ceremonies, honors, and salutes	U350-365	355.17	Military law—Africa	UB715-729	343.601
Military currency	HG353.5	332.4	Military law—Argentina	UB530-534	343.8201
Military decorations	VB330-335	359.1342	Military law—Asia	UB685-710	343.501
Military decorations	UB430-435	355.134	Military law—Australia	UB730-734	343.9401
Military dependents	UB400-405	355.12	Military law—Canada	UB505-509	343.7101
Military discipline	UB790-795	343.014	Military law—Central America	UB515-519	343.72801
Military education	U400-714	355.0071			
Military education—[By region or country]	U407-714	355.00710(4-9)	Military law—Chile	UB545-549	343.8301
			Military law—China	UB690-694	343.5101
Military education—Africa	U670-695	355.007106	Military law—Colombia	UB550-554	343.86101
Military education—Asia	U635-660	355.007105	Military law—Europe	UB590-684	343.401
Military education—Australia	U700-704	355.0071094	Military law—France	UB615-619	343.4401
			Military law—Germany	UB620-624	343.4301
Military education—Austria	U550-554	355.00710436	Military law—Greece	UB630-634	343.49501
Military education—Canada	U440-444	355.0071071	Military law—India	UB695-699	343.5401
Military education—Central America	U450-454	355.00710728	Military law—Italy	UB640-644	343.4501
			Military law—Japan	UB700-704	343.5201
Military education—China	U640-644	355.0071051	Military law—Mexico	UB510-514	343.7201
Military education—Europe	U505-630	355.007104	Military law—Oceania	UB735-736	343.9(5-6)01
Military education—Germany	U570-574.54	355.0071043	Military law—Portugal	UB650-654	343.46901
			Military law—Russia	UB655-659	343.4701
Military education—Great Britain	U510-549.3	355.0071041	Military law—South America	UB530-589	343.801
			Military law—Spain	UB660-664	343.4601
Military education—India	U645-649	355.0071054	Military law—Venezuela	UB585-589	343.8701
Military education—Iran	U655-659	355.0071055	Military law—West Indies	UB520-524	343.72901
Military education—Japan	U650-654	355.0071052	Military maneuvers	U250-255	355.4
Military education—Mexico	U445-449	355.0071072	Military maneuvers	UD460-465	356.4
Military education—South America	U465-499	355.007108	Military missions	UA16	355.032
			Military museums	U13	355.0074
Military education—United States	U408-439	355.0071073	Military museums	UF6	358.12074
			Military music	M1270	781.599
Military education—[United States, By state]	U409	355.007107(4-9)	Military music	VG30-35	781.599
			Military nursing	UH490-495	355.345
Military education—West Indies	U455-459	355.00710729	Military oceanography	V396-.5	359.8
			Military offenses	UB780-789	355.1334
Military engineering	UG	358.22	Military passes	UB280-285	355.113
Military engineering—Congresses	UG5	358.2206	Military pensions	UB370-375	331.25291355
			Military pensions	VB280-285	362.86
			Military police	VB920-925	359.13323
			Military police	UB820-825	355.13323

Subject Heading	LC	Dewey
Military policy	UA11	355.0335
Military prisons	VB890-895	365.48
Military prisons	UB800-805	365.48
Military railroads	UG345	623.63
Military readiness—Law and legislation	K4720-4760	343.01
Military readiness—Law and legislation—Canada	KE6800-7240	343.7101
Military readiness—Law and legislation—England	KD6000-6355	343.4201
Military reconnaisance	U220	355.413
Military research	U390-395	355.07
Military reservations	UB390-395	355.7
Military roads	UG330	623.62
Military sealift	VC530-535	359.985
Military service, Voluntary	UB320-325	355.22362
Military social work	UH750-769	306.27
Military statistics	UA19	355.0021
Military supplies	UC260-267	355.8
Military telecommunication	UG590-610.5	623.73 (2-3)
Military telegraph	UG590-613.5	623.732
Military training camps	VE430-435	359.965
Military training camps	U290-295	355.5
Military uniforms	VC300-345	359.81
Military uniforms	UC480-485	355.14
Militia	UA13	355.37
Milk	SF251-262.5	636.2142
Milk—Pasteurization	SF259	637.141
Milk—Sterilization	SF259	637.141
Milk-free diet	RM234.5	613.26
Milk programs	HV868	363.83
Milking	SF250	637.124
Milking machines	SF247	637.1240284
Millennium	BT890-891	236.9
Millerite movement	BX6101-6193	286.7
Millinery	TT650-665	687.42
Milling-machines	TJ1225-1227	621.91
Millipedes	QL449.6-.65	595.66
Milwaukee (Wi.)	F589.M6	977.595
Mime	PN2071.G4	792.3
Mind and body	BF150-172	150
Mine accidents	TN311-320	622.8
Mine explosions	TN313	622.82
Mine fires	TN315	622.82
Mine gases	TN305-306	622.82
Mine lighting	TN306.5-309	622.47
Mine railroads	TN336	622.66
Mine rescue work	TN297	622.89
Mine surveying	TN273	622.14
Mine timbering	TN289	622.28
Mine ventilation	TN301-306	622.42
Mine water	TN318	622.5
Mineral industries—Congresses	TN5	338.206
Mineral industries—Dictionaries	TN9-10	338.203
Mineral industries—Directories	TN12	338.2025
Mineral industries—Exhibitions	TN6	338.2074
Mineral industries—History	TN15-124	338.209

Subject Heading	LC	Dewey
Mineral industries—Periodicals	TN1-4	338.205
Mineral lands	HD242.5	333.850973
Mineral oils	TP685-699	665.4
Mineral waters	RA793-954	613.287
Mineral waters	TN923-929.7	622.373
Mineralogical chemistry	QE371	549.13
Mineralogy	QE351-399.2	549
Mineralogy, Determinative	QE367-369	549.1
Mineralogy—Periodicals	QE351	549.05
Minerals—Classification	QE388	549.012
Minerals in the body	QP533	572.51
Miners	HD8039.M6-.M7	331.7622
Mines (Military explosives)	UG490	623.45115
Mines and minelaying	V856-.5	623.26
Mines and mineral resources	TN	622
Mines and mineral resources—[By region or country]	TN21-127	622.09(4-9)
Mines and mineral resources—Africa	TN115-119	622.096
Mines and mineral resources—Arctic regions	TN125-.5	622.0998
Mines and mineral resources—Argentina	TN36-37	622.0982
Mines and mineral resources—Asiatic Russia	TN109-110	622.0957
Mines and mineral resources—Australia	TN121-122	622.0994
Mines and mineral resources—Austria	TN65-.2	622.09436
Mines and mineral resources—Balkan Peninsula	TN95.A2	622.09496
Mines and mineral resources—Bolivia	TN38-39	622.0984
Mines and mineral resources—Brazil	TN41-42	622.0981
Mines and mineral resources—Canada	TN26-27	622.0971
Mines and mineral resources—Central America	TN30-31	622.09728
Mines and mineral resources—Chile	TN43-44	622.0983
Mines and mineral resources—China	TN101-102	622.0951
Mines and mineral resources—Colombia	TN45-46	622.09861
Mines and mineral resources—Czechoslovakia	TN65.3-.4	622.09437
Mines and mineral resources—Denmark	TN69-70	622.09489
Mines and mineral resources—Ecuador	TN47	622.09866
Mines and mineral resources—Egypt	TN117-118	622.0962

Subject Heading	LC	Dewey	Subject Heading	LC	Dewey
Mines and mineral resources—Finland	TN95.F5	622.094897	Mines and mineral resources—Sweden	TN89-90	622.09485
Mines and mineral resources—France	TN71-72.5	622.0944	Mines and mineral resources—Switzerland	TN91-92	622.09494
Mines and mineral resources—French Guiana	TN50	622.09882	Mines and mineral resources—Turkey	TN111-112	622.09561
Mines and mineral resources—Germany	TN73-74.5	622.0943	Mines and mineral resources—United States	TN23-25	622.0973
Mines and mineral resources—Great Britain	TN57-64	622.0941	Mines and mineral resources—Uruguay	TN53	622.09895
Mines and mineral resources—Greece	TN75-76	622.09495	Mines and mineral resources—Venezuela	TN54	622.0987
Mines and mineral resources—Guyana	TN48	622.09881	Mines and mineral resources—West Indies	TN32-33	622.09729
Mines and mineral resources—Hungary	TN65.5-66	622.09439	Mines and mineral resources—Yugoslavia	TN95.Y8	622.09497
Mines and mineral resources—India	TN103-104	622.0954	Miniature electronic equipment	TK7870	621.3810228
Mines and mineral resources—Indonesia	TN113.I55	622.09598	Miniature horses	SF293.M56	636.109
Mines and mineral resources—Iran	TN107-108	622.0955	Miniature objects	NK8470-8475	745.0228
Mines and mineral resources—Iraq	TN113.I7	622.09567	Miniature objects	NK492	745.5928
Mines and mineral resources—Israel	TN113.I75	622.095694	Miniature weapons	NK8475.A7	739.70228
Mines and mineral resources—Italy	TN79-80	622.0945	Minibikes	TL443	629.2275
Mines and mineral resources—Japan	TN105-106	622.0952	Minimum wage	HD4917-4924	331.23
Mines and mineral resources—Mexico	TN28-29	622.0972	Minimum wage—[By region or country]	HD4918-4924	331.2309(4-9)
Mines and mineral resources—Netherlands	TN77-78	622.09492	Mining engineering	TN	622
Mines and mineral resources—New Zealand	TN122.5-.6	622.0993	Mining engineers	TN139-140	622.092
Mines and mineral resources—Norway	TN81-82	622.09481	Mining law—Canada	KE1790-1802	343.71077
			Mining law—England	KD2331-2370	343.42077
Mines and mineral resources—Oceania	TN123-124	622.099(5-6)	Mining law—United States	KF1801-1873	343.73077
Mines and mineral resources—Pakistan	TN104.5-.6	622.095491	Mining machinery	TN345-347	622.0284
Mines and mineral resources—Paraguay	TN51	622.09892	Mining schools and education	TN165-213	622.071
Mines and mineral resources—Peru	TN52	622.0985	Ministerial responsibility	JF341	352.293
Mines and mineral resources—Philippines	TN113.P6	622.09599	Mink farming	SF405.M6	636.97662701
			Minneapolis (Minn.)	F614.M5	977.6579
Mines and mineral resources—Portugal	TN83-84.5	622.09469	Minnesota	F601-615	977.6
Mines and mineral resources—Russia	TN85-86	622.0947	Minnesota—Gazetteers	F604	917.76003
Mines and mineral resources—Scandinavia	TN88.5	622.0948	Minnesota—History—To 1858	F606	977.60(1-4)
Mines and mineral resources—Spain	TN87-88	622.0946	Minnesota—History—1858-	F606	977.60(4-5)
			Minnesota—Maps	G4140-4144	912.776
Mines and mineral resources—Sri Lanka	TN104.7-.8	622.095493	Minnesota—National Guard	UA270-279	355.3709776
			Minnesota—Periodicals	F601	977.6005
Mines and mineral resources—Surinam	TN49	622.09883	Minnesota Multiphasic Personality Inventory	BF698.8.M5	155.283
			Minnesota Multiphasic Personality Inventory	RC473.M5	616.89075
			Minorities	JC312	323.1
			Minorities—Education	LC3701-3740	371.829
			Minorities—Employment	HD6304	331.6
			Minotaur (Greek mythology)	BL820.M63	292.13
			Minstrel music	M1365	791.12
			Minstrels	GT3650	390.478
			Mints	HG321-329	332.4
			Minuet	GV1796.M5	793.3
			Miracles	BT97-.2	231.73
			Miracles	BS2545.M5	231.73
			Miracles	BS1199.M5	231.73
			Mirrors	NK8440-.2	748.8

Subject Heading	LC	Dewey
Mirrors	TP867	681.428
Miscarriage	RG648	618.392
Miscegenation	E185.62	306.846
Miscegenation	GN254	306.846
Missals	BX2015-2016	264.023
Missing link	GN282.5	569.9
Mission of the church	BV601.8	261
Missionaries	BV3700-3705	266.0092
Missions	BV2000-3705	266
Missions—Interdenominational cooperation	BV2082.I6	266
Missions—Africa	BV3500-3630	266.0096
Missions—Asia	BV3149-3487	266.0095
Missions—Australia	BV3650-3660	266.00994
Missions—Canada	BV2810-2820	266.00971
Missions—European	BV2855-3145	266.0094
Missions—France	BV2940-2945	266.00944
Missions—Germany	BV2950-2957	266.00943
Missions—Great Britain	BV2860-2895	266.00941
Missions—Japan	BV3440-3457	266.00952
Missions—Oceania	BV3640-3680	266.0099(3-6)
Missions—Spain	BV3120-3127	266.00946
Missions, Medical	RA390-392	362.1
Missions to Jews	BV2619-2623	266
Missions to Muslims	BV2625-2626.4	266
Missions to lepers	BV2637	266
Mississippi	F336-350	976.2
Mississippi—History—To 1803	F341	976.20(1-4)
Mississippi—History—Civil War, 1861-1865	E516	976.205
Mississippi—History—Civil War, 1861-1865	E568	976.205
Mississippi—Gazetteers	F339	917.62003
Mississippi—Maps	G3980-3984	912.762
Mississippi—National Guard	UA280-289	355.3709762
Mississippi—Periodicals	F336	976.2005
Mississippi River Valley	F350.5-358.2	977
Missouri	F461-475	977.8
Missouri—Gazetteers	F464	917.78003
Missouri—History—Civil War, 1861-1865	E517	977.803
Missouri—History—Civil War, 1861-1865	E569	977.803
Missouri—Maps	G4160-4164	912.778
Missouri—National Guard	UA290-299	355.3709778
Missouri—Periodicals	F461	977.8005
Missouri compromise	E373	973.7113
Missouri River	F598	978
Miter-gages	TH5618	694.0284
Mites as carriers of disease	RA641.M5	614.433
Mitosis	QH605.2	571.844
Mitral valve insufficiency	RC685.V2	616.125
Mixing	TA357.5.M59	620.1064
Mnemonics	BF380-387	153.14
Mobile Bay (Ala.), Battle of, 1864	E476.85	973.75
Mobile home living	TX1100-1105	643.2
Mobiles (Sculpture)	NB1315	731.55
Mobs	HM281-283	302.33
Mobs	HV6474-6485	364.143
Moccasins	E98.C8	391.413008997
Model airplane racing	GV761.5	796.154
Model car racing	GV1570	796.156
Model theory	QA9.7	511.801
Modeling	NB1180-1185	731.42
Models (Patents)	T324	608.0228
Models (Persons)	HD6073.M7	746.92092
Models and modelmaking	TT154-.5	688.1
Modems	TK7887.8.M63	621.39814
Modern dance	GV1783	792.8
Modernism	BT82	273.9
Modernism (Art)	N6490	700.4112
Modesty	BJ1533.M73	179.9
Modular arithmetic	QA247.35	513.6
Modular construction	TH1098	729.2
Modular programming	QA76.6	005.112
Mogul Empire	DS461-.9	954.025
Mohave Indians	E99.M77	973.049757
Mohawk Indians	E99.M8	973.049755
Mohawk language	PM1881-1884	497.55
Mohegan Indians	E99.M83	973.04973
Mohegan language	PM1885	497.3
Moisture	QC915-929	551.57
Moisture index	QC915	551.57
Moisture index	S594	631.432
Mole (Dermatology)	RL793	616.(042/55)
Molecular astrophysics	QB462.6	523.019
Molecular biology	QH506	572.8
Molecular cloning	QH442.2	660.65
Molecular structure	QD461	541.22
Molecular theory	QD461	541.2
Molecular weights	QD463-464	541.222
Molecules	QC179	539.6
Molecules	QC173	539.6
Mollusks	QL401-432	594
Moments of inertia	QA839	531.12
Moments of inertia	TG265-267	624.25
Mon-Khmer languages	PL4301-4309	495.93
Monaco	DC941-947	944.949
Monaco—Maps	G5980-5984	912.44949
Monarchy	JC375-393	321.6
Monarchy—Great Britain	KD4430-4531	342.4206
Monasteries	BX2460-2749	255.(1-7)
Monasteries	NA4850	726.7
Monastic and religious life	BX2435	255.(1-7)
Monastic and religious life—History	BX2460-2749	255.(1-7)009
Monasticism and religious orders	BX580-583	255.819
Monasticism and religious orders	BX2400-4560	255.(1-7)
Monasticism and religious orders	BX385	255.819
Monasticism and religious orders—Rules	BX2436-2437	255.(1-7)06
Monasticism and religious orders—Africa	BX2732-2740	255.(1-7)0096
Monasticism and religious orders—Asia	BX2677-2731	255.(1-7)0095
Monasticism and religious orders—Canada	BX2527-2529	255.(1-7)00971

151

Subject Heading	LC	Dewey
Monasticism and religious orders—Central America	BX2533-2547	255.(1-7)009728
Monasticism and religious orders—Europe	BX2631-2676	255.(1-7)0094
Monasticism and religious orders—Mexico	BX2530-2532	255.(1-7)00972
Monasticism and religious orders—[New Zealand/Australia]	BX2743-2745	255.(1-7)0099 (3/4)
Monasticism and religious orders—South America	BX2561-2589	255.(1-7)0098
Monasticism and religious orders—United States	BX2505-2525	255.(1-7)00973
Monasticism and religious orders, Anglican	BX5970-5974	255.83
Monasticism and religious orders, Buddhist	BQ6001-6160	294.3657
Monasticism and religious orders, Hindu	BL1238	294.5657
Monasticism and religious orders, Orthodox Eastern	BX385-388	255.819
Monasticism and religious orders, Protestant	BV4405-4408	255.8
Monasticism and religious orders for women	BX4200-4563	255.9(1-7)
Money	HG201-1496	332.4
Money—Law and legislation—England	KD5284-5286	343.42032
Money—Law and legislation—United States	KF6201-6219	343.73032
Money—Tables	HG3854-3858	332.4021
Money—[By region or country]	HG451-1496	332.49(4-9)
Money—United States	HG451-645	332.4973
Mongolia—Census	HA4630.8	315.17
Mongolia—Maps	G7895-7899	912.517
Mongolian language	PL401-409	494.23
Mongolian languages	PL400-431	494.23
Mongolian literature	PL410-419	894.23
Mongols	DS19-23	950.04942
Mongols	GN548	305.8942
Monitorial system of education	LB1029.M7	371.39
Monmouth, Battle of, 1778	E241.M7	973.334
Monologue	PN1530	808.8245
Monologues	PN4305.M6	808.8245
Mononucleosis	RC147.G6	616.925
Monopolies	HD2709-2932	338.82
Monopolies—United States	KF1631-1657	343.73072
Monorail railroads	TF694	625.103
Monotheism	BL221	211.34
Monotype	Z253	686.22542
Monsoons	QC939.M7	551.5184
Monsters	GR825-830	398.45
Montana	F726-740	978.6
Montana—Gazetteers	F729	917.86003
Montana—History—1951-	F735-.2	978.603(3-4)
Montana—Maps	G4250-4254	912.786
Montana—National Guard	UA300-309	355.3709786
Montana—Periodicals	F726	978.6005
Montenegro	DR1802-1928	949.745

Subject Heading	LC	Dewey
Montenegro—History	DR1827-1928	949.745
Montenegro—Maps	G2020-2022	912.49745
Monterrey (Mexico), Battle of, 1846	E406.M7	973.623
Montessori method of education	LB1029.M75	371.392
Montserrat	F2082	972.975
Montserrat—Maps	G5055-5059	912.72975
Monuments	NA9335-9355	725.94
Monuments	NB1330-1685	731.76
Monuments—[By region or country]	NB1501-1685	731.7609(4-9)
Moon	QB580-595	523.3
Moon worship	BL438	291.212
Moon—Maps	G3195-3199	912.991
Moon—Maps	G1000.3-.5	912.991
Moon—Surface	QB591	523.3
Moon—Tables	QB399	523.3021
Moon—Tables	VK563-567	523.3021
Moor ecology	QH541.5.M6	577.38
Mooring of ships	VK361-365	387.54044
Moors and heaths	QH87.5	578.738
Moral development	BF723.M54	155.25
Moral education	LC251-318	370.114
Moral re-armament	BJ10.M6	267.16
Morale	U22	355.123
Moravia	DB2300-2421	943.72
Moravia (Czech Republic)—History—To 906	DB2385-2391	943.72021
Moravia (Czech Republic)—Civilization	DB2335	943.72
Moravia (Czech Republic)—Ethnography	DB2340-2342	943.72004
Moravia (Czech Republic)—History	DB2345-2421	943.72
Moravians	BX8551-8593	284.6
Moravians—Biography	BX8591-8593	284.6092
Moravians—Education	BX8561-8564.5	268.846
Moravians—History	BX8565-8569	284.609
Moravians—Sermons	BX8577	252.046
Moravians—Societies, etc.	BX8553	284.606
Mordvin language	PH751-779	494.56
Mordvin literature	PH781-785	894.56
Mormon Church	BX8601-8695	289.3
Mormon Church—Education	BX8610	268.893
Mormon Church—History	BX8611-8617	289.309
Mormon Church—Missions	BX8661	266.93
Mormon Church—Sacred books	BX8621-8631	289.32
Mormon Church—Sermons	BX8639	252.093
Mormon cosmology	BX8643.C68	231.765
Mormon temples	BX8643.T4	246.6
Morocco	DT301-330	939.71/964
Morocco—Census	HA4682	316.4
Morocco—Civilization	DT312	939.71/964
Morocco—Description and travel	DT307-310.2	913.97104/916.404
Morocco—Economic conditions	HC810	330.964
Morocco—Gazetteers	DT304	913.971003/916.4003

Subject Heading	LC	Dewey
Morocco—History	DT313.7-325.92	939.71/964
Morocco—History—To 647	DT318	939.71
Morocco—History—647-1516	DT319	964.02
Morocco—History—1516-1830	DT321-323.5	964.02
Morocco—History—19th century	DT324	964.0(2-3)
Morocco—History—20th century	DT324-325.92	964.0(4-5)
Morocco—Maps	G8230-8234	912.64
Morphemics	P241-259	415
Morphine	RM666.M8	615.7822
Morphine habit	HV5813	362.293
Morphine habit	RC568.06	616.8632
Morphology	QH351	571.3
Morphology (Animals)	QL799-.5	571.3
Morrisite War, 1862	F826	979.202
Mortality	HB1321-1528	304.64
Mortality—Tables	HG8783-8785	368.3201
Mortality—Tables	HB1322	304.64021
Mortality—[By region or country]	HB1335-1526	304.645(4-9)
Mortgage banks	HG2039.5-2040.5	332.32
Mortgage guarantee insurance	HG9992	368.852
Mortgage loans, Reverse	HG2039.5-2040.5	332.72
Mortgages	HD1443	332.72
Mortgages	HG4655	332.63244
Mortgages—England	KD1010-1016	346.4204364
Mosaics	NA3750-3860	729.7
Mosaics	NK5430	748.50285
Mosaics	NK8500	738.5
Moscow (Russia)	DK588-609	947.31
Moscow, Battle of, 1941-1942	D764.3.M	940.5421731
Moses (Biblical leader) in the Koran	BP133.7.M67	297.122092
Mosques	NA4670	726.2
Mosquitoes as carriers of disease	RA640	614.4323
Mosquitoes—Control	RA640	614.4323
Mossi languages	PJ4149	496.35
Mother goddesses	BL325.M6	291.2114
Mother goddesses, Greek	BL820.M65	292.2114
Mother-of-pearl	SH377.5	639.412
Mother's Day	HQ759.2	394.262
Motherhood	HQ759-.6	306.8743
Mothers	HQ759-.6	306.8743
Motion	QC122-168	531.11
Motion	QA801-935	531.11
Motion picture plays	PN1996-1997	791.437
Motion picture theaters	NA6845-6846	725.823
Motion pictures	PN1993-1999	791.43
Motion pictures—Editing	TR899-.5	778.535
Motion pictures—Moral and ethical aspects	PN1995.5	175
Motion pictures—Religious aspects	PN1995.5	791.43682
Motion pictures—Reviews	PN1995	791.4375
Motion sickness	RC103.M6	616.9892

Subject Heading	LC	Dewey
Motion study	T60.7	658.542
Motivation (Psychology)	BF199	153.8
Motor vehicles	TL	629.2
Motor vehicles—Electronic equipment	TL272.5-.55	629.2549
Motor vehicles—Pollution control devices	TL214.P6	629.25
Motor vehicles, Amphibious	V880	359.83
Motorboats	GV833.5-835.9	797.125
Motorboats	VM340-349	623.81
Motorcycles	TL439-448	629.2275
Motorization, Military	UC340-345	355.83
Motors	TJ	621.4
Mottoes	CR73-75	929.6
Mounds	GN795-796	930.1
Mountain climate	QC993.6	551.69143
Mountain gods	BL325.M63	291.212
Mountain life	GT3490	390.09143
Mountain plants	QK937	581.7538
Mountain railroads	HE4051-4071	385.6
Mountain roads	TE229.8	625.709143
Mountain sickness	RC103.A4	616.9893
Mountain warfare	UD460-465	356.164
Mountain wave	QC939.M8	551.5185
Mountain worship	BL447	291.212
Mountaineering	GV199.8-200.3	796.522
Mountains	GR660	398.3209143
Mountains	GB501-555	551.432
Mourning customs, Jewish	BM712	296.445
Mourning etiquette	BJ2071-2075	395.23
Mouth	QM306	611.31
Mouth	QL857	573.35
Mouth—Cancer	RC280.M6	616.99431
Mouth—Diseases	RC815-.6	616.31
Mouth—Surgery	RK529-535	617.605
Mouth protectors	GV749.M6	796.0284
Movement (Philosophy)	B105.M65	573.701
Movement, Psychology of	BF295-.5	152.3
Moving target indicator radar	TK6592.M67	621.3848
Mowing machines	S695-697	631.3
Mozambique—Census	HA4698	316.79
Mozambique—Civilization	DT3320	967.9
Mozambique—Description and travel	DT3308-3312	916.7904
Mozambique—Economic conditions	HC890	330.9679
Mozambique—Gazetteers	DT3294	916.79003
Mozambique—History	DT3330-3398	967.9
Mozambique—History—To 1505	DT3345-3348	967.901
Mozambique—History—1505-1698	DT3350-3359	967.90(1-2)
Mozambique—History—1698-1891	DT3361-3374	967.902
Mozambique—History—1891-1975	DT3376-3387	967.90(2-3)
Mozambique—History—War of 1894-1895	DT3381	967.902
Mozambique—History—Revolution, 1964-1975	DT463-.3	967.903

Subject Heading	LC	Dewey	Subject Heading	LC	Dewey
Mozambique—History—1975-	DT3389-3398	967.905	Municipal ownership	HD4421-4730.9	352.266
			Municipal revenue	HJ9115-9123	336.2014
Mozambique—History—To 1505	DT3345-3348	967.901	Municipal universities and colleges	LB2329	378.052
Mozambique—History—1505-1698	DT3350-3359	967.90(1-2)	Municipal water supply	TD201-500	628.1
Mozambique—History—1698-1891	DT3361-3374	967.902	Mural painting and decoration	ND2550-2877	751.73
Mozambique—History—1891-1975	DT3376-3387	967.90(2-3)	Mural painting—[By region or country]	ND2601-2877	751.7309(4-9)
Mozambique—History—War of 1894-1895	DT3381	967.902	Murder	HV6499-6542	364.1523
			Murder—[By region or country]	HV6518-6535	364.152309(4-9)
Mozambique—History—Revolution, 1964-1975	DT463-.3	967.903	Murder—United States	HV6518-6534	364.15230973
Mozambique—History—1975-	DT3389-3398	967.905	Murder—[Other regions or countries]	HV6535	364.152309(4-9)
Mozambique—Maps	G8450-8454	912.679	Muscles	QP321-322	612.74
Muffins	TX770.M83	641.815	Muscles	QM151-170	611.73
Muffs	GT2190	391.412	Muscles	QM571	611.73
Mugging	HV6646-6665	364.1552	Muscles	QL831	573.75
Muhammad, Prophet, d. 632	BP75-77.5	297.63	Muscles—Diseases	RD688	616.74
			Muscles—Diseases	RC925-935	616.7
Muhammad, Prophet, d. 632—Miracles	BP75.8	297.63	Muscles—Diseases	RD925-927	616.74
			Muscular atrophy	RC935.A8	616.74
Mulattoes	GN645	305.8044	Muscular sense	BF285	152.182
Mulching	S661.5	631.451	Musculoskeletal banks	RD128	362.1783
Mules	SF362	636.183	Musculoskeletal system	QL821-831	573.7
Multicultural education	LC1099-.5	370.117	Musculoskeletal system	QP301-336	612.7
Multidimensional Aptitude Battery	BF432.5.M85	153.94	Musculoskeletal system	QM100-170	611.7
			Musculoskeletal system—Effect of drugs on	RM312	615.773
Multihull sailboats	GV811.53-.58	797.1246	Musculoskeletal system—Wounds and injuries	RD680-688	617.47044
Multilevel marketing	HF5415.126	381.1			
Multilinear algebra	QA199.5	512.5	Museum conservation methods	AM141-145	069.53
Multimedia systems	QA76.575	006.7			
Multiphase flow	TA357.5.M84	620.1064	Museum finance	AM122	069.0681
Multiple birth	RG696-698	618.25	Museums	AM	069
Multiple-choice examinations	LB3060.32.M85	371.271	Museums—Law and legislation—England	KD3736	344.42093
Multiple cropping	S603.7	631.58			
Multiple personality	RC569.5.M8	616.85236	Museums—Law and legislation—United States	KF4305	344.73093
Multiple pregnancy	RG567	618.25			
Multiple psychotherapy	RC489.M85	616.8914	Museums—Methodology	AM111-157	069.01
Multiple sclerosis	RA645.M82	614.59834	Museums—[By region or country]	AM10-101	069.09
Multiple sclerosis	RC377	616.834			
Multiple stars	QB821-830	523.841	Museums—Africa	AM80-91	069.096
Multiplication	QA115	513.213	Museums—Asia	AM71-79	069.095
Multiprocessors	QA76.5	004.35	Museums—Australia	AM93-95	069.0994
Multipurpose trees	SB172	634.99	Museums—Balkan Peninsula	AM69	069.09496
Mumps	RC168.M8	616.313			
Munda languages	PL4501-4509	495.95	Museums—Canada	AM21-22	069.0971
Municipal bonds	HG4726	332.63233	Museums—Central America	AM25-27	069.09728
Municipal buildings	NA4430-4437	725.13	Museums—China	AM72	069.0951
Municipal corporations	JS	320.85	Museums—Europe	AM40-70	069.094
Municipal engineering	TD159-168	628	Museums—France	AM46-48	069.0944
Municipal government	JS	320.85	Museums—Germany	AM49-51	069.0943
Municipal government—[U.S. by city]	JS504-1583	352.16097(4-9)	Museums—Great Britain	AM41-43	069.0941
			Museums—Greece	AM52-53	069.09495
Municipal government by commission	JS342-343	352.250973	Museums—Italy	AM54-55	069.0945
			Museums—Japan	AM77-78	069.0952
Municipal home rule	JS113	320.85	Museums—Mexico	AM23-24	069.0972
Municipal officials and employees	JS148-155	352.16092	Museums—New Zealand	AM96-98	069.0993
			Museums—Oceania	AM99-100	069.099(5-6)

Subject Heading	LC	Dewey	Subject Heading	LC	Dewey
Museums—Portugal	AM66	069.09469	Musical instruments—Central America	ML484	784.19728
Museums—Russia	AM60-61	069.0947	Musical instruments—China	ML531	784.195
Museums—Scandinavia	AM61.5-64	069.0948	Musical instruments—Czechoslovakia	ML493	784.19437
Museums—South America	AM33-35	069.098	Musical instruments—Denmark	ML514	784.19489
Museums—Spain	AM65	069.0946	Musical instruments—Europe	ML489-522	784.194
Museums—United States	AM11-13	069.0973	Musical instruments—France	ML497	784.1944
Mushrooms, Edible	QK617	579.6	Musical instruments—Germany	ML499-500	784.1943
Mushrooms, Hallucinogenic	QK600-635	579.6	Musical instruments—Great Britain	ML501	784.1941
Mushrooms, Hallucinogenic	SB293-295	633.88	Musical instruments—Hungary	ML494	784.19439
Mushrooms, Poisonous	QK617	581.659	Musical instruments—India	ML533	784.1954
Music	M	780	Musical instruments—Iran	ML539	784.1955
Music—Bibliography	ML111-158	016.78	Musical instruments—Italy	ML503	784.1945
Music—Bio-bibliography	ML385-429	780.92	Musical instruments—Japan	ML535	784.1952
Music—Bio-bibliography	ML105-107	780.12	Musical instruments—Korea	ML537	784.19519
Music—Dictionaries	ML100-110	780.3	Musical instruments—Mexico	ML482	784.1972
Music—Examinations, questions, etc.	MT9	780.76	Musical instruments—Netherlands	ML505	784.19492
Music—History and criticism	ML159-3799	780.9	Musical instruments—[New Zealand/Australia/Oceania]	ML547	784.199(3-6)
Music—Instruction and study	MT	780.7	Musical instruments—Norway	ML515	784.19481
Music—Manuscripts	ML93-98	780	Musical instruments—Portugal	ML519	784.19469
Music—Memorizing	MT82	781.426	Musical instruments—Saudia Arabia	ML527	784.19538
Music—Performance	ML457	780.7809	Musical instruments—Scandinavia	ML513-516	784.1948
Music—Philosophy and aesthetics	ML3800-3920	780.1	Musical instruments—South America	ML486	784.198
Music—Psychology	ML3830-3838	781.11	Musical instruments—Spain	ML518	784.190946
Music—Societies, etc.	ML25-28	780.6	Musical instruments—Sweden	ML516	784.19485
Music—Terminology	ML108	780.14	Musical instruments—Switzerland	ML520	784.19494
Music—Theory	MT6-7	781	Musical instruments—United States	ML476	784.1973
Music, Origin of	ML3800	780.9	Musical instruments—West Indies	ML480	784.19729
Music and mythology	ML3849	780.0398	Musical instruments, Ancient	ML162-169	784.1901
Music appreciation	MT90-145	781.17	Musical instruments, Electronic	MT724	786.707
Music box	ML1065-1066	786.6509	Musical instruments (Mechanical)	MT700	786.607
Music festivals	ML35-38	780.79	Musical intervals and scales	ML3809	781.246
Music-halls (Variety-theaters, cabarets, etc.)	PN1960-1969	792.7	Musical notation	MT35	780.148
Music in churches	ML3001	782.3209	Musical pitch	ML3807-3809	781.232
Music in prisons	ML3920	780.0365	Musical shorthand	MT35	780.1407
Music in the army	UH40-45	781.599	Musical temperament	ML3809	784.1928
Music recorder	ML1055	788.3609	Musicals	M1500-1508	782.14
Music therapy	ML3919-3920	615.85154			
Musical Meter and rhythm	ML3850	781.22(4/6)			
Musical accompaniment	MT239	786.214707			
Musical accompaniment	MT190	786.14707			
Musical accompaniment	MT68	781.4707			
Musical dictation	MT35	780.14			
Musical films	PN1995.9.M86	791.43657			
Musical instruments	ML459-1093	784.1909			
Musical instruments	MT170-805	784.1907			
Musical instruments—Catalogs, Manufacturers'	ML155	784.190294			
Musical instruments—[By region or country]	ML475-1354	784.19(4-9)			
Musical instruments—Africa	ML544	784.196			
Musical instruments—Asia	ML525-541	784.195			
Musical instruments—Austria	ML491	784.19436			
Musical instruments—Belgium	ML496	784.19493			
Musical instruments—Canada	ML478	784.1971			

Subject Heading	LC	Dewey
Musicals—History and criticism	ML1700-1751	782.1409
Musicians	ML385-403	780.92
Musicians—Autographs	ML93-98	780.262
Musicians—Salaries, etc.	ML3795	331.28178
Musico-callisthenics	GV464	613.714
Musicology	ML	780.72
Muskogean Indians	E99.M95	973.04973
Muskogean languages	PM1971-1974	497.3
Muslim converts	BP170.5	297.574
Muslim converts from Christianity	BP170.5	297.574
Muslim pilgrims and pilgrimages	BP187	297.35
Muslim pilgrims and pilgrimages—Saudi Arabia—Mecca	BP187.3	297.352
Muslim saints	BP189.33	297.4092
Muslim teachers	LC905.T42	371.100882971
Muslim women	HQ1170	305.486971
Muslims, Black	BP62.N4	297.87
Mussel fisheries	SH371-374.52	639.42
Mussels	SH372.5-.52	639.42
Mustache	GT2318	391.5
Mustard gas	RA1247.M8	615.91
Mustard gas	UG447.5.M8	358.34
Mustard seed (Parable)	BT378.M8	226.8
Mutagens	QH465-.5	576.549
Mutation (Biology)	QH460-468	576.549
Mutilation	GN419.2	391.65
Mutiny	UB787	355.1334
Mutiny	VB860-867	359.1334
Mutual funds	HG4530	332.6327
Mutual security program, 1951-	UA12	355.031
Mutualism (Biology)	QH548.3	577.852
Mycobacterial diseases	RC116.M8	616.92
Mycoses	RC117	616.969
Myocardial depressants	RM347	615.716
Myocardial infarction	RC685.I6	616.1237
Myocarditis	RC685.M92	616.124
Myocardium	QP113.2	612.17
Myocardium	QM181	611.12
Myocardium—Diseases	RC685.M9	616.124
Mysteries and miracle-plays	PN1761	809.2527
Mysteries of the Rosary	BT303	242.74
Mysticism	B828	149.3
Mysticism	BV5070-5095	248.22
Mysticism	BL625	291.422
Mysticism	B728	189.5
Mysticism in literature	PN49	808.804291
Mysticism—Hinduism	BL1215.M9	294.5422
Mysticism—Islam	BP189	297.4
Mysticism—Jainism	BL1378.8	294.4422
Mystics	BV5095	248.22
Myth in literature	PN56.M94	808.8015
Myth in the Bible	BS520.5	220.68
Myth in the Old Testament	BS1183	221.68
Mythology	BL300-325	291.13
Mythology, Buddhist	BQ5741-5755	294.333
Mythology, Classical	BL700-820	292.13

Subject Heading	LC	Dewey
Mythology, European	BL689-980	291.13094
Mythology, Indic	BL2000-2016	294
Mythology, Oriental	BL1000-2370	299.5
Mythology, Polynesian	BL2620.P6	299.924
Mythology in literature	PN56.M95	808.8037
N stars	QB843.N12	523.88
Naga languages	PL3881-3884	495.4
Nahuas	F1219.73-.75	972.00497452
Nahuatl Language	PM4061-4069	497.452
Nails (Anatomy)	QM488	611.78
Nails (Anatomy)	QL942	573.59
Nails, Ingrowing	RD563	616.547
Naktong River (Korea), Battle of, 1950	DS918.2	951.904242
Nama langue	PL8541	496.1
Names, Personal	CS2300-3090	929.4
Names, Personal—Islamic	CS2970	929.42971
Names, Personal—Jewish	CS3010	929.4296
Names, Personal—[By region or country]	CS2395-3090	929.409(4-9)
Namibia—Census	HA4708	316.881
Namibia—Civilization	DT1552	968.81
Namibia—Description and travel	DT1532-1536	916.88104
Namibia—Gazetteers	DT1514	916.881003
Namibia—History	DT1564-1648	968.81
Namibia—History—To 1884	DT1587-1601	968.8101
Namibia—History—1884-1915	DT1603-1622	968.8102
Namibia—History—Herero Revolt, 1904-1907	DT1618	968.8103
Namibia—History—1915-1946	DT1625-1636	968.8103
Namibia—History—1946-1990	DT1638-1648	968.8103
Namibia—History—1990-	DT1648	968.8104
Namibia—Maps	G8620-8624	912.6881
Nanotechnology	T174.7	620.5
Naples (Kingdom)—History	DG845.8-851	945.73
Narcissism	RC553.N36	616.8585
Narcolepsy	RC549	616.8498
Narcotherapy	RC489.N3	616.8918
Narcotic habit	HV5800-5840	362.293
Narcotic habit	RC566	616.8632
Narcotics	GT3010	394.14
Narcotics	RM328	615.7822
Narration (Rhetoric)	PE1425	820.8023
Narrative poetry	PN6110.N17	808.813
Narrow gap semiconductors	QC611.8.N35	537.6223
Nasopharynx	QM505	611.21
Nasoscopy	RF345	616.21207545
Natal (South Africa)—Maps	G8530-8533	912.684
National characteristics	CB195-197	305.8
National music	M1627-1853	781.599
National music—History and criticism	ML3545	781.59909
National parks and reserves	SB481-484	363.68
National parks and reserves—United States	E160	333.780973
National socialism	DD253-256.5	943.086
Nationalism	JC311-314	320.54

Subject Heading	LC	Dewey
Native element minerals	QE389.1	549.2
Native language and education	LC201.5-.7	370.117
Native plant gardening	SB439-.26	635.951
Natural childbirth	RG661-662	618.45
Natural family planning	RG136.5	613.9434
Natural foods	TX369	641.302
Natural gas	TN880-884	622.3385
Natural gas	TP350	665.7
Natural gas pipelines	TN880.5	665.744
Natural history	QH	508
Natural history—Dictionaries	QH13	508.03
Natural history—Periodicals	QH1-7	508.06
Natural history—Pictorial works	QH46	508.0222
Natural history—Study and teaching	QH51-58	508.071
Natural history—Terminology	QH83	508.014
Natural history—[By region or country]	QH101-199	578.09(4-9)
Natural history—Africa	QH194-195	578.096
Natural history—Asia	QH179-193	578.095
Natural history—Australia	QH197	578.0994
Natural history—Canada	QH106-.2	578.0971
Natural history—Central America	QH108	578.09728
Natural history—Europe	QH135-178	578.094
Natural history—Mexico	QH107	578.0972
Natural history—South America	QH111-130	578.098
Natural history—United States	QH104-105	578.0973
Natural history—West Indies	QH109	578.09729
Natural history illustration	QH46.5	508.022
Natural history museums	QH70	508.074
Natural immunity	QR185.2	571.96
Natural landscaping	SB439-.26	719
Natural language processing (Computer science)	QA76.9.N38	006.35
Natural pesticides	SB951.145.N37	632.95
Natural products in agriculture	S587.45	631.86
Natural resources—Law and legislation	K3478-3486	346.044
Natural resources—Law and legislation—England	KD1035	346.42046
Natural selection	QH375	576.82
Natural theology	BL175-190	210
Naturalism	B828.2	146
Naturalism in literature	PN56.R3	808.8012
Naturalism in literature	PN601	808.8012
Naturalists	QH26-35	508.092
Nature (Aesthetics)	BH301.N3	700.46
Nature conservation	QH75-77	333.7816
Nature in literature	PN48	808.8036
Nature in the Bible	BS660-667	220.85
Nature photography	TR721-733	778.93
Nature study	QH51-58	508.071

Subject Heading	LC	Dewey
Nature worship	BL435-457	291.212
Naturopaths	RZ440	615.535092
Naturopathy	RZ433-445	615.535
Nautical alamancs	QB8	528
Nautical astronomy	VK549-587	527
Nautical charts	G1059-1061	912.1962
Nautical instruments	VK573-587	623.89(2-3)
Nautical training-schools	VK525-529	623.880971
Navajo Indians	E99.N3	973.04972
Navajo language	PM2006-2009	497.2
Naval architecture—Study and teaching	VM165-276	623.81071
Naval art and science	V	359
Naval art and science	VB	359.6
Naval art and science—Congresses	V7	359.006
Naval art and science—Dictionaries	V23-24	359.003
Naval art and science—History	V25-55	359.009
Naval art and science—Periodicals	V1-5	359.005
Naval art and science—[By region or country]	VB21-124	359.609(4-9)
Naval art and science—Africa	VB115-119	359.6096
Naval art and science—Argentina	VB36-37	359.60982
Naval art and science—Asia	VB99-113	359.6095
Naval art and science—Australia	VB121-122	359.60994
Naval art and science—Canada	VB26-27	359.60971
Naval art and science—Central America	VB30-31	359.609728
Naval art and science—Chile	VB43-44	359.60983
Naval art and science—China	VB101-102	359.60951
Naval art and science—Colombia	VB45-46	359.609861
Naval art and science—Europe	VB55-96	359.6094
Naval art and science—France	VB71-72	359.60944
Naval art and science—Germany	VB73-74.5	359.60943
Naval art and science—Great Britain	VB57-64	359.60941
Naval art and science—Greece	VB75-76	359.609495
Naval art and science—Italy	VB79-80	359.60945
Naval art and science—Japan	VB105-106	359.60952
Naval art and science—Mexico	VB28-29	359.60972
Naval art and science—Pacific Islands	VB123-124	359.6099(5-6)
Naval art and science—Portugal	VB83-84	359.609469

| --- | --- | --- | --- | --- | --- |
Naval art and science—Russia	VB85-86	359.60947	Naval research	V390-395	359.07
Naval art and science—South America	VB34-54	359.6098	Naval reserves	VA45	359.37
			Naval strategy	V160-165	359.42
Naval art and science—Spain	VB87-88	359.60946	Naval tactics	V167-178	359.42
Naval art and science—Terminology	V23-24	359.003	Navies	VA37-42	359
			Navies—Officers	VB310-315	359.332
Naval art and science—United States	VB23-25	359.60973	Navies, Cost of	VA20-25	359.6229
Naval art and science—West Indies	VB32-33	359.609729	Navigation—Safety measures	VK200	623.890289
Naval auxiliary vessels	V865	359.985	Navigation—Study and teaching	VK401-529	623.89071
Naval aviation	VG90-95	359.94	Navigation—Tables	VK563-567	527.021
Naval battles	D27	359.4	Navigation (Aeronautics)	TL586-589	629.13251
Naval biography	V61-65	359.0092	Navigation (Astronautics)	TL1065-1080	629.453
Naval ceremonies, honors, and salutes	V310	359.17	Navy Cross (Medal)	VB333	355.13420973
Naval discipline	VB840-845	343.014	Navy-yards and naval stations	V230	359.7
Naval districts	VA	359	Navy-yards and naval stations—Great Britain	VA460	359.370941
Naval education	V400-695	359.0071			
Naval education—[By region or country]	V411-695	359.00710(4-9)	Navy-yards and naval stations—United States	VA66	359.70973
Naval education—Africa	V660-680	359.007106	Neanderthals	GN285	569.9
Naval education—Asia	V625-650	359.007105	Near-death experiences	BF1045.N4	133.9013
Naval education—Australia	V690-694	359.0071094	Nebraska—Gazetteers	F664	917.82003
Naval education—Canada	V440-444	359.0071071	Nebraska—History	F661-675	978.2
Naval education—Central America	V450-453	359.00710728	Nebraska—Maps	G4190-4194	912.782
			Nebraska—National Guard	UA310-319	355.3709782
Naval education—China	V630-634	359.0071051	Nebraska—Periodicals	F661	978.2005
Naval education—Confederate States of America	V438	973.0071075	Necessity (Philosophy)	BD417	123.7
			Necessity, Fort, Battle of, 1754	E199	973.26
Naval education—Europe	V500-623	359.007104	Neck	QM535	611.93
Naval education—Germany	V570-574.54	359.0071043	Necklaces	GT2260	391.7
Naval education—Great Britain	V510-530	359.0071041	Necks (Geology)	QE611-.5	551.88
			Neckties	GT2120	391.44
Naval education—India	V635-639	359.0071054	Neckties	TT616	687.19
Naval education—Iran	V645-649	359.0071055	Needlework	NK8800-9505.5	746.4
Naval education—Japan	V640-644	359.0071052	Needlework	TT700-845	746.4
Naval education—Mexico	V445-449	359.0071072	Negativism	BF698.35.N44	155.232
Naval education—South America	V465-496	359.007108	Negotiable instruments	K1054-1065	346.096
			Negotiable instruments—Canada	KE980-986	346.71096
Naval education—United States	V411-437	359.0071073	Negotiable instruments—England	KD1695-1699	346.42096
Naval education—West Indies	V455-458	359.00710729			
			Negotiable instruments—United States	KF956-962	346.73096
Naval history	D27	359.009	Negotiation	BF637.N4	158.5
Naval history, Ancient	D95	359.00901	Negotiation in business	HD58.6	658.4052
Naval history, Modern—20th century	D436	359.0094	Negritos	GN664.N3	305.8096
			Neith (Egyptian deity)	BL2450.N45	299.31
Naval hygiene	VG470-475	359.345	Neo-Confucianism	B127.N4	181.112
Naval law	VB350-785	343.019	Neo-Scholasticism	B839	149.91
Naval maneuvers	V245	359.41	Neo-impressionism (Art)	N6465.N44	709.0345
Naval militia—Canada	VA402	359.370971	Neoclassicism (Architecture)	NA600	724.2
Naval museums	V13	359.0074	Neon	QD181.N5	546.752
Naval museums	VF6	359.82/623.8251 + (074)	Neon lamps	TK4383	621.3275
			Neon tubes	TK4383	621.3275
Naval offenses	VB850-880	359.1334	Neonatal emergencies	RJ253.5	618.9201
Naval prints	NE957-.3	769.437	Neonatal gastroenterology	RJ268.8	618.9201
Naval reconnaissance	V190	359.413	Neonatal hematology	RJ269.5-271	618.9215
			Neonatal infections	RJ275	618.929

Subject Heading	LC	Dewey	Subject Heading	LC	Dewey
Neonatal intensive care	RJ253.5	618.9201	Netherlands—Emigration and immigration	JV8150-8159	325.(2492/492)
Neonatology	RJ251-325	618.9201	Netherlands—Gazetteers	DJ14	913.63003/ 914.92003
Neoplatonism	B645	186.4			
Neoplatonism	B517	186.4	Netherlands—Gazetteers	DH14	913.63003/ 914.92003
Nepal—Census	HA4570.9	315.496			
Nepal—Civilization	DS493.7	954.96	Netherlands—History	DH95-207	936.3/949.2
Nepal—Description and travel	DS493.5-.53	915.49604	Netherlands—History	DJ95-292	936.3/949.2
			Netherlands—History, Military	DJ124	355.309492
Nepal—Economic conditions	HC425	330.95496			
Nepal—Gazetteers	DS493.3	915.496003	Netherlands—History, Military	DH113	355.309492
Nepal—History	DS494.4-495.592	954.96			
Nepal—History—To 1768	DS495	954.96	Netherlands—History, Naval	DJ130-138	359.309492
Nepal—History— 1768-1951	DS495.3	954.96			
			Netherlands—History, Naval	DH121	359.309492
Nepal—Maps	G7760-7764	912.5496			
Nepal—Maps	G2295-2299	912.5496	Netherlands—History— To 1384	DJ151-152	936.3/949.201
Nepalese War, 1814-1816	DS485.N4	954.0313			
Nepali language	PK2595-2599	491.495	Netherlands—History— To 1384	DH141-162	936.3/949.201
Nephrology	RC902	616.61			
Neptune (Planet)	QB691	523.481	Netherlands—History— House of Burgundy, 1384-1477	DH171-177	949.201
Neptune (Planet)	QB388	523.481			
Neptune (Planet)—Satellites	QB407	523.9881			
Nerve tissue	QM575	611.0188	Netherlands—History— House of Habsburg, 1477-1556	DH179-184	949.202
Nerves	QP361-375.5	612.81			
Nerves	QM471	611.83			
Nerves	QL939	573.85	Netherlands—History— House of Habsburg, 1477-1556	DJ151-152	949.202
Nervous system	QP351-430	612.81			
Nervous system	QM451-471	611.8			
Nervous system	QL921-939	573.8	Netherlands—History— Charles V, 1506-1555	DH182	949.202
Nervous system— Abnormalities	RJ290-.5	618.928043			
			Netherlands—History— Charles V, 1506-1555	DJ151-152	949.202
Nervous system—Diseases	RC346-429	616.8(1-4)			
Nervous system— Diseases—Eclectic treatment	RV241-246	616.806	Netherlands—Wars of Independence, 1556-1648	DH185-207	949.20(2-3)
Nervous system— Diseases— Homeopathic treatment	RX281-301	616.806	Netherlands—History— Twelve Years' Truce, 1609-1621	DJ170	949.203
Nervous system—Surgery	RD592.5-596	617.48059	Netherlands—History— Twelve Years' Truce, 1609-1621	DH201	949.203
Nervous system—Tumors	RD663	616.9948			
Nervous system—Wounds and injuries	RD592.5-596	617.48044			
			Netherlands—History— 1648-1795	DJ180-209	949.204
Nestorian Church	BX150-159	281.8			
Nestorians	BT1440	281.8	Netherlands—History— Batavian Republic, 1795-1806	DJ211	949.205
Netherlands	DH	936.3/949.2			
Netherlands	DJ	936.3/949.2			
Netherlands Antilles— Census	HA917-.78	317.2986	Netherlands—History— 1815-1830	DJ241	949.205
Netherlands—Biography	DH103	920.0363/ 920.0492	Netherlands—History— 1830-1849	DJ241-251	949.206
Netherlands—Biography	DJ103-106	920.0363/ 920.0492	Netherlands—History— William II, 1840-1849	DJ251	949.206
Netherlands—Census	HA1381-1390	314.92	Netherlands—History— William III, 1849-1890	DJ261	949.206
Netherlands—Civilization	DH71	936.3/949.2			
Netherlands—Civilization	DJ71	936.3/949.2	Netherlands—History— Wilhelmina, 1898-1948	DJ281-287	949.20(6-71)
Netherlands—Description and travel	DJ33-41	913.6304/ 914.9204			
			Netherlands—History— German occupation, 1940-1945	DJ287	949.2071
Netherlands—Description and travel	DH31-40	913.6304/ 914.9204			
Netherlands—Economic conditions	HC321-329.5	330.9492			

Subject Heading	LC	Dewey	Subject Heading	LC	Dewey
Netherlands—History— 1945-	DJ288-292	949.207(1-3)	New England—Gazetteers	F2	917.4003
			New England—History	F1-15	974
Netherlands—History— Juliana, 1948-1980	DJ288-289	949.2072	New England—History— Colonial period, ca. 1600-1775	F7-.75	974.0(1-2)
Netherlands—History— Beatrix, 1980-	DJ290-292	949.2073	New England—History— French and Indian War, 1755-1763	E199	974.02
Netherlands—Manufactures	TS77-78	670.9492			
Netherlands—Maps	G6000-6004	912.492	New England—History— 1775-1865	F8	974.0(2-3)
Netherlands—Periodicals	DJ1	936.3005/ 949.2005			
			New England—History— Revolution, 1775-1783	F8	974.0(2-3)
Netherlands—Periodicals	DH1	936.3005/ 949.2005	New England—History— War of 1812	E357-359	974.03
Netherlands—Politics and government	JN5701-5999	320.9492	New England—Maps	G3720-3784	912.74
Network analysis (Planning)	T57.85	658.4032	New England—Periodicals	F1	974.005
Neuengamme (Hamburg, Germany: Concentration camp)	D805.G3	940.5318	New Guinea	DU739-747	995
			New Guinea—Maps	G8140-8142	912.95
			New Hampshire— Gazetteers	F32	917.42003
Neural computers	QA76.87	006.32			
Neural networks (Computer science)	QA76.87	006.32	New Hampshire—History	F31-45	974.2
			New Hampshire—History— Colonial period, ca. 1600-1775	F37	974.20(1-2)
Neural stimulation	RC350.N48	616.806			
Neurasthenia	RC552.N5	616.8528			
Neuritis	RC416	616.87	New Hampshire—History— King George's War, 1744-1748	E198	974.202
Neuroblastoma	RC280.N4	616.9948			
Neurochemistry	QP356.3	612.8042			
Neurocutaneous disorders	RL701-751	616.5	New Hampshire—History— 1775-1865	F38	974.203
Neurologic examination	RC348-349	616.804075			
Neurological intensive care	RC350.N49	616.8028	New Hampshire—History— Revolution, 1775-1783	E263.N4	974.20(2-3)
Neurological nursing	RC350.5	610.7368			
Neurological nursing	RD596	610.7368	New Hampshire—History— Civil War, 1861-1865	E520	974.203
Neurology	RC346-429	616.8(1-4)			
Neuromuscular blocking agents	RM312	615.773	New Hampshire—History— 1951-	F40	974.2043
Neuroophthalmology	RE725-780	617.732	New Hampshire—Maps	G3740-3744	912.742
Neuropharmacology	RM315-334	615.78	New Hampshire—National Guard	UA330-339	355.3709742
Neuropsychopharmacology	RM315-334	615.78			
Neuroses	RC530-552	616.852	New Hampshire— Periodicals	F31	974.2005
Neutrality, Armed	D295	940.253			
Neutrinos	QC793.5.N42- .N429	539.7215	New Jersey—Gazetteers	F132	917.49003
			New Jersey—History	F131-145	974.9
Neutron bomb	UG1282.N48	358.428251	New Jersey—History— Colonial period, ca. 1600-1775	F137	974.90(1-2)
Neutron counters	QC787.C6	539.77			
Neutron sources	QC793.5.N4629	539.7213			
Neutron stars	QB843.N4	523.8874	New Jersey—History— 1775-1865	F138	974.90(2-3)
Neutrons	QC793.5.N462- .N4622	539.7213			
			New Jersey—History— Revolution, 1775-1783	E263.N5	974.90(2-3)
Nevada	F836-850	979.3			
Nevada—Gazetteers	F839	917.93003	New Jersey—History— War of 1812	F138	974.903
Nevada—Maps	G4350-4354	912.793			
Nevada—National Guard	UA320-329	355.3709793	New Jersey—History— Civil War, 1861-1865	E521	974.903
Nevada—Periodicals	F836	979.3005			
New Age movement	BP605.N48	299.93	New Jersey—History— 1865-	F139-140.22	974.904
New Brunswick—Gazetteers	F1041.4	917.151003			
New Brunswick—Maps	G3430-3434	912.7151	New Jersey—Maps	G3810-3814	912.749
New Brunswick—Periodicals	F1041	971.51005	New Jersey—National Guard	UA340-349	355.3709749
New Caledonia	DU720	995.97	New Jersey—Periodicals	F131	974.9005
New Caledonia—Census	HA4015	319.597	New Jerusalem Church	BX8701-8749	289.4
New Caledonia—Maps	G9340-9344	912.9597	New Jerusalem Church— Biography	BX8747-8749	289.4092
New Caledonian literature (French)	PQ3998.5.N	840			

Subject Heading	LC	Dewey	Subject Heading	LC	Dewey
New Jerusalem Church—Congresses	BX8705	289.406	New Zealand prose literature	PR9637.25-.92	828.08
New Jerusalem Church—Education	BX8714	268.894	New Zealand prose literature	PR9632.2-.6	828.08
New Jerusalem Church—Government	BX8737	262.094	New Zealand—Biography	CT2880-2888	920.0993
			New Zealand—Census	HA3171-3190	319.3
New Jerusalem Church—History	BX8715-8719	289.409	New Zealand—Civilization	DU418	993
New Jerusalem Church—Periodicals	BX8701	289.405	New Zealand—Description and travel	DU409-413	919.304
New Jerusalem Church—Sermons	BX8724	252.094	New Zealand—Economic conditions	HC661-670	330.993
New Mexico	F791-805	978.9	New Zealand—Emigration and immigration	JV9260-9269	325.(293/93)
New Mexico—Gazetteers	F794	917.89003	New Zealand—Gazetteers	DU405	919.3003
New Mexico—History—To 1848	F799-800	978.90(1-3)	New Zealand—Genealogy	CS2170-2179	929.393
New Mexico—History—1848-	F801-.2	978.90(4-5)	New Zealand—History	DU419-422	993
New Mexico—History—Civil War, 1861-1865	E571	978.904	New Zealand—History—To 1840	DU420.12-.14	993.01
New Mexico—History—Civil War, 1861-1865	E522	978.904	New Zealand—History—1840-1876	DU420.16-.18	993.02(1-2)
New Mexico—Maps	G4320-4324	912.789	New Zealand—History—Maori War, 1845-1847	DU420.16	993.021
New Mexico—National Guard	UA350-359	355.3709789	New Zealand—History—Taranaki War, 1860-1861	DU420.22-.34	993.022
New Mexico—Periodicals	F791	978.9005			
New Orleans (La.)	F379.N5	976.335	New Zealand—History—1876-1918	DU420.22-.24	993.0(23-31)
New Orleans (La.), Battle of, 1815	E356.N5	973.5239	New Zealand—History—1918-1945	DU420.26-.28	993.032
New Thought	BF638-648	299.93	New Zealand—History—1945-	DU420.32-.34	993.03(5-7)
New Year	GT4905-4908	394.2614			
New Year sermons	BV4282	252.68	New Zealand—Manufactures	TS122.5-.6	670.993
New York (N.Y.)	F128-.9	974.71	New Zealand—Maps	G9080-9084	912.93
New York (State)—Gazetteers	F117	917.47003	New Zealand—Maps	G2795-2799	912.93
			New towns	HT169.55-.57	307.768
New York (State)—History	F116-130	974.7	New towns	NA9053.N	711.45
New York (State)—History—Colonial period, ca. 1660-1775	F122-.1	974.70(1-2)	Newfoundland—Gazetteers	F1121.4	917.18003
			Newfoundland—History	F1121-1124	971.8
			Newfoundland—Maps	G3600-3604	912.718
New York (State)—History—King William's War, 1689-1697	E196	974.702	Newfoundland—Periodicals	F1121	971.8005
			Newsletters	PN4784.N5	070.175
New York (State)—History—Queen Anne's War, 1702-1713	E197	974.702	Newspapers	AN	070.172
			Newspapers—Indexes	AI21	016.07
			Nez Perce Indians	E99.N5	973.049741
New York (State)—History—French and Indian War, 1755-1763	F123	974.702	Nicaragua	F1521-1537	972.85
			Nicaragua—Census	HA831-840	317.285
New York (State)—History—1775-1865	F123	974.70(2-3)	Nicaragua—Civilization	F1523.8	972.85
			Nicaragua—Description and travel	F1524-.3	917.28504
New York (State)—History—Revolution, 1775-1783	E263.N6	974.70(2-3)	Nicaragua—Emigration and immigration	JV7426	325.(27285/7285)
New York (State)—History—War of 1812	E359.5.N6	974.703	Nicaragua—Gazetteers	F1522	917.285003
New York (State)—History—1865-	F124-125	974.74	Nicaragua—History	F1525.5-1528.22	972.85
			Nicaragua—History—To 1838	F1526.25	972.850(1-42)
New York (State)—Maps	G3800-3804	912.747	Nicaragua—History—English Invasion, 1780-1781	F1526.25	972.8503
New York (State)—National Guard	UA360-369	355.3709747			
New York (State)—Periodicals	F116	974.7005	Nicaragua—History—1838-1909	F1526.27	972.850(44-51)

161

Subject Heading	LC	Dewey	Subject Heading	LC	Dewey
Nicaragua—History—Filibuster War, 1855-1860	F1526.27	972.85044	Nigeria—History—Civil War, 1967-1970	DT515.836	966.9052
Nicaragua—History—1909-1937	F1526.3	972.8505(1-2)	Nigeria—History—Coup d'etat, 1983	DT515.84	966.9053
Nicaragua—History—Revolution, 1909-1910	F1526.3	972.85051	Nigeria—Maps	G8840-8844	912.669
Nicaragua—History—Revolution of 1912	F1526.3	972.85051	Night fighter planes	UG1242.F5	358.4303
			Night flying	TL711.N5	629.1325214
Nicaragua—History—Revolution, 1926-1929	F1526.3	972.85051	Night photography	TR610	778.719
Nicaragua—History—1937-1979	F1527	972.85052	Night work	HD5113-.2	331.2574
			Nightmares	BF1099.N53	154.63
Nicaragua—History—San Carlos Barracks Attack, 1977	F1527	972.85052	Nihilism	HX914-917	149.8
			Nile, Battle of the, 1798	DC226.N5	940.27
Nicaragua—History—Uprising, 1978	F1527	972.85052	Nineteenth century	CB415-417	909.81
			Nineteenth century	D351-400	940.2(7-87)
Nicaragua—History—1979-1990	F1528	972.85053	Nitrates	TP237-238	661.65
			Nitrates	S651-.3	631.842
Nicaragua—History—Revolution, 1979	F1528	972.85052	Nitrates	TN911	622.364
			Nitrogen	QD181.N1	546.711
Nicaragua—History—1990-	F1528	972.85054	Nitrogen fertilizers	S651-.3	631.84
Nicaragua—Maps	G4850-4854	912.7285	Nitrogen in agriculture	S587.5.N5	631.84
Nicaragua—Periodicals	F1521	972.85005	Nitrogen in the body	QP535.N1	572.54
Nicaragua—Politics and government	JL1600-1619	320.97285	Niumi (Kingdom)	DT532.23	966.(3/51)
			No first use (Nuclear strategy)	U264	355.0217
Nicaraguan literature	PQ7510-7519.2	860	No-tillage	S604	631.5814
Nickel	TA480.N6	620.188	Noah's ark	BL325.D4	222.11
Nicknames	CT108	929.44	Noah's ark	BS658	222.1109505
Nicotine	TS2255	679.7	Nobility	HT647-653	305.5223
Nicotine	RC567	616.865	Nobility, Papal	CR5547-5577	262.13
Niger—Census	HA4724	316.626	Nobility—Social life and customs	GT5350-5490	390.23
Niger—Civilization	DT547.4	966.26			
Niger—Description and travel	DT547.27	916.62604	Nobility—Social life and customs	GT5010-5090	390.23
Niger—Economic conditions	HC1020	330.96626	Noise	BF205.N6	152.15
Niger—History	DT547.5-.83	966.26	Noise barriers	TD892	620.23
Niger—History—To 1960	DT547.65-.75	966.260(1-3)	Noise pollution	TD891-893.6	620.23
Niger—Maps	G8770-8774	912.6626	Noise—Physiological effect	QP82.2.N6	571.444
Niger-Congo languages	PL8026.N44	496.3	Noise—Psychological aspects	BF353.5.N65	152.15
Nigeria—Census	HA4731	316.69	Nomads	GN387	305.90691
Nigeria—Civilization	DT515.4	966.9	Nominations for office	JK2063-2075	324.273015
Nigeria—Description and travel	DT515.27	916.6904	Nominations for office	JF2085	324.5
			Nomography (Mathematics)	QA90	511.5
Nigeria—Economic conditions	HC1055	330.9669	Non-Verbal Ability Tests	BF432.5.N64	153.9324
			Non-destructive testing	TA417.2-.55	620.1127
Nigeria—Gazetteers	DT515.15	916.69003	Non-importation agreements, 1768-1769	E215.3	973.3112
Nigeria—History	DT515.53-.84	966.9			
Nigeria—History—To 1851	DT515.65-.67	966.901	Non-insulin-dependent diabetes	RC660-662.18	616.462
Nigeria—History—1851-1899	DT515.7-.72	966.90(1-3)	Nonarticular rheumatism	RC927.5.N65	616.723
Nigeria—History—1900-1960	DT515.7-.77	966.903	Nonclassical mathematical logic	QA9.4-.5	511.3
			Nonets	M900-986	785.19
Nigeria—History—1960-	DT515.8-.84	966.905	Nonferrous metals	TA479.3	620.18
Nigeria—History—Coup d'etat, 1966 (January 15)	DT515.832	966.9051	Nonferrous metals	TN758-799	669.(2-7)
			Nongraded schools	LB1029.N6	371.255
			Nonimpact printing	Z252.5.N46	686.233
			Nonionizing radiation	QP82.2.N64	571.45
Nigeria—History—Coup d'etat, 1966 (July 29)	DT515.832	966.9051	Nonlethal weapons	HV7936.E7	363.20284
			Nonlinear control theory	QA402.35	515.64
			Nonlinear functional analysis	QA321.5	515.7248

Subject Heading	LC	Dewey
Nonlinear optics	QC446.15-.3	535.2
Nonlinear programming	T57.8-.825	519.76
Nonlinear wave equations	QA927	532.593
Nonmetallic steel	TA478	620.18
Nonmetals	QD161-169	546.7
Nonparametric statistics	QA278.8	519.5
Nonprescription drug industry	HD9665-9675	338.476151
Nonprofit organizations— Law and legislation— England	KD2061-2062	346.42064
Nonprofit organizations— Law and legislation— United States	KF1388-1390	346.73064
Nonstandard mathematical analysis	QA299.82	515
Nontariff trade barriers	HF1430	382.9
Nonverbal communication (Psychology)	BF637.N66	153.69
Nonverbal communication in education	LB1033.5	370.14
Nonverbal intelligence tests	BF432.5.N65	153.9324
Nonwoven fabrics	TS1828	677.6
Noodles	TX809.N65	641.822
Norm-referenced tests	LB3060.32.N67	371.271
North America	E31-45	970
North America—Biography	E36	920.07
North America—Civilization	E40	970
North America—Description and travel	E41	917.04
North America—Gazetteers	E35	917.003
North America—History	E45-46	970
North America—Maps	G1105-1692	912.7
North America—Maps	G3300-4884	912.7
North America—Periodicals	E31	970.005
North Carolina	F251-265	975.6
North Carolina—Gazetteers	F252	917.56003
North Carolina—History— Colonial period, ca. 1600-1775	F257	975.60(1-2)
North Carolina—History— Regulator Insurrection, 1766-1771	F257	975.602
North Carolina—History— 1775-1865	F258	975.60(2-3)
North Carolina—History— Revolution, 1775-1783	E263.N8	975.70(2-3)
North Carolina—History— Civil War, 1861-1865	E573	975.603
North Carolina—History— Civil War, 1861-1865	E524	975.603
North Carolina—History— 1865-	F259-260.42	975.604
North Carolina—Maps	G3900-3904	912.756
North Carolina—National Guard	UA370-379	355.3709756
North Carolina—Periodicals	F251	975.6005
North Dakota	F631-645	978.4
North Dakota—Gazetteers	F634	917.84003
North Dakota—Maps	G4170-4174	912.784
North Dakota—National Guard	UA380-389	355.3709784
North Dakota—Periodicals	F631	978.4005
Northern boundry of the United States	F551	977
Northern Hemisphere	G912-916	910.021813
Northern Hemisphere— Maps	G3210-3212	912.19813
Northern Hemisphere— Maps	G1050	912.19813
Northern Ireland—Census	HA1141-1150	314.16
Northern Ireland— Constitutional law	KDE410-462	342.416
Northern Ireland—Maps	G5790-5794	912.416
Northern Ireland—Politics and government	JN1572	320.9416
Northern War, 1700-1721	DL733-743	947.05
Northwest, Canadian	F1060-.97	971.92
Northwest, Old	F476-485	977
Northwest Passage	G640-665	910.0216327
Northwest Territories— Maps	G3530-3564	912.7192
Norway—Biography	DL444	920.0363/ 920.0481
Norway—Census	HA1501-1520	314.81
Norway—Civilization	DL431-433	936.3/948.1
Norway—Description and travel	DL415-419.2	913.6304/ 914.8104
Norway—Economic conditions	HC361-370	330.9481
Norway—Emigration and immigration	JV8210-8219	325.(2481/481)
Norway—Gazetteers	DL405	913.63003/ 914.81003
Norway—Historiography	DL445	936.30072/ 948.10072
Norway—History	DL401-596	936.3/948.1
Norway—History—To 1030	DL460-478	936.3/948.101
Norway—History— 1030-1397	DL480-502	948.101
Norway—History— 1397-1814	DL485-502	948.102
Norway—History— Christian IV, 1588-1648	DL490	948.102
Norway—History—Scottish Expedition, 1612	DL490	948.102
Norway—History— Hannibal's War, 1644-1645	DL490	948.102
Norway—History— Frederick III, 1648-1670	DL490	948.102
Norway—History— Christian V, 1670-1699	DL495-.8	948.102
Norway—History—War of 1807-1814	DL499	948.102
Norway—History— 1814-1905	DL503-526	948.103
Norway—History—Christian Frederick, 1814	DL500-502	948.10(2-3)

Subject Heading	LC	Dewey	Subject Heading	LC	Dewey
Norway—History—1905-1940	DL530-532	948.1041	Nuclear counters	QC787.C6	539.77
			Nuclear crisis stabililty	U263	355.0217
Norway—History—Separation from Sweden, 1905	DL525	948.1041	Nuclear energy	TK9001-9401	621.48
			Nuclear energy	QC791.9-792.8	539.7
			Nuclear engineering	TK9001-9401	621.48
Norway—History—German Occupation, 1940-1945	DL532	948.1041	Nuclear engineering—Periodicals	TK9001	621.4805
Norway—History—1945-	DL533	948.104(5-9)	Nuclear engineering—Safety measures	TK9152-.16	621.480289
Norway—Manufactures	TS81-82	670.9481			
Norway—Maps	G6940-6944	912.481	Nuclear fission	QC789.7-790.8	539.762
Norway—Maps	G2065-2069	912.481	Nuclear fuel rods	TK9207	621.4833
Norway—Periodicals	DL401-403	936.3005/ 948.1005	Nuclear fuels	TK9360	621.4833
			Nuclear fusion	QC790.95-791.8	539.764
Norway—Politics and government	JN7401-7695	320.9481	Nuclear industry	HD9698-.5	333.7924
			Nuclear magnetic resonance	QC762	538.362
Norwegian drama	PT8699-8718	839.822008	Nuclear medicine	R895-920	616.07575
Norwegian drama	PT8500-8534	839.822009	Nuclear physics	QC770-798	539.7
Norwegian fiction	PT8555-8567	839.823009	Nuclear power plants	TK1078	621.483
Norwegian fiction	PT8720-8722	839.823008	Nuclear power plants—Instruments	TK9178-9183	621.480284
Norwegian language	PD2571-2699	439.82			
Norwegian language—Dialects	PD2696-2699	439.827	Nuclear propulsion	TK9230	621.485
			Nuclear reactors	QC786.4-786.8	621.483
Norwegian language—Dictionaries	PD2688-2695	439.823	Nuclear reactors	TK9202-9230	621.483
			Nuclear reactors—Computer programs	QC783.3-.4	621.4830285
Norwegian language—Etymology	PD2683-2684	439.822			
			Nuclear reactors—Cooling	TK9212	621.48336
Norwegian language—Grammar	PD2619-2673	439.825	Nuclear rockets	TL783.5	629.4753
			Nuclear saline water conversion plants	TD479.6	628.16723
Norwegian language—Lexicography	PD2687-2695	439.823028			
			Nuclear ships	VM317	623.8728
Norwegian language—Slang	PD2699	439.827	Nuclear ships	VM774-777	623.8728
Norwegian language—Study and teaching	PD2611-2612	439.82071	Nuclear structure	QC793.3.S8	539.74
			Nuclear submarines	V857.5	359.93834
Norwegian literature	PT8301-9155	839.82	Nuclear warfare	U263	355.0217
Norwegian literature—Study and teaching	PT8340-8344	839.82071	Nuclear weapons	U264	355.825119
			Nucleic acids	QP620-625	572.8
Norwegian literature (Nynorsk)	PT9000-9094	839.83	Nucleotide sequence	QP625.N89	572.8633
			Nude in art	N7572	704.9421
Norwegian philology	PD2501-2999	439.82	Nudism	GV450	613.194
Norwegian poetry	PT8675-8695	839.821008	Nudist camps	GV451-.4	613.19406
Norwegian poetry	PT8460-8490	839.821009	Nullification	E384.3	973.561
Norwegian prose literature	PT8719-8722	839.82808	Number concept	QA141.15	512.7
Norwegian prose literature	PT8540-8567	839.82808	Number theory	QA241-247.5	512.7
Nose	QP458	612.86	Numbers, Divisibility of	QA242	512.72
Nose—Diseases	RF341-437	616.212	Numbers, Prime	QA246	512.72
Nose—Diseases—Eclectic treatment	RV341-347	617.52306	Numeration	QA141-.8	513.5
			Numerical analysis	QA297-299.4	515
Nose—Diseases—Homeopathic treatment	RX451	617.52306	Numerical calculations	QA297	519.4
			Numerical differentiation	QA355	515.623
Note-taking	LB2395	378.170281	Numerical functions	QA246	512
Nothing (Philosophy)	BD398	111.5	Numerical integration	QA299.3-.4	515.624
Notices to mariners	VK798	623.8922	Numerical weather forecasting	QC996	551.634
Nova Scotia—Gazetteers	F1036.4	917.16003			
Nova Scotia—History	F1036-1040	971.6	Numerology	BF1623.P9	133.335
Nova Scotia—Maps	G3420-3424	912.716	Numismatics	CJ	737
Nova Scotia—Periodicals	F1036	971.6005	Nunamiut Eskimos	E99.E7	973.04971
Nowcasting (Meteorology)	QC997.75	551.6362	Nurse and patient	RT86.3	610.730699
Nozzles	TC173	532.52	Nurse and physician	RT86.4	610.730699
Nubian languages	PL8571-8574	496.5	Nurse practitioners	RT82.8	610.730692
Nuclear astrophysics	QB463-464.2	523.019	Nurseries (Horticulture)	SB118.48-.75	635
Nuclear chemistry	QD601-608	541.38	Nursery rhymes	PZ8.3	398.8

Subject Heading	LC	Dewey
Nursery rhymes	PN6110.C4	398.8
Nurses	RT34-37	610.73092
Nurses' aides	RT84	610.730698
Nurses—Directories	RT25	610.73025
Nursing	RT	610.73
Nursing—Congresses	RT3	610.7306
Nursing—Data processing	RT50.5	610.730285
Nursing—History	RT31	610.7309
Nursing—Philosophy	RT84.5	610.7301
Nursing—Practice	RT86.7-.75	610.73069
Nursing—Psychological aspects	RT86	610.73019
Nursing—Research	RT81.5	610.73072
Nursing—Societies, etc.	RT1	610.7306
Nursing—Study and teaching	RT71-81	610.73071
Nursing—[By region or country]	RT4-17	610.7309(4-9)
Nursing assessment	RT48-.6	610.73069
Nursing diagnosis	RT48.6	610.73069
Nursing ethics	RT85	174.2
Nursing homes	RA997-999	362.16
Nursing schools	RT71-81	610.730711
Nutation	QB165	521.9
Nutrition	RA784	613.2
Nutrition	TX341-641	363.8
Nutrition	QP141-185.3	612.3
Nutrition disorders	RC620-627	616.39
Nutrition disorders	RA645.N87	614.5939
Nutrition disorders in animals	SF851-855	636.089639
Nutrition—Study and teaching	TX364-365	363.8071
Nutritionally induced diseases	RC622	616.39
Nutritionally induced diseases	RA645.N87	614.5939
Nuts	SB401	634.5
O'Donnell Camp (Philippines : Concentration camp)	D805.P5	940.5317599
Oaths	GT3085	394
Ob-Ugric languages	PH1251-1254	494.51
Obesity	RC628-.5	616.398
Object constancy (Psychoanalysis)	RC489.024	616.8917
Object relations (Psychoanalysis)	RC489.025	616.8917
Object-oriented programming (Computer science)	QA76.64	005.117
Objective tests	LB3060.32.035	371.271
Objectivity	BD220	121.4
Obligations (Law)	K830-968	346.02
Oboe	MT360-378	788.5207
Oboe music	M65-69	788.52
Obsessive-compulsive disorders	RC533	616.85227
Obstacles (Military science)	UG375	358.22
Obstetrical emergencies	RG571-591	618.3025
Obstetrical extraction	RG741	618.82
Obstetrical forceps	RG739	618.20284

Subject Heading	LC	Dewey
Obstetricians	RG509-510	618.2092
Obstetricians—Directories	RG504-505	618.20025
Obstetrics	RG	618.2
Obstetrics—Apparatus and instruments	RG545	618.200284
Obstetrics—Case studies	RG529	618.209
Obstetrics—History	RG511-518	618.209
Obstetrics—Research	RG155	618.20072
Obstetrics—Surgery	RG725-791	618.8
Obstetrics, Eclectic	RV361-365	618.206
Obstetrics, Homeopathic	RX476	618.206
Occasional sermons	BV4254.2	252
Occasional services	BV199	265.9
Occcupational training	HD5715-.5	370.113
Occluded fronts (Meteorology)	QC880.4.F7	551.5512
Occultism	BF1404-2050	133
Occultism—Congresses	BF1404	133.06
Occultism—Dictionaries	BF1407	133.03
Occultism—Directories	BF1409	133.025
Occultism—History	BF1421-1429	133.09
Occultism—[By region or country]	BF1434	133.09(4-9)
Occultists	BF1408-.2	133.092
Occupational dermatitis	RL241	616.5
Occupational health services	RC968-969	613.62
Occupational neuroses	RC552.03	616.8521
Occupational therapy	RM735-.7	615.8515
Occupational therapy	RC487	616.89165
Occupations—Folklore	GR890-910	398.355
Occupations—Statistics	HB2581-2787	331.7
Ocean bottom	GC87-.6	551.46083
Ocean circulation	GC228.5-.6	551.47
Ocean currents	GC229-299	551.4701
Ocean engineering	TC1501-1800	620.4162
Ocean engineering—Congresses	TC1505	620.416206
Ocean engineering—Periodicals	TC1501	620.416205
Ocean temperature	GC160-177	551.4601
Ocean travel	G540-550	910.45
Ocean wave power	TC147	621.20422
Ocean waves	GC205-226	551.4702
Ocean-atmosphere interation	GC190-.5	551.5246
Oceania	DU	995/996
Oceania—Biography	CT2900-3090	920.099(5-6)
Oceania—Church history	BR1490-1495	279.9(5-6)
Oceania—Description and travel	DU19-23.5	919.(5-6)04
Oceania—Emigration and immigration	JV9290-9470	325.(29(5-6)/9(5-6))
Oceania—Gazetteers	DU10	919.(5-6)003
Oceania—Genealogy	CS2191-2209	929.39(5-6)
Oceania—History	DU28.11-66	995-996
Oceania—Manufactures	TS123-124	670.99(5-6)
Oceania—Politics and government	JQ5995-6651	320.9(5-6)
Oceania—Religion	BL2600-2630	299.92
Oceanographic instruments	GC41	551.460284

Subject Heading	LC	Dewey	Subject Heading	LC	Dewey
Oceanographic research ships	VM453	623.8226	Oil reservoir engineering	TN871	622.3382
			Oil storage tanks	TP692.5	665.542
Oceanographic submersibles	GC67	387.2045	Oil well drilling	TN871.2-.3	622.3381
			Oil well drilling, Submarine	TN871.3	622.33819
Oceanography	GC	551.46	Oil well drilling rigs	TN871.5	622.3381
Oceanography—Research	GC57-59	551.46072	Oil-shales	TN858-859	662.3383
Oceanography—Antarctic Ocean	GC461-462	551.469	Oils and fats	TP669-699	664.3
			Oilseed plants	SB298-299	633.85
Oceanography—Arctic Ocean	GC401-455	551.468	Ointments	RS201.03	615.45
			Ojibwa Indians	E99.C6	973.04973
Oceanography—Atlantic Ocean	GC481-711	551.461	Ojibwa language	PM851-854	497.3
			Oklahoma	F691-705	976.6
Oceanography—Indian Ocean	GC721-761	551.467	Oklahoma—Gazetteers	F692	917.66003
			Oklahoma—History— Land Rush, 1889	F699	976.604
Oceanography—Pacific Ocean	GC771-871	551.465	Oklahoma—History— Land Rush, 1893	F699	976.604
Octets	M800-886	785.18	Oklahoma—Maps	G4020-4024	912.766
Ocular pharmacology	RE994	617.7061	Oklahoma—National Guard	UA400-409	355.3709766
Odes	PN6110.04	808.8143	Oklahoma—Periodicals	F691	976.6005
Odessa (Ukraine), Battle of, 1941	D764.3	940.5421772	Old Norse Language— Dialects	PD2483-2489	439.67
Odors	QP458	612.86	Old Norse Poetry	PT7170-7175	839.61009
Odors	BF271	152.166	Old Norse language	PD2201-2392	439.6
Offenses against property	HV6635-6700	364.16	Old Norse language— Dialects	PD2387-2392	439.67
Offenses against property— United States	KF9350-9379	345.73026			
			Old Norse language— Etymology	PD2361-2369	439.62
Offenses against public safety	HV6419-6433	364.142	Old Norse language— Grammar	PD2229-2331	439.65
Offenses against the person	HV6493-6633	364.15			
Offenses against the person—United States	KF9304-9329	345.73025	Old Norse language— Lexicography	PD2376-2385	439.63028
Office Management	HF5546-5548	651.3	Old Norse literature	PT7101-7338	839.6
Office buildings	NA6230-6234	725.23	Old Norse literature— Study and teaching	PT7135-7139	839.6071
Office equipment and supplies	HF5548-.115	651.2			
			Old Norse philology	PD2201-2392	439.6
Office practice—Automation	HF5548.125-.6	651.8	Old Norse poetry	PT7230-7252	839.61008
Offshore support vessels	VM466.035	623.826	Old Norse prose literature	PT7177-7211	839.6808
Oglala Indians	E99.03	973.049752	Old Norse prose literature	PT7255-7262	839.6808
Ohio	F486-500	977.1	Old Order Mennonites	BX8129.043	289.7092
Ohio River Valley	F516-520	977	Old Persian inscriptions	PK6128	491.5111
Ohio—Gazetteers	F489	917.71003	Old Persian language	PK6121-6129	491.51
Ohio—History—To 1787	F495	977.10(1-2)	Old Saxon language	PF3992-4000	439.4
Ohio—History—Revolution, 1775-1783	E263.0	977.102	Old Turkic language	PL31	494.31
			Old age	HV1450-1493	362.6
Ohio—History—1787-1865	F495	977.103	Old age	QP86	612.67
Ohio—History—War of 1812	E359.5.02	977.103	Old age homes	HV1454-.2	362.61
Ohio—History—Civil War, 1861-1865	E525	977.103	Old age pensions	HD7105.3-.35	331.252
			Old growth forests	SD387.043	333.75
Ohio—History—1865-	F496-.2	977.104	Oligarchy	JC419	321.5
Ohio—Maps	G4080-4084	912.771	Oligopolies	HD2757-2768	338.82
Ohio—National Guard	UA390-399	355.3709771	Olympia (Greece : Ancient sanctuary)	DF261.05	938.8
Ohio—Periodicals	F486	977.1005			
Oil burners	TH7466.06	697.044	Olympics—Records	GV721.8	796.48
Oil fields—Production methods	TN870	622.338	Oman—Census	HA4565	315.353
			Oman—Economic conditions	HC415.35	330.95353
Oil filters	TJ1081	621.890284	Oman—Maps	G7560-7564	912.5353
Oil gasification	TP759	665.773	Oman—Politics and government	JQ1843	320.95353
Oil hydraulic machinery	TJ843	621.20424			
Oil industries	HD9490-.5	338.476655	Omens	BF1777	133.334
Oil pollution of soils	TD879.P4	628.55	Oncogenic DNA viruses	QR372.058	579.2569
Oil pollution of water	TD427.P4	628.16833			

Subject Heading	LC	Dewey
Oncology	RC254-282	616.994
Onions	SB341	635.25
Online data processing—Downloading	QA76.55-.57	005.7
Ontario—Gazetteers	F1056.4	917.13003
Ontario—History	F1056-1059.7	971.3
Ontario—Maps	G3460-3464	912.713
Ontario—Periodicals	F1056	971.3005
Ontology	BD300-450	111
Opals	QE394.07	549.68
Open and closed shop	HD6488-.2	331.8892
Open plan schools	LB1029.06	371.256
Open-hearth furnaces	TN740-742	669.1422
Opera	ML3858	782.1
Operant conditioning	BF319.5.06	153.1526
Operas	M1500-1508	782.1
Operating systems (Computers)	QA76.76.063	005.43
Operational art (Military science)	U161-163	355.4
Operator algebras	QA326	512.55
Operatta	ML1900	782.1209
Ophthalmic drugs	RE994	617.7061
Ophthalmic lenses	RE961-962	617.7522
Ophthalmic nursing	RE88	610.73677
Ophthalmologic emergencies	RE48	617.7026
Ophthalmologists	RE31-36	617.70232
Ophthalmologists—Directories	RE22	617.70025
Ophthalmology	RE	617.7
Ophthalmology—Congresses	RE11	617.7006
Ophthalmology—History	RE26-30	617.709
Ophthalmology—Instruments	RE73	617.700284
Ophthalmology—Periodicals	RE6	617.7005
Ophthalmology—Societies, etc.	RE1	617.7006
Ophthalmology—Study and teaching	RE56	617.70071
Ophthalmology—Terminology	RE20	617.70014
Opioid habit	RC568.058	616.8632
Opium	SB295.06	633.75
Opium habit	HV5816	362.293
Opium habit	RC568.06	616.8632
Opium poppy	SB295.065	633.75
Opposition (Political science)	JF518	328.369
Ops (Roman deity)	BL820.06	292.2113
Optic nerve	QL949	573.88
Optic nerve	QM511	611.84
Optical communications	TK5103.59	621.3827
Optical gyroscopes	TL589.2.06	681.753
Optical instruments	QC370.5-379	535.028
Optical instruments	RE73	616.700284
Optical measurements	QC367	535.0284
Optical storage devices	TK7895.M4	621.39767
Opticians	RE940-981	681.4092
Optics	QC350-467	535
Optimism	BF698.35.057	155.232

Subject Heading	LC	Dewey
Optimism	B829	149.5
Optimum ship routing	VK570	387.52
Optometry	RE940-981	617.75
Oracles	BL613	291.32
Oracles	BF1745-1779	133.3248
Oracles, Greek	DF125	133.32480938
Oral contraceptives	RG137.5	613.9432
Oral interpretation	PN4145-4151	808.54
Oral medication	RM162	615.6
Oral medicine	RC815-.6	616.31
Oral reading	LB1573.5	372.452
Oratorios	M2000-2007	782.23
Oratory	PN4001-4355	808.85
Oratory—History	PN4021-4055	809.5
Oratory, Ancient	PA3479-3842	885.108
Orbiting astronomical observatories	QB500.267-.268	522.29
Orbits	QB355-357	521.3
Orbs	CR4485.07	929.7
Orchards	SB354-402	634
Orchestra	ML1200-1251	784.209
Orchestral music	M1000-1075	784.2
Orchestral music—Analysis, appreciation	MT125	784.2117
Order (Philosophy)	B105.07	117
Orders of knighthood and chivalry	CR4501-6305	929.71
Orders of knighthood and chivalry—[By region or country]	CR4801-6305	929.7(2-3/094)
Orders of knighthood and chivalry—Austria	CR4951-5005	929.736
Orders of knighthood and chivalry—France	CR5025-5085	929.74
Orders of knighthood and chivalry—Germany	CR5100-5475	929.73
Orders of knighthood and chivalry—Great Britain	CR4801-4917	929.72
Orders of knighthood and chivalry—Greece	CR5485-5489	929.795
Orders of knighthood and chivalry—Italy	CR5500-5580	929.75
Orders of knighthood and chivalry—Poland	CR5713-5737	929.738
Orders of knighthood and chivalry—Portugal	CR5900-5925	929.769
Orders of knighthood and chivalry—Russia	CR5657-5703	929.77
Orders of knighthood and chivalry—Scandinavia	CR5745-5809	929.78
Orders of knighthood and chivalry—Spain	CR5819-5889	929.76
Orders of knighthood and chivalry, Papal	CR5547-5575	255.7
Orders of knighthood and chivalry, Papal	CR4701-4731	255.791
Ordinary-language philosophy	B828.36	149.94
Ordination	BV685	262.14
Ordination	BV830	262.14
Ordination—Catholic Church	BX2240	264.02084
Ordination of women	BV676	262.14

Subject Heading	LC	Dewey
Ordnance	UF520-780	358.1282
Ordnance, Naval	VF	359.82
Ordnance, Naval—History	VF15	359.82/ 623.8251 + (09)
Ordnance, Naval—Societies, etc.	VF1	359.82/ 623.82510 + 6
Ordnance, Naval—[By region or country]	VF21-124	359.82/623.8251 + 09 09(4-9)
Ordnance, Naval—Africa	VF115-119	359.82/ 623.8251 + (096)
Ordnance, Naval—Argentina	VF36-37	359.82/623.8251 + (0982)
Ordnance, Naval—Asia	VF101-113	359.82/623.8251 + (095)
Ordnance, Naval—Australia	VF121-122	359.82/623.8251 + (0994)
Ordnance, Naval—Canada	VF26-27	359.82/623.8251 + (0971)
Ordnance, Naval—Central America	VF30-31	359.82/623.8251 + (09728)
Ordnance, Naval—Chile	VF43-44	359.82/623.8251 + (0983)
Ordnance, Naval—Colombia	VF45-46	359.82/623.8251 + (09861)
Ordnance, Naval—Europe	VF55-96	359.82/623.8251 + (094)
Ordnance, Naval—France	VF71-72	359.82/623.8251 + (0944)
Ordnance, Naval—Germany	VF73-74.5	359.82/623.8251 + (0943)
Ordnance, Naval—Great Britain	VF57-64	359.82/623.8251 + (0941)
Ordnance, Naval—Italy	VF79-80	359.82/623.8251 + (0945)
Ordnance, Naval—Japan	VF105-106	359.82/623.8251 + (0952)
Ordnance, Naval—Mexico	VF28-29	359.82/623.8251 + (0972)
Ordnance, Naval—New Zealand	VF122.5	359.82/623.8251 + (0993)
Ordnance, Naval—Portugal	VF83-84	359.82/623.8251 + (09469)
Ordnance, Naval—Russia	VF85-86	359.82/623.8251 + (0947)
Ordnance, Naval—Scandinavia	VF86.5	359.82/623.8251 + (0948)
Ordnance, Naval—South America	VF34-54	359.82/623.8251 + (098)
Ordnance, Naval—Spain	VF87-88	359.82/623.8251 + (0946)
Ordnance, Naval—Turkey	VF111-112	359.82/623.8251 + (09561)
Ordnance, Naval—United States	VF23-25	359.82/623.8251 + (0973)
Ordnance, Naval—West Indies	VF32-33	359.82/623.8251 + (09729)
Ordnance testing	VF540	359.80287
Ordnance testing	UF890	358.1280287
Ordnance, Rapid-fire	UF560-565	358.128
Ore carriers	VM457	623.8245
Oregon	F871-885	979.5

Subject Heading	LC	Dewey
Oregon Trail	F880	979.503
Oregon—Gazetteers	F874	917.95003
Oregon—History—To 1859	F879-880	979.50(1-3)
Oregon—History—1859-	F881-.35	979.504
Oregon—History—1951-	F881.2-.35	979.504(3-4)
Oregon—Maps	G4290-4294	912.795
Oregon—National Guard	UA410-419	355.3709795
Oregon—Periodicals	F871	979.5005
Ores	TN400-580	622.34
Organ	ML550-649	786.509
Organ—Instruction and study	MT180	786.507
Organ donors	RD129.5	362.1783092
Organ music	M6-14	786.5
Organic acids	TP247.2	661.86
Organic compounds	TP247-248	661.8
Organic compounds—Synthesis	QD262	547.2
Organic farming	S605.5	631.584
Organic fertilizers	S654	631.86
Organic gardening	SB453.5	635.0484
Organic semiconductors	QC611.8.O7	537.6223
Organic solid state chemistry	QD478	541.0421
Organic wastes as feed	SF99.W34	636.0855
Organic wastes as fertilizer	S654	631.86
Organic water pollutants	TD427.O7	628.1682
Organizational behavior	HD58.7	658.019
Organizational change	HD58.8	658.406
Organized crime investigation	HV8079.O73	363.25906
Organometallic compounds	QD410-412.5	547.05
Oriental antiquities	DS11	950
Oriental antiquities	N5343-5345	709.31
Oriental drama	PJ371	895.2008
Oriental languages	PJ	490
Oriental languages—Etymology	PJ183	490.2
Oriental languages—Grammar	PJ120-171	490.5
Oriental languages—Lexicography	PJ187	490.3028
Oriental languages—Study and teaching	PJ65-69	490.071
Oriental literature	PJ306-489	895
Orientation (Psychology)	BF299.O7	152.1882
Orienteering	GV200.4	796.58
Origami	TT870	736.982
Oriya language	PK2561-2569	491.45
Ornamental evergreens	SB435	635.97715
Ornamental grasses	SB431.7	635.9
Ornamental trees	SB435-437	635.977
Ornithology	QL671-699	598
Orphanages	HV959-1420.5	362.732
Orphanages—[By region or country]	HV971-1420.5	362.73209(4-9)
Orphanages—United States	HV971-995	362.7320973
Orphans	HV959-1420.5	362.73
Orthodonic appliances	RK527-528	617.64300284
Orthodontics	RK520-528	617.643
Orthodontics, Corrective	RK527-528	617.643

Subject Heading	LC	Dewey
Orthodox Eastern Church	BX200-754	281.9
Orthodox Eastern Church	BX460-605	281.947
Orthodox Eastern Church—Government	BX520-558	262.01947
Orthodox Eastern Church—History	BX485-492	281.94709
Orthodox Eastern Church—Liturgy	BX350-376	264.019
Orthodox Eastern Church—[Austria/Hungary]	BX630-639	281.943(6/9)
Orthodox Eastern Church—Greece	BX610-619	281.9495
Orthodox Eastern Church—Russia	BX560-563	264.01947
Orthopedic apparatus	RD755-757	617.9
Orthopedic emergencies	RD750	616.7025
Orthopedic hospitals	RD705-706	362.11
Orthopedic hospitals—United States	RD705.5	362.110973
Orthopedic implants	RD755.5-.7	617.470592
Orthopedic nursing	RD753	610.73677
Orthopedic shoes	RD757.S45	616.70284
Orthopedic slings	RD757.S5	617.9
Orthopedic surgery	RD701-789	617.47
Orthopedic traction	RD736.T7	617.9
Orthopedics	RD701-811	616.7
Orthopedics—Diagnosis	RD734-.5	616.70754
Orthopedics—History	RD725-726	616.709
Orthopedics—Periodicals	RD711	616.7005
Orthopedics—Pictorial works	RD733.2	617.300222
Orthopedists	RD727-728	616.70232
Osage Indians	E99.08	973.049752
Oscillations	QA865-867.5	531.32
Oscillators, Electric	TK6565.O7	621.38412
Osiris (Egyptian deity)	BL2450.O7	299.31
Osmosis	QD543	541.3415
Osteitis	RC931.O64	616.712
Osteoarthritis	RC931.O67	616.7223
Osteopathic hospitals	RZ302-304	362.11
Osteopathic medicine	RZ301-397.5	615.533
Osteopathic medicine—Congresses	RZ313	615.53306
Osteopathic medicine—History	RZ321-325	615.53309
Osteopathic medicine—Periodicals	RZ311	615.53305
Osteopathic medicine—Societies, etc.	RZ301	615.53306
Osteopathic medicine—Study and teaching	RZ337-338	615.533071
Osteopathic medicine—Vocational guidance	RZ336	615.533023
Osteopathic physicians—Biography	RZ331-332	615.533092
Osteopathic physicians—Directories	RZ333	615.533025
Osteopathic schools	RZ337-338	615.5330711
Osteoporosis	RC931.073	616.716
Osteosarcoma	RC280.B6	616.9947
Otolaryngologic examination	RF48-.5	617.51075
Otolaryngological nursing	RF52.5	610.736
Otolaryngologists	RF37-38	617.51092
Otolaryngologists—Directories	RF28	617.510025
Otolaryngology	RF	617.51
Otolaryngology—Congresses	RF16	617.51006
Otolaryngology—Diagnosis	RF48-.5	617.51075
Otolaryngology—History	RF25-26	617.5109
Otolaryngology—Periodicals	RF11	617.51005
Otolaryngology—Societies, etc.	RF1	617.51006
Otolaryngology—Study and teaching	RF62	617.80071
Otolaryngology—Wounds and injuries	RF50	617.51044
Otolaryngology, Operative	RF51-52	617.51059
Otology	RF110-320	617.8
Outdoor cookery	TX823	641.578
Outdoor education	LB1047	371.384
Outdoor furniture	TT197.5.09	684.18
Outdoor life	GV191.2-200.56	796.5
Outdoor photography	TR659.5	778.71
Outlaws	HV6441-6453	364.3
Outlet stores	HF5429.2-.215	381.15
Outline maps	GA101-130	912
Outrigger canoes	GN440.2	386.229
Ovaries	QL881	573.665
Ovaries	QM421	611.65
Overhead projection	LB1043.5	371.335
Overlay dentures	RK656-666	617.692
Overtime	HD5111	331.2162
Overtures	M1004	784.18926
Oxidation	QD281.09	547.23
Oxygen	TP245.09	661.0721
Oxygen	QD181.01	546.721
Oxygen therapy	RM666.08	615.836
Oxygen—Physiological effect	QP913.01	572.53
Oyster fisheries	SH371	639.41
Oyster shell	SH379.5	639.41
Ozone layer	QC881.2.09	551.5142
Oyster fisheries	SH371	639.41
Oyster shell	SH379.5	639.41
Pacemaker, Artificial (Heart)	RC684.P3	617.4120645
Pacific Coast Indians, Wars with, 1847-1865	E83.84	979.02
Pacific Island literature	PN849.026	899
Pacific Ocean—Maps	G2860-2867	912.1964
Pacific States—Maps	G4230-4232	912.79
Pacific railroads	HE2763	385.0979
Pacific railroads	HE1062	385.0979
Pacific railroads—Early projects	HE2763	385.0979
Pack transportation	UC300-305	358.25
Packaging	TS195-198.8	688.8
Packet switching (Data transmission)	TK5105	621.38216
Packhorse camping	GV199.7	796.54
Paddle steamers	HE566.P3	387.2044
Paddle tennis	GV1006	796.346
Paddleball	GV1003.2	796.34
Pageants	GT3980-4099	394.5
Pageants	PN3202-3299	791.62

Subject Heading	LC	Dewey	Subject Heading	LC	Dewey
Pagodas	NA1540-1547	720.951	Painting—Iran	ND980-989	759.955
Pagodas—Design and construction	TH4224	690.61	Painting—Israel	ND977-979	759.95694
			Painting—Italy	ND611-623.3	759.5
Pahari languages	PK2591-2610	491.49	Painting—Jamaica	ND309-311	759.97292
Pain	QP401	612.88	Painting—Japan	ND1050-1059.6	759.952
Pain	RB127	616.0472	Painting—Jordan	ND979-.8	759.95695
Pain	RC73-.2	616.0472	Painting—Korea	ND1060-1070.3	759.9519
Paint	TP934-937.5	667.6	Painting—Laos	ND1016-.3	759.9594
Paint mixing	TT310	667.0283	Painting—Lebanon	ND976.6-.8	759.95692
Painting	ND	750	Painting—Libya	ND1089-.3	759.9612
Painting—Biography	ND34-38	759	Painting—Malaysia	ND1025-.8	759.9595
Painting—Catalogs	ND40-45	750.294	Painting—Mexico	ND250-259	759.972
Painting—Conservation and restoration	ND1630-1662	751.6	Painting—Morocco	ND1090-.3	759.964
			Painting—New Zealand	ND1106-1108	759.993
Painting—History	ND49-813	759	Painting—Nicaragua	ND282-284	759.97285
Painting—Study and teaching	ND1115-1120	750.71	Painting—Norway	ND761-773.3	759.81
			Painting—Oceania	ND1110-1113	759.99(5-6)
Painting—[By region or country]	ND204-1113	759.(1-9)	Painting—Pakistan	ND1010.7-.73	759.95491
			Painting—Panama	ND285-287	759.97287
Painting—Afghanistan	ND992-.3	759.9581	Painting—Paraguay	ND400-409	759.9892
Painting—Africa	ND1080-1099	759.96	Painting—Peru	ND410-419	759.985
Painting—Africa, East	ND1097-.6	759.9676	Painting—Philippines	ND1027-1029	759.9599
Painting—Africa, Southern	ND1091.7-1096.6	759.968	Painting—Poland	ND999.P6	759.38
Painting—Africa, West	ND1098-1099	759.966	Painting—Portugal	ND821-833.3	759.69
Painting—Algeria	ND1088-.3	759.965	Painting—Puerto Rico	ND312-314	759.97295
Painting—Argentina	ND330-339	759.982	Painting—Russia	ND681-699	759.7
Painting—Asia	ND960-1070.3	759.95	Painting—Saudi Arabia	ND970-972	759.9538
Painting—Asiatic Russia	ND992.4-999	759.957	Painting—Scandinavia	ND701-793.3	759.8
Painting—Australia	ND1100-1105.3	759.994	Painting—South America	ND320-439	759.98
Painting—Austria	ND501-511.6	759.36	Painting—Spain	ND801-813.3	759.6
Painting—Bahamas	ND300-302	759.97296	Painting—Sri Lanka	ND1010.6-.63	759.95493
Painting—Bolivia	ND340-349	759.984	Painting—Surinam	ND396	759.9883
Painting—Brazil	ND350-359	759.981	Painting—Sweden	ND781-793.3	759.85
Painting—Burma	ND1012-.3	759.9591	Painting—Syria	ND989.6-.8	759.95691
Painting—Cambodia	ND1015-.3	759.9596	Painting—Thailand	ND1021-1023	759.9593
Painting—Canada	ND240-249.5	759.11	Painting—Tunisia	ND1091-.3	759.9611
Painting—Central America	ND260-290	759.9728	Painting—Turkey	ND861-873.3	759.9561
Painting—Chile	ND360-369	759.983	Painting—United States	ND205-238	759.13
Painting—China	ND1040-1049.6	759.951	Painting—Uruguay	ND420-429	759.9895
Painting—Colombia	ND370-379	759.9861	Painting—Venezuela	ND430-439	759.987
Painting—Costa Rica	ND273-275	759.97286	Painting—Vietnam	ND1014-.63	759.9597
Painting—Cuba	ND303-305	759.97291	Painting—West Indies	ND291-315	759.9729
Painting—Denmark	ND711-723.3	759.89	Painting, Ancient	ND70-130	759.01
Painting—Ecuador	ND380-389	759.9866	Painting, Industrial	TT300-380	667.6
Painting—Egypt	ND1081-1085.3	759.962	Painting, Iraqi	ND967-969	759.9567
Painting—El Salvador	ND288-290	759.97284	Painting, Islamic	ND146	750.882971
Painting—Ethiopia	ND1086-.3	759.963	Painting, Japanese	ND1050-1059.6	759.952
Painting—Europe	ND450-955	759.(2-8)	Painting, Korean	ND1060-1070.3	759.9519
Painting—Finland	ND955.F5	759.897	Painting, Medieval	ND140-146	759.02
Painting—France	ND541-553.3	759.4	Painting, Modern	ND160-196	759.06
Painting—French Guiana	ND397	759.9882	Painting, Modern— 17th-18th centuries	ND177-188	759.04
Painting—Germany	ND568-589	759.3			
Painting—Great Britain	ND461-481	759.2	Painting, Modern— 19th century	ND190-192	759.05
Painting—Greece	ND591-603.3	759.3			
Painting—Guatemala	ND276-278	759.97281	Painting, Modern— 20th century	ND195-196	759.06
Painting—Guyana	ND395	759.9881			
Painting—Haiti	ND306-308	759.97294	Painting, Renaissance	ND170-172	759.03
Painting—Honduras	ND279-281	759.97283	Paired-association learning	BF319.5.P34	153.1526
Painting—Hungary	ND512-522.6	759.39	Pakistan—Census	HA4590.5	315.491
Painting—India	ND1001-1010.3	759.954	Pakistan—Civilization	DS379	934/954.91
Painting—Indonesia	ND1026-.8	759.9598			

Subject Heading	LC	Dewey		Subject Heading	LC	Dewey
Pakistan—Description and travel	DS377	913.4/ 915.491(04)		Paleontology—Central America	QE751	560.9728
Pakistan—Economic conditions	HC440.5	330.95491		Paleontology—Europe	QE753-755	560.94
Pakistan—Gazetteers	DS376.8	934/ 915.491(003)		Paleontology—Mexico	QE749	560.972
				Paleontology—South America	QE752	560.98
Pakistan—History	DS381.7-388.2	934/954.91		Paleontology—United States	QE746-747	560.973
Pakistan—Manufactures	TS104.5-.6	670.95491		Paleontology—West Indies	QE750	560.9729(9)
Pakistan—Maps	G7640-7644	912.5491		Palestine—History— 70-638	DS109.913	956.9402
Pakistan—Maps	G2270-2274	912.5491		Palestine—History— 638-1917	DS109.916-.925	956.9403
Pakistan—Politics and government	JQ629	320.95491		Palestine—History— 1799-1917	DS125	956.9403
Pakistan—Religion	BL2035	299.14122		Palestine—History— 1917-1948	DS125.5-126.4	956.9404
Palaces	NA7710-7786	728.82		Palestine—History— Arab riots, 1920	DS109.93	956.9404
Palaces	NA320	728.8209376				
Palaces	NA277	728.820938		Palestine—History— 1929-1948	DS126-.4	956.9404
Paleobotany—Africa	QE947	561.196				
Paleobotany—Antarctic regions	QE950	561.19989		Palestine—History— Arab riots, 1929	DS126	956.9404
Paleobotany—Arctic regions	QE934	561.1998(1-8)		Palestine—History—Arab rebellion, 1936-1939	DS126	956.9404
Paleobotany—Asia	QE946	561.195		Palestine—History— Proposed partition, 1937	DS109.93	956.9404
Paleobotany—Australia	QE948	561.1994				
Paleobotany—Canada	QE938	561.1971				
Paleobotany—Central America	QE941	561.19728		Palestine—History— Partition, 1947	DS109.93	956.9404
Paleobotany—Europe	QE943-945	561.194		Pali language	PK1001-1095	491.37
Paleobotany—Mexico	QE939	561.1972		Pali language—Dictionaries	PK1089-1095	491.373
Paleobotany—New Zealand	QE948.2	561.1993		Pali language—Etymology	PK1083-1086	491.372
Paleobotany—Oceania	QE949	561.199(5-6)		Pali language—Grammar	PK1017-1073	491.375
Paleobotany—South America	QE942	561.198		Pali language—Lexicography	PK1087-1093	491.373028
Paleobotany—United States	QE936-937	561.1973		Pali literature	PK4501-4681	891.37
				Pali philology	PK1001-1095	491.37
Paleobotany—West Indies	QE940	561.19729		Palm Sunday	BV53	263.92
Paleoclimatology	QC884-.2	551.69		Palm frond weaving	TT877.5	746.41
Paleogeography	QE501.4.P3	551.7		Palmistry	BF910-940	133.6
Paleography	Z105-115.5	411.7		Palms	SB413.P17	635.9345
Paleolithic period, Lower	GN771	930.12		Palpitation	RC685.A65	616.128
Paleomagnetism	QE501.4.P35	538.727		Pan (Greek deity)	BL820.P2	292.2113
Paleontology	QE701-996.5	560		Panama	F1561-1577	972.87
Paleontology—Periodicals	QE701	560.5		Panama—Census	HA851-854	317.287
Paleontology—Cambrian	QE726	560.1723		Panama—Civilization	F1563.8	972.87
Paleontology—Cenozoic	QE735-741.3	560.178		Panama—Description and travel	F1564-.3	917.28704
Paleontology—Cretaceous	QE734	560.177				
Paleontology—Devonian	QE728	560.174		Panama—Emigration and immigration	JV7429	325.(27287/ 7287)
Paleontology—Eocene	QE737	560.1784				
Paleontology—Jurassic	QE733	560.1766		Panama—Gazetteers	F1562	917.287003
Paleontology—Mesozoic	QE731-734	560.176		Panama—History	F1565.5-1567	972.87
Paleontology—Miocene	QE739	560.1787		Panama—History—To 1903	F1566.45	972.870(1-3)
Paleontology—Oligocene	QE738	560.1785		Panama—History— 1903-1946	F1566.5	972.87051
Paleontology—Paleozoic	QE725-730	560.172				
Paleontology—Precambrian	QE724	560.171		Panama—History— Revolution, 1903	F1566.5	972.87051
Paleontology—Africa	QE757	560.96				
Paleontology—Antarctic regions	QE760	560.9989		Panama—History— 1946-1981	F1566.5-1567	972.8705(1-3)
				Panama—History—Coup d'etat, 1968	F1566.5	972.87051
Paleontology—Arctic regions	QE744	560.9981				
Paleontology—Asia	QE756	560.95		Panama—History—1981-	F1567	972.87053
Paleontology—Australia	QE758	560.994				
Paleontology—Canada	QE748	560.971				

Subject Heading	LC	Dewey	Subject Heading	LC	Dewey
Panama—History—American Invasion, 1989	F1567	972.87053	Paraguay—Civilization	F2670	989.2
Panama—Maps	G4870-4874	912.7287	Paraguay—Description and travel	F2671-2676	918.9204
Panama—Periodicals	F1561	972.87005	Paraguay—Economic conditions	HC221-225	330.9892
Panamanian literature	PQ7520-7529.2	860			
Panarabism	DS38	320.5409174927	Paraguay—Emigration and immigration	JV7500-7509	325.(2892/892)
Panbabylonism	BL1625.P3	299.21			
Pancakes, waffles, etc.	TX770.P34	641.815	Paraguay—Gazetteers	F2664	918.92003
Pancreas	QL866	573.377	Paraguay—History	F2679.35-2689.23	989.2
Pancreas	QP188.P26	612.34			
Pancreas	QM353	611.37	Paraguay—History—To 1811	F2683-2684	989.20(1-3)
Pancreas—Diseases	RC857-858	616.37	Paraguay—History—Revolution of the Comuneros, 1721-1735	F2683	989.203
Pancreas—Secretions	QP195	612.34			
Pandora (Greek mythology)	BL820.P	292.13			
Panhandle culture	E99.P244	976.481	Paraguay—History—War of Independence, 1810-1811	F2683	989.203
Panic disorders	RC535	616.85223			
Panjabi language	PK2631-2639	491.42			
Pannonia Region	DJK77	939.8	Paraguay—History—1811-1870	F2686-2687	989.20(4-5)
Panoramas	N7436.5-.53	745.8			
Panoramas	ND2880-2881	751.74	Paraguay—History—1870-1938	F2688-.5	989.20(6-71)
Pantheism	BL220	211.2			
Pantomines	PN6120.P3-.P4	792.3	Paraguay—History—20th century	F2688	989.20(6-7)
Paoli Massacre, 1777	E241.P2	973.333			
Papacy	BX950-961	262.13	Paraguay—History—Revolution, 1904	F2688	989.2071
Papacy—History—To 1309	BX965-1263	262.13090(1-23)			
Papacy and Christian union	BX9.5.P29	280.042	Paraguay—History—Revolution, 1922-1923	F2688	989.2071
Papal States	DG791-800	945.6			
Papal States—History	DG796-800	945.6	Paraguay—History—Revolution, 1936	F2688	989.2071
Papal decorations	CR5547-5577	255.791			
Papal visits	BX958.V7	262.13	Paraguay—History—1938-1989	F2689	989.207(1-3)
Paper	TS1080-1268	676			
Paper	Z247	676	Paraguay—History—Revolution, 1947	F2689	989.2072
Paper airplanes	TL778	745.592			
Paper coatings	TS1118.F5	676.235	Paraguay—History—1989-	F2689.2-.23	989.2073
Paper-cutting machines	Z249	686.20284	Paraguay—History—Coup d'etat, 1989	F2689.2	989.2073
Paper finishing	TS1118.F5	676.234			
Paper money	HG348-353.5	332.4044	Paraguay—Manufactures	TS51	670.9892
Paper products	TS1080-1268	676	Paraguay—Maps	G5380-5384	912.892
Paper sculpture	NB1270.P3	731.2	Paraguay—Periodicals	F2661	989.2005
Paperhanging	TH8441	698.6	Paraguay—Politics and government	JL3200-3299	320.9892
Papermaking	TS1080-1268	676			
Papermaking—History	TS1090-1096	676.09	Paraguayan literature	PQ8250-8259	860
Paperweights	NK5440.P3	748.84	Parallel computers	QA76.5	004.35
Papillomavirus diseases	QR201.P26	571.992445	Paralysis	RJ496.P2	618.92842
Papovaviruses	QR406-.2	579.2445	Paralysis	RJ301	618.92842
Papua New Guinea	DU740	995.3	Paralytic shellfish poisoning	SH177.R4	615.954
Papua New Guinea—Census	HA4013	319.53	Paranoid schizophrenia	RC514	616.898
Papuan languages	PL6601-6621	499.12	Paraplegics	RC406.P3	616.837
Papuans	GN664.P2	305.89912	Parapsychology	BF1001-1389	133
Parabola	QA485	516.15	Parapsychology—Biography	BF1026-1027	133.092
Parachute troops	UD480-485	356.166	Parapsychology—Congresses	BF1021	133.06
Parachutes	TL750-758	629.134386			
Parachutes—Rigging	TL753	629.134386	Parapsychology—Dictionaries	BF1025	133.03
Parachuting	GV769.5-770.2	797.56			
Parachuting	TL750-758	629.134386	Parapsychology—History	BF1028-.5	133.09
Parades	GT3980-4096	394.5	Parapsychology—Periodicals	BF1001-1008	133.05
Paradise	BT844-849	236.24	Parapsychology—Religious aspects—Christianity	BR115.P85	261.513
Paradise (Islam)	BP166.87	297.23			
Paradox	BC199.P2	165			
Paraguay	F2661-2699	989.2	Parapsychology—Study and teaching	BF1040.5	133.071
Paraguay—Census	HA1041-1050	318.92			

Subject Heading	LC	Dewey	Subject Heading	LC	Dewey
Parasites	QL757	591.65	Passion-plays	PN3203-3299	792.16
Parasitic diseases	RC119-.7	616.96	Passivity (Psychology)	BF698.35.P36	155.232
Parasitic diseases	RA643-644	614.55	Passover	BM675.P3	296.437
Parasitic plants	SB610-615	632.52	Passover	BM695.P3	296.437
Parasitology	QL757	591.65	Passover cookery	TX739.2.P37	641.5676437
Parathyroid glands	QP188.P3	612.44	Passover sermons	BM747.P3	296.4737
Parcel post	HE6171-6173	383.125	Passports—United States	KF4794-.5	342.73082
Parcel post—United States	HE6471-6473	383.1250973	Pasta products	TX394.5	641.822
Pardon	HV8692	364.65	Pastel drawing	NC880	741.235
Pardon—United States	KF9695	345.73077	Pastoral art	N8205	700.421734
Parent and adult child	HQ755.86	306.874084	Pastoral counseling	BV4012.2	253.5
Parent and teenager	HQ799.15	306.874	Pastoral counseling	BM652.5	296.61
Parent-teacher conferences	LC225.5	371.103	(Judaism)		
Parental behavior in animals	QL762	591.563	Pastoral counseling centers	BV4012.25	253.5
Parental leave	HD6065-.5	331.25763	Pastoral medicine	BV4335	253
Parenteral solutions	RS201.P37	615.6	Pastoral prayers	BV250-254	264.13
Parenteral solutions	RM149	615.855	Pastoral psychology	BV4012-.3	253.52
Parenteral therapy	RM149	615.855	Pastoral systems	SF140.P38	636.0845
Parenthood	HQ755.7-759.92	306.874	Pastoral theology	BV4000-4470	253
Parenting	HQ755.7-759.92	306.874	Pastoral theology (Islam)	BP184	297.61
Parents of exceptional	HQ759.913	306.874	Pastry	TX773	641.8659
children			Pastures	SB199	633.202
Parents of handicapped	HQ759.913	306.874	Patchwork	NK9100-9499	746.46
children			Patent laws and	KD1361-1413.3	346.420486
Parents' and teachers'	LC230-235	371.19206	legislation—England		
associations			Patent laws and	KF3091-3193	346.730486
Paris (France)	DC701-790	944.36	legislation—United States		
Parish missions	BX2375	269.6	Patent medicines	RM671-.5	615.886
Parkinsonism	RC382	616.833	Patents	T201-342	608
Parkinsonism, Symptomatic	RC382	616.833	Patents—History	T221-323.7	608.7
Parks	SB481-485	363.68	Pathogenic bacteria	QR201	579.3
Parks—Management	SB481-485	363.68068	Pathogenic fungi	QR245-248	571.995
Parks—United States	SB482-483	363.680973	Pathogenic microorganisms	QR201	579.165
Parks—[Other countries	SB484-485	363.6809(4-9)	Pathology	RB	616.07
or regions]			Pathology—Congresses	RB3	616.0706
Parmesan cheese	SF272.P3	637.354	Pathology—History	RB15-.2	616.0709
Parodies	PN6110.P3	808.87	Pathology—Periodicals	RB1	616.0705
Parody	PN6149.P3	808.87	Pathology—Study and	RB123-124	616.07071
Parole	HV9278	364.63	teaching		
Parsees	BL1500-1590	295	Patience	BJ1533.P3	179.9
Part-songs	M1578-1600	783.1	Patient compliance	R727.43	615.5
Part-time employment	HD5110-.2	331.2572	Patient education	RT90-.3	615.507
Parthian War, 113-117	DG294	937.07	Patio gardening	SB473.2	635.9671
Partial dentures	RK664-666	617.692	Patios	NA8375	728.93
Partial dentures, Removable	RK665	617.692	Patriarchs (Bible)	BS573	222.110922
Partial differential operators	QA329.42	515.7242	Patriarchs and patriarchate	BX400-440	262.13
Partial sums (Series)	QA295	515.243	Patriarchy	GN479.6	321.1
Particle accelerators	QC787.P3	539.73	Patriotic societies	HS2301-2460.7	369
Particle accelerators	TK9340	539.73	Patriotic societies—	HS2321-2330	369.1
Particle beams	QC793.3.B4	539.73	United States		
Particles (Nuclear physics)	QC793-.5	539.72	Patriotism—United States	JK1758-1759	323.60973
Parties to actions—United	KF8890-8896.5	347.73052	Patriots' Day	E231	394.26973
States			Pattern perception	BF311	152.1423
Partitions (Mathematics)	QA165	512.73	Pattern perception	Q327	006.4
Partnership—England	KD2049-2054	346.420682	Pattern perception	QP360	152.1423
Parts of speech	P270-288	415	Pavements	TE250-278.8	625.8
Party decorations	TT900.P3	745.5941	Pavements, Asphalt	TE266-276	625.85
Parvovirus infections	QR201.P33	571.99247	Pavements, Concrete	TE278-.8	625.84
Parvoviruses	QR408-.2	579.247	Pavements, Mosaic	NA3750-3860	729.7
Paschal mystery	BV55	263.93	Pavements, Wooden	TE253	625.83
Passenger ships	VM381-383	623.8243	Pawnbrokers	HG2070-2106	332.34

Subject Heading	LC	Dewey	Subject Heading	LC	Dewey
Pawnbroking	HG2070-2106	332.34	Pendulum	QA862.P4	531.324
Pawnee Indians	E99.P3	973.04979	Penetration mechanics	TA354.5	620.1126
Pay equity	HD6061-.2	331.2153	Penicillin	RS165.P38	615.3295654
Pearl Harbor (Hawaii), Attack on, 1941	D767.92	940.5426	Penicillin	RM666.P35	615.3295654
			Peninsular Campaign, 1862	E473.6-.68	973.73(1-2)
Pearl fisheries	SH375-377	639.412	Peninsular War, 1807-1814	DC231-233.5	940.27
Pearl of great price (Parable)	BT378.P	226.8	Penis	QM416	611.64
Peasantry	HD1336-1339	333.32	Penis—Diseases	RC896	616.66
Peasantry	HD1521-1542	331.763	Penmanship	LB1590	372.634
Peasantry	GT1850	391.024	Penmanship	LB1536	372.634
Peasantry—Social life and customs	GT5650-5680	390.24	Penmanship	Z43-45	652.1
			Pennsylvania Dutch	F160.G3	974.8004310748
Peat soils	S592.85	631.826	Pennsylvania—Gazetteers	F147	917.48003
Pedantry	BF698.35.P43	155.232	Pennsylvania—History	F146-160	974.8
Peddlers and peddling	HF5457-5459	381.092	Pennsylvania—History— Colonial period, ca. 1600-1775	F152-.2	974.80(1-2)
Pediatric anesthesia	RD139	617.960083			
Pediatric cardiology	RJ421-426	618.9212			
Pediatric clinics	RJ27-28	362.12	Pennsylvania—History— 1865-	F154-155.3	974.804
Pediatric clinics—United States	RJ27.2-.3	362.110973			
			Pennsylvania—Maps	G3820-3824	912.748
Pediatric emergencies	RJ370	618.920025	Pennsylvania—National Guard	UA420-429	355.3709748
Pediatric endocrinology	RJ418-420	618.924			
Pediatric gastroenterology	RJ446-456	618.9233	Pennsylvania—Periodicals	F146	974.8005
Pediatric hematology	RJ411-416	618.9215	Pens	TS1262-1266	681.6
Pediatric intensive care	RJ370	618.920028	Pentecost	BT122.5	263.94
Pediatric neurology	RJ486-496	618.928	Pentecost Festival	BV60	263.94
Pediatric nursing	RJ245-247	610.7362	Pentecost Festival	GT4995.P45	394.266
Pediatric ophthalmology	RE48.2.C5	618.920977	Pentecost season	BV61-63	263.94
Pediatric oral medicine	RJ460-463	618.9231	Pentecostal churches	BX8762-8780	289.94
Pediatric pharmacology	RJ560-570	615.1083(2-4)	Pentecostalism	BR1644-.5	270.82
Pediatric respiratory diseases	RJ431-436	618.922	People (Constitutional law)	K3290-3304	342.08
			People (Constitutional law)	K3224-3229	342.08
Pediatric urology	RJ466-478.5	618.926	People (Constitutional law)—United States	KF4881-4921	342.7308
Pediatricians	RJ43	618.9200092			
Pediatricians—Directories	RJ29	618.9200025	Peptic ulcer	RC821	616.343
Pediatricians—Societies, etc.	RJ1	618.920006	Peptide hormones	QP572.P4	572.65
			Peptides	QD431-.7	547.756
Pediatrics	RJ	618.92	Peptides	QP552.P4	572.65
Pediatrics—Congresses	RJ21	618.920006	Perceptual-motor learning	BF295-.5	152.334
Pediatrics—History	RJ36-42	618.920009	Percussion drilling	TN279	622.23
Pediatrics—Periodicals	RJ16	618.920005	Percussion drilling	TD412	628.114
Pediatrics—Practice	RJ33.5-.8	618.920232	Percussion instruments	ML1030-1040	786.809
Pediatrics—Psychosomatic aspects	RJ47.5-.53	618.9200019	Percussion music	M146	786.8
			Perennials	SB434	635.932
Pedodontics	RK55.C5	617.645	Perfectionism (Personality trait)	BF698.35.P47	155.232
Peer counseling of students	LB1027.5	371.4047			
Pegasus (Greek mythology)	BL820.P4	292.13	Performance contracts in education	LB2806.2	371.393
Peking man	GN284.7	569.9			
Pelvic bones—Fractures	RD549-.5	617.158	Performance practice (Music)	ML457	781.4409
Pelvic inflammatory disease	RG411	618.142			
Pelvic pain	RG483.P44	618.1	Performing arts	PN1560-1590	790.2
Pelvis—Diseases	RC946	617.55	Performing arts—History	PN1581	790.209
Pelvis—Diseases— Eclectic treatment	RV297	617.5506	Performing arts—Law and legislation—England	KD3720-3731	344.42097
			Perfumes	GT2340	391.63
Pen-based computers	QA76.89	004.16	Pericardium	QM181	611.11
Pen drawing	NC905	741.26	Pericardium	RC685.P5	616.11
Penal colonies	HV8935-8962	365.34	Perinatal cardiology	RG618	618.3261
Penance	BX2260-2283	264.02086	Perinatal death	RG631-633	618.32
Penance	BV840-850	265.6	Perinatology	RG600-650	618.32
Penance (Jainism)	BL1375.P	294.434	Periodic law	QD467	541.24
Pencil drawing	NC890-895	741.24			

Subject Heading	LC	Dewey
Periodicals	AP	050
Periodicals	PN4700-5650	050
Periodicals—Indexes	AI	050
Periodontal disease	RK361-450	617.632
Periodontics	RK361-450	617.645
Periodontitis	RK450.P4	617.632
Peripheral vascular diseases	RC694	616.131
Peritoneum	QM367	611.38
Peritonitis	RC867.5	618.73
Perjury	HV6326	364.134
Permaculture	S494.5.P47	631.58
Permic languages	PH1001-1004	494.53
Permutations	QA165	512.925
Perpetual calendars	CE91-92	529.3
Persecution	BR1600-1609	272
Persephone (Greek deity)	BL820.P7	292.2114
Perseus (Greek mythology)	BL820.P5	292.13
Persian Gulf War, 1991	DS79.72	956.70442
Persian cat	SF449.P4	636.832
Persian drama	PK6421-6422	891.552009
Persian language	PK6201-6399	491.55
Persian literature	PK6400-6599	891.55
Persian poetry	PK6416-6420	891.551009
Persian prose literature	PK6423	891.55808
Persian prose literature	PK6443	891.55808
Personal archives	CD977	027.1
Personal property	K783-793	341.48
Personal property—Canada	KE765-781	346.71047
Personal property—England	KD1205-1465	346.42047
Personal property—United States	KF701-720	346.73047
Personalism	B828.5	141.5
Personality	BD331	126
Personality	BF698-.9	158.1
Personality assessment	BF698.4-.8	155.28
Personality development	BF723.P4	155.41825
Personality disorders	RC554-569.5	616.858
Personality questionnaires	BF698.8.P48	155.283
Personnel management	HF5549-.5	658.3
Persons (Canon law)	BX1939.P47	262.932
Persons (Law)—Canada	KE498-606	346.71012
Persons (Law)—England	KD723-785	346.42012
Persons (Law)—Ireland	KDK185-205	346.415012
Persons (Law)—Northern Ireland	KDE90-98	346.416012
Persons (Law)—Scotland	KDC350-378	346.411012
Persons (Law)—United States	KF465-553	346.73012
Perspective	NC749-750	742
Perspective	T369	604.245
Perspiration	QP221	612.7921
Perturbation (Astronomy)	QB361-407	521.4
Perturbation (Mathematics)	QA871	515.35
Peru	F3401-3619	985
Peru—Census	HA1051-1070	318.5
Peru—Civilization	F3410	985
Peru—Description and travel	F3410.5-3425	918.504
Peru—Economic conditions	HC226-230	330.985
Peru—Emigration and immigration	JV7510-7519	325.(285/85)
Peru—Gazetteers	F3404	918.5003
Peru—History	F3430.3-3448.4	985
Peru—History—To 1548	F3442	985.0(1-2)
Peru—History—To 1820	F3442-3444	985.0(1-4)
Peru—History—Conquest, 1522-1548	F3442	985.02
Peru—History—1548-1820	F3444	985.0(2-4)
Peru—History—Insurrection of Tupac Amaru, 1780-1781	F3444	985.03
Peru—History—War of Independence, 1820-1829	F3446	985.0(4-5)
Peru—History—1829-1919	F3447	985.0(5-631)
Peru—History—Spanish question, 1864	F3447	985.05
Peru—History—Revolution of 1872	F3447	985.061
Peru—History—1919-1968	F3448	985.063(1-2)
Peru—History—Revolution, 1930	F3448	985.0631
Peru—History—1968-1980	F3448.2	985.0633
Peru—History—Coup d'etat, 1968	F3448.2	985.0633
Peru—History—1980-	F3448.2	985.0633
Peru—Manufactures	TS52	670.985
Peru—Maps	G5310-5314	912.85
Peru—Periodicals	F3401	985.005
Peru—Politics and government	JL3400-3499	320.985
Peruvian literature	PQ8300-8498.36	860
Pessimism	B829	149.6
Pessimism	BF698.35.P49	155.232
Pesticidal plants	SB292	633.898
Pesticide residues in feeds	SF98.P46	636.0855
Pesticide resistance	SB957	632.95042
Pesticides	SB950.9-970.4	632.95
Pesticides—Application	SB952.8-955	632.94
Pesticides—Government policy	SB970-.4	344.04633
Pesticides—Physiological effect	QP801.P38	571.49
Pests	SB599-1100	632.(6-7)
Pests—Biological control	SB975-989	632.96
Pests—Control	SB950-989	632.9
Pet boarding facilities	SF414.3	636.0887
Pet grooming salons	SF427.55	636.70833
Pet shows	SF411.5	636.0811
Petit mal epilepsy	RC374.5	616.853
Petition, Right of	JK1731	323.480973
Petition, Right of	JC609	323.48
Petrified forests	QE991	561.16
Petroleum	TN860-879	622.3382
Petroleum	TP690-692.5	665.5
Petroleum—Prospecting	TN271.P4	622.1828
Petroleum—Refining	TP690-692.5	665.53
Petroleum—Storage	TP692.5	665.542
Petroleum as fuel	TP355	665.5
Petroleum pipelines	TN879.5-.6	665.544
Petroleum products	TP690-692.5	665.5
Petroleum waste	TD800	628.16837
Petroleum waste	TD899.P4	628.16836

Subject Heading	LC	Dewey
Philosophy—Periodicals	B1-8	105
Philosophy—Societies, etc.	B11-18	106
Philosophy—Study and teaching	B52-.65	107.1
Philosophy—Terminology	B49-50	103
Philosophy, African	B5300-5320	199.6
Philosophy, American	B850-945	191
Philosophy, Ancient	B108-708	180
Philosophy, Ancient	B630-708	189
Philosophy, Arab	B740-753	181.92
Philosophy, Arab	B5295	181.92
Philosophy, Babylonian	B145-148	181.6
Philosophy, Belgian	B4151-4175	199.493
Philosophy, Buddhist	B162	181.043
Philosophy, Canadian	B981-995	191
Philosophy, Central American	B1025-1026	199.728
Philosophy, Chinese	B125-128	181.11
Philosophy, Chinese	B5230-5234	181.11
Philosophy, Confucian	B127.C65	181.112
Philosophy, Czech	B4801-4805	199.437
Philosophy, Danish	B4325-4395	198.9
Philosophy, Dutch	B4041-4095	199.492
Philosophy, Egyptian	B140-143	181.2
Philosophy, English	B1111-1674	192
Philosophy, Finnish	B4711-4800	198.8
Philosophy, French	B1801-2430	194
Philosophy, German	B2521-3396	193
Philosophy, Greek (Modern)	B3500-3515	199.495
Philosophy, Hungarian	B4811-4815	199.439
Philosophy, Iranian	B150-153	181.5
Philosophy, Islamic	B740-753	181.07
Philosophy, Israeli	B5055-5059	181.3
Philosophy, Italian	B3551-3656	195
Philosophy, Japanese	B5243-5244	181.12
Philosophy, Japanese	B135-138	181.12
Philosophy, Jewish	B755-759	181.3
Philosophy, Jewish	B154-157	181.06
Philosophy, Korean	B139.1-.4	181.119
Philosophy, Medieval	B720-785	189
Philosophy, Mexican	B1015-1019	199.72
Philosophy, Middle Eastern	B5025-5099	181.(3/6-8)
Philosophy, Modern	B790-5739	190
Philosophy, Norwegian	B4411-4445	198.1
Philosophy, Oriental	B121-162.7	181
Philosophy, Oriental	B5000-5295	181
Philosophy, Polish	B4687-4691	199.438
Philosophy, Portuguese	B4591-4598	196.9
Philosophy, Renaissance	B770-785	190
Philosophy, Romanian	B4821-4825	199.498
Philosophy, Russian	B4201-4279	197
Philosophy, Shinto	B162.6	181.09561
Philosophy, South American	B1030-1084	199.8
Philosophy, Spanish	B4561-4568	196.1
Philosophy, Swedish	B4455-4495	198.5
Philosophy, Swiss	B4628-4651	199.494
Philosophy, Taoist	B163	181.114
Philosophy, Turkish	B4871-4875	199.561
Philosophy, West Indian	B1028-1029	199.729
Philosophy of mind	BD418-.5	128.2
Philosophy of nature	BD581	113

Subject Heading	LC	Dewey
Phlebitis	RC696	616.142
Phobias	RC535	616.85225
Phobias in children	RJ506.P38	618.9285225
Phoenician antiquities	DS80.3	939.44
Phoenician language	PJ4171-4187	492.6
Phoenicians	DS81-89	939.44
Phoenicians	HF370	380.1089926
Phoenix (Ariz.)	F819.P57	979.173
Phoenix Islands (Kiribati)	DU790	996.81
Phonetic alphabet	PE1151	421
Phonetic spelling	PE1151	421
Phonetics	P221-232	414.8
Phonograph	ML1055	780.26609
Phosphate minerals	QE389.64	549.72
Phosphate mines and mining	TN913-914	622.364
Phosphatic fertilizers	S647	631.85
Phosphorus	QD181.P1	546.712
Photobiochemistry	QP517.P45	572.435
Photochemistry	QD701-731	541.35
Photoconductivity	QC612.P5	537.54
Photocopying	TR824-835	686.4
Photoelasticity	TA418.12	620.11295
Photoelectric cells	TK8300-8360	621.381542
Photoelectric multipliers	TK8314	621.381542
Photoelectricity	QC611	537.54
Photoemission	QC715.15	537.54
Photoengraving	TR970-977	686.2327
Photoengraving—Halftone process	TR975	686.2327
Photogrammetry	TR693-696	526.982
Photogrammetry	TA593	526.982
Photograph collections	N4000-4042	779.074
Photographers	TR139	770.92
Photographic chemicals	TR212	771.5
Photographic chemistry	TR210-212	771.5
Photographic interpretation (Military science)	UG476	623.72
Photographic lenses	TR270-271	771.352
Photographic reproduction of plans, drawings, etc.	TR920-923	686.4
Photographic surveying	TA592-593.9	526.982
Photographs—Conservation and restoration	TR465	779.0288
Photographs—Trimming, mounting, etc.	TR340	771.44
Photography	TR	770
Photography—Artificial light	TR600	778.72
Photography—Biography	TR139-140	770.92
Photography—Congresses	TR5	770.6
Photography—Developing and developers	TR295	771.49
Photography—Encyclopedias	TR9	770.3
Photography—Enlarging	TR475	771.44
Photography—Enlarging	TR905	771.44
Photography—Equipment and supplies	TR196-199	771
Photography—Exhibitions	TR6	770.74
Photography—Films	TR283	771.5324
Photography—History	TR15	770.9
Photography—Lighting	TR590-620	778.72
Photography—Negatives	TR290-312	771.43

Subject Heading	LC	Dewey	Subject Heading	LC	Dewey
Photography—Periodicals	TR1	770.5	Photography, Pinhole	TR268	771
Photography—Peru	TR52	770.985	Photography of sports	TR821	070.49796
Photography—Plates	TR281	771.5322	Photogravure	TR980	686.2327
Photography—Printing processes	TR330-333	772.774	Photojournalism	TR820	070.49
Photography—Processing	TR287-500	772.774	Photolithography	TR940-950	686.2325
Photography—Studios and dark rooms	TR550-581	771.1	Photomechanical processes	TR925-997	686.232
Photography—Study and teaching	TR161	770.71	Photometry	QC391	535.220287
Photography—Tables	TR151	770.21	Photon beams	QC173	539.7217
Photography—Wastes, Recovery of	TR225	771.47	Photon rockets	TL783.57	629.4754
Photography—[By region or country]	TR21-127	770.9(4-9)	Photonics	TA1501-1820	621.36
			Photons	QC793.5.P42-.P429	539.7217
Photography—Africa	TR115-119	770.96	Photonuclear reactions	QC794.8.P4	539.756
Photography—Argentina	TR36-37	770.982	Photosensitivity disorders	RL247	616.5
Photography—Asia	TR99-113	770.95	Photosnythesis	QK882	572.46
Photography—Asiatic Russia	TR109-110	770.957	Photostat	TR470	686.45
Photography—Australia	TR121-122	770.994	Phototherapy	RM835-844	615.831
Photography—Austria	TR65-.2	770.9436	Phototypesetting	TR1010	686.22544
Photography—Bolivia	TR38-39	770.984	Phrenology	BF866-885	139
Photography—Brazil	TR41-42	770.981	Physical anthropology	GN49-298	599.9
Photography—Canada	TR26-27	770.971	Physical diagnosis	RC76-.5	616.0754
Photography—Central America	TR30-31	770.9728	Physical distribution of goods	HF5415.6-.9	380.1
Photography—Chile	TR43-44	770.983	Physical education and training	GV201-555	796.07
Photography—China	TR101-102	770.951	Physical education and training, Military	U320-325	355.5
Photography—Colombia	TR45-46	770.9861	Physical education for children	GV443	613.7042
Photography—Ecuador	TR47	770.9866			
Photography—Egypt	TR117-118	770.962	Physical fitness—Testing	GV436	613.70287
Photography—Europe	TR55-95	770.94	Physical fitness centers	GV428-433	613.706
Photography—France	TR71-72.5	770.944	Physical geography	GB	910.02
Photography—Germany	TR73-74.5	770.943	Physical geology	QE28.2	551
Photography—Great Britain	TR57-64	770.941	Physical instruments	QC53-55	530.7
Photography—Greece	TR75-76	770.9495	Physical laboratories	QC51	530.072
Photography—India	TR103-104	770.954	Physical metallurgy	TN690	669.9
Photography—Iran	TR107-108	770.955	Physical optics	QC392-449.5	535.2
Photography—Ireland	TR59-60	770.9415	Physical sciences	Q	500.2
Photography—Italy	TR79-80	770.945	Physical therapists	RM699.5-.7	615.82092
Photography—Japan	TR105-106	770.952	Physical therapists—Directories	RM697	615.82025
Photography—Mexico	TR28-29	770.972	Physical therapy	RM695-893	615.82
Photography—Netherlands	TR77-78	770.9492	Physical therapy—Congresses	RM696	615.8206
Photography—New Zealand	TR122.5-.6	770.993			
Photography—Norway	TR81-82	770.9481	Physical therapy—Societies, etc.	RM695	615.8206
Photography—Oceania	TR123-124	770.99(5-6)			
Photography—Paraguay	TR51	770.9892	Physical therapy—Study and teaching	RM706-707	615.82071
Photography—Russia	TR85-86	770.947			
Photography—Spain	TR87-88	770.946	Physically handicapped children—Education	LC4201-4580	371.91
Photography—Sweden	TR89-90	770.9485			
Photography—Switzerland	TR91-92	770.9494	Physically handicapped children—Vocational education	LC4219.7	370.113087
Photography—Turkey	TR111-112	770.9561			
Photography—United States	TR22-25	770.973			
Photography—Uruguay	TR53	770.9895	Physically handicapped—Services for	HV3011-3024	362.48
Photography—Venezuela	TR54	770.987			
Photography—West Indies	TR32-33	770.9729	Physically handicapped—[By region or country]	HV3023-3024	362.4809(4-9)
Photography, Artistic	TR640-688	770			
Photography, Artistic	TR183	770	Physically handicapped—United States	HV3023	362.480973
Photography, High-speed	TR593	778.37			
Photography, Military	TR785	623.72			
Photography, Panoramic	TR661	778.36			

Subject Heading	LC	Dewey	Subject Heading	LC	Dewey
Physically handicapped—[Other regions or countries]	HV3024	362.4809(4-9)	Pilot guides	VK798-997	623.8922
			Pilot guides—[By body of water]	VK804-997	623.892216(3-7)
Physician and patient	R727.3-.45	610.696	Pilot guides—Atlantic Ocean	VK810-880	623.89223
Physicians	R707-.4	610.6952	Pilot guides—Baltic Sea	VK819-821.8	623.8922334
Physicians	UH400	355.345092	Pilot guides—English Channel	VK839-844	623.8922336
Physicians—Biography	R134-.5	610.92			
Physicians—Directories	R711-713.97	610.25	Pilot guides—Indian Ocean	VK885-901	623.89225
Physicists	QC15-16	530.092	Pilot guides—Mediterranean Sea	VK853-874	623.892238
Physics	QC	530			
Physics—Congresses	QC1	530.06	Pilot guides—North Pacific Ocean	VK917	623.892244
Physics—Encyclopedias	QC5	530.03			
Physics—History	QC6.9-9	530.09	Pilot guides—North Sea	VK815-818	623.8922336
Physics—Laboratory manuals	QC35-37	530.078	Pilot guides—Pacific Ocean	VK915-956	623.89224
			Pilot guides—South Pacific Ocean	VK925	623.892248
Physics—Philosophy	QC5.56-6.4	530.01			
Physics—Study and teaching	QC30-48	530.071	Pilot guides—United States	VK947-948	623.89223(4/6)
Physics—Vocational guidance	QC29	530.071	Pilots and pilotage	VK1500-1661	623.8922
			Pilots and pilotage—History	VK1515	623.892209
Physiognomy	BF839.8-861	138	Pilots and pilotage—[By region or country]	VK1521-1624	623.892(2-9) + (4-9)
Physiological apparatus	QP55	571.0284			
Physiology	QP	571	Pima Indians	E99.P6	973.049745
Physiology—Periodicals	QP1	571.05	Pima languages	PM2175	497.45
Physiology—Study and teaching	QP39-47	571.071	Pins and needles	GT2280	391.44
			Pins and needles, Prehistoric	GN799.P5	646.2040284
Physiology—Terminology	QP13	571.014			
Physiology, Comparative	QP31-33	571.1	Pinto horse	SF293.P5	636.13
Physiology, Pathological	RB113	571.9	Pipe fitting	TH6703-6729	696.2
Phytogeography	QK101-474.5	581.9	Pipelines	TJ930-934	621.8672
Piano	ML649.8-747	786.209	Pirate radio broadcasting	HE8697.P57	384.54
Piano—Instruction and study	MT220-255	786.207	Pirates	G535-537	910.45092
			Pisces (Astrology)	BF1727.75	133.5277
Piano music	M20-39	786.2	Pistol shooting	GV1175	799.31
Piccolo	ML935-937	788.3309	Pistols	UD410-415	356.1182432
Piccolo music	M110.P5	788.33	Pistols	VD390	359.82432
Picketing	HD5468	331.8927	Pistons	TJ533	621.84
Picnicking	GT2955	394.15	Pita bread	TX770.P56	641.815
Picture books	NC965.85	741.6	Pitcairn Island	DU800	996.18
Picture frames and framing	N8550-8553	684	Pitcairn Island—Maps	G9660-9664	912.9618
Picture-writing, Indian	E98.P6	497	Pituitary gland	QP188.P58	612.492
Pictures	ND1142-1146	750	Pituitary gland	QL868	573.45
Pictures—Copying	N8580	702.872	Pituitary gland	QM371	611.47
Pictures in education	LB1043.67	371.3352	Pituitary gland—Diseases	RC658-.7	616.47
Pidgin English	PM7891	427.9	Pituitary gland—Transplantation	RD599.5.P58	617.440592
Pidgin languages	PM7801-7895	417.22			
Piece of eight	CJ3189	737.4946	Placenta	RG591	618.34
Piece-work	HD4928.P5	331.2164	Placenta praevia	RG715	618.56
Piers	TC357	627.31	Placental extracts	RM298.P5	615.39
Pietism	BR1650-1653	273.7	Plagiarism	PN167-168	808
Piety	BV4647.P5	241.4	Plague	RC171-179	616.9232
Pig Latin	PE3729.U	427	Plague—Vaccination	RA644.P7	614.5732
Pigments	ND1510	751.2	Plain People	BX4950-4951	289.(6-7)
Pigments	TN948.P5	622.3662	Plains	GB571-578	551.453
Pigments	TP934-937.5	667.29	Plane trigonometry	QA533	516.242
Pigments (Biology)	QP670-671	572.59	Planetary nebulae	QB855.5	523.1135
Pilgrim Festivals (Judaism)	BM693.P5	296.481	Planetary quarantine	TL943	629.455
Pilgrims (New Plymouth Colony)	F68	974.402008825	Planetary rings	QB603.R55	523.4
			Planetary theory	QB361-389	523.4
Piling (Civil engineering)	TA780-787	624.154	Planets	QB600-701	523.4
Pillars of Islam	BP176	297.31	Planing hulls	VM341-349	623.84
Pills	RS201.P5	615.43	Planing-machines	TJ1205-1210	621.91

Subject Heading	LC	Dewey	Subject Heading	LC	Dewey
Plankton	QH90.8.P5	578.776	Plants, Protection of	SB950-989	632.9
Planned communities	HT169.55-.57	307.768	Plants, Sex in	QK827-830	575.6
Plant biochemical genetics	QK981.3	581.35	Plants, Sex in	QK658-659	575.6
Plant biotechnology	SB106.B56	631.5233	Plants, Useful	QK98.4	581.63
Plant breeding	SB123-.5	631.52	Plants for land reclamation	S621.5.P59	631.64
Plant cell development	QK725	571.7236	Plants for soil conservation	S627.P55	631.45
Plant cells and tissues	QK725	571.7236	Plasma (Ionized gases)	QC717-.8	530.44
Plant chromosomes	QK725	571.72366	Plasma astrophysics	QB462.7-.72	523.019
Plant competition	QK911	577.83	Plasma chemistry	QD581	541.0424
Plant conservation	QK86-.4	333.953	Plasma exchange	RC271.P54	616.99406
Plant diseases	SB599-989	632.3	(Therapeutics)		
Plant ecology	QK900-938	581.7	Plasma exchange	RM175-176	615.39
Plant enzymes	QK898.E58	572.72	(Therapeutics)		
Plant genetic engineering	SB123.57	631.5233	Plasma rockets	TL783.6	629.4755
Plant genetic regulation	QK981.4	581.35	Plaster	TH8135-8139	693.6
Plant growing media	S589.8	631.4	Plaster casts	NB1190	731.452
Plant hormones	QK898.H67	571.742	Plastic analysis	TA652	620.11233
Plant introduction	SB108-109	631.523	(Engineering)		
Plant maintenance	TS192	670.288	Plastic foams	TP1183.F6	668.493
Plant molecular biology	QK728	572.82	Plastic sculpture	NB1270.P5	731.2
Plant parasites	SB601	632	Plasticity	QA931-939	531.385
Plant physiology	QK710-899	575	Plasticity	QC191	531.385
Plant pigments	QK898.P7	572.592	Plastics	TP1101-1185	668.4
Plant propagation	SB119-124	631.52	Plastics	TA455.P5-.P55	620.1923
Plant quarantine	SB979.5-985	632.93	Plastics—Congresses	TP1105	668.406
Plant shutdowns	HD5708.5-.55	338.6042	Plastics—Encyclopedias	TP1110	668.403
Plant viruses	QR351	579.28	Plastics—Extrusion	TP1175.E9	668.413
Plantation workers	HD8039.P496	630.92	Plastics—History	TP1116-1118	668.409
Planting (Plant culture)	SB121	631.53	Plastics—Molding	TP1150	668.412
Planting time	SB185.8	631.53	Plastics—Patents	TP1114	668.4027
Planting time	SB454.3.P7	635.043	Plastics—Periodicals	TP1103	668.405
Planting time	S600.7.P53	631.53	Plastics—Societies, etc.	TP1101	668.406
Plants	GR780-790	398.368	Plastics—Study and	TP1127-1129	668.4071
Plants	QK	580	teaching		
Plants—Absorption of water	QK871	575.76	Plastics—Welding	TP1160	668.415
Plants—Collection and	QK61	580.75	Plastics craft	TT297-.5	745.572
preservation			Plastics in building	TA668	624.18923
Plants—Disease and	SB750	632.95042	Plastics machinery	TP1135	668.41
pest resistance			Plate tectonics	QE511.4-.48	551.8
Plants—Evolution	QK980-989	581.38	Plateaus	GB571-578	551.434
Plants—Frost resistance	QK756	632.11	Plating	TS662-693	671.732
Plants—Habitat	QK900-938	577	Plating	TS213	671.732
Plants—Metabolism	QK881-897	572.42	Plato's cave (Allegory)	B398.C34	184
Plants—Nutrition	QK867-898	572.42	Platonic love	B398.L9	184
Plants—Reproduction	QK825-830	575.6	Play (Philosophy)	B105.P54	790.01
Plants—Respiration	QK891	572.472	Play behavior in animals	QL763.5	591.563
Plants, Edible	QK98.5	581.632	Player-piano music	M20-32	786.66
Plants, Effect of acid	QK751	577.2752	Playgrounds	GV421-433	796.068
precipitation on			Playgrounds—Equipment	GV426-.5	796.0680284
Plants, Effect of acid	SB745	632.19	and supplies		
precipitation on			Plazas	NA9070-9072	711.55
Plants, Effect of air	QK751	577.276	Pleading—United States	KF8866-8885	347.73072
pollution on			Pleasure	BF515	152.42
Plants, Effect of air	SB745	632.19	Pleurisy	RC751	616.25
pollution on			Plots (Drama, novel, etc.)	PN3378	809.924
Plants, Effect of	QK750-751	577.27	Plows	S683-685	631.3
pollution on			Plumbing	TH6101-6729	696.1
Plants, Flowering of	QK830	575.6	Plumbing—Repairing	TH6681-6685	696.10288
Plants, Motion of fluids in	QK871	575.75	Pluralism	BD394	147.4
Plants, Ornamental	SB403-450.87	635.9	Plush	TS1680	677.617
Plants, Potted	SB415	635.986	Pluto (Planet)	QB701	523.482

Subject Heading	LC	Dewey	Subject Heading	LC	Dewey
Plywood	TS870	674.834	Poland—History—Parititon period, 1763-1796	DK4328.9-4348	943.8025
Pneumatic machinery	TJ950-1030	621.51	Poland—History—Stanislaus II Augustus, 1764-1795	DK4330-4348	943.8025
Pneumatic presses	TJ1465	621.98			
Pneumatic tools	TJ1005-1007	621.904			
Pneumatics	QC161-166.5	533	Poland—History—Revolution of 1794	DK4338-4345	943.8025
Pneumonia	RA644.P8	614.59241	Poland—History—Revolution, 1830-1832	DK4359-4363	943.8032
Pneumonia	RC771-772	616.241			
Poaching	SK36.7	799.2028	Poland—History—Partisan Campaign, 1833	DK4363.2	943.8032
Podiatry	RD563	617.585			
Poetics	PN1039-1049	808.1	Poland—History—Revolution, 1846	DK4364	943.8032
Poetry	PN1010-1525	808.1			
Poetry—Collections	PN6099-6110	808.108	Poland—History—Revolution, 1863-1864	DK4366-4378	943.8033
Poetry—History and criticism	PN1105-1279	809.1			
			Poland—History—1864-1918	DK4379.5-4395	943.8033
Poetry—Study and teaching	PN1101	808.81071	Poland—History—Revolution, 1905-1907	DK4383-4389	943.8033
Poetry, Medieval	PN688-691	808.82			
Poisoning	HV6549-6555	364.1791	Poland—History—German occupation, 1914-1918	DK4390-4395	943.8033
Poisoning	RA1190-1270	615.9			
Poisoning, Accidental, in children	RA1225	615.90083	Poland—History—Austrian occupation, 1915-1918	DK4394-4395	943.8033
Poisonious animals	QL100	591.65	Poland—History—1918-1945	DK4397-4420	943.804(4-53)
Poisonous fishes	QL618.7	597.165			
Poisonous plants	QK100	581.659	Poland—History—Wars of 1918-1921	DK4404-4409	943.804
Poisonous snakes—Venom	RA1242.S53	615.942			
Poisons	RA1190-1270	615.9	Poland—History—Coup d'etat, 1926	DK4409.4	943.804
Poker	GV1251-1255	795.412			
Poland	DK4010-4800	943.8	Poland—History—Occupation, 1939-1945	DK4410-4415	943.8053
Poland—Biography	DK4130-4138.5	920.0438			
Poland—Census	HA1451-1460	314.38	Poland—History—1945-	DK4429-4442	943.805(4-7)
Poland—Civilization	DK4110-4115	943.8	Poland—History—1980-1989	DK4443	943.8056
Poland—Congresses	DK4018	943.8006			
Poland—Description and travel	DK4047-4081	914.3804	Poland—History—1989-	DK4442	943.8057
			Poland—Maps	G1950-1954	912.438
Poland—Economic conditions	HC340.3	330.9438	Poland—Maps	G6520-6524	912.438
			Poland—Periodicals	DK4010	943.8005
Poland—Emigration and immigration	JV8195	325.(2438/438)	Poland—Politics and government	JN6750-6769	320.9438
Poland—Gazetteers	DK4030	914.38003	Polar regions	G575-597	910.0211
Poland—Historiography	DK4139-.25	943.80072	Polar regions—Maps	G3260-3272	912.191
Poland—History—To 1795	DK4186-4348	943.802	Polar regions—Maps	G1054-1055	912.191
Poland—History—To 1572	DK4186-4289	943.802(2-3)	Polarization (Light)	QC440-446	535.52
Poland—History—To 960 (ca.)	DK4210-.7	943.8022	Police	HV7551-8280.7	363.2
			Police—Directories	HV7900	363.2025
Poland—History—Piast period, 960-1386	DK4211-4249.5	943.8022	Police—Drug testing	HV7936.D78	363.2
			Police—History	HV7903-7909	363.209
Poland—History—Mieszko II, 1025-1034	DK4222	943.8022	Police—Job stress	HV7936.J63	363.22019
			Police—Study and teaching	HV7923	363.2071
Poland—History—Casimir I, 1040-1058	DK4223	943.8022	Police—[By region or country]	HV8130-8280.7	363.209(4-9)
Poland—History—1138-1305	DK4227-4246.5	943.8022	Police—Africa	HV8267-8279.3	363.2096
			Police—Asia	HV8241.85-8263	363.2095
Poland—History—Mongol Invasion, 1241	DK4245.7	943.8022	Police—Australia	HV8280	363.20994
			Police—Benelux countries	HV8215.5-8223.5	363.209492
Poland—History—Jagellons, 1386-1572	DK4249.7-4289	943.8023	Police—Canada	HV8157-8160	363.20971
			Police—Central America	HV8163-8169	363.209728
Poland—History—16th century	DK4276	943.802(3-4)	Police—China	HV8260	363.20951
			Police—Europe	HV8194-8261.84	363.2094
Poland—History—Elective monarchy, 1572-1763	DK4289.5-4328	943.802(4-5)	Police—France	HV8203-8206	363.20944
Poland—History—18th century	DK4314.5	943.80(25-3)			

Subject Heading	LC	Dewey	Subject Heading	LC	Dewey
Police—Germany	HV8207-8210	363.20943	Political persecution	JC585-599	323.044
Police—Great Britain	HV8195-8197.5	363.20941	Political rights—Great Britain	JN900-1088	323.0941
Police—Greece	HV8241.83	363.209495			
Police—India	HV8247-8250	363.20954	Political rights—United States	JK1717-2217	323.0973
Police—Italy	HV8212-8215	363.20945			
Police—Japan	HV8257	363.20952	Political science	B65	320
Police—Mexico	HV8161	363.20972	Political science	JA	320
Police—Middle East	HV8241.9-8242.56	363.20956	Political science	J	320
			Political science	HM33	320
Police—Philippines	HV8255	363.209599	Political science—Congresses	JA35.5	320.06
Police—Portugal	HV8239	363.209469			
Police—Russia	HV8224-8227	363.20947	Political science—History	JA81-84	320.09
Police—South America	HV8176-8193	363.2098	Political science—Periodicals	JA1-26	320.05
Police—Spain	HV8235-8238	363.20946			
Police—United States	HV8130-8148	363.20973	Political science—Societies, etc.	JA27-34	320.06
Police—West Indies	HV8170-8175.9	363.209729			
Police, Private	HV8290-8291	363.289	Political science—Study and teaching	JA86-88	320.071
Police, Rural	HV7965-7985	363.2091734			
Police administration	HV7935-8025	353.36	Polka (Dance)	GV1796.P55	793.31
Police artists	HV8073.4	363.258	Pollen	QK658	571.845
Police chiefs	HV8012	363.22	Pollination	QK828	575.65
Police communication systems	HV7936.C8	363.24	Pollination	QK926	571.8642
			Polling places	JF1125	324.65
Police divers	HV8080.D54	363.22	Pollution	TD172-193.5	628.5
Police dogs	HV8025	636.70886	Pollution—History	TD179	628.509
Police patrol—Field interrogation	HV8080.P2	363.232	Pollution—Physiological effect	QP82.2.P6	571.49
Police patrol—Surveillance operations	HV8080.P2	363.232	Pollution—Research	TD178.5-.7	628.5072
			Pollution—[By region or country]	TD179.5-191	628.509(4-9)
Police power	JK371.P7-.P8	342.0418			
Police power—Canada	KE5006-5010	342.710418	Pollution—Africa	TD188-.5	628.5096
Police power—United States	KF5399-.5	342.730418	Pollution—Arctic regions	TD190-.5	628.50998
Police power—United States	KF4695	342.730418	Pollution—Asia	TD187-.5	628.5095
Police psychiatrists	HV7936.P75	363.22	Pollution—Canada	TD182-.4	628.50971
Police psychologists	HV7936.P75	363.22	Pollution—Europe	TD186-.5	628.5094
Police reports	HV7936.R53	363.24	Pollution—Mexico	TD182.6-.7	628.50972
Police social work	HV8079.2-.3	363.22	Pollution—[New Zealand/ Australia/Oceania]	TD189.5.A8	628.5099(3-6)
Police stations	NA4490-4497	725.18			
Policewomen	HV8023	363.22082	Pollution—South America	TD185-.5	628.5098
Poliomyelitis	RC180-181	616.835	Pollution—United States	TD180-181	628.50973
Poliomyelitis—Nursing	RC180.8	610.73699	Pollution control equipment	TD192	628.5028
Polish language	PG6001-6790	491.85	Poltergeists	BF1483	133.142
Polish language—Dialects	PG6700-6790	491.857	Polyandry	GN480.6	306.8423
Polish language—Lexicography	PG6625-6638	491.853028	Polycarbonates	TP1180.P57	668.423
			Polyester fibers	TS1548.7.P58	677.4743
Polish literature	PG7001-7446	891.85	Polyesters	TP1180.P6	668.4225
Polish philology	PG6001-6790	491.85	Polygamy	GN480.33-.36	306.8423
Polishes	TP940	667.72	Polygamy	HQ981-996	306.8423
Political anthropology	GN492-495	306.2	Polyglot glossaries, phrase books, etc.	PB73	418
Political clubs	JF2101	324.3			
Political conventions	JK2255-2261	324.2730156	Polyglot glossaries, phrase books, etc.	P361	413
Political corruption	JF1081-1083	324.66			
Political crimes and offenses	HV6254-6322.7	364.131	Polygons	QA482	516.15
			Polygraph operators	HV8078	363.254092
Political customs and rites	GN492.3	398.27	Polymerization	QD281.P6	547.28
Political geography	JC319-323	320.12	Polymerization	TP156.P6	668.92
Political parties	JF2011-2112	324.2	Polymers	QD380-388	547.7
Political parties—Great Britain	JN1111-1129	324.241	Polymers	TA455.P58	620.192
			Polynesia	DU510	996
Political parties—United States	KF4788	342.73087	Polynesia—Maps	G9500-9652	912.96
			Polynesia—Maps	G2970-2984	912.96

Subject Heading	LC	Dewey
Polynesian languages	PL6401-6551	499.4
Polytheism	BL217	211.32
Ponies	SF315	636.16
Pontoon bridges	TG450	624.87
Pontoon bridges	UG335	623.67
Pool (Game)	GV891-899	794.73
Poor	HV4023-4470.7	362.5
Poor—[By region or country]	HV4041-4173	362.509(4-9)
Poor—Africa	HV4157-4169.3	362.5096
Poor—Asia	HV4131.85-4156.5	362.5095
Poor—Australia	HV4170	362.50994
Poor—Benelux countries	HV4105.5-4113.5	362.509492
Poor—Canada	HV4047-4050	362.50971
Poor—Central America	HV4053-4059	362.509728
Poor—China	HV4150	362.50951
Poor—Developing countries	HV4173	362.5091724
Poor—Europe	HV4084-4131.84	362.5094
Poor—France	HV4093-4096	362.50944
Poor—Germany	HV4097-4100.5	362.50943
Poor—Great Britain	HV4085-4087.5	362.50941
Poor—India	HV4137-4140	362.50954
Poor—Italy	HV4102-4105	362.50945
Poor—Japan	HV4147	362.50952
Poor—Mexico	HV4051	362.50972
Poor—Russia	HV4114-4117	362.50947
Poor—South America	HV4066-4083	362.5098
Poor—Spain	HV4125-4128	362.50946
Poor—United States	HV4043-4046	362.50973
Poor—West Indies	HV4060-4065.9	362.509729
Popcorn	SB191.P64	635.677
Popes	BX1805-1810	262.13
Popes	BX1001-1378	262.13
Popes—Abdication	BX958.A23	262.13
Popes—Infallibility	BX1806	262.131
Popular instrumental music	ML3469-3541	784.16309
Popular music	ML3469-3541	781.6309
Popular music	M1627-1844	781.63
Population	HB848-3697	304.6
Population Research	HB850-.5	304.6072
Population assistance	HB884.5	363.96091724
Population biology	QH352	577.88
Population density	HB1953	304.61
Population genetics	QH455	576.58
Population geography—Aghanistan	HB2096.6	304.609581
Population geography—Albania	HB2086.5	304.6094965
Population geography—Algeria	HB2121.4	304.60965
Population geography—American Samoa	HB2153.7	304.6099613
Population geography—Angola	HB2124.4	304.609673
Population geography—Anguilla	HB2016.72	304.60972973
Population geography—Antigua	HB2016.74	304.60972974
Population geography—Arctic regions	HB2155	304.60998(1-8)
Population geography—Argentina	HB2019-2020	304.60982
Population geography—Aruba	HB2017.35	304.60972986
Population geography—Australia	HB2135-2136	304.60994
Population geography—Austria	HB2051-2052	304.609436
Population geography—Azores	HB2127.5	304.6094699
Population geography—Bahamas	HB2007-2008	304.6097296
Population geography—Bahrain	HB2095.9	304.6095365
Population geography—Bangladesh	HB2100.6	304.6095492
Population geography—Barbados	HB2016.57	304.60972981
Population geography—Belgium	HB2063-2064	304.609493
Population geography—Belize	HB1995-1996	304.6097282
Population geography—Benin	HB2125.7	304.6096683
Population geography—Bermuda Islands	HB2128	304.6097299
Population geography—Bhutan	HB2100.3	304.6095498
Population geography—Bolivia	HB2021-2022	304.60984
Population geography—Bonaire	HB2017.36	304.60972986
Population geography—Botswana	HB2123.9	304.6096883
Population geography—Brazil	HB2023-2024	304.60981
Population geography—Bulgaria	HB2087-2088	304.609499
Population geography—Burkina Faso	HB2126.4	304.6096625
Population geography—Burma	HB2096.7	304.609591
Population geography—Burundi	HB2122.8	304.60967572
Population geography—Cambodia	HB2104.3	304.609596
Population geography—Cameroon	HB2125.4	304.6096711
Population geography—Canada	HB1989-1990	304.60971
Population geography—Canary Islands	HB2129	304.609649
Population geography—Cape Verde	HB2129.5	304.6096658
Population geography—Chad	HB2125.3	304.6096743
Population geography—Chile	HB2025-2026	304.60983
Population geography—China	HB2114	304.60951

Subject Heading	LC	Dewey	Subject Heading	LC	Dewey
Population geography—Colombia	HB2027-2028	304.609861	Population geography—Greece	HB2092.5	304.609495
Population geography—Comoro Islands	HB2132.5	304.609694	Population geography—Greenland	HB2156	304.609982
Population geography—Congo (Brazzaville)	HB2125	304.6096724	Population geography—Grenada	HB2016.95	304.609729845
Population geography—Cook Islands	HB2153.65	304.6099623	Population geography—Guadeloupe	HB2017.7	304.60972976
Population geography—Costa Rica	HB1997-1998	304.6097286	Population geography—Guam	HB2152.7	304.609967
Population geography—Cote d'Ivoire	HB2126	304.6096668	Population geography—Guatemala	HB1999	304.6097281
Population geography—Cuba	HB2009-2010	304.6097291	Population geography—Guinea	HB2126.2	304.6096652
Population geography—Curacao	HB2017.37	304.60972986	Population geography—Guinea-Bissau	HB2127.3	304.6096657
Population geography—Cyprus	HB2093.5	304.6095693	Population geography—Guyana	HB2032.3	304.609881
Population geography—Czechoslovakia	HB2052.3	304.609437	Population geography—Haiti	HB2011	304.6097294
Population geography—Denmark	HB2071-2072	304.609489	Population geography—Honduras	HB2000	304.6097283
Population geography—Developing countries	HB2160	304.6091724	Population geography—Hong Kong	HB2117	304.6095125
Population geography—Djibouti	HB2122.3	304.6096771	Population geography—Hungary	HB2052.5	304.609439
Population geography—Dominica	HB2016.93	304.609729841	Population geography—Iceland	HB2073-2074	304.6094912
Population geography—Dominican Republic	HB2012	304.6097293	Population geography—India	HB2099-2100	304.60954
Population geography—Ecuador	HB2029-2030	304.609866	Population geography—Indonesia	HB2107-2108	304.609598
Population geography—Egypt	HB2121.7	304.60962	Population geography—Iran	HB2096.4	304.60955
Population geography—El Salvador	HB2004	304.6097284	Population geography—Iraq	HB2096.3	304.609567
			Population geography—Ireland	HB2049-2050	304.609415
Population geography—England and Wales	HB2045-2046	304.60942(9)	Population geography—Israel	HB2094	304.6095694
Population geography—Equatoria Guinea	HB2124.6	304.6096718	Population geography—Italy	HB2059-2060	304.60945
Population geography—Ethiopia	HB2122	304.60963	Population geography—Jamaica	HB2013-2014	304.6097292
Population geography—Falkland Islands	HB2131	304.6099711	Population geography—Japan	HB2111-2112	304.60952
Population geography—Fiji	HB2153.5	304.6099611	Population geography—Jordan	HB2094.3	304.6095695
Population geography—Finland	HB2068.3	304.6094897	Population geography—Kenya	HB2122.5	304.6096762
Population geography—France	HB2053-2054	304.60944	Population geography—Kerguelen Islands	HB2134	304.609699
Population geography—French Guiana	HB2032.7	304.609882	Population geography—Kiribati	HB2152.9	304.6099681
Population geography—French Polynesia	HB2153.9	304.609962	Population geography—Korea	HB2112.5-.6	304.609519
Population geography—Gabon	HB2124.9	304.6096721	Population geography—Kuwait	HB2096	304.6095367
Population geography—Gambia	HB2127	304.6096651	Population geography—Laos	HB2104.4	304.609594
Population geography—Germany	HB2055-2056	304.60944949	Population geography—Lebanon	HB2093.9	304.6095692
Population geography—Ghana	HB2126.8	304.609667	Population geography—Lesotho	HB2123.7	304.6096885

Subject Heading	LC	Dewey	Subject Heading	LC	Dewey
Population geography—Liberia	HB2127.2	304.6096662	Population geography—Panama	HB2002-2003	304.6097287
Population geography—Libya	HB2121.6	304.609612	Population geography—Papua New Guinea	HB2152.8	304.609953
Population geography—Liechtenstein	HB2052.9	304.60943648	Population geography—Paraguay	HB2033-2034	304.609892
Population geography—Luxembourg	HB2066.5	304.6094935	Population geography—Peru	HB2035-2036	304.60985
Population geography—Macao	HB2115	304.6095126	Population geography—Philippines	HB2109-2110	304.609599
Population geography—Madagascar	HB2123.2	304.609691	Population geography—Poland	HB2068.7	304.609438
Population geography—Madeira Islands	HB2128.5	304.6094698	Population geography—Portugal	HB2081-2082	304.609469
Population geography—Malawi	HB2124	304.6096897	Population geography—Qatar	HB2095.7	304.6095363
Population geography—Malaysia	HB2104.6	304.609595	Population geography—Reunion	HB2133.5	304.6096981
Population geography—Maldives	HB2131.5	304.6095495	Population geography—Romania	HB2091-2092	304.609498
Population geography—Mali	HB2126.3	304.6096623	Population geography—Russia	HB2067-2068.2	304.60947
Population geography—Martinique	HB2017.9	304.60972982	Population geography—Rwanda	HB2122.7	304.60967571
Population geography—Mauritania	HB2126.6	304.609661	Population geography—Saint Eustatius (Netherlands Antilles)	HB2017.385	304.60972977
Population geography—Mauritius	HB2133	304.6096982	Population geography—Saint Helena	HB2130	304.609973
Population geography—Mexico	HB1991-1992	304.60972	Population geography—Saint Kitts and Nevis	HB2016.78	304.60972973
Population geography—Mongolia	HB2112.8	304.609517	Population geography—Saint Lucia	HB2016.97	304.609729843
Population geography—Monserrat	HB2016.76	304.60972975	Population geography—Saint Martin	HB2017.39	304.60972977
Population geography—Morocco	HB2121.3	304.60964	Population geography—Saint Vincent	HB2016.99	304.609729844
Population geography—Mozambique	HB2123	304.609679	Population geography—Sao Tome and Principe	HB2124.7	304.6096715
Population geography—Namibia	HB2124.2	304.6096881	Population geography—Saudi Arabia	HB2094.7	304.609538
Population geography—Nepal	HB2096.9	304.6095496	Population geography—Scotland	HB2047-2048	304.609411
Population geography—Netherlands	HB2065-2066	304.609492	Population geography—Senegal	HB2126.5	304.609663
Population geography—New Caledonia	HB2153.3	304.6099597	Population geography—Seychelles	HB2132	304.609696
Population geography—New Zealand	HB2152.5	304.60993	Population geography—Sierra Leone	HB2126.9	304.609664
Population geography—Nicaragua	HB2001	304.6097285	Population geography—Solomon Islands	HB2153	304.6099593
Population geography—Niger	HB2125.9	304.6096626	Population geography—Somalia	HB2122.2	304.6096773
Population geography—Nigeria	HB2126.7	304.609669	Population geography—South Africa	HB2123.4	304.60968
Population geography—Northern Ireland	HB2048.5	304.609416	Population geography—Spain	HB2079-2080	304.60946
Population geography—Norway	HB2075-2076	304.609481	Population geography—Sri Lanka	HB2096.8	304.6095493
Population geography—Oman	HB2095.3	304.6095353	Population geography—Sudan	HB2121.8	304.609624
Population geography—Pakistan	HB2100.5	304.6095491			

185

Subject Heading	LC	Dewey	Subject Heading	LC	Dewey
Population geography—Surinam	HB2032.5	304.609883	Population geography—Zambia	HB2123.6	304.6096894
Population geography—Swaziland	HB2123.8	304.6096887	Population policy	HB883.5	363.9
Population geography—Sweden	HB2077-2078	304.609485	Porcelain	NK4370-4584	738.2
Population geography—Switzerland	HB2083-2084	304.609494	Porches	NA7125	721.84
			Pornography	HQ471-472	363.47
Population geography—Syria	HB2093.7	304.6095691	Pornography	NX650.E7	704.9428
Population geography—Taiwan	HB2116	304.60951249	Pornography—Social aspects	HQ471	363.47
Population geography—Tanzania	HB2122.9	304.609678	Port wine	TP559.P8	663.223
			Portfolio management	HG4529.5	332.6
Population geography—Thailand	HB2104.55	304.609593	Portland cement	TA680-683.94	624.1833
Population geography—Togo	HB2125.8	304.6096681	Portrait miniatures	N7616	704.942
			Portrait miniatures	ND1329.8-1337	757.7
Population geography—Tonga	HB2153.6	304.6099612	Portrait painting	ND1300-1337	757
			Portrait painting	ND2200-2202	751.42242
Population geography—Trinidad and Tobago	HB2017	304.60972983	Portrait painting—Biography	ND1328-1329	759
Population geography—Tristan da Cunha	HB2130.5	304.609973	Portrait painting—15th century	ND1308	757.090(24-31)
Population geography—Tunisia	HB2121.5	304.609611	Portrait painting—16th century	ND1308	757.09031
Population geography—Turkey	HB2093.4	304.609561	Portrait painting—17th century	ND1309.3	757.09032
Population geography—Ubangi-Shari	HB2125.2	304.6096741	Portrait painting—18th century	ND1309.4	757.09033
Population geography—Uganda	HB2122.6	304.6096761	Portrait painting—19th century	ND1309.5	757.09034
Population geography—United Arab Emirates	HB2095.5	304.6095357	Portrait painting—20th century	ND1309.6	757.0904
Population geography—United States	HB1965-1987	304.60973	Portrait painting—Asia	ND1325-1326.8	757.095
Population geography—[United States, By city]	HB1987	304.6097(4-9)	Portrait painting—Europe	ND1313-1324	757.0904
			Portrait painting—France	ND1316-.6	757.0944
Population geography—[United States, By state]	HB1985	304.6097(4-9)	Portrait painting—Germany	ND1317-.7	757.0943
Population geography—Uruguay	HB2037-2038	304.609895	Portrait painting—Great Britain	ND1314-.6	757.0941
Population geography—Vanuatu	HB2153.4	304.6099595	Portrait painting—Italy	ND1318-.6	757.0945
Population geography—Venezuela	HB2039-2040	304.60987	Portrait painting—Netherlands	ND1319-.6	757.09492
			Portrait painting—Russia	ND1320-.6	757.0947
Population geography—Vietnam	HB2104.5	304.609597	Portrait painting—Spain	ND1322-.6	757.0956
Population geography—Virgin Islands of the United States	HB2016.3	304.609729722	Portrait painting—United States	ND1311-.9	757.0973
			Portrait photography	TR680-681	778.92
			Portrait photography	TR575-581	778.92
Population geography—Western Sahara	HB2127.4	304.609648	Portrait sculpture	NB1293-1310	731.82
			Portraits	N7575-7649	704.942
Population geography—Western Samoa	HB2153.8	304.6099614	Portugal—Biography	DP536	920.0366/ 920.0469
Population geography—Yemen	HB2094.9-2095	304.609533	Portugal—Census	HA1571-1580	314.69
			Portugal—Civilization	DP532-.7	936.6/946.9
Population geography—Yugoslavia	HB2088.5	304.609497	Portugal—Colonies	JV4200-4299	325.3469
			Portugal—Description and travel	DP520-526.5	913.6604/ 914.6904
Population geaphry—Zaire	HB2124.5	304.6096751	Portugal—Economic conditions	HC391-394.5	330.9469
			Portugal—Emigration and immigration	JV8260-8269	325.(2469/469)
			Portugal—Gazetteers	DP514	913.66003/ 914.69003
			Portugal—Historiography	DP536.8-.96	936.60072/ 946.90072

Subject Heading	LC	Dewey	Subject Heading	LC	Dewey
Portugal—History	DP501-900	936.6/946.9	Portugal—History—John VI, 1816-1826	DP650-651	946.903(4-5)
Portugal—History, Military	DP547	355.309469	Portugal—History—Conspiracy of 1817	DP650	946.9034
Portugal—History, Naval	DP550-551	359.309469	Portugal—History—Revolution, 1820	DP650	946.9035
Portugal—History—To 1385	DP558-618	936.6/946.901	Portugal—History—1826-1853	DP653-660	946.903(5-6)
Portugal—History—Alfonso Henriques, 1139-1185	DP570	946.90(1-2)	Portugal—History—Civil War, 1846-1847	DP659	946.9035
Portugal—History—Sancho I, 1185-1211	DP571	946.902	Portugal—History—Uprising, 1846	DP659	946.9035
Portugal—History—Alfonso II, 1211-1223	DP572	946.902	Portugal—History—Peter V, 1853-1861	DP665-.5	946.9036
Portugal—History—Sancho II, 1223-1248	DP573	946.902	Portugal—History—Charles I, 1889-1908	DP668-669	946.9036
Portugal—History—Alfonso III, 1248-1279	DP574	946.902	Portugal—History—Revolution, 1891	DP662	946.9036
Portugal—History—Denis, 1279-1325	DP575-.3	946.902	Portugal—History—20th century	DP670-682.2	946.904
Portugal—History—Alfonso IV, 1325-1357	DP576	946.902	Portugal—History—1910-1974	DP675-680.5	946.904(1-3)
Portugal—History—Pedro I, 1357-1367	DP577	946.902	Portugal—History—Revolution, 1910	DP674-682.2	946.9041
Portugal—History—Fernando, 1367-1383	DP578	946.902	Portugal—History—Revolution, 1926	DP680	946.9042
Portugal—History—Interregnum, 1383-1385	DP580	946.902	Portugal—History—1974-	DP680	946.9044
Portugal—History—Period of discoveries, 1385-1580	DP582-618	946.902	Portugal—History—Revolution, 1974	DP681	946.9044
Portugal—History—John I, 1385-1433	DP585-590	946.902	Portugal—History—Coup d'etat, 1975	DP681	946.9044
Portugal—History—Edward, 1433-1438	DP592-594	946.902	Portugal—Manufactures	TS83-84.5	670.9469
Portugal—History—Alfonso V, 1438-1481	DP596-598	946.902	Portugal—Maps	G6690-6694	912.469
Portugal—History—John II, 1481-1495	DP600-602	946.902	Portugal—Maps	G1975-1979	912.469
Portugal—History—Manual, 1495-1521	DP604-606	946.902	Portugal—Periodicals	DP501	936.6005/ 946.9005
Portugal—History—John III, 1521-1557	DP608-610	946.902	Portugal—Politics and government	JN8423-8661	320.9469
Portugal—History—Sebastian, 1557-1578	DP612-616	946.902	Portuguese drama	PQ9083-9095	869.2009
Portugal—History—Henry I, 1578-1580	DP618	946.902	Portuguese drama	PQ9164-9170	869.2008
Portugal—History—Modern, 1580-	DP620-682.2	946.90(2-4)	Portuguese language	PC5001-5498	469
Portugal—History—Spanish dynasty, 1580-1640	DP622-629	946.902	Portuguese language—Dialects	PC5350-5498	469.7
Portugal—History—John IV, 1640-1656	DP634-.8	946.9032	Portuguese language—Dictionaries	PC5325-5348	469.3
Portugal—History—Revolution, 1640	DP628	946.902	Portuguese language—Etymology	PC5301-5315	469.2
Portugal—History—Alfonso VI, 1656-1683	DP636	946.9032	Portuguese language—Grammar	PC5061-5231	469.5
Portugal—History—Peter II, 1683-1706	DP636-.8	946.9032	Portuguese language—Lexicography	PC5320-5348	469.3028
Portugal—History—John V, 1706-1750	DP638	946.9032	Portuguese language—Slang	PC5498	469.709
Portugal—History—Joseph I, 1750-1777	DP639-641.9	946.9033	Portuguese language—Study and teaching	PC5035-5039	469.0071
Sortugal—History—Maria I, 1777-1816	DP642-644.9	946.903(3-4)	Portuguese literature	PQ9000-9999	869
			Portuguese literature—Foreign countries	PQ9421	869
			Portuguese literature—Study and teaching	PQ9008-9009.5	869.071
			Portuguese periodicals	PN5321-5330	056.9

Subject Heading	LC	Dewey	Subject Heading	LC	Dewey
Portuguese philology	PC5001-5041	469	Poultry—Feeding and feeds	SF494	636.508(4-5)
Portuguese poetry	PQ9149-9163	869.1008	Poultry—Hatcheries	SF495-497	636.5082
Portuguese poetry	PQ9061-9081	869.1009	Poverty	HC79.P6	339.46
Portuguese prose literature	PQ9172-9188	869.808	Poverty	HV1-4630	362.5
Portuguese prose literature	PQ9097-9119	869.808	Powder metallurgy	TN695-697	671.37
Position-finders	UF853	623.46	Powders (Pharmacy)	RS201.P8	615.43
Positivism	B831	146.4	Power (Mechanics)	TJ163.6-.95	621
Possession (Law)—England	KD810-815	346.420437	Power-plants	TJ164	621.3121
Post office buildings	NA4450-4457	725.16	Power-plants	TH4581-4591	690.54
Post-traumatic stress disorder	RC552.P67	616.8521	Power of attorney—England	KD2022	346.42029
			Power transmission	TJ1045-1119	621.85
Postage stamps	HE6182-6228	383.23	Power transmission	S711-713	631.372
Postage-stamp albums	HE6221	769.56075	Powwows	E98.P86	394.2608997
Postal rates	HE6125-6148	383.23	Practical nursing	RT62	610.730693
Postal savings banks	HG1951-1956	332.22	Pragmatics	B831.5	144.3
Postal service	HE6000-7500	383.1	Pragmatics	P99.4.P72	401.9
Postal service	UH80-85	355.693	Pragmatism	B832	144.3
Postal service	VG60-65	359.34	Prague (Czech Republic)	DB2600-2650	943.712
Postal service—Biography	HE6061	383.492	Prairie Provinces—Maps	G3470-3504	912.712
Postal service—Directories	HE6031	383.1025	Prairie ecology	QH541.5.P7	577.44
Postal service—History	HE6041-6055	383.49	Prairies	GB571-578	551.453
Postal service—International cooperation	HE6246-6278	383.41	Prairies	QK938.P7	581.744
			Prakrit languages	PK1201-1429	491.3
Postal service—Law and legislation	K4245-4254	343.0992	Prakrit languages—Dictionaries	PK1223-1225	491.33
Postal service—Study and teaching	HE6036	383.1071	Prakrit languages—Grammar	PK1206-1215	491.35
Postal service—Unclaimed mail	HE6149	383.1	Prakrit literature	PK4990-5001.8	891.309
			Prakrit literature	PK5003-5009	891.308
Postal service—[By region or country]	HE6300-7496	383.49(4-9)	Prayer	BL560	291.43
			Prayer—Buddhism	BQ5595-5630	294.3443
Postal service—United States	HE6300-6500	383.4973	Prayer—Christianity	BV205-287	264.13
			Prayer—Islam	BP178	297.382
Postal service—[Other regions and countries]	HE6651-7496	383.49(4-9)	Prayer—Judaism	BM669	296.45
			Prayer-books	BV245-283	242.8
Postcards	HE6184.P65	383.122	Prayer groups	BV287	242.2
Postcards	NC1870-1879	741.683	Prayers	BL560	291.43
Posters	HF5843-.5	659.132	Prayers	BV228-284	264.13
Posters	NC1800-1850	741.674	Pre-trial procedure—United States	KF8900-8902	347.73072
Postmarks	HE6182-6228	383.1			
Postnatal care	RG801-871	618.7	Preaching	BV4200-4317	251
Postoperative pain	RD98.4	617.01	Preaching—History	BV4207-4208	251.009
Postpartum depression	RG852	618.76	Precedence	CR3575	929.7
Postpartum psychiatric disorders	RG850-852	618.76	Precious metals	HG258-312	332.4042
			Precious metals	TN410-439	622.342
Posture	GN231-232	599.947	Precious stones	NK7650-7690	739.27
Posture	RA781.5	613.78	Precious stones	TN980-997	622.38
Posture disorders	RD762	616.7	Precious stones, Artificial	TP873-.5	666.88
Potassium salts	TN919	622.3636	Precipitation (Meteorology)	QC929	551.577
Potters	NK4200-4210	738.092	Precipitation gauges	QC926	551.5770284
Pottery	NK3700-4695	738	Precipitation hardening	TN672	669.8
Pottery	TP785-842	666.3	Predestination	BT809-810.2	234.9
Pottery—Collectors and collecting	NK4230	738.075	Predestination—Islam	BP166.3	297.227
			Prefabricated houses	TH4819.P7	643.2
Pottery—[By region or country]	NK4001-4184	738.09(4-9)	Pregnancy	RG551-591	618.2
			Pregnancy—Nutritional aspects	RG559	618.24
Pottery, Ancient	NK3800-3855	738.0901			
Pottery, Medieval	NK3870-3885	738.0902	Pregnancy—Psychological aspects	RG560	618.20019
Potting soils	S589.8-.85	631.4			
Poultry—Breeding	SF492-493	636.5082	Pregnancy—Signs and diagnosis	RG563-564	618.2075
Poultry—Diseases	SF995-.4	636.50896			

Subject Heading	LC	Dewey	Subject Heading	LC	Dewey
Prisms	QA491	516.15	Procedure (Law)—United States	KF8700-9075	347.7305
Prison administration	HV8756-8763	365.068	Processes, Infinite	QA295	515.24
Prison discipline	HV8766-8778	365.643	Processions	GT3980-4099	394.5
Prison homocide	HV9025	365.64	Proctology	RC864-866	616.35
Prison industries	HV8888-8931	365.65	Producer cooperatives	HD3120-3260.9	334.6
Prison libraries	Z675.P8	027.665	Producer cooperatives— [By region or country]	HD3131-3260.9	334.609(4-9)
Prison nurses	HV8833-8844	365.66	Product coding	HF5416	380.1
Prison physicians	HV8833-8844	365.66	Product management	HF5415.15-.157	658.5
Prison psychology	HV6089	155.962	Product recall	HF5415.9	363.19
Prison reformers	HV8971-8978	365.7	Product safety—Law and legislation—United States	KF3945-3965	344.73042
Prison sentences	HV8708-8719	365	Production (Economic theory)	HD	338
Prison violence	HV9025	365.6	Production control	T56	658.5
Prison visits	HV8884	365.6	Production management	TS155-194	658.5
Prisoners, Transportation of	HV8935-8962	365.64	Profession (Buddhist monastic orders)	BL1478	294.3657
Prisons	HV8301-9960	365	Professional education	LC1051-1071	378.013
Prisons—History	HV8497-8654	365.09	Professional employees	HD8038	331.712
Prisons—Statistics	HV8482-8488	365.021	Professional ethics	BJ1725	174
Prisons—[By region or country]	HV9441-9649	365.9(4-9)	Professions	GT6110-6390	395.52
Prisons—Africa	HV9836-9868.5	365.96	Professions—Law and legislation	K4360-4375	344.01712
Prisons—Australia	HV9871-9875	365.994	Professions—Law and legislation—United States	KF2900-2940	344.7301712
Prisons—Benelux countries	HV9696-9710.5	365.9492	Profit	HC79.P7	338.516
Prisons—Canada	HV9501-9510	365.971	Profit	HB601	338.516
Prisons—Central America	HV9516-9550	365.9728	Profit-sharing	HD2970-3110.9	331.2164
Prisons—China	HV9816-9820	365.951	Profit-sharing—[By region or country]	HD2981-3110.9	331.216409(4-9)
Prisons—Europe	HV9636-9775.7	365.94	Progesterone	QP572.P7	612.405
Prisons—France	HV9661-9670	365.944	Prognosis	RC80	616.075
Prisons—Germany	HV9671-9680.5	365.943	Program music	ML3855	781.56
Prisons—Great Britain	HV9641-9650	365.941	Program music	ML3300-3354	781.5609
Prisons—Greece	HV9776-831	365.9495	Programmed instruction	LB1028.5	371.334
Prisons—India	HV9791-9795	365.954	Programming (Electronic computers)	QA76.6-.66	005.1
Prisons—Italy	HV9686-9695	365.945	Programming (Mathematics)	QA402.5	519.7
Prisons—Japan	HV9811-9815	365.952	Programming languages (Electronic computers)	QA76.7-.73	005.13
Prisons—Mexico	HV9511-9515	365.972	Progress	CB155	303.44
Prisons—Middle East	HV9776.5-9785.2	365.956	Progress	HM101-121	303.44
Prisons—Philippines	HV9806-9810	365.9599	Progressive taxation	HJ2326-2327	336.293
Prisons—Russia	HV9711-9715	365.947	Projectiles	VF480-500	359.8251
Prisons—South America	HV9576-9635	365.98	Projectiles	UF750-770	358.1282513
Prisons—Spain	HV9741-9745	365.946	Projectiles, Aerial	UF767	358.128251
Prisons—United States	HV9456-9481	365.973	Projection	QA501-521	516.5
Prisons—West Indies	HV9551-9575.95	365.9729	Projection	T362-369	604.245
Private banks	HG1978-2031	332.123	Projective techniques	BF698.7	155.284
Private duty nursing	RT104	610.732	Projective techniques	RC473.P7	616.890028
Private investigators	HV8081-8099	363.289	Prolactin	QP572.P74	612.405
Private masses	BX2231.7	264.02036	Proletariat	HD4801-8943	331.11
Private revelations	BV5091.R4	248.29	Promises	BJ1500.P7	177.3
Private schools	LC47-57	371.02	Promotions	HF5549.5.P7	658.3126
Private security services	HV8290-8291	363.289	Proof theory	QA9.54	511.3
Prize contests in advertising	HF6146.P75	659.17	Proofreading	Z254	686.2255
Probabilities	BC141	121.63	Propaganda	HM263	303.375
Probabilities	QA273-274.8	519.2	Propellers	VM753-757	623.873
Probation	HV9278	364.63			
Problem-solving therapy	RC489.P68	616.8914			
Procedure (Law)	K2100-2385	347.05			
Procedure (Law)—Canada	KE8341-8605	347.7105			
Procedure (Law)—England	KD6850-7640	347.4205			
Procedure (Law)—Ireland	KDK1580-1713	347.41505			
Procedure (Law)— Northern Ireland	KDE510-530	347.41605			
Procedure (Law)—Scotland	KDC840-915	347.41105			

Subject Heading	LC	Dewey	Subject Heading	LC	Dewey
Propellers, Aerial	TL705-708	629.13436	Protestant churches—West Indies	BX4835	280.409729
Property	HB701-715	330.17	Protestantism	BX4800-4946	280.4
Property tax	HJ4101-4936	336.22	Protestantism—History	BX4804-4807	280.409
Property tax—Law and legislation	K4560-4564	343.054	Protestantism—Periodicals	BX4800	280.405
Property tax—Law and legislation—United States	KF6525-6558	343.73054	Protestants	BX4800-9890	280.4092
			Protohistory	CB305	930
Property tax—[By region or country]	HJ4120-4460	336.2309(4-9)	Protozoa	QL366-369.2	579.4
			Protozoan diseases	RC118.7	616.936
Prophets	BS1501-1675.5	224	Provencal language	PC3201-3299	449
Prophets (Mormon theology)	BX8643.P7	231.745	Provencal language—Dialects	PC3296	449.77
Prophets, Pre-Islamic	BP166.4	297.246	Provencal language—Etymology	PC3283-3286	449.2
Proportion (Anthropometry)	GN66-69	599.949			
Proportion (Art)	NC745	741.018	Provencal language—Grammar	PC3219-3273	449.5
Proportional representation	JF1071-1075	328.3347	Provencal language—Lexicography	PC3287-3295	449.3028
Proposition (Logic)	BC181	160			
Proprietary libraries	Z675.P85	027.2	Provencal language—Slang	PC3299	449.7
Prospecting	TN270-271	622.18	Provencal literature	PC3301-3359	849
Prostate	QM416	611.63	Proverbs	PN6400-6525	398.9
Prostate	QL878	573.658	Providence and government of God	BT95-96.2	231.5
Prostate—Diseases	RC899	616.65			
Prosthesis	RD130	617.95	Providence and government of God	BT135	231.5
Prosthodontics	RK641-667	617.69			
Prostitution	HQ101-440.7	306.74	Prudence	BJ1533.P9	179.9
Prostitution—History	HQ111-117	306.7409	Prussia (Germany)	DD301-491	936.3/943
Prostitution—[By region or country]	HQ141-270.7	306.7409(4-9)	Prussia (Germany)—Biography	DD343-.8	920.043/ 920.043
Protective clothing	HD7395.C5	363.1172	Prussia (Germany)—Civilization	DD331	936.3/943
Protective coatings	TA418.76	667.9			
Protective coloration (Biology)	QL767	591.472	Prussia (Germany)—Description and travel	DD314-320	913.6304/ 914.304
Proteins	QD431-.7	547.75	Prussia (Germany)—Gazetteers	DD308	913.63003/ 914.3003
Protest songs	M1977.P75	781.592			
Protestant church buildings	NA4828.5	726.58(1-9)	Prussia (Germany)—Historiography	DD345	936.30072/ 943.0072
Protestant churches	BX4800-9999	280.4			
Protestant churches—Missions	BV2350-2595	266	Prussia (Germany)—History	DD341-454	936.3/943
			Prussia (Germany)—History, Military	DD354	355.30943
Protestant churches—Missions—History	BV2400-2595	266.009			
Protestant churches—Relations	BX4818-.3	280.4	Prussia (Germany)—History, Naval	DD358	359.30943
			Prussia (Germany)—History—1640-1740	DD394-399.8	943.0(41-52)
Protestant churches—Asia	BX4857	280.4095			
Protestant churches—Central America	BX4833.5-4834	280.409728	Prussia (Germany)—History—Frederick William I, 1713-1740	DD399-.8	943.052
Protestant churches—Europe	BX4837-4854	280.4094			
Protestant churches—France	BX4843	280.40944	Prussia (Germany)—History—1740-1789	DD406-413.2	943.05(3-7)
Protestant churches—Germany	BX4844-.5	280.40943	Prussia (Germany)—History—Frederick II, 1740-1786	DD401-413.2	943.053
Protestant churches—Great Britain	BX4838-4840	280.40941			
			Prussia (Germany)—History—Frederick William II, 1786-1797	DD414-416	943.06
Protestant churches—Italy	BX4847	280.40945			
Protestant churches—Mexico	BX4833	280.40972	Prussia (Germany)—History—Frederick William IV, 1840-1861	DD424-.9	943.07
Protestant churches—South America	BX4836	280.4098			
			Prussia (Germany)—History—Revolution, 1848-1849	DD424	940.284
Protestant churches—Spain	BX4851	280.40946			

Subject Heading	LC	Dewey
Prussia (Germany)—History—William I, 1861-1888	DD425-446	943.0(76-83)
Prussia (Germany)—History—1870-	DD446-454	943.08(2-8)
Prussia (Germany)—Periodicals	DD301	936.3005/ 943.005
Prussian language	PG8201-8208	491.91
Prussian language—Dictionaries	PG8206	491.913
Pseudomonas	QR82.P78	579.332
Psoriasis	RL321	616.526
Psychiatric aides	RC440.5	616.890092
Psychiatric day treatment	RC439.2	616.891
Psychiatric emergencies	RC480.6	616.89025
Psychiatric ethics	RC455.2.E8	174.2
Psychiatric hospitals—Emergency service	RC480.6	362.2881
Psychiatric nursing	RC440	610.7368
Psychiatric referral	RC455.2.R43	362.172
Psychiatric social work	HV689-690	362.20425
Psychiatry—Differential therapeutics	RC480.52	616.891
Psychiatry—Methodology	RC455.2.M4	616.89001
Psychiatry, Comparative	RC455.4.C6	616.89
Psychoanalysis	BF173-175.5	150.195
Psychoanalysis	RC500-510	616.8917
Psychoanalytic counseling	BF175.4.C68	150.195
Psychodiagnostics	RC469-473	616.89075
Psychodrama	RC489.P7	616.891523
Psychohistory	D16.16	901.9
Psychokinesis	BF1371-1389	133.88
Psycholinguistics	P37	401.9
Psychological child abuse	RC569.5.P75	616.858223
Psychological consultation	BF637.C56	158.3
Psychological tests	BF176-.5	150.287
Psychological warfare	UB275-277	355.3434
Psychologists	BF109	150.92
Psychologists—Professional ethics	BF76.4	174.915
Psychology	BF	150
Psychology—Congresses	BF20	150.6
Psychology—Dictionaries	BF31	150.3
Psychology—History	BF81-105	150.9
Psychology—Methodology	BF38.5-39.8	150.1
Psychology—Periodicals	BF1-8	150.5
Psychology—Research	BF76.5-.6	150.72
Psychology—Study and teaching	BF77-80.7	150.71
Psychology—Terminology	BF32	150.14
Psychology, Applied	BF636-637	158
Psychology, Comparative	BF660-685	156
Psychology, Forensic	RA1148	614.1
Psychology, Industrial	HF5548.7-.85	158.7
Psychology, Pathological	RC435-571	616.89
Psychology, Religious	BL53	291.175
Psychopharmacology	RM315-334	615.78
Psychoses	RC512-528	616.892
Psychosexual development	BF723.S4	155.3
Psychosexual disorders	RC556-560	616.8583
Psychosurgery	RD594-.15	617.481
Psychotherapists—Professional ethics	RC455.2.E8	174.2
Psychotherapy	RC475-489	616.8914
Psychotherapy—Failure	RC489.F27	616.8914
Psychotherapy—Moral and ethical aspects	RC455.2.E8	616.8914
Psychotherapy—Termination	RC489.T45	616.8914
Psychotherapy patients—Abuse of	RC455.2.A28	616.89140092
Psychotropic drugs	RM315-334	615.788
Pteridophyta	QK520-532	587
Puberty	QP84.4	612.661
Public administration	JF	350
Public administration—Decision making	JF1525.D4	352.33
Public administration—Canada	JL1-500	351.71
Public administration—Europe	JN	354.094
Public administration—Great Britain	JN309-678	351.41
Public administration—United States	JK404-1685	353
Public administration—[United States, By state]	JK2443-2525	352.1309(4-9)
Public architecture	NA9050.5	725
Public buildings	NA4170-5095	725
Public buildings—Access for the physically handicapped	NA2545.P5	725.087
Public buildings—[By region or country]	NA4201-4385	725.09(4-9)
Public buildings—United States	NA4205-4228.3	725.0973
Public contracts	HD3860-3861	346.023
Public defenders	JK1548.P8	345.7301
Public domain	K3476-3558	343.02
Public health	RA	614
Public health—Research	RA440.85-.87	614.072
Public health—[By region or country]	RA442-558	614.09(4-9)
Public health—Africa	RA545-552	614.096
Public health—Asia	RA525-541	614.095
Public health—Canada	RA449-450	614.0971
Public health—Central America	RA453-454	614.09728
Public health—Developing countries	RA441.5	614.091724
Public health—Europe	RA483-523	614.094
Public health—Mexico	RA451-452	614.0972
Public health—North America	RA443-450	614.097
Public health—South America	RA457-482	614.098
Public health—United States	RA445-448.5	614.0973
Public health—West Indies	RA455-456	614.09729
Public health laws	K3566-3597	344.04
Public health laws—Canada	KE3575-3635	344.71041
Public health laws—England	KD3351-3375	344.4204

Subject Heading	LC	Dewey
Public health laws—United States	KF3775-3816	344.7304
Public health nursing	RT97	610.734
Public health surveillance	RA652.2.P82	614.42
Public hospitals	RA960-996	362.11
Public hospitals—Outpatient services	RA974-.5	362.12
Public housing—Law and legislation	K3550-3553	344.063635
Public law	K3150	342
Public libraries	Z675.C8	027.5
Public opinion	HM261	303.38
Public opinion polls	HM261	303.380723
Public policy (Law)	K3220-3225	342.041
Public relations	HD59-.6	659.2
Public school closings	LB2832.2	379.1535
Public schools	LC	371.01
Public service employment	HD5713.5-.6	352.63
Public speaking	PN4121-4130	808.851
Public utilities	HD2763-2768	363.6
Public utilities—Law and legislation	K3978-3990	343.09
Public utilities—Law and legislation—Canada	KE2020-2061	343.7109
Public utilities—Law and legislation—England	KD2535-2560	343.4209
Public welfare	HV	361.6
Public welfare—Law and legislation	KD3291-3315	344.420316
Public welfare—Law and legislation	K1960-2000	344.0316
Public welfare—Law and legislation—United States	KF3720-3745	344.730316
Public works	HD3840-4420.8	363
Public works—Law and legislation—England	KD1195	343.420256
Public works—Law and legislation—United States	KF5865	344.7306
Public worship	BV5-25	264
Publishers and publishing	Z278-550	070.5
Publishers and publishing—[By region or country]	Z289-550	070.509(4-9)
Puddings	TX773	641.864
Pueblo Indians	E99.P9	973.04974
Pueblo Indians—Antiquities	E78	973.04974
Pueblos	E99.P9	973.04974
Puerperal convulsions	RG831	618
Puerperal disorders	RG801-871	618.7
Puerperal psychoses	RG851	618.76
Puerto Rican literature	PQ7420-7440	860
Puerto Rico	F1951-1983	972.95
Puerto Rico—Census	HA901-910	317.295
Puerto Rico—Civilization	F1960	972.95
Puerto Rico—Description and travel	F1961-1965.3	917.29504
Puerto Rico—Emigration and immigration	JV7380-7389	325.(27295/7295)
Puerto Rico—Gazetteers	F1954	917.295003
Puerto Rico—History	F1970-1976.3	972.95

Subject Heading	LC	Dewey
Puerto Rico—History—To 1898	F1973	972.950(1-4)
Puerto Rico—History—Insurrection, 1868	F1973	972.9504
Puerto Rico—History—1898-1952	F1975	972.950(4-52)
Puerto Rico—History—Nationalist Insurrection, 1950	F1975	972.95052
Puerto Rico—History—1952-	F1976-.3	972.95053
Puerto Rico—Maps	G4970-4974	912.7295
Puerto Rico—Periodicals	F1951	972.95005
Puerto Rico—Politics and government	JL1040-1059	320.97295
Pulleys	TJ1103	621.85
Pullman cars	TF457	625.23
Pulmonary artery	QM191	611.13
Pulmonary circulation	QP107	612.2
Pulmonary embolism	RC776.P85	616.249
Pulmonary function tests	RC734.P84	616.2075
Pulmonary pharmacology	RM388-.7	615.72
Pulse	QP101	612.14
Pumping machinery	TJ899-927	621.69
Pumping stations	TD485-487	628.144
Punic War, 1st, 264-241 B.C.	DG243-244	937.04
Punic War, 2nd, 218-201 B.C.	DG247-249.4	937.04
Punic War, 3rd, 149-146 B.C.	DG252.6	937.04
Punishment	HV7231-9960	364.6
Pupil (Eye)	QM511	611.84
Pupil (Eye)	QL949	573.88
Pupil (Eye)	QP476	612.84
Puppets	PN1970-1979	791.53
Puppies	SF421-435	636.707
Purchasing power	HG229-.5	332.41
Pure Land Buddhism	BQ8500-8769	294.3926
Purgatory	BT840-842	236.5
Puritans	BX9301-9359	285.9
Puritans	F7	974.02008825
Puritans—[By region or country]	BX9331-9359	285.909(4-9)
Purity, Ritual—Islam	BP184.4	297.38
Puzzles	GV1491-1507	793.73
Pyramids	DT63-.5	932.01
Pyromania	RC569.5.P9	616.85843
Pyrometers	QC277	536.520287
Qatar—Census	HA4567	315.363
Qatar—Economic conditions	HC415.37	330.95363
Qatar—Maps	G7580-7584	912.5363
Qatar—Politics sand government	JQ1845	320.95363
Quadrant	VK583	623.890284
Quadrant	QB105	522.4
Quadruple Alliance, 1718	D287.5	940.253
Quadruple Alliance, 1815	D383	940.27
Quadruplets	GN63.6	306.875
Quakers—Biography	BX7790-7795	289.6092

194

Subject Heading	LC	Dewey
Radio direction finders	TL696.D5	629.1352
Radio in aeronautics	TL693-696	629.1355
Radio in education	LB1044.5-.6	371.3331
Radio in navigation	VK397	623.8932
Radio meteorology	QC972.6-973.8	551.635
Radio music	M176.5	781.544
Radio on boats	VM325	623.85641
Radio plays	PN6120.R2	808.8222
Radio plays—Technique	PN1991.73	808.222
Radio telescopes	QB479.2	522.682
Radio waves	QC676-678.6	537.534
Radio waves—Polarization	QC665.P6	537.534
Radioactive dating	QE508	551.701
Radioactive pollution of the atmosphere	TD887.R3	628.535
Radioactive pollution of water	TD427.R3	628.1685
Radioactive substances	QE364.2.R3	549.528
Radioactive substances—Toxicology	RA1231.R2	616.9897
Radioactive substances in rivers, lakes, etc.	TD427.R3	628.1685
Radioactive waste disposal	TD812-.4	628.42
Radioactivity	QC794.95-798	539.752
Radioactivity—Instruments	QC785.5-787	539.770284
Radiochemistry	QD601-608	541.38
Radioecology	QH543.5-.6	577.277
Radiography, Medical	RC78-.5	616.07572
Radiotherapy	RM845-862.5	615.842
Radium—Therapeutic use	RM859	615.8423
Radon	QD181.R2	546.756
Raeto-Romance language	PC901-949	459.9
Raeto-Romance language—Dialects	PC941-949	459.97
Raeto-Romance language—Dictionaries	PC937	459.93
Raeto-Romance language—Etymology	PC931	459.92
Raeto-Romance language—Grammar	PC911-923	459.95
Raeto-Romance language—Slang	PC949	459.97
Raeto-Romance language—Study and teaching	PC907	459.9071
Raeto-Romance literature	PC951-986	859.9
Rafts	VM352	623.8202
Ragtime music	M1366	781.645
Raids (Military science)	U167.5.R34	355.422
Railroad accidents	HE1779-1795	363.122
Railroad conductors	HE1811	385.092
Railroad engineering	TF	625.1
Railroad engineering—Tables	TF205	625.10021
Railroad engineers	TF139-140	625.10092
Railroad law	K4061-4070	343.095
Railroad museums	TF6	625.10074
Railroad stations	HE1613-1614	385.314
Railroad terminals	TF300-308	625.18
Railroads	HE1001-5600	385
Railroads	TF	625.1

Subject Heading	LC	Dewey
Railroads—Baggage handling	HE2556	385.22
Railroads—Baggage handling	TF656	625.23
Railroads—Cars	HE1830	385.37
Railroads—Cars	TF371-499	625.2
Railroads—Congresses	TF5	625.1006
Railroads—Continuous rails	TF262	625.15
Railroads—Crossings	HE1617-1618	385.312
Railroads—Crossings	TF263	625.163
Railroads—Design and construction	TF200-320	625.1
Railroads—Design and construction—Costs	TF193	625.11299
Railroads—Directories	HE1009	385.025
Railroads—Directories	TF12	625.10025
Railroads—Earthwork	TF220-226	625.12
Railroads—Electrification	TF858-859	621.33
Railroads—Employees	HE1741-1759	331.761385
Railroads—Employees	HD8039.R1-.R45	385.092
Railroads—Equipment and supplies	TF340-499	625.100284
Railroads—Fares	HE1951-2100	385.22
Railroads—Finance	HE2231-2261	385.1
Railroads—Freight	HE2301-2547	385.24
Railroads—Freight	TF662-667	625.24
Railroads—Freight-cars	TF470-481	625.24
Railroads—History	HE1021	385.09
Railroads—History	TF15-20	625.1009
Railroads—Livestock transportaton	HE2321.L7	385.24
Railroads—Maintenance and repair	TF530-548	625.100288
Railroads—Management	HE1621-1813	385.068
Railroads—Models	TF197	625.19
Railroads—Passenger traffic	HE2561-2591	385.22
Railroads—Passenger traffic	TF653	385.22
Railroads—Passenger-cars	TF455-461	625.23
Railroads—Periodicals	HE1001	385.05
Railroads—Periodicals	TF1-4	625.1005
Railroads—Rails	TF258-262	625.15
Railroads—Research	TF171-183	625.10072
Railroads—Safety measures	TF610	625.100289
Railroads—Signaling	TF615-640	625.165
Railroads—Snow-plows	TF542	625.100288
Railroads—Societies, etc.	HE1003	385.06
Railroads—Specifications	TF195	625.100212
Railroads—Statistics	HE2271-2273	385.021
Railroads—Surveying	TF210-217	625.11
Railroads—Switching	TF592	625.163
Railroads—Track	TF240-268	385.312
Railroads—Traffic	HE1821-2591	385.2
Railroads—Yards	TF590-593	625.18
Railroads—[By region or country]	HE2701-3560	385.09(4-9)
Railroads—[By region or country]	TF21-127	625.1009(4-9)
Railroads—Algeria	HE3412	385.0965
Railroads—Angola	HE3433	385.09673

Subject Heading	LC	Dewey	Subject Heading	LC	Dewey
Railroads—Argentina	HE2901-2910	385.0982	Railroads—Morocco	HE3411	385.0964
Railroads—Australia	HE3461-3550	385.0994	Railroads—Mozambique	HE3424	385.09679
Railroads—Austria	HE3051-3059.2	385.09436	Railroads—Namibia	HE3432.3	385.096881
Railroads—Bangladesh	HE3300.6	385.095492	Railroads—Netherlands	HE3121-3130	385.09492
Railroads—Belgium	HE3111-3120	385.09493	Railroads—New Zealand	HE3550.5	385.0993
Railroads—Belize	HE2825.5	385.097282	Railroads—Nicaragua	HE2846-2850	385.097285
Railroads—Benin	HE3444	385.096683	Railroads—Niger	HE3446	385.096626
Railroads—Bolivia	HE2911-2920	385.0984	Railroads—Nigeria	HE3453	385.09669
Railroads—Botswana	HE3431	385.096883	Railroads—Norway	HE3171-3180	385.09481
Railroads—Brazil	HE2921-2930	385.0981	Railroads—Pakistan	HE3300.5	385.095491
Railroads—Bulgaria	HE3231-3240	385.09499	Railroads—Paraguay	HE2966-2970	385.09892
Railroads—Burkina Faso	HE3450	385.096625	Railroads—Peru	HE2971-2980	385.0985
Railroads—Burundi	HE3422	385.0967572	Railroads—Philippines	HE3341-3350	385.09599
Railroads—Cameroon	HE3442	385.096711	Railroads—Poland	HE3060.5	385.09438
Railroads—Canada	HE2801-2810	385.0971	Railroads—Portugal	HE3201-3210	385.09469
Railroads—Chad	HE3441	385.096743	Railroads—Romania	HE3251-3260	385.09498
Railroads—Chile	HE2931-2940	385.0983	Railroads—Russia	HE3131-3140.2	385.0947
Railroads—China	HE3281-3290	385.0951	Railroads—Rwanda	HE3421	385.0967571
Railroads—Colombia	HE2941-2950	385.09861	Railroads—Sao Tome and Principe	HE3436	385.096715
Railroads—Congo (Brazzaville)	HE3439	385.096724	Railroads—Saudi Arabia	HE3380.3	385.09538
Railroads—Costa Rica	HE2831-2835	385.097286	Railroads—Senegal	HE3451	385.09663
Railroads—Cote d'Ivoire	HE3447	385.096668	Railroads—Sierra Leone	HE3455	385.09664
Railroads—Czechoslovakia	HE3059.3	385.09437	Railroads—Somalia	HE3417	385.096773
Railroads—Denmark	HE3151-3160	385.09489	Railroads—South Africa	HE3426	385.0968
Railroads—Ecuador	HE2951-2960	385.09866	Railroads—South America	HE2891-3000	385.098
Railroads—Egypt	HE3401-3410	385.0962	Railroads—Spain	HE3191-3200	385.0946
Railroads—El Salvador	HE2851-2855	385.097284	Railroads—Sri Lanka	HE3300.3	385.095493
Railroads—Equatoria Guinea	HE3435	385.096718	Railroads—Sudan	HE3415	385.09624
Railroads—Ethiopia	HE3416	385.0963	Railroads—Surinam	HE2963	385.09883
Railroads—France	HE3061-3070	385.0944	Railroads—Swaziland	HE3430	385.096887
Railroads—French Guiana	HE2964	385.09882	Railroads—Sweden	HE3181-3190	385.09485
Railroads—Gabon	HE3438	385.096721	Railroads—Switzerland	HE3211-3220	385.09494
Railroads—Gambia	HE3456	385.096651	Railroads—Tanzania	HE3423	385.09678
Railroads—Germany	HE3071-3080.5	385.0943	Railroads—Togo	HE3445	385.096681
Railroads—Ghana	HE3454	385.09667	Railroads—Tunisia	HE3413	385.09611
Railroads—Great Britain	HE3011-3040	385.0941	Railroads—Uganda	HE3420	385.096761
Railroads—Guatemala	HE2836-2840	385.097281	Railroads—United States	HE2704-2791	385.0973
Railroads—Guinea	HE3448	385.096652	Railroads—Uruguay	HE2981-2990	385.09895
Railroads—Guinea-Bissau	HE3458	385.096657	Railroads—Venezuela	HE2991-3000	385.0987
Railroads—Guyana	HE2962	385.09881	Railroads—Vietnam	HE3320.3	385.09597
Railroads—Honduras	HE2841-2845	385.097283	Railroads—West Indies	HE2856-2889	385.09729
Railroads—Hungary	HE3059.5	385.09439	Railroads—Western Sahara	HE3458.2	385.09648
Railroads—Iceland	HE3161-3170	385.094912	Railroads—Yugoslavia	HE3241-3245	385.09497
Railroads—India	HE3291-3300	385.0954	Railroads—Zaire	HE3434	385.096751
Railroads—Indonesia	HE3331-3340	385.09598	Railroads—Zambia	HE3428	385.096894
Railroads—Ireland	HE3041-3050	385.09415	Railroads, Cable	TF835	625.5
Railroads—Italy	HE3091-3100	385.0945	Railroads, Elevated	HE4201-5300	388.44
Railroads—Japan	HE3351-3360	385.0952	Railroads, Elevated	TF840-841	625.44
Railroads—Kenya	HE3419	385.096762	Railroads, Elevated—[By region or country]	HE4401-5260	388.4409(4-9)
Railroads—Korea	HE3360.5	385.09519	Railroads, Elevated— United States	HE4401-4491	388.440973
Railroads—Laos	HE3320.4	385.09594	Railroads, Elevated— [Other regions or countries]	HE4500-5260	388.4409(4-9)
Railroads—Lesotho	HE3429	385.096885			
Railroads—Liberia	HE3457	385.096662			
Railroads—Libya	HE3414	385.09612			
Railroads—Madagascar	HE3425	385.09691			
Railroads—Malawi	HE3432	385.096897	Railroads, Industrial	TF677	385.54
Railroads—Malaysia	HE3321-3330	385.09595	Railroads, Local and light	HE3601-4043	388.42
Railroads—Mali	HE3449	385.096623	Railroads, Local and light	TF670-1124	385.5/625.(4-6)
Railroads—Mauritania	HE3452	385.09661	Railroads, Local and light—Periodicals	HE3601	388.4205
Railroads—Mexico	HE2811-2820	385.0972			

Subject Heading	LC	Dewey	Subject Heading	LC	Dewey
Railroads, Local and light—[By region or country]	HE3651-4043	388.4209(4-9)	Real estate business	HD1361-1395.5	333.33
			Real property	HD251-279	333.30973
			Real property—Canada	KE625-754	346.71043
Railroads, Narrow-gage	TF675	385.52	Real property—England	KD821-1195	346.42043
Railway mail service	HE6175-.5	383.143	Real property—United States	KF566-698	346.73043
Railway mail service—United States	HE6475-.3	383.1430973	Real-time data processing	QA76.54-.545	004.33
Rain and rainfall	QC924.5-926.2	551.577	Realism	B835	149.2
Rain forest ecology	QH541.5.R27	577.34	Realism in literature	PN56.R3	808.8012
Rain gauges	QC926	551.5770284	Reality	BD331	111
Rain-making	QC928.6	551.68	Rearguard action (Military science)	U215	355.422
Rain-water (Water-supply)	TD418	628.11			
Rainbow	QC976.R2	551.567	Reasoning	BC177	160
Rajasthani language	PK2701-2709	491.479	Reasoning (Psychology)	BF442	153.43
Ramadan sermons	BP183.6	297.362	Recall	JF247.R4	324.68
Raman effect	QC454.R36	535.846	Recall	JK1533	324.680973
Random access memory	TK7895.M4	621.3973	Recall	JS344.R4	324.680973
Random noise theory	TK5101	621.38224	Receivers	HG3773	332.75
Range ecology	QH541.5.R3	577.4	Recidivism	HV6049	364.3
Range management	SF84.82-98	636.0845	Recipes	TX151-162	641.5
Range-finding	VF550	359.422	Reciprocating pumps	TJ915	621.65
Range-finding	UF850-857	623.46	Reciprocity	HF1721-1733	382.9
Rangelands	SF84.82-85.6	636.0845	Recitation (Education)	LB1039	371.37
Rangelands	SB193-.55	633.202	Recitations	PN4199-4355	808.54
Rape	HV6558-6569	364.1532	Reclamation of land	TC801-937	627.5
Rape—Investigation	HV8079.R35	363.259532	Reclamation of land	TC970-978	627.5
Rape trauma syndrome	RC560.R36	616.8521	Reclamation of land	TC343-345	627.54
Rape victims	RC560.R36	362.883	Reclamation of land	S604.8-621.5	631.6
Rappelling	GV200.19.R34	796.522	Reclamation of land—[By region or country]	TC815-927	627.509(4-9)
Rare birds	QL676.7	597.168			
Rare breeds	SF105.27-.275	636.082	Recognition (Psychology)	BF378.R4	153.124
Rare earth metals	QD172.R2	546.41	Recoilless rifles	UF656	358.1282
Rare mammals	QL706.8-.83	599.168	Recombinant blood proteins	RM171.4	615.39
Rationalism	BL2700-2790	211.4	Reconnaissance aircraft	UG1242.R4	358.45
Rationalism	B833	149.7	Reconstruction (1914-1939)	D652-659	940.5 (1-2)
Rationalism	BT1209-1211	239.7			
Rationing	HF5415	381.3	Reconstruction (1939-1951)	D824-829	940.53144
Raw food diet	RM237.5	613.26			
Raw materials	HF1051-1054	333.7	Recorder music	M110.R4	788.36
Rayon	TS1688	677.46	Recording instruments	QC53	530.7
Razors	TT967	646.7240284	Recording instruments	TK393	621.373
Reactor fuel reprocessing	TK9360	621.4838	Recreation centers	GV182-.5	790.068
Read-only memory	TK7895.M4	621.3973	Recreation leadership	GV14.5	790.092
Readers	PE1417	428.6	Recreational therapy	RC489.R4	616.891653
Readers	PE1117-1130	428.6	Recreational therapy	RM736.7	615.85153
Reading	LB1050	372.4	Recruiting and enlistment	VB260-275	359.2236
Reading	PN83	808.54509	Recruiting and enlistment	UB320-345	355.223
Reading—Ability testing	LB1050.46	372.48	Recycling (Waste, etc.)	TD794.5	628.4458
Reading—Phonetic method	LB1573.3	372.465	Red Brigades	HV6433.I	323.0440951
Reading—Remedial teaching	LB1050.5	372.43	Red Cross	HV560-583	361.77
Reading (Elementary)	LB1525	372.4	Red Cross	UH535-537	361.77
Reading (Elementary)	LB1573	372.4	Red Cross	VG457	361.77
Reading (Elementary)—Whole-word method	LB1573.37	372.462	Red Cross—[By region or country]	HV575-580	361.7709(4-9)
			Red dwarfs	QB843.R4	523.88
Reading (Kindergarten)	LB1181.2	372.4	Red fescue	SB413.R43	633.28
Reading (Preschool)	LB1140.5.R4	372.4	Red giants	QB843.R42	523.88
Reading (Primary)	LB1525-.8	372.4	Red tide	SH177.R4	639.964
Reading comprehension	LB1050.45	372.47	Redemption	BT775	234.3
Reading disability and crime	HV6166	364.25	Reducing diets	RM222.2	613.25
Reading machines	LB1050.37	372.40284	Reduction (Chemistry)	QD63.R4	541.393
Reading readiness	LB1050.43	372.414			

Subject Heading	LC	Dewey	Subject Heading	LC	Dewey
Redwood	SD397.R3	634.9758	Refuse collection—United States	TD788-.4	628.440973
Reed-organ	ML597	786.5509	Refuse collection—[Other countries]	TD789	628.4409(3-9)
Reed-organ—Methods—Self-instruction	MT208	786.5507	Refutation (Logic)	B491.R44	184
Reed-organ music	M15-17	786.55	Regattas	GV775	797.14
Reefs	GB461-468	551.424	Regeneration (Biology)	QH499	571.889
Reference books	Z711	028.7	Regeneration (Botany)	QK840	571.8892
Referendum	JF491-497	328.23	Regeneration (Theology)	BT790	234.4
Reflecting telescopes	QB88	522.2	Regional planning	NA9000-9428	711.3
Reflection (Optics)	QC425	535.323	Regional planning—Law and legislation	K3531-3544	346.045
Reflection (Optics)	QC385	535.323	Regional planning—Law and legislation—Canada	KE5258-5284	346.71045
Refloating of ships	VK1259	363.3481			
Reforestation	SD409	634.956	Regional planning—[By region or country]	HT392-395	307.1209(4-9)
Reformation	BR300-420	270.6			
Reformation—Causes	BR307	270.6	Regional planning—United States	HT392-394	307.120973
Reformation—Early movements	BR295	270.6			
Reformatories	HV9051-9230.7	365.34	Regular Baptists	BX6388.3-.38	286.1
Reformatories for women	HV8738	365.34082	Rehabilitation counselors	HD7255-7256	362.0425
Reformed Church	BX9401-9640	284.2	Rehabilitation technology	RM950	617.03
Reformed Church—Doctrines	BX9420-9422.2	230.42	Reincarnation	BP573.R5	299.934
			Reincarnation	BL515	291.237
Reformed Church—Government	BX9425	262.042	Reinforced concrete construction	TH1501	693.54
Reformed Church—History	BX9415	284.209	Reinforced concrete construction	TA683-683.94	624.18341
Reformed Church—Liturgy	BX9427-.5	264.042			
Reformed Church—Sermons	BX9426	252.042	Reinforcement (Psychology)	BF319.5.R4	153.85
Reformed Church—Societies, etc.	BX9403	284.206	Reinforcement learning (Machine learning)	Q325.6	006.31
			Reining (Horsemanship)	SF296.R4	798.2028
Reformed Church—Africa	BX9618-9640	284.26	Relapsing fever	RC182.R3	616.9244
Reformed Church—Asia	BX9615	284.25	Relationism	B836	111
Reformed Church—Canada	BX9596-9598	284.271	Relativity (Physics)	QC173.5-.65	530.11
Reformed Church—Europe	BX9430-9480	284.24	Relaxation	RA785	613.79
Reformed Church—France	BX9450-9459	284.244	Relics	BX2315	235.2
Reformed Church—Netherlands	BX9470-9479	284.2492	Relics	BV890	235.2
			Relics	BX577	235.2
Reformed Church—Switzerland	BX9430-9439	284.2494	Religion	BL48-50	200
			Religion—Directories	BL35	200.25
Reformed Church—United States	BX9495-9593	284.273	Religion—Periodicals	BL1-10	200.5
			Religion—Philosophy	BL51	210
Reformed Church in the United States	BX9551-9593	285.733	Religion—[Societies/Congresses]	BL11-21	200.6
Reformed Presbyterian Church	BX8990-8998.38	285.136	Religion—Study and teaching	BL41	200.71
Refraction, Astronomical	QB155-156	522.9	Religion, Prehistoric	GN799.R4	291.13
Refraction, Double	QC425	535.324	Religion and civilization	BL55	291.17
Refrigeration and refrigerating machinery	TP490-497	621.56	Religion and culture	BL65.C8	291.17
			Religion and ethics	BJ47	291.5
Refrigerator cars	TF477	625.24	Religion and justice	BL65.J87	291.5622
Refrigerator ships	VM459	623.8245	Religion and law	BL65.L33	291.177
Refrigerators	TP496-497	621.57	Religion and politics	BL65.P7	291.177
Refugees	HV640-.5	362.87	Religion and science	BL239-265	291.175
Refugees, Political	HV640-.5	362.87	Religion and sociology	BL60	291.17
Refuse and refuse disposal	TD785-812.5	628.44	Religion and state	BL65.S8	291.177
Refuse and refuse disposal—Research	TD793.3	628.44072	Religion in the public schools	LC107-120	379.28
Refuse and refuse disposal, Rural	TD929-930.4	628.744	Religions	BL74-98	230-299
Refuse collection	TD794	628.442	Religious calendars—Judaism	BM690	296.43

Subject Heading	LC	Dewey
Religious communities	BL632	291.65
Religious education—Audio-visual aids	BV1535	268.635
Religious education—Home training	BV1590	249
Religious education—Teaching methods	BV1534-1536	268.6
Religious ethics	BJ1188-1295	291.5
Religious life	BL624-627	291.4
Religious life—Buddhism	BQ5360-5680	294.3444
Religious life—Hinduism	BL1228	294.544
Religious life—Islam	BP188	297.57
Religious literature	BL29	291.175
Religious medals	CJ5793.R34	737.224
Religious tolerance	BR1610	241.4
Remarriage	HQ1018-1019	306.84
Remedial teaching	LB1029.R4	374.012
Reminiscing	BF378.R44	153.123
Remote handling (Radioactive substances)	TK9151.6-.7	621.4835
Remote submersibles	TC1662	623.8205
Remount service	UC600-695	357.2
Renaissance	CB351-369	909.07
Renaissance	PN715-749	808.800(24-32)
Renal anemia	RC641.7.R44	616.152
Renal hypertension	RC918.R38	616.132
Renewable energy sources	TJ807-830	621.042
Rent	HB401	333.5/339.21
Rental libraries	Z675.R4	027.3
Repairing	TT151	745.50288
Reparation	K970	342.03288
Repentance	BT800	234.5
Reporters and reporting	PN4781	070.43
Representation (Philosophy)	B105.R4	324.6301
Representations of groups	QA176	512.2
Representative government and representation	JF1051-1075	324.63
Reproduction	QP251-285	612.6
Reproduction	QH471-489	571.8
Reproduction (Psychology)	BF365-395	153.123
Reproduction, Asexual	QH475-479	571.89
Reptiles	GR740	398.36979
Reptiles	QL641-669	597.9
Republics	JC421-458	321.86
Requiems	M2010-2014	782.3238
Requisitions, Military	UC15	355.28
Rescue dogs	SF428.55	636.70886
Research	Q180	507.2
Research	T65	607.2
Research—Law and legislation	K3770	344.09
Research, Industrial	T175-178	607.2
Research, Industrial—Laboratories	TP187-197	660.072
Research aircraft	TL567.R47	629.130072
Research natural areas	QH75-77	508.072
Reservoir sedimentation	TD396	628.132
Reservoirs	TC167	627.86
Reservoirs	TD395-397	628.132
Residents (Medicine)	RA972	610.6952
Respiration	QP121-125	612.2

Subject Heading	LC	Dewey
Respiratory agents	RM388-.7	615.72
Respiratory allergy	RC589-596	616.202
Respiratory infections	RC740	616.2
Respiratory insufficiency in children	RJ312	618.922
Respiratory organs	QP121-125	612.2
Respiratory organs	QL845-855	573.2
Respiratory organs	QM251-265	611.2
Respiratory organs—Diseases	RC705-779	616.2
Respiratory organs—Diseases—Eclectic treatment	RV261-266	616.206
Respiratory organs—Diseases—Homeopathic treatment	RX321-326	616.206
Respiratory organs—Diseases—Nursing	RC735.5	610.73692
Respiratory organs—Foreign bodies	RD137	616.244
Respiratory organs—Obstructions	RC776.03	616.24
Respiratory therapy	RM161	615.836
Respiratory therapy	RC735.I5	615.836
Respiratory therapy for children	RJ434	615.542
Responsive worship	BV199.R5	265
Rest	RA785	613.79
Rest periods	HD5112	331.2576
Restaurants	TX945-.5	647.95
Restaurants—Personnel management	TX911.3.P4	647.950683
Restorationism	BX9901-9996	289.134
Resumes (Employment)	HF5383	650.14
Resurrection	BT870-872	236.8
Resurrection	BL503	291.23
Resurrection (Islam)	BP166.83	297.23
Resuscitation	RC87	615.8043
Retail trade	HF5428-5429.6	381.1
Retaining walls	TG325	624.284
Retaining walls	TA760-772	624.164
Retina	QP479	612.843
Retina	QL949	573.88
Retina	QM511	611.84
Retina—Diseases	RE551-661	617.735
Retinal detachment	RE603	617.735
Retirement age	HD7105-7108.4	331.252
Retreats	BV5068.R4	269.6
Retreats—Catholic Church	BX2375-2376	269.6
Retroviruses	QR414.5-.6	579.2569
Reunion—Census	HA2307	316.981
Reunion—Civilization	DT469.R37	969.81
Reunion—Description and travel	DT469.R35	916.98104
Reunion—Gazetteers	DT469.R32	916.981003
Reunion—History	DT469.R42-.R458	969.81
Reunion—History—To 1764	DT469.R44-.R443	969.8102
Reunion—History—1764-1946	DT469.R45-.R453	969.8102
Reunion—History—British occupation, 1810-1815	DT469.R45	969.8102

Subject Heading	LC	Dewey	Subject Heading	LC	Dewey
Reunion—History—1946-	DT469.R455-.R458	969.8104	Riemann surfaces	QA333-337	515.93
			Rif language	PJ2377	493.3
Reunion—Maps	G9190-9194	912.6981	Rifle practice	GV1177	799.31
Revelation	BS646	228	Rifles	SK274.2-.4	799.202832
Revelation	BV5091.R4	248.29	Rifles	UD390-395	356.1182425
Revelation	BT126-127.5	231.74	Rifles	VD370	359.82425
Revelation (Islam)	BP166.6	297.2115	Rifles, Bolt action	TS536.6.B6	683.422
Revelation (Mormon theology)	BX8643.R4	231.74	Right and wrong	BJ1410-1418	170
			Right to labor	HD4903-.5	331.8892
Revenge	BV4627.R4	241.3	Right to life	K3252	342.085
Revenue	HJ2240-7395	336.02	Rings	GT2270	391.7
Revenue-stamps	HJ5315	336.272	Rings	NK7440-7459	739.2782
Revivals	BV3750-3799	269.24	Rings	TS720-770	739.2782
Revolutions	HM281-283	303.64	Rings (Algebra)	QA247	512.4
Revolutions	JC491	321.094	Rings (Gymnastics)	GV539	613.714
Revolvers	UD410-415	356.1182436	Ringworm	RL780	616.57
Revolvers	TS537	683.436	Rio de la Plata, Battle of the, 1939	D772.G7	940.5428
Revolvers	VD390	359.82436	Riot helmets	HV7936.E7	363.20284
Revues	M1500-1508	782.14	Riots	HM281-283	303.623
Reward (Psychology)	BF505.R48	153.85	Riots	HV6474-6485	364.143
Rhetoric	PN171.4-229	808	Riots	U230	355.351
Rhetoric	P301-.5	808	Risk	HB615	338.5
Rhetoric, Ancient	PA3265	808.0481	Risk (Insurance)	HG8054.5	368
Rhetorical criticism	PN4096	809	Risk management	HD61	658.155
Rheumatic fever	RC182.R4	616.991	Rites and ceremonies	GN473	291.38
Rheumatism	RC927-.5	616.723	Rites and ceremonies	BL600-619	291.38
Rheumatoid arthritis	RC933	616.7227	Rites and ceremonies	GT	390
Rhode Island—Gazetteers	F77	917.45003	Rites and ceremonies	BV169-199	264
Rhode Island—History	F76-90	974.5	Ritual	BL600-619	291.38
Rhode Island—History—Colonial period, ca. 1600-1775	F82	974.50(1-2)	Ritualism	BX5123	264.03
			Ritualism	BV180-181	264
Rhode Island—History—King George's War, 1744-1748	E198	974.502	River boats	VM461-.5	623.82436
			River engineering	TC401-558	628.112
Rhode Island—History—Revolution, 1775-1783	E263.R4	974.50(2-3)	River engineering—[By region or country]	TC415-527	628.109(4-9)
			River steamers	VM461-.5	623.82436
Rhode Island—History—Civil War, 1861-1865	E528	974.503	Rivers	GR680	398.32091693
			Rivers	GB1201-1399.5	551.483
Rhode Island—Maps	G3770-3774	912.745	Rivers	TC401-558	628.112
Rhode Island—National Guard	UA430-439	355.3709745	Riviera (France)	DC608.1-.9	944.9
			Riviera (Italy)	DG975.R6	945.18
Rhode Island—Periodicals	F76	974.5005	Road drainage	TE215	625.734
Rhodesia—Census	HA4702	316.89	Road machinery	TE223-227	625.70284
Rhodesia—Economic conditions	HC910	330.9689	Road materials	TE200-205	625.8
			Road-rollers	TE223-227	625.70284
Rhythm	BF475	153.753	Roads	HE331-380	388.1
Ribosomes	QH603.R5	571.658	Roads	TE	625.7
Ribs	GN70	599.947	Roads—Congresses	TE5	625.706
Ribs	QM113	611.712	Roads—Design and construction	TE175	625.725
Rice	TX558.R5	641.3318			
Rich man and Lazarus (Parable)	BT378.D5	226.8	Roads—Foundations	TE210-212	625.733
			Roads—History	TE15-19	625.709
Rickets	RJ396	618.92395	Roads—Location	TE206-209.5	625.7
Rickettsia	QR353.5.R4	571.99327	Roads—Maintenance and repair	TE220-.63	625.76
Riddles	PN6366-6377	808.882			
Rider-gods	BL1590.R5	299.15	Roads—Periodicals	TE1-4	625.705
Ridesharing	HE5620.R53	388.413212	Roads—Specifications	TE180	625.70212
Ridgway's revolving battery	VF440	359.820973	Roads—Study and teaching	TE191	625.7071
Riding clubs	SF310-.5	798.2306	Roads—Surveying	TE209-.5	625.723
Riding schools	SF310.4	798.23071			

Subject Heading	LC	Dewey	Subject Heading	LC	Dewey
Roads—[By region or country]	TE21-127	625.709(4-9)	Romania—Description and travel	DR207-210	913.9804/ 914.9804
Roads, Brick	TE255	625.82	Romania—Economic conditions	HC405	330.9498
Roads, Concrete	TE278-.8	625.84			
Roads, Earth	TE230	625.74	Romania—Gazetteers	DR204	913.98003/ 914.98003
Roads, Gravel	TE233	625.82			
Roads, Macadamized	TE243	625.86	Romania—Historiography	DR216.7-.92	939.80072/ 949.80072
Roads, Plank	TE245	625.83			
Roads, Roman	DG28-29	388.10937	Romania—History	DR215-267.5	939.8/949.8
Roadside ecology	QH541.5.R62	577.55	Romania—History, Military	DR219	355.309498
Roadside improvement	TE177	625.77	Romania—History, Naval	DR225	359.309498
Roadside marketing	S571.5	380.141	Romania—History—To 1711	DR238-241	939.8/949.801 (3-5)
Roadside rest areas	TE178.8	625.77			
Roadsteads	VK321	387.12	Romania—History— 1711-1821	DR241	949.8015
Roasting (Cookery)	TX690	641.71			
Robbery investigation	HV8079.R62	363.259552	Romania—History— 1821-1859	DR242-250	949.8016
Robotics	TJ210.2-211.49	629.892			
Robots	TJ210.2-211.49	629.892	Romania—History— Revolution, 1821	DR241	949.8016
Rock climbing	GV200.2	796.5223			
Rock deformation	QE604	551.8	Romania—History— Revolution, 1848	DR244	940.284
Rock-drills	TA745-747	621.952			
Rock-drills	TN279-281	622.23	Romania—History— 1859-1866	DR244	949.80(16-2)
Rock excavation	TA740-747	624.152			
Rock gardens	SB459	635.9672	Romania—History— Charles I, 1866-1914	DR250-266	949.802
Rock glaciers	GB641-648	551.312			
Rock music	ML3533.8-3534	784.16609	Romania—History—War of Independence, 1876-1878	DR248	949.802
Rockabilly music	ML3535	784.16609			
Rockets (Aeronautics)	TL780-785.8	629.475			
Rockets (Aeronautics)— Guidance systems	TL784.C63	629.433	Romania—History— Peasants' Uprising, 1888	DR256	949.802
Rockets (Aeronautics)— Models	TL844	621.43560228			
			Romania—History— Peasants' Uprising, 1907	DR252-258	949.802
Rockets (Ordnance)	UF767	358.1282356			
Rocks	GR800	398.365	Romania—History— 1914-1918	DR263	949.802
Rocks	QE420-499	552			
Rocks, Carbonate	QE471.15.C3	552.58	Romania—History— Uprising, 1941	DR264-266	949.802
Rocks, Igneous	QE461-462	552.1			
Rocks, Metamorphic	QE475	552.4	Romania—History— 1944-1989	DR267	949.80(2-31)
Rocks, Sedimentary	QE471-.15	552.5			
Rockslides	QE599	551.307	Romania—History—1989-	DR267-.5	949.8031
Rocky Mountains	F721-722	978	Romania—History— Revolution, 1989	DR269.5-.6	949.8032
Rodeos	GV1834	791.84			
Roll-mill	TS340	671.32	Romania—Maps	G2035-2039	912.498
Roll-on/roll-off ships	HE566.R64	387.5442	Romania—Maps	G6880-6884	912.498
Roll-on/roll-off ships	VM393.R64	623.8245	Romania—Periodicals	DR201	939.8005/ 949.8005
Roller bearings	TJ1071	621.822			
Roller-skating	GV858.2-859.7	796.21			
Rollers (Printing)	Z256	686.20284	Romanian language	PC601-799	459
Rolling (Aerodynamics)	TL574.M6	629.132364	Romanian language— Etymology	PC761-767	459.2
Roman emperors	DG124	937.0099			
Romance fiction	PN816	808.80145	Romanian language— Grammar	PC631-725	459.5
Romance languages	PC	440			
Romance languages— Periodicals	PC1-5	440.05	Romanian language— Lexicography	PC775-784	459.3028
			Romanian language—Slang	PC799	459.7
Romance languages— Study and teaching	PC35-39	440.071	Romanian language— Study and teaching	PC619	459.071
Romance philology	PC	440	Romanian literature	PC800-872	859
Romania	DR201-296	939.8/949.8	Romanian philology	PC601-872	459
Romania—Census	HA1641-1650	314.98	Romanticism	PN750-759	808.80145
Romania—Civilization	DR212	939.8/949.8	Romanticism	PN603	808.80145

Subject Heading	LC	Dewey	Subject Heading	LC	Dewey
Romanticism	PN56.R7	808.80145	Rome—History—Constantine I, the Great, 306-337	DG315	937.08
Romanticism in art	N70	709.0342			
Romanticism in music	ML196	780.9034			
Romany language	PK2896-2899	491.497	Rome—History—Conference of Carnuntum, 308	DG314	937.08
Rome	DG11-365	937			
Rome (Italy)—History	DG803-818	945.632			
Rome—Biography	DG203-204	920.037	Rome—History—Theodosians, 379-455	DG330-338	937.06
Rome—Civilization	DG75-142	937			
Rome—Congresses	DG12.5	937.006	Rome—History—Romulus Augustulus, 475-476	DG365	937.09
Rome—Geography	DG27-31	913.7			
Rome—Historiography	DG205	937.0072	Rome—Periodicals	DG11	937.005
Rome—History	DG61-365	937	Rome—Politics and government	JC81-89	320.9376
Rome—History—To 510 B.C.	DG221-233.9	937.0(1-2)			
			Rome—Religion	BL800-820	292.07
Rome—History—Republic, 510-30 B.C.	DG235-269	937.0(2-5)	Rome—Study and teaching	DG206.5	937.0071
			Roof gardening	SB419.5	635.9671
Rome—History—Servile Wars, 135-71 B.C.	DG252.9	937.05	Roofing	TH2431-2459	690.15
			Roofs	TH2391-2495	690.15
Rome—History—First Triumvirate, 60-53 B.C.	DG263	937.05	Roofs, Open-timbered	NA2900	721.5
			Roofs, Shell	TH2416-2417	690.15
Rome—History—Civil War, 43-31 B.C.	DG268-269	937.05	Root crops	SB351.R65	635.1
			Root crops	SB209-211	635.1
Rome—History—Empire, 30 B.C.-476 A.D.	DG269.5-365	937.06	Roots (Botany)	QK776	581.498
			Roots (Botany)	QK644	575.54
Rome—History—Augustus, 30 B.C.-14 A.D.	DG279	937.06	Roots, Numerical	QA119	513.23
			Rope	TS1784-1787	677.71
Rome—History—Tiberius, 14-37	DG282.5	937.07	Rorschach Test	BF698.8.R5	155.2842
			Rorschach Test	RC473.R6	616.89075
Rome—History—Caligula, 37-41	DG283	937.07	Rosary	BX2310.R7	242.74
			Rose gardens	SB411	635.933734
Rome—History—Claudius, 41-54	DG284	937.07	Roses	SB410.9-411.7	635.933734
			Rosh ha-Shanah	BM695.N5	296.4315
Rome—History—Nero, 54-68	DG285	937.07	Rotary converters	TK2796	621.313
			Rotary drilling	TN281.5	622.23
Rome—History—Civil War, 68-69	DG286	937.07	Rotary pumps	TJ917	621.66
			Rotating masses of fluid	QA913	532.5
Rome—History—Revolt of Civilis, 69-70	DG288	937.07	Roulette	GV1309	795.23
			Route choice	HE336.R68	388.1
Rome—History—Vitellius, 69	DG289	937.07	Route surveying	TA625	526.9
			Roving vehicles (Astronautics)	TL475-480	629.295
Rome—History—Titus, 79-81	DG290	937.07			
			Row houses	NA7520	728.312
Rome—History—Domitian, 81-96	DG291	937.07	Rowing	GV790.9-807.5	797.123
			Royal Psalms	BS1445.M4	223.2
Rome—History—Antonines, 96-192	DG292-299	937.07	Royal houses	D226.7	321.6
			Royal houses	D352.1	321.03094
Rome—History—Trajan, 98-117	DG294	937.07	Royal houses	D412.7	321.03094
			Rubber bands	TS1920	678.35
Rome—History—Hadrian, 117-138	DG295	937.07	Rubber bearings	TJ1073.R8	621.822
			Rubber industry and trade	TS1870-1935	678.2
Rome—History—Severans, 193-235	DG300-304	937.07	Rubber plants	SB289-291	633.8952
			Rubber, Articifical	TS1925-1927	678.72
Rome—History—Maximimus, 235-238	DG306	937.07	Rubbing	NC915.R8	760
			Rubella	RA644.R8	614.524
Rome—History—Gallienus, 260-268	DG307.5	937.07	Rubella	RC182.R8	616.916
			Ruby lasers	TA1705	621.366
Rome—History—Empire, 284-476	DG310-365	937.06	Rugby football	GV945	796.333
			Rugs	NK2775-2898	747.5
Rome—History—Constantines, 306-363	DG315-317	937.08	Rugs—Private collections	NK2790	747.5074
			Rugs, Braided	TT850	746.73
			Rugs, Islamic	NK2809.I8	746.70882971

Subject Heading	LC	Dewey
Rugs, Oriental	NK2808-2810	746.75095
Rule of law—United States	KF382	340.11
Rule of the road at sea	VK371	623.8884
Rum	TP607.R9	663.59
Rummy (Game)	GV1295.R8	795.418
Running	GV1061-1069	796.42
Runways (Aeronautics)	TL725.3.R8	629.1363
Rural aged	HV1450-1494	362.6091734
Rural aged	HQ1060-1064	305.26091734
Rural churches	BV638-.8	250.91734
Rural free delivery—United States	HE6455-6456	383.1450973
Rural geography	GF127	910.021734
Rural health	RA771-.7	613.091734
Rural hospitals	RA975.R87	362.11091734
Rural libraries	Z675.V7	027.091734
Rural population	HB2371-2578	304.6091734
Rural roads	HE336.R85	388.12091734
Rural roads	TE229-.9	625.7091734
Rural-urban migration	HB1955	307.24
Russia	DK1-290.3	947
Russia	DK510-651	947
Russia—Armed Forces—Management	UB85-86	355.60947
Russia—Census	HA1431-1450.12	314.7
Russia—Church history	BR930-939	274.7
Russia—Civilization	DK32-.7	947
Russia—Commerce	HF3621-3630	380.10947
Russia—Congresses	DK2.5	947.006
Russia—Description and travel	DK19-29	914.7(04)
Russia—Economic conditions	HC331-340	330.947
Russia—Emigration and immigration	JV8180-8189	325.(247/47)
Russia—Gazetteers	DK14	914.7003
Russia—Genealogy	CS840-869	929.347
Russia—History	DK65-290.3	947
Russia—History, Naval	DK55-59	359.00947
Russia—History—To 1533	DK70-104	947.0(1-42)
Russia—History—Ivan IV, 1533-1584	DK106-107	947.043
Russia—History—Time of Troubles, 1598-1613	DK111-112	947.045
Russia—History—1613-1689	DK112.8-126	947.04(6-9)
Russia—History—1613-1917	DK112.8-264.8	947.0(47-83)
Russia—History—Aleksei Mikhailovich, 1645-1676	DK116-122.5	947.048
Russia—History—Rebellion of Stenka Razin, 1667-1671	DK118.5	947.048
Russia—History—Sofia Alekseevna, 1682-1689	DK125	947.049
Russia—History—Peter I, 1689-1725	DK128-148	947.05
Russia—History—Streltsy Revolt, 1698	DK133	947.05
Russia—History—Catherine II, 1762-1796	DK168-183	947.063
Russia—History—Rebellion of Pugachev, 1773-1775	DK183	947.063
Russia—History—Alexander I, 1801-1825	DK190-201	947.072
Russia—History—1801-1917	DK188-264.8	947.0(72-83)
Russia—History—December Uprising, 1825	DK212	947.073
Russia—History—Nicholas I, 1825-1855	DK209-215.97	947.073
Russia—History—Alexander II, 1855-1881	DK219-223	947.081
Russia—History—Alexander III, 1881-1894	DK234-243	947.082
Russia—History—Nicholas II, 1894-1917	DK251-264.8	947.083
Russia—History—Revolution, 1905-1907	DK263-264.7	947.083
Russia—History—February Revolution, 1917	DK265.19	947.0841
Russia—Manufactures	TS85-86	670.947
Russia—Maps	G7060-7342	912.47
Russia—Maps	G2110-2193	912.47
Russia—Periodicals	DK1	947.005
Russia—Politics and government	JN6500-6598	320.947
Russia (Federation)—History—Revolution, 1917-1921	DK265.8.R85	947.084
Russian language	PG2001-2847	491.7
Russian language—Dialects	PG2700-2850	491.77
Russian language—Dictionaries	PG2625-2693	491.73
Russian language—Etymology	PG2571-2591	491.72
Russian language—Grammar	PG2097-2127	491.75
Russian language—Lexicography	PG2601-2693	491.73028
Russian language—Morphology	PG2171-2197	491.75
Russian language—Parts of speech	PG2199-2321	491.75
Russian language—Phonology	PG2131-2161	491.715
Russian language—Slang	PG2850	491.7709
Russian language—Study and teaching	PG2065-2069	491.7071
Russian literature	PG2900-3580	891.7
Russian periodicals	PN5271-5280	059.9171
Russian philology	PG2001-2069	491.7
Russo-Finnish War, 1939-1940	DL1095-1105	948.97032
Russo-Japanese War, 1904-1905	DS516-517.9	952.031
Rwanda—Census	HA4695	316.7571
Rwanda—Civilization	DT450.22	967.571

Subject Heading	LC	Dewey	Subject Heading	LC	Dewey
Rwanda—Description and travel	DT450.2	916.757104	Sagas	PT7181-7193	839.6309
Rwanda—Economic conditions	HC875	330.967571	Sagittarius (Astrology)	BF1727.6	133.5274
			Sahara	DT331-346	966
Rwanda—Gazetteers	DT450.115	916.7571003	Sailboat living	GV811.65	643.2
Rwanda—History	DT450.26-.437	967.571	Sailboats	VM351-361	623.8223
Rwanda—History—Civil War, 1994	DT450.435	967.57104	Sailing	GV811	797.124
			Sailing	VK543	623.88203
Rwanda—Maps	G8430-8434	912.67571	Sailing ships—Models	VM298	623.8201043
Ryukyu Islands—History	DS895.R97	952.29	Sailing, Single-handed	GV811	797.124
Saba (Netherlands Antilles)	F2088	972.977	Sailors	HD8039.S4	387.5092
Sabbatarians	BX9680.S3	296.82092	Sailors	VD	359.0092
Sabbath	BM685	296.41	Sailors—History	VD15	359.0092
Sabbathaians	BM199.S3	296.82	Sailors—Services for	HV3025-3163	362.858
Sabbatical year (Judaism)	BM720.S2	296.4391	Sailors—[By region or country]	VD21-124	359.0092
Sabers	UE420-425	357.0482			
Sabers	U850-863	355.8241	Sailors—United States	VD23-25	359.009
Sabotage	HD5473	331.893	Sails	VM532	623.862
Sacramentals	BV875-885	264.9	Saint Bartholomew's Day, Massacre of, France, 1572	DC118	944.028
Sacramentals	BX2295-2310	264.0209			
Sacramentaries	BX2037	264.023			
Sacraments	BV800-873	265	Saint Croix (V.I.)	F2096	972.9722
Sacraments—Adventists	BX6124.3-.6	264.06708	Saint Eustatius (Netherlands Antilles)	F2097	972.977
Sacraments—Church of England	BX5148-5149	264.035			
			Saint Helena—Census	HA2291	319.73
Sacraments—Congregational churches	BX7238-7239	264.05808	Saint Helena—Maps	G9170-9174	912.973
			Saint John (V.I.)	F2098	972.9722
Sacraments—Lutheran Church	BX8072-8073.5	264.04108	Saint Kitts (Island)—Maps	G5040-5044	912.72973
			Saint Kitts and Nevis	F2091	972.973
Sacraments—Methodist Church	BX8338	264.0708	Saint Louis (Mo.)	F474.S2	977.866
			Saint Lucia	F2100	972.9843
Sacraments—Mormon Church	BX8655-.3	264.09308	Saint Lucia—Maps	G5110-5114	912.729843
			Saint Martin	F2103	972.976
Sacraments—New Jerusalem Church	BX8736	264.09408	Saint Patrick's Day	GT4995.P3	394.262
			Saint Thomas (V.I.)	F2105	972.9722
Sacraments—Orthodox Eastern Church	BX377-378	264.019	Saint Vincent—Maps	G5120-5124	912.729844
			Saintes Islands (Guadeloupe)	F2070	972.976
Sacraments—Presbyterian Church	BX9188-9189	264.05			
			Saints	BT683-694	235.2
Sacraments—Unitarianism	BX9854	264.0913308	Salad dressing	TX819.S27	641.814
Sacraments—Universalism	BX9954	264.0913408	Salads	TX807	641.83
Sacraments (Liturgy)	BX2200-2292	264.0208	Salads	TX740	641.83
Sacred books	BL70-71	291.82	Sales executives	HF5439.25-.8	381.092
Sacred meals	BL619.S3	291.36	Sales meetings	HF5438.8.M4	658.8106
Sacred vocal ensembles	M2018-2019.5	782.221438	Sales personnel	HF5439.25-.8	381.092
Sacred vocal music	M1999-2199	782.3	Sales presentations	HF5438.8.P74	658.82
Sacred vocal music	ML2900-3275	782.2209	Sales tax	HJ5711-5721	336.2713
Sacrifice	BL570	291.34	Saline water conversion	TD478-480.7	628.167
Sacrifice	BL1236.76.S23	294.534	Saline water conversion—Electrodialysis process	TD480.5	628.1674
Sacrilege	BV4726.S2	241.3			
Saddlery	TS1030-1035	685.1	Saline water conversion—Reverse osmosis process	TD480.4	628.16744
Sadducees	BM175.S2	296.813			
Sadism	HQ79	306.775	Salinity	GC121-127	551.4601
Sadomasochism	HQ79	306.775	Saliva	QP191	612.313
Sadomasochism	RC560.S23	616.85835	Salivary glands	QM325-371	611.316
Safaris	G516	916.04	Salivary glands	QP188.S2	612.313
Safe-deposit boxes	HG2251-2256	332.178	Salmon fishing	SH684-686.7	799.1755
Safety appliances	HD7273	363.107	Salmonellosis	RC182.S12	616.927
Safety factor in engineering	TA656.5	624.10289	Salon-orchestra music	M1350	784.4
Safety-lamps	TN307	622.473	Salt	GT2870	394.12
Sagas	PT7261-7262	839.6308	Salt	TN900-909	622.3632
			Salt—Physiological effect	QP913.N2	572.5238224

Subject Heading	LC	Dewey
Salt-free diet	RM237.8	613.285
Salt lake ecology	QH541.5.S22	577.639
Salt mines and mining	TN900-909	622.3632
Salts	QD189-193	546.34
Saltwater fishing	SH457-.5	799.16
Salutations	GT3050	394
Salvadoran literature	PQ7530-7539.2	860
Salvage	HE971	387.55
Salvage	VK1491	387.55
Salvation	BT750-810.2	234
Salvation Army	BX9701-9743	287.96
Salvation Army	HV4330-4470.7	287.96
Salvation outside the Catholic Church	BT755	234
Salvation outside the church	BT759	234
Samaria Region	DS110.S3	933/956.953
Samaritan Aramaic language	PJ5271-5279	492.29
Samaritan theology	BM945	296.3
Samoan Islands	DU810-819	996.1(3-4)
Samoan Islands—Maps	G9555-9557	912.961(3-4)
Samoan question	DU817	996.1(3-4)
Sampling (Statistics)	HA31.2	310.0723
Sampling (Statistics)	QA276.6	519.52
San Francisco (Calif.)	F869.S3	979.461
Sanatoriums	RA960-993	362.16
Sand	TN939	622.3622
Sand and gravel plants	TN939	622.3622
Sand Creek Massacre, Colo., 1864	E83.863	978.802
Sand dune ecology	QH541.5.S26	577.583
Sand dune planting	S621.5.S3	631.64
Sand dunes	GB631-638	551.375
Sand waves	GB649.S3	551.375
Sandstone	QE471.15.S25	552.5
Sandstone	TN957	622.353
Sandwich construction	TA492.S25	624.1779
Sandwiches	TX818	641.84
Sanitary engineering	TD	628
Sanitary engineering— History	TD15-20	628.09
Sanitary engineering— Periodicals	TD1-4	628.05
Sanitary engineering— [By region or country]	TD21-127	628.09(4-9)
Sanitary engineers— Biography	TD139-140	628.092
Sanitary engineers— Directories	TD12	628.025
Sanitary landfills	TD795-.7	628.44564
Sanitation, Household	GT472	392.36
Sanitation, Household	TH6014-7696	648
Sanitation, Rural	TD920-931	628.7
Sanskrit language	PK401-976	491.2
Sanskrit language— Dictionaries	PK925-969	491.23
Sanskrit language— Etymology	PK901-919	491.22
Sanskrit language— Grammar	PK501-811	491.25
Sanskrit language— Lexicography	PK920-969	491.23028
Sanskrit literature	PK3591-4485	891.2
Sanskrit philology	PK401-418	491.2
Sao Tome and Principe	G8675-8679	912.6715
Sao Tome and Principe— Census	HA4713	316.715
Sao Tome and Principe— Description and travel	DT615.2	916.71504
Sao Tome and Principe— History	DT615.5-.8	967.15
Sapphires	TN997.S24	622.384
Sardine fisheries	SH351.S3	639.2745
Saskatchewan—Gazetteers	F1070.4	917.124003
Saskatchewan—History	F1070-1074.7	971.24
Saskatchewan—Maps	G3490-3494	912.7124
Saskatchewan—Periodicals	F1070	971.24005
Sasquatch	QL89.2.S2	001.944
Satanism	BL480	291.216
Satanism	BF1546-1550	133.422
Satellite master antenna television	HE8700.7-.72	384.555
Satellites	QB401-407	523.98
Sati	GT3370	393.9
Satin	TS1640-1688	677.39
Satire	PN6231.S2	808.87
Satis (Egyptian deity)	BL2450.S27	299.31
Saturn (Planet)	QB671	523.46
Saturn (Planet)	QB384	523.46
Saturn (Planet)—Orbit	QB384	623.263
Saturn (Planet)—Ring system	QB405	523.986
Saturn (Roman deity)	BL870.S29	292.2113
Sauces	TX819	641.814
Saudi Arabia	DS201-248	939.49/953.8
Saudi Arabia—Census	HA4563	315.38
Saudi Arabia—Civilization	DS215	939.49/953.8
Saudi Arabia—Description and travel	DS204.5-208	913.94904/ 915.3804
Saudi Arabia—Economic conditions	HC415.33	330.9538
Saudi Arabia—History	DS221-244.63	939.49/953.8
Saudi Arabia—Maps	G2249.3-.34	912.538
Saudi Arabia—Maps	G7530-7534	912.538
Saudi Arabia—Politics and government	JQ1841	320.9538
Savanna ecology	QH541.5.P7	577.48
Savannas	GB561-568	551.453
Savannas	QH87.7	578.748
Saving and thrift	HG7920-7933	332.0415
Savings accounts	HG1660	332.1752
Savings and loan associations	HG2121-2156	332.32
Savings banks	HG1881-1966	332.21
Sawmills	TS850	674.2
Saws	TS850-851	674.0284
Saws	TJ1233-1255	621.93
Saxons	DA150-162	942.017
Saxony (Germany)—History	DD801.S31-.S59	943.21
Saxophone music	M105-109	788.7
Scabies	RL764.S28	616.57
Scaffold burial	GT3350	393.4
Scale insects	SB939	632.752

Subject Heading	LC	Dewey	Subject Heading	LC	Dewey
Scales (Fishes)	QL639	597.1477	Scholarships	LB2848-2849	371.223
Scales (Weighing instruments)	QC107	530.7	Scholarships	LB2338-2339	378.34
			Scholasticism	B734	189.4
Scalping	E98.W2	399.08997	Scholasticism	B839	149.91
Scandinavia	DL	936.3/948	Scholasticism	BD125	149.91
Scandinavia—Biography	CT1240-1328	920.048	School accidents	LB2864.6.A25	363.119371
Scandinavia—Church history	BR970-1019	274.8	School administrators	LB2831.8-.876	371.2011
			School attendance	LC142-148.5	371.294
Scandinavia—Civilization	DL30-33	936.3/948	School attendance	LB3081-3087	371.294
Scandinavia—Congresses	DL1.5	936.3006/ 948.006	School boards	LB2831	379.1531
			School bonds	HG4951-4953	379.130973
Scandinavia—Description and travel	DL6.7-11.5	913.6304/ 914.804	School bonds	LB2824-2830	379.13
			School breakfast programs	LB3473-3479	371.716
Scandinavia—Economic conditions	HC341-380	330.948	School buildings	LB3205-3295	371.6
			School children—Food	LB3473-3479	371.716
Scandinavia—Gazetteers	DL4	913.63003/ 914.8003	School children—Substance use	HV4999.C45	362.290834
Scandinavia—Genealogy	CS890-939	929.1072048	School children—Transportation	LB2864	371.872
Scandinavia—History	DL43-87	936.3/948	School choice	LB1027.9	379.111
Scandinavia—History— 15th century	DL61-65	948.03	School closings	LB2823.2	379.1535
			School discipline	LB3011-3095	371.5
Scandinavia—History— The Count's War, 1534-1536	DL75-81	948.04	School districts	LB2817-.5	379.1535
			School employees	LB2831.5-.585	371.201
Scandinavia—History— 20th century	DL83-87	948.08	School employees— Legal status, laws, etc.—United States	KF4192-.5	344.7307
Scandinavia—Manufactures	TS88.5	670.948	School enrollment	LC130-139	371.219
Scandinavia—Maps	G6910-6963	912.48	School facilities	LB3205-3325	371.6
Scandinavia—Periodicals	DL1	936.3005/ 948.005	School field trips	LB1047	371.384
			School grounds	LB3251	371.61
Scandinavia—Politics and government	JN7011-7066	320.948	School health services	LB3401-3495	371.71
Scandinavian languages	PD1501-5929	439.(5-6)	School hygiene	LB3401-3495	371.71
Scandinavian languages— Dialects	PD1850-1893	439.(5-6)7	School integration	LC214-.3	379.263
			School libraries	Z675.S3	027.8
Scandinavian languages— Etymology	PD1801-1819	439.(5-6)2	School management and organization	LB3011-3095	371.2
Scandinavian languages— Grammar	PD1559-1701	439.(5-6)5	School management and organization	LB2801-2997	378.1
Scandinavian languages— Lexicography	PD1823	439.(5-6)3028	School management teams	LB2806.3	371.2
			School milk programs	LB3473-3479	371.716
Scandinavian languages— Study and teaching	PD1535-1539	439.(5-6)071	School personnel management	LB2831.5- 2844.4	371.201
Scandinavian literature	PT7001-9999	839.5	School photography	TR818	371.897
Scandinavian literature— Study and teaching	PT7035-7039	839.5071	School principals	LB2831.9-.976	371.2012
			School psychology	LB1027.55	371.713
Scandinavian periodicals	PN5280.5-5310	058	School safety patrols	LB2865	363.1257
Scandinavian philology	PD1501-1541	439.(5-6)	School social work	LB3013.4	371.46
Scarabs	NK5561	736.20932	School sports	GV346	796.042
Scarlatina	RC182.S2	616.917	School superintendents	LB2831.7-.776	371.2011
Scattering (Physics)	QC794.6.S3	539.758	School supervision	LB2806.4	371.203
Scattering amplitude (Nuclear physics)	QC794.6.S3	539.758	School vandalism	LB3249	371.58
			School violence	LB3013.3	371.78
Scene painting	ND2885-2888	751.75	School year	LB3034	371.23
Schism, The Great Western, 1378-1417	BX1301	284.8	School-age child care	HQ778.6	305.234
			Schools	L	371
Schism—Eastern and Western Church	BX303	270.38	Schools—Centralization	LB2861	379.1535
			Schools—Decentralization	LB2862	379.1535
Schizophrenia	RC514	616.898	Schools—Furniture, equipment, etc.	LB3261-3281	371.63
Scholarly publishing	Z286.S37	070.594			
Scholars	CT	001.2092	Schools—Prayers	BV283.S3	242.2

Subject Heading	LC	Dewey
Schools—United States	LD	371.00973
Sciatica	RC420	616.87
Science	Q	500
Science—Data processing	Q183.9	502.85
Science—Dictionaries	Q123	503
Science—Exhibitions	Q105	507.4
Science—History	Q124.6-127.2	509
Science—Methodology	Q174-175.32	501
Science—Nomenclature	Q179	501.4
Science—Periodicals	Q1-9	505
Science—Philosophy	Q174-175.32	501
Science—Social aspects	Q175.5	303.483
Science—Societies, etc.	Q10-99	506
Science—Study and teaching	Q181-183.4	507.1
Science—Terminology	Q179	501.4
Science—[By region or country]	Q127-.2	509.(4-9)
Science, Ancient	Q124.95	509.01
Science, Medieval	Q124.97	509.02
Science, Renaissance	Q125.2	509.0(24-31)
Science and astrology	BF1729.S34	133.585
Science fiction	P96.S34	808.838762
Science fiction	PN6120.95.S33	808.838762
Science fiction	PN3433-.8	808.838762
Science projects	Q182.3	507.8
Scientific apparatus and instruments	Q184-185.7	502.84
Scientific illustration	Q222	502.2
Scientific surveys	Q148-149	508
Scientists—Biography	Q141-143	509.2
Scientists—Directories	Q145	502.5
Scintillation counters	QC787.S34	539.775
Sclera—Diseases	RE328	617.719
Scleroderma (Disease)	RL451	616.544
Scones	TX770.B55	641.815
Scorpio (Astrology)	BF1727.5	133.5273
Scotland	DA750-890	936.1/941.1
Scotland—Census	HA1151-1160	314.11
Scotland—Constitutional law	KDC750-785	342.411
Scotland—Description and travel	DA850-878	914.1104
Scotland—Emigration and immigration	JV7700-7709	325.(2411/411)
Scotland—History— To 1057	DA777-778.9	941.101
Scotland—History— 1057-1603	DA779-790	941.10(2-5)
Scotland—History— 1649-1660	DA803.8	941.1063
Scotland—History— 18th century	DA809-814.5	941.10(69-73)
Scotland—History— 19th century	DA815-818	941.1081
Scotland—History— 20th century	DA821-826	941.1082
Scotland—Maps	G5770-5774	912.411
Scotland—Periodicals	DA750	936.1005/ 941.1005
Scotland—Politics and government	JN1187-1371	320.9411
Scots language	PE2101-2364	427.9411
Scottish deerhound	SF429.S39	636.7532
Scottish literature	PR8510-8553	820.9
Scottish literature	PR8631-8644	820
Scouts and scouting	U190	355.413
Scrap metals	TS214	363.7288
Scrapbooks	AC999	Varies
Scrapers (Earthmoving machinery)	TA725	624.1520284
Screen doors	TH2278	690.1822
Screen process printing	TT273	686.2316
Screens	NK2910	749.3
Screws	TJ1338-1340	621.882
Scribes, Jewish	BM659.S3	296.4615
Scrotum—Diseases	RC897	616.67
Sculptors	NB1115	730.92
Sculpture	NB	730
Sculpture—Appreciation	NB1142.5	730.11
Sculpture—Catalogs	NB35	730.216
Sculpture—Conservation and restoration	NB1199	731.48
Sculpture—Exhibitions	NB16-17	730.74
Sculpture—History	NB60-615	730.9
Sculpture—Periodicals	NB1	730.5
Sculpture—Technique	NB1170-1195	731.028
Sculpture—[By region or country]	NB201-1114	730.9(4-9)
Sculpture—Afghanistan	NB992-.3	730.9581
Sculpture—Africa	NB1080-1099	730.96
Sculpture—Africa, East	NB1097-.6	730.9676
Sculpture—Africa, Southern	NB1091.7-1096.6	730.968
Sculpture—Africa, West	NB1098-1099	730.966
Sculpture—Algeria	NB1088.3	730.965
Sculpture—Argentina	NB330-339	730.982
Sculpture—Asia	NB960-1070.3	730.95
Sculpture—Asiatic Russia	NB992.4-999	730.957
Sculpture—Australia	NB1100-1105.3	730.994
Sculpture—Austria	NB501-511.6	730.9436
Sculpture—Bahamas	NB300-302	730.97296
Sculpture—Belgium	NB661-673.3	730.9493
Sculpture—Bolivia	NB340-349	730.984
Sculpture—Brazil	NB350-359	730.981
Sculpture—Burma	NB1012-.3	730.9591
Sculpture—Cambodia	NB1015-.3	730.9596
Sculpture—Canada	NB240-249.5	730.971
Sculpture—Central America	NB260-290	730.9728
Sculpture—Chile	NB360-369	730.983
Sculpture—Colombia	NB370-379	730.9861
Sculpture—Costa Rica	NB273-275	730.97286
Sculpture—Cuba	NB303-305	730.97291
Sculpture—Czechoslovakia	NB523-534.5	730.9437
Sculpture—Denmark	NB711-723.3	730.9489
Sculpture—Ecuador	NB380-389	730.9866
Sculpture—Egypt	NB1081-1085.3	730.962
Sculpture—El Salvador	NB288-290	730.97284
Sculpture—Ethiopia	NB1086.3	730.963
Sculpture—Europe	NB450-955	730.94
Sculpture—Finland	NB955.F5	730.94897
Sculpture—France	NB541-553.3	730.944

Subject Heading	LC	Dewey	Subject Heading	LC	Dewey
Sculpture—French Guiana	NB397	730.9882	Sculpture, Gothic	NB180	734.25
Sculpture—Germany	NB561-589	730.943	Sculpture, Greek	NB90-105	733.3
Sculpture—Great Britain	NB461-481	730.941	Sculpture, Japanese	NB1050-1059.6	730.952
Sculpture—Greece	NB591-603	730.9495	Sculpture, Medieval	NB170-180	734
Sculpture—Guatemala	NB276-278	730.97281	Sculpture, Modern	NB185-198.5	735
Sculpture—Guyana	NB395	730.9881	Sculpture, Prehistoric	GN799.S4	732
Sculpture—Haiti	NB306-308	730.97294	Sculpture, Primitive	NB62-64	732.2
Sculpture—Honduras	NB279-281	730.97283	Sculpture, Renaissance	NB190	735.21
Sculpture—Hungary	NB512-522.6	730.9439	Sculpture, Rococo	NB193	735.21
Sculpture—Iceland	NB741-753.3	730.94912	Sculpture, Roman	NB115-120	733.5
Sculpture—India	NB1001-1010.3	730.954	Sea breeze	QC939.L37	551.5185
Sculpture—Indonesia	NB1026-.8	730.9598	Sea-floor spreading	QE511.7	551.136
Sculpture—Iran	NB980-989	730.955	Sea ice drift	GB2401-2598	551.343
Sculpture—Iraq	NB967-969	730.9567	Sea Islands Creole dialect	PM7875.G8	427.9
Sculpture—Israel	NB977-979	730.95694	Sea kayaking	GV788.5	797.1224
Sculpture—Italy	NB611-623.3	730.945	Sea songs	M1977.S2	782.421595
Sculpture—Jamaica	NB309-311	730.97292	Sea-walls	TC335	627.24
Sculpture—Jordan	NB979.6-.8	730.95695	Seafaring life	G540-550	910.45
Sculpture—Korea	NB1060-1070.6	730.9519	Seafaring life	VK149	387.54044
Sculpture—Laos	NB1016-.3	730.9594	Seafood	TX385-388	641.392
Sculpture—Lebanon	NB976.6-.8	730.95692	Seafood gathering	SH400-.8	639.22
Sculpture—Libya	NB1089.3	730.9612	Seafood poisoning	RA1242.S48	615.954
Sculpture—Malaysia	NB1025-.8	730.9595	Seagrasses	SH393	639.89
Sculpture—Mexico	NB250-259	730.972	Sealing	SH360-363	639.29
Sculpture—Morocco	NB1090.3	730.964	Seals (Numismatics)	CD5001-6471	737.6
Sculpture—Netherlands	NB641-653.3	730.9492	Seals (Numismatics)	JC345-347	929.(82/92)
Sculpture—New Zealand	NB1106-1108	730.993	Seals (Numismatics)—Biography	CD5051-5052	737.6092
Sculpture—Nicaragua	NB282-284	730.97285	Seals (Numismatics)—Congresses	CD5009	737.606
Sculpture—Norway	NB761-773.3	730.9481			
Sculpture—Oceania	NB1110-1113	730.99(5-6)	Seals (Numismatics)—Exhibitions	CD5017-5018	737.6074
Sculpture—Pakistan	NB1010.7-.73	730.95491			
Sculpture—Panama	NB285-287	730.97287	Seals (Numismatics)—History	CD5049	737.609
Sculpture—Paraguay	NB400-409	730.9892			
Sculpture—Peru	NB410-419	730.985	Seals (Numismatics)—Periodicals	CD5001	737.605
Sculpture—Philippines	NB1027-1029	730.9599			
Sculpture—Poland	NB955.P6	730.9438	Seals (Numismatics)—Societies, etc.	CD5005	737.606
Sculpture—Portugal	NB821-833.3	730.9469			
Sculpture—Puerto Rico	NB312-314	730.97295	Seals (Numismatics)—Study and teaching	CD5045	737.6071
Sculpture—Romania	NB921-933.3	730.9498			
Sculpture—Russia	NB681-699	730.947	Seals (Numismatics)—Techniques	CD5085-5175	737.6028
Sculpture—Saudi Arabia	NB970-972	730.9538			
Sculpture—Scandinavia	NB701-793.3	730.948	Seals (Numismatics)—[By region or country]	CD5592-6471	737.609(4-9)
Sculpture—South America	NB320-439	730.98			
Sculpture—Spain	NB801-813.3	730.946	Seals (Numismatics)—Canada	CD5619	737.0971
Sculpture—Sri Lanka	NB1010.6-.63	730.95493			
Sculpture—Surinam	NB396	730.9883	Seals (Numismatics)—Central America	CD5621-5700	737.09728
Sculpture—Sweden	NB781-793.3	730.9485			
Sculpture—Switzerland	NB841-853.3	730.9494	Seals (Numismatics)—Mexico	CD5620	737.0972
Sculpture—Syria	NB989.6-.8	730.95691			
Sculpture—Thailand	NB1021-1023	730.9593	Seals (Numismatics)—United States	CD5601-5617	737.60973
Sculpture—Tunisia	NB1091.6	730.9611			
Sculpture—Turkey	NB861-873.3	730.9561	Seamanship	VK541-547	623.88
Sculpture—United States	NB205-238	730.973	Seaplane bases	TL725.6	629.1361
Sculpture—Uruguay	NB420-429	730.9895	Seaplanes	TL684-.3	629.133347
Sculpture—Venezuela	NB430-439	730.987	Search and rescue operations	TL553.8	363.3481
Sculpture—Vietnam	NB1014-.63	730.9597			
Sculpture—West Indies	NB291-315	730.9729	Search dogs	SF428.73	636.70886
Sculpture—Yugoslavia	NB941-953.3	730.9497	Search-lights	VM493	623.852
Sculpture, Ancient	NB69-169	732.2	Searches and seizures—United States	KF9630	345.730522
Sculpture, Byzantine	NB172	734.224			
Sculpture, Chinese	NB1040-1049.6	730.951			

Subject Heading	LC	Dewey
Seashore	GB451-460	551.458
Seashore ecology	QH541.5.S35	577.69
Seasonal unemployment	HD5855-5856	331.137044
Seasons	GR930	398.33
Seasons	QB637.2-.8	525.5
Seattle (Wash.)	F899.S4	979.7772
Seawater	GC100-103	551.4601
Seawater—Distillation	VM505	623.854
Secession	JK310-331	342.73042
Secession—Southern States	E458-459	973.713
Second Advent	BT885-886	236.9
Second language acquisition	P118.2	401.93
Second-born children	HQ777.22	306.87
Secondary recovery of oil	TN871.37	622.3382
Secret service	HV7961	363.283
Secret societies	GN495.2	366.(1-5)
Secret societies	HS101-330.7	366.(1-5)
Secret societies—Congresses	HS110	366.(1-5)06
Secret societies—Directories	HS121-123	366.(1-5)03
Secret societies—History, organization, etc.	HS125-148	366.(1-5)09
Secret societies—Periodicals	HS101-106	366.(1-5)05
Secret societies—Rituals	HS155-158	366.(1-5)
Secret societies—[By region or country]	HS201-330.7	366.(1-5)09(4-9)
Secret societies—United States	HS203-206	366.(1-5)0973
Secret societies—[Other regions or societies]	HS207-330.7	366.(1-5)09(4-9)
Secretion	QP190-246.5	612.4
Secular Franciscans	BX3651-3653	255.3
Secularism	BL2700-2790	211.6
Securities	HG4650-4930.5	332.632
Securities—Canada	KE1042-1056	346.71092
Securities fraud	HV6763-6771	364.168
Securities theft	HV6763-6771	364.168
Security (Law)	K1100-1108	346.092
Security (Law)—United States	KF1046-1062	346.73092
Sedatives	RM325	615.782
Seder	BM695.P35	296.437
Sediment transport	TC175.2	551.353
Sedimentary structures	QE472	552.5
Sedimentation and deposition	QE571-597	551.303
Sedimentology	QE471-.15	552.5
Sedition	HV6285	364.131
Seduction	HV6584-6589	364.153
Seed adulteration and inspection	SB114	631.521
Seed crops	SB183-187	633
Seed technology	SB113.2-118.45	631.521
Seedlings—Transplanting	SB121	631.536
Seeds	SB113.2-118.45	631.521
Segregation in education	LC212.5-.73	379.26
Seismology	QE531-541	551.22

Subject Heading	LC	Dewey
Seismometry	QE541	551.220287
Selection (Plant breeding)	SB123-.25	631.52
Self	BF697-.5	155.2
Self-actualization (Psychology)	BF637.S4	158.1
Self-confidence	BF575.S39	155.232
Self-control	BJ1533.D49	179.9
Self-control	BF632	153.8
Self-control in children	BF723.S25	155.4138
Self-defense	GV1111	613.66
Self-denial	BV4647.S4	241.4
Self-destructive behavior	RC569.5.S45	616.8582
Self-destructive behavior in children	RJ506.S39	618.928582
Self-esteem	BF697.5.S46	158.1
Self-help groups	HV547	374.22
Self in children	BF723.S24	155.4182
Self-injurious behavior	RC569.5.S48	616.8582
Self-insurance	HG8082	368
Self-interest	BJ1474	171.9
Self-mutilation	RA1146	616.8582
Self-mutilation	RC552.S4	616.8582
Self-organizing systems	Q325-390	003.7
Self-presentation	BF697.5.S44	155
Self psychology	BF697-.5	155.2
Self-reliance	BJ1533.S27	179.9
Selling	HF5438-5439	380.1
Selling—Automobiles	HF5439.A8	380.145388342
Selling—Drugs	HF5439.D75	380.1456151
Semantics	P325-.5	401.43
Semantics, Historical	P325.5.H57	401.4309
Semen	QP255	612.61
Semiconductor storage devices	TK7895.M4	621.39732
Semiconductor wafers	TK7871.85-.99	621.38152
Semiconductors	QC610.9-611.8	537.6226
Seminars	LB2393.5	378.177
Seminary extension	BV4164	230.0711
Seminole Indians	E99.S28	973.04973
Seminole War, 1st, 1817-1818	E83.817	975.03
Seminole War, 2nd, 1835-1842	E83.835	973.57
Semiotics	P99-.4	401.41
Semites	GN547	305.892
Semites—Religion	BL1600-1710	299.2
Semitic languages	PJ3001-9278	492
Semitic languages—Dictionaries	PJ3004	492.043
Semitic languages—Etymology	PJ3065	492.042
Semitic languages—Grammar	PJ3021-3041	492.045
Semitic languages—Lexicography	PJ3071-3075	492.043028
Semitic languages—Study and teaching	PJ3011-3013	492.04071
Semitic languages, Northwest	PJ4121-4129	492.047
Semitic literature	PJ3097	892.009
Senegal—Census	HA4729	316.63

Subject Heading	LC	Dewey	Subject Heading	LC	Dewey
Senegal—Civilization	DT549.4	966.3	Serbo-Croatian language— Slang	PG1399	491.827
Senegal—Description and travel	DT549.27	916.6304	Serbo-Croatian philology	PG1201-1223	491.82
Senegal—Gazetteers	DT549.15	916.63003	Serfdom	HT751-815	306.365
Senegal—History	DT549.47-.83	966.3	Serfdom—[By region or country]	HT781-815	306.36509(4-9)
Senegal—History—To 1960	DT549.7-.73	966.30(1-3)	Serfdom—Austria	HT803	306.3650943(6/9)
Senegal—History—1960-	DT549.8-.83	966.305	Serfdom—France	HT785	306.3650944
Senegal—History—Coup d'etat, 1962	DT549.8	966.305	Serfdom—Germany	HT791-801	306.3650943
			Serfdom—Great Britain	HT781	306.3650941
Senegal—Maps	G8810-8814	912.663	Serfdom—Russia	HT807-809	306.3650947
Senile dementia	RC524	616.8983	Sericulture	SF541-560	638.2
Seniority, Employee	HF5549.5.S4	658.312	Series, Infinite	QA295	515.243
Sense organs	QL945-949	573.87	Serigraphy	NE1843-1844	764.8
Sense organs	QM501-511	611.8	Sermon on the mount	BT380-.2	226.9
Senses and sensation	BD214	121.35	Sermons	BV4239-4316	252
Senses and sensation	BF231-299	152.1	Serotherapy	RM270-282	615.37
Senses and sensation	QP431-495	612.8	Serpent worship	BL441	291.212
Sensory stimulation in newborn infants	BF720.S45	155.42221	Service, Compulsory non-military	HD4871-4875	331.1173
Sentences (Criminal procedure)	K5510-5560	345.0772	Service, Compulsory non-military	HD4905.5	331.1173
Separation of powers	JF229	320.404	Service industries	HD9980-9990	338.4
Separation of powers	JK305	342.73044	Service stations	TL153	629.286
Separation of powers— England	KD4000-4010	342.42044	Setters (Dogs)	SF429.S5	636.7526
			Seven Days' Battles, 1862	E473.68	973.732
Separation of powers— United States	KF4565-4579	342.73044	Seven Years' War, 1756-1763	DD409-412.8	940.2534
Septets	M700-786	785.17	Seventeenth century	D242-283.5	940.2 (3-5)
Septic tanks	TD778	628.742	Seventh-Day Adventists	BX6151-6155	286.732
Sepulchral monuments	NB1800-1895	736.5	Seventh-Day Baptists	BX6390-6408	286.3
Serbia	DR1932-2125	949.71	Severance pay	HD4928.D5	331.216
Serbia—History	DR343	949.71	Sewage	S657	631.869
Serbia—History—To 1456	DR1977-1999.5	949.71013	Sewage	TD730-737	628.3
Serbia—History— 1456-1804	DR2000-2005	949.71013	Sewage—Purification	TD745-758.5	628.3
			Sewage disposal	TD741-780	628.36
Serbia—History—Great Emigration, 1690	DR2004.8	949.71013	Sewage disposal, Rural	TD929-930.4	628.742
			Sewage irrigation	TD760	628.3623
Serbia—History— Insurrection, 1788	DR2005	949.71013	Sewage lagoons	TD746.5	628.351
Serbia—History— 1804-1918	DR2006-2032	949.7101(4-5)	Sewage sludge— Conditioning	TD769.7	628.364
Serbia—History— Insurrection, 1804-1813	DR343	949.71014	Sewage sludge— Incineration	TD770-.3	628.37
Serbia—History—Milos Obrenovic, 1814-1839	DR2016	949.71014	Sewer design	TD678-688	628.2
			Sewerage	TD511-780	628.3
Serbia—History—Revolt, 1883	DR2026.8	949.71015	Sewerage—History	TD515-520	628.309
Serbia—History—1918-	DR2033-2047	949.710(2-3)	Sewerage—[By region or country]	TD521-627	628.309(4-9)
Serbia—History— 1918-1945	DR2033-2040	949.7102	Sewerage, Rural	TD929-930.4	628.742
			Sewers, Concrete	TD682	628.2
Serbia—History— 1945-1992	DR2041-2047	949.710(2-3)	Sewing	TT700-715	646.2
			Sewing machines	TJ1501-1519	646.2044
Serbia—History—1992-	DR2047	949.7103	Sex	HQ12-449	306.7
Serbia—Maps	G6850-6853	912.4971	Sex—Folklore	GR462	398.354
Serbia—Maps	G2015-2017	912.4971	Sex—Religious aspects—Christianity	BT708	233.5
Serbo-Croatian language	PG1224-1399	491.82			
Serbo-Croatian language— Dictionaries	PG1374-1384	491.823	Sex—Religious aspects—Islam	BP190.5.S4	297.577
			Sex (Psychology)	BF692-.5	155.3
Serbo-Croatian language— Grammar	PG1229-1313	491.825	Sex addition	RC560.S43	616.8583
			Sex crimes	HQ71-72	364.153

Subject Heading	LC	Dewey
Sex crimes	HV6558-6569	364.153
Sex crimes—Investigation	HV8079.S48	363.25953
Sex customs	GN484.3	392.6
Sex customs	HQ12-18	306.73
Sex discrimination in education	LC212.8-.83	379.26
Sex discrimination in employment	HD6060-.5	331.4133
Sex distribution (Demography)	HB1741-1948	305.3
Sex distribution (Demography)— United States	HB1755-1777	305.30973
Sex distribution (Demography)—[United States, By state]	HB1775	305.3097(4-9)
Sex in the Bible	BS680.S5	220.83067
Sex instruction	HQ56-59	613.9071
Sex instruction for boys	HQ41	613.9071
Sex instruction for children	HQ53	613.9071
Sex instruction for girls	HQ51	613.9071
Sex instruction for the aged	HQ55	613.9071
Sex instruction for the handicapped	HQ54-.4	613.9071
Sex offenders	HQ71-72	364.153
Sex role	HQ1075-.5	305.3
Sex role in children	BF723.S42	155.3
Sex role in mass media	P96.S5	305.3
Sexadecimal system	QA141.8.S4	513.57
Sexism in communication	P96.S48	305.3
Sexism in religion	BL458	291.178344
Sexism in textbooks	LB3045.66	379.156
Sexology—Research	HQ60	613.9072
Sextant	VK583	623.890284
Sextets	M600-686	785.16
Sexual animosity	BF692.15	155.3
Sexual aversion disorders	RC560.S45	616.8583
Sexual behavior in animals	QL761	591.562
Sexual disorders in children	RJ476.5-478.5	618.92098
Sexual ethics	HQ31-64	176
Sexual ethics for teenagers	HQ35	176.0835
Sexual ethics for women	HQ46	176.082
Sexual instinct	HQ19-30.7	306.7
Sexual selection in animals	QL761	591.562
Sexually abused children	RJ507.S49	618.9285836
Sexually transmitted diseases	RC200-203	616.951
Sexually transmitted diseases	RA644.V4	614.547
Sexually transmitted diseases—Prevention	RA644.V4	614.547
Seychelles—Census	HA2301	316.96
Seychelles—Civilization	DT469.S44	969.6
Seychelles—Description and travel	DT469.S427	916.9604
Seychelles—Gazetteers	DT469.S415	916.96003
Seychelles—History	DT469.S452-.S483	969.6
Seychelles—History— Coup d'etat, 1977	DT469.S48	969.6

Subject Heading	LC	Dewey
Seychelles—History— Coup d'etat, 1981	DT469.S48	969.6
Seychelles—Maps	G9200-9204	912.696
Shade-tolerant plants	SB434.7	635.9543
Shades and shadows	NC755	742
Shadow prices	HB143	338.52
Shadow shows	PN1979.S5	791.53
Shaft sinking	TN283	622.25
Shakers	BX9751-9793	289.8
Shakers—Biography	BX9791-9793	289.8092
Shakers—Congresses	BX9755	289.806
Shakers—Education	BX9761-9764	268.898
Shakers—Government	BX9776	262.098
Shakers—History	BX9765-9769	289.809
Shakers—Sermons	BX9777	252.098
Shakers—United States	BX9766-9768	289.80973
Shakers—[By region or country]	BX9766-9769	289.809(4-9)
Shakespeare, William, 1564-1616	PR2750-3112	822.33
Shaktism	BL1282.2-.292	294.5514
Shale	QE471.15.S5	552.5
Shamanism	BF1585-1623	291.144
Shamanism	BL2370.S5	291.144
Shampoos	TT969	646.7240284
Sharecropping	HD1478	333.335563
Shareware (Computer software)	QA76.76.S46	005.3
Sharpshooting (Military science)	UD330-335	356.114
Shaving	TT970	646.724
Shaving (Jewish law)	BM523.5.S53	340.18
Shawnee Indians	E99.S35	973.04973
Sheep	SF371-379	636.3
Sheep-shearing	SF379	636.30833
Sheet-metal	TS250	671.823
Shell money	HG235	332.4
Shell money	GN435.7-450.5	332.4
Shellcraft	NK8643	745.55
Shellcraft	TT862	745.55
Shellfish	QL401-445.2	594
Shellfish culture	SH365-380.92	639.4
Shellfish culture—[By region or country]	SH365-367	639.409(4-9)
Shellfish gathering	SH400.4-.8	639.4
Shells	QL401-432	591.477
Shells, Concrete	TA683.5.S4	624.1834
Shelving (Furniture)	NK2740	749.3
Shenandoah Valley Campaign, 1862	E473.7	973.732
Shenandoah Valley Campaign, 1864 (August-November)	E477.33	973.737
Shenandoah Valley Campaign, 1864 (May-August)	E476.66	973.73(6-7)
Shenandoah Valley Campaign, 1865	E477.65	973.738
Sherman's March to the Sea	E476.69	973.7378
Shields	CR91-93	929.6

Subject Heading	LC	Dewey	Subject Heading	LC	Dewey
Signal lights	TA1250	629.040289	Sino-Tibetan languages	PL3521-3529	495
Signals and signaling	HE9723-9737	384	Sins	BV4625-4627	241.3
Signals and signaling	V280-285	623.8561	Sisterhoods	BX4200-4556	255.9(1-7)
Signals and signaling	UG570-613.5	358.24	Sisterhoods	BX5185	255.983
Signals and signaling	VK381-397	623.8561	Sitar music	M142.S5	787.82
Signatures (Writing)	Z41-42	929.88	Sitting customs	GT3005.3-.4	392
Signs and symbols	BV150-168	246.55	Sixteenth century	CB367-401	909.5
Sikh sects	BL2018.7	294.69	Sizing (Textile)	TS1488	677.028
Sikhism	BL2017-2018.7	294.6	Skating	GV848.9-852	796.91
Sikhism—Sacred books	BL2017.2-.4	294.682	Skeet shooting	GV1181.3	799.3132
Sikhs	BL2020.S5	294.6	Skeleton	GN70	599.947
Silage	SB195	633.2	Skeleton	QL821-827	573.76
Silent film music	M176	781.542	Skeleton	QM101-117	611.71
Silent films—Musical	MT737	781.54207	Skepticism	B837	149.73
accompaniment			Skepticism	BD201	121.2
Silent reading	LB1050.55	418.4	Skepticism	B779	149.73
Silesia, Lower (Poland	DK4600.S44	943.85	Skepticism	BL2700-2790	211.4
and Germany)			Skeptics (Greek philosophy)	B525	186
Silesia, Upper (Poland	DK4600.S46	943.(72/85)	Ski racing	GV854.9.R3	796.935
and Czech Republic)—			Ski resorts	GV854.35	796.93068
History			Ski troops	UD470-475	356.164
Silhouettes	NC910-.5	741.7	Skin	GN191-199	599.945
Silicone rubber	TS1927.S55	668.4227	Skin	QM481-484	611.77
Silk	SF541-560	638.2	Skin	QL941-943	573.5
Silk	TS1640-1688	677.39	Skin—Cancer	RC280.S5	616.99477
Silk	TS1546	677.39	Skin—Care and hygiene	RL87	613.4
Silk-printing	TP901	686.2316	Skin—Inflammation	RL231-241	616.51
Silkworms	SF541-560	638.2	Skin divers	GV837.9-838	797.23092
Silkworms, Non-mulberry	SF559.5-560	638.2	Skin-grafting	RD121	617.4770592
Silos	TH4935	690.892	Skipjacks	VM331	623.8226
Silva Mind Control	RZ403.S56	615.851	Skirmishing	U210	355.422
Silver	HG301-309	332.4223	Skis and skiing	GV854	796.93
Silver	TA480.S5	620.18923	Skull	GN71-131	599.948
Silver flatware	NK7234-7235	739.2383	Skull	QM105	611.715
Silver mines and mining	HD9536	622.3423	Skull—Abnormalities	RD763	616.71043
Silver mines and mining	TN430-439	622.3423	Skull—Fractures	RD529	617.155
Silverpoint drawing	NC900-902	741.25	Skydiving	GV769.5-770	797.56
Silverwork	NK7100-7695	739.23	Slabs	TA660.S6	624.1772
Silvicultural systems	SD392	634.95	Slander	BV4627.S6	241.3
Simulated environment	LB1029.S5	371.397	Slander	BJ1535.S6	177.3
(Teaching method)			Slang	P409-410	417.2
Sin	BT715-722	233.14	Slaughtering and	TS1960-1967	664.9029
Sin	BV4625	241.3	slaughter-houses		
Sin, Original	BT720	233.14	Slave labor	HD4861-4865	331.11734
Sin, Unpardonable	BT721	241.3	Slave-trade	HT975-1445	380.144
Sin, Venial	BV4625.6-.7	241.31	Slavery	E441-453	973.711
Sin (Islam)	BP166.75	297.22	Slavery	HT851-1444	305.567
Sin (Judaism)	BM630	296.32	Slavery—History	HT863-867	305.56709
Sindhi language	PK2781-2794	491.41	Slavery—Africa	HT1321-1427	305.567096
Singapore—Maps	G8040-8044	912.5957	Slavery—Asia	HT1240.5-1315	305.567095
Singing—Methods	MT882	782.001	Slavery—Australia	HT1431	305.5670994
Singing—Methods	MT825-850	782.001	Slavery—Benelux countries	HT1196-1203	305.56709492
Single people	HQ800-.4	305.90652	Slavery—Canada	HT1051-1052	305.5670971
Single tax	HD1311-1313	330.155	Slavery—Central America	HT1055-1056	305.56709728
Single women	HQ800.2	305.489652	Slavery—China	HT1241-1244	305.5670951
Single-session	RC480.55	616.8914	Slavery—Europe	HT1155-1240	305.567094
psychotherapy			Slavery—France	HT1176-1180	305.5670944
Sinkholes	GB609.2	551.447	Slavery—Germany	HT1181	305.5670943
Sinking-funds	HJ8052	336.363	Slavery—Great Britain	HT1161-1165	305.5670941
Sino-Indian Border	DS480.85	954.042	Slavery—Greece	HT1234	305.56709495
Dispute, 1957-			Slavery—Italy	HT1191-1194	305.5670945

Subject Heading	LC	Dewey
Snow and ice climbing	GV200.3	796.52
Snow camping	GV198.9	796.54
Snow loads	TA654.4	624.172
Snow loads	TG304	624.252
Snow loads	TH895	690.21
Snow removal	TD868-870	625.763
Snow removal	TF542	625.22
Snow White (Tale)	GR75.S6	398.21
Snowboarding	GV857.S57	796.95
Snowmobiling	GV857.S6	796.94
Snowshoes and showshoeing	GV853	796.92
Snuff	GT3030	394.14
Soap	TP990-992.5	668.12
Soap box derbies	GV1029.7	796.6
Soap operas	PN1992.8.S4	791.456
Soap operas	PN1991.8.S4	791.446
Soccer	GV943-944	796.334
Soccer—Tournaments	GV943.45-.54	796.33464
Soccer referees	GV942.7	796.3343
Social adjustment	RC455.4.S67	302.14
Social change	HM101-121	303.4
Social classes	HT601-1444	305.5
Social classes—History	HT607	305.509
Social classes—Research	HT608	305.5072
Social contract	JC336	320.11
Social contract	JA81-84	320.11
Social ecology	HM206-208	304.2
Social ethics	HM216	303.372
Social group work	HV45	361.4
Social groups	HM131-134	305
Social hierarchy in animals	QL775	591.56
Social influence	HM259	303.34
Social interaction	HM291	302.(3/4)
Social legislation	K1701-2000	344
Social legislation—Canada	KE3098-3542	344.71
Social legislation—England	KD3000-3315	344.42
Social legislation—Ireland	KDK800-895	344.415
Social legislation—Northern Ireland	KDE320-348	344.416
Social legislation—Scotland	KDC635-674	344.411
Social legislation—United States	KF3300-3771	344.73
Social norms	GN493.3	306
Social perception	BF323.S63	302.12
Social problems	HN	361.1
Social problems—Congresses	HN3	361.106
Social problems—History	HN8-19	361.109
Social problems—Periodicals	HN1	361.105
Social psychology	HM251-291	302
Social responsibility of business	HD60-.5	658.408
Social sciences	H	300
Social sciences—Biography	H57-59	300.92
Social sciences—Congresses	H21-29	300.6
Social sciences—Experiments	H62	300.724
Social sciences—History	H51-53	300.9
Social sciences—Methodology	H61-.4	300.1
Social sciences—Periodicals	H1-8	300.5
Social sciences—Research	H62-.5	300.72
Social sciences—Study and teaching	H62-.5	300.71
Social security	HD7088-7250.7	368.4
Social security—Law and legislation	K1861-1929	344.05242
Social security—Law and legislation—England	KD3241-3250	343.4205242
Social security—[By region or country]	HD7121-7250.7	368.4009
Social security—United States	HD7123-7126	368.400973
Social security—United States	KF3641-3664	343.7305242
Social service	HV1-696	361
Social service—Directories	HV7	361.025
Social service—History	HV16-25	361.709
Social service—Societies, etc.	HV6	361.006
Social service—Vocational guidance	HV10.5	361.3023
Social service—[By region or country]	HV85-520.5	361.9(4-9)
Social service—United States	HV85-99	361.973
Social service—[United States, By state or city]	HV98-99	361.97(4-9)
Social service—[Other regions or countries]	HV101-520.5	361.9(4-9)
Social service, Rural	HV67	361.91734
Social structure	GN478-491.7	305
Social surveys	HN29	361.10723
Social work education	HV11-.8	361.3071
Social work with criminals	HV7428	361.3
Social work with gays	HV1449	361.308664
Social work with juvenile delinquents	HV9051-9230.7	364.6
Social workers—Supervision of	HV40.54	361.3092
Socialism	HX1-550	335
Socialism—History	HX21-54	335.009
Socialism—Study and teaching	HX19-.2	335.0071
Socialism—[By region or country]	HX80-517.5	335.009(4-9)
Socialism, Christian	HX51-54	335.7
Socialist ethics	BJ1388	171.7
Socialization	GN510	303.32
Socialization	HQ783	303.32
Socially handicapped children—Education	LC4051-4100	371.82694
Societies	HS	366
Societies—Congresses	HS5	366.006
Societies—Directories	HS17	366.0025
Societies—Encyclopedias	HS12	366.003

Subject Heading	LC	Dewey	Subject Heading	LC	Dewey
Societies—History, organization, etc.	HS25-35	366.009	Sociology, Urban—Great Britain	HT133	307.760941
Societies—Periodicals	HS1	366.005	Sociology, Urban—Mexico	HT127.7	307.760972
Society Islands	DU870	996.21	Sociology, Urban—South America	HT129	307.76098
Society Islands—Maps	G9640-9644	912.9621			
Society of Friends	BX7601-7795	289.605	Sociology, Urban—United States	HT123-.5	307.760973
Society of Friends—Congresses	BX7606.5-7608	289.606	Sociometry	HM253	302.015195
			Sofia (Bulgaria)	DR97	949.99
Society of Friends—Education	BX7619-7627	268.896	Softball	GV881-.4	796.3578
			Software compatibility	QA76.76.C64	005
Society of Friends—Government	BX7740-7746	262.096	Software documentation	QA76.76.D63	005.3
			Software engineering	QA76.758	005.1
Society of Friends—History	BX7630-7728	289.609	Software maintenance	QA76.76.S64	005.16
Society of Friends—Periodicals	BX7601	289.605	Software protection	QA76.76.P76	005.8
			Soil acidity	S592.575	631.42
Society of Friends—Sermons	BX7733	252.096	Soil biochemistry	S592.7-.85	631.417
			Soil biology	QH84.8	578.757
Society of Friends—Africa	BX7720-7723	289.66	Soil chemistry	S592.5-.6	631.41
Society of Friends—Asia	BX7715-7716	289.65	Soil conservation	S622-627	631.45
Society of Friends—Australia	BX7725-7726	289.694	Soil conservation projects	S627.P76	631.45
			Soil ecology	QH541.5.S6	577.57
Society of Friends—Canada	BX7650-7653	289.671	Soil management	S590-592	631.4
Society of Friends—Europe	BX7675-7710	289.64	Soil mechanics	TA710-711.5	624.15136
Society of Friends—Great Britain	BX7676-7693	289.641	Soil microbiology	QR111-113	579.1757
			Soil moisture	S594	631.432
Society of Friends—South America	BX7671-7673	289.68	Soil pollution	TD878-880	363.7396
			Soil pollution	RA571	614.59
Society of Friends—United States	BX7635-7649	289.673	Soil protection	TD878-880	628.5
			Soil science	S590-599.9	631.4
Society, Primitive	GN406-498	301.7	Soil surveys	TE208-.5	625.732
Sociobiology	GN365.9	304.5	Soil surveys	S592.14-.147	631.47
Sociolinguistics	P40	306.44	Soils	S590-599.9	631.4
Sociological jurisprudence	K368-380	340.115	Soils—Agricultural chemical content	S592.6.A34	631.41
Sociology	HM	301			
Sociology—Congresses	HM13	301.06	Soils—Analysis	S593	631.4
Sociology—Dictionaries	HM17	301.03	Soils—Pesticide content	TD879.P37	628.55
Sociology—History	HM19-22	301.09	Soils, Irrigated	S599-.9	631.587
Sociology—Methodology	HM24-37	301.01	Solar activity	QB524-526	523.72
Sociology—Periodicals	HM1-7	301.05	Solar cells	TK2960	621.31244
Sociology—Study and teaching	HM45-47	301.071	Solar collectors	TJ812	621.472
			Solar compass	QB105	522
Sociology, Biblical	BS670	220.8301	Solar cosmic rays	QC485	539.7223
Sociology, Christian	BT738-.5	261.5	Solar cycle	QB526.C9	523.73
Sociology, Hindu	BL1215.S64	294.517	Solar eclipses	QB541-545	523.78
Sociology, Islamic	BP173.25-.45	297.27	Solar energy	TJ809-812.8	621.47
Sociology, Rural	HT401-485	307.72	Solar energy—Research	TJ811-.5	621.47072
Sociology, Rural—History	HT415	307.7209	Solar energy industries	HD9681	333.7923
Sociology, Urban	HT101-395	307.76	Solar engines	TJ812.5	621.473
Sociology, Urban—History	HT111-150	307.7609	Solar flares	QB516.F6	523.75
Sociology, Urban—Research	HT110	307.76072	Solar greenhouses	SB415-416.3	631.583
Sociology, Urban—Africa	HT148	307.76096	Solar heating	TH7413-7414	697.78
Sociology, Urban—Asia	HT147	307.76095	Solar houses	TH7414	697.78
Sociology, Urban—Australia	HT149	307.760994	Solar magnetic fields	QB539.M23	523.72
Sociology, Urban—Canada	HT127	307.760971	Solar noise storms	QB539.N6	523.72
Sociology, Urban—Central America	HT128	307.7609728	Solar power plants	TK1085-1087	621.31244
			Solar power plants	TK1545	621.31244
Sociology, Urban—Developing countries	HT149.5	307.76091724	Solar radiation	QB531	523.72
			Solar radiation	QC910.2-911.82	551.5271
Sociology, Urban—Europe	HT131-145	307.76094	Solar saline water conversion plants	TD479.7	628.16725
Sociology, Urban—France	HT135	307.760944			
Sociology, Urban—Germany	HT137	307.760943			

Subject Heading	LC	Dewey
Solar system	QB500.5-785	523.2
Solar wind	QB529	523.58
Soldiers	U1-145	355.0092
Soldiers	U750-773	355.0092
Soldiers—Billeting	UC410	355.71
Soldiers—Education, Non-military	U715-717	355.5071
Soldiers of fortune	G539	355.354
Soldiers' homes	UB380-385	362.1608697
Soldiers' monuments	NA9325-9355	725.94
Solid fuel reactors	TK9203.S65	621.4834
Solid propellants	TL785	629.47524
Solid state chemistry	QD478	541.0421
Solid state physics	QC176-.9	531
Solidification	QC303	536.42
Solo instrument music	M175.5	785
Solo man	GN284.4	569.9
Solomon Islands	DU850	995.93
Solomon Islands—Census	HA4014	319.593
Solomon Islands—Maps	G9280-9284	912.9593
Solubility	QD543	541.342
Solution (Chemistry)	QD541-549	541.34
Solutions (Pharmacy)	RS201.S6	615.42
Solvents	TP247.5	661.807
Somali language	PJ2531-2534	493.54
Somalia	DT401-409	967.73
Somalia—Census	HA4690	316.773
Somalia—Civilization	DT402.2	967.73
Somalia—Description and travel	DT401.8	916.77304
Somalia—Economic conditions	HC850	330.96773
Somalia—Gazetteers	DT401.2	916.773003
Somalia—History	DT402.5-407.3	967.73
Somalia—History— 1960-1991	DT407-.3	967.7305
Somalia—History—1991-	DT407	967.73053
Somalia—Maps	G8350-8354	912.6773
Somatization disorder	RC552.S66	616.8524
Somatotypes	GN66	599.949
Son of Man	BT232	232.9
Sonar	VK560	623.8938
Sonar	VK388	623.8938
Sonata	MT62	784.18307
Song cycles	M1621.4	782.47
Songbooks	M1977.C5	782.42
Songhai Empire	DT551.45.S	966.23
Songs—Accompaniment	MT68	781.4707
Songs—History and criticism	ML2500-2862	782.4209
Sonnet	PN1514	808.8142
Sontay Raid, 1970	DS557.8.S6	959.704342
Sophists (Greek philosophy)	B288	183.1
Sopono (Cult)	BL2480.Y6	299.6869
Sorbian languages	PG5631-5698	491.88
Sorbian literature	PG5661-5698	891.88
Sotho language	PL8689	496.3977
Soul	BD419-428	128.1
Soul	BT740-743	233.5
Soul	BL290	291.22
Soul (Hinduism)	BL1215.S8	294.522

Subject Heading	LC	Dewey
Soul (Islam)	BP166.73	297.225
Sound	QC220-246	534
Sound—Equipment and supplies	QC228.3	534.0284
Sound—Measurement	QC243	534.0287
Sound production by animals	QL765	591.594
Sound recordings— Album covers	NC1882-1883.3	741.66
Sound-waves—Damping	QC235	534.208
Sound-waves—Damping	QC243	534.208
Sounding and soundings	VK584.S6	623.8938
Soundproofing	TH1725	693.834
Source reduction (Waste management)	TD793.95	628.44
South Africa—Census	HA4701	316.8
South Africa—Civilization	DT1752	968
South Africa—Description and travel	DT1730-1738	916.804
South Africa—Economic conditions	HC905	330.968
South Africa—Gazetteers	DT1714	916.8003
South Africa—History	DT1772-1969	968
South Africa—History— To 1836	DT1807-1845	968.0(2-42)
South Africa—History— Frontier Wars, 1811-1878	DT1837	968.0(3-45)
South Africa—History— 1836-1909	DT1848-1922	968.04(2-9)
South Africa—History— Great Trek, 1836-1840	DT1853	968.044
South Africa—History— Xhosa Cattle-Killing, 1856-1857	DT1863	968.045
South Africa—History— Usutu Uprising, 1888	DT1888	968.045
South Africa—History— 1906-1961	DT1924-1941	968.0(49-5)
South Africa—History— Rebellion, 1914-1915	DT1933	968.052
South Africa—History— 1961-	DT1945-1970	968.06
South Africa—History— Soweto Uprising, 1976	DT1959	968.0627
South Africa—Maps	G8500-8504	912.68
South America	F2201-3799	980
South America—Armed Forces—Supplies and stores	UC106-154	355.8098
South America—Biography	CT640-758	920.08
South America—Church history	BR660-730	278
South America—Climate	QC988	551.698
South America— Commmerce	HF3371-3480	380.1098
South America— Economic conditions	HC161-239.5	330.98
South America—Genealogy	CS270-409	929.38
South America—History	F2201-2239	980
South America—Maps	G5200-5668	912.8

Subject Heading	LC	Dewey
Spain—Colonies	JV4000-4099	325.346
Spain—Commerce	HF3681-3690	380.10946
Spain—Congresses	DP2	936.6006/ 946.006
Spain—Description and travel	DP27-43.2	913.6604/ 914.604
Spain—Directories	DP11	946.0025
Spain—Economic conditions	HC381-390	330.946
Spain—Emigration and immigration	JV8250-8259	325.(246/46)
Spain—Gazetteers	DP12	913.66003/ 914.6003
Spain—Historiography	DP63-.83	936.60072/ 946.0072
Spain—History, Military	DP76-78	355.30946
Spain—History, Naval	DP80-81	359.30946
Spain—History—To 711	DP91-96	936.6/946.01
Spain—History—Roman period, 218 B.C.- 414 A.D.	DP94-95	936.603
Spain—History—Gothic period, 414-711	DP96	946.01
Spain—History—711-1516	DP97.3-160.8	946.0(2-3)
Spain—History—Ferdinand and Isabella, 1479-1516	DP161.5-166	946.03
Spain—History—House of Austria, 1516-1700	DP170-189	946.04
Spain—History—Charles I, 1516-1556	DP172-175	946.042
Spain—History—Philip II, 1556-1598	DP176-181	946.043
Spain—History—Philip III, 1598-1621	DP182-183.9	946.051
Spain—History—Philip IV, 1621-1665	DP184-185.9	946.052
Spain—History—Charles II, 1665-1700	DP186-189	946.053
Spain—History—18th century	DP194-200.8	946.054
Spain—History— Bourbons, 1700-	DP192-200.8	946.054
Spain—History—Louis I, 1724	DP195	946.055
Spain—History— Ferdinand VI, 1746-1759	DP198-.7	946.056
Spain—History— Charles IV, 1788-1808	DP200-.8	946.058
Spain—History—19th century	DP201-232.6	946.0(58-7)
Spain—History— Ferdinand VII, 1813-1833	DP214-215.9	946.072
Spain—History—Bourbon Restoration, 1814-1868	DP212-220	946.072
Spain—History— Revolution, 1820-1823	DP215	946.072
Spain—History— Isabella II, 1833-1868	DP216-220	946.072
Spain—History—Carlist War, 1833-1840	DP219-.2	946.072
Spain—History— Revolution, 1854	DP217	946.072
Spain—History— Revolutionary period, 1868-1875	DP222-232.6	946.073
Spain—History—Carlist War, 1873-1876	DP228-231.5	946.07(3-4)
Spain—History—Republic, 1873-1875	DP230-231.5	946.073
Spain—History— Alfonso XII, 1875-1885	DP232-.6	946.074
Spain—History— Alfonso XIII, 1886-1931	DP233-272.4	946.074
Spain—History— Dictatorship, 1923-1930	DP247	946.074
Spain—History—Republic, 1931-1939	DP250-269.9	946.081
Spain—History— Revolution, 1931	DP250	946.08
Spain—History—Civil War, 1936-1939	DP269.A1-.9	946.081
Spain—History— 1939-1975	DP270-271	946.082
Spain—History—1975-	DP272-.4	946.083
Spain—History—Coup d'etat, 1981	DP272	946.083
Spain—Manufactures	TS87-88	670.946
Spain—Maps	G1965-1969	912.46
Spain—Maps	G6560-6564	912.46
Spain—Periodicals	DP1	936.6005/ 946.005
Spain—Politics and government	JN8101-8399	320.946
Spanish Succession, War of, 1701-1714	D281-283.5	940.2526
Spanish Succession, War of, 1701-1714	DP196	940.2526
Spanish drama	PQ6099-6129	862.009
Spanish drama	PQ6217-6241	862.008
Spanish fiction	PQ6251-6257	863.008
Spanish fiction	PQ6138-6147	863.009
Spanish language	PC4001-4977	460
Spanish language— Dialects	PC4700-4941	467
Spanish language— Dictionaries	PC4620-4645	463
Spanish language— Etymology	PC4571-4580	462
Spanish language— Grammar	PC4099-4400	465
Spanish language— Lexicography	PC4620-4693	463.028
Spanish language—Slang	PC4951-4977	467
Spanish language—Study and teaching	PC4065	460.71
Spanish literature	PQ6001-8929	860
Spanish literature— Foreign countries	PQ7020-8921	860

Subject Heading	LC	Dewey	Subject Heading	LC	Dewey
Spanish literature—History and criticism	PQ6022-6167	860.009	Spice plants	SB305-307	633.8(3-4)
Spanish literature—Study and teaching	PQ6013-6020	860.71	Spice trade	HD9210-9211	380.141383
			Spices	GT2870	394.12
Spanish literature— To 1500	PQ6057-6060	860.900(1-2)	Spices	TX406-407	641.3383
			Spies	UB270-271	355.3432092
Spanish literature— Classical period, 1500-1700	PQ6063-6072	860.900(2-3)	Spies	VB250	359.3432092
			Spillways	TC555	627.883
			Spin excitations	QC794.6.E9	539.725
Spanish periodicals	PN5317.P4	056.1	Spinal adjustment	RZ265.S64	616.73062
Spanish philology	PC4001-4071	460	Spinal canal	QM111	611.711
Spanish poetry	PQ6174.95-6215	861.008	Spinal cord	QM465	611.82
Spanish poetry	PQ6075-6098	861.009	Spinal cord	QP370-375	612.83
Spanish prose literature	PQ6131-6153	868.08	Spinal cord	QL938.S6	573.869
Spanish prose literature	PQ6247-6264	868.08	Spinal cord—Diseases	RC400-406	616.87
Spatial analysis (Statistics)	HA30.6	310.1	Spinal cord—Surgery	RD594.3	617.482059
Spatial behavior	BF469	153.752	Spine	QP330	612.83
Spears	GN498	623.441	Spine	QM111	611.711
Special districts—United States	JS426	324.973	Spine—Abnormalities	RD768-771	616.73043
			Spine—Instability	RD771.I58	616.73
Special education	LC3950-3990.4	371.9	Spine—Wounds and injuries	RD533	617.482044
Special libraries	Z675.A2	026	Spinning	GN432	677.02822
Specific gravity	QC111-114	531.14	Spinning	TS1480-1487	677.02822
Specifications	TA180-181	620.00212	Spires	NA2930	721.5
Spectroscope	QC465	535.84	Spirits	BT960-962	235
Spectrum analysis	QC450-467	543.0858	Spirits (Islam)	BP166.89	297.21
Spectrum analysis	QD95-96	544.6	Spiritual direction	BX2350.7	253.53
Spectrum analysis— Instruments	QC451	535.840284	Spiritual direction	BX382.5	253.53
			Spiritual direction	BV5053	253.53
			Spiritual healing	BT732.5-.56	234.131
Speculation	HG6001-6051	332.645	Spiritual life—Zen Buddhism	BQ9288	294.3444
Speech	BF455-463	153.6			
Speech	LB1139.L3	153.6	Spiritual works of mercy	BV4647.M4	241.4
Speech	QP306	612.78	Spiritualism	BF1228-1389	133.9
Speech disorders	RC423-428.8	616.855	Spiritualism (Philosophy)	B841	133.9
Speech synthesis	TK7882.S65	621.399	Spiritualism (Philosophy)	BD331	110
Speech therapy	RC423-428.8	616.85506	Spirituals (Songs)	M1670-1671	782.253
Speeches, addresses, etc.	PN6121-6129	808.85	Spithead Mutiny, 1797	DA87.7 1797	942.073
Survival after airplane accidents, shipwrecks, etc.	TL553.7	613.69	Spleen	QL868	573.1555
			Spleen	QP187	612.41
			Spleen	QM371	611.41
			Sponges	QL370.7-374.2	593.4
Speeches, addresses, etc., American	PS660-668	815.008	Spontaneous generation	QH325	576.83
			Spores (Botany)—Dispersal	QK929	571.847
Speeches, addresses, etc., American	PS400-408	815.009	Sporting goods	GV743-749	796.0284
			Sporting guns	SK274	799.20283
Speeches, addresses, etc., English	PR1321-1329	825.008	Sporting prints	NE960-.3	769.49796
			Sports	GN454-455	306.483
Speeches, addresses, etc., English	PR901-907	825.009	Sports	GV561-1198.995	796
			Sports—Economic aspects	GV716	796.0681
Speeches, addresses, etc., French	PQ1281-1283	845.008	Sports—Law and legislation—England	KD3525	344.42099
Speeches, addresses, etc., German	PT1344-1345	835.008	Sports—Law and legislation—United States	KF3989	344.73099
Speeches, addresses, etc., German	PT801	835.009			
Speechwriting	PN4142	808.5	Sports administration	GV713	796.06
Spellers	PE1144-1146	428.1	Sports facilities	GV401-433	796.068
Spelling ability	LB1574	372.632	Sports for the handicapped	GV709.3	796.087
Spent reactor fuels	TK9360	621.48335	Sports journalism	PN4784.S6	070.449796
Spermicides	RG137.2	613.9432	Sports medicine	RC1200-1245	617.1027
Spherical astronomy	QB140-237	522.7	Spotsylvania Court House, Battle of, Va., 1864	E476.52	973.736
Spherical trigonometry	QA535	516.244			

Subject Heading	LC	Dewey
Spraying and dusting in agriculture	SB953	632.94
Spring festivals	GT4504-.995	394.262
Springboard diving	GV838.67.S65	797.24
Springs	GB1198-.4	551.498
Springs—Folklore	GR690	398.364
Springs (Mechanism)	TJ210	621.824
Squall lines	QC880.4.S65	551.55
Squalls	QC880.4.S65	551.55
Square root	QA49	513.23
Square root	QA119	513.23
Squatter sovereignty	E415.7	973.711
Squatter sovereignty	JK318	346.043
Sri Lanka	DS488-490	954.93
Sri Lanka—Census	HA4570.8	315.493
Sri Lanka—Description and travel	DS489-.15	915.49304
Sri Lanka—Economic conditions	HC424	330.95493
Sri Lanka—Gazetteers	DS488.9	915.493003
Sri Lanka—History	DS489.5-490	954.93
Sri Lanka—History— To 1505	DS489.6-.63	954.9301
Sri Lanka—History— 1505-1948	DS489.7-.73	954.930(1-2)
Sri Lanka—History— Rebellion, 1818	DS489.7	954.9302
Sri Lanka—History— Rebellion, 1848	DS489.7	954.9302
Sri Lanka—History—1948-	DS489.8-.86	954.9303
Sri Lanka—History— Rebellion, 1971	DS489.8	954.93031
Sri Lanka—Manufactures	TS104.7-.8	670.95493
Sri Lanka—Maps	G7750-7754	912.5493
Sri Lanka—Maps	G2290-2294	912.5493
Sri Lanka—Politics and government	JQ650-659	320.95493
Stability	QA871	515.35
Stability of airplanes	TL574.S7	629.13236
Stability of ships	VM159	623.81
Stadiums	GV415-416	796.068
Stadiums	NA6860-7010	725.827
Staff rides	U280-285	355.4(8)
Staff, Pastoral	BV168.S7	254
Staffs (Sticks, canes, etc.)	GT2220	391.44
Stains and staining (Microscopy)	QH237	570.2827
Staircases	TH5667-5680	690.1832
Stairs	NA3060	721.832
Stalingrad, Battle of, 1942-1943	D764.3.S7	940.5421721
Stamp collecting	HE6187.6230	769.56
Standardbred horse	SF293.S72	636.13
Standardization	HD62	658.562
Standardization	T59-.2	658.562
Standards, Engineering	TA368	620.00218
Standards, Military	UC590-595	355.15
Staphylococcal infections	QR201.S68	571.99353
Staphylococcal infections	RC116.S8	616.92
Starch	TP415-416	664.2
Stars	GR625	398.362

Subject Heading	LC	Dewey
Stars	QB799-903	523.8
Stars—Atlases	QB65	520.223
Stars—Catalogs	QB6	523.80216
Stars—Clusters	QB851-855.9	523.85
Stars—Evolution	QB806	523.88
Stars—Formation	QB806	523.88
Stars—Masses	QB814	523.81
Stars—Observations	QB6	523.8
Stars—Photographic measurements	QB121	523.87
Stars—Radiation	QB817	523.82
Stars—Rotation	QB810	523.83
Stars, New	QB895	523.88
Stars, New	QB841	523.88
Starvation	RA1116	616.39
State, The	JC	320.011
State, The—Origin	GN492.6	320.11
State aid to private schools	LB2828	379.32
State bankruptcy	HJ8061	336.368
State departments of education	LB2809	379.152
State farms	HD1493-.5	334.683
State governments— United States	JK2403-9593	352.130973
State governments— [United States, By state]	JK2701-9593	352.1309(4-9)
State universities and colleges	LB2329.5	378.053
States rights	JK311-325	342.73042
States, Small	JC365	321.06
Statics	QA821-835	531.12
Stationery	TS1228-1268	676.2823
Stations of the Cross	BX2040	264.0274
Statistical astronomy	QB149	520.21
Statistical consultants	QA276.17	310.92
Statistical mechanics	QC174.7-175.36	530.13
Statistical weather forecasting	QC996.5	551.633
Statistics	HA	310
Statistics—Dictionaries	HA17	310.3
Statistics—Graphic methods	HA31	001.4226
Statistics—History	HA19	310.9
Statistics—Methodology	HA29-32	310.1
Statistics—Periodicals	HA1	310.5
Statistics—Research	HA35	310.72
Statues	NB	731.7
Status offenders	HV9051-9230.7	365.6
Statutes	K7010-7011	348.022
Statutes—England	KD125-150	348.42022
Statutes—England	KD8850-9355	349.42
Statutes—London	KD8996-9142	342.421
Statutes—United States	KF50-70	348.73022
Statutes—Wales	KD9407	348.429022
Stealth aircraft	UG1240	385.4183
Steam	TJ268-280.7	621.1
Steam as a disinfectant	RA766.S8	614.48
Steam-boilers	TJ281-393	621.183
Steam-boilers, Marine	VM741-750	623.8722
Steam-boilers—Safety appliances	TJ350-357	621.1830289

Subject Heading	LC	Dewey	Subject Heading	LC	Dewey
Steam engineering	TJ268-748	621.1	Stomache	QL862	573.36
Steam-engines	TJ461-740	621.1	Stomache—Diseases	RC816-840	616.33
Steam generating heavy water reactors	TK9203.H4	621.483	Stomache—Secretions	QP193	612.32
			Stomache—Surgery	RD540.5-.57	617.553059
Steam-heating	TH7561-7599	697.5	Stone	TN950-997	622.35
Steam-heating, Low pressure	TH7570-7578	697.5	Stone age	GN775-768	930.1(2-4)
			Stone carving	NB1208-1210	731.463
Steam-pipe coverings	TJ427	621.185	Stone money	GN436.2	332.4
Steam-pipes	TJ415-444	621.185	Stone walls	TH2249	690.12
Steam power plants	TJ395-444	621.312132	Stonemasonry	TH5401-5440	693.1
Steam-turbines	TJ735-740	621.165	Stoneware	NK4360-4367	738.3
Steamboat disasters	VK1250-1299	363.123	Storage batteries	TK2941	621.31242
Steamboat lines	HE945	387.2044	Stores or stock-room keeping	HF5495	381.1
Steamboats—Passenger accommodation	HE599-601	387.2044	Storm sewers	TD665	628.212
Steaming (Cookery)	TX691	641.73	Storm surges	GC225-226	551.47022
Steel—Fatigue	TA473	620.176	Storms	HV635.5-636	363.3492
Steel, Galvanized	TA472-473	620.17	Storms	QC940.6-959	551.55
Steel, Stainless	TA479.S7	620.16	Storytelling	GR72.3	808.543
Steel, Structural	TA684-695	624.1821	Storytelling	LB1042	372.677
Steel boats	V880	359.82	Stoves	TH7435-7458	697.22
Steel boats	VM320-361	623.843	Stoves	TX657.S3-.S8	641.5028
Steel houses	NA7180	728	Stoves, Coal	TH7443-7446	697.22
Steel I-beams	TA660.S67	624.17723	Stoves, Electric	TX827	641.586
Steel-works	TS300-360	672	Stoves, Gas	TH7454-7457	697.043
Steel-works	TN755	669.142	Stoves, Wood	TH7437-7441	697.22
Steeplechasing	SF359-.7	798.45	Stowage	VK235	387.544
Steering-gear	VM841-845	623.862	Strains and stresses	QA931-939	531.381
Stellar oscillations	QB812	523.83	Strains and stresses	TG265-267	624.252
Stencil work	TT270-273	745.73	Strains and stresses	TH845-895	690.21
Step aerobics	GV501.5	613.71	Strange particles	QC793.5.S72-.S729	539.7216
Stepfathers	HQ756	306.8742			
Steppes	GB571-578	551.453	Strategic planning	HD30.28	658.4012
Sterilization of women	RG138	618.12059	Strategy	U161-163	355.42
Sterilization reversal	RD585	618.145	Stream crossing, Military	U205	355.423
Sterilization reversal	RG138	618.12059	Stream ecology	QH541.5.S7	577.64
Sterilization reversal	RD585.5	617.463	Stream measurements	GB1201-1398	551.4830287
Sterilization, Eugenic—Law and legislation—United States	KF3832	344.73048	Streamflow	GB1207	551.483
			Street children	HV873-887	362.708691
			Street cleaning	TD813-870	628.46
Stethoscopes	RC76.3	616.0754028	Street cleaning—Equipment and supplies	TD860	628.460284
Stevedores	HD8039.L8	387.5092			
Stewardship, Christian	BV772	248.6	Street cleaning—[By region or country]	TD815-849	628.4609(3-9)
Stews	TX693	641.73			
Still-life painting	ND2290-2305	751.422435	Street-railroads	TF701-1124	625.66
Still-life painting	ND1390-1400	758.4	Street-railroads—Fares	HE4341-4345	388.46
Still-life photography	TR656.5	778.935	Street-railroads—Finance	HE4351	388.46
Stillbirth	RG631-633	618.4	Streets	HE331-380	388.411
Stimulants	RM332-.3	615.785	Strength of materials	TA405	620.112
Stir frying	TX689.5	641.77	Strength of materials	TA410-417.7	620.112
Stochastic processes	QA274-.8	519.23	Streptococcus	QR82.S78	579.355
Stock companies	HD2709-2932	338.86	Stress (Psychology)	BF575.S75	155.9042
Stock-exchanges	HG4551-4598	332.642	Stress fractures (Orthopedics)	RD104.S77	617.15
Stock index futures	HG6043	332.63228			
Stock options	HG6042	332.63228	Stress in children	BF723.S75	155.418
Stockbrokers	HG4621	332.62	Strikes and lockouts	HD5306-5474	331.892
Stockholm (Sweden)	DL976	948.73	Strikes and lockouts—[By region or country]	HD5321-5450.7	331.892(4-9)
Stocks	HG4661	332.6322			
Stoics	B528	188	Strikes and lockouts, Sympathetic	HD5309	331.8923
Stomache	QP151	612.32			
Stomache	QM341	611.33	String instrument music	M59.5	787

Subject Heading	LC	Dewey
String-orchestra music	M1100-1160	784.7
String quartets	M450-454	784.4
String trios	M349-353	785.13
Stringed instruments	MT259-338	787.07
Stringed instruments	ML750-927	787.09
Strip mining	TN291	622.292
Structural analysis (Engineering)	TG260-270	624.25
Structural analysis (Engineering)	TA645-656.5	624.171
Structural design	TA658-.8	624.1771
Structural drawing	T355	604.2
Structural dynamics	TA654-656.5	624.176
Structural engineering	TA630-901	624.1
Structural engineering—Computer programs	TA641	624.10285
Structural engineering—Periodicals	TA630	624.105
Structural engineering—Research	TA638.2	624.1072
Structural frames	TG260	624.257
Structural frames	TA660.F7-.F73	624.1773
Structural unemployment	HD5708.46-.47	331.137041
Structuralism	B841.4	149.96
Stucco	NA7160	728
Student activities	LB3605	371.8
Student adjustment	LB1139.S88	370.158
Student aid	LB2337.2-2340.8	378.3
Student ethics	LB3609	174.9375
Student exchange programs	LB2375-2378	378.016
Student flying	TL711.S8	629.1325071
Student government	LB3092-3095	371.59
Student housing	LB3226-3228	371.871
Student loan funds	LB2340-.4	378.362
Student movements	LA186	371.81
Student publications	LB3621	371.897
Student registration	LB2341	378.161
Student suspension	LB3089-.4	371.543
Student teachers	LB2157	370.71
Students	LB3602-3618	371.8
Students—Crimes against	HV6250.4.S78	362.88088375
Students—Language	LB3604	371.8
Students—Legal status, laws, etc.—United States	KF4150-4166	344.73079
Students—Sexual behavior	HQ27	306.7088375
Students, Transfer of	LB3064	371.2914
Stunt performers	PN1995.9.S7	791.43028092
Stuttering	RC424	616.8554
Stuttering in children	RJ496.S8	618.928554
Style, Literary	PN203	808
Styrene	TP1180.S7	668.4233
Subconsciousness	BF315	154.2
Subconsciousness	BF1001-1389	127
Subjectivity	BD222	121.4
Sublimation	BF175.5.S92	154.24
Subliminal perception	BF323.S8	153.736
Subliminal perception	RC499.S92	153.736
Sublittoral ecology	QH541.5.S87	577.78
Submarine boat combat	V214.5	359.93
Submarine boats	V857-859	359.9383
Submarine disasters	VK1265	363.123
Submarine geology	QE39	551.4608
Submarine medicine	RC1000-1020	616.98022
Submarine topography	GC83-87.6	551.46084
Submarine trenches	GC87.6	551.4608
Submarine warfare	V210-214.5	359.93
Submarines (Ships)	V857-859	359.933
Submarines (Ships)	VM365-367	623.8257
Substance (Philosophy)	BD331	111.1
Substance abuse	HV4997-5840	362.29
Substance abuse	RC563-568	616.86
Substance abuse—[By region or country]	HV4999.2-5000	362.2909(4-9)
Substance abuse in pregnancy	RG580.S75	618.3268
Substitutions, Linear	QA190-201	512.5
Subtraction	QA115	513.212
Suburban churches	BV637.7	250.91733
Suburban homes	NA7570-7572.5	728.091733
Suburban life	HT351-352	307.74
Subways	TF845-851	625.42
Success	BF637.S8	158
Success in business	HF5386	650.1
Sudan	DT154.1-159.9	962.4
Sudan—Census	HA4687	316.24
Sudan—Civilization	DT154.9	962.4
Sudan—Description and travel	DT154.7-.75	916.2404
Sudan—Economic conditions	HC835	330.9624
Sudan—Gazetteers	DT154.4	916.24003
Sudan—History	DT155.3-157.67	962.4
Sudan—History—To 1820	DT156-.3	962.40(1-2)
Sudan—History—1820-	DT156.4-157.67	962.40(3-4)
Sudan—History—1862-1899	DT156.6	962.403
Sudan—History—1899-1956	DT156.7-157.67	962.403
Sudan—History—Civil War, 1955-1972	DT157.67	962.40(3-4)
Sudan—History—Coup d'etat, 1985	DT156.7	962.404
Sudden infant death syndrome	RJ320.S93	618.92
Suez Canal (Egypt)	TC791	627.1370962
Suffering of God	BT153.S8	231
Suffrage	JC75.S8	324.620938
Suffrage	JS215	324.62
Suffrage	JC85.S8	324.6209376
Suffrage	JF831-851	324.62
Suffrage—United States	JK1846-1929	324.60973
Sufi meditations	BP189.62	297.4382
Sufism	BP189	297.4
Sugar	SB215-230	633.6
Sugar—Manufacture and refining	TP375-414.5	664.1
Sugar-free diet	RM237.85	613.26
Sugar in the body	QP702.S85	572.565
Sugars	QD320-327	547.781
Sugars	QP702.S85	572.565
Sugars in human nutrition	TX553.S8	613.283

Subject Heading	LC	Dewey	Subject Heading	LC	Dewey
Suicidal behavior	RC569	616.858445	Suretyship and guaranty—England	KD1752	346.42074
Suicide	HV6543-6548	364.1522	Suretyship and guaranty—United States	KF1045	346.73074
Suicide	RC569	616.858445	Surface chemistry	QD506-509	541.33
Suicide	RA1136-1137	616.858445	Surface tension	QC183	530.427
Suicide—Statistics	HB1323.S8	362.28021	Surface-to-air missiles	UF625	358.174
Suite (Music)	ML1258	784.18509	Surfaces	QA631-638	516.36
Suite (Music)	ML1158	784.18509	Surfaces	QA571-573	516.352
Sullivan's Indian Campaign, 1779	E235	973.335	Surfaces	QA641-672	516.36
Sulphites	TP240	661.63	Surgery—Complications	RD98-.4	617.01
Sulphur	TN890	622.3668	Surgery, Homeopathic	RX366-376	617
Sumerian language	PJ4001-4041	499.95	Surgery, Military	RD151-498	617.99
Sumerian language—Dictionaries	PJ4037	499.953	Surgery, Military—Africa	RD481-489	617.99096
			Surgery, Military—Asia	RD445-476	617.99095
Sumerian language—Grammar	PJ4011-4025	499.955	Surgery, Military—Australia	RD493	617.990994
Sumerian literature	PJ4045-4083	899.95	Surgery, Military—Canada	RD216	617.990971
Sumerians	DS72	935.01	Surgery, Military—Central America	RD224-225	617.9909728
Summer (Jewish law)	BM729.S85	296.18			
Summer employment	HD6271-.2	331.137044	Surgery, Military—Europe	RD268-441	617.99094
Summer schools	LC5701-5760	371.232	Surgery, Military—Mexico	RD221	617.990972
Sun	GR625	398.362	Surgery, Military—New Zealand	RD493.5	617.990993
Sun	QB520-545	523.7			
Sun—Corona	QB529	523.75	Surgery, Military—Oceania	RD498	617.99099(5-6)
Sun—Internal structure	QB539.I5	523.76	Surgery, Military—South America	RD235-267	617.99098
Sun—Rising and setting	QB216	525.317			
Sun—Rotation	QB551	523.73	Surgery, Military—United States	RD200-214	617.990973
Sun—Rotation	QB523	523.73			
Sun—Tables	QB374	523.7021	Surgery, Military—West Indies	RD231-232	617.9909729
Sun-baths	RM843	613.193			
Sun dance	E98.D2	299.74	Surgery, Minor	RD111-114	617.024
Sun worship	BL438	291.212	Surgery, Naval	RD151-498	617.99
Sunday	BV107-133	263.3	Surgery, Plastic	RD118-120.5	617.95
Sunday school literature	BV4560-4579	268.6	Surgery, Primitive	GN477.5-.7	617.0901
Sunday schools	BV1500-1578	268	Surgical dressings	RD113-.4	617.93
Sunday schools—Hymns	BV520	246.75	Surgical nursing	RD99-.35	610.73677
Sundials	QB215	529.7	Surgical wound infections	RD98.3	617.01
Sunflowers	SB299.S9	635.93399	Surinam	F2401-2431	988.3
Sunnites	BP175.S8	297.81	Surinam—Census	HA1035	318.83
Sunshine	QC910.2-913.2	551.5271	Surinam—Civilization	F2409.8	988.3
Sunspots	QB525	523.75	Surinam—Description and travel	F2410-2413	918.8304
Supercomputers	QA76.88	004.11			
Superconducting Super Collider	QC787.S83	539.736	Surinam—Gazetteers	F2404	918.83003
			Surinam—History	F2420.3-2425.23	988.3
Superconductivity	QC611.9-.98	537.623	Surinam—History—To 1814	F2423	988.301
Superego	BF175.5.S93	154.22			
Superfluidity	QC175.4-.47	530.42	Surinam—History—1814-1950	F2424	988.30(1-31)
Supergravity	QC174.17.S9	530.1423			
Superheating reactors	TK9203.S86	621.4834	Surinam—History—1950-	F2425-.23	988.303(1-2)
Supernatural	BF1001-1999	133	Surinam—History—Coup d'etat, 1980	F2425	988.3032
Supernatural	GR500-510	398.45			
Supersonic transport planes	TL685.7	358.44	Surinam—History—Coup d'etat, 1982	F2425	988.3032
Superstition	AZ999	001.96	Surinam—Manufactures	TS49	670.9883
Superstition	BF1001-1999	001.96	Surinam—Maps	G5260-5264	912.883
Superstition	GR81	398.41	Surinam—Periodicals	F2401	988.3005
Supervision of employees	HF5549.12	658.302	Surinam—Politics and government	JL780-789	320.9883
Supply and demand	HB201-206	338.521			
Supply-side economics	HB241	330.15	Surplus military property	UC260-267	355.62137
Supportive psychotherapy	RC489.S86	616.8914	Surrealism	NX600.S9	709.04062
Suppuration	RB131-.5	571.9379	Surrealism (Literature)	PN56.S87	808.801163

Subject Heading	LC	Dewey
Surrogate mothers	HQ759.5	306.8743
Surveying	TA501-625	526.9
Surveying—Instruments	TA562-581	526.90284
Surveying—Study and teaching	TA535-538	526.9071
Surveyors	TA515-531	526.9
Surveyors' chains	TA579	526.90284
Surveys	GA51-87	526.9
Surveys	QE61-350	551.0723
Surveys	QB301-328	526.3
Surveys—Plotting	TA611	526.9
Survival after airplane accidents, shipwrecks, etc.	TL553.7	613.69
Survival swimming	GV838.76	797.21
Suspension bridges	TG400	624.5
Swahili language	PL8701-8704	496.392
Swamp camping	GV198.95	796.54
Swamp ecology	QH541.5.S9	577.68
Swamps	GB621-628	551.41
Swamps	QH87.3	578.768
Swastika	BL604.S8	291.37
Swaziland—Census	HA4705	316.887
Swaziland—Civilization	DT2742	968.87
Swaziland—Description and travel	DT2732	916.88704
Swaziland—Economic conditions	HC925	330.96887
Swaziland—Gazetteers	DT2714	916.887003
Swaziland—History	DT2754-2806	968.87
Swaziland—Maps	G8590-8594	912.6887
Swearing	BV4627.S9	241.3
Swearing	BJ1535.S9	179.5
Swearing	GT3080	394
Sweatshops	HD2337-2339	331.117
Sweden—Biography	DL644	920.0363/ 920.0485
Sweden—Census	HA1521-1540	314.85
Sweden—Civilization	DL631-635	936.3/948.5
Sweden—Description and travel	DL614.55-619.5	913.6304/ 914.8504
Sweden—Economic conditions	HC371-380	330.9485
Sweden—Emigration and immigration	JV8220-8229	325.(2485/485)
Sweden—Gazetteers	DL605	913.63003/ 914.85003
Sweden—Historiography	DL645	936.30072/ 948.50072
Sweden—History	DL601-991	936.3/948.5
Sweden—History—To 1397	DL660-700.9	936.3/948.501
Sweden—History—Magnus II Ericksson, 1319-1363	DL689	948.501
Sweden—History—1397-1523	DL696-700.9	948.5018
Sweden—History—1523-1718	DL701-879	948.50(2-5)
Sweden—History—Gustavus I Vasa, 1523-1560	DL703	948.502
Sweden—History—Eric XIV, 1560-1568	DL703.8	948.502
Sweden—History—17th century	DL704.6-.7	948.50(2-3)
Sweden—History—Charles IX, 1604-1611	DL704.8	948.502
Sweden—History—Gustavus II, Adolphus, 1611-1632	DL705.A2-715	948.502
Sweden—History—Charles X Gustavus, 1654-1660	DL725.7	948.503
Sweden—History—Charles XI, 1660-1697	DL727-729	948.503
Sweden—History—Charles XII, 1697-1718	DL730-743	948.503
Sweden—History—1718-1814	DL747-805	948.503
Sweden—History—Ulrika Eleonora, 1718-1720	DL753	948.503
Sweden—History—Frederick I, 1720-1751	DL755-759	948.503
Sweden—History—Insurrection, 1743	DL757	948.503
Sweden—History—Gustavus III, 1771-1792	DL766-770	948.503
Sweden—History—Revolution, 1772	DL766	948.503
Sweden—History—1814-1905	DL807-859	948.50(3-4)
Sweden—History—20th century	DL860-879	948.505
Sweden—History—Gustavus V, 1907-1950	DL867-870	948.505(1-5)
Sweden—History—Farmers' Demonstration, 1914	DL868	948.5051
Sweden—History—Gustavus VI Adolphus, 1950-1973	DL872-876	948.505(5-7)
Sweden—History—Carl XVI Gustav, 1973-	DL877-879	948.505(7-6)
Sweden—Manufactures	TS89-90	670.9485
Sweden—Maps	G2070-2074	912.485
Sweden—Maps	G6950-6954	912.485
Sweden—Periodicals	DL601	936.3005/ 948.5005
Sweden—Politics and government	JN7721-7995	320.9485
Swedish drama	PT9415-9449	839.72009
Swedish drama	PT9605-9625	839.72008
Swedish fiction	PT9480-9492	839.73009
Swedish fiction	PT9627-9630	839.73008
Swedish language	PD5001-5929	439.7
Swedish language—Dialects	PD5700-5929	439.77
Swedish language—Dictionaries	PD5625-5693	439.73
Swedish language—Etymology	PD5571-5599	439.72

Subject Heading	LC	Dewey
Syriac language	PJ5701-5809	492.3
Syriac language—Dictionaries	PJ5490-5493	492.33
Syriac language—Etymology	PJ5483	492.32
Syriac langue—Grammar	PJ5419-5471	492.35
Syriac literature	PJ5601-5695	892.3
Syriac philology	PJ5401-5411	492.3
Syrups	RS201.S8	615.42
Syrups	TP375-414.5	664.1
System analysis	QA402-.37	003
System theory	Q295	003.01
Systems engineering	TA168	620.001171
Systems software	QA76.76.S95	005.43
T-ball	GV881.5	796.3578
T cells	QR185.8.T2	571.966
T-shirts	TT675	687.21
Tabla music	M146	786.93
Table	TX871-885	642
Table etiquette	BJ2041	395.54
Table-moving (Spiritualism)	BF1375	133.92
Table setting and decoration	TX871-885	642.7
Table tennis	GV1005	796.346
Tables	TS880	684.13
Tables	TT197.5.T3	684.13
Tablets (Medicine)	RS201.T2	615.43
Taboo	GN494	390
Tactics	U164-167.5	355.42
Tagalog language	PL6051-6059	499.211
Tagalog literature	PL6058	899.211
Tahiti	DU870	996.211
Tahitian language	PL6515	499.444
Tailoring	TT570-630	687.044
Taiwan—Census	HA4646-4650	315.1249
Taiwan—Description and travel	DS799.15-.24	913.104/915.124904
Taiwan—Economic conditions	HC430.5	330.951249
Taiwan—Emigration and immigration	JV8710-8719	325.(251249/51249)
Taiwan—Gazetteers	DS798.96	931.003/915.1249003
Taiwan—History	DS799.99-.833	931/951.249
Taiwan—History—To 1895	DS799.64-.66	931/951.2490(2-3)
Taiwan—History—1895-1945	DS799.69-.72	951.2490(3/4)
Taiwan—History—Insurrection, 1895	DS799.69	951.24904
Taiwan—History—1945-	DS799.77-.833	951.24905
Taiwan—History—February Twenty Eighth Incident, 1947	DS799.823	951.24905
Taiwan—History—1975-	DS799.83-.833	951.24905
Taiwan—History—Kaohsiung Incident, 1979	DS799.834	951.24905
Taiwan—Maps	G2340-2344	912.51249
Taiwan—Politics and government	JQ1520-1539	320.951249
Tajikistan	DK921-929.5	958.6

Subject Heading	LC	Dewey
Tales	GR74-76	398.2
Talismans	GR600	398.45
Talismans	BF1561	133.44
Tall buildings	NA6230-6234	720.483
Tall buildings	TH6057.T23	690
Talmud	BM500-509	296.12
Tambourine music	M175.T	786.95
Tamil language	PL4751-4759	494.811
Tank engineers	UG127-128	358.22092
Tankers	HE566.T3	387.245
Tankers	VM455	623.8245
Tanks (Military science)	UG446.5	358.1883
Tannaim	BM177	296.120092
Tanning	TS940-1047	675.23
Tantrism	BL1141.2-1142.6	294.5514
Tanzania—Census	HA4697	316.78
Tanzania—Civilization	DT442.5	967.8
Tanzania—Description and travel	DT439-440.5	916.7804
Tanzania—Economic conditions	HC885	330.9678
Tanzania—Gazetteers	DT437	916.78003
Tanzania—History	DT443.5-448.25	967.8
Tanzania—History—To 1964	DT443.5-448.25	967.8
Tanzania—Maps	G8440-8444	912.678
Taoism	BL1900-1940	299.514
Taoist ethics	BL1290.8	299.5145
Taos Indians	E99.T2	973.049749
Tap dancing	GV1794	792.78
Tapa	GN432	641.812
Tapestry	NK2975-3049	746.3
Tapestry	TS1780	677.64
Taps and dies	TJ1335	621.984
Tarawa, Battle of, 1943	D767.917	940.5426
Target practice	UF340-345	358.125
Target practice	VF310-315	359.547
Tariff	HF1701-2701	382.7
Tariff preferences	HF1721-1733	382.7
Tariff—Law and legislation	K4600-4640	343.056
Tariff—Law and legislation—England	KD5641-5694	343.42056
Tariff—Law and legislation—United States	KF6651-6708	343.73056
Tariff—[By region or country]	HF1745-2580.9	382.709(4-9)
Tariff—United States	HF1750-1757	382.70973
Tariff—[Other regions or countries]	HF1761-2580.9	382.709(4-9)
Tarot	BF1879.T2	133.32424
Tartar emetic	RM666.T2	615.731
Taste	BF261	152.167
Taste	QP456	612.87
Tatar language	PL65.T3	494.387
Tatar literature	PL65.T35-.T39	894.387
Tatars	DS25	950.0494387
Tatting	TT840.T38	746.436
Taurus (Astrology)	BF1727.2	133.5263
Tautomerism	QD471	541.2252
Tax assessment	HJ3241	336.2

Subject Heading	LC	Dewey	Subject Heading	LC	Dewey
Tax evasion—United States	KF6334	345.730233	Technical education	T61-173	607.1
Tax exemption	HJ2336-2337	336.206	Technical education	LC1041-1047	370.113
Tax exemption—Law and legislation—United States	KF6329-6330	343.7304	Technical education—[By region or country]	T71-170	607.10(4-9)
Tax incidence	HJ2321-2323	336.294	Technical illustration	T11.8	602.2
Tax revenue estimating	HJ2351.4	336.20015195	Technological forecasting	T174	601.12
Taxation	HJ2240-7395	336	Technological unemployment	HD6331-.2	331.137042
Taxation—History	HJ2250-2279	336.2009	Technology	T	600
Taxation—Law and legislation	K4456-4590	343.04	Technology—Abbreviations	T8	601.48
Taxation—Law and legislation—England	KD5351-5605	343.4204	Technology—Congresses	T6	606
			Technology—Dictionaries	T9-10	603
Taxation—Law and legislation—United States	KF6271-6636	343.7304	Technology—History	T14.7-33	609
			Technology—Language	T11-.3	601.4
Taxation—[By region or country]	HJ2361-3192.7	336.2009(4-9)	Technology—Periodicals	T1-5	605
			Technology—Philosophy	T14	601
Taxation—United States	HJ2361-2442	336.200973	Technology—Social aspects	T14.5	303.483
Taxation—[United States, By state]	HJ2391-2442	336.20097(4-9)	Technology—Sociological aspects	HM221	306.46
Taxation—[Other regions or countries]	HJ2449-3192.7	336.2009(4-9)	Technology—Terminology	T9-10	601.4
			Technology assessment	T174.5	303.483
Taxation (Roman law)	KJA3210	343.37604	Technology transfer	T174.3	338.926
Taxation of personal property	HJ4581-4601	336.23	Teddy bears	GV1220.7	790.133
			Teenage girls	HQ798	305.23508352
Taxicabs	HE5601-5725	388.34232	Teenage mothers	HQ759.4	306.87430835
Taxidermy	QL63	590.752	Teenage parents	HQ759.64	306.8740835
Tea	GT2905-2916	394.12	Teenage pregnancy	RG556.5	618.200835
Tea tax (American colonies)	E215.7	973.3115	Teenagers—Growth	RJ140	612.661
Teacher exchange programs	LB2283-2285	370.1163	Teeth	GN209	599.943
			Teeth	QL858	573.356
Teacher-student relationships	LB1033	371.1023	Teeth	QM311	611.314
			Teeth—Care and hygiene	RK61	617.601
Teachers	LB2832-2844.47	371.1	Teeth—Diseases	RK301-493	617.63
Teachers	LA2301-2397	370.92	Teeth—Diseases— Diagnosis	RK308-310	617.630754
Teachers	LB1755-1779	371.11			
Teachers—Certification	LB1771-1773	371.12	Teeth—Extraction	RK531-.5	617.66
Teachers—In-service training	LB1731	370.711	Teeth—Polishing	RK60.7	617.601
			Teeth—Transplantation	RK533	617.60592
Teachers—Leaves of absence	LB2843.L4	371.104	Teeth—Wounds and injuries	RK490-493	617.6044
			Telecommunication	TK5101-5105.9	621.382
Teachers—Legal status, laws, etc.—United States	KF4175-4190	344.73078	Telecommunication—Law and legislation	K4301-4339	343.0994
			Telecommuting	HD2331-2336.35	331.25
Teachers—Salaries, etc.	LB2842-2844	331.2813711	Telegraph	HE7601-8635	384.1
Teachers—Tenure	LB2836	371.104	Telegraph	TK5105-5865	621.383
Teachers—Training of	LB1705-2286	370.711	Telegraph—Directories	HE7621	384.1025
Teachers—Workload	LB2844.1.W6	371.1412	Telegraph—Periodicals	TK5107	621.38305
Teachers, Part-time	LB2844.1	371.14	Telegraph—Rates	HE7681-7691	384.13
Teachers, Probationary	LB2844.1.P7	371.144	Telegraph—Societies, etc.	HE7603	384.106
Teachers colleges	LB1805-2151	370.711	Telegraph—[By region or country]	HE7761-8630.7	384.109(4-9)
Teachers' unions	LB2844.52-.53	331.88113711			
Teaching	LB1025-1050.7	371.1	Telegraph—United States	HE7761-7798	384.10973
Teaching	LB1775-1785	371.1	Telegraph, Wireless	HE8660-8688	384.52
Teaching, Freedom of	LC72-.5	371.104	Telegraph, Wireless	TK5700-5865	621.3842
Teaching machines	LB1029.A85	371.334	Telegraph, Wireless— Installation on ships	VK397	623.85642
Team learning approach in education	LB1032	371.148	Telegraph, Wireless— Marconi system	TK5811-5865	621.3842
Team nursing	RT90.5	610.73028	Telegraph lines	TK5301-5481	384.15
Tear gas munitions	HV7936.E7	363.20284	Telemarketing	HF5415.1265	381.1

Subject Heading	LC	Dewey	Subject Heading	LC	Dewey
Teleology	BD530-595	124	Temporary marriage	HQ803	306.84
Telepathy	BF1161-1171	133.82	Temptation	BT725	241.3
Telephone	HE8701-9685	384.6	Ten commandments	BV4655-4710	241.52
Telephone	TK6001-6571.5	621.385	Ten commandments	BS1281-1285.5	222.16
Telephone—Directories	TK6011	621.385025	Tender offers (Securities)	HG4028.T4	332.6322
Telephone—Periodicals	TK6001	621.38505	Tendinitis	RC935.T4	616.76
Telephone answering services	HD9999.T34-.T344	651.73	Tendons	QM170	611.74
Telephone cables	TK6381-6383	621.38784	Tennessee	F431-445	976.8
Telephone companies	HE8701-9685	384.6	Tennessee—Gazetteers	F434	917.68003
Telephone companies— [By region or country]	HE8801-9685	384.609(4-9)	Tennessee—History— Civil War, 1861-1865	E579	976.804
Telephone companies— United States	HE8801-8846	384.60973	Tennessee—History— Civil War, 1861-1865	E531	976.804
Telephone companies— [Other regions or countries]	HE8861-9685	384.609(4-9)	Tennessee—Maps	G3960-3964	912.768
			Tennessee—National Guard	UA460-469	355.3709768
			Tennessee—Periodicals	F431	976.8005
Telephone etiquette	BJ2195	395.59	Tennis	GV990-1005	796.342
Telephone lines	TK6201-6285	621.38784	Tension headache	RB128	616.8491
Telephone switchboards	TK6391-6397	621.385	Term loans	HG1641-1643	332.1753
Telephone switching systems, Electronic	TK6397	621.3857	Terminal care	RT87.T45	610.7361
Telephone systems	TK6401-6505	621.387	Terminal care	R726.8	616.029
Telephone wire	TK6381-6383	621.38784	Terminally ill	R726.8	616.029
Telescopes	QB88	522.2	Terminals (Transportation)	TA1225	388.47
Telescopes	UF845	358.128	Terra-cotta sculpture	NB1265	731.2
Telescopic sights	UF855	623.46	Terra-cotta sculpture	NB145-159	731.2
Television	TK6630-6720	621.388	Terrariums	QH68	635.9824
Television—Periodicals	TK6630.A1	621.388005	Terrestrial radiation	QC809.T4	551.5272
Television—Equipment and supplies	TK6650-6655	621.38800284	Testing	TA401-492	620.110287
			Testing	QC100-111	530.8
Television, Master antenna	TK6676	621.38835	Testing-machines	TA413-.5	620.11260287
Television actors and actresses	PN1992.4	791.45028092	Testosterone	QP572.T4	612.405
Television advertising	HF6146.T42	659.143	Tetanus	RC185	616.9318
Television broadcasting	HE8700-.95	384.55	Teton Indians	E99.T34	973.049752
Television comedies	PN1992.8.C66	791.45617	Teutonic Knights	CR4759-4775	255.7914
Television in education	LB1044.7	371.3358	Teutonic Knights	DK4600.P77	255.7914
Television programs	PN1992-.92	384.5532	Teutonic race	GN549.T4	305.83
Television programs— Rating	HE8700.65-.66	384.5532	Texas	F381-395	976.4
			Texas—Gazetteers	F384	917.64003
Television weathercasting	QC877.5	551.632	Texas—History—To 1846	F389-390	976.40(1-4)
Telugu language	PL4771-4779	494.827	Texas—History— 1810-1821	F389	976.402
Temper	BF575.A5	152.47			
Temper tantrums in children	BF723.A4	155.41247	Texas—History— Revolution, 1835-1836	F390	976.403
Temperament	BF795-811	155.26	Texas—History— Republic, 1836-1846	F390	976.404
Temperance	HV5001-5720	362.2928	Texas—History— 1846-1950	F391	976.40(5-63)
Temperance—History	HV5020-5025	362.2920709	Texas—History—Civil War, 1861-1865	E532	976.405
Temperance—Societies, etc.	HV5006	362.2928	Texas—History—Civil War, 1861-1865	E580	976.405
Temperance (Virtue)	BV4647.T4	241.4			
Temperature measurements	QC270-278.6	536.50287	Texas—History—1951-	F391.2-.4	976.406(3-4)
			Texas—Maps	G4030-4034	912.764
Tempering	TS320	671.36	Texas—National Guard	UA470-479	355.3709764
Temples	NA4610-4710	726.1	Texas—Periodicals	F381	976.4005
Temples, Buddhist	BQ5130-5137	294.3435	Text processing (Computer science)	QA76.9.T48	005
Temples, Buddhist— Dedication	BL1477.8.D4	294.3435	Textbook bias	LB3045.6	371.32
Temples, Hindu	BL1243.72-.78	294.535	Textbooks	LB3045-3048	371.32
Tempo (Music)	MT42	781.2207	Textbooks	LT	371.32

Subject Heading	LC	Dewey	Subject Heading	LC	Dewey
Textile chemistry	TP890-933	677	Therapeutics—Congresses	RM21	615.506
Textile crafts	TT699-854.5	746	Therapeutics—History	RM41-47	615.509
Textile design	NK8800-9505.5	746	Therapeutics—Periodicals	RM16	615.505
Textile fabrics	TS1300-1865	677	Therapeutics—Societies,	RM1	615.506
Textile fibers	TS1540-1549	677	etc.		
Textile finishing	TS1510	677.02825	Therapeutics—Study	RM108-.5	615.5071
Thai language	PL4111-4251	495.91	and teaching		
Thai literature	PL4200-4209	895.911	Therapeutics—Terminology	RM38	615.5014
Thailand—Census	HA4600.55	315.93	Therapeutics, Experimental	RM111	615.5072
Thailand—Civilization	DS568	959.3	Therapeutics, Physiological	RM695-931	615.82
Thailand—Description	DS564-566.2	915.9304	Therapeutics, Suggestive	RC490-499	616.89162
and travel			Theravada Buddhism	BQ7100-7285	294.391
Thailand—Economic	HC445	330.9593	Thermal analysis	QD79.T38	544.2
conditions			Thermal analysis	QD117.T4	545.4
Thailand—Gazetteers	DS563	915.93003	Thermal stresses	TA418.58	620.1121
Thailand—History	DS570.95-586	959.3	Thermochemistry	QD510-536	541.36
Thailand—Maps	G2375-2379	912.593	Thermodynamics	TJ265	621.4021
Thailand—Maps	G8025-8029	912.593	Thermodynamics	QC310.15-319	536.7
Thailand—Politics and	JQ1740-1749	320.9593	Thermoelectricity	QC621-625	537.65
government			Thermometers	QC270-278.6	536.50287
Thallium	QD181.T7	546.678	Thermonuclear fuels	TK9360	621.484
Thanatology	HQ1073-.5	306.9	Thermotherapy	RM865-868.5	615.832
Thanksgiving cookery	TX739.2.T45	641.568	Thieves	HV6653	364.162
Thanksgiving Day	GT4975	394.2649	Thin films	QC176.82-.9R37	530.4175
Thanksgiving Day	BV75	263.97	Thirst	QP139	612.391
The Grenadines	F2061	972.9844	Thirteen (The number)	GR933	398.41
Theater	PN2000-3299	792	Thirty Years' War,	D251-271	940.24
Theater—History	PN2100-2193	792.09	1618-1648		
Theater—History—To 500	PN2131-2145	792.0901	Thought and thinking	BF441-449.5	153.42
Theater—History—	PN2152-2160	792.0902	Thought and thinking	LB1590.3-.5	153.42
Medievel, 500-1500			Thrace	DR50-.84	949.61
Theater—History—18th	PN2171-2179	792.09033	Thread	TS1590	677.02862
century			Threshing machines	S699-701	631.3
Theater—History—20th	PN2181-2193	792.09034	Throat	QM535	611.32
century			Throat—Diseases	RF460-547	616.31
Theater—Greece	PN2660-2668	792.09495	Throat—Examination	RF476	616.31075
Theater—Japan	PN2920-2928	792.0952	Throat—Wounds and	RF547	617.531044
Theater—United States	PN2220-2298	792.0973	injuries		
Theater, Open-air	PN2219.08	792.022	Thrombosis	RE651	617.74
Theater architecture	NA6820-6846	725.822	Thunderstorms	GR630	398.363
Theaters	NA6820-6845	725.822	Thunderstorms	QC968-.2	551.554
Theaters—Accidents	PN2091.A	792.028	Thyroid gland	QM371	611.44
Theaters—Stage-setting	PN2091.S8	792.025	Thyroid gland—Diseases	RC655-657	616.44
and scenery			Tibetan language	PL3601-3651	495.4
Theism	BL200	211.3	Tibetan literature	PL3701-3775	895.4
Theism	BD555	211.3	Tibeto-Burman languages	PL3551-4001	495.4
Theocracy	JC20-89	321.5	Tick-borne diseases	RA641.T5	614.433
Theodicy	BT160-162	231.8	Ticonderoga, Battle of,	E199	973.26
Theological seminaries	BV4019-4160	230.0711	1758		
Theological virtues	BV4635-4639	241.4	Tidal currents	GC308-309	551.4708
Theology—History	BT1313-1480	270	Tidal power	TC147	621.20422
Theology—Study and	BV4019-4180	230.071	Tidal power-plants	TK1081	621.312134
teaching			Tide pool ecology	QH541.5.S35	577.69
Theology, Doctrinal	BT65-84	231-239	Tides	GC300-376	551.4708
Theology, Doctrinal—	BT20-30	230.09	Tigers	QL737.C23	599.756
History			Tile construction	TH1077-1083	693.3
Theology, Practical	BV1-4	240-248	Tiles	NA3705	721.0443
Theory of distribution	QA324	515.7	Tillage	S604	631.51
(Functional analysis)			Timber	SD430-557	338.17498
Theosophy	BP500-585	299.934	Timber	TA419-424.6	620.12
Therapeutics	RM	615.5	Timberline	QK938.F6	581.73

Subject Heading	LC	Dewey
Time	BD638	115
Time	QB209-224	529
Time—Systems and standards	QB223	529.0218
Time, Equation of	QB217	529.1
Time measurements	QB213	529.7
Time perception	BF468	153.753
Time-series analysis	QA280	519.55
Time study	T60.4-.47	658.5421
Timpani music	M146	786.93
Tin	TA480.T5	620.185
Tin mines and mining	TN470-479	622.3453
Tin ores	TN470-479	622.3453
Tires, Rubber	TS1912	678.32
Tissue banks	RD127-128.5	362.1783
Tissue-integrated prostheses	RK667.T57	617.69
Tissues	QM551-575	611.018
Tissues	QP88-.6	611.018
Titanium	TA480.T54	620.18932
Titans (Mythology)	BL820.T6	292.13
Tithes	BX5165	248.6
Tithes	BV771	254.8
Tithes—Mormon Church	BX8643.T5	248.6
Titles of honor and nobility	CR3499-4420	929.7
Toasts	PN6340-6348	808.851
Tobacco	GT3020-3030	394.14
Tobacco	SB273-278	633.71
Tobacco—Physiological effect	RC567	616.865
Tobacco—Physiological effect	RM666.T6	616.865
Tobacco habit	HV5725-5770	362.296
Tobacco habit	RC567	616.865
Tobacco industry	HD9130-9149	336.27863371
Tobacco industry	TS2220-2283	679.7
Tobacco-pipes	TS2270	688.42
Tobogganing	GV856	796.95
Toddlers	HQ774.5	305.232
Toenails	QL942	573.59
Toes	QM549	611.98
Toes—Abnormalities	RD786-789	617.585043
Tofu	TX401.2.S69	641.35655
Togo—Census	HA4723	316.681
Togo—Civilization	DT582.4	966.81
Togo—Description and travel	DT582.27	916.68104
Togo—Gazetteers	DT582.15	916.681003
Togo—History	DT582.5-.82	966.81
Togo—History—1922-1960	DT582.75	966.8103
Togo—Maps	G8760-8764	912.6681
Toilets	GT476	392.36
Toilets	TH6498	696.182
Tokelau	DU910	996.15
Tokelau—Maps	G9550-9554	912.9615
Tokens	CJ4801-5450	737.3
Tokens—Exhibitions	CJ4805-4808	737.3074
Tokens—Museums	CJ4805-4806	737.3074
Tokens—Periodicals	CJ4801	737.305
Tokens—[By region or country]	CJ4901-5336	737.309(4-9)
Tokens—United States	CJ4901-4906	737.30973
Toll roads	HE336.T64	388.122
Tomatoes	SB349	635.642
Tombs	NA6120-6199	726.8
Tombs—[By region or country]	NA6149-6199	726.809
Tomography	RC78.7.T6	616.0757
Tone (Phonetics)	P223	414.8
Tonga	DU880	996.12
Tonga—Census	HA4017	319.612
Tonga—Maps	G9570-9574	912.9612
Tonga language (Tonga Islands)	PL6531	499.48
Tongue	QM503	611.313
Tongue	QL946	573.357
Tonnage	HE565	387.2
Tonsillectomy	RF484.5	617.531059
Tonsillitis	RF491	616.314
Tonsils	QM331	611.32
Tonsils	QP146	612.312
Tonsils—Diseases	RF481-499	616.32
Tools	GN436.8-437	621.9
Tools	TJ1180-1313	621.9
Toothpicks	GT2952	394.12
Topaz	QE391.T6	549.62
Topical preaching	BV4235.T65	251
Topographical drawing	TA616	526.98
Topographical surveying	TA590	526.3
Topology	QA611-614.97	514
Torah scrolls	BM657.T6	296.4615
Tories, English	JN1129.T7	324.24102
Tornadoes	QC955-.5	551.553
Torpedo-boats	V830-840	359.3258
Torpedoes	V850-855	359.82517
Torts	K923-968	346.03
Torts—Canada	KE1232-1309	346.7103
Torts—England	KD1941-1980	346.4203
Torts—Ireland	KDK450-469	346.41503
Torts—United States	KF1246-1329	346.7303
Torture	HV8593-8599	364.67
Total hip replacement	RD549	617.4720592
Total knee replacement	RD561	617.5820592
Total quality management	HD62.15	658.4013
Totalitarianism	JC480-481	321.9
Totemism	GN489	291.211
Totems	GN491	291.211
Touch	BF275	152.182
Touch	QP451	612.88
Tourist camps, hostels, etc.	TX901-941	647.94
Tourist trade	G154.9	338.4791
Tournaments	GV1191-.75	790.134
Tournaments	CR4553	929.6
Towboats	VM464	623.8232
Towers	TH2180	690.15
Towers	NA2930	721.5
Toxemia of pregnancy	RG575-576	618.75
Toxicity testing	RA1199-.5	615.907
Toxicological emergencies	RA1224.5	615.908
Toxicology	RA1190-1270	615.9
Toxicology—Research	RA1199-.5	615.90072

Subject Heading	LC	Dewey	Subject Heading	LC	Dewey
Toxicology—Study and teaching	RA1198-.3	615.90071	Transfiguration (Spiritualism)	BF1389.T7	133.9
Toys	GN799.T75	790.1330901	Transformations (Mathematics)	QA601-608	516.1
Toys	GN454-456	394.3	Transgenic plants	SB123.57	631.5233
Toys	TT174-.5	745.592	Transients (Electricity)	TK3226	621.31921
Trace elements in the body	QP534	572.515	Transistor amplifiers	TK7871.2-.58	621.381535
Tracheotomy	RF517	617.533059	Transition metal compounds	QD172.T6	546.6
Track system (Education)	LB3061.8	371.25			
Track-athletics	GV1060.5-1098	796.42	Transits	QB175-185	523.9
Tracked landing vehicles	UG615-620	623.7472	Transliteration	P226	411
Traction-engines	TL233-.8	629.2252	Transmigration	BL525	291.21
Trade associations—Law and legislation—England	KD2228	346.4206	Transnational crime	HV6252	364.135
			Transpersonal psychology	BF204.7	150.198
Trade associations—Law and legislation—United States	KF1661	346.73064	Transplantation of organs, tissues, etc.	RD120.6-129.8	617.95
Trade regulation	K3842-3862	343.08	Transport theory	QC175.2-.25	530.138
Trade regulation—Canada	KE1591-1660	343.7108	Transportation	HE	388
Trade regulation—England	KD2204-2231	343.4208	Transportation	GT5220	394.53
Trade-unions	HD6350-6940.7	331.88	Transportation—Biography	HE151.4-.5	388.092
Trade-unions—History	HD6451-6481.2	331.8809	Transportation—Congresses	HE11	388.06
Trade-unions—Organizing	HD6490.07	331.8912			
Trade-unions—Recognition	HD6490.R4	331.8912	Transportation—History	HE159-181	388.09
Trade-unions—[By region or country]	HD6500-6940.7	331.8809(4-9)	Transportation—Law and legislation	K4021-4025	343.093
Trade-unions—United States	HD6500-6519	331.880973	Transportation—Law and legislation—Canada	KE2071-2649	343.71093
Trade winds	QC939.T7	551.5183	Transportation—Law and legislation—England	KD2571-2838	343.42093
Trademarks	T325	602.75			
Traditional farming	GN407.4-.8	630	Transportation—Law and legislation—United States	KF2161-2654	343.73093
Traditional medicine	GR880	615.882			
Traditional medicine	GN477-.7	615.882			
Trafalgar, Battle of, 1805	DA88.5 1805	942.073	Transportation—Periodicals	HE1-8	388.05
Traffic accidents	RC1040-1045	613.69	Transportation—Rates	HE1831-2220	388.042
Traffic accidents	RA772.T7	363.125	Transportation—Rates	HE195.4-.5	388.049
Traffic circles	TE176.5	625.7	Transportation—Statistics	HE191.4-.5	388.021
Traffic congestion	HE336.C64	388.314	Transportation—Study and teaching	HE191.9-192	388.071
Traffic police	HV8079.5-.55	363.2332			
Traffic regulations	HE369-373	388.312	Transportation—Theory	HE147.5-149	388.01
Traffic safety	HE5613.5-5614.6	363.125	Transportation, Military	VC550-580	359.985
Traffic surveys	HE369-373	388.310723	Transportation, Military	UC270-360	358.25
Traffic violations	HV6422-6425	364.147	Transportation, Military	UH500-505	355.83
Tragedy	PN6111-6120	808.820512	Transportation engineering	TA1001-1280	629.04
Trail riding	SF309.28	798.23	Transportation engineering—History	TA1015	629.0409
Trails	TE303	625.88			
Trails	TE304	625.88	Transportation engineering—Periodicals	TA1001-1004	629.0405
Training-ships	V435-436	359.50973			
Tramps	HV4480-4630	362.5	Transportation engineering—Study and teaching	TA1163	629.04071
Trance	BV5090-5091	248.29			
Tranquilizing drugs	RM333	615.7882			
Transactional analysis	RC489.T7	616.89145	Transportation engineering—[By region or country]	TA1021-1127	629.0409(3-9)
Transcendental Meditation	BF637.T68	158.125			
Transcendentalism	B823	141.3			
Transcendentalism (New England)	B905	141.3	Transportation medicine	RC1030-1035	616.9802
			Transportation noise	TD893.6.T7	620.23
Transfer RNA	QP623.5.T73	572.886	Transports	UC320-325	355.83
Transfer factor (Immunology)	RM282.T7	615.37	Transsexualism	HQ77.7-.95	305.3
			Transubstantiation	BX2220	264.02036
Transfer of training	LB1059	153.154	Transvaal—Maps	G8540-8543	912.682
Transference (Psychology)	RC489.T73	154.24	Transvestites	HQ76.97-77.2	306.77
			Transylvania (Romania)	DR279-280.74	949.84

Subject Heading	LC	Dewey
Trapping	SK283-.6	799.2
Trapshooting	GV1181-.3	799.3132
Trauma centers	RA975.5.T83	362.18
Travel	GT5220-5285	394.53
Travel	G149-180	910
Travel—Guidebooks	G153	910.202
Travel etiquette	BJ2137-2156	395.5
Travel posters	NC1849.T68	741.674
Travelers	G200-336	910.92
Traveling sales personnel	HF5441-5444	381.092
Treadmill exercise tests	RC683.5.E94	616.12075
Treason	JC328	323.6
Treason	HV6275	364.131
Tree crops	SB170-171	634.99
Tree planting	SD391	634.9565
Tree planting	SB435-437	635.977
Tree worship	BL444	291.212
Trees	SD391-535	634.9
Trees	QK474.8-494	582.16
Trees—Folklore	GR785	398.368216
Trees in cities	SB436	635.977
Trench mortars	UF563.A77	358.1282
Trestles	TG365-370	624.32
Trial practice (Canon law)	BX1939.T65	262.934
Trial practice—United States	KF8911-8925	347.73075
Trials	K540-546	347.07
Trials	K5460-5492	345.075
Trials—Canada	KE225-237	347.7107
Trials—England	KD370-379.5	347.4207
Trials—Ireland	KDK102-106	347.41507
Trials—Scotland	KDC184-188	347.41107
Trials—United States	KF8910-8986	347.7307
Trials—United States	KF219-224	345.7307
Trials—Wales	KD9423	345.42907
Trials (Bribery)—United States	KF221.B74	345.7302
Trials (Conspiracy)—United States	KF221.C6	345.730207
Triangle	QA482	516.15
Triangle music	M175.T	786.8842
Triangulation	QB311	526.33
Triangulation	TA583	526.33
Tribes	GN492.5	306.08
Trick photography	TR148	778.8
Trick riding	SF296.T75	798.23
Tricks	GV1541-1561	793.8
Tricycles	GV1040-1058	796.6(2-4)
Trigonometry	QA531-538	516.24
Trigonometry—Tables	QA55	516.24021
Trinidad and Tobago	F2116-2123	972.983
Trinidad and Tobago—Census	HA867	317.2983
Trinidad and Tobago—Maps	G5150-5162	912.72983
Trinidad and Tobago—Politics and government	JL650-659	320.972983
Trinity	BT109-115	231.044
Trios	M300-386	785.13
Tripitaka	BQ1100-3340	294.382
Triple Entente, 1907	D443	940.288
Triple Entente, 1907	D511	940.288
Triplets	GN63.6	306.875
Triumphal arches	NA9360-9380	725.96
Trolley buses	TL232	629.22233
Trolls	GR555	398.45
Trombone music	M90-94	788.93
Tropical crops	SB111	631.913
Tropical medicine	RC960-962	616.9883
Tropical plants	QK936	581.748
Tropics	G905-910	910.0213
Tropics—Climate	QC993.5	551.6913
Tropics—Maps	G3240-3241	912.193
Tropics—Maps	G1053	912.193
Troposphere	QC881.2.T75	551.513
Troubadours	GT3650	390.478
Troubadours	PC3304-3330	849.104
Trousers	TT605	687.113
Trout fishing	SH687-688	799.1755
Truck drivers	TL230.3	629.224092
Trucking	HE5601-5725	388.324
Trucking—[By region or country]	HE5623-5725	388.32409(4-9)
Trucks	TL230-.5	629.224
Trumpet music	M85-89	788.92
Trumpet-calls	UH40-45	781.599
Trumpet-calls	M1270	788.92
Truncheons	HV7936.E7	363.20284
Trusses	TA660.T8	624.1773
Trust companies	HG4301-4480.9	332.26
Trust companies—Directories	HG4307	332.26025
Trust companies—History	HG4311	332.2609
Trust companies—[By region or country]	HG4341-4480.9	332.2609(4-9)
Truth	BC171	121
Truthfulness and falsehood	BJ1420-1428.3	177.3
Tsetse-flies	RA641.T7	614.4322
Tuba music	M95-99	788.98
Tuberculin test	RC311.2	616.995075
Tuberculosis	RA644.T7	614.542
Tuberculosis	RC306-320.5	616.995
Tuberculosis—Chemotherapy	RC311.3.C45	616.995061
Tuberculosis—Diet therapy	RC311.D5	616.9950654
Tuberculosis—Hospitals	RC309-.5	362.196995
Tuberculosis—Vaccination	RA644.T7	614.542
Tugboats	VM464	623.8232
Tumors	RC254-282	616.992
Tumors	RD651-678	616.992
Tungsten ores	QE390.2.T85	549.74
Tungus-Manchu languages	PL450	494.1
Tunisia	DT241-269	939.73/961.1
Tunisia—Census	HA4684	316.11
Tunisia—Civilization	DT252	939.73/961.1
Tunisia—Description and travel	DT248-250.2	913.97304/ 916.1104
Tunisia—Economic conditions	HC820	330.9611
Tunisia—Gazetteers	DT244	913.973003/ 916.11003
Tunisia—History	DT253.4-264.49	939.73/961.1

Subject Heading	LC	Dewey	Subject Heading	LC	Dewey
Turkish literature	PL201-272	894.35	Ultrasonic waves	QC244	534.55
Turkmen language	PL331-334	494.364	Ultrasonic waves— Therapeutic use	RM862.7	615.83
Turkmenistan	DK931-939.5	958.5	Ultrasonics in medicine	R857.U48	616.07543
Turnover tax	HJ5711-5715	336.27	Ultrasonics in obstetrics	RG527.5.U48	618.207543
Turpentine	TP977-979.5	665.332	Ultraviolet radiation	QC459-.5	535.014
Turquoise	QE394.T8	549.72	Ultraviolet spectroscopy	QC459-.5	535.844
Turtle fisheries	SH399.T9	639.392	Umbilical cord—Prolapse	RG719	618.58
Tuscany (Italy)	DG731-759.3	945.5	Umbrellas and parasols	GT2210	391.44
Tutors and tutoring	LC41	371.394	Underemployment	HD5709-.2	331.13
Twelfth century	D201.7-.8	909.1	Underground architecture	NA2542.7	720.473
Twelfth century	CB353	909.1	Underground construction	TA712	624.19
Twentieth century	D410-893	940.(288-5)	Underground electric lines	TK3251-3261	621.31923
Twentieth century	CB425-430	909.82	Underground railroad	E450	973.7115
Twentieth century— Forecasts	CB160-161	003.20904	Undertakers and undertaking	HD9999.U5-.U54	363.75
Twins	GN63.6	306.875	Undertakers and undertaking	RA622-623.6	363.75
Twins—Psychology	BF723.T9	155.444	Underwater acoustics	QC242-.5	534.23
Two-body problem	QB362.T9	521.4	Underwater archaeology	CC77.U5	930.102804
Two-dimensional echocardiography	RC683.5.U5	616.1207543	Underwater childbirth	RG663	618.4
Two-tier wage payment systems	HD4928.T93	331.216	Underwater construction	TC195-201	627.7
Tympanic membrane— Diseases	RF210	617.85	Underwater demolition teams	VG86-88	359.984
Typewriters	Z49-50.5	652.3	Underwater demolition teams—United States	VG87	359.9840973
Typhoid fever	RC187-197	616.9272	Underwater drilling	TC193	627.75
Typhoid fever	RA644.T8	614.5112	Underwater exploration	GC65-78	551.4607
Typhoid fever—Vaccination	RA644.T8	614.5112	Underwater photography	TR800	778.73
Typhoon modification	QC948	551.68	Underwater pipelines	TC1800	627.7
Typhoons	QC948	551.552	Underwater welding and cutting	VM965	623.8432
Typhus fever	RC199-.9	616.9222	Underwear	GT2073	391.42
Typology (Theology)	BT225	232.1	Underwear	TT669-678	687.2
Typology (Theology)	BS478	220.64	Unemployed	HD5707.5-5710.2	331.137
Uganda—Census	HA4694	316.761	Unemployment	HD5707.5-5710.2	331.137
Uganda—Civilization	DT433.24	967.61	Uneven parallel bars	GV536	613.714
Uganda—Description and travel	DT433.227	916.76104	Unicorns	GR830.U6	398.469
Uganda—Economic conditions	HC870	330.96761	Unidentified flying objects	TL789-.6	001.942
Uganda—Gazetteers	DT433.215	916.761003	Unified operations (Military science)	U260	366.46
Uganda—History	DT433.252-.287	967.61	Uniform state laws	KF165	348.7(4-9)
Uganda—History—To 1890	DT433.265-.267	967.6101	Unincorporated societies—Canada	KE1351-1361	346.71064
Uganda—History— 1890-1962	DT433.27-.273	967.610(1-3)	Unincorporated societies—England	KD2046-2054	346.42064
Uganda—History— 1971-1979	DT433.282	967.61042	Unincorporated societies—United States	KF1361-1381	346.73064
Uganda—History—1979-	DT433.284-.286	967.6104(2-4)			
Uganda—Maps	G8420-8424	912.6761	Unit method of teaching	LB1029.U6	371.36
Ugaritic language	PJ4150	492.67	Unitarian Universalist churches	BX9801-9869	289.1
Ukraine	DK508-.95	947.7	Unitarian Universalist churches—Congresses	BX9805-9807	289.106
Ukrainian language	PG3801-3899	491.79	Unitarian Universalist churches—Education	BX9817-9823	268.891
Ukrainian language— Grammar	PG3819-3881	491.795	Unitarian Universalist churches—Government	BX9850	262.091
Ukrainian literature	PG3900-3987	891.79	Unitarian Universalist churches—History	BX9831-9835	289.109
Ukranian language— Dictionaries	PG3888-3894.5	491.793			
Ukranian language— Lexicography	PG3887-3894.5	491.793028			
Ukulele music	M142.U5	787.89			
Ultrasonic encephalography	RC386.6.U45	616.8047543			
Ultrasonic testing	TA417.4	620.11274			

235

Subject Heading	LC	Dewey
Unitarian Universalist churches—Sermons	BX9843	252.091
Unitarianism	BX9801-9869	289.133
Unitarianism—United States	BX9833	289.173
Unitarianism—[By region or country]	BX9833-9835	289.1(4-9)
Unitarians	BX9867-9869	289.1092
United Arab Emirates	JQ1844	320.95357
United Arab Emirates—Census	HA4566	315.357
United Arab Emirates—Economic conditions	HC415.36	330.95357
United States	E151-887	973
United States—Antiquities	E159.5	973.1
United States—Antiquities	E75-99	973.1
United States—Appropriations and expenditures	HJ2050-2053	352.530973
United States—Armed Forces—Afro-Americans	E185.63	355.3008996073
United States—Armed Forces—Airborne troops	UD483	356.1660973
United States—Armed Forces—Headquarters	UB233	355.306073
United States—Armed Forces—Management	UB23-25	355.60973
United States—Armed Forces—Messes	UC723	355.3410973
United States—Armed Forces—Officers' clubs	U56-59	355.3460973
United States—Armed Forces—Parachute troops	UD483	356.1660973
United States—Armed Forces—Procurement	UC260-267	355.62120973
United States—Armed Forces—Reserves	UA42-560	355.370973
United States—Armed Forces—Reserves [By state]	UA50-549	355.37097(4-9)
United States—Armed Forces—Warrant officers	UB408-.5	355.3320973
United States—Armed Forces—Warrant officers	VB308	359.3320973
United States—Armed Forces—Women's reserves	UA45	355.3480973
United States—Biography	E176	920.073
United States—Capital and capitol	NA4411-4413	725.110973
United States—Census	HA201-730	317.3
United States—Civilization	E169.1-.12	973
United States—Civilization	E162-168	973
United States—Climate	QC983-984	551.6973
United States—Commerce	HF3000-3163	380.10973
United States—Commerce—History	HF3021-3031	380.10973

Subject Heading	LC	Dewey
United States—Commerce—Statistics	HF3001-3006	380.10973
United States—Constitutional history	JK	342.73029
United States—Constitutional law	KF4546-4554	342.73
United States—Constitutional law	KF4501-5130	342.73
United States—Constitutional law—Amendments	KF4555-4558	342.73032
United States—Defenses	UA23	355.450973
United States—Description and travel	E161.5-169.04	917.304
United States—Directories	E154.5-.7	973.025
United States—Economic conditions	HC101-110	330.973
United States—Emigration and immigration	JV6403-7127	325.(273/73)
United States—Ethnic relations	E184.A1	305.8073
United States—Gazetteers	E154	917.3003
United States—Genealogy	CS42-71	929.1072073
United States—Historical geography—Maps	G3701	911.73
United States—Historiography	E175-.7	973.072
United States—History	E171-183.9	973
United States—History, Military	E181	355.30973
United States—History, Naval	E182	359.30973
United States—History—Colonial period, ca. 1600-1775	E186-199	973.(1-2)
United States—History—King William's War, 1689-1697	E196	973.25
United States—History—Queen Anne's War, 1702-1713	E197	973.25
United States—History—King George's War, 1744-1748	E198	973.26
United States—History—French and Indian War, 1755-1763	E199	973.26
United States—History—Revolution, 1775-1783	E201-298	973.3
United States—History—Revolution, 1775-1783—Campaigns	E230-241	973.33
United States—History—1783-1865	E301-655	973.3
United States—History—Confederation, 1783-1789	E303-309	973.318
United States—History—Constitutional period, 1789-1809	E310-337	973.4

Subject Heading	LC	Dewey	Subject Heading	LC	Dewey
United States—History—1801-1809	E331-337	973.4(6-8)	United States—Politics and government	JK	320.973
United States—History—Tripolitan War, 1801-1805	E335	973.47	United States—Politics and government—To 1775	JK54-103	320.9730903
United States—History—1809-1817	E341-370	973.5(1-4)	United States—Politics and government—Civil War, 1861-1865	JK320	320.97309034
United States—History—War of 1812	E351-364.9	973.52	United States—Politics and government—1865-1877	JK321	320.97309034
United States—History—1815-1861	E338	973.(51-68)	United States—Race relations	E184-185.98	305.8073
United States—History—War with Algeria, 1815	E365	973.53	United States—Religion	BR513-569	277.3
United States—History—1817-1825	E371-375	973.54	United States—Seal	CD5610	737.60973
United States—History—1825-1829	E376-380	973.55	United States—Social conditions	HN51-90	973
United States—History—1849-1877	E671-680	973.(63-82)	United States—Statistics	HA201-214	317.3
United States—History—1849-1877	E415.6-680	973.(63-82)	United States—Statistics, Vital	HA201-214	317.3
United States—History—Civil War, 1861-1865	E456-655	973.7	United States—Territorial expansion	E179.5	973
United States—History—1865-	E660-887	973.(8-9)	United States—Territories and possessions	JK2556	320.120973
United States—History—1865-1921	E660-783	973.(8-913)	United States—Territories and possessions	JV500-599	325.373
United States—History—1865-1898	E660-735	973.8(1-8)	United States—Territories and possessions—Maps	G3690-3691	912.73
United States—History—20th century	E740-887	973.91	United States. Air Force	UG633-634.5	358.400973
United States—History—1901-1909	E740-760	973.911	United States. Army	UA24-39	355.30973
United States—History—1909-1913	E761-765	973.912	United States. Army—Airborne troops	D769.346	940.541273
United States—History—1913-1921	E766-783	973.913	United States. Army—Appropriations and expenditures	UA24.A7	355.30973
United States—History—1919-1933	E784-805	973.91(3-6)	United States. Army—Artillery	UA32-33	358.120973
United States—History—1933-1945	E806-812	973.917	United States. Army—Artillery	UF23	358.120973
United States—History—1945-1953	E813-816	973.918	United States. Army—Artillery—Drill and tactics	UF160-162	358.1240973
United States—History—1953-1961	E835-837.7	973.921	United States. Army—Commissariat	UC40-44	355.620973
United States—History—1961-1969	E838-851	973.92(2-3)	United States. Army—Equipment	UC523	355.80973
United States—Manufactures	TS23-25	670.973	United States. Army—Field service	U173	355.350973
United States—Manufactures—Law and legislation	KF1875-1893	343.73078	United States. Army—Handbooks, manuals, etc.	U113	355.5470973
United States—Maps	G3690-4383	912.73	United States. Army—History	UA23-25	355.30973
United States—Maps	G1200-1534.24	912.73	United States. Army—History	E181	355.30973
United States—Militia	UA42-560	355.370973	United States. Army—Inspection	UB243	355.6850973
United States—National Guard	UA42-560	355.370973	United States. Army—Maneuvers	U253	355.40973
United States—Officials and employees—Salaries, etc.	JK771-794	352.630973			
United States—Periodicals	E151	973.05			

Subject Heading	LC	Dewey	Subject Heading	LC	Dewey
United States. Army—Medals, badges, decorations, etc.	UC533	355.13420973	United States. Navy—Boats	V880	359.3220973
			United States. Navy—Boatswains	VG953	359.3380973
United States. Army—Officers	UB412-414	355.3320973	United States. Navy—Chaplains	VG23	359.3470973
United States. Army—Ordnance and ordnance stores	UF523-563	355.80973	United States. Navy—Communication systems	VG73	359.9830973
United States. Army—Parachute troops	D769.347	940.541273	United States. Navy—Draftsmen	VG913	359.3380973
United States. Army—Pay, allowances, etc.	UC70-75	355.640973	United States. Navy—Field service	V175	359.350973
United States. Army—Physical training	U323	355.50973	United States. Navy—Fire control technicians (Missile)	VF347	359.98170973
United States. Army—Procurement	UC263	355.62120973	United States. Navy—Firearms	VF350-420	359.8240973
United States. Army—Records and correspondence	UB163	355.60973	United States. Navy—Firearms	VD360-390	359.8240973
United States. Army—Recruiting, enlistment, etc.	UB323	355.2230973	United States. Navy—History	E182	359.30973
United States. Army—Registers	U11	355.309730216	United States. Navy—Inspection	VB223	359.6850973
United States. Army—Transportation	UC273	358.250973	United States. Navy—Intelligence specialists	VG1020	359.34320973
United States. Army. Cavalry	UA30-31	357.10973	United States. Navy—Machinist's mates	VG803	359.3380973
United States. Army. Infantry	UD23	356.10973	United States. Navy—Maneuvers	V245	359.410973
United States. Army. Infantry	UA28-29	356.10973	United States. Navy—Officers	VB313-314	359.3320973
United States. Coast Guard	V437	359.9709073	United States. Navy—Officers' handbooks	V133	359.3320973
United States. Coast Guard	VG53	359.970973	United States. Navy—Ordnance and ordnance stores	VF353-420	359.80973
United States. Congress	JK1012-1432	328.73			
United States. Congress—Directories	JK1012	328.73025	United States. Navy—Organization	VA49-395	359.30973
United States. Congress—History	JK1033-1059	342.730509	United States. Navy—Pay, allowances, etc.	VC50-65	359.80973
United States. Congress. House	JK1308-1432	328.320973	United States. Navy—Personnel management	VB258	359.610973
United States. Congress. Senate	JK1154-1259	328.310973	United States. Navy—Petty officers' handbooks	V123	359.3320973
United States. Continental Army—History	E259	973.34(4-5)	United States. Navy—Physical training	V263	359.50973
United States. Dept. of Defense	UA23.2-.6	355.60973	United States. Navy—Postal service	VG63	359.340973
United States. Marine Corps	VE23-25	359.9630973	United States. Navy—Procurement	VC260-267	359.62120973
United States. Marine Corps—Drill and tactics	VE160-162	359.9650973	United States. Navy—Recruiting, enlistment, etc.	VB263	359.22360973
United States. Navy	VC20-65	359.80973			
United States. Navy—Accounting	VC503	359.6220973	United States. Navy—Safety measures	V383	359.00289
United States. Navy—Appropriations and expenditures	VA53	359.6220973	United States. Navy—Sailors' handbooks	V143-144	359.3380973
United States. Navy—Aviation	VG93	359.940973	United States. Navy—Sailors' handbooks	VD150-155	359.3380973
United States. Navy—Barracks and quarters	VC423	359.710973	United States. Navy—Small-boat service	VD403	359.310973

Subject Heading	LC	Dewey	Subject Heading	LC	Dewey
United States. Navy—Songs and music	VG33	781.599/784.84 (0973)	Upland game bird shooting—[By region or country]	SK324	799.24609(4-9)
United States. Navy—Submarine forces	V858	359.9330973	Uranium	TP245.U7	661.0431
United States. Navy—Supplies and stores	VC263	359.80973	Uranium	QD181.U7	546.431
United States. Navy—Transportation	VC553	359.9850973	Uranus (Planet)	QB387	523.47
United States. Navy—Weapons systems	VF347	359.820973	Uranus (Planet)	QB681	523.47
			Urban agriculture	S494.5.U72	630.91732
United States. Navy—Yeomen	VG903	359.3380973	Urban anthropology	GN395	307.76
			Urban climatology	QC981.7.U7	551.691732
Universalism	BX9901-9969	289.134	Urban ecology	HT241-243	577.56
Universalism—Congresses	BX9905-9907	289.13406	Urban ecology (Biology)	QH541.5.C6	577.56
Universalism—Education	BX9917-9923	268.89134	Urban economics	HT321-325	330.91732
Universalism—History	BX9931-9935	289.13409	Urban geography	GF125	910.021732
Universalism—Sermons	BX9943	252.09134	Urban health	RA566.7	613.091732
Universalists	BX9967-9969	289.134092	Urban homesteading	HD7289.4-.42	363.5091732
Universities and colleges	LB2300-2411	378	Urban poor	HV4023-4470.7	362.5091732
Universities and colleges—Accreditation	LB2331.6-.615	353.88284	Urban renewal	HT170-178	307.3416
Universities and colleges—Admission	LB2351-2359	378.161	Urban renewal—United States	HT175-177	307.34160973
Universities and colleges—Curricula	LB2361-2365	378.199	Urban renewal—[Other regions or countries]	HT178	307.341609(4-9)
Universities and colleges—Entrance requirements	LB2351-2360	378.1617	Urban runoff	TD657-.5	628.21
			Urban-rural migration	HB1956-2157	307.26
Universities and colleges—Examinations	LB2367	378.1662	Urban-rural migration	HT381	307.26
			Urban schools	LC5101-5143	370.91732
Universities and colleges—Examinations	LB2353	378.1662	Urban transportation	HE305-311	388.4
			Urban transportation	TA1205-1207	388.4
Universities and colleges—Faculty	LB2331.7-.74	378.12	Urban universities and colleges	LB2328.4	378.052
Universities and colleges—Finance	LB2342	378.106	Urdu language	PK1975-1987	491.439
			Urdu literature	PK2030-2058	891.439
Universities and colleges—Graduate work	LB2371	378.155	Uremia	RC915	616.635
			Urethra—Diseases	RC892	616.62
Universities and colleges—Africa	LG401-681	378.6	Urinary organs	QM401-413	611.61
			Urinary organs	QL872-881	573.49
Universities and colleges—America	LE	378.(7/8)	Urinary organs	QP247-250.8	612.46
			Urinary organs—Calculi	RC916	616.622
Universities and colleges—Asia	LG21-395	378.5	Urinary organs—Diseases	RC900-923	616.6
Universities and colleges—Canada	LE3-5	378.71	Urinary organs—Examination	RC901	616.6075
Universities and colleges—Europe	LF	378.4	Urinary tract infections	RC901.8	616.6
			Urination disorders	RC901.75	616.6
Universities and colleges—United States	LD13-7251	378.73	Urology	RC870-923	616.6
			Uruguay	F2701-2799	989.5
University cooperation	LB2331.5	378.104	Uruguay—Census	HA1071-1090	318.95
University extension	LC6201-6401	378.175	Uruguay—Civilization	F2710	989.5
Unmarried fathers	HV700.7	362.8294	Uruguay—Description and travel	F2711-2715	918.9504
Unmarried mothers	HV700.5	362.8394			
Unsteady flow (Aerodynamics)	TL574.U5	629.13232	Uruguay—Economic conditions	HC231-235	330.9895
Unsteady flow (Fluid dynamics)	TA357.5.U57	620.1064	Uruguay—Emigration and immigration	JV7520-7529	325.(2895/895)
Upland game bird shooting	SK323-325	799.246	Uruguay—Gazetteers	F2704	918.95003
			Uruguay—History	F2720-2729.52	989.5
			Uruguay—History—To 1810	F2723	989.50(1-3)
			Uruguay—History—1810-1830	F2725	989.50(1-4)
			Uruguay—History—1830-1875	F2726	989.505

Subject Heading	LC	Dewey	Subject Heading	LC	Dewey
Vegetation surveys	QK62	580.723	Venus (Planet), Transit of	QB509-513	523.423
Veils	GT2112	391.43	Venus (Planet)—Orbit	QB372	523.423
Veins	QM191	611.14	Venus (Planet)—Surface	QB621	523.42
Veins	QL835	573.186	Veps language	PH541-549	494.54
Veins—Diseases	RC695-697	616.14	Verdun, Battle of, 1914	D545.V25	940.421
Veins—Puncture	RM182-190	617.414059	Verdun, Battle of, 1916	D545.V3	940.4272
Veins (Geology)	QE611-.5	551.88	Verdun, Battle of, 1940	D756.5.V3	940.54214
Vellum printed books	Z1030	096.2	Vermont—Gazetteers	F47	917.43003
Velvet	TS1675	677.617	Vermont—History	F46-60	974.3
Venda language	PL8771	496.397	Vermont—History—To 1791	F52	974.303
Vendetta	HV6441-6453	364.256	Vermont—History— Revolution, 1775-1783	E263.V5	974.30(2-3)
Vending machines	TJ1560	629.82	Vermont—History—War of 1812	E359.5.V3	974.303
Veneers and veneering	TS870	674.83			
Veneration of saints and Christian union	BX9.5.V45	280.042	Vermont—History—Civil War, 1861-1865	E533	974.303
Venezuela	F2301-2349	987	Vermont—Maps	G3750-3754	912.743
Venezuela—Census	HA1091-1100	318.7	Vermont—National Guard	UA490-499	355.3709743
Venezuela—Civilization	F2310	987	Vermont—Periodicals	F46	974.3005
Venezuela—Description and travel	F2311-2315	918.704	Versification	PN1031-1035	808.1
			Versification	P311	808.1
Venezuela—Economic conditions	HC236-239.5	330.987	Vertebrae	QM111	611.711
			Vertebrates	QL605-739.8	596
Venezuela—Emigration and immigration	JV7530-7539	325.(287/87)	Vertebrates, Fossil	QE841-899	566
			Vertically rising aircraft	TL685	629.13335
Venezuela—Gazetteers	F2304	918.7003	Vestals	BL815.V4	292.61
Venezuela—History	F2319.5-2328.52	987	Vestibular apparatus	QP471	612.858
Venezuela—History— To 1810	F2322	987.0(1-3)	Veterans	UB356-375	362.1608697
			Veterans—Education	UB356-359	371.82697
Venezuela—History— To 1556	F2322	987.0(1-3)	Veterans—Employment	UB356-359	331.52
			Veterans—Medical care	UB368-369.5	362.108697
Venezuela—History— 1556-1810	F2322	987.03	Veterans, Disabled	UB360-366	362.408697
			Veterinarians	SF612-613	636.089092
Venezuela—History— Insurrection of the Comuneros, 1781	F2322	987.03	Veterinarians—Directories	SF611	636.089025
			Veterinarians— Professional ethics	SF756.39	174.2
Venezuela—History— Miranda's Expedition, 1806	F2322	987.03	Veterinary acupuncture	SF914.5	636.0895892
			Veterinary anatomy	SF761-767	636.0891
Venezuela—History—1810-	F2322.8	987.0(4-6)	Veterinary anesthesia	SF914	636.089796
Venezuela—History— 1810-1830	F2324	987.0(4-5)	Veterinary autopsy	SF769	636.08960759
			Veterinary bacteriology	SF780.3	636.0896014
Venezuela—History— War of Independence, 1810-1823	F2324	987.0(4-5)	Veterinary cardiology	SF811	636.089612
			Veterinary colleges	SF756.3-.37	636.0890711
			Veterinary critical care	SF778	636.0896028
Venezuela—History— 1830-1935	F2325	987.061	Veterinary disinfection	SF757.15	636.089448
			Veterinary emergencies	SF778	636.0896025
Venezuela—History— Federal Wars, 1858-1863	F2325	987.061	Veterinary epidemiology	SF780.9	636.08944
			Veterinary genetics	SF756.5	636.0821
			Veterinary hospitals	SF604.4-.7	636.089
Venezuela—Manufactures	TS54	670.987	Veterinary hygiene—Law and legislation	K3615-3617	344.049
Venezuela—Maps	G5280-5284	912.87			
Venezuela—Periodicals	F2301	987.005	Veterinary hygiene—Law and legislation—England	KD3420-3422	344.42049
Venezuela—Politics and government	JL3800-3899	320.987			
			Veterinary hygiene—Law and legislation— United States	KF3835-3838	344.73049
Venezuelean literature	PQ8530-8550.36	860			
Venice (Italy)	DG670-684.72	945.31			
Ventilation	TH7647-7699	697.92	Veterinary medicine	SF600-1100	636.089
Ventricular fibrillation	RC685.V43	616.128	Veterinary medicine— Congresses	SF605	636.08906
Ventriloquism	GV1557	793.89			
Venus (Planet)	QB621	523.42			
Venus (Planet)	QB372	523.42			

Subject Heading	LC	Dewey
Veterinary medicine—Diagnosis	SF771-774	636.0896075
Veterinary medicine—History	SF615-724	636.08909
Veterinary medicine—Societies, etc.	SF600-604	636.08906
Veterinary medicine—Terminology	SF610	636.089014
Veterinary nursing	SF774.5	636.089073
Veterinary obstetrics	SF887	636.08982
Veterinary oncology	SF910.T8	636.0896992
Veterinary orthopedics	SF910.5	636.08967
Veterinary physiology	SF768-.2	636.0892
Veterinary prescriptions	SF916.5	636.08951
Veterinary public health	SF740	636.0894
Veterinary service, Military	UH650-655	355.345
Veterinary surgery	SF911-914.4	636.0897
Veterinary vaccines	SF918.V32	636.0895372
Veterinary virology	SF780.4	636.08960194
Vibraphone music	M175.X6	786.843
Vibration	QC235-241	534.5
Vibration	QA935-939	531.32
Vibration (Aeronautics)	TL574.V5	629.132362
Vicars apostolic	BX1910	262.142
Vicars-general	BX1910	262.142
Vice	BV4630-4647	241.3
Vice	BJ1534-1535	179.8
Vice (Buddhism)	BQ4425-4430	294.35
Vice control	HV8067	363.
Vice-Presidents—United States	JK609.5	352.2390973
Viceroyalty	JV431	353.15092
Vices	BV4625-4627	241.3
Vices	BJ1534-1535	179.8
Victims of crimes	HV6250-.4	362.88
Victims of crimes—United States	KF9763	344.7303288
Victims of crimes surveys	HV6250	362.880723
Video cassette recorders	TK6655.V5	621.38833
Video games	GV1469.3	794.8
Video recordings	PN1992.95	791.45
Video recordings for the hearing impaired	HV2503	362.4283
Video tapes	LB1044.75	371.33523
Video tapes in education	LB1044.75	371.33523
Videocassette recorders	TK6655.V5	621.38833
Videodisc players	TK6685	384.558
Vienna (Austria)	DB841-860	943.613
Vietnam	DS556-559.916	959.7
Vietnam—Census	HA4600.5	315.97
Vietnam—Civilization	DS556.42	959.7
Vietnam—Description and travel	DS556.34-.39	915.9704
Vietnam—Economic conditions	HC444	330.9597
Vietnam—Gazetteers	DS556.25	915.97003
Vietnam—History—To 939	DS556.6-.63	959.703
Vietnam—History—Later Le dynasty, 1428-1787	DS556.7-.73	959.703
Vietnam—History—19th century	DS556.8-.83	959.70(3-4)
Vietnam—History—August Revolution, 1945	DS556.815	959.703
Vietnam—Maps	G2370-2374	912.597
Vietnam—Maps	G8020-8024	912.597
Vietnam—Politics and government	JQ800-899	320.9597
Vietnamese Conflict, 1961-1975	DS557-559.8	959.7043
Vietnamese language	PL4371-4379	495.922
Vietnamese literature	PL4378	895.922
Vietnamese literature (French)	PQ3960-3979	840
Vietnamese reunification question (1954-1976)	DS556.9-.93	959.704(2-44)
Viking ships	V46	359.3220948
Vikings	DL65	948.5014
Viol music	M59	787.6
Viola music	M45-49	787.3
Violence	RC569.5.V55	616.8582
Violence	HM281-283	303.6
Violence in mass media	P96.V5	303.6
Violence in psychiatric hospitals	RC439.4	362.21
Violetta d'amore music	M59.V	787.66
Violin	ML800-897	787.209
Violin music	M40-44	787.2
Violoncello music	M50-54	787.4
Viral carcinogenesis	RC268.57	616.994071
Viral pollution of water	TD427.V55	628.168
Virgin Islands of the United States	F2136	972.9722
Virgin Islands of the United States—Census	HA911-915	317.29722
Virgin Islands of the United States—History—1775-1783	E263.W5	972.9722
Virgin Islands of the United States—History—1775-1793	E263.W5	972.9722
Virgin Islands of the United States—Maps	G5010-5014	912.729722
Virgin birth	BT317	232.921
Virginia—Gazetteers	F224	917.55003
Virginia—History	F221-235	975.5
Virginia—History—Colonial period, ca. 1600-1775	F229	975.50(1-2)
Virginia—History—1775-1865	F230	975.50(2-3)
Virginia—History—Revolution, 1775-1783	E263.V8	975.50(2-3)
Virginia—History—War of 1812	E359.5.V8	975.503
Virginia—History—Civil War, 1861-1865	E534	975.503
Virginia—History—Civil War, 1861-1865	E581	975.503
Virginia—Maps	G3880-3884	912.755
Virginia—National Guard	UA500-509	355.3709755
Virginia—Periodicals	F221	975.5005

Subject Heading	LC	Dewey
Virginity	BV4647.C5	241.66
Virgo (Astrology)	BF1727.4	133.5267
Virtue	BJ1518-1691	179.9
Virtue	BV4630-4647	241.4
Virtues	BV1518-1533	241.4
Virtues	BV4625-4627	241.4
Virtues (Buddhism)	BQ4401-4430	294.35
Virus diseases	RC114-.7	616.92
Virus diseases	RA644.V55	614.57
Virus diseases in children	RJ401-406	618.92925
Viruses	QR355-502	579.2
Viscosity	QC189-.2	531.1134
Vision	QP474-495	612.84
Vision disorders	RE91-95	617.75
Vision, Monocular	RE95	617.712
Visions	BV5091.V6	248.29
Visions	BT650-660	232.917
Visiting nurses	RT98	610.7343
Visiting teachers	LB3013.5	371.46
Visual aids	LB1043.5-1044	371.335
Visual learning	LB1067.5	153.152
Visual perception	BF241	152.14
Visually handicapped—Means of communication	HV1631.5	362.418
Vital statistics	HA154-4737	310
Vitamin therapy	RM259	615.328
Vitamins	TX553.V5	613.286
Vitreous body—Diseases	RE501	617.746
Vocabulary	P305-.18	401.4
Vocal cords—Diseases	RF526	616.22
Vocal ensembles	M1528-1529.5	782.0438
Vocal music	M1495-5000	782
Vocal music—History and criticism	ML1400-3275	782.009
Vocational education	LC1041-1047	370.113
Vocational guidance	HF5381-5382.5	331.702
Voice	QL765	591.594
Voice	QP306	612.78
Voice disorders	RF510-540	616.855
Volcanic ash, tuff, etc.	QE461-462	552.23
Volcanic gases	QE545	551.23
Volcanoes	QE521.5-527.5	551.21
Volleyball	GV1015-.57	796.325
Voltameter	TK331	621.3744
Voltameter	QC615	621.3743
Voltmeter	TK321	621.3743
Volumetric analysis	QD111	545.2
Voluntarism	HN49.V64	302.14
Volunteer workers in long-term care facilities	RA997-998	362.16092
Voodooism	BL2490	299.675
Vortex-motion	QC159	532.595
Vortex-motion	QA925	532.59
Votic language	PH561-569	494.54
Voting	JF825-1141	324.62
Voting, Compulsory	JF1031	324.62
Voting age	JF841	324.62
Voting-machines	JF1128	324.65
Voyages and travels	G149-922	910
Voyages around the world	G420-445	910.41
Voyeurism	RC560.V68	616.8583
Vulcanization	TS1891	678.24
Vulva—Diseases	RG261-266	618.16
Wages	HD4909-5100.7	331.21
Wages—Tables	HF5705-5707	658.32021
Wages—Canada	HD4977-4980	331.210971
Wages—Central America	HD4983-4989	331.2109728
Wages—Developing countries	HD4967	331.21091724
Wages—Europe	HD5014-5061.84	331.21094
Wages—Mexico	HD4981	331.210972
Wages—South America	HD4996-5013	331.21098
Wages—United States	HD4973-4976	331.210973
Wages—West Indies	HD4990-4995.9	331.2109729
Wagons	HD9709.5	388.341
Wake services	BX2045.W34	264.02085
Wakes (Fluid dynamics)	QA913	532.593
Waldenses	BX4872-4883	284.4
Wales	DA700-745	942.9
Wales—Biography	DA710	920.0429
Wales—Census	HA1161-1170	314.29
Wales—Civilization	DA711.5	942.9
Wales—Description and travel	DA725-731.2	914.2904
Wales—History	DA714-722.1	942.9
Wales—Maps	G5760-5764	912.429
Wales—Periodicals	DA700	942.9005
Wales—Politics and government	JN1150-1159	320.9429
Walking (Sports)	GV1071	796.51
Wall Street	HG4571-4575.3	332.64273
Wall hangings	NK2910	746.3
Wall hangings	TT850.2	746.3
Wallis and Futuna Islands	DU920	996.16
Wallis and Futuna Islands—Maps	G9515-9517	912.9616
Wallpaper	TH8461-8463	676.2848
Wallpaper	NK3375-3496.3	747.3
Walls	TH2201-2251.5	690.12
Walls	NA2940-2942	721.2
Waltz	GV1761	793.33
Wampum	E98.M7	332.4089973
War	U	355.02
War	V	359
War—Casualties (Statistics, etc.)	UH215-325	355.345021
War—Relief of sick and wounded	UH201-551	355.345
War, Cost of	UA17	355.622
War and civilization	CB481	909
War and crime	HV6189	364.2
War and emergency legislation—United States	KF5900-6075.5	343.7301
War correspondents	PN4823	070.4333092
War crimes	D625-626	364.13809041
War games	U310	355.48
War games, Naval	V250	359.48
War horses	UE460-475	357.2
War memorials	NA9325-9330	725.94
War relief	HV639	363.34988
War wounds	RD156	617.044

243

Subject Heading	LC	Dewey	Subject Heading	LC	Dewey
Warehouses	HF5484-5495	380.1	Water in landscape architecture	SB475.8	714
Warehouses	NA6340-6343	725.35	Water in the body	QP535.H1	572.539
Warehouses—Design and construction	TH4451-4499	690.535	Water jets	TC173	532.52
Wars of Liberation, 1813-1814	DC236-238.5	940.27	Water mills	TJ859	621.21
			Water-pipes	TD491	628.15
Warsaw (Poland)	DK4610-4645	943.84	Water-power	TJ840-890	621.21
Warsaw, Battle of, 1945	D765.2.W3	940.5421384	Water-power	TC147	621.20422
Warships	V750-995	359.32	Water quality	TD370-375	628.16
Warships—Camouflage	V215	359.41	Water quality management	TD365-.5	628.16
Warships—Turrets	VF440	359.32	Water resources development	HD1690-1702	333.91
Warts	RL471	616.544			
Warves	TC357	627.31	Water resources development	TC401-558	627
Washington (D.C.)	F191-205	975.3			
Washington (D.C.)—Gazetteers	F192	917.53003	Water resources development—Law and legislation	KF5551-5590	346.7304691
Washington (D.C.)—History—Capture by the British, 1814	E356.W3	975.302	Water reuse	TD429	628.162
			Water skiing	GV840.S5	797.35
Washington (D.C.)—Maps	G3850-3854	912.753	Water-supply	GB651-2998	551.48
Washington (D.C.)—National Guard	UA120-129	355.3709753	Water-supply	TD201-500	628.1
			Water-supply—History	TD215-220	628.109
Washington (D.C.)—Periodicals	F191	975.3005	Water-supply—Law and legislation	K3496-3501	343.0924
Washington (State)	F886-900	979.7	Water-supply—[By region or country]	TD221-327	628.109(4-9)
Washington (State)—Gazetteers	F889	917.97003			
Washington (State)—History—To 1889	F891	979.70(1-3)	Water-supply, Rural	TD927	628.72
			Water towers	TD489	628.13
Washington (State)—History—1889-	F891	979.704	Water towers	TH9332-9334	628.9252
			Water treatment plants	TD434	628.162
Washington (State)—Maps	G4280-4284	912.797	Water waves	TC172	532.59
Washington (State)—National Guard	UA510-519	355.3709797	Water-wheels	TJ860-880	621.21
			Watercolor painting	ND1700-2495	751.422
Washington (State)—Periodicals	F886	979.7005	Watercolor painting—Study and teaching	ND2110-2115	751.422071
Washington's Birthday	E312.6	394.26973			
Waste lands	HD1665-1671	333.73137	Waterfalls	GB1401-1597	551.484
Waste products	TP995-996	658.567	Waterfowl	SK331-335	799.244
Waste products	HD9975	658.567	Watergate Affair, 1972-1974	E860	973.924
Watchdogs	SF428.8	636.70886			
Watchmen	HV8290-8291	363.289	Watergate Trial, Washington, D.C., 1973	KF224.W	345.730231
Water	QD169.W3	546.22			
Water	QC920	551.57	Waterloo, Battle of, 1815	DC241-244.7	940.27
Water	GB651-2998	551.48	Waterproofing	TH9031	693.892
Water—Aeration	TD458	628.165	Waterproofing of fabrics	TS1520	677.682
Water—Analysis	QD142	546.22	Watersheds	GB561-568	551.45
Water—Distribution	TD481-493	628.144	Waterspouts	QC957	551.553
Water—Law and legislation—England	KD1070	346.4204691	Waterways	HE380.8-560	386
			Waterways—Canada	HE399-401.25	386.0971
Water—Pollution	TD419-428	628.168	Waterways—Latin America	HE401.5-402	386.098
Water—Purification	TD429.5-477	628.162	Waterways—United States	HE392.8-398	386.0973
Water chemistry	GB855	546.22	Waterways—[Other regions or countries]	HE403.5-520.9	386.09(4-9)
Water conservation	TD388-.5	628.13			
Water conservation projects	TD388-.5	628.13	Wave guides	QC661	621.381331
Water-electrolyte imbalances	RC630	616.3992	Wave makers	TC172	532.59
			Wave mechanics	QC174.2-.26	530.124
Water gardens	SB423	635.9674	Wave-motion, Theory of	QA935	531.33
Water hammer	TC174	620.1064	Wave-motion, Theory of	QA927	532.593
Water heaters, Gas	TH6561	696.6	Wavelets (Mathematics)	QA403.3	515.2433
			Waves	QC157	532.593
			Waves	GC211-222	551.4702
			Waxes	TP669-695	665.1

Subject Heading	LC	Dewey
Weak interactions (Nuclear physics)	QC794.8.W4	539.7544
Weapons	NK6600-6999	739.7
Weapons	U800-897	355.8
Weapons—Law and legislation	K3661	344.0533
Weapons—Law and legislation—England	KD3492	344.420533
Weapons—Law and legislation—United States	KF3941-3942	344.730533
Weapons, Prehistoric	GN799.W3	623.441
Weather	QC980-999	551.6
Weather—Periodicals	QC980	551.605
Weather—Physiological effect	QP82.2.C5	571.49
Weather—Psychological aspects	BF353.5.W4	155.915
Weather, Influence of the moon on	QC883-.2	551.5
Weather broadcasting	QC877.5	551.632
Weather control	QC926.6-928.74	551.68
Weather control—Law and legislation—United States	KF5594	344.730655168
Weather forecasting	QC994.95-999	551.63
Weather radar networks	QC973.8.W	551.6353
Weather reporting, Radio	QC877.5	551.632
Weathering	QE570	551.302
Weavers	HD8039.T4	677.028242092
Weavers	GN432	677.028242092
Weaving	GN432	677.028242
Weaving	TS1490-1500	677.028242
Wedding anniversaries	GT2800	394.2
Wedding cakes	GT2797	392.5
Wedding decorations	SB449.5.W4	745.926
Wedding etiquette	BJ2051-2065	395.22
Weddings, Military	U350-355	355.17
Weeds	SB610-615	632.5
Weeds—Control	SB610-615	632.5
Week-day church schools	BV1580-1583	371.071
Weekly rest-day	HD5114	331.2576
Weighing-machines	QC107	530.7
Weight lifting	GV546.3	613.713
Weights and measures	QC81-114	530.81
Weights and measures—History	QC83-86	530.8109
Weights and measures—Law and legislation—United States	KF1665-1666	343.73075
Welding	TS227-228.96	671.52
Wells	TD405-414	628.114
Wells	GR690	398.364
Welsh language	PB2101-2199	491.66
Welsh literature	PB2206-2499	891.66
West (U.S.)—History	F590.3-596.3	978
West (U.S.)—History—To 1848	F592-.7	978.0(1-2)
West (U.S.)—History—1848-1860	F593	978.02
West (U.S.)—History—1860-1890	F594	978.02
West (U.S.)—History—Civil War, 1861-1865	E470.9	978
West (U.S.)—History—1890-1945	F595	978.0(2-32)
West (U.S.)—History—1945-	F595-.3	978.033
West (U.S.)—Maps	G4050-4052	912.78
West Indian literature (French)	PQ3940-3949	840
West Indies	F1601-1629	972.9
West Indies—Biography	CT329-448	920.0729
West Indies—Civilization	F1609.5	972.9
West Indies—Climate	QC987	551.69729
West Indies—Commerce	HF3311-3369	380.109729
West Indies—Description and travel	F1610-1613	917.2904
West Indies—Economic conditions	HC151-158.6	330.9729
West Indies—Emigration and immigration	JV7320-7397	325.(2729/729)
West Indies—Gazetteers	F1604	917.29003
West Indies—Genealogy	CS200-261	929.3729
West Indies—History	F1620-1623	972.9
West Indies—Manufactures	TS32-33	670.9729
West Indies—Maps	G1600-1692	912.729
West Indies—Maps	G4900-5184	912.729
West Indies—Periodicals	F1601	972.9005
West Virginia	F236-250	975.4
West Virginia—Gazatteers	F239	917.54003
West Virginia—History—1951-	F245-.42	975.404(3-4)
West Virginia—History—Civil War, 1861-1865	E536	975.403
West Virginia—History—Civil War, 1861-1865	E582	975.403
West Virginia—National Guard	UA520-529	355.3709754
West Virginia—Periodicals	F236	975.4005
West Virignia—Maps	G3890-3894	912.754
Western Hemisphere—Maps	G1100-1779	912.19812
Western Sahara—Census	HA4737	316.48
Western Samoa	DU819.A2	996.14
Western riding	SF309.3	798.23
Western saddle	SF309.9	636.13037
Western swing (Music)	ML3541	784.16409
Wetland conservation	QH75-77	333.91816
Wetland ecology	QH541.5.M3	577.68
Wetlands	QH87.3	578.768
Whaling	SH381-385	639.28
Whaling	G545	910.45
Wheat-free diet	RM237.87	613.26
Wheelchairs	RD757.W4	617.9
Wheels	TJ181.5	621.837
Whiskey	TP605	663.52
Whiskey Rebellion, Pa., 1794	E315	973.43
Whistling	MT949.5	782.98

Subject Heading	LC	Dewey	Subject Heading	LC	Dewey
White collar crime investigation	HV8079.W47	363.25968	Will	BF608-635	153.8
White collar workers	HD8039.M39	331.792	Wind ensembles	M955-959	785.43
White dwarfs	QB843.W5	523.887	Wind erosion	QE597	551.372
Whole and parts (Philosophy)	BD396	111.82	Wind forecasting	QC931	551.6418
Wholesale trade	HF5419-5422	381.2	Wind instrument music	M111	788
Whooping cough	RC204	616.204	Wind instruments	ML929-990	788.09
Whooping cough	RA644.W6	614.543	Wind power	TJ820-828	621.45
Wide area networks (Computer networks)	TK5105.87-.888	004.67	Windlasses	VM811	621.864
			Windmills	TJ823-828	621.453
Wide gap semiconductors	QC611.8.W53	537.6223	Window gardening	SB419-.3	635.9678
Wide-screen processes (Cinematography)	TR855	778.53	Windows	TH2261-2276	690.1823
			Windows	NA3000-3030	721.823
Widow suicide	GT3370	393.9	Winds	QC930.5-959	551.518
Widowers	HQ1058-.5	305.389654	Winds aloft	QC935	551.518
Widows	HQ1058-.5	305.489654	Windsurfing	GV811.63.W56	797.33
Wife abuse	HV6626-.23	364.15553	Windward Islands	F2011	972.98
Wife abuse	RC569.5.F3	616.85822	Windward Islands—Maps	G5090-5184	912.7298
Wife abuse—Investigation	HV8079.S67	363.2595553	Wine and wine making	TP544-559	663.2
Wigs	GT2310	391.5	Winter grain	SB188-192	633.1
Wigs	TT975	646.7248	Winter sports	GV841-857	796.9
Wild men	GN372	305.31	Winter warfare	U167.5.W5	355.423
Wild plants, Edible	QK98.5	581.632	Wisconsin	F576-590	977.5
Wild women	GN372	305.4	Wisconsin—Gazetteers	F579	917.75003
Wildcat strikes	HD5311	331.8924	Wisconsin—History— To 1848	F584	977.50(1-3)
Wilderness survival	GV200.5-.56	796.5			
Wildlife cinematography	TR893.5	778.53859	Wisconsin—History— 1848-	F586-.42	977.50(3-4)
Wildlife conservation	QL81.5-84.7	333.95416			
Wildlife management— Congresses	SK352	639.906	Wisconsin—History— Civil War, 1861-1865	E537	977.503
Wildlife management areas	SK351-579	639.9	Wisconsin—Maps	G4120-4124	912.775
Wildlife management areas—[By region or country]	SK361-579	639.909(4-9)	Wisconsin—National Guard	UA530-539	355.3709775
			Wisconsin—Periodicals	F576	977.5005
			Wit and humor	PN6147-6231	808.87
Wildlife management areas—Africa	SK571-575	639.9096	Wit and humor, Pictorial	PC1300-1766	857.00222
			Witchcraft	GR530	398.45
Wildlife management areas—Australia	SK577	639.90994	Witchcraft	BF1562.5-1584	133.43
			Witness bearing (Christianity)	BV4520	248.5
Wildlife management areas—Canada	SK470-471	639.90971			
			Wok cookery	TX840.W65	641.589
Wildlife management areas—Central America	SK475	639.909728	Wok cookery	TX724.5.C	641.589
			Wolf ritual	E98.R2	299.74
Wildlife management areas—Europe	SK503-543	639.9094	Woman (Buddhism)	BQ4570.W6	294.3378344
			Woman (Christian theology)	BT704	233
Wildlife management areas—Great Britain	SK505-511	639.90941	Women	GT2520-2540	390.082
			Women	HQ1101-2030.7	305.4
Wildlife management areas—Mexico	SK473	639.90972	Women—Biography	CT3200-3830	920.72
			Women—Crimes against	HV6250.4.W65	362.88082
Wildlife management areas—South America	SK479-501	639.9098	Women—Diseases	RC48.6	618
			Women—Education	LC1401-2571	371.822
Wildlife management areas—United States	SK361-465	639.909(4-9)	Women—Education (Higher)	LC1551-1651	378.19822
Wildlife management areas—West Indies	SK477	639.909729	Women—History	HQ1121-1172	305.409
			Women—Psychology	HQ1206-1216	155.633
Wildlife managers	SK354	639.9092	Women—Services for	HV1442-1448	362.83
Wildlife photography	TR729.W54	778.932	Women—Sexual behavior	HQ29	306.7082
Wildlife rehabilitation	SF996.45	333.95416	Women—Social conditions	HQ1121-1870.5	305.42
Wildlife reintroduction	QL83.4	333.95416	Women—Socialization	HQ1201-1216	302.32082
Wildlife rescue	QL83.2	636.0832	Women—Societies and clubs	HQ1871-2030.7	305.4(06/8)/367
Will	LB1071	153.8			
			Women—Suffrage	JF847-855	324.623

Subject Heading	LC	Dewey
Women—Vocational education	LC1500-1506	370.113082
Women—[By region or country]	HQ1400-1870.5	305.409(4-9)
Women, Prehistoric	GN799.W66	569.9
Women clergy	BV676	262.14
Women physicians	R692	610.82
Women's rights	HQ1236-.5	323.34
Women's studies	HQ1180-1186	305.407
Wood—Chemistry	TS932-934	674.386
Wood-carving	NK9700-9799	736.4
Wood-engraving	NE1000-1325	761.2
Wood-engraving—15th century	NE1050-1075	761.209024
Wood-engraving—16th century	NE1050-1075	761.209031
Wood-engraving—17th century	NE1050-1075	761.209032
Wood-engraving—18th century	NE1085-1088	761.209033
Wood-engraving—19th century	NE1090-1093	761.209034
Wood-engraving—20th century	NE1095-1097	761.20904
Wood-engraving—Exhibitions	NE1010-1012	761.2074
Wood-engraving—History	NE1030-1196.3	761.209
Wood-engraving—Periodicals	NE1000	761.205
Wood-engraving—[By region or country]	NE1101-1196.3	761.209(4-9)
Wood-pulp	TS1171-1177	676.12
Woodlots	SD387.W6	634.99
Woodwind ensembles	M955-959	785.8
Woodwork	NK9600-9955	745.51
Woodwork	TT180-203.5	745.51
Wool	TS1547	677.31
Woolen and worsted manufacture	TS1600-1631	677.31
Word of God (Islam)	BP166.2	297.211
Word processing	HF5548.115	652.5
Work	BJ1498	174
Work	BF481	158.7
Work	HD4801-8943	331
Work—Psychological aspects	BF481	158.7
Work environment	RC963-969	616.9803
Work environment	HD7260-7780.8	331.25
Work ethic	HD4905-.3	306.3613
Work groups	HD66-.2	658.402
Work sharing	HD5110.5-.6	331.2572
Workhouses	HV8748-8749	365.34
Working animals	SF170-180	636.0886
Working class	HD4801-8943	331.11
Working class—Education	LC5001-5060	371.82623
Working class—Religious life	BV4593	248.88
Working class women—[By region or country]	HD6091-6220.7	331.409(4-9)
Working dogs	SF428.2	636.73
Working mothers	HQ759.48	306.8743

Subject Heading	LC	Dewey
Workshops	TT152-153.7	684.08
World War, 1914-1918	D501-680	940.3
World War, 1914-1918—Aerial operations	D600-607	940.44
World War, 1914-1918—Atrocities	D625-626	940.405
World War, 1914-1918—Biography	D507	940.3092
World War, 1914-1918—Campaigns	D529-578	940.4
World War, 1914-1918—Campaigns—Belgium	D541-542	940.414
World War, 1914-1918—Campaigns—Eastern front	D550-569.5	940.4147
World War, 1914-1918—Campaigns—France	D548-549.5	940.4144
World War, 1914-1918—Campaigns—France	D544-545	940.4144
World War, 1914-1918—Campaigns—Germany	D531-538.5	940.4143
World War, 1914-1918—Campaigns—Italy	D569	940.4145
World War, 1914-1918—Campaigns—Turkey	D566-568.9	940.415
World War, 1914-1918—Campaigns—Western front	D530-549.5	940.4144
World War, 1914-1918—Naval operations	D580-589	940.45
World War, 1914-1918—Peace	D613-614	940.439
World War, 1914-1918—Peace	D642-651	940.439
World War, 1914-1918—Registers of dead	D609	940.467
World War, 1939-1945	D731-838	940.53
World War, 1939-1945—Aerial operations	D785-792	940.544
World War, 1939-1945—Armistice	D812	940.5312
World War, 1939-1945—Atrocities	D803-804.35	940.5405
World War, 1939-1945—Biography	D736	940.53092
World War, 1939-1945—Blockades	D770-784	940.5452
World War, 1939-1945—Campaigns	D755-769.87	940.54
World War, 1939-1945—Campaigns—Africa, North	D766.82	940.5423
World War, 1939-1945—Campaigns—Eastern front	D764-766.7	940.5425
World War, 1939-1945—Campaigns—France	D761-762	940.54214
World War, 1939-1945—Campaigns—Germany	D757-.9	940.54213

Subject Heading	LC	Dewey	Subject Heading	LC	Dewey
Yiddish language—Grammar	PJ5115-5116.5	439.15	Yugoslavia—History—1918-1945	DR1281-1312	949.70(2-3)
Yiddish literature	PJ5120-5192	839.09	Yugoslavia—History—Axis occupation, 1941-1945	D802.Y8	949.7022
Yoga	B132.Y6	181.45	Yugoslavia—History—Coup d'etat, 1941	DR1297-1298	949.7022
Yoga (Jainism)	BL1375.Y63	294.4436	Yugoslavia—History—1945-1980	DR1300	949.7023
Yom Kippur	BM675.A8	296.432	Yugoslavia—History—1980-1992	DR1306-1313.8	949.70(24-3)
Yom Kippur	BM695.A8	296.432	Yugoslavia—History—1992-	DR1306-1312	949.7103
Young American Medal for Bravery	CR6253.Y	929.8173	Yugoslavia—Manufactures	TS95.Y8	670.9497
Young Men's Christian associations	BV1000-1220	267.3	Yugoslavia—Maps	G6840-6844	912.497
Young Women's Christian associations	BV1300-1393	267.5	Yugoslavia—Periodicals	DR1202	939.8005/ 949.7005
Young adults	HQ799.5-.9	305.235	Yukon Territory—Gazetteers	F1092	917.191003
Young adults—Sexual behavior	HQ27-.5	306.70835	Yukon Territory—History	F1091-1095.5	971.91
Young men	HV1423	362.7083	Yukon Territory—Maps	G3520-3524	912.7191
Young women	HV1425	362.7083	Yukon Territory—Periodicals	F1091.A1	971.91005
Young women—Psychology	HQ1229	155.533	Yupik Eskimos	E99.E7	973.04971
Youth	HQ793-799.9	305.235	Zaire—Census	HA4711	316.751
Youth—Crimes against	HV6250.4.Y68	362.88083	Zaire—Civilization	DT649	967.51
Youth—Employment	HD6270-6276	331.34	Zaire—Description and travel	DT645-647.5	916.75104
Youth—Physiology	RJ140-145	612.661	Zaire—Economic conditions	HC955	330.96751
Youth—Religious life	BV4530-4579	248.83	Zaire—History	DT650.2-663	967.51
Youth—Societies and clubs	HS3250-3270	367.4	Zaire—History—To 1908	DT654-655.2	967.510(1-22)
Youth—Substance use	HV4999.Y68	362.29083	Zaire—History—1908-1960	DT657-.2	967.51024
Youth—Travel	G156.5.Y6	910.83	Zaire—History—1960-	DT658-.25	967.5103
Youth—[By region or country]	HQ799	305.23509(4-9)	Zaire—History—Civil War, 1960-1965	DT658	967.51031
Youth, Buddhist—Conduct of life	BJ1289.5.Y6	294.35	Zaire—History—Shaba Invasion, 1977	DT658.25	967.51033
Youth, Muslin—Religious life	BP188.3.Y6	297.57	Zaire—History—Shaba Uprising, 1978	DT658.25	967.51033
Youth hostels	TX907-910	647.94	Zaire—Maps	G8650-8654	912.6751
Youth in church work	BV4427-4430	258.0835	Zambia—Census	HA4703	316.894
Youth in missionary work	BV2617	266.0083	Zambia—Civilization	DT3052	968.94
Youth in the ecumenical movement	BX9.5.Y68	280.0420835	Zambia—Description and travel	DT3050	916.89404
Youth sermons	BV4310	252.55	Zambia—Economic conditions	HC915	330.96894
Youthfulness	BF724-.3	155.5	Zambia—Gazetteers	DT3037	916.894003
Youths' periodicals	AP200-230	050.835	Zambia—History	DT3064-3119	968.94
Yugoslavia	DR1202-2285	939.8/949.7	Zambia—History—To 1890	DT3079-3089	968.9401
Yugoslavia—Biography	DR1233-1235	920.0398/ 920.0497	Zambia—History—1890-1924	DT3091-3101	968.9402
Yugoslavia—Census	HA1631-1635	314.97	Zambia—History—1924-1953	DT3103-3106	968.9402
Yugoslavia—Civilization	DR1228	939.8/949.7	Zambia—History—1953-1964	DT3108-3111	968.940(3-4)
Yugoslavia—Congresses	DR1205	939.8006/ 949.7006	Zambia—History—1964-	DT3113-3119	968.9404
Yugoslavia—Description and travel	DR1218-1224	913.9804/ 914.9704	Zen Buddhism	BQ9250-9519	294.3927
Yugoslavia—Economic conditions	HC407	330.9497	Zen Buddhism—Psychology	BL1493	294.3375
Yugoslavia—Gazetteers	DR1209	913.98003/ 914.97003	Zimbabwe—Civilization	DT2908	968.91
Yugoslavia—Historiography	DR1239-1243	939.80072/ 949.70072	Zimbabwe—Description and travel	DT2900-2904	916.89104
Yugoslavia—History	DR1232-1321	939.8/949.7	Zimbabwe—Gazetteers	DT2884	916.891003
Yugoslavia—History, Military	DR1250-1251	355.309497	Zimbabwe—History	DT2914-3000	968.91
Yugoslavia—History, Naval	DR1252-1253	359.309497			

Subject Heading	LC	Dewey	Subject Heading	LC	Dewey
Zimbabwe—History—1890-1965	DT2959-2979	968.910(2-4)	Zoologists	QL26-31	591.5092
			Zoology	QL	590
Zimbabwe—History—Shona Insurrection, 1896-1897	DT2970	968.9102	Zoology—Experiments	QL52.6	590.724
			Zoology—Pictorial works	QL46	590.222
			Zoology—Societies, etc.	QL1	590.6
Zimbabwe—History—Ndebele Insurrection, 1896	DT2968	968.9102	Zoology—Study and teaching	QL51-58	590.71
Zimbabwe—History—1965-1980	DT2981-2994	968.9104	Zoology—Terminology	QL10	590.14
			Zoology—[By region or country]	QL155-339	590.9
Zimbabwe—History—Chimurenga War, 1966-1980	DT2988	968.9104	Zoology, Economic	SF84-.45	591.6
			Zoology, Economic	SB922-998	591.6
Zimbabwe—History—1980-	DT2996-3000	968.9105	Zoology, Economic—[By region or country]	SB993.3-.34	591.609(4-9)
			Zoonoses	SF740	636.0896959
Zionism	DS149-151	320.54095694	Zoonoses	RC113.5	616.959
Zither music	M135-137	787.7	Zoonoses	RA639-641	614.56
Zither—Instruction and study	MT620-634	787.707	Zoos	QL76-77.5	590.73
			Zorastrianism	BL1500-1590	295
Zodiac	QB15-26	523	Zoroastrianism—Sacred books	BL1510-1525	295.82
Zodiac	QB802	523	Zulu War, 1879	DT1875-1882	968.045
Zoning	HT169.6-.9	333.7717	Zulu language	PL8841-8844	496.3986
Zoning law—England	KD1125-1162	346.42045	Zuni Indians	E99.Z9	973.04979
Zoogeography	QL101-345	590.9(3-9)	Zuni language	PM2711	497.9
Zoological museums	QL71	590.74			